Children's Thinking About
Cultural Universals

Children's Thinking About Cultural Universals

Jere Brophy
Janet Alleman
Michigan State University

 LAWRENCE ERLBAUM ASSOCIATES, PUBLISHERS
2006   Mahwah, New Jersey   London

Lawrence Erlbaum Associates, Inc., Publishers
10 Industrial Avenue
Mahwah, New Jersey 07430
www.erlbaum.com

Cover art by Jered Brophy and Chris Speier
Cover design by Kathryn Houghtaling Lacey

Library of Congress Cataloging-in-Publication Data

Brophy, Jere E.
   Children's thinking about cultural universals / Jere Brophy, Janet Alleman.
     p. cm.
   Includes bibliographical references and indexes.
   ISBN 0-8058-4893-2 (cloth : alk. paper)
   ISBN 0-8058-4894-0 (pbk. : alk paper)
   1. Social sciences—Study and teaching (Primary)—United States—Case studies.
2. Social learning—Case studies.   3. Child development—United States—Case studies.
I. Alleman, Janet. II. Title.

LB1530.B76   2005
372.83—dc22   2004062504
                                                                   CIP

Printed in the United States of America
10 9 8 7 6 5 4 3 2 1

Contents

Preface

This book summarizes findings from interview studies probing K–3 students' knowledge and thinking (including misconceptions) about topics commonly addressed in the primary-grades social studies curriculum. The interview questions addressed a great many topics, but they were organized around activities relating to *cultural universals*—domains of human experience that have existed in all cultures, past and present. Specifically, the questions probed students' understandings related to nine cultural universals: food, clothing, shelter, communication, transportation, family living, government, money, and childhood. Most of the findings come from samples of primarily lower-middle-class suburban students, stratified by gender and achievement level.

The book is intended for two primary audiences: people interested in child development generally and people interested in early social learning specifically. Child development researchers and course instructors, preschool and elementary teachers, and parents of young children will find a great deal of information about what children ages 5 to 9 know (or think they know) about a great many aspects of social knowledge, as well as information about how such children think about these topics when they do not yet possess accurate and well-articulated knowledge.

In recent decades, attention to children's cognitive development has shifted from a focus on presumably generic stages and processes to a focus on the acquisition of knowledge in specific domains. To date, much more research has been done on trajectories of knowledge development in mathematics and science than in social studies. Furthermore, most of the available research that does relate to topics addressed in social studies has been organized around concepts or principles emphasized in history, geography, or the social sciences, so it has not paid much attention to the pre- or pandisciplinary topics addressed in the primary grades. Of the nine cultural universals addressed in our studies, only "government" has received much prior research attention. Consequently, this book contains a great deal of information that will be new to people interested in general developments in cognition and domain knowledge across childhood.

Our findings will have special relevance, however, for teachers, teacher educators, researchers, curriculum developers, museum designers, parents, policymakers, and others with particular interests in social studies teaching and learning in the primary grades. This is because contemporary depictions of best practice in school teaching and learning emphasize the importance of teaching school subjects for understanding, appreciation, and life application, using methods that connect with students' prior experience and engage them in actively constructing new knowledge and correcting existing misconceptions. Accomplishing this requires detailed information about what children typically know (or think they know) about the content taught at their grade levels. This will enable curriculum developers and teachers to draw on what is known about common trajectories in children's developing understanding in a content domain so as to plan instruction that will both build on existing valid knowledge and address common misconceptions. This book represents a quantum leap in the availability of information relating to trajectories of knowledge concerning topics commonly addressed in primary social studies.

OVERVIEW

Chapter 1 describes the nature and purpose of this line of work, locating it with reference to previous research on developmental trajectories in children's cognition generally and social knowledge specifically. It also introduces the concept of cultural universals, outlines our position on why cultural universals have been and should continue to be basic organizers for primary social studies, and contrasts this position with several alternatives. The chapter also summarizes some general characteristics of children's social knowledge and draws contrasts with the kinds of scientific knowledge featured in most previous studies (in particular, noting that social knowledge consists primarily of verbally mediated observations of social phenomena, whereas much scientific knowledge is based on manipulation of objects in the physical environment).

Chapter 2 through chapter 8 summarize findings from large interview studies of K–3 students' thinking about food, clothing, shelter, transportation, communication, family living, and government. These chapters focus on progressions across the K–3 grade range in students' thinking about these topics, subsuming both tables presenting quantitative data on commonly observed response categories and supplementary information in the text on noteworthy rare and unique responses. References to technical reports and other publications on these data are given for researchers or others who want more detailed information. In addition, these chapters include our ideas about implications for early social studies curriculum and instruction, with references to resource units we have developed about the topics for social studies educators and others interested in more detail.

Chapter 9 summarizes findings and potential teaching implications from two smaller studies of first and second graders' thinking about the topics of money and childhood. Chapter 10 addresses issues that cut across the studies, particularly the degree to which students' socioeconomic status (SES), achievement level, or gender create variation around the general trends described in the previous chapters. We believe that the general trends observed across the entire K–3 range and the grade level progressions observed within this range are the findings of primary magnitude and significance, but we did identify some SES, achievement level, and gender differences worth noting, and these are described in chapter 10.

Finally, chapter 11 concludes the volume with an extended discussion of potential implications for curriculum and instruction in primary social studies. Rather than repeat the material on potential implications for teaching specific topics that were included in chapter 2 through chapter 9, chapter 11 focuses on findings that cut across the interview topics and carry implications about general characteristics of social studies teaching in the early grades. This chapter also includes a more extended argument for and explanation of our approach to developing resource units capable of supporting powerful social studies teaching in these grades, contrasting it with approaches that we believe to be less effective.

ACKNOWLEDGMENTS

The authors wish to acknowledge and thank Donna Anderson and Ruth Bell, who conducted the interviews; Jill Schaberg, who verified the interview transcriptions; Nelia Mendez, who helped to establish reliability of the coding; Carolyn O'Mahony and Tracy Reynolds, who coded the interview transcriptions; and June Benson, who transcribed the interviews and assisted in all aspects of data and manuscript preparation. We also wish to express our appreciation to Keith Barton and Steve Thornton, who provided reviews of the initial version of the manuscript. Finally, we offer special thanks to kindergartener Jered Brophy and third grader Chris Speier, who contributed the original artwork used in the cover design.

—*Jere Brophy*
—*Janet Alleman*

1

Introduction

Interviewer:	Why did some Indians live in tipis?
Kindergartener:	Maybe they just had a small family and only needed a little house.
First grader:	You could build a fire in a tipi and the smoke would go out the hole in the top, so it was cozy warm in there and they could cook.
Second grader:	They liked them because they could paint designs on them to decorate them.
Second grader:	Maybe they were poor people and didn't have enough money to get a better house.
Third grader:	The Indians never wasted anything, and building tipis gave them a way to use all of their leftover animal skins.

This question about tipis was included in an interview about shelter as a cultural universal that was administered to students in Grades K–3. A previous question established that the vast majority of the students could supply the name "tipi" when shown a drawing of a tipi and asked what it was. Most of them also were able to generate one or more reasons why some Indians lived in tipis, as the examples indicate. Despite this familiarity with tipis and ability to reason about them, however, very few students understood that the main reason that the tribes who constructed tipis used this form of housing was its portability. These were plains tribes who followed the buffalo on which they were dependent for meeting most of their basic needs, so they had to pack up and move periodically, taking everything that they owned with them, including their shelter. The students' interview responses imply a need for instruction about tipis to include emphasis on the tipis' portability, as well as a need for teaching about the nature of and reasons for nomadic societies (a concept unfamiliar to most K–3 students).

Another one of our interviews dealt with clothing. Responses to initial questions indicated that most K–3 students could describe business, work, and play clothes accurately and talk knowledgeably about why these different types of clothing are worn in their respective contexts. When asked about cloth itself, however, many were unable to describe how it is made and most of the rest talked about "smishing" fluffy cotton in order to flatten it into cloth, putting wool into a machine that makes it into cloth (or even, makes it into shirts or other specific clothing items), or cutting material into the appropriate shapes for parts of a shirt (trunk, sleeves, collar, etc.) and then sewing them together to make the shirt (without explaining where the material came from in the first place). Probing often indicated that the students thought of cloth as a solid akin to leather or plastic, not realizing that it is a fabric woven from threads, which in turn are spun from raw material. These findings imply that K–3 students do not need much instruction about different kinds of clothes and when they are worn, but they do need instruction in the basic processes involved in creating cloth (spinning threads or yarn from raw material and then weaving or knitting these into fabric).

Tipis and cloth are just two of over 100 topics addressed in interviews that we conducted with students in Grades K–3. These interviews were designed to identify aspects of students' prior knowledge and thinking about these topics that might be taken into account in planning social studies curriculum and instruction in the primary grades. Ideally, such instruction will connect with students' prior knowledge, both by building on their valid knowledge and by addressing their misconceptions.

K–3 students' thinking about food, clothing, shelter, communication, transportation, family living, and government was explored in seven large interview studies. In addition, first and second graders' thinking about two additional topics—childhood and money—was explored in smaller studies. Along with a great many specific ideas unique to just one of these nine topics, our interviews elicited several general response tendencies that cut across topics but also had implications for teaching. For example:

1. When talking about the past, students often displayed historical presentism (disparaging the thinking or technologies of people of the past because they viewed them only with hindsight instead of appreciating them within the context of the time and place studied).

2. When talking about other cultures, they frequently displayed chauvinism (depicting unfamiliar customs as "funny," "weird," etc.).

3. When seeking to explain why particular people use certain food or forms of shelter or emphasize certain economic activities, they seldom showed much awareness of the role of climate and geography in creating affordances and constraints that affect the lives of people living in the area.

The presentism and chauvinism tendencies highlight the need for instruction that will help students to empathize with people from the past or from other cultures, so as to be able to view them within the context of their time and place and to appreciate their activities as sensible adaptations to that context. The paucity of geographical components in the students' explanations indicates the need for a general consciousness-raising concerning the role of geography in creating affordances and constraints for human activities in particular places, as well as for more specific highlighting of climate and location influences on the diets, clothing styles, shelter forms, and economic activities developed in particular societies. The social studies curriculum in the primary grades is the logical "home" for these and other basic social understandings. However, primary students in most American elementary schools are not systematically introduced to such content, nor to much, if any, significant social education content at all.

DEARTH OF CONTENT IN EARLY SOCIAL STUDIES

The social studies curriculum in the primary grades tends to be a loose amalgam of three main sources of content: (a) socialization of students concerning the prosocial attitudes and behavior expected of them as members of the classroom community; (b) introduction to map concepts and skills; and (c) introduction to basic social knowledge drawn mostly from history and the social sciences. Good materials are available for teaching about maps (in several textbook series) and about becoming a prosocial member of the learning community (in widely distributed ancillary materials). However, there is much dissatisfaction with the social knowledge component of early social studies, especially as it is represented in the leading textbook series (Alter, 1995; Beck & McKeown, 1988; Beck, McKeown, & Gromoll, 1989; Brophy, 1992; Brophy & Alleman, 1992–1993; Egan, 1988; Woodward, 1987).

The content of primary-grade social studies texts is often criticized as overly limited in scope, trivial in import, and lacking connection to major social education goals or structuring around key ideas. Much of it focuses on (ostensibly) human activities related to basic needs or other universal domains of human experience, and some critics believe that the problems with the textbook series are rooted in their focus on this content base. In contrast, we believe that cultural universals are viable topics around which to organize the primary-grade social studies curriculum, and that the problems with textbooks are rooted in inadequate development of this content base, not in the choice of the content base itself.

For example, treatments of shelter in these textbooks typically feature several pages of colorful photographs of a wide variety of shelter forms: tipis, igloos, stilt houses, tropical huts, modern homes, apartment buildings, and so forth. However, the text accompanying these photographs typically says little or nothing more than "People around the world live in many different kinds of homes." Furthermore, little or nothing is said in the teacher's manual about big ideas to develop in helping students understand the reasons for this variety in housing forms. Students will not gain much understanding from looking at or even discussing photographs unless they are taught something about the reasons why different forms of shelter have been constructed in past and present societies.

Some basic ideas that we would emphasize in units on shelter in the primary grades include:

1. People's shelter needs are determined in large part by local climate and geographical features.
2. Most housing is constructed using materials made from natural resources that are plentiful in the area.
3. Certain forms of housing reflect local cultural, economic, or geographic conditions (e.g., tipis and tents as easily movable shelters used by nomadic societies, stilt houses as adaptation to periodic flooding used by rice farmers who live in marshes or flood plains, high-rise apartment buildings as adaptation to land scarcity in urban areas).
4. Inventions, discoveries, and improvements in construction knowledge and materials have enabled many modern people to live in housing that offers better durability, weatherproofing, insulation, and temperature control, with fewer requirements for maintenance and labor, than anything that was available to even the richest of their ancestors.
5. In the process, people's orientations have shifted from merely meeting basic shelter needs to acquiring comfortable internal living environments that offer a great many labor-saving devices and other conveniences.
6. Modern industries and transportation make it possible to construct almost any kind of shelter almost anywhere on earth, so it is now possible for those who can afford it to live comfortably in very hot or very cold climates.
7. Forms of shelter that existed in the past and that still exist in some societies today are much simpler than the modern homes that most American students live in, but they typically represent intelligent use of locally available materials to fashion homes that not only meet basic shelter needs but are well adapted to the local climate and reflective of the culture of the inhabitants.

CULTURAL UNIVERSALS

Anthropologists and other social scientists often refer to *cultural universals* (sometimes called *social universals* or *basic categories of human social experience*) as useful dimensions for understanding a given society or making comparisons across societies (Banks, 1990; Brown, 1991; Cooper, 1995; Payne & Gay, 1997). Cultural universals are domains of human experience that have existed in all cultures, past and present. They include activities related to meeting the basic needs of food, clothing, and shelter, as well as family structures, government, communication, transportation, money or other forms of economic exchange, religion, occupations, recreation, and perhaps others as well. The term implies that activities relating to each cultural universal can be identified in all societies, but not that these activities necessarily have the same form or meaning in each society. On the contrary, it recognizes variations among societies (as well as among individuals within societies) in orientation toward or handling of common life events associated with each cultural universal (e.g., family structures are universal, but different cultures and individuals within cultures have different notions of what constitutes a family).

Cultural universals have special importance for the early elementary social studies curriculum because although it is usually described as an "expanding horizons" or "expanding communities" curriculum, much of its basic content actually focuses on the universals. The traditional reasoning has been that teaching students about how their own and other societies have addressed the human purposes associated with cultural universals is an effective way to establish an initial, predisciplinary knowledge base in social studies, preparing the way for the more discipline-based courses of the middle and upper grades. Organizing early social studies around cultural universals provides a sound basis for developing fundamental understandings about the human condition for two main reasons: First, human activities relating to cultural universals account for a considerable proportion of everyday living and are the focus of much of human social organization and communal activity, so a curriculum organized around cultural universals provides many natural starting points for developing initial social understandings. Until children understand the motivations and cause-and-effect explanations that underlie these activities, they do not understand much of what is happening around them all the time. As they develop such understandings, the previously mysterious behavior of their parents and other people significant in their lives becomes comprehensible to them, and they acquire intellectual tools for developing efficacy in these domains themselves.

Second, children begin accumulating direct personal experiences with most cultural universals right from birth, and they can draw on these experiences as they construct understandings of social education concepts and principles in the early grades. This is true for all children, regardless of their family's ethnicity or socioeconomic status. If cultural universals are taught with appropriate focus on powerful ideas and their potential life applications, students should develop basic sets of connected understandings about (a) how our social system works (with respect to each cultural universal); (b) how and why it got to be that way over time; (c) how and why related practices vary across locations and cultures; and (d) what all of this might mean for personal, social, and civic decision making.

Not everyone agrees with this rationale, or even with the notion of social studies as a pre- or pandisciplinary school subject organized primarily as preparation for citizenship. Advocates of basing school curricula directly on the academic disciplines would offer separate courses in history, geography, and the social sciences, simplified as needed but designed primarily to pursue disciplinary goals rather than citizenship education goals. With particular reference to the primary grades, Egan (1988), Ravitch (1987), and others advocated replacing topical teaching about cultural universals with a heavy focus on chronological history and related children's literature (not only historical fiction but myths and folktales).

We agree that K–3 students can and should learn certain aspects of history, but we also believe that these students need a balanced and integrated social education curriculum that includes sufficient attention to powerful ideas drawn from geography and the various social sciences, subsumed within citizenship education purposes and goals. Furthermore, we see little social education value in replacing reality-based social studies with myths and folklore likely to create misconceptions, especially during the primary years when children are struggling to determine what is real (vs. false/fictional) and enduring (vs. transitory/accidental) in their physical and social worlds.

Recent trends in U.S. education have increased the applicability of this argument. So-called reform movements built around high-stakes testing programs have increased the curricular "air time" allocated to language arts (and to a lesser extent, mathematics) at the expense of science and social studies (Haas & Laughlin, 2001). As a result, contemporary American children are getting even more exposure to the fictional (and often fanciful) content emphasized in primary language arts, and even less exposure to information about physical and social realities. This imbalance might be justified if research supported the argument that it would establish a solid literacy foundation that ultimately would enhance achievement in all subjects. Ironically, however, relevant research indicates that children show more progress in literacy (as well as in other subjects) when their reading and writing opportunities emphasize content-area texts and reality-based tradebooks, not fanciful fiction (Duke, 2000; Pappas, 1993).

NEED FOR INFORMATION ABOUT CHILDREN'S KNOWLEDGE AND THINKING

Some of those who are opposed to a focus on cultural universals in early social studies have asserted, without presenting evidence, that there is no need to teach this content because students already know it from everyday experience (Larkins, Hawkins, & Gilmore, 1987; Ravitch, 1987). We have disputed this assertion, suggesting that the knowledge about cultural universals that children develop through everyday experience tends to be tacit rather than well articulated. Furthermore, much of it is confined to knowledge about how things are without accompanying understandings about why they got to be that way, how and why they vary across cultures, or the mechanisms through which they accomplish human purposes (Brophy & Alleman, 1996).

Recent developments in research on teaching suggest the need for data that speak to this issue. Increasingly, educational theory and research have been emphasizing the importance of teaching school subjects for understanding, appreciation, and life application, using methods that connect with students' prior experience and engage them in actively constructing new knowledge and correcting existing misconceptions. In mathematics and science, rich literatures have developed describing what children typically know (or think they know) about the content taught at their grade levels. These literatures allow curriculum developers and teachers to draw on what is known about common trajectories in children's developing understanding of a content domain (including knowledge about false starts or distorted paths associated with common misconceptions), so as to scaffold students' learning optimally. Drawing on information about students' prior knowledge and thinking about a topic, a teacher can "work in the zone of proximal development" by asking questions, suggesting problems, or providing feedback that will be most helpful in enabling students to construct accurate understandings, make connections, and see the need to question invalid assumptions or other misconceptions.

PRIOR RESEARCH IN CHILD DEVELOPMENT

Unfortunately, very little information of this kind exists about topics addressed in K–3 social studies (Brophy, Alleman, & O'Mahony, 2000; Marker & Mehlinger, 1992; Schug & Hartoonian, 1996). There have been some studies of stages in the development of economic, political, and social knowledge (Barrett & Buchanan-Barrow, 2002, 2005; Berti & Bombi, 1988; Furnham & Stacey, 1991; Furth, 1980; Moore, Lare, & Wagner, 1985), but most child development research has concentrated on cognitive structures and strategies that children acquire through general life experiences rather than on their developing understanding of knowledge domains learned primarily at school. Furthermore, when child development researchers have addressed topics taught at school, they have focused on mathematical and scientific knowledge rather than on social knowledge.

Furthermore, they have focused on attempts to support or dispute the claim that preschool and early-primary-grade children have intuitive theories of biology, physics, psychology, and possibly other disciplines, even before they acquire connected knowledge in these domains. Carey (1999), for example, argued that even by 12 months of age, infants show abilities to represent concepts in at least three core domains: intuitive mechanics, intuitive psychology, and number. These core domains are structures that determine the cores of ontologically important concepts, embody causal and explanatory principles, and support infer-ences. Intuitive mechanics, for example, features physical objects as its central ontological kind (i.e., kind of entity included in the domain) and contact causal-ity as its basic causal principle, whereas intuitive psychology features person as its central ontological kind and intentional causality as its basic causal principle. In-tuitive knowledge of these domains provides frameworks within which children generate causal explanations (i.e., explaining mechanical events with reference to contact between physical objects but explaining psychological events with ref-erence to people's goal-oriented intentions and actions).

Many investigators of these phenomena claim that children develop intuitive theories in several domains over the first several years of life, and that these do-mains frame their thinking even before their domain-relevant knowledge be-comes organized and before they are able to verbalize much of it (Atran, 1998; Carey, 1985, 1999; Gopnik & Meltzoff, 1997; Siegal & Peterson, 1999; Wellman & Gelman, 1992). Others have disputed these claims, arguing that so-called in-tuitive theories are not sufficiently well articulated and explicit to merit the name *theories*, or alternatively, are not sufficiently specific to the domain to merit description as domain-specific theories. Au and Romo (1999), for example, argued that much of children's early thinking about biological phenomena rec-ognizes inputs and outputs but lacks clarity about causal mechanisms, and fur-thermore includes causal ideas that are fundamentally psychological (rooted in goal-oriented intentions) rather than mechanistic, and thus is not specifically biological. They believe that children and even adults do not spontaneously construct uniquely biological causal explanations from everyday experience, and do not acquire them until they are exposed to formal science education.

Keil, Levin, Richman, and Gutheil (1999) argued that this dispute is essen-tially semantic—that the degree to which evidence supports claims that children develop intuitive theories in particular domains depends on how the term *theory* is defined. We find this position persuasive. Consequently, although we some-times cite findings developed by participants in this dispute and although we have generated new findings that are relevant to aspects of it, we do not discuss our findings as evidence either for or against claims that children possess intuitive theories of biology, physics, psychology, and so forth. Instead, our discussions fo-cus on what we have learned about developments in children's trajectories of knowledge (including misconceptions) about the topics addressed in our inter-views, and on the implications of this for curriculum and instruction in primary-grade social studies.

We also wish to note another contrast between the work reported here and much of the work on children's intuitive domain theories. Many of the investiga-tors who have done the latter work believe that clinical interviews underestimate children's knowledge because that knowledge includes intuitive preconceptions that influence their thinking, even though they cannot articulate these ideas verbally. Consequently, these investigators have developed choice tasks (e.g.,

"Which is the best explanation for why we eat food—because we like tasty food, because we get vital energy from the food, or because we need the substance to build new muscle and bone as we grow?") and other methods of tapping into children's thinking without requiring them to articulate their ideas at length. We have not used these methods in our research, partly out of validity concerns, but mostly because children in the K–3 grade range are old enough to be able to respond to clinical interviews, particularly when the questions focus on familiar experiences rather than abstract, remote, or hypothetical content. In addition, our primary interest is in aspects of children's social knowledge that are relatively easy for them to access and verbalize because it is this knowledge base that early social studies curriculum and instruction needs to connect with and build on.

PRIOR RESEARCH ON CHILDREN'S SOCIAL KNOWLEDGE

Even scholars concerned with curriculum and instruction in social studies have not developed much information about trajectories of development of social knowledge. There have been occasional surveys of knowledge about particular social studies topics (Guzzetta, 1969; Lapp, Grigg, & Tay-Lim, 2002; Ravitch & Finn, 1987; U.S. Department of Education, 1995a, 1995b). However, these have concentrated mostly on isolated facts such as names, dates, places, or definitions, with reporting of findings limited to percentages of students able to answer each item correctly. To be more useful to educators, the research needs to emphasize (a) questions that probe children's understanding of connected networks of knowledge and (b) analyses that focus on qualitative aspects of their thinking about the topic, including identification of commonly held misconceptions.

Political Knowledge

Most such studies done to date have been couched within the academic disciplines of history, geography, or the social sciences. Significant progress has been made in studying children's developing knowledge of politics and government. For example, children are much more aware of the executive than the legislative or judicial aspects of government and they tend to view presidents as godlike figures notable for their power to get things done and their benevolence or caring about the needs of each individual citizen (Connell, 1971; Greenstein, 1969; Hess & Torney, 1967; Moore et al., 1985; Stevens, 1982). See chapter 8, this volume, for more details on this topic.

Economic Knowledge

Research on economic knowledge has begun to uncover stages in children's development of understanding of, as well as common misconceptions in their ideas about, such concepts as *supply*, *demand*, *cost*, and *price*, as well as such topics as the

functions of banks and the operations of retail stores (Berti & Bombi, 1988; Berti
& Monaci, 1998; Burris, 1983; Byrnes, 1996; Jahoda, 1984; Leiser, 1983; Schug,
1991; Thompson & Siegler, 2000). Aspects of these findings are cited in several
chapters because most of our interviews included questions about economic aspects of the topic.

Historical Knowledge

Several teams of investigators have studied children's historical learning (Barton
& Levstik, 1996, 2004; Brophy & VanSledright, 1997; Lee & Ashby, 2001;
McKeown & Beck, 1994). This work has demonstrated, for example, that much
of the historical knowledge of fifth graders is organized in narrative form, so that
it tends to feature stories focused around a few hero figures rather than less per-
sonalized causal analyses of historical trends. The students' narratives also tend to
compress time and space by depicting face-to-face interactions between people
whose life spans did not overlap (e.g., Columbus and the Pilgrims), by personalizing complex events involving many people and institutions around the motives
and actions of a few individuals (e.g., the Revolutionary War as a dispute between the English king and a few colonial leaders, fought by the same two armies
that kept meeting periodically in battles), or by treating slow, evolutionary
changes as quantum leaps or single events (e.g., immigrants to the New World
came in a single ship; discrimination against African Americans stopped when
Martin Luther King, Jr., made his speech).

    These and other investigators have also established that children are inter-
ested in the past and able to understand those aspects of it that can be connected
to their existing experiences and concepts, especially when the content is rendered in narrative formats structured around the motives and actions of key individuals. Although they have trouble with the mathematical aspects of dates, they
can understand sequences using terms such as *very long ago*, *old timey*, or *recently*,
and they perform mostly accurately when asked to place photos from the past in
historical sequence. They tend to think about history as being just about the past
(and particularly about important people and events in the past), not realizing
that it includes everything up to the present and the routine activities of everyday people along with the exploits of the famous. American children tend to tell
tales of continuous progress, depicting people as acting rationally and thus gradually improving things by adopting new insights (e.g., slavery is wrong) or invent-
ing technological improvements. However, they tend to attribute seemingly in-
explicable actions to ignorance or stupidity rather than to view them as rational
given the time, place, and information available to the actors. Speaking from
hindsight, they tend to display presentism rather than empathy, depicting life in
the past as drab and difficult or boring (Barton, 1996, 1997a, 1997b; Davis,
Yeager, & Foster, 2001; Dickenson, Lee, & Rogers, 1984; Downey & Levstik,

1991; Foster, Hoge, & Rosch, 1999; Hallden, 1994; Lee & Ashby, 2001; Levstik & Barton, 1996; Masterman & Rogers, 2002; Seixas, 1994; VanSledright & Brophy, 1992; Willig, 1990).

Geographic Knowledge

Research on children's geography knowledge indicates that it accumulates gradually across the elementary years. Preschool and early elementary children tend to identify with their own country and to be aware of at least some other countries, although they usually do not possess much specific knowledge unless they have traveled abroad. Their beliefs combine accurate information with stereotypes and misconceptions. This is especially true of their ideas about Africa, which tend to emphasize images of jungles, wild animals, witch doctors, and people starving, living in huts, and living primitive lives generally (Palmer, 1994; Wiegand, 1993).

Primary-grade children have difficulty understanding nested geographical relationships (e.g., local community within the state, within the region, within the nation, within the hemisphere). However, they can learn these relationships through exposure to map-based instruction, and there is some evidence that their understandings have improved in recent decades (Harwood & McShane, 1996; Jahoda, 1963; Wiegand, 1993).

Until about age 5, children often have little knowledge of their own country or national group, and may even be unable to name their country (Piaget & Weil, 1951). Thereafter, they tend to be able to name their country and to classify themselves as members of their own national group. Early knowledge is focused around symbols such as the flag, the national anthem, and salient buildings, landscapes, or historical figures, depending on what is emphasized in their nation. For example, one study found that in talking about their country, Argentine children emphasized its geographical territory but English children talked more about the queen and the values of freedom and democracy. In general, primary-grade children's knowledge about their own country is mostly vague and symbolic, and their knowledge about other countries is even vaguer and often riddled with stereotypes or misconceptions (Barrett & Buchanan-Barrow, 2002).

Beginning when they are still preschoolers, and often before they have acquired much specific knowledge, American and English children typically develop positive attitudes toward their country, say that they are happy to live in it, and select positive adjectives as descriptive of it. These tendencies are less pronounced among minority group members in these countries and are not always observed among children from other countries (much depends on the country's history and the kinds of messages about it to which children are exposed).

These early positive attitudes toward the home country are not necessarily accompanied by negative attitudes toward other countries, so they are best interpreted as manifestations not of chauvinism but of an apparently universal tendency to prefer the familiar to the unfamiliar (Zajonc, 2001). As children begin and progress through elementary school, however, many of them do acquire at least temporary negative stereotypes of particular nations or world regions. As they learn more, their perceptions about the home country and other countries tend to become more differentiated, and they come to appreciate that there are both positives and negatives about any nation (Barrett & Buchanan-Barrow, 2002; Barrett & Short, 1992; Bennett, Lyons, Sani, & Barrett, 1998; Cameron, Alvarez, Ruble, & Fuligni, 2001; Rutland, 1999). Parallel developments occur in children's attitudes toward and beliefs about their own and other racial and ethnic groups (Aboud, 1988; Sears & Levy, 2003).

CHARACTERISTICS OF SOCIAL KNOWLEDGE

Compared to knowledge of the physical world, knowledge of the social world is often harder to grasp and less reliable (i.e., less immutable or fully predictable in its manifestations). A much smaller percentage of it is anchored in direct experience with physical objects, and a much larger percentage depends on verbal mediation or inferential learning from social observations or experiences. This kind of learning often is ambiguous or otherwise difficult because the meanings of people's social activities usually need to be inferred from the verbal discourse that accompanies them, rather than being transparent from the nature and outcomes of their object manipulations. Most of the discourse to which young children are exposed is informal, in which the language referents and the causal relationships that underlie the meanings of the communications are tacitly understood by the speakers but often not by an observing child (Bernstein, 1962). Finally, many of the concepts used to make sense of the social sphere are fuzzy sets that overlap with related concepts, and many of the principles are rules of thumb that admit to frequent exceptions, not fully reliable rules or algorithms.

A further complication that has assumed increasing importance in recent decades is that much of children's input concerning the social world comes from books, movies, television, and other media, and much of this input is fanciful, distorted, or in other respects likely to complicate their attempts to determine which aspects of the social world are real (vs. false or fictional) and enduring (vs. transitory or accidental). Contemporary children are exposed to a greater variety of verbally and visually mediated input than ever before, but most of it is too incoherent to be retained as anything but disconnected fragments and images, and much of it is fictional content of dubious value. Stereotypes and other distortions abound, for example, in depictions of life in the past and in other cultures. We suspect that the "mile wide but inch deep" characterization used to criticize contemporary U.S. school curricula (Schmidt et al., 2001) is even more applicable to the informal curriculum conveyed in media directed at children.

OUR SERIES OF INTERVIEW STUDIES

As a first step toward developing information about the extent and accuracy of primary-grade students' knowledge about cultural universals, we interviewed one class of students late in the spring of second grade on various aspects of the topic of shelter. Shelter is not only a cultural universal but a basic need, and second graders have had experience with it throughout their lives. Thus, if assertions that children develop clear knowledge about such topics through everyday experience were correct, we would see such knowledge demonstrated by middle-class children approaching the upper end of the primary-grade range. Instead, we found that the students' knowledge about topics relating to shelter was limited and spotty, tacit rather than well articulated, composed of loose collections of observations rather than well-integrated knowledge networks that included awareness of connections and understanding of cause–effect relationships, and often distorted by inaccurate assumptions or outright misconceptions (Brophy & Alleman, 1997).

These findings motivated us to launch a series of studies on developments across Grades K–3 in students' knowledge and thinking about cultural universals. Seven of these studies involved interviewing large samples of students stratified according to grade level (K–3), prior achievement level (high, average, low), and gender (boys, girls). We later added four smaller studies. Two of these probed the thinking of special samples of third graders that we suspected might have unusual perspectives on food (students from farm families) and shelter (students living in the high-rise, high-density neighborhoods of the borough of Manhattan in New York City). The other two studies probed knowledge of two additional topics—money/economics and childhood across time and cultures—in small samples of first and second graders.

Most of the questions on our interviews addressed topics readily identified with the social studies curriculum, but a few spilled over into science, especially when we asked about historical developments (e.g., inventions) or causal mechanisms that explain contemporary practices involved in addressing cultural universals. With regard to shelter, for example, we wondered what children knew or thought about the mechanisms involved in equipping modern homes with comfort/convenience features such as temperature control, running water, and light at the flip of a switch.

Predisciplinary Topical Focus

By organizing our interviews around cultural universals, we featured topics rather than disciplines in identifying knowledge domains. One reason for this was our interest in primary social studies, which typically is organized around cultural universals and designed to establish an initial, predisciplinary knowledge base before shifting to the more discipline-based courses in history, geography, and the social sciences taught in the middle and upper grades.

Also, we were concerned about overemphasis on the disciplines as the bases for identifying knowledge domains. The purposes and activities of the disciplines are different from those of the K–12 school subjects. The disciplines are communities devoted to generating and structuring knowledge in particular domains, typically differentiating into subdomains as they extend the frontiers of knowledge. School subjects, in contrast, are designed to provide children and youth with broad preparation for life in contemporary society. They place more emphasis on synthesizing knowledge and considering its practical applications than on extending or differentiating it. They also place more emphasis on the consumption than the production of knowledge, so that in developing curricula they look not only to knowledge of enduring value (including but not restricted to disciplinary knowledge) but also to the learners (their current interest in and readiness to learn particular content) and society (what knowledge, skills, and values it most wants to see developed in its citizens). From this perspective, restricting oneself to the disciplines in identifying knowledge domains limits one's thinking about the topics that might be raised with children and the kinds of questions that might be posed. Consequently, we preferred a broader purview that subsumed pre- and pandisciplinary knowledge as well as knowledge organized within particular disciplines.

Samples

Most of our interviews were conducted with students who attended the public schools of a middle/working class bedroom suburb of a small city (population about 160,000) in Michigan. The community is average or slightly above average on most socioeconomic and educational indices. During the years when the interviews were conducted, its high school graduation rate was 83% and the percentages of its fourth graders who achieved "satisfactory" scores on the state's achievement tests were 49% for reading and 65% for mathematics. Reflecting the population of the community, most of the students we interviewed were White.

We did not consider race or ethnicity in identifying students to interview. However, we excluded students who had spent most of their preschool years in other countries, because an assumption underlying the work was that what the students knew about the topic (other than what they learned at school) had been learned in the process of growing from infancy in the contemporary United States (particularly through home and neighborhood experiences and exposure to television and other media). Interviewees were selected from among students whose parents gave us permission to do so. They were characterized by their teachers, within gender groups, as being within the upper third, the middle third, or the lower third in general academic achievement.

Plans for our first two large studies (on shelter and clothing) called for interviewing 216 students, 54 in each of Grades K–3, stratified not only by gender and prior achievement level but by the socioeconomic status (SES) level of the community. SES variation was introduced by conducting one third of the interviews in an upper-middle-class suburb, one third in the middle/working-class suburb already described, and one third in lower-middle/working-class neighborhoods of the city. High school graduation rates were 94% in the upper-middle-class suburb, 76% of its fourth graders achieved "satisfactory" scores on the state's mathematics test, and 72% did so on the reading test. Corresponding figures for the city's schools were 76%, 50%, and 37%.

The SES differences observed in these two studies were relatively small and not especially interesting or informative. Students from higher SES backgrounds tended to have more, or more accurate, knowledge than students from lower SES backgrounds, but the same general age trends were observed in each group. We did not find contrasts suggesting the existence of qualitatively different trajectories of knowledge development that were unique to particular SES groups. Consequently, we discontinued further systematic sampling across the SES range, and focused subsequent studies on samples of 96 students drawn from the middle/working-class suburb, because this location was the most representative of the population as a whole (with regard to SES).

Where we suspected that different subpopulations might have different response patterns to some of our interviews, we conducted follow-up studies in specially chosen locations. For example, we followed up the shelter study by interviewing students who lived in Manhattan, a high-rise, high-density residence area that contrasts with the low-rise, low-density communities in which the students interviewed for the initial study resided. Also, because our food interview included several questions on farming and the origins of food, we followed up the initial study with interviews of students from farm families.

Interview Development

The content base for each interview was synthesized from three general sources: (a) social studies teacher education textbooks and other sources (e.g., Project 2061, 2001; Wiegand, 1993) that identified key ideas about the topic that are rooted in the social science disciplines; (b) information about the topic typically included in elementary social studies textbook series or in children's tradebooks; and (c) our own ideas about the key features of elementary social studies units that focus on cultural universals and are designed to teach the material for understanding, appreciation, and life application (Brophy & Alleman, 1996). Our questions first probed the degree to which students understood the topic as a cultural universal, then addressed some of its historical, geographic, economic, and decision-making aspects, with particular attention to the human goals and motives and the cause-and-effect relationships underlying topic-related practices.

The interviews never included all aspects of the topic that we considered to be important and worth teaching in the primary grades because we knew from others' research or our own pilot work that the vast majority of K–3 students would be unable to say much if anything about aspects with which they had little or no prior experience (e.g., forms of government or transportation found in other parts of the world but not in the United States; details of the steps involved in constructing a house and the work performed by people whose jobs are associated with the housing industry). Thus, the content of our interviews was limited by the students' ability to provide substantive responses to our questions, and the levels of sophistication and detail built into our systems for coding their responses were limited by the range of content included in those responses.

The "funnel" interview technique was used, in which initial broad questions encouraged students to make extended statements about a topic, attending to whatever aspects they selected for focus on their own initiative, and explaining themselves in their own words. Probing then began with follow-up questions asking (if necessary) for clarification or elaboration of these initial statements. Finally, more specific questions were asked (if necessary) to call students' attention to aspects of the topic that they did not address spontaneously. This approach maximized the degree to which students' responses reflected their own unique stances toward and construction of knowledge about the topic, but also ensured that all students addressed certain key aspects.

Successive drafts of each interview were piloted with students who were not involved in the later study. This pilot work led to revisions designed to make sure that all questions were clear, to specify probing and follow-up questions more completely, and to eliminate questions that were too easy or difficult to be useful.

Collection and Preparation of Data

Students were interviewed individually. The interviews typically lasted 20 to 30 minutes and were conducted in small offices or empty classrooms at their schools. To facilitate rapport and make sure that responses were preserved verbatim, the interviews were tape-recorded, using a microphone that could be placed unobtrusively on the table and did not require either the interviewer or the student to handle it or speak directly into it. Interviewers were instructed to establish a good rapport with the student before beginning and then to conduct the interview in a relaxed and conversational style rather than a more formal or testlike style.

Coding the Transcripts

The tape-recorded interviews were transcribed by one person and then corrected by another. Data for statistical analyses were then developed by coding the corrected transcripts. We did not attempt to force students' responses into predetermined coding categories. Instead, we allowed the categories to arise from the data, using what have been called analytic induction methods for developing grounded theory (Bogdan & Biklen, 1982; Glaser & Strauss, 1979; Patton, 1990).

Coding schemes were developed by reading responses to each question and identifying common ideas that represented alternative ways to respond to the question. Responses then were coded for the presence or absence of these common ideas. Multiple codes were assigned if the student mentioned more than one such idea. In addition, each coding scheme contained an "other" category for flagging rare or unique responses.

Coding categories were considered reliable if independent coders achieved at least 60% exact agreement. If this did not occur initially, the categories were revised or the instructions were elaborated until satisfactory agreement was reached. Eventually, all transcripts were coded twice and all discrepancies were resolved. Across studies, exact agreement ranged from 60% to 100% for individual categories, averaging 80%.

Once the coding was completed, the codes were converted into scores that became the bases for statistical analyses. In most cases the categories were used as is. However, categories that were only coded rarely were either omitted from statistical analyses or combined to create new scores (where the combination scores would be meaningful). If the "other" category included an idea mentioned frequently enough to be worth analyzing in its own right, codes representing this idea were removed from the "other" category and placed into a newly created specific category.

Data Analysis and Reporting

Scores derived from the codes were subjected to statistical analyses. These began with frequency distributions reflecting the degree to which common ideas were expressed across the sample as a whole and within its stratified grade level, SES level, achievement level, and gender subgroups. These data then were subjected to chi-square analyses to identify coding categories for which variation across subgroups was large enough to reach statistical significance. We also performed correlational analyses across the coding categories to identify response clusters reflecting themes that reappeared in the responses of certain students to certain questions. Detailed technical reports that present all of these quantitative data along with complete lists of rare and unique responses are available from the Educational Resource Information Center (ERIC).

Across interviews, the statistical analyses typically indicated that (a) the response patterns to most questions featured statistically significant and often quite dramatic grade-level progressions showing increases in amount and accuracy of knowledge across the K–3 range; (b) the SES, achievement, and (especially) gender differences were much smaller and less likely to reach statistical significance; (c) although not always completely linear, those trends that were statistically significant almost always showed, as expected, that students who were higher in SES or achievement level had more, or more accurate, knowledge than students who were lower in SES or achievement level; and (d) significant gender differences were infrequent, but when they did appear, they were somewhat likely to confirm and highly unlikely to contradict expectations based on what is known about differences in American children's gender roles and related socialization.

SOME GENERAL FINDINGS

Many of the findings reflect generic characteristics of children's thinking. These generic characteristics resemble Piagetian operations in some respects but seem better described as implicit assumptions about the human condition (e.g., things are getting better all the time due to inventions and other scientific advances) and predispositions toward particular approaches to thinking and reasoning (e.g., teleological explanations rooted in assumptions that everything that exists has been designed to fulfill some function).

Within this context, the interviews generated interesting similarities and contrasts both with earlier Piagetian work and with more recent studies of children's domain-specific knowledge. For example, children develop considerable knowledge about food (foods vs. nonfoods, types and groupings of foods, healthy vs. junk foods, cooking and preserving foods). Although this knowledge subsumes considerable vocabulary and can be conveyed verbally, it also shares many characteristics associated with sensorimotor and pre-operational knowledge as described by Piaget: Much of it is learned through personal experience or direct observation of significant others (e.g., their food-related behavior), and it is focused on what one does with the objects in question (e.g., defining food as what we eat and talking about culturally prescribed norms governing when and how it is consumed), rather than on its fundamental nature (as our source of energy) or on causal mechanisms that explain its place in the human condition (including developments across time and variations across culture and location).

Children have accessible schemas for recognizing and using objects (e.g., food items) in relevant situations, but these schemas are not yet integrated within well-connected knowledge networks structured around big ideas. Parallel examples appeared in responses to our clothing interview, in which the children showed good knowledge of different kinds of clothing worn in different contexts (business, work, play), but little knowledge of the fundamental nature of clothing (they tended to think of it as a solid akin to plastic or leather, not knowing that cloth is woven from threads that in turn are spun from raw material).

Although our interviews were organized topically around cultural universals, many of the questions and related responses can be considered with reference to relevant disciplines, such as biology, geography, or anthropology. Most biological questions pose greater challenges to children than the questions about the physical world that have been used to study developments in logical and mathematical operations. This is because the phenomena involved are stretched over longer timelines (so there are fewer opportunities to observe immediate results of manipulations or events), many of the events are unobservable or only partially observable (e.g., what happens inside bodies when food is ingested or what happens inside foods to cause spoilage over time), and the most sophisticated explanatory concepts and principles appeal to tiny material entities (e.g., germs) or theoretical abstractions (e.g., energy).

Lacking articulated knowledge to bring to bear on such questions, children extrapolate from their experience, usually reasoning by analogy. Carey (1985) showed that children often extrapolate from what they know about people, offering theories built around human intentions as explanations for biological phenomena. That is, children begin thinking like psychologists before they begin thinking like biologists. Our data indicate that young children also are not yet well developed as geographers or historians, and to the extent that they are social scientists, they are primarily psychologists rather than anthropologists, sociologists, economists, or political scientists. Their knowledge tends to be organized as narratives of the goal-oriented actions of individuals, not analyses structured around scientific concepts and principles.

The children showed little knowledge of reasons for developments through time or variations across locations and cultures. Across our interviews, they showed little awareness of the degree to which humans have reshaped landforms, imported flora and fauna, created built-environment infrastructures, and developed transportation and delivery systems that support life in contemporary first-world societies.

Au and Romo (1999) noted that children's explanations typically fall short of scientific explanations because they describe input and output states but do not include causal mechanisms explaining how the former became transformed into the latter. We frequently encountered such explanations in our interviews, referring to them as "black box" explanations. Berti and Bombi (1989) and Lee and Ashby (2001) reported similar responses in interviews about social and historical phenomena.

To explain cultural differences (in food, clothing, shelter, etc.), the students we interviewed generated explanations at several levels of sophistication. Those least prepared to answer the questions were unable to offer any explanation (i.e., they would say, "I don't know"). Among the explanations offered, the least sophisticated were appeals to a "Different people want/do different things" principle (e.g., American and Chinese people eat different foods because they are different people). Slightly more sophisticated versions of this idea made reference to culture or religion (e.g., people eat different foods because they come from different cultures or practice different religions). More sophisticated as an explanation, although naive with regard to modern communication and transportation systems, was the idea that certain people do not do something (eat particular foods, wear certain kinds of clothes, etc.) because they have no knowledge of these things—they weren't invented within their cultures and they lack awareness of what is going on in other parts of the world.

The most sophisticated explanations appealed to differences in economic/technical development or geography. Economic/technical development explanations were rooted in the idea that certain people lack access to certain foods, clothing, and so forth because their societies or the parts of the world that they live in have not yet developed the machines or other technology needed to produce the products or the economies necessary to afford them (K–3 students typically do not articulate such explanations at this level of sophistication—they talk about the people being poor, lacking machines or factories to manufacture the products, or lacking stores in which they can be purchased). Geographical explanations appealed to the basic idea that the local geography does not provide needed raw materials or support the raising of needed crops or animals.

A parallel range of explanations was seen in children's historical thinking, especially when they tried to explain developments over time. Again, the students least prepared to address such questions (e.g., "Why didn't people eat pizza back in 1920?") were simply unable to respond to them. Among those who did offer explanations, some of the least sophisticated endorsed extreme forms of presentism (e.g., "The people were not as smart as we are today," or "They didn't have scientists then," etc.). Somewhat more sophisticated explanations did not assume quantum leaps in intelligence or other fundamental changes in human nature, but recognized that people living at a given point in the past were limited by the technological developments available at the time, either in the world in general or in their specific locales. Some of these were relatively primitive black box explanations (e.g., "They didn't eat pizza because there were no food stores/pizzerias then," or even "They didn't have stores then because they didn't have the bricks, construction equipment, etc., needed to build them"). Another intermediate class of explanations was rooted in the idea that the people couldn't make a particular food because they lacked one or more key ingredients. Some of these explanations were based on mistaken assumptions about when certain plant and animal species evolved (e.g., "They didn't have milk because there were no cows then").

More sophisticated versions recognized that the major categories of plants and animals existed long before recorded human history, but appealed to the idea that their geographic distributions were uneven (e.g., "Bananas didn't grow in their part of the world"). Still more sophisticated historical explanations incorporated the idea that tools, machines, or other technology needed to process the raw materials and manufacture the product in question had not yet been developed. Perhaps the most sophisticated explanations were those rooted in the idea that the basic concept (or in the case of foods, the recipe) for the product had not yet been conceived.

We also frequently observed teleological explanations akin to those reported by Keil (1992) and Keleman (1999). Often these were rooted in assumptions such as that things must necessarily be as they are, everything that exists has been designed to fulfill some function, or this is a just world where everything happens for a reason. Examples included the observation that if foods were not good for you, they wouldn't have been invented, and the idea that Chinese people eat clumped rice because it is convenient to pick up with chopsticks. The latter idea also illustrates a form of reversed logic that we frequently encountered, in which children confused causes and effects. Examples included stating (a) that a substance is food because you can eat it with a fork or spoon; (b) that you have to pay at a restaurant because there is a cash register there, but you don't have to pay at home because there is no cash register; (c) that a local restaurant raised its prices because it was getting too crowded; or (d) that the existence of stoves proves that some foods need to be cooked. Sometimes different students used different aspects of the same basic idea to explain different phenomena (e.g., that people in the past didn't have access to certain foods because there were no stores at which to buy them; farmers in the past grew just enough for their families because there were no stores to sell surpluses to).

Expressions of presentism and especially chauvinism appeared frequently in the children's responses. They are not surprising, given the general tendency for people of all ages to develop preferences for the familiar through repeated exposure (Zajonc, 2001). They are worrisome, however, because they impede development of the kinds of empathic understandings of other people that are desirable from both a disciplinary and a civic education perspective. A major implication for curriculum and instruction is to make sure that what is taught about people in the past or in other cultures is presented in ways that encourage students to empathize with the people being studied and thus appreciate their activities as intelligent adaptations to time and place (rather than as stupid, weird, etc.). These and other teaching implications will be addressed in detail in chapter 11, this volume.

OVERVIEW OF THE BOOK

Rather than duplicate the level of detail of the technical reports, we have focused this book on the data likely to be of most interest and use to most readers: trends observed in the sample as a whole and trajectories observed across Grades K–3 in students' knowledge and thinking about the topics addressed, discussed with reference to their implications for curriculum and instruction in the primary grades. Chapters 2 through 8, respectively, present this information for each of the seven cultural universals addressed in our large interview studies. Chapter 9 summarizes findings from the two smaller studies of first and second graders' thinking about childhood and money. Chapter 10 looks across the interviews to summarize noteworthy SES, achievement level, and gender differences. Chapter 11 then concludes the volume with discussion of the teaching implications of several generic aspects of the students' thinking.

2

Food

Our interview about food asked students:

- to define the nature of food and distinguish food from nonfood;
- to explain why people need food;
- to discuss food groups, and explain why some foods are healthful and some are junk foods;
- to compare foods eaten in the United States with foods typically eaten in other parts of the world and explain the reasons for the contrasts in diets;
- to explain why some foods are cooked and others are refrigerated;
- to explain why foods last longer in cans and bottles;
- to describe the land-to-hand progressions involved in bringing several common foods to our tables;
- to identify products derived from common farm animals;
- to explain why a pound of cereal costs more than a pound of apples and a restaurant meal costs more than the same meal eaten at home;
- to describe the steps involved in growing corn;
- to explain why there are few farms in Alaska;
- to identify inventions that have modernized farming, and explain why many fewer farmers per capita are needed today than in the past.

For details of the findings, see the technical report (Brophy, Alleman, & O'Mahony, 2001).

CHILDREN'S KNOWLEDGE
AND THINKING ABOUT FOOD

Children learn very early to distinguish food from nonfood items, and they learn "cuisine rules" about what foods are eaten in what combinations at what times of day (Birch, Fisher, & Grimm-Thomas, 1999; Rozin, 1990). They link eating with consequences that include growth, health, strength, and energy, but their knowledge tends to be vague and spotty. They know that food is important because it is needed to keep us alive but they cannot explain how it does so, such as by referring to its role in metabolism (Driver, Squires, Rushworth, & Wood-Robinson, 1994).

By the time they start school, children usually have general knowledge about nutritious (good for you) versus junk (not good for you) foods, although they usually cannot explain the reasons for the difference (Coulson, 1990; Driver et al., 1994). Studies of children's ideas about food groupings have produced varying results concerning general levels of knowledge to be expected at different ages. However, all of these studies indicate that older students, especially those from higher SES backgrounds, tend to identify categorical groupings like those in food pyramids used in nutrition education, whereas younger students, especially those from lower SES backgrounds, are more likely to suggest context-specific groupings (i.e., placing together foods that are commonly eaten together, such as meat and potatoes; Hart, Bishop, & Truby, 2002; Michela & Contento, 1984; Turner, 1997).

When asked about what happens to food in the body, children typically depict the food traveling from the mouth through a gullet to the stomach, and from there all around the body. Those below age 5 tend to think that the food stays in the body, those ages 6 through 8 tend to think that it comes out after being transformed into waste material, and older children tend to speak of food as composed of a good part that stays in the body and a bad part that is eliminated. The children talk about food getting smaller, becoming liquefied, or turned into blood or waste material, but not undergoing chemical transformations that change its basic composition (Contento, 1981; Ramadas & Nair, 1996; Teixeira, 2000). Most do not understand that food is processed by the human digestive system to extract needed nutrients.

Studies of children's thinking about food have focused on their knowledge of its biological aspects, rather than food production, geographical or cultural influences on diets, or other societal aspects of the topic. Mugge (1963) found that urban second graders were able to report only limited and imprecise information about farming, even though they had studied the farm in first grade. She attributed this to the children's lack of direct experience with farms. Barrett and Short (1992) studied English schoolchildren's images of people from other European countries. They found that the younger children (ages 5 to 7) had limited factual knowledge about these countries but nevertheless did have some idea of their diets. For example, they associated the French with snails, garlic, and French bread and the Italians with pasta, seafood, and pizza.

Berti and Bombi (1989) reported that when young children first become aware of farmers as holding a distinct economic role, they attribute no production function to them. That is, they believe that plants grow by themselves and the farmers' only tasks are to watch over them and every so often harvest the fruit and vegetables to eat or take to market.

OUR FOOD INTERVIEWS

Food interviews were conducted with 96 students, 24 in each of Grades K–3, stratified within each grade by prior achievement level and gender. Descriptive statistics and information from analyses of scores derived from the coding are given in Table 2.1. The Mantel–Haenszel chi-square test was used to assess the statistical significance of grade-level trends in the frequency of use of a response category. Significant Mantel–Haenszel chi-squares do not imply that the difference between each successive grade level is statistically significant, or even necessarily consistent with the overall trend. However, they do indicate that a rising or dropping trend was detected across Grades K–3. When significant chi-squares were obtained, the corresponding sets of grade-level scores have been underlined in the table. In addition, phi coefficients (similar to correlation coefficients) have been included to indicate the direction and strength of the significant relationships observed between grade level (K–3) and certain categories of student responses.

The first question assessed students' understanding that food is a universal human need. Following the question are examples representative of responses elicited from average achievers in Grades K–3. They are quoted verbatim but edited to eliminate extraneous material (mostly final probes that failed to elicit further response).

WHY PEOPLE NEED FOOD

1. People all over the world eat food. Is that just because they like to or do they need food? Why? What does food do for us?

K   They need food to live. (What does it do for us?) It makes us strong.

1st   They need food. (Why do they need food?) To keep them alive.

2nd   They need food. (Why do they need food?) So they can get protein that helps them and so they can stay alive [One of many responses that included scientific terminology but not scientific explanation].

3rd   They need food to help them grow.

Over 90% of the students understood that food is a universal need. Over 70% (68) said that we need food to keep us alive. Other common responses were that we need food to be healthy (27), to grow (16), for the energy or fuel that it provides (13), or because it gives us strength or helps our bones, muscles, or other

Number of Students	Total	K	1	2	3	Phi
	96	24	24	24	24	
1. Why do people need food? What does food do for us?						
0. Doesn't know/no relevant response	6	5	1	1	0	–36
1. Food provides energy or fuel	13	0	2	6	5	˙ 29
2. To avoid starvation, death; to stay alive	68	10	20	19	19	37
3. To grow (no further explanation)	16	5	2	3	6	
4. To be healthy (no further explanation)	27	3	8	10	6	
5. Food provides strength or assists body functioning (helps grow bone or muscle)	10	3	1	1	5	
2A. What is food?						
0. Doesn't know/no relevant response	18	9	6	3	0	–36
1. Lists food items without defining food	21	5	4	4	8	
2. Food is something that people eat	54	8	12	18	16	32
3. Other (response not codable in other categories)	16	1	2	3	10	40
4. Food is good for you, makes you healthy, contains things good for the body, and so on.	12	3	2	5	2	
2B. How is food different from things that are not food?						
0. Doesn't know/no relevant response	31	13	8	7	3	–32
1. Lists nonessential food characteristics (looks like food, doesn't walk, not hard, has seeds, etc.)	16	3	1	4	8	29
2. Food is healthy, good for you (no further explanation)	10	2	4	3	1	
3. Food has taste/tastes different from nonfood	14	3	0	5	6	27
4. Food is eaten, nonfood items are not eaten	25	2	11	4	8	
5. Food provides health benefits, contains vitamins and minerals, and so on	11	0	2	3	6	28
6. Lists food and nonfood examples (candy, bugs, flowers, rocks, etc.)	21	3	4	6	8	19
7. At some point in responding to the first two questions, the student describes food as a source of energy for the body	14	1	2	5	6	24
3. What are some of the food groups?						
0. Cannot list any food groups	34	17	9	2	6	–48
1. Lists food items (cheese, apples, pears) or unconventional food groups (purple, green, etc.; breakfast/lunch/dinner; meat/deli/fruit)	20	5	3	7	5	
2. Lists one, two, or three conventional food groups	29	3	12	8	6	
3. Lists four or more conventional food groups	25	0	3	12	10	47

(Continued)

TABLE 2.1
(Continued)

Number of Students	Total	K	1	2	3	Phi
	96	24	24	24	24	
4A. Certain foods are healthful and nutritious. What foods are especially good for you?						
1. Lists one or more foods that are not nutritious	6	0	3	2	1	
2. Lists specific nutritious foods other than fruits and vegetables	37	11	11	8	7	
3. Lists specific fruits or vegetables	66	17	18	17	14	
4. Lists categories of food or food groups	45	5	14	14	12	31
4B. Why are these foods good for you?						
0. Doesn't know/no relevant response	17	10	5	1	1	−40
1. They keep you healthy	24	3	8	7	6	
2. They make you strong	6	0	2	3	1	
3. They help you grow/make you big	11	4	3	2	2	
4. They help specific parts of the body: heart, teeth, bones, and so on	11	2	2	3	4	
5. They give you energy	8	0	1	3	4	24
6. They do not have fats or sugars	8	1	1	2	4	19
7. They contain healthy stuff/nutrition	21	5	4	7	5	
8. They contain vitamins, minerals, proteins, fiber, and so on	18	1	2	7	8	33
5A. Other foods are not very healthful or nutritious. What are some of these junk foods?						
1. Candy, gum, chocolate, potato chips (snack foods)	79	11	22	23	23	55
2. Pop/soda	9	0	3	3	3	
3. Ice cream/milk shakes	19	6	4	5	4	
4. Heavy fried or fatty foods (burgers, bacon, pizza, French fries)	7	0	2	2	3	
5. Baked dessert foods (cakes, cookies, brownies, donuts)	25	7	3	5	10	
6. Sugar/honey	9	1	4	2	2	
7. Other (bones, alcohol, seaweed, peanut butter and jelly, fish, butter, caffeine)	9	3	2	1	3	
5B. Why aren't these foods good for you?						
0. Doesn't know/no relevant response	16	7	7	2	0	−35
1. They don't keep you healthy/make you strong	12	2	3	1	6	
2. Bad for your teeth, give you cavities, rot your teeth	21	5	5	5	6	
3. Have a lot of sugar	36	6	4	12	14	36
4. Have a lot of fat	15	2	1	3	9	36
5. Make you hyperactive	6	0	0	1	5	36
6. Make you sick or could make you die	16	4	3	5	4	
7. Lack "healthy stuff" in them (vitamins, protein, nutrients, etc.)	17	2	5	6	4	

(Continued)

TABLE 2.1
(*Continued*)

	Total	K	1	2	3	
Number of Students	96	24	24	24	24	Phi

6. Do we have foods today that they didn't have in 1920? Why didn't they have those things back then?

	Total	K	1	2	3	Phi
0. Doesn't know/no relevant response	15	7	5	1	2	–27
1. No—there are no foods now that they didn't have in 1920	14	6	3	2	3	
2. Says "yes" but cannot explain or give examples	14	5	4	4	1	
3. Incorrectly lists foods that were available in 1920	47	5	12	15	15	34
4. Correctly lists foods that were not available in 1920 (fast food, pizza, junk foods, candies, etc.)	19	1	2	8	8	34
5. The foods existed but were not available locally (chocolate)	6	0	1	2	3	19
6. The foods were unavailable because they hadn't been invented yet	12	1	1	4	6	27
7. The foods were unavailable because people didn't know how to make them or lacked the technological capabilities to do so	17	0	5	6	6	27

7. Back then did they eat some foods that we don't eat today?

	Total	K	1	2	3	Phi
1. No—they ate the same foods that we eat	18	8	2	3	5	
2. Says "yes" but cannot give examples	36	4	12	11	9	
3. Incorrectly lists foods still eaten today	12	2	6	3	1	
4. Mentions a food not typically eaten today, although still available (buffalo, squash/gourds, brains, molasses)	16	1	1	6	8	35

8. Are there some countries where people eat different foods than we eat? What do they eat? What do we eat that they don't eat?

	Total	K	1	2	3	Phi
0. Doesn't know/no relevant response	13	6	5	2	0	–29
1. No—everyone else eats the same foods	6	2	1	3	0	
2. Says "yes" or lists countries but gives no examples	36	10	8	10	8	
3. Lists American foods that people in other countries presumably do not eat (common meats and sandwiches, junk food, fruit, vegetables, cereals, etc.)	22	4	5	5	8	
4. (For those coded 3) Mentions one or more typical American food that actually is not eaten in many places (peanut butter, packaged cereals, hot dogs)	12	1	2	2	7	30
5. They eat exotic or questionable foods (cheetahs, tigers, spiders, slugs, snow)	7	1	4	1	1	
6. They eat generic ethnic foods (Chinese, Italian food)	9	1	3	1	4	
7. Lists specific foods conventionally associated with other countries (hot peppers, egg rolls, pizza, Chinese chicken dishes, fortune cookies, French bread)	27	2	5	7	13	37

(*Continued*)

TABLE 2.1
(Continued)

	Total	K	1	2	3	
Number of Students	96	24	24	24	24	Phi

9. Do the Japanese people eat different foods than we do? What do the Japanese people eat? What do we eat that the Japanese people don't eat?

	Total	K	1	2	3	Phi
0. Doesn't know/no relevant response	10	3	2	4	1	
1. No—we eat the same foods	6	3	2	1	0	−19
2. Says "yes" but cannot explain or give examples	15	7	5	1	2	−27
3. Americans eat candy and other processed junk foods	15	1	3	6	5	22
4. Americans eat fruits and vegetables or Japanese people do not	32	6	9	9	8	
5. Americans eat family meal food (macaroni and cheese, steak and mashed potatoes, chicken, barbecue, pizza, ravioli)	33	6	8	7	12	20
6. Lists conventional Japanese foods (noodles, rice, fish, sushi, tofu)	22	3	2	5	12	39
7. (If coded 3, 4, or 5): Lists one or more American foods that Japanese people ordinarily would not eat	40	7	10	9	14	22

10. American people eat a lot of beef but Chinese people eat a lot of chicken. Why is that?

	Total	K	1	2	3	Phi
0. Doesn't know/no relevant response	28	12	6	4	6	−28
1. Simply because they are different people	14	5	5	1	3	
2. Chinese people like chicken but Americans like beef	35	6	10	10	9	
3. Chinese people have more access to chicken or raise more chickens; Americans raise more beef/cattle	29	3	5	11	10	30
4. Chinese people do not know anything about beef or do not know how to cook it	6	0	2	2	2	

11. American people eat a lot of bread but Chinese people eat a lot of rice. Why is that?

	Total	K	1	2	3	Phi
0. Doesn't know/no relevant response	31	11	9	6	5	−21
1. Simply because they are different people	14	5	4	2	3	
2. Chinese people like rice; Americans like bread	31	7	7	8	9	
3. Chinese people have greater access to rice, grow more rice; Americans more wheat/bread	33	3	6	8	16	42

12. We eat some vegetables raw, but we cook meats and many vegetables before we eat them. Why do we cook these foods?

	Total	K	1	2	3	Phi
0. Doesn't know/no relevant response/"for health" (unexplained)	9	7	0	1	1	−40
1. To soften the foods; so they will be easier to eat, won't break your teeth	24	3	7	9	5	
2. So eating the foods will not make you sick; to kill germs or bacteria	26	3	7	7	9	20
3. So they will taste better	55	11	12	13	19	26
4. So they will be warm or hot when we eat them	39	6	11	13	9	

(Continued)

TABLE 2.1
(Continued)

	Total	K	1	2	3	
Number of Students	96	24	24	24	24	Phi

13. We eat many vegetables and most fruits raw. Why don't we cook these foods?

	Total	K	1	2	3	Phi
0. Doesn't know/no relevant response	13	7	4	2	0	−32
1. "Other" responses not coded in the following categories	8	1	1	2	4	19
2. People don't want to cook them; don't like them cooked; like to eat them raw	9	1	3	3	2	
3. These foods are not supposed to be cooked	20	3	7	5	5	
4. These foods don't need to be cooked	24	6	4	8	6	
5. These foods taste good already; cooking will make them taste bad	29	4	4	11	10	30
6. The current state of these foods is OK; they are already good	18	5	1	3	9	
7. Cooking these foods will change them in an undesirable way (gross, yucky, too hot, burned, melted, not fresh)	21	3	6	7	5	
8. Eating these foods cooked can make people sick	6	1	2	1	2	

14. We put many foods in the refrigerator to keep them cold. Why do we do that?

	Total	K	1	2	3	Phi
0. Doesn't know/no relevant response	9	5	2	2	0	−26
1. Some foods need to stay cold (unexplained further— no codes in 2–6)	11	5	4	0	2	−25
2. To save the foods for later; keep leftovers	11	2	4	3	2	
3. To keep the foods tasting good	19	5	2	7	5	
4. To keep the foods from melting	17	3	4	4	6	
5. To keep the foods fresh; keep them from getting stale/rotten/yucky	52	5	12	18	17	43
6. To keep them from making people sick	17	0	3	5	9	36

15. Before electricity was discovered, people didn't have refrigerators. Where did they keep their foods then?

	Total	K	1	2	3	Phi
0. Doesn't know/no relevant response	26	9	11	4	2	−34
1. In storage places or cold places (no further explanation)	10	1	4	3	2	
2. In cupboards or a pantry	19	8	3	5	3	
3. In cold water	9	4	2	3	0	−21
4. On ice or in ice boxes	27	1	3	7	16	53
5. Outside	18	1	4	6	7	25
6. Other (underground, cooked the food or ate it quickly, protected it from bugs, covered or wrapped it)	16	1	1	9	5	37

16. Some foods keep for a long time in bottles or cans without spoiling. Why is that?

	Total	K	1	2	3	Phi
0. Doesn't know/no relevant response	56	22	18	12	4	−57
1. Bottles and cans are cold or retain cold	7	1	2	0	4	

(Continued)

TABLE 2.1
(Continued)

Number of Students	Total	K	1	2	3	Phi
	96	24	24	24	24	
2. Bottles and cans are closed (no further explanation)	10	1	2	2	5	21
3. Bottles and cans are closed so that no air/nothing can get to the food	14	0	1	7	6	36
17. How is applesauce made?						
0. Doesn't know/no relevant response	8	6	2	0	0	−37
1. You need apples (no further explanation)	6	3	0	3	0	
2. Crush, mush, stir apples	67	11	15	20	21	37
3. Cut up apples	16	3	7	2	4	
4. Remove peel, core, seeds	22	3	5	7	7	
5. Cook apples	21	2	7	4	8	24
6. Add other ingredients (sugar, water, cinnamon, sauce, butter)	21	3	7	6	5	
7. Use an appliance (mixer, blender, machine in factory to crush apples)	19	2	3	6	8	25
8. Store the applesauce in a container or refrigerator	20	4	4	7	5	
18. How is cheese made?						
0. Doesn't know/no relevant response	46	18	13	9	6	−38
1. It's made from milk	40	4	9	11	16	36
2. Adds something acceptable to the idea that it's made from milk (the milk has to be stirred or mixed, the material needs to be pressed into the shape of cheese, etc.)	10	2	2	4	2	
19. How is bread made?						
0. Doesn't know/no relevant response	30	13	9	5	3	−35
1. Made from dough	16	5	4	3	4	
2. Made from grain (wheat, corn, etc.)	41	3	8	14	16	43
3. Grind the wheat	12	0	3	5	4	24
4. Mix flour, milk, and other common bread ingredients	28	1	6	9	12	37
5. Bake	28	3	7	8	10	23
6. Use a bread maker or other machine	9	1	1	3	4	19
7. Gives a good explanation that includes making and then baking dough	21	1	4	6	10	33
20A. Where does the meat in a hamburger come from?						
0. Doesn't know/no relevant response	39	19	11	7	2	−53
1. Animals other than cows	18	1	6	6	5	
2. Cows	39	4	7	11	17	41

(Continued)

TABLE 2.1
(Continued)

	Total	K	1	2	3	
Number of Students	96	24	24	24	24	Phi
20B. What is the process of making the hamburger patty?						
0. Doesn't know/no relevant response	36	17	10	9	0	−52
1. Kill the animal	34	1	7	10	16	47
2. Cut up the animal or take the meat off of it	34	3	6	10	15	39
3. Fry, grill, cook the meat	26	7	6	10	3	
4. Shape the meat into patties	10	0	2	0	8	45
21. Why do some farmers raise chickens?						
0. Doesn't know/no relevant response	7	4	2	1	0	−24
1. To eat them or get chicken meat	62	15	14	16	17	
2. For the eggs	50	7	14	14	15	27
3. To get baby chickens	9	1	4	1	3	
4. To sell them to stores	13	0	1	4	8	38
22. Some farmers raise cows. What do we get from cows?						
1. Milk	87	22	22	24	19	
2. Other dairy products (butter, cheese, ice cream, etc.)	12	0	1	6	5	32
3. Meat (hamburger, steak, beef, etc.)	49	8	9	13	19	36
23. Some farmers raise pigs. What do we get from pigs?						
0. Doesn't know/no relevant response	20	8	4	6	2	−23
1. Mud	6	4	2	0	0	−29
2. Meat	37	10	9	8	10	
3. Bacon	21	2	4	5	10	30
4. Ham	27	2	6	10	9	29
5. Pork, pork chops	13	0	3	2	8	36
6. Sausages, hot dogs	9	2	0	3	4	
7. Mentions specific pork product (coded in 3, 4, 5, or 6)	51	5	12	14	20	45
24. Some farmers raise sheep. What do we get from sheep?						
0. Doesn't know/no relevant response	26	14	7	3	2	−44
1. Meat	23	1	5	7	10	32
2. Fur, fuzz, fluff, hair	8	2	3	2	1	
3. Wool	22	3	6	5	8	
4. Clothing, mittens, blankets, wool fabric	39	5	9	13	12	26
25. A pound of cereal costs more than a pound of apples. Why is that?						
0. Doesn't know/no relevant response	38	16	11	6	5	−37
1. You get more cereal; bigger box, lasts longer	43	8	10	14	11	
2. Cereal is better for you than apples	7	0	0	2	5	33

(Continued)

TABLE 2.1
(Continued)

	Total	K	1	2	3	
Number of Students	96	24	24	24	24	Phi
3. Cereal has additional or more expensive stuff in it: sugar, marshmallows, honey, food coloring, toys in the box, the box itself	15	2	5	4	4	
4. Cereal needs to be manufactured but apples can be picked	8	0	0	3	5	32
26. It costs more to eat a meal in a restaurant than it does to have the same meal at home. Why is that?						
0. Doesn't know/no relevant response	31	19	8	3	1	−62
1. You have to pay for food at a restaurant, but at home it's free (used only if 4 or 5 are not coded)	22	2	11	5	4	
2. Restaurants offer better food or greater selection of food	12	3	2	3	4	
3. Restaurants are special, fancy places to eat out	7	0	0	1	6	40
4. You pay people for cooking and serving the food	34	1	3	13	17	58
5. The people at the restaurant have already bought the food and you have to reimburse that	8	1	0	2	5	28
27. What are the steps that farmers go through to grow corn?						
0. Doesn't know/no relevant response	7	4	2	1	0	−24
1. Plant the seeds	85	17	22	23	23	33
2. Weed, rake, hoe the soil	11	2	2	3	4	
3. Water the plants	63	15	18	16	14	
4. Wait for the plants to grow enough	72	13	17	20	22	33
5. Pick, cut, or harvest the corn	65	12	14	18	21	31
6. Shuck or clean the corn	18	6	4	3	5	
7. Make sure the corn gets enough sunshine	12	2	2	5	3	
8. Fertilize the corn or spray pesticides	7	1	0	2	4	24
9. After harvest, clear the field/plow for next planting	9	0	0	4	5	33
28. There are lots of farmers around here but there are not so many farmers in Alaska. Why not?						
0. Doesn't know/no relevant response	39	19	12	7	1	−56
1. Not as many people live in Alaska	10	3	5	1	1	
2. It is too cold/snowy in Alaska (unexplained further)	18	1	2	7	8	33
3. It is too cold/snowy to grow crops in Alaska	26	1	4	7	14	45
4. It is too cold for animals to survive in Alaska	7	0	1	1	5	31
5. There is not enough sunlight in Alaska	7	0	0	2	5	33
29. How is farming today different from farming 100 years ago?						
0. Doesn't know/no relevant response	45	22	13	6	4	−59
1. They didn't have the range or quality of animals/plants/seeds we have now	7	0	3	2	2	
2. We have better tools (nonmechanized hand tools)	8	0	1	5	2	28

(Continued)

TABLE 2.1
(Continued)

	Total	K	1	2	3	
Number of Students	96	24	24	24	24	Phi
3. We have machines (tractors and other large machines)	29	0	4	11	14	50
4. Farming is easier now/harder then (not explained or explained without referral to machines)	7	0	3	3	1	
30. What are some inventions that have helped farmers?						
0. Don't know/no relevant response	29	20	4	3	2	-67
1. Horses, cows, or other animals	7	1	2	2	2	
2. Hand tools (pitchforks, rakes, shovels, hoes, etc.)	17	2	7	3	5	
3. Generic machines or motors	15	1	4	6	4	
4 Tractors	37	0	10	14	13	47
5. Farm machines besides tractors (tillers, combines, etc.)	27	0	5	11	11	43
31. Long ago, most people had to be farmers in order to produce enough food to feed everyone. But today, only a few farmers produce all the food we need. Why is that?						
0. Doesn't know/no relevant response	60	24	20	12	4	-66
1. Farmers have more knowledge now	7	0	2	2	3	
2. Farms are bigger now/have more land/have more animals	17	0	3	5	9	36
3. Farmers have better equipment now (tractors, etc.)	22	0	0	7	15	61
4. Machines allow a person to get more done in the same time	14	0	0	7	7	41

Note.   Numbers in the frequencies columns show how many students in each group were coded for mentioning the ideas represented by the response category described on the left side of the table. Underlining indicates that the chi-square for the underlined distribution was statistically significant at or below the .05 level. In these instances the phi coefficients (with decimal points omitted) are given in the phi column as indicators of the magnitudes of linear trends.

body parts or functions (10). These trends are similar to those reported for British children by Turner (1997).

THE NATURE OF FOOD

2. What is food? How is food different from things that are not food?

K   Stuff you eat. (How is food different from other things that are not food?) I don't know.

1st   It's healthy. (How is food different from other things that are not food?) Well, you can eat food, and you can't eat like a chunk off of stuff. You can eat apples and you can't eat rocks.

2nd Food is something that you eat, like meat, bread, and vegetables and fruit.

3rd It's something that you eat. (How is food different from other things that are not food?) Because it makes you grow and get healthy and strong.

Our second question assessed students' understanding of the nature of food, in terms of both defining what it is (2A) and contrasting it with nonfood (2B). Almost all of the students understood that we need food to sustain life and remain healthy, and majorities were able to define or describe food and distinguish it from nonfood. However, only 15% ever described food as a source of energy for the body. Many responses were based on appearances or external characteristics (food has taste, contains juice or seeds, etc.) or involved circular reasoning (you eat things because they are food and food is food because you eat it) or reversed logic (foods are things you can eat with a fork or spoon).

Older students were more likely to note that food provides health benefits or energy, but also more likely to simply list examples or suggest distinctions based on nonessential characteristics. Although relatively unsophisticated, these responses indicated that most older students at least were able to generate answers to Question 2B, whereas many younger students were not.

Responses to the first two questions were generally free of misconceptions and accurate as far as they went, although most knowledge about food was limited to its surface appearances and gross physical characteristics. Like those interviewed by Driver et al. (1994), these students knew that we need food to survive but did not understand much about nutrition or how food exerts its effects on our bodies, even though some used scientific terms such as *energy, protein,* or *vitamins.* Most said that we need food to stay alive or that it provides energy, keeps us healthy, or helps us grow.

Some made further reference to these same characteristics when asked to define food or distinguish it from nonfood. However, others referred to nonessential characteristics, displayed circular reasoning or reversed logic, or classified potentially edible substances (bugs, flowers, clover, horses, sunflower seeds) as nonfoods on the basis of cultural convention rather than fitness as an energy source. Other confusions included classifying pills or vitamins as food; drawing rigid distinctions between human and animal food; defining food as solids (including pills) but classifying liquids (e.g., soup) as nonfoods; and contrasting good versus bad food instead of food versus nonfood. Students who emphasized that foods are healthy and good for us sometimes excluded sugar, junk foods, or poisoned food as foods.

A few responses conveyed hints of the vitalistic thinking reported by Inagaki and Hatano (1993), in which people speak of internal organs such as the stomach as if they possessed "agency" or the ability to initiate and sustain goal-directed activity. The Japanese children they studied also conveyed only occasional hints of vitalistic thinking in their free responses to questions like "Why do we eat food?," although they often made vitalistic selections when forced to choose between intentional explanations (we want to eat tasty food), vitalistic explanations (our stomach takes in vital power from food), or mechanical explanations (we take food into our body after its form is changed in the stomach and bowels). However, in studies done with American children, Miller and Bartsch (1997) and Au and Romo (1999) found no evidence of vitalistic thinking in free response explanations, and Miller and Bartsch (1997) and Morris, Taplin, and Gelman (2000) found less evidence of it in forced choices than Inagaki and Hatano (1993) had found. Our findings support the conclusion that vitalistic causal explanations are not typical of children's freely constructed explanations for biological phenomena.

They also suggest that primary-grade students stand to benefit from exposure to the scientific definition of food (as a source of energy) and some of the concepts and causal explanations associated with it. They are not yet ready for the details of the biochemistry involved, but they can understand that, just as cars need fuel (gas) to burn to supply the energy that keeps them moving, people need fuel (food) to energize their activities.

FOOD GROUPS AND NUTRITIONAL VALUE

3. Scientists talk about different food groups. Have you heard of food groups? What are some of the food groups?

K   No.

1st   The food groups are fruit, vegetables, grain, and juices.

2nd   My health teacher taught me: There are vegetable groups, meat groups, the grain groups, the . . . I can't get the rest of them.

3rd   I've heard of all of them. There's the sweet at the top, there's the grain, fruits, veggies, the dairy, and the meat.

More than one third (34) of the students had not heard of food groups or were unable to list any. Most of the rest referred to conventional food groups, although they sometimes used alternative terms: bread or wheat for grains, sugars for carbohydrates, milk for dairy, and "the ones like candy and butter," "desserts and stuff," or "other—chocolate and all that" for fats. However, 20 students instead listed individual food items (cheese, apples, etc.) or unconventional food groups (purple, green, etc.; breakfast/lunch/dinner; meat/deli/fruit). Five students referred to food pyramids, either directly or indirectly (i.e., through references to "at the top"). In addition, a few explained that you are supposed to eat more of the better foods and less of the bad foods.

Most of the kindergarteners knew little or nothing about conventional food groups, whereas most of the second and third graders could name at least some of them. Second graders knew the most, perhaps because food groups were taught late in first grade or early in second grade. On all of our interviews, second graders communicated as much or more information about some topics as third graders did.

Responses to this and subsequent questions about healthful versus junk foods suggested that the students were a little more knowledgeable about the relationships between food and health than were the students interviewed by Michela and Contento (1984), as well as more likely to name conventional food groups than the British children interviewed by Turner (1997). This reflects the increased emphasis on nutrition education in recent years, featuring food pyramids and discussion of food groups and recommended diets.

4. Certain foods are healthful and nutritious. What are some of the foods that are especially good for you? Why are these foods good for you?

5. Other foods—often called junk foods—are not very healthful and nutritious. What are some of these junk foods? Why aren't these foods good for you?

K   4. Meat, potatoes, salad. There's a lot of food. (Why are they good for you?) That's a good question. I don't know.

5. Marshmallows, chocolate. (Why aren't marshmallows and chocolate good for you?) 'Cause chocolate has bad stuff in it and so does marshmallows. Junk . . . they put junk inside of it. (What does the bad stuff in marshmallows and chocolate do to you?) They'll make you throw up. (Can you think of other junk food?) Oreo cookies. Chocolate chip cookies.

1st 4. Chicken noodle soup, beans, rice, bread, fish . . . that's all I can think of. (Why are these foods good for you?) 'Cause they have nutrition in them. (What do you mean by nutrition?) Nutrition is stuff that helps you grow. It's like a kind of vitamin.

5. That's like candy and peanuts and all that stuff. (Why are these foods not so good for you?) 'Cause they have a lot of sugar in them. Good foods don't have any sugar in them. Junk foods have a bunch of sugar in them. (What's so bad about sugar?) It could get in your teeth and rottens them instead of making you grow.

2nd 4. Fruit is good for you, vegetables, bread, breakfast—like cereal. (Why are these foods good for you?) Because it gives you lots of energy.

5. Chocolate chip cookies, candy bars, chocolate chips, the gum that's not sugarless. That's all I can think of. (Why aren't these foods good for you?) Because you could get hyper and you could faint.

3rd 4. Meat, fruits, yogurt, dairies, grains. (Why are these foods especially good for you?) 'Cause they keep your body healthy and they can give you . . . if you don't have any medicine and you need some vitamins, like bananas, and they give you protein.

5. Sweets, candy canes, Pop Tarts, Reese's. (Why are these foods not so good for you?) 'Cause they don't keep you in shape. It doesn't make your body good and stuff, but sometimes we do need sweets if we feel like it, but we can't have them all the time.

Most of the students displayed good basic knowledge about healthful versus junk foods. Even the youngest understood that fruits and vegetables are better for you than snack foods and desserts. However, their abilities to explain the reasons for the difference were limited or nonexistent. The general patterns resemble those reported by Michela and Contento (1984), Driver et al. (1994), and other investigators, although they indicate that students are much more attuned to potential problems with sugars than with fats.

Many students understood foods as mixtures or compounds subsuming both healthful and unhealthful components. They tended to assume that anything added to processed foods makes these foods less healthful ("They put junk inside of it"). A few other misconceptions appeared (that carrots make you see better in the dark or turn your skin orange; apples keep the doctor away; ice cream is bad for you because it's cold; carrots, meat, and eggs are good for you because otherwise "they wouldn't be invented" [teleological thinking]; good or bad foods have immediate effects on the body, such as healing wounds or making you vomit). There also were a few unusually knowledgeable statements (fat can clog your arteries; cookies and potato chips contain a lot of unhealthful grease, oils, sugars, fats, and calories).

Overall, most students could distinguish healthful from junk foods, but even the third graders did not yet possess enough knowledge about body metabolism to be able to say much about why nutritious foods are good for us or junk foods are bad for us. Building on the scientific definition of food as the energy source fueling the body's activities, primary-grade teachers can develop basic knowledge about why particular foods are relatively good or bad for us in the process of using food pyramids to teach about food groups.

CHANGES OVER TIME IN AMERICAN DIETS

6. Think about the foods that people ate about 80 years ago, around 1920. Do we have foods today that they didn't have in 1920? Why didn't they have those things back then?

7. Back then, did they eat some foods that we don't eat today?

K   6. Marshmallows. (Why didn't they have marshmallows?) I don't know. They probably weren't done with them [i.e., they hadn't finished inventing/developing them].

7. There was no milk or stuff, so they had to drink mud.

1st 6. Macaroni and cheese or plain old cheese. (OK. And why didn't they have them back then?) Because they didn't know how to make them.

7. They ate the same kind of food that we do.

2nd 6. They had vegetables and fruit . . . (But do we have anything that they didn't have?) Yeah, like grains, meat . . . no they had meat. I'm not really sure.

7. Yeah, I think so. (Can you think of anything?) No.

3rd 6. Cake, donuts, ice cream . . . candy. (Why didn't they have candy or ice cream or cake back then?) Because it wasn't really healthy for them. (Can you think of any other reasons?) Because they didn't have a lot of medicine back then if you got sick [i.e., we can eat these things now because we have better medicine].

7. Yes. (Can you think of some examples?) . . . No.

The students had difficulty with these questions about how patterns of food consumption in the United States evolved during the 20th century. When asked about foods that we eat today that were not around in 1920, most couldn't respond or incorrectly listed foods that already were available then. Some recognized packaged junk foods as modern inventions, along with pizza, fast foods, and a few others. Only a minority were able to offer explanations for their responses and many of these were explanations for incorrect statements. The most naive explanations suggested that certain foods were unavailable because "there were no stores then" (children commonly invoke this idea as an explanation of the lack of availability of consumer items in the past) or because the source (seed, plant, animal) of a key ingredient didn't yet exist. More sophisticated responses referred to the lack of a key invention (the basic concept/recipe for the food or special technology used in making it).

Many students answered in terms much farther back than 1920. Some referred to the pioneers or to Native Americans, and a few to prehistoric times. Others referred not to foods themselves but to activities involved in obtaining them, such as gathering berries or hunting game. At least a few, unaware of contemporary food production and distribution practices, thought that meat and produce sold in supermarkets is obtained from individual hunters or gatherers who bring it to the store to sell. Rare and unique responses included "Jesus didn't have that much food, so he didn't put much food out"; they didn't have eggs because nothing that laid eggs there was big enough; they didn't have mashed potatoes because there were no stoves or microwaves; they didn't have enough food back then so they had to eat animals; and they didn't know a lot but we have scientists and also news media to spread the word about inventions (presentism).

The students found Question 7 even more difficult. They generated many fewer answers and most of these incorrectly identified foods that are still eaten commonly today. However, a minority did mention foods no longer eaten commonly, such as buffalo, gourds, sheep brains, or molasses, and a few indicated that the same foods were eaten but in less satisfactory condition (hard strawberries, icy ice cream). Many of the incorrect answers came from students who understood that fruits and vegetables have always been basic foods (eaten with little or no transformation from their harvested form) and reasoned that in the past, people ate food that they grew or raised themselves, so they were limited by the range of seeds and animals available to them. This reasoning would have been well suited to comparisons with the 18th century or earlier, but it led to incorrect responses for the reference year of 1920. Only a handful of students showed much awareness of the relatively recent vintage of modern food processing and packaging methods or of the degree to which certain foods that we now take for granted (especially frozen foods and other convenience foods) have become commonplace only in recent decades. As with all of the topics addressed in our interviews, primary-grade students could benefit from learning about historical, geographical, and technological aspects of food that explain change over time and variation across locations and cultures.

FOODS EATEN IN AMERICA AND OTHER PARTS OF THE WORLD

8. Are there some countries where people eat different foods than we eat? What do they eat? What do we eat that they don't eat?

9. Think about Japan. Do the Japanese people eat different foods than we do? What things do the Japanese people eat? What do we eat that the Japanese people don't eat?

K　8. Yeah. (Can you give me some examples?) No.

9. Yes. (What things do the Japanese people eat that we don't eat?) I don't know what they eat.

1st　8. Some countries eat just . . . I don't know what, but I know that some countries have different food. (Can you think of particular countries?) No.

9. Yup. (What do they eat that we don't eat?) I don't know. (What do we eat that they don't eat?) Macaroni and cheese and chicken noodle soup.

2nd　8. In the rain forest, people just eat plants. (What do they eat that we don't eat?) We eat like macaroni and all that other stuff, but they eat like plants and coconuts, fruits. Sometimes we eat fruits, but they just eat them without cleaning them.

9. Sometimes they eat chicken and rice a lot, but sometimes they eat with these things [pantomimes chopsticks]. Yeah, chopsticks, and

they eat fish. (What things do we eat that the Japanese people don't eat?) We don't eat with numchucks [sic], they don't eat ice cream or Popsicle sticks or macaroni.

3rd 8. Well, there are lots but I can't think of the names of them.

9. They eat like bowls . . . with coconut bowls and stuff. They eat coconut food. Let's see here. . . . They have water, they could have crab 'cause there's lots of sand. (Do we eat anything that they don't eat?) We eat canned peaches. They eat coconuts and drink coconuts, and they eat crab and we eat crab. We eat meat, we eat soup, and they drink water, and they sometimes get stuff by trees.

The students had as much trouble with these geographical/cultural comparisons as they did with the historical comparisons addressed in Question 6 and Question 7. Given the remarkable cultural diffusion that has occurred in recent decades, national contrasts in diets and eating patterns are much less clear-cut than they used to be (especially for industrialized countries). Even so, certain foods are associated with certain countries and emphasized in the meals consumed there, and other foods are considered foreign by the countries' residents. Thus, it is still possible to make relative comparisons.

When asked to compare American food with food eaten in other countries, only small minorities of the students were able to do so. Most examples of foreign foods were Mexican, Italian, or Chinese. Interestingly, many responses that mentioned Asian foods contrasted them with spaghetti and meatballs, macaroni and cheese, pizza, or Mexican food as typical American fare. These responses are accurate; certain foods originally considered ethnic are now eaten so commonly in the United States that it makes sense to talk of them as American foods.

A common accurate response was that Americans eat candy and other processed foods or traditional family meals (meat and potatoes) but Japanese people eat rice, fish, and so forth. A common mistake was to name fruits and vegetables as foods that the Japanese people do not eat. The students found it easier to talk about foods eaten commonly in other countries but not in the United States than to talk about foods eaten commonly in the United States but not in other countries. This is understandable given that they were American children with little or no direct experience with life in other countries.

Elements of chauvinism appeared in some of the responses, most notably those that made reference to what Americans would regard as exotic foods (tiger hamburgers, parts of animals that we don't eat today, little green stuff that looks like seaweed, brains—"It's probably like spaghetti to them"). In addition, certain students viewed American practices as more appropriate than their counterparts in other countries, such as those who referred to "weird" sauce for chicken or tendencies to eat raw rather than cooked fish. In all of our interviews, children commonly displayed chauvinism when drawing comparisons with other cultures.

Elaboration of the findings for Question 8 appeared in responses to a related question about foods brought to America. The 1992 quincentennial of Columbus's first voyage to the Americas stimulated scholarly activity on what at first was called the Columbian Exchange but later simply the Encounter—the diffusion that occurred when previously isolated peoples and cultures met and began influencing each other. The National Council for the Social Studies (1992), as well as individual scholars (Davis & Hawke, 1992; Wooster, 1992) published guidelines for teaching about the Encounter, and these typically included information about crops or foods introduced to America from Europe and Africa (and vice versa). We wondered if students interviewed just a few years after this flurry of interest in the Encounter would display any evidence of exposure to it (e.g., in connection with teaching about Columbus Day), so we asked about foods that had been brought to America from other parts of the world. However, their responses (not shown here) were similar to those made in response to Question 8. That is, the students talked about Italian, Mexican, Asian, and other ethnic foods introduced (or at least, popularized) in America in recent decades. None mentioned Columbus or the Encounter, although a few spoke of the Pilgrims or other early English colonists. Thus, the students' thinking was based on an Anglocentric version of America's past.

GEOGRAPHIC INFLUENCES ON DIETS

Questions 10 and 11 were designed to assess the degree to which the students were aware of geographic (and related economic) factors that underlie two key contrasts between American and Chinese diets.

10. American people eat a lot of beef but Chinese people eat a lot of chicken. Why is that?

11. American people eat a lot of bread but Chinese people eat a lot of rice. Why is that?

K   10. Because they're different people.

11. Because rice is made in Chinese [*sic*].

1st   10. 'Cause they like chicken more than beef, and we like beef more than chicken.

11. Because rice is better for the chopsticks to pick up. And bread they can't pick up very good with chopsticks, and they don't even have bread where China is.

2nd   10. 'Cause they might have more chicken there, and we have more beef here. (Why might that be?) I'm not sure about that.

11. We have bread—we can make bread, and rice is not like a kind of food that American people eat, and they have more rice there or

something, and more bread here. (Why isn't it something that many Americans eat?) 'Cause usually they can't find it because they don't grow it here, I don't think.

3rd 10. 'Cause they can't find much beef around where they live. (Why might that be?) [very long pause, no response]

   11. Because in another country they need iron. [couldn't explain]

Only about one third of the students were able to supply substantive responses to these two questions. Most lacked awareness of the role of geography in influencing regional crop- and animal-raising patterns, so they were unable to explain these contrasts in Chinese versus American diets or attributed them to differences in taste preferences or in access to the foods involved. The latter responses usually were limited to statements that Chinese people have more chicken/rice and American people have more beef/wheat, made without explanation of why this might be so.

A few students, particularly older ones responding to Question 11, did attempt to explain the role of geography (they might not have the same animals because of their surroundings; cows need a lot of fresh grass to eat but in China it's usually hot weather and it's harder for the grass to stay fresh; rice grows better there; there are more wheat fields in America because of the amount of rain and we have something called the Great Plains where half our grains grow; they eat stuff that they can raise well over there and we eat what we can raise well over here— like if it's sunny, you can raise tropical things). However, these few geographical explanations were the only ones elicited, and several were accompanied by confused or incorrect statements (things made of beef live here and things made of chicken live there; chickens like to live there and pigs like to live here; maybe they don't have enough mud there for pigs).

Other unusual responses suggested nongeographical reasons for the diet difference (the Chinese have never heard of beef because no one has told them about it yet; they don't know how to cook it; it could have something to do with their culture or religion [children commonly invoke culture or religion, without elaboration, as explanations for group differences in behavior patterns]; they have less money and don't have stores that sell beef; cows are heavy, so how would they get all of that meat all the way to China; they probably don't have stoves or ovens; they prefer foods that you can eat with chopsticks because they don't want to get sick from passing germs by handling food with their hands; they don't have knives to spread butter, so they don't eat a lot of bread). Most of these responses reflected naiveté about modern communication and transportation systems, reversed reasoning, or chauvinistically tinged misconceptions.

The students were more likely to cite geography as an influence on crop farming than animal ranching. Only four cited geography in talking about the contrast in chicken versus cattle raising, and only two suggested possible explanations. In contrast, nine alluded to geographical influences on rice versus wheat production, and several suggested explanations. Units on plants are often in-cluded in primary-grade science teaching, so this difference may have reflected the effects of experimentation with environmental conditions (e.g., exposure to sunlight) that affect plant growth.

WHY SOME FOODS ARE COOKED

12. We eat some vegetables raw, but we cook meats and many vegetables before we eat them. Why do we cook these foods?

13. We eat many vegetables and most fruits raw. Why don't we cook these foods?

K   12. Because they're raw before we eat them. (But why do we cook them? Why can't we eat them raw?) Because it would taste yucky!

       13. Because it comes from a different country. (Why does that make a difference?) I don't know.

1st   12. So they're warm and hot and soft and stuff.

       13. Because they want them to be raw.

2nd 12. 'Cause if you eat them raw, sometimes you can get sick from them. (Are there other reasons for cooking these foods?) Sometimes if they're frozen and you bite on it, you could lose a tooth or some-thing—permanent.

       13. You don't need to cook them because sometimes you can eat them just regular. (Why can we do that?) 'Cause they won't hurt you, 'cause they don't like to freeze them like meats and stuff. They don't freeze them.

3rd 12. (pause) You cook them because . . . so we can be strong instead of not strong, and if you don't cook them, they're not healthy for you.

       13. Because you don't have to when they're already healthy for us.

Most students described the purpose of cooking as softening foods or making them taste better. Only a few mentioned killing germs or bacteria ("Germs die re-ally fast when they're cooked"), although 26 indicated that eating some foods raw could make us sick because they contain blood, poison, minerals, bugs, diseases, or other "bad stuff" that needs to be eliminated through cooking. Rather than killing the "bad stuff," some thought that cooking boils it away or causes it to dis-solve in the water.

The responses were generally accurate as far as they went, although they usu-ally did not include scientific terminology. There were occasional tendencies to-ward reversed logic (the existence of stoves proves the need to cook certain foods) or minor misconceptions (that ham is eaten raw, heating meat "pressures the blood out," the major reason for cooking is to prevent choking, animal blood is bad for you, people with colds shouldn't eat cold food, the "bad stuff" is on the outside of the meat rather than dispersed throughout it, and cooking certain foods could make you sick).

REFRIGERATION AND PRESERVATION OF FOODS

14. We put many foods in the refrigerator to keep them cold. Why do we do that?

15. Before electricity was discovered, people didn't have refrigerators. Where did they keep their foods then?

16. Some foods keep for a long time in bottles or cans without spoiling. Why is that?

K   14. To keep them fresh.

    15. On the table . . . on the counter. (Can you think of anywhere else they might keep them?) In the cupboards.

    16. I don't know.

1st 14. So they won't get warm and gross. (What's wrong with them getting warm?) Because when they get warm, they might get little white stuff on them and sometimes if you leave bread out too long, it'll turn green.

    15. I don't know.

    16. I don't know.

2nd 14. So they won't spoil. Keep them cold. Some foods like juices and stuff need to be cold.

    15. Well, shady spots. They could make one out of rocks and then find something to keep it cold and put it in there.

    16. 'Cause nothing gets to them because they're in a can. (What do you mean by nothing gets to them?) Like spoiling . . . I'm not very sure.

3rd 14. 'Cause we have a place to store them and they won't get rotten.

    15. A cabinet or a cupboard. (How did they preserve their foods to keep them from spoiling?) A cloth or something over them so they wouldn't dry out.

    16. It might have a lid on it so it won't spoil. (How does that keep the food from spoiling?) I don't know.

Once again, most students had experience-based practical knowledge (understanding that foods spoil and that steps such as refrigeration, wrapping, or sealing can retard spoilage), but few understood much about the causal mechanisms underlying these transformations. Those with no knowledge were unable to offer substantive explanations, those with beginnings of understanding spoke of protecting food from "bugs" (insects), and those who were starting to develop more scientific understanding spoke of protecting foods from germs, bacteria, or things in the air (including oxygen and air itself). Only one student referred to decomposition ("Drinking spoiled milk could make you sick because there's things called decomposers that if they get into the milk, they can make you sick, like bacteria") and none explicitly noted that this process occurs more quickly at higher temperatures.

Because most of the steps that can be taken to preserve foods involve covering them or placing them in sealed containers, the students typically spoke of protecting foods from external entities but not of retarding spoilage tendencies inherent within foods themselves. As with children interviewed by Au and Romo (1999), even those who were able to generate an explanation focused on mechanical causality (keeping germs away from the food) rather than biological causality (killing the germs).

A majority of the students either were unable to say anything about how people preserved foods prior to electricity or could only make vague references to storage places. However, many (especially third graders) knew about iceboxes and could even describe them in some detail. In addition, a few made references to underground cellars or the hanging of meat, although none mentioned salt or other preservation methods. A few mentioned wrapping or covering foods to protect them from insects or the air.

Lacking knowledge about decomposition, the students also had difficulty explaining why foods don't spoil in bottles or cans. Some knew that it was important to keep bottles and cans tightly closed but could not explain why, and a few noted that certain beverages contain "fizz" and reasoned that the fizz must be responsible for keeping the beverages from spoiling. The best responses made reference to tight sealing to keep harmful things away from the food, but most described these harmful things as air or bugs rather than germs or bacteria. Children could acquire and connect several basic understandings about cooking and preserving foods if taught about decomposers and their relationship to temperature (i.e., refrigeration retards decomposition because germs thrive in warmer temperatures, but very hot temperatures kill them, which is one reason why we cook certain foods).

LAND-TO-HAND PROGRESSIONS IN PRODUCING COMMON FOODS

Questions 17 through 20 addressed students' knowledge about the origins of common foods and the processes involved in bringing them to the table in ready-to-eat form. The questions progressed from simpler to more complex, in terms of the degree to which the foods are transformed from their original physical state, combined with other ingredients, or subjected to cooking or other processing.

17. Let's talk about how we get different foods. We'll start with apple-sauce. How is applesauce made?

18. How is cheese made?

19. How is bread made?

20. How is the meat in a hamburger made? Where does this meat come from? What is the process of making the hamburger patty?

K 17. From apples. (What do you do to the apples?) You crunch the inside up—really mash it up.

18. You sit the melted cheese in the refrigerator for a really long time and let the cheese freeze. (Where does cheese come from?) I don't know.

19. I don't know.

20. From a cow or something. (How does it get from the cow to the hamburger?) I don't know.

1st 17. They're made out of apples, and you get this pot and you peel off the skin and put them in this water and put in a jar of applesauce. That's how it's made.

18. There's this cheese store and these guys . . . I don't know.

19. It's made out of white milk. (White milk and what else?) That's all.

20. You've got two breads—one on the bottom, one on the top, and you have lettuce inside. (How is the meat made?) It's made out of chicken and it turns into meat.

2nd 17. It's out of apples. You take the apple peeling off and then you smish the inside of the apple and then you put it in a jar, and that's applesauce.

18. I don't really know how cheese is made. (What's it made from?) Eggs.

19. Out of wheat and stuff. They put it in a bread baker, then they take it out and slice it up and then they put it in a bag.

20. Some of them are made out of cows. (How do you get from cows to hamburger meat?) I don't really know.

3rd 17. It's made by machines. You pick the apples just before you put it in the machines.

18. It's made from milk and the milk's put into a machine. (What does the machine do?) I don't know.

19. It's made by [from] wheat and the wheat comes from farmers, and they put the wheat into a machine and it turns into flour, and then they put the flour in a machine and lots of other stuff—water and . . . I don't know what else.

20. They kill a pig and then they take the meat from the pig and cook it and then they put it in a bun.

As expected, students' knowledge of what is involved in bringing common foods to our tables varied with grade level, with the degree to which raw ingredients are transformed and combined with other ingredients in the process of creating the foods, and with the degree to which steps involved in preparing the foods are done at home and thus available for observation (making bread or hamburgers) versus on farms or in factories and thus outside of most children's experience (making cheese, grinding meat). The students knew the most about making applesauce, which among the foods considered involves the fewest transformations or combinations with other ingredients. Also, many primary-grade students experience making applesauce firsthand as part of a social studies/literacy unit. More than two thirds understood that applesauce is basically crushed/mushed apples, although fewer than one fourth were able to identify any of the specific steps involved in manufacturing it. Only 22% noted that cooking is involved and only 22% mentioned ingredients other than apples. Confused responses included: Crush apples and then add sauce; stir the apples and wait until they turn into applesauce; smush the apples, then put them into a can that makes applesauce [magical response]; squash the apples, then can them and store them until they get mushy; crush the apples and then add "taste of apple."

Primary-grade students in Michigan often visit (with their families) or make field trips (as classes) to apple orchards, especially at harvest time when they can taste freshly made cider. Students who had made such visits may have been more likely to talk about crushing the apples (because they had seen crushing being done at an orchard), but less likely to mention cooking the apples (because making cider does not require cooking).

About half (50) of the students knew that cheese is made from milk, but only 10 were able to add something else to this basic idea. Only a few offered anything like an explanation, and several advanced misconceptions (that cheese is made by cooking milk or stirring something into it, by freezing milk or "melted cheese," or that it is made from eggs or wheat). The patterns of responses to this and several other questions confirm previous findings that urban and suburban children tend to know very little about what occurs on farms because they lack direct personal experience with farming.

Creating bread involves somewhat radical transformations and combinations in moving from its raw ingredients to the final product. Perhaps this is why almost one third (30) of the students were unable to respond when asked how bread is made, and several generated misconceptions: Gather corn and squish it together; put butter in the stove and cook it (it comes out bread); made from potatoes; made from pigs and stuff from farms; cook water and "little pieces of bread" together to make bread; made of vitamins, minerals, and milk; a machine changes wheat into bread [directly]; made of yeast, salt, and eggs [no mention of grain or flour]. Most of what the other students said was valid as far as it went, although frequently oversimplified or distorted in some way. Many students thought that bread is made simply by grinding up grain and then cooking it. They had learned that bread is made from wheat (or other grains), but knew little or nothing about the process (they probably didn't understand, for example, that flour is milled grain).

The more knowledgeable students made reference to flour or dough and talked about mixing the ingredients and then baking the bread. Many of these students had seen bread made at home (if not from scratch, then at least at the level of baking loaves of frozen dough purchased at the supermarket). In general, knowledge progressed from knowing nothing at all, to knowing that bread is made from grain but lacking further information about the processes involved, to knowing that flour is milled grain and must be mixed with other ingredients to form dough and then baked to make bread.

Some of the confused responses concerning applesauce, cheese, or bread at some point called for including the ostensible final product (i.e., applesauce, cheese, or bread) instead of creating this product by mixing and processing its basic ingredients. These responses are parallel to responses reported by Berti and Bombi (1989), in which children suggested that clothes are made from old rags and new glass is made from broken shards.

Fewer than half (39) of the students understood that the meat in a hamburger comes from cattle, and they all used the word "cow" rather than "cattle," "steer," or any other term suggesting awareness of a distinction between dairy cows and beef cattle. About 20% mentioned animals other than cows, typically pigs or chickens. These statements are understandable given that the term *burger* has been applied by fast food chains to a range of meat concoctions and even meatless *veggie burgers*. Surprisingly, despite frequent mention of pigs, only one student mentioned ham and none stated that hamburgers are made from ham.

When asked to describe the steps involved in making a hamburger patty, 36 students were unable to respond and the rest limited their responses to killing the animal, removing the meat, cutting it up, and then cooking it. Ten mentioned forming the meat into patties, but only one referred to grinding (calling it "squashing"). Thus, the students were not aware of grinding as a process or the distinction between grinding meat and merely cutting it into small pieces. Furthermore, very few students used the word *beef*, and none spoke of ground beef. Perhaps more would have shown awareness of grinding if we had asked them to distinguish between steak and hamburger meat.

In general, the students displayed not only a lack of specific knowledge but a more fundamental lack of awareness of many of the land-to-hand progressions that bring foods to our tables, especially processes that occur on farms or in factories. Most of what they knew about cheese or hamburger meat began with purchase of these products in supermarkets, with little awareness of the processing involved in developing them from their bovine origins. Like the responses to most of the questions in all of our interviews, the students' responses to these land-to-hand progression questions indicated that although they possessed practical knowledge about the general nature, appearance, and uses of things in their environment, they often had little knowledge of their essential nature (e.g., flour is milled grain, hamburger meat is ground beef), or the processes involved in manufacturing them. They stand to benefit from instruction about the raw materials from which common foods are made and the processes (e.g., grinding, milling) involved in transforming them to recipe-ready form.

PRODUCTS DERIVED FROM FARM ANIMALS

21. **Many farmers grow crops but others raise animals. For example, some farmers raise chickens. Why do these farmers raise chickens?**
22. **Some farmers raise cows. What do we get from cows?**
23. **Some farmers raise pigs. What do we get from pigs?**
24. **Some farmers raise sheep. What do we get from sheep?**

K   21. They want to eat them. (What else do we get from chickens?) Eggs.

22. Milk. (Do we get anything else from cows?) [no response]

23. Milk—no, mud. (So, pigs sometimes live in mud, but why would farmers raise pigs?) I don't know.

24. Wool. They cut the wool off. (What else do we get from sheep?) I don't know.

1st   21. So they can eat eggs. (Is there anything else we get from chickens?) I don't know.

22. Milk. (What else do we get from cows?) Cheese.

23. Meat. (What else do we get from pigs?) I don't know.

24. Clothes. (What sort of clothes?) Wool clothes. (Do we get anything else from sheep?) I don't know.

2nd   21. So they can get eggs for cooked eggs or a lot of different kind of eggs. (What else do we get from chickens?) I don't know.

22. Milk and hamburgers, burgers.

23. We get fat out of pigs. . . . We get ham out of pigs.

24. We get their fur for like blankets so we can keep warm. I don't really know anything else. (Do we get meat from sheep?) No.

3rd   21. So they can get money for them so like if they get bigger and they don't want them, they could sell them for money, or they could get the eggs from them and then they could make eggs out of them—the kind that you eat—or they could sell the eggs and get money for them.

22. Milk, meat, and I think that's all.

23. Bacon, more meat. Stuff that's smushed. I think it's pork or something, and then when you eat it, it's like you're eating a pig or something. [Thinking of Spam or sausages?]

24. Wool, and I think meat. (We do get meat. Do you know what it's called?) No.

Knowledge about products derived from farm animals was more developed for chickens and cows than for pigs and sheep. Common responses included meat and eggs from chickens, milk and meat from cows, meat from pigs, and wool/cloth and meat from sheep. Responses concerning cows and pigs focused on edibles, with very little mention of leather, but responses concerning sheep made more frequent mention of wool or woolen fabrics and clothing than of meat. Although the students showed some confusion about which meats come from which animals (especially regarding pigs), most of what they said was accurate as far as it went and free of significant misconceptions. However, six students had no idea that pigs were good for anything other than "slopping in the mud," and at least some of them seemed to believe that pigs actually make mud.

Also, a few students spoke of certain forms of meat, especially chicken, as if it were something other than flesh removed from dead animals. That is, despite the common name, some students did not appear to have made the connection yet between the chicken that they eat and the chickens found in barnyards. Among students who were aware that meats are flesh from dead animals, some were under the impression that the flesh is taken from these animals only after they have died natural deaths. The responses typically implied images of small family farms with small numbers of animals (perhaps even known individually and treated as pets by family members), not large, corporately owned farms or ranches. Only 13 students, for example, indicated that chickens were raised to sell to stores, and most implied that the meat and eggs derived from the chickens would be consumed primarily if not solely by the family. To the extent that the students were working from images here, they were thinking of family farms as subsistence operations, not of large ranches raising animals as profit-making businesses. Even the third graders seemed to have little awareness of feedlots, slaughterhouses, or other "macro" aspects of meat production.

THE COSTS OF FOOD PROCESSING

25. A pound of cereal costs more than a pound of apples. Why is that?

26. It costs more to eat a meal in a restaurant than it does to have the same meal at home. Why is that?

K   25. I don't know.

26. I don't know.

1st   25. Because of the box. (What about the box?) It might be more. (Can you think of any other reasons why?) 'Cause there's more cereal in cereal boxes than apples.

26. 'Cause you gotta pay for the food. (Yes, but at home you pay for the food because you go to the store and buy it, so why does it still cost more at the restaurant?) I don't know.

2nd 25. 'Cause it has more stuff to eat instead of just one apple, so you could have five or six apples in a box of cereal. (But they weigh the same amount.) 'Cause they're big and the other ones are little ones and there's lots of them. (Why would that mean that they cost more? They're only little. You'd think they'd cost less.) 'Cause you can eat one apple and it would be gone, but you can eat one bowl of cereal and it wouldn't be gone.

26. 'Cause they cook the food instead of you.

3rd 25. I think 'cause apples weigh less than the cereal does because you could put lots of cereal in one of them boxes up there, and then you could get like a little box and put the apples in there, but I think apples would still weigh a lot. (Yeah, they're both the same weight, but the cereal costs more. Why is that?) Maybe they like you to pay more for it or maybe it's more nutritious than apples.

26. Because sometimes restaurants can be expensive, but like McDonald's and Burger King and Hot N' Now—they're not that expensive because they just serve hamburgers and French fries, and sometimes they give out toys, but I think that sometimes Murphy's [a local family steakhouse] can be more better but it costs more because maybe they have too many customers and they like to put up their prices so they don't get so many customers, because sometimes Murphy's is packed [reversed logic]. (But why would you pay more for eating at Murphy's than you would for eating at home?) Maybe because their food is like eating at bars and at home, it's just on your plate and you don't have to get up, and your house is for you to live in, but at Murphy's you have to pay to go there and you don't get to live in it.

The students showed little awareness of the fact that food prices must cover the costs of labor involved in manufacturing, packaging, shipping, and other processing of the food, and in the case of food eaten at restaurants, the services of the restaurant staff. Nor was there much awareness of food production, manufacturing, distribution, or service as major industries driven by large corporations. To the extent that responses were based on images of the processes involved, these images featured small family farms supplying food to local stores and restaurants, where any needed processing was accomplished on site.

Students' difficulties in answering Question 25 were compounded by confusions surrounding *mass, volume, density,* and related concepts. Some students visualized a box of cereal compared to just one apple rather than a bag of apples, and even those who did visualize a bag of apples often had difficulty retaining the idea that the cereal and the apples weighed the same because the larger size of the cereal box made it seem that there must be more cereal than apples. For example, one first grader said, "Cereal comes in a box and apples come in a bag and the box makes it heavier and the cereal helps a little to make it heavy, and it makes it heavier than the apples."

Some students determined that the costs involved in manufacturing the cereal box would exceed the costs involved in manufacturing whatever container (if any) held the apples, and some raised the possibility that the box might contain a toy or trinket in addition to the cereal. Thirty-eight students could not respond, and another 43 attempted to deny the premise of the question by suggesting that despite the equivalent weight, you get more cereal because it comes in a bigger box or is not consumed as quickly as the apples. Only eight directly stated the idea that cereal is more expensive because it has to be manufactured, although this idea was implicit in several other students' statements that cereal has additional ingredients in it (sugar, marshmallows, honey, food coloring).

John (1999), in a review of research on children's consumer knowledge, noted that younger children view prices in terms of the concrete physical features of products, whereas adults see prices as reflecting the utility of the item to the consumer, the costs of manufacturing it, and its relative scarcity. Thus, it is not surprising to find that children think cereal costs more than apples because the box is bigger or you get more cereal.

The students showed more awareness of the labor costs involved in restaurant meals; more than one third indicated that we have to pay the staff for cooking and serving the food. This is not surprising, given that they had much more direct experience with restaurants than with the processes (and payrolls) involved in food manufacturing and distribution. Students who lacked this basic insight struggled to construct explanations for why eating the same meal is more expensive in a restaurant. Some pointed to the "specialness" of the ambiance of eating out, whereas others suggested that the food is of better quality than what you have at home, that there is more of it, that extras come with it, or that it is prepared more elegantly or "perfectly" than at home.

Older students were more likely to give the most sophisticated responses, but also more likely to say that cereal costs more because it is better for you than apples or that a meal costs more in a restaurant because restaurants are fancy places to eat out. These were not sophisticated answers to the questions posed, but they indicate that the older students were more able to generate substantive (and reasonable) guesses in the absence of knowledge, whereas the younger students were more likely to be forced to say "I don't know."

STEPS IN GROWING CORN

27. Many farmers grow corn. Tell me about the steps that farmers go through to grow corn.

K   Seeds. (What about the seeds?) You can have corn seeds. (Then what
      would you do?) Grow them . . . you stick them in the dirt and you grow
      them. (Do you have to do anything to them once you stuck them in the
      dirt?) Water them, and then you have to make sure you have sunshine on
      them.

1st   Usually they get corn seeds and grow them. (OK. What do they do with
      the seeds?) They put them in the dirt. (Then what do they do?) They put
      dirt on the seed, they water it, then it will grow for a long time, for all day,
      and then it will be corn, and then you pick the corn, then you eat it. (Be-
      tween picking the corn and planting the new corn, do they need to do
      anything?) Yeah, put the seed back in there, put the dirt on there, and
      water it, and then there'll be more corn.

2nd   They grow it by seeds. (They plant the seeds. Then what do they do?)
      They get it in deep, deep soil—good soil—then they cover the seed up
      and water it and then it will grow up. (Then what do they do?) They pick
      and then they cook it. (After the corn is picked and taken away, what
      does the farmer do before planting the next year's crop?) He makes sure
      that his soil is ready for it.

3rd   First you have to plant it, you have to water it, let it get sunshine, you
      have to put it where it gets lots and lots of sunshine so you can grow big
      crops of corn, and like if you get not that big a corn, maybe you didn't
      give it enough water or you didn't give it enough sunlight. (Then what do
      you do?) When it gets bigger, you pick it off the stalk and you peel it and
      eat it.

We asked about steps involved in raising corn because it is grown locally, the
plants are salient because of their size, and the corn served at our tables is only
minimally transformed from its appearance when harvested from the fields. Most
responses were valid as far as they went but confined to the popular categories:
Plant the seeds (85), water the plants (63), wait for them to mature (72), and
then harvest them (65). Even so, almost all of the students depicted farmers as
active in planting and caring for their corn crops, not just as waiting for the corn
to be ready for harvesting (cf. Berti & Bombi, 1989).

A few responses were both knowledgeable and detailed, such as the following
comments by a third grader:

> They first plow the ground flat, make little hills to plant the seeds in, plant the
> seeds, plow it flat, and if you were an Indian, you'd put dead fish in it. That just
> makes the soil better. Then you plow, let the corn grow, weed it and tend it and care
> for it, and pretty soon it comes harvesting season and you go out with your big trac-
> tor and just go over the corn and somehow it picks out the corn. (What does the
> farmer do before planting the following year's crop?) He takes out the roots and the
> stalks that are left.

The most detailed knowledge appeared to have been acquired outside of school by students whose neighbors or relatives grew corn in gardens or on farms. However, some students communicated knowledge probably picked up at school, especially the idea that Indians used fish as fertilizer (a common detail in stories about how local Native Americans helped the Pilgrims learn to raise crops, included in units on Thanksgiving or America in the 17th century). Several students referred to the "knee high by the Fourth of July" saying.

Throughout our interviews, the students showed relatively little awareness of the role of geography and climate in affecting people's lives. In this case, some of them did show knowledge that crops require optimal amounts of both sunshine and rain (or irrigation), and that corn plants are grown from seeds. However, only small minorities spoke of the need to prepare the soil prior to planting, to protect the plants from pests, or to clear the field as part of the preparation for the next planting.

CLIMATES SUITABLE FOR FARMING

28. There are lots of farmers around here but there are not so many farmers in Alaska. Why not?

K   I don't know.

1st   I don't know.

2nd 'Cause it's not a good place to harvest food. (Why?) They don't have good soil and dirt.

3rd   Because it snows continuously in Alaska.

This question more directly addressed the students' knowledge that possibilities for farming are affected by climate and geography. About 40% (39) of the students were unable to respond, and many others could only say that it is too cold/snowy in Alaska (18) or that not many people live there (10). The remaining students specified that it is too cold/snowy to grow crops in Alaska (26), that it is too cold for animals to survive (7), or that there is not enough sunlight (7).

Many students did not know where Alaska is and thus did not get the point of the question. Others made comments about Alaska that did not address the question or communicated misconceptions about why there is less farming there: that Alaska must be small; there is not much dirt up there—just snow and ice; polar bears would eat all the crops. Two third graders talked about cycles of day and night (one saying that Alaska has 60 and the other 66 straight days of light, then 60 or 66 straight days of dark). However, neither brought this idea to bear on the question (i.e., by saying that crops require lots of sunlight).

Once again we see limitations in the students' knowledge about how geography and climate constrain human activities. Only about half provided substantive responses that spoke to the question, and most of these were limited to the idea that it is too cold/snowy in Alaska to allow plants to grow well. Few students mentioned factors such as the availability of sunshine or the quality of the soil.

MODERNIZATION OF FARMING

29. How is farming today different from farming 100 years ago?

30. What are some inventions that have helped farmers?

31. Long ago, most people had to be farmers in order to produce enough food to feed everyone. But today, only a few farmers produce all the food we need. Why is that?

K 29. A hundred years ago, there weren't very much people who hunted. (Why was that?) Because there weren't very much farmers who hunted.

30. I don't know.

31. 'Cause you can buy it from people who have the store. You could hunt for the store and then you can bring it to the store and then they can put it in a plastic jar or something or in a glass jar. (So the hunters can take their food to the store. What about the farmers? Why can they feed everybody?) 'Cause they hunt.

1st 29. 'Cause there's all these big machines that help the farmers.

30. I don't know.

31. I don't know.

2nd 29. They didn't have farming 100 years ago . . . they'd hunt animals.

30. Tractors.

31. 'Cause people have more money and they can buy houses instead of farms, and they can buy food, but some people can't. (Right, but where does the food come from?) From other countries. They get it on a boat and then they sail it over to here and give it to the company and then they give it to the store.

3rd 29. Well, I think sometimes they didn't have the food that we have now, and maybe sometimes them kind of farmers did not have a lot of money to buy the seeds that we have now, and maybe they didn't have enough money to, but maybe for selling their crops or something, they could trade in the crops and get money and then they could go buy more seeds for it.

30. The plow and the tractor.

31. Because maybe long ago, farmers didn't have enough crops or enough stuff to feed everybody, but maybe now they have like a huge area of land. (Why do they have more room now?) Because maybe

some people don't need that much room to live on or that much land, but probably long ago they did because maybe they had more stuff than we have now. (But why is it those few farmers are still able to produce all that food?) Because maybe some houses got knocked down or got struck by lightning, and maybe the farmer just moved right on to the land next door and used the land for crops.

The last three questions addressed students' knowledge about the ways in which machines and other inventions have revolutionized farming, in terms of both changing the methods used and multiplying the yields per acre. Kindergarteners and first graders had little or no knowledge about the revolution in farming (except for one first grader who lived next to a farm). In contrast, about half of the second and third graders generated responses that were valid as far as they went, and a few displayed considerable knowledge about modern farming. Knowledgeable students were aware of tractors and other large machines as inventions that have helped farmers, but only a few mentioned seeds, fertilizers, or sprays, and none mentioned crop rotation or other specific techniques. Finally, only 14 noted that machines multiply what a single worker can accomplish in a day (e.g., machines do the work faster; they didn't have big machines to go as far) and only one indicated awareness that modern farms are more productive not only because they are bigger but because they produce greater yields per acre.

One third grader offered an interesting economic explanation:

Because land back then cost a lot of money, [but today an acre is] cheaper than my portable TV. So you can buy thousands of acres of land and harvest it all in one shot . . . with all those inventions. So today they can have lots of acres of land because they have the money to do that, and the more acres of land, the more you plant, and the more you can harvest.

Another third grader displayed noteworthy knowledge about the modernization of farming. Her answer to Question 29 was:

One hundred years ago when they had to plant their corn, they would have to walk up and down and make the rows with those old fashioned plows, and as they were making the rows, they would drop the seeds behind them. That's what Pa did on Laura Ingalls Wilder. Today, all they have to do is have machines with a sharp blade at the end and they just drive up and down the field.

Later, when asked about inventions, she said: "There's the manure spreader and the thing that makes the rows, and those really long sprinklers and like a wheat picker or something and a corn picker and I think there's a seed spreader." Finally, when asked why a few farmers can produce all the food that we need today, she said: "Because they have a lot more room than people did in the past and they have inventions where they can go a lot faster up and down and it only takes them a little bit of time and they make their rows really close together so they can have a lot."

Misconceptions were infrequent, although several students thought that we have more types of animals now than they did in the past, one that there was more rain in the past, and one that all farmers at one time were Indians. More common than clear misconceptions were elaborations on valid ideas that included some invalid elements: that the ground was harder in the past because it was less worked, most farm work was done by slaves, all farms were the same size, farmers had to produce their own seeds because they lacked the money to buy seeds at a store, today's big farm machines are steam powered, farmers welcome rabbits and gophers because they eat chaff, farmers can get more land now because it is left by people who move to cities, and we need fewer farmers today because we import food from other countries. Many of these ideas reflect the larger trend noted earlier: To the extent that responses were guided by particular images of farming, those images were centered on small family farms like those depicted in children's literature (e.g., *Little House on the Prairie*), not large corporate operations.

A FOLLOW-UP STUDY

The students we interviewed lived in a suburb, and few had had any contact with farmers or farming. Given that our food interview contained questions about farming and land-to-hand operations in food production, we wondered if students from farm families might provide generally more sophisticated responses. To assess this, we conducted a follow-up study in which we interviewed a stratified sample of 24 third graders who came from farm families and attended schools in rural areas of mid-Michigan. Comparisons with the suburban third graders indicated that the farm students were more successful in describing the steps involved in making bread, noting that farmers get eggs from chickens, describing the steps involved in growing corn, and naming inventions that have helped farmers, whereas the suburban students were more successful in identifying foods eaten elsewhere in general and in Japan in particular and in explaining why junk foods are bad for us.

Concerning the price of a pound of apples compared to a pound of cereal, most of the farm students implied that the prices of things reflect their true value or cost (just as the suburban students had). However, five of the farm students suggested that prices also reflect the motivations of the people who set them. Three of them suggested that cereal prices might be higher than they need to be because the cereal companies or the supermarkets want to maximize their profits, and two suggested that apple prices are kept low because the supermarkets (or physicians who pressure them) want people to eat more apples because they are good for you.

The only instances in which students' family circumstances appeared to confer a specific advantage in answering some of our questions occurred with the questions about steps in growing corn and inventions that have helped farmers. Most of the farm students answered these questions notably more successfully and in much more specific detail than the suburban students. However, their direct experiences with farming did not enable them to respond any more successfully to questions about land-to-hand relationships involved in bringing common foods to our table, and they actually were less successful than the suburban students in explaining why there are fewer farms in Alaska and why fewer farmers per capita are needed today than in the past (Brophy, O'Mahony, & Alleman, 2001). Thus, once again we see that the students' experience-based knowledge is mostly tacit and context specific, not articulated into a network of connected ideas that can provide a basis for reasoning about related questions. This points up the need to help students see these connections and thus develop more meaningful understandings of their experiences with cultural universals.

DISCUSSION

Responses to the food interview displayed several common patterns seen in all of our interviews: The students knew more about the physical appearances of things than their underlying natures, and more about the uses of finished products than about the land-to-hand transformations involved in creating those products. Sophistication of responses often was related more closely to personal experiences out of school than to school experiences or achievement levels. Knowledge about the past was limited and often tinged with presentism, knowledge about other cultures was limited and often tinged with chauvinism, and there was only limited evidence of historical or cultural empathy (i.e., understanding people's behavior from their perspectives and thus viewing it as sensible adaptation to their time and place rather than as weird, stupid, or incomprehensible). These recurring limitations in the students' responses imply the need to promote empathy in teaching about the historical and cultural aspects of topics.

Data presented in this chapter support and extend previous findings indicating that children's knowledge about food is focused on what one does with it (e.g., defining food as what we eat and talking about consuming it according to "cuisine rules"), rather than on its fundamental nature (source of energy) or on causal mechanisms that explain its place in the human condition (including developments across time and variations across culture and location).

Lacking articulated knowledge of these topics, children extrapolate from their experience, usually reasoning by analogy. Carey (1985) showed that children often extrapolate from what they know about people, offering psychological theories built around human intentions as explanations for biological phenomena.

Inagaki and Hatano (1993) suggested that vitalistic explanations that attribute energy and/or intentionality to bodily organs emerge as preferred forms of biological explanation in between less mature intentional explanations and more scientific mechanical explanations. We found only rare and vague hints of intentional or vitalistic explanations for biological phenomena in our K–3 interviewees' ideas about food.

Even in the early grades, students should be able to construct meaningful knowledge about biological aspects of food, provided that the instruction connects with their prior knowledge, addresses their misconceptions, is structured around key ideas, and is developed using activities calling for comparison, explanation, and problem solving or decision making rather than just workbook exercises calling for nothing more than discriminating foods from nonfoods. Primary-grade students are capable of understanding many things about decomposers, for example, including the ideas that the germs or bacteria involved are tiny organisms very different from "bugs" (insects), and that refrigeration helps retain foods because decomposers thrive in warmer temperatures. They also can understand that people and animals require fuel (food) as a source of energy, and that the key characteristic distinguishing foods from nonfoods is that foods contain nutrients that supply energy.

Answers to questions about food in the past and about food production and distribution indicated that the students were working from images of small family farms on which the families ate most of the crops or animals they raised, and sold the rest to local stores. They showed little or no awareness of large corporate farms, ranches, feedlots, orchards, and so on, or of the network of large trucking, food processing, and supermarket companies that dominate the modern food industry.

The children also showed little knowledge of reasons for developments through time or variations across cultures and locations. They understood that individual inventions can make a difference but had little awareness of mega-businesses as industries driven by consumer demand. Consequently, they suggested such things as that people don't eat much porridge now because it is harder to find (rather than because it has been eclipsed by manufactured breakfast cereals), or that we don't eat much deer or buffalo these days because there aren't many of them around to hunt and hunting is restricted (not realizing that demand for cattle and pig meats largely eclipsed demand for deer and buffalo meats, and that production of deer and buffalo meats would be major industries today if consumer demand dictated).

The questions in our interview reflect our notions about key ideas that might be emphasized in teaching about food. Some of them might be classified more readily as science than social studies, but they all tap networks of knowledge that we believe to be basic for developing initial understandings of the topic. Experimentation may be needed to find appropriate levels of explanation and elaboration. For example, telling students only that butter is made "by shaking cream" is likely to confuse or mislead them, but an extended explanation that included reference to chemical transformations would exceed their readiness to learn with understanding.

Sometimes, emotional readiness also needs to be considered. For example, experiences with pets, zoos, fanciful children's literature, Disney movies, cartoons, and other child-oriented input sources conditions children to personify animals and think in terms of nurturing them and enjoying their companionship. As part of acquiring realistic social knowledge in the primary grades, children need to learn that many animals are basic sources for common foods (and other products). However, this instruction need not include the gorier details of slaughterhouse operations or other content likely to upset some students unnecessarily.

Black and Harlen (1993) suggested organizing instruction about food around the idea that it has both physiological and cultural functions. Its physiological functions are mediated by its component nutrients that are absorbed into the body after the food is digested and reduced to its component elements. These processes, and the nutrients involved, are universal. The particular foods eaten, however, and especially the combinations in which they are eaten, the recipes used to prepare them, and any associated cuisine rules or rituals, vary within and across societies and reflect people's cultural heritages.

Wiegand (1992) suggested teaching children basic ideas about farming as a market-driven enterprise adapted to local geographical conditions. That is, decisions about what crops to raise must take into account both the existing markets (likelihood of selling one's entire crop at an acceptable price) and the farming potential of one's land (likelihood of raising a particular crop cost-effectively, given the soil, the local rainfall and growing season, etc.). No crops can be grown profitably in extreme climates, and within temperate zones that support farming, it is easier or more profitable to raise some crops than others because of local rainfall, temperature, sunshine, hilliness of terrain, and so forth. Farmers may be able to use technology to compensate for unfavorable local geography (e.g., irrigation, greenhouses), but this adds cost and thus reduces or even eliminates potential profitability.

Payne and Gay (1997) suggested that whenever students are taught about regional or cultural foods, they should be invited to speculate about why particular types of foods developed in particular regions or cultures (e.g., abundance of particular spices, dependence on the sea for most food, diffusion from neighbors).

The *Atlas of Science Literacy* (Project 2061, 2001) is a good source of basic ideas (with graphic depictions of their connections) concerning environmental influences, food production, preservation, and transportation, effects on society, diet and nutrition, and other scientific aspects of food as a cultural universal.

Our own unit on food, developed for use in the primary grades, can be found in Alleman and Brophy (2001). It emphasizes social studies rather than science aspects of the topic, including all of the aspects addressed in our food interview.

This concludes our discussion of issues specific to food, although the discussion in chapter 11 of more generic aspects of teaching social studies to young children also contains implications for food units. The conventions for presenting our findings established in this chapter (organization of text and tables) is repeated in chapter 3 through chapter 8, because similar methods were used in our other six large studies (on clothing, shelter, communication, transportation, family living, and government, respectively).

3

Clothing

Our clothing interview asked students:

- to explain why people need clothes;
- to distinguish between business, work, and play clothes and explain why these different forms of clothing are worn;
- to explain what clothes are made from, what cloth is made from, and where threads come from;
- to describe clothes worn by people in the distant past;
- to describe clothes worn when their great-grandparents were children and explain how today's clothes are improved over those clothes;
- to talk about inventions that have made clothes better;
- to talk about whether clothes are easier or harder to take care of today than in the past;
- to identify steps involved in manufacturing a shirt or a dress;
- to talk about where clothes are made and explain why they are made there;
- to explain why people in other parts of the world may dress differently than we do;
- to talk about where to go to purchase a shirt and what criteria to consider in deciding which shirt to purchase;
- to talk about what shoes are made of and what are some steps involved in manufacturing them.

For details of the findings, see the technical report (Brophy & Alleman, 1999a).

CHILDREN'S KNOWLEDGE AND THINKING
ABOUT CLOTHING

Even though clothing is a basic and universal human need and was included as a topic in primary social studies throughout most of the 20th century, we were unable to locate any studies that explored children's thinking about this topic. However, questions relating to clothing were included in a few studies designed to address some broader topic.

For example, Ordan (1945) reviewed surveys of children's knowledge of social concepts. He reported a steady grade-to-grade increase in the number of concepts understood, but also a great deal of individual variation, due primarily to out-of-school experiences. Misconceptions were common among children in the early grades. Even fifth through eighth graders often had vague or incorrect notions of terms they used routinely in schoolwork. For example, they could answer true–false items such as "Massachusetts has many textile factories" correctly, but could not define a textile factory accurately.

Berti and Bombi (1989) interviewed Italian children about the origins and production of three objects (a peach, a clothing item, and a glass) selected to represent increasing degrees of land-to-hand transformation undergone as raw materials are fashioned into final products. They identified three stages in children's understanding of the production cycles involved in combining and transforming raw materials to create products such as clothing items or drinking glasses:

Level 1: No idea about production. Doesn't know where manufactured items come from or believes that they have always been in the home or store.

Level 2: Knows that production exists but not how it is carried out. Is unable to explain or says that the objects were made by machines but without mentioning materials or details. May say that the objects are made out of used materials, without realizing the circularity of this explanation (e.g., collect old rags to make clothes or broken glass to make new glass).

Level 3: Understands that production involves transforming raw materials existing in nature into manufactured products, and knows at least something about the materials or details of production.

The only other references to clothing we found in reviewing literature on children's understanding of social concepts were found in studies of children's consumer knowledge and behavior. These studies will be referenced in discussing the findings from our question about the considerations to take into account in buying a shirt.

OUR CLOTHING INTERVIEWS

Clothing interviews were conducted with 213 students, 54 in kindergarten, 54 in Grade 1, 53 in Grade 2, and 52 in Grade 4, stratified within grade by SES, prior achievement level, and gender. Descriptive statistics and information from analyses of scores derived from the coding are given in Table 3.1.

WHY PEOPLE NEED CLOTHES

1. All over the world, people wear clothes. Do they wear clothes because they need to, or just because they want to? Why? Are there any other reasons why people wear clothes?

2. [If student's response to Question 1 only mentions keeping warm:] **Do they wear clothes in warm places like Hawaii? Why?**

Question 1 assessed understanding that clothing is a universal need. The research was done in Michigan, and we anticipated that many students would respond to Question 1 by saying that people need clothes to protect them from cold or winter weather. Consequently, we included Question 2 to prompt these students to think about other functions of clothing.

K   1. They want to. (Why do you think they want to?) Because they don't want to go around and see everybody naked.

    2. Yes. (Why do they wear clothes?) I don't know.

1st 1. They need to keep them warm from the winter, and in the summer to keep them cool 'cause they need summer clothes 'cause it's really hot. (Are there other reasons why people wear clothes?) So . . . like they need to so people won't see their body parts 'cause they don't want people to see that.

    2. Bathing suits, and sometimes they wear clothes.

2nd 1. Because they need to. (Why do you think they need to?) To keep warm. (What else?) I don't know.

    2. Yeah. (Why do you think that?) Because, sometimes it's probably cold and sometimes it's probably hot. (Are there places where people don't wear clothes?) Africa.

3rd 1. Because they need to because back . . . way back—my mom told me this—people did not have clothes and now today probably you don't feel like walking around without no clothes on. (Why else would you wear clothes?) To keep you warm.

    2. Once in a while if they would get a cold breeze or a chilly day.

More than 90% (193) of the 213 students stated without qualification that people do need clothes. However, 12 said that people do not need clothes and another 8 said that their need depends on the climate in which they live. Perhaps these students had seen photos in *National Geographic* or other sources of information about life in the tropics suggesting that people in some environments do not actually need clothes.

TABLE 3.1
Distributions and Phi Coefficients Showing Relationships
of Coding Categories to Grade Level

Response Categories	Total 213	K 54	1 54	2 53	3 52	Phi
1. Do people need clothes?						
0. No	12	5	1	1	5	
1. Depends on the climate	8	4	1	1	2	
2. Yes (unqualified)	193	45	52	51	45	
2. Why do people need clothes?						
0. Doesn't know	18	7	10	0	1	−28
1. Protect against cold	153	32	34	44	43	24
2. Protect against dirt, sun, insects, injury	35	6	6	7	16	22
3. Modesty	99	21	24	25	29	
4. Decoration/they look good on you	10	2	1	2	5	
5. Number of B1–B4 categories coded[a]	1.4	1.1	1.2	1.5	1.8	37
3. What are business clothes?						
0. Doesn't know/no relevant response	44	32	6	6	0	−57
1. Formal or semiformal clothes	159	14	44	43	48	57
2. Work clothes/uniforms	20	8	4	4	4	
4. Why do business people wear business clothes?						
0. Doesn't know/no relevant response	71	38	19	8	6	−50
1. Protection/no business-specific reason	22	7	4	7	4	
2. Present good appearance to public	120	9	31	38	42	50
5. What are work clothes?						
0. Doesn't know	32	18	10	3	1	−35
1. Old, worn clothes that you can get dirty	170	34	42	47	47	27
2. Heavy, protective clothes	73	13	22	19	19	
3. Uniforms	10	2	1	3	4	
6. Why do workers wear work clothes?						
0. Doesn't know/no relevant response	62	26	22	10	4	−36
1. So people will know that you work there	11	2	3	2	4	
2. Protection from dirt (keep you clean)	111	22	24	29	36	22
3. Protection from hazards (keep you safe)	43	5	11	14	13	17
4. Required by company/boss	8	0	2	4	2	
7. What are play clothes?						
1. Describes casual/play clothes (jeans, t-shirts, sweatshirts, shorts, etc.)	205	46	54	53	52	34
8. Why do we wear play clothes?						
0. Doesn't know/no relevant response	26	16	7	3	0	−34
1. Protection/no play-specific reason	15	7	6	1	1	−20
2. You can get them dirty/they're washable	148	27	36	44	41	28

(Continued)

TABLE 3.1
(Continued)

Response Categories	Total	K	1	2	3	Phi
	213	54	54	53	52	
3. They're comfortable, soft, easy to relax in	21	2	5	5	9	
4. Other (they look nice, they're what you always wear except when dressing up)	14	2	5	2	5	
9. Why do some workers wear uniforms?						
0. Doesn't know/no relevant response	32	23	6	2	1	−46
1. Specific examples (tool belts/pockets, police equipment, etc.)	7	1	4	1	1	
2. So people will know that they work there	141	18	32	46	45	47
3. Protection against dirt or hazards	36	5	14	10	7	
4. Company/boss requires it	31	5	11	6	9	
5. Other	22	4	5	7	6	
10. What are clothes made from?						
0. Doesn't know/no relevant response	25	20	3	2	0	−46
1. Cloth, material, fabric	85	7	27	25	26	32
2. Thread, string, yarn, knitting, stitching	75	19	22	17	17	
3. Wool, fur, animal skin, leather	88	11	25	28	24	25
4. Silk, cotton, linen, polyester, denim	69	6	18	17	28	32
5. Other	9	4	3	1	1	
11. What is cloth made from?						
0. Doesn't know/no relevant response	52	24	15	8	5	−31
1. Woven or knitted from thread, yarn, and so on	57	6	14	17	20	23
2. Pieces of cloth are sewn together (no knowledge that cloth is woven)	23	2	7	7	7	
3. Raw materials are processed directly (e.g., fluffy cotton is ironed or flattened by machines)	27	2	8	9	8	
4. Made by recycling old clothes, socks, and so on	7	2	1	2	2	
5. Animal or plant sources (fur, wool, feathers, cotton, silk, etc.; no knowledge of weaving)	36	8	9	10	9	
6. Other (wood, straw, paper, gel, spider webs, etc.)	17	9	3	4	1	−20
7. Says that cloth is made from thread, yarn, and so on, but can't explain how	24	5	8	5	6	
12. Where do threads come from?						
0. Doesn't know/no relevant response	79	23	19	20	17	
1. Spun from raw material	27	1	6	11	9	22
2. Stores, factories, machines	39	14	10	2	13	
3. Cut/unravel cloth	18	3	4	8	3	
4. Found materials (hair, animal skin, string, whatever silkworms produce, etc.)	44	10	17	7	10	
5. Other (feathers, paper, silk, wool, weaving, etc.)	15	6	2	6	1	

(Continued)

TABLE 3.1
(Continued)

Response Categories	Total	K	1	2	3	Phi
	213	54	54	53	52	
13. What did cave dwellers wear?						
0. Doesn't know/no relevant response	37	26	5	5	1	−48
1. Clothes fashioned from animal skins (not woven)	130	15	31	39	45	45
2. Other (wool, woven cloth, made from leaves or branches, Pilgrim clothes, etc.)	45	13	18	8	6	−21
14. What did the Pilgrims wear?						
0. Doesn't know/no relevant response	49	31	11	6	1	−50
1. Conventional description of Pilgrim clothes	66	4	18	23	21	31
2. Conventional description of pioneer clothes	54	3	9	18	24	36
3. Other, partly correct (wool clothes, Indian clothes, ruffled shirts and coats, etc.)	41	12	15	8	6	
4. Other, incorrect (animal skins, clothes just like ours, suits, uniforms, etc.)	16	6	2	4	4	
5. Described both Pilgrim and pioneer clothes	12	2	1	5	4	
15. How did the pioneers get their clothes?						
0. Doesn't know/no relevant response	90	34	28	15	13	−32
1. Made all or most clothes themselves	74	7	18	20	29	32
2. Bought from stores or clothing merchants	35	13	6	11	5	
3. Made some, bought some	14	0	2	7	5	21
16. Describe clothes when great-grandparents were children						
0. Doesn't know/no relevant response	71	35	21	10	5	−45
1. Generally correct response (woven but heavier, less comfortable, less colorful, etc.)	98	10	22	30	36	38
2. Too far back in time (describes cave dweller, Middle Ages, Pilgrim, or pioneer clothes)	14	1	3	4	6	
3. No difference (just like today's clothes)	21	7	7	4	3	
4. Other incorrect responses (fancy clothes, no clothes, uniforms, etc.)	9	1	1	5	2	
17. How are today's clothes improved?						
0. Doesn't know/no relevant response	93	44	29	16	4	−55
1. Aesthetics (more colorful, decorated with pictures, beads, designs, etc.)	67	8	16	19	24	24
2. Warmer, better at keeping us warm	15	0	0	7	8	28
3. More comfortable (better fits, shorts and informal clothes)	31	2	8	10	11	19
4. Lighter/softer due to finer threads, and so on	20	2	5	4	9	17
5. Mass produced/good quality and variety	31	0	3	5	23	49
6. Durable (less likely to fall apart, sewn better from better materials)	14	0	2	8	4	23

(Continued)

TABLE 3.1
(Continued)

Response Categories	Total	K	1	2	3	Phi
	213	54	54	53	52	
18. What inventions have made clothes better?						
0. Doesn't know/no relevant response	158	49	42	41	26	−34
1. Sewing machines	40	4	6	11	19	29
2. Other (spinning machines, looms, ironing or pressing machines, washers or dryers, better needles, sheep-shearing equipment)	26	2	8	4	12	23
19. Are clothes easier or harder to take care of today?						
0. Doesn't know/no relevant response	14	7	1	2	4	
1. Harder	58	16	16	13	13	
2. Easier	143	31	38	38	36	
20. Why are clothes harder to take care of today?						
1. Doesn't know/no relevant response	15	8	4	2	1	−20
2. We have more clothes today, so it is harder to keep track of them and take care of them	12	0	4	2	6	
3. Machine washing and drying is harder or takes longer than hand washing and drying	9	1	1	4	3	
4. Today's (business) clothes are harder to keep clean than the clothes of the past	8	3	1	3	1	
5. Other	15	4	5	2	4	
6. Student is coded in Categories 2, 3, and/or 4	27	4	6	9	8	
21. Why are clothes easier to take care of today?						
0. Doesn't know/no relevant response	28	15	6	4	3	−27
1. Correct statement that is not germane to the question (today's clothes are easier to put on and take off, etc.)	19	6	4	4	5	
2. Machines (today we have washers, dryers, etc.)	51	4	14	17	16	23
3. Fabrics (ours are lighter and more foldable, wash and wear without ironing, etc.)	13	1	5	3	4	
4. Storage (we have hampers, closets, hangers, etc.)	30	4	11	9	6	
5. Other (our environment is cleaner so clothes don't get as dirty, you can buy new clothing instead of mending, etc.)	27	4	5	7	11	
6. Gives at least one valid reason	92	8	27	29	28	34
22. Steps in manufacture of student's shirt or dress						
0. Doesn't know/no relevant response	22	16	3	3	0	−38
1. Process raw material (shear sheep, pick and clean cotton, etc.)	19	4	3	6	6	
2. Dye to add color	34	9	9	11	5	
3. Spin thread or yarn from raw material	10	0	1	5	4	19

(Continued)

TABLE 3.1
(Continued)

Response Categories	Total 213	K 54	1 54	2 53	3 52	Phi
4. Weave cloth from thread or yarn	63	7	21	17	18	22
5. Cut cloth into shaped pieces of garment	24	4	7	8	5	
6. Sew, stitch, or knit pieces together to form garment	99	25	22	36	16	
7. Add trim, ruffles, belt loops, buttons, pockets, collar, and so on	31	3	13	7	8	19
8. Add decorative design, logo, and so on	47	3	17	17	10	
9. Black box responses that combine Steps 4 through 6 (e.g., make it into a shirt)	58	7	11	7	33	47
10. Number of steps mentioned (0 = 0, 1 = 1, 2 = 2, 3 = 3 or more)[a]	1.7	1.1	1.8	2.0	2.0	38
23. Where student thinks shirt or dress was made						
0. Doesn't know/no relevant response	64	23	18	10	19	
1. Handmade by individual	7	0	2	4	1	
2. Machine-made at a factory	107	14	23	34	36	35
3. Machine-made at the store where it was purchased	35	17	11	5	2	−29
24. Student's explanation for where shirt or dress was made						
0. Doesn't know/no relevant response	69	27	21	15	6	−30
1. It was made somewhere near where it was purchased	63	20	19	15	9	−17
2. It was made in a factory located where raw materials are plentiful	58	6	11	16	25	31
3. It could have been made almost anywhere, clothes are made in many places	23	1	3	7	12	26
25. Why people in other parts of the world dress differently than we do						
1. Doesn't know if people dress differently, or thinks that everyone dresses the same everywhere	12	6	5	1	0	−20
2. Says that there are places where people dress differently, but cannot give examples or explanations	70	29	19	15	7	−31
3. Identifies types of people who dress differently (poor or homeless, boys vs. girls, Pilgrims, etc.)	49	10	13	11	15	
4. Identifies styles of clothing (bathing suits, smocks, strips of cloth wrapped around you, etc.)	15	2	4	6	3	
5. Climate explanations (fewer/lighter clothes in hot climates, more/heavier clothes in cold climates)	40	1	8	12	19	32
6. Economic development explanations (third world lacks access to variety of clothes, some people make clothes from leaves or found materials)	12	1	7	2	2	

(Continued)

TABLE 3.1
(Continued)

Response Categories	Total 213	K 54	1 54	2 53	3 52	Phi
7. Culture/custom examples (sombreros or blankets in Mexico, Chinese robes, Indian saris, etc.)	50	5	6	13	26	38
8. Gives at least two substantive responses (coded in Categories 3, 5, 6, or 7)	28	0	6	3	19	41
26. Reasons for choice of store in which to purchase shirt						
0. Doesn't know/no relevant response	4	3	1	0	0	
1. A store that sells clothes (no elaboration)	81	30	21	16	14	−23
2. Store offers good quality clothes	64	12	11	20	21	20
3. Store offers large selection	62	8	21	17	16	20
4. Store offers reasonable prices, good sales	21	2	3	6	10	20
5. Student gives two or more reasons (among quality, selection, or price)	18	1	3	6	8	19
27. Reasons for choice of shirt to purchase						
0. Doesn't know/no relevant response	27	16	8	3	0	−34
1. Appearance (shirt is nice, pretty, attractive, etc.)	69	13	20	17	19	
2. Shirt "looks good on me" when tried on	17	1	1	6	9	24
3. Price (reasonable)	34	5	11	9	9	
4. Color (favorite color, likes the color)	53	7	15	16	15	
5. Design/print (it has an animal on it, etc.)	51	15	13	11	12	
6. Fabric (likes silk, flannel, a jersey, etc.)	20	4	3	6	7	
7. Size/fit (just right)	58	5	10	18	25	33
8. Season (light shirt for warm weather, etc.)	12	1	4	2	5	
9. Other (clean, same as shirt being replaced, etc.)	15	2	4	5	4	
10. Gender (wants a shirt made for a boy/girl)	6	1	1	1	3	
11. Matches wardrobe (goes with other clothes)	8	0	1	4	3	
12. Quality (well made, will last, won't shrink)	9	0	3	2	4	
13. Style/fashion (matches student's taste, "in" now, etc.)	7	0	1	1	5	21
14. Number of reasons given (0 = 0, 1 = 1, 2 = 2, 3 = 3 or more)[a]	2.4	1.1	2.2	2.5	3.8	17
28. What are shoes made of?						
0. Doesn't know/no relevant response	21	13	4	4	0	−30
1. Leather, suede, snakeskin, alligator skin, and so on	119	12	30	32	45	46
2. Wood	29	8	8	8	5	
3. Rubber	62	9	14	16	23	22
4. Plastic (elastic), styrofoam, polyester	43	5	11	14	13	17
5. Fabric (material, cloth, soft stuff, wool sewing, etc.)	97	18	26	27	26	
6. String, laces	37	4	9	11	13	17

(Continued)

TABLE 3.1
(Continued)

Response Categories	Total 213	K 54	1 54	2 53	3 52	Phi
7. Metal	28	3	8	6	11	
8. Other valid responses (Velcro, hard material for sole, etc.)	21	6	4	6	5	
9. Incorrect responses (paper, feathers, etc.)	10	4	5	0	1	−18
10. Number of shoe materials mentioned in Categories 1–8 (0 = 0, 1 = 1, 2 = 2, 3 = 3, 4 = 4 or more)[a]	2.0	1.2	2.0	2.2	2.7	44
29. Does the student know that leather is animal hide?						
0. Not applicable (student never mentioned leather or was not asked what it is)	110	46	29	24	11	−46
1. Doesn't know	35	5	10	8	12	
2. Incorrect (says it's made from rubber, wood, etc.)	19	0	5	9	5	
3. Correct (says it's animal skin, cowhide, deer skin, etc.)	49	3	10	12	24	35
30. Steps in manufacturing shoes						
0. Doesn't know/no relevant response	32	20	7	3	2	−37
1. Process raw materials (tan hides, clean or soften leather, process rubber or plastic to right degree of hardness, etc.)	12	1	1	6	4	18
2. Measure/cut/fashion the parts	103	15	19	34	35	35
3. Sew/glue/nail the parts together to form shoe	160	25	43	43	49	41
4. Add extras (laces, bows, buckles, polish, designs, labels, etc.)	125	25	35	33	32	
5. Student mentions both making the parts and combining them	92	12	19	27	34	33

Note. Underlining indicates that the chi-square for the underlined distribution was statistically significant at or below the .05 level. In these instances the phi coefficients (with decimal points omitted) are given in the phi column to indicate the magnitudes of linear trends.

[a]Numbers in these rows are means. Numbers in all other rows are frequency scores showing how many students in each group were coded for mentioning the ideas represented by the response category.

In our shelter interview, all of the students stated that people need homes, even in Hawaii, but in these clothing interviews, 20 students maintained that people do not need clothes if they live in a warm climate. They appeared unaware of functions of clothing beyond protection from cold, so they viewed clothing as a social convention or personal preference rather than a fundamental need. Thus, even though 90% of them did recognize that clothing is a basic need, this need was less obvious to K–3 students than our needs for food or shelter.

The rationales that the students gave in explaining their answers help us to understand why some of them viewed clothing as an option rather than a need.

Clothing has at least four noteworthy functions (protection, modesty, appearance enhancement/decoration, and identification with a social group or cultural reference), but the students' responses were focused almost exclusively on the first two of these functions. The most popular explanation for why people need clothes was for protection against cold (given by 153 students). In addition or instead, 99 gave modesty explanations and 35 spoke of protection against dirt, sun, insects, injury, or other hazards, but only 10 said that we wear clothes for decorative purposes or because they look good on us, and only one even hinted at the notion of identification. It would be interesting to see how students living in a warm climate (e.g., Florida or Hawaii) would respond to Question 1. We would expect such students to put less emphasis on clothing's protective function than our Michigan students did, and to the extent that they did talk about clothing as protective, to emphasize protection against the sun or insects rather than against cold.

Some students, notably those who said that people need clothes but could not explain why, may have been embarrassed to talk about modesty, especially if the only ways that they could think of to express this idea involved using words they did not feel comfortable using (e.g., "because then people could see your booty"). Among students who did bring up modesty, the younger ones tended to talk about the reactions of other people who might see you naked, whereas the older ones tended to talk more about your own internal feelings of embarrassment.

Responses to Questions 1 and 2 were mostly correct as far as they went and lacking in noteworthy misconceptions. However, some of the younger students spoke from a childish or egocentric purview: so no one will see their underwear; so people won't see them naked—"because if you go out and do that, everyone will think that it's terrible"; because other people would see their private parts and think that they weren't very nice people; they'll see your behind and make fun of you; going naked is illegal and will get you sent to jail.

These findings suggest that K–3 students could benefit from instruction clarifying that clothing is considered a basic need for all people, regardless of the climate in which they reside, and that clothing has at least four noteworthy functions: (a) protection (not only against cold but against injury, dirt, insects, the sun, and various other hazards); (b) modesty; (c) appearance enhancement/decoration; and (d) identification with a social group or cultural reference (expressed through one's general style of clothing or through designs or logos associated with favorite sports teams, hobbies, artists, etc.). Students would learn that expectations regarding these functions of clothing vary with climate and culture, but the functions themselves (and presumed needs that underlie them) are universal.

TYPES OF CLOTHES

3. Bankers and lawyers and certain other business people wear business clothes. Can you describe these business clothes that bankers or lawyers wear? Why do they wear business clothes?

4. People who work on farms or in factories wear work clothes. Can you describe these work clothes? Why do workers wear work clothes?

5. When we are just relaxing at home, we wear casual clothes, or play clothes. Can you describe these play clothes? Why do we wear play clothes?

6. Some workers wear uniforms, like the police or the people who work at McDonald's. Why do some workers wear uniforms?

K   3. I don't know that one.

4. Yes, because so they won't get their other clean clothes dirty. (What do the work clothes look like?) I don't know.

5. If you didn't have play clothes, then you'd get all dirty. (Why do we wear play clothes when we want to play?) Because so you won't get them all messed up and you can probably wash it.

6. Because they have to dress up in a uniform or they don't know which job they're in.

1st   3. Bankers wear these clothes . . . like breakers [blazers] and they're gray and they wear ties. They just got to look good for the customers that come to the bank. (Why do they wear these clothes?) Because if they don't wear them, the customers will laugh at them and their boss says they have to wear them so they'll be nice at the bank because the bank is a nice place.

4. They're clothes that have big things that you hook them on and then they wear like shirts and they walk around picking up eggs and milking cows or making food. They gotta sell pigs for hot dogs and lots of food. (So why do workers wear work clothes?) Because they're workers. (Any other reason why?) No.

5. Yeah, they're like clothes like I'm wearing. (Yes. Tell me what you're wearing.) Like I'm wearing my brother's shirt because it fits me good and it gots Looney Tunes on them and shorts are cool, and like jeans, some people think jeans are cool. (Why do we wear play clothes when we want to relax and play?) Because they just want to be cool or they just want to look nice to play.

6. 'Cause they want to know they really do work at McDonald's or for the police. If they don't wear them, they don't know they're really police. Like one person calls the police and they think he's the police but he really ain't. (All right. Are there other reasons why people wear uniforms?) Probably they wear uniforms is because they just need to so they'll know they work at the place.

2nd   3. Um . . . they're nice and they're dressy and they like to dress up in them. (Why do they wear these clothes?) Because they have to look nice to go to work.

4. Well, they're . . . they wear farmer clothes that has straps around their arms and people who work in factories have pants with holes in them and stuff. (OK. Why do workers wear work clothes?) Because . . . I think they just want to.

5. They're dirtier than the new ones and they're just . . . I don't know. (Well, why do we wear play clothes when we want to relax?) Because our moms don't want us to get our new clothes dirty.

6. Because people who work at like McDonald's and stuff like that— they have to wear uniforms for people to know that they work there.

3rd 3. Yeah, it's like a suit that has dress pants, a vest with a tie and a white shirt. (Why do they wear these clothes?) Because the boss doesn't want them to be all grubby and walking in with shorts on. Probably they want them to wear the suit because maybe they've got hairy legs.

4. They've got overalls that hold the pants up, probably a short sleeve or a long sleeve, probably a hat to keep the sun from shining in their eyes. (Well, why do workers and farmers wear work clothes?) To show their boss or whoever they work for that they can be this nice.

5. Yeah, like dirty clothes or old clothes and probably shorts or something like that. (Why do we wear play clothes when we want to play?) Because probably your mother don't want you getting your school clothes or party clothes all dirty so that she has to wash them all over again.

6. To show that they're not like some other person that could sneak in there and act like they work there because some people . . . like the police gotta wear uniforms so that people know they're police, not like some guy walking out and saying "Hey, I'm on the police side."

Question 3 through Question 6 probed students' knowledge of major types of clothing worn in different situations (business clothes, work clothes, play clothes, and uniforms). Almost three fourths (159) accurately described business clothes as semiformal attire (although some referred to "tuxedos" instead of suits or sport jackets). However, 20 described business clothes as work clothes or uniforms, and another 44 (including 32 kindergarteners) were unable to respond to the question. When asked why business people wear business clothes, 120 spoke of wanting to make a good appearance to the public or to one's business clients, 71 could not respond, and 22 could only give explanations that applied to clothing in general rather than business clothing in particular (e.g., business people wear clothes to protect them from the cold).

The students were more successful in talking about work clothes. More than three fourths (170) described work clothes as old, worn clothes that you do not mind getting dirty. In addition or instead, 73 said that work clothes are heavy and provide protection to workers and another 10 described them as uniforms. Only 32 were unable to respond.

When asked why workers wear work clothes, 111 students said that these clothes protect workers from dirt, grease, and so on, and thus help them to keep clean. Responses generated less frequently included the ideas that work clothes protect workers from hazards or injury (43), identify workers to the public as employees of the company (11), or are worn simply because they are required by the company or the boss (8). Most of the explanations focusing on identifying the worker as an employee of the company were made by students who described work clothes as uniforms. Finally, 62 students were unable to explain why workers wear work clothes.

The students were most successful in talking about play clothes. All but eight (205) accurately described play clothes as jeans, t-shirts, sweat shirts, shorts, or other casual clothes (several of the younger students included pajamas). Furthermore, only 26 could not explain why play clothes are worn, although another 15 only mentioned protection from cold or some other rationale that was not specific to the play setting. A majority (148) described play clothes as washable or clothes that you don't mind getting dirty, 21 said that they are worn because they are comfortable, soft, or easy to relax in, and 14 gave other reasons (including the notion that play clothes are the default choice—you always wear them except when dressing up).

Finally, even though only 10 students had mentioned uniforms spontaneously when asked about work clothes, all but 32 were able to provide some explanation when asked why some workers wear uniforms. The most popular responses were that uniforms identify workers to the public as employees of the company (141), uniforms protect workers against dirt or hazards (36), and the company or boss requires them (31). The remaining students gave miscellaneous "other" reasons, except for 7 who gave specific examples of the functional value of certain aspects of certain uniforms (tool belts or pockets, police holsters, etc.).

In general, the students knew more about the clothes with which they had personal experience (play clothes) than about types of clothing worn primarily in adult work settings. Even when they did have general knowledge about business or work clothes, their ability to talk about them often was hampered by limited expressive vocabularies (e.g., terms such as *suit, sport coat, jacket, blazer,* or *overalls*).

Several naive notions appeared among the rare and unique responses: Bankers and lawyers wear suits and ties because "it's their uniform so people will know if they see them driving and will get out of the way because they're going to work and they might be late"; farmers wear farmer clothes so that other people will know that they are farmers; farmers wear protective clothes so animals don't lick their skin; farmers wear sunhats because they're usually redheads who sweat a lot; McDonald's workers wear uniforms so that people who are confused about how to work the machines (apparently, soda dispensers) will know whom to ask for help and won't end up breaking the machines by trying to do things on their own.

There was a fascination on the part of several students with police uniforms and equipment. In general, however, the rare and unique responses to Question 3 through Question 6 contained fewer naive ideas or misconceptions than most of the data sets in most of our interviews. Kindergarten students frequently were unable to respond, but most older students were able to describe business clothes, work clothes/uniforms, and play clothes accurately and explain their key characteristics and functions, even though they often lacked precise vocabulary for describing business and work clothes.

These findings indicate that K–3 students are able to draw on tacit knowledge of transparent features in order to draw comparisons of different forms of clothing and their respective functions, even when they don't understand the "land-to-hand" connections and causal relationships that underlie what is visible to the eye. Similar findings emerged in our shelter study, in which students made many valid statements of comparing and contrasting different types of housing, even though most of them lacked understanding of the geographical and cultural reasons why the different forms of housing were constructed by the people who lived in them.

CLOTH AND THREAD

7. What are our clothes made from? [If necessary, rub your own shirt/blouse and pants/skirt and ask:] **What do we call this material that clothes are made out of?**

8. [If child has not said so already, say:] **Our clothes are made out of cloth. What is cloth made from? How is _____ made into cloth?**

9. Most cloth is made by weaving it from threads. Where do threads come from? [If necessary, probe by asking:] **How is thread made from _____?**

K 7. A factory on a machine. (What are they made out of?) I don't know.

8. Um . . . I don't know.

9. I don't know. (How is thread made?) I don't know.

1st 7. From like wool or like fluffy stuff. Jeans are from wool, and then they get this machine and make the jeans hooked together on the side. (What do we call this material that your shirt is made out of?) Like really flat wool.

8. Cloth is made out of . . . it can be made out of other things like people who cut off sheep's fur and make it into cloth. (How is wool made into cloth?) See, you take this thing and when you put it in and when it goes around this thing and it's like shaking the cloth and flatten it and make it into clothes.

9. (That's what you were describing for me—weaving it—weaving it from threads like this.) Yup. (Where does the thread come from?)

Thread—it probably comes from . . . they probably cut off an animal's fur and it's really long and then they make it into colors and then they wrap it around one of those things.

2nd 7. Cloth.

8. From a factory. (It probably is made in a factory—and how do they do it in that factory?) They probably have a big machine and it like just sews it all up.

9. I don't know.

3rd 7. Silk, wool, cloth.

8. Spider webs and . . . that's all. (How is cloth made out of spider webs?) You take the webs and give it to a factory, then they change it to cloth or silk.

9. Sheep. (OK, you mean the sheep's wool.) Yeah, their wool. (OK, so then, how does it come from the sheep's wool to this—the thread?) First the farmer shaves the wool off the sheep, then they give it to their wives, if they're old fashioned, and she'll spin the wool and it'll come out really skinny, and if they wanted different colors, they'd probably dye it.

Students' responses to Question 7 through Question 9 were much less knowledgeable than their responses to Question 1 through Question 6. Most knew that clothing is a basic need and could talk about different kinds of clothing and why they are worn, but most did not know what clothing actually is (i.e., cloth woven from thread that is spun from raw material). Only 57 (27%) understood that cloth is woven from thread, and fewer than half of these (13%) understood that thread is manufactured through a process of spinning.

Lacking knowledge that cloth is woven, a majority of the students envisioned cloth as a solid membrane (i.e., animal skin) or manufactured substance (akin to plastic, rubber, or paper). Many understood that thread is used in manufacturing clothing because they understood that thread is used to stitch together pieces of cloth to form the garment. However, most did not realize that the garment pieces themselves were woven from thread. These ideas sometimes were seen even in students who correctly stated that clothes are made from wool, silk, or cotton, because they thought that these raw materials were processed by "smishing" them into flat cloth membranes or substances (rather than by spinning threads from them). In attempting to describe clothing manufacture, these students sometimes depicted (presumably solid) pieces of wool or cotton being glued, sewn, or otherwise attached to a (presumably solid) cloth substrate of undescribed origins.

Among students who did understand that clothing is woven, some were confined to a "knitting" model in which the entire garment is woven/knitted in one continuous operation from beginning to end. The others articulated a "parts assembly" model in which patterns are used to cut pieces of woven cloth to create components, which then are stitched together to form the complete garment.

Students who had no knowledge of "land-to-hand" relationships in obtaining thread from plant or animal sources and then weaving the thread into cloth were forced to develop alternative explanations when asked where cloth and thread come from. Some talked about gathering and processing naturally found material such as animal hair. Others, echoing students classified by Berti and Bombi (1989) as at Level 2 in their understanding of production cycles, spoke of unraveling and reusing old clothing. One carried the "recycling" notion even further by suggesting that clothing is made from lint collected from clothes dryers.

In summary, although responses to Question 1 through Question 6 were generally knowledgeable (beyond kindergarten) and most responses to Question 7 gave an initial impression that students understood the basic nature of cloth and clothing, responses to Question 8 and Question 9 made it clear that this was not the case. Even though a majority of the students made accurate statements about the plant or animal sources of clothing (e.g., wool, silk, cotton, etc.), only one fourth of them understood that cloth is a fabric woven from thread or yarn and only one eighth understood that thread or yarn is spun from its raw material.

One common misconception held by half or more of the students was that cloth is a solid akin to soft plastic, rubber, or paper. Some expressed this notion directly in talking about machines that iron or flatten fluffy cotton. Others were vague about how cloth is manufactured but talked about making clothes by sewing together pieces of (presumably solid) cloth.

Other misconceptions concerning cloth included statements that spinning wheels are used to spin "cloth" into "sweaters"; pieces of cotton are sewn inside two pieces of "fabric" (unexplained further); cloth is raw silk that has been washed; and "cotton" is sewn inside of the cloth, to make it soft. Several students spoke of attaching raw wool to a (woven) cloth substrate or sewing the wool in between two layers of cloth (like insulation). Others spoke of a cotton "pocket" inside cloth covers, or a cloth substrate covered over with layers of cotton, wool, and so on. These responses came from students who did not understand that cloth is woven threads and were seeking to explain the relationship between raw wool or cotton (as they envisioned it) and fabric.

Many students spoke of "sewing" a garment from start to finish—like knitting a sweater (and maybe cutting out neck or arm holes)—as opposed to assembling cut pieces and then stitching them together. Some of those who knew that cloth is made from thread, yarn, and so on, but were not able to explain how, probably were working from this model.

Most of the students who did not know that thread is spun from raw material were unable to explain at all, but 44 thought that thread was (or was made from) found material such as hair, string, or "what silkworms produce." Concerning both cloth and thread, some students could only suggest a recycling notion (new cloth is made from old clothes, socks, and so on; new thread is obtained by cutting up or unraveling already-existing cloth). Other misconceptions concerning thread included: Use a shredder to shred rope into threads; iron the wool and then spread it out to make it soft; machines separate thick from thin sheep hairs, then dye the thin ones for thread; made from horse tails; made from strings found in hay; pull out loose threads hanging from garments; sheep hairs are fused using heat or else tied together in tiny knots; cotton is forced through a small hole to make thread; silk strings are made from horsetail hair; a machine "takes the extra stuff off" that makes the wool too fluffy.

In summary, even though the students were familiar with different types of clothing, most of them were vague or confused about the nature of cloth itself. The majority who did not realize that cloth is woven fabric had to "reach" from what they did know in order to generate explanations. Those who knew that cloth is wool or cotton sometimes spoke of attaching the raw wool or cotton to a presumably solid substrate (without indicating what this substrate was). Those who knew that clothing is made from thread or yarn sometimes suggested a "knitting" model, envisioning the sewing of a garment from start to finish as one continuous operation, as opposed to assembling pieces and then stitching them together.

EVOLUTION IN CLOTHING OVER TIME

10. Let's talk about clothing in the past. Way back when people lived in caves—what kind of clothes did they wear? What were their clothes made of? How did they make the _____ into clothes?

11. Back in the days of the Pilgrims and the pioneers, what kind of clothes did people wear? What were these clothes made of? Where did the pioneers get their clothes?

12. Back when your great-grandparents were children, what were people's clothes like? How were clothes back then different from today's clothes?

13. How have today's clothes been improved over clothes in the past? Do you know about any inventions that have made clothes better than they used to be?

17. Are clothes today easier or harder to take care of than they used to be? Why?

    K   10. I don't know.

           11. Different kind of clothes. They have white hats. I don't know anything else. (What were those clothes made out of?) I don't know. (Where did they get their clothes?) Probably just made them.

           12. Different. (How were they different?) I don't know.

           13. I don't know. (Do you think the clothes we wear today are better than they used to be?) Yeah. (How are they better?) 'Cause they look gooder. (All right. Do you know of any invention that has made

clothes better than they used to be?) No. I know how they make white stuff from lambs.

17. Harder to take care of. (What makes them harder to take care of now?) If they get all dirty, the dirt can't come off.

1st 10. Probably they just had to cut off a tooth from a saber tooth tiger and then they go up to some animal that has fur, like a mouse, they could cut off their fur and then they wrapped it and then they cut off another part of it and then they wrapped it around, but way back then, they didn't have stuff to hook it together so they took some bones and they curl it so the bone will hook the clothes together.

11. The Indians wear just these clothes and the Pilgrims—they wore these . . . the girls had these two things tied back there and it made a hat and then they walked around with these clothes with red stripes . . . the owner, he took some of those Pilgrims and made them into slaves and then he made the slaves make clothes. (So where did the pioneers get their clothes?) They get the clothes like from the prisoners [slaves]. (The pioneers are the people who settled in the west. We see picture of pioneers going out west to new land in their covered wagons. What do you think they wore?) They wore probably like stuff, like important clothes. (Where do you think they got their clothes?) Probably they got their clothes from fur cloth too.

12. I don't know but they probably were like mixed up like blue jeans weren't blue—they were red, and they looked . . . my mom once gave me these pants that my dad weared when he was a kid and they were red so I think they just got their pants turned red. (Do you know of any other differences between the clothes that we wear today and clothes they wore back then?) Yeah, their pants were red and our pants or blue jeans are blue. And the clothes were just different. That was a long time ago, and now is now and they make our clothes like this.

13. Like kids' clothes back in the past, their clothes had to be fancy and nice. But in our times, they made our clothes kind of nice. (Do you know about any inventions that have made clothes better than they used to be?) I think a long time ago there wasn't anything where you make cloth. Now there is stuff to make cloth.

17. Easier, 'cause a long time ago, like when there was those people, probably they just had one clothes and they would get teared off or something, but now we have a lot of clothes and we can put our dirty clothes downstairs to get washed and put our clean clothes in a dresser so they'll be safe.

2nd 10. They wore skins from animals. (How did they make the skins into clothes?) They killed the animals and cut off their fur and made clothes with them.

11. They wore dresses and pants just like we do. (Where did they get their clothes—the pioneers? Where did they get their clothes?) They made them. (What do you think they made them out of?) [no response]

12. Just like ours. (There were no differences between their clothes and what we wear today?) The girls always had to wear dresses and the boys always had to wear pants.

13. They're warmer than the others. (Are there any other differences?) No. (Are there any inventions that you know of that have made clothes better than they used to be?) No.

17. Easier. (Why do you say that?) Because we have like . . . [no further response]

3rd 10. Animal skins and . . . that's all. (How did they make the animal skins into clothes?) They probably took something sharp, like an arrow, and shot the animal and killed it and brung it to their cave and took something sharp and cut it out like they wore back in the old times.

11. Some of them wore shoes—some didn't, probably 'cause they couldn't afford it—long socks, short pants, and a shirt and—this is for boys—and a little hat, not today's hat. (What were these clothes made of?) Probably sheep or something. (Where did the pioneers get their clothes?) Probably they make them for their own self, the people that can't afford it, and probably some other people bought it from people. (Do you have any idea where they'd get the fabric to make them?) Wool from sheeps.

12. Probably the same, like the Pilgrims. Yeah. (How were clothes back then different from today's clothes?) We got short socks and they still had long socks and now we have new hats like basketball hats and baseball and football, and back in the old times, they just had brown hats, nothing like today. Plus, we got shorts and they just had long pants and we've got different colored pants and they just had one color of pants, like that.

13. Color. (Any other improvements?) Nope. (Do you know about any inventions that have made clothes better than they used to be?) No.

17. Easier. (Why do you say that?) Because we got like machines, like washers and we can just throw them in there and just wash them, and back in the old times it would take like one hour just to get the dirt out and get it clean—the clothes. That's why I think it's easier.

At first glance, responses to Question 10 through Question 12 seem to indicate that the students knew more about clothing far back in time than in more recent eras; more were able to respond, and more accurately, concerning the clothing of cave dwellers and Pilgrims and pioneers, compared to clothing when their great-grandparents were children. However, the latter responses were more detailed. Most responses concerning cave dwellers' clothing simply depicted the stereotype of clothing fashioned from animal skins shown in the Flintstones™ and Alley Oop™ cartoons. Students who did not possess this stereotyped image tended to produce misconceptions: that clothes in the distant past were made from trees, wood, branches, leaves, bark, acorns, newspaper, rock, moss, straw, or "junk found in rivers"; that they were made from "soft rocks" and material, using a design pattern; that people didn't wear clothes because they didn't know how to make them; that clothes were made from leaves or dinosaur skin; and that they wore sewn togas.

Although fewer students were able to respond when asked about the clothing of the Pilgrims, the pioneers, or the early 20th century, those who did respond provided more lengthy and less stereotyped descriptions. Descriptions of Pilgrim clothing clearly were based on illustrations shown in history texts, children's literature, or movies and television programs about the Pilgrims (men wearing black, gray, or green hats, coats worn over a white shirt, and pants with a big belt buckle; women wearing long dresses, often with aprons, as well as bonnets or shawls). Descriptions of pioneers' clothing were more varied. Many were influenced by the buckskin outfits shown in history texts, children's literature, and movies and television programs about Daniel Boone, Davy Crockett, or other pioneer heroes. Others emphasized homespun work or "farmer" clothes for men and dresses for women. Responses that did not conform to either the conventional Pilgrim or the conventional pioneer clothing stereotypes but could be considered at least partly correct included wool clothes, Indian clothes, and ruffled shirts and coats.

Several students described pioneer clothing as army uniforms, probably as a result of watching movies and television programs featuring clashes between the U.S. Army and Native Americans. For these students, the term *pioneer* apparently conjured images of the U.S. Army fighting Indians along the frontier, rather than nonmilitary families developing homesteads. Similarly, several suggested that the Pilgrims were given clothes by local Native Americans, probably extrapolating from the traditional First Thanksgiving story or accounts of Squanto or other Native Americans helping the early European immigrants to survive.

Several students noted that pioneer women made their families' clothes. One first grader initially said that maybe Indians taught the Pilgrims how to make their clothes out of acorns, string, and newspaper, then said that the pioneers always wore black clothes which they got from "the animals and trees and leather and wool and maybe they learned how to make it out of bark."

Concerning clothing when their great-grandparents were children, the students did not have a clear stereotype to work from, yet their responses were mostly accurate and the inaccurate ones contained only minor misconceptions. Thus, the students were more able to make reasonable inferences about clothing in the relatively recent past than they were about clothing in the days of the cave dwellers.

If the students did possess a stereotype of clothing early in the 20th century, it was the idea that such clothing was rather drab, formal, heavy, and uncomfortable. Many students celebrated the proliferation of shorts and comfortable play clothes and the waning of the expectation that girls would always be expected to wear dresses. One surprise was that five students identified bell bottoms as clothing typical of the period. We suspect that these students were thinking of clothes worn to dress up as hippies for Halloween or 1960s days at school (and in the process, thinking that the 1960s were so long ago that their great-grandparents would have been children then).

The students generally viewed modern clothes as improved over earlier clothes in every way. Many were under the impression that earlier clothes were sewn poorly and prone to unravel or fall apart easily. Other common observations included that today's fabrics are more aesthetically pleasing, lighter yet stronger and better at keeping us warm, and more comfortable because they include shorts and other play clothes; that many modern fabrics are softer and thus less stiff or scratchy; and that today we have larger and more varied wardrobes that allow us to adjust more completely to seasonal variations in temperature. A few students attributed our enjoyment of a wide variety of good-quality clothing choices to mass production and other modern manufacturing inventions and techniques, but most simply noted this abundance of choices without attempting to explain it. Students who viewed clothes of the early 20th century as more formal than ours may have been influenced by family photos or other photos taken in an era in which photographs were expensive so most people rarely had them taken and usually dressed formally when they did.

The students had only limited knowledge of inventions, but what was said (by the 25% who were able to respond) was accurate. The only misconception was one student's description of machines that flatten and press wool into cloth, which obviously was connected to the common misconception that cloth is a solid made by "smishing" raw materials rather than a fabric made by weaving threads.

The question about whether clothes are easier or harder to take care of today unexpectedly led to bifurcated lines of responses, with good reasoning shown in support of both conclusions. This occurred because the phrase "to take care of" was interpreted by most students in the way we intended (i.e., referring to laundering and storage of clothes), but was understood by a minority to refer to "keeping track of." Thus, in addition to students who showed good reasoning by stating that clothes are easier to take care of today because of washers and dryers, better fabrics, modern storage, and so on, other students showed good reasoning by stating that clothes are harder to take care of today because we have more clothes to keep track of and higher cleanliness expectations in modern business environments. For the most part, however, the students expressed clear preferences for contemporary clothing and clothing-related cultural expectations over those of the past. This was part of the pervasive presentism that has appeared in all of our studies whenever the students are asked to talk about the past or to make comparisons between the past and the present.

Many of the rare and unique responses also showed good reasoning: Clothes are harder to take care of today because we are expected to wash them more often; we have whiter or brighter colored clothes that are harder to keep clean; modern stains are difficult to eradicate; and many modern fabrics are delicate and require special handling. Clothes are easier to take care of today because modern soaps and cleaning agents are better; the clothes come with cleaning instructions; and many of our clothes are shorter, lighter, more easily foldable, or otherwise easier to handle than the heavier clothes of the past. Other unusual responses included: Pioneer women often had to struggle to sew clothes while seated in bumpy wagons, whereas modern clothing workers sit on stable seats; they didn't have turtlenecks then, or rubber to make rubber items; clothes are more reliable now due to machines and patterns; we have belts; girls can now wear pants or whatever they want, not just hoop skirts; some of our clothes are waterproof; our clothes are tested for safety and freedom from ants and bugs; we now have sturdier threads for making stronger clothes; and we have machines that press wool into cloth, add plastic trim and designs, or "make clothes smooth and design them and everything."

MODERN CLOTHING MANUFACTURE

14. How do you think your shirt (dress) was made? What was the first step in making it? Then what? [Probe for specifics of process, not just statements about what it was made from.]

15. Where do you think your shirt (dress) was made? [If child says "in a factory," ask:] **Where do you think the factory is?**

16. Are there people in other parts of the world who dress differently than we do? Tell me about that. [Repeat for as many examples as the child can generate, and for each example ask:] **Why do they dress like that?**

K   14. I don't know.

     15. (no response)

     16. In India—it's a different country. I don't know anything else.

1st   14. Probably they took a black sheep and they took it off and then they rolled it together and inside of there they probably sewed on this side white, and they sewed on the other side blue. (I see. Then what?) And then probably they took that big gold pin and they just stuck it on.

     15. In Africa because a lot of stuff is made in Africa. I found trolls made in Africa, trash cans . . . all kinds of stuff is made in Africa.

16. Yeah, everybody has different clothes. See, you're wearing different clothes than I'm wearing. That's because you're a grown up and I'm a kid. All the kids my age in my class wear different clothes than I wear. (Well, think about people in other parts of the world.) Well, like in Africa, their clothes are a lot different than our clothes. Like in Chicago, their clothes are kinda same as our clothes. (Why is it that the people in Africa wear different kinds of clothes than we do?) 'Cause probably some people who live there don't know how to make our clothes and we don't know how to make their clothes.

2nd 14. Um . . . out of like . . . a caterpillar, like for silk. (OK, you get silk from a caterpillar. What was the first step in making your blouse?) They had to buy the stuff, like the cloth. Then they had to buy the buttons and the thread to sew it up with. (Then what?) And then they put like some designs on it.

15. I think at a factory. (Where do you suppose that factory is?) Like um . . . in a building that makes stuff.

16. Some people have just pants and some people just have dresses. That's all I can think of.

3rd 14. Probably from thread from sheep—wool, I mean. They probably dyed it and just made it. You can see some of it here.

15. I forgot. I've got to cheat and look [at the tag in his shirt]. It doesn't tell. (Well, where do you think?) Probably China. (Could be.) Aha. U.S.A. (It's made in the U.S.A., but you said you guessed it was made in China. Why did you say that?) Because it looks like China. (What makes you think it looks like China or the Chinese made it?) Because the Chinese like dark colors and you can see there's a lot of dark colors in it. That's why I thought it was made in China, but it's not.

16. Like China and Europe and Africa. In Africa, they got like under-wear but not the kind we have in the U.S.A. We have different col-ored underwear but not with designs on them, and in China they wear like real big hats and real heavy stuff, and in Europe—I have no idea. (Well, why do the people in China, for instance, dress differ-ently?) Probably they dress for their gods because one of my friends named Mei, she's part China—she is full China actually, and she dresses like she does because they dress for the gods. That's what I be-lieve.

Almost 90% of the students were able to name one or more steps in the manu-facture of a shirt or dress, and most of these responses were accurate as far as they went. However, they were not particularly impressive. Table 3.1 identifies eight steps in the clothing manufacture process, in the order in which they ordinarily would be performed. No student included all of these steps, although many included several of them.

The most common responses made some reference to sewing, stitching, or knitting pieces together to form a garment (99); weaving the cloth in the first place (63); dyeing the cloth to add color (34); adding trim, ruffles, belt loops, buttons, pockets, collars, or other elaborations of the basic garment (31); or adding a decorative design or logo (47). Fewer students referred to processing raw material (shearing sheep, picking and cleaning cotton, etc.; 19); spinning thread or yarn from the raw material (10); or cutting clothing into shaped pieces corresponding to the major sections of the garment (24). More than one quarter (58) gave "black box" descriptions of the manufacturing process. These students spoke of weaving (or simply obtaining) cloth and then using machines to "make it into a shirt/dress," without specifically mentioning cutting cloth into shaped pieces or stitching the pieces together to form the garment.

Only minorities of students mentioned the key processes of spinning thread (10) and weaving cloth (63). The rest omitted those steps or finessed them by generating "black box" theories. The majority thought of cloth as a solid and thread only as a means for stitching the pieces of a garment together (not as the basic material from which the garment itself was manufactured). Instead of focusing on steps involved in manufacturing the basic garment, many responses focused on dyeing for color or on adding finishing touches that create features that are especially noticeable to children (trim, ruffles, belt loops, buttons, pockets, collar, etc., or decorative designs or logos). Misconceptions included: smush the cloth into little pieces and make it soft, then sew it; "slam" thread together to make cloth; glue the pieces together; "get the wool inside of the shirt" (one of several students to suggest a vague template to which wool, cotton, etc., is attached, sometimes as lining); sew it first, then add cotton (substrate plus layer notion); after the dress is made, it is machine shrunk or stretched to size.

Descriptions of the steps involved in manufacturing the basic garment often were vague or incorrect, for two basic reasons. First, many students thought of cloth as a solid created by "smishing" material rather than as a fabric woven from thread. Second, the students who knew the most about the nature of cloth and clothing (the third graders) understood that manufacturing clothing in factories is not the same as making garments at home using patterns and a simple sewing machine, but they had not yet developed clear images of the processes or steps involved in mass production. Consequently, these students tended to give black box explanations of automated clothing manufacture by machines in factories. Many of them did not realize that these machines perform essentially the same steps that are performed by individuals making clothing at home (cutting cloth to form major parts of the garment following pattern specifications, then stitching these together to form the basic garment, etc.).

Although black box theories referred to machines "making" the shirt or dress but without specifying the steps involved, these explanations actually were more sophisticated than explanations based on the notion of an individual making the entire garment using a simple sewing machine. Even so, they were vague about the nature of the machines or processes used in mass production of clothing. A few students thought that a basic garment manufacturing machine produced garments that were all the same size, and these then were moved on to other machines for shrinking or stretching to create other sizes.

Only half (107) of the students were able to say that their shirt or dress was probably machine made at a factory, and of these, only 58 said that the factory was probably located where raw materials are plentiful. Among the other half (106), some could not respond and most of the rest (63) thought that the garment was made near where it was purchased (including 35 who thought it was made at the store itself). Only one attempted to explain the conclusion that clothing is made at or near the store at which it is purchased by suggesting that this arrangement minimizes shipping costs.

Wiegand (1993) argued that primary-grade children can profit from instruction depicting farms and factories as subsystems within large economic systems, including principles for making decisions about what crops to farm or where to locate one's factory. Students would learn that transportation costs are one contributor to the latter decision. Depending on whether a major raw material or the ultimate finished product was heavier, bulkier, or otherwise more difficult and expensive to transport, it might make sense to locate a factory either near the source of the raw material (e.g., a steel factory) or near a concentration of consumers who buy the product (e.g., a soft drink bottling plant).

Data from responses to Question 15 and Question 16 provide more evidence that K–3 students have little awareness of the geographic and economic reasons why particular types of human artifacts (shelter, clothing, etc.) are favored in particular climates and locations. Some did display glimmerings of understanding that geographical locations differ in their natural resources and societies differ in their degrees of economic development, but few were able to generate specific explanations about why clothing is manufactured in particular places or why certain people have more clothing options available to them than other people.

Students who raised the possibility that the garment had been made in another country tended to nominate Asian countries, especially China. It was not clear whether they actually understood that much contemporary clothing is made in Asia or whether they just named China as their default choice for "a foreign country."

Most of the younger students had trouble responding to the question about how people in other parts of the world dress differently than we do, but most of the older students answered it by generating climate explanations or culture/custom examples. The latter responses identified particular examples of clothing (sombreros or serapes in Mexico, robes in China, saris in India, etc.) and attributed them simply to differences in customs or culture. Overall, only about one fourth of the students were able to respond to this question knowledgeably by citing one or more specific examples of clothing commonly worn in other places or cultures, and many of these struggled to do so because they lacked specific vocabulary (e.g., serape, sombrero, sari, third world, economically underdeveloped).

This question yielded quite a variety of responses, including several noteworthy naive ideas and misconceptions (references to Santa Claus and his elves, machines melting down because of the heat in Africa, places where there are no clothes because there are no animals or only homemade clothes because there are no factories, a lack of colored thread in Mexico, people who "believe in crime" and dress dirty, and an abundance of gold, rubies, and riches in China).

Most of the rare and unique responses could be considered accurate as far as they went. However, many of them reflected stereotyped images: Chinese and Hawaiians wear grass skirts; Chinese women wear little dresses, put up their hair, and wear unusual makeup and jewelry; in India they wear robes because they never saw our clothes; in Japan they wear kimonos and weird hats; they use big hats and blankets to protect them from the sun in Mexico; in Africa they wrap a blanket around their upper bodies and wear shorts with no shoes; Chinese wear long dresses and funny little hats that look like pan tops. In addition, some responses suggested ethnocentrism (those that boiled down to "they don't dress like us because they don't have what we have or know how to do what we know how to do"). A few suggested incipient bias toward Mexicans, Africans, or African Americans: Black people dress like teenagers; Indians, the homeless, and Mexicans dress differently because they don't know how to dress like we do; Africans—we had the idea about how to make our clothes, but they didn't; in Somalia, they dress sort of like Indians because they're poor; in Africa they don't have machines because all the machines melt down because it's so hot; Indians and poor people don't have clothes, so they have to make them from animals; they wear white shirts and white clothes in Mexico (maybe they don't have colored thread like we do); in Africa people don't wear shirts—it's their religion; in Africa they sometimes wear whatever cloth they can find, even leaves. These responses underscore the importance of choosing cultural illustrations with care and helping students to get past stereotypes and learn about other cultures and customs in ways that encourage understanding and empathy rather than chauvinism.

SHOPPING FOR A SHIRT

18. Let's talk about shopping for clothes. If you were going to buy a shirt, where would you go to buy it? Why? How would you decide what shirt to buy? Would you think about anything besides _____ when deciding what shirt to buy?

K   At a store. (What store?) Any kind of store. (How would you decide what
     shirt to buy?) I would look at what color they are. (What else besides
     color?) I don't know.
1st Kmart. (Why would you go there?) 'Cause they have lots of nice clothes
     there and they look nice and they don't have another state's clothes but
     our clothes. I think it's just nicer. (How would you decide what shirt to
     buy?) I would probably buy the nicest, the coolest, and my favorite.
2nd At the mall. (Why would you go to the mall?) Because they have good
     clothes, I guess. (How would you decide which shirt to buy?) Because
     one's prettier than the other. (OK, so you'd want one that was pretty.
     What else?) Um . . . and it's cool to wear.
3rd Probably a mall. Yeah, a mall and see what size it is, try it on, see what it
     looks like, and if it fits you, buy it if you want to. (So if it fits, you'd buy it.
     Is there anything else you'd consider in choosing a shirt?) Yeah, if it has
     the stuff you want—you can't just walk in and say "I want this shirt. Can
     you change the design?"

Responses to our questions about shopping for clothes were accurate as far as
they went and free of misconceptions. Concerning where to buy the shirt, only
four students were unable to respond but 81 could do no more than name a store
(e.g., Kmart) or say that they would go to a mall or store that sells clothes. The remaining 60% were able to supply one or more reasons to explain why they would
go to a particular store to buy a shirt. These explanations concentrated on quality, selection, and price—all reasonable criteria. However, the unique responses
often did not include compelling rationales explaining why the selected store
would be a good place to buy a shirt (e.g., it's the closest store). One kindergartener offered the charming explanation that the family patronizes a certain store
because "My grandma told her son to go there, and he's my dad."

Almost 90% of the students were able to identify one or more criteria they
would use in deciding which shirt to purchase, and all of these responses showed
good reasoning: Students would buy shirts that matched their appearance or style
preferences, that fit them well or looked good on them, and/or that were well
made or reasonably priced. As a set, these responses showed more emphasis on
the shirt's appearance, color, or decorative design or logo, and less emphasis on its
quality or price, than a comparable set of responses from adults might show. Otherwise, however, all of the students' responses (including all of the rare and
unique responses) reflected valid assumptions and good reasoning about the decision making involved in purchasing a shirt.

These findings are consistent with previous research on developments in children's knowledge and behavior as consumers. Carruth and Skinner (2001) sur-
veyed middle- and upper-class mothers of children ages 5 to 9 about their consumer education practices with their children. The mothers reported frequent

modeling and socializing regarding consumer practices, especially during "co-shopping" with the child. They wanted their children to learn about getting the best buy and quality for the money, making cost/unit comparisons, being knowledgeable about products, and avoiding impulse buying. Despite this reported emphasis on price by mothers, however, neither the students we interviewed nor students studied in other research placed much emphasis on price in talking about decision making in buying clothing.

Product evaluation and comparison studies indicate that with age, children focus on more important and relevant attributes, attend to more of these attributes in forming preferences, more carefully consider them in making choices, and become more successful in comparing brands on dimensions such as price and quality. Younger children (ages 3 to 7) are primarily perceptual—oriented toward immediate and readily observable features such as size, style, or color. They often suggest decisions that are simple, expedient, and egocentric, such as purchasing a shirt based on size alone. Older children (ages 7 to 11) are more analytical—considering multiple dimensions and perspectives beyond their own in making purchase decisions. They are more likely to take into account brand name, peer preferences (e.g., current popularity of a particular item or style of clothing), and quality or value for price. However, pricing knowledge develops slowly. By age 8 or 9, children know that products have prices and even where to look for the price information, as well as that there are price variations among products and stores. However, few of them know the specific prices of frequently purchased items or ask about price when listing information they would want to know about a new product (John, 1999; Shim, Snyder, & Gehrt, 1995). Similarly, children asked to draw whatever came to mind when they thought about shopping typically showed brand consciousness but not price consciousness, except for toys they had been saving for (McNeal, 1992). Our findings were consistent with these previously reported trends.

THE MANUFACTURE OF SHOES

19. **Along with our clothes, we wear shoes. What are our shoes made from?** [If student says "leather," ask:] **What is leather? Are there other shoes that are made out of different materials?**

Because there are many different kinds of shoes made of many different materials, for Question 20, we showed a photo of a man's black dress shoe. The question asked students to describe the steps involved in manufacturing such a shoe.

20. [Show picture of shoe.] **How do you think this shoe was made? What was the first step? Then what?**

K   19. Wood. Do you know how I know? (How?) They have a little game
          on the computer and in a little book you can see people in it, and um
          . . . you can do it. And in the book I saw the little guy . . . he carved
          wood. (And made a shoe?) Yeah. (Are shoes made out of other mate-
          rials?) I don't know. (Well, look at your shoes. Are your shoes the
          same thing as mine?) No, mine are made out of threads up here.
          That's all I know. (Are the bottoms the same?) No, because they're
          harder and they're made of wood too.

      20. I don't know. (What would be the first thing they'd do?) They would
          find a little book of a shoe and then they'll put it on. (Why would
          they want a little book?) 'Cause then they could see how they make
          shoes.

1st   19. Probably they take some fur from any animal and they put it inside
          the shoes and they put this stuff hooked on the outside of the shoes
          so the inside of the shoes will feel good. And also the shoes would be
          nice and hard so nobody could damage our feet. (Are there shoes
          made out of other material?) Probably shoes are made out of other
          material . . . like some shoes are sandals and they got flat bottoms.

      20. Probably people took the bottom part . . . they took a animal and
          then they cut around it and made the bottom part and then they
          took some more apart and then they hooked it up and then they put
          this furry stuff all on the inside and then they put this belt, the black
          belt and hooked it through it and then took this metal belt and
          hooked it.

2nd   19. Some shoes are made from like leather. (What is leather?) Leather is
          a type of cloth that you can buy at a store. (Are they made out of any
          other kinds of material? Look at your shoes.) They're made out of
          jeans material. (All right. What else?) They're made out of thread.

      20. They got . . . it looks like they got a little needle and . . . in all sizes
          and like poked them in there . . . little holes, and then they fin-
          ished the rest of the shoe. (How would they finish the rest of the
          shoe?) They'd put . . . (Is the top of the shoe the same piece of ma-
          terial that the bottom is?) No. (Well, how do they get them at-
          tached?) They have like a machine, I guess, to make that attached
          to the top. (All right. Then what?) And then they get some buckles
          and put it on the top. (OK, then what?) Then they put the inside of
          the shoe in there.

3rd   19. Probably leather. (What is leather?) I have no idea. Some shoes are
          made in China. Mine are. (OK. Some shoes are made out of leather.
          Are there other things that shoes are made out of?) Yeah, but I don't
          remember what they're made of. (Well, look at your shoes. Look at
          mine.) Probably . . . I forgot the name . . . like um . . . not silk. I still

have no idea. All I know is that I have no shoes that are made out of leather.

20. Size them. (What do you mean "size them"?) Like put a thing that looks like a foot but it's not—it's a flat thing. It's a foot but not a real foot, and they like put it in there and cut the material that it's made out of around like that, and probably get more stuff and you put it around it and get more leather, not a whole lot, probably a little bit, and probably make designs in it, then sew it right down here at the bottom where it's all sewed because there's leather going down to make it tightly made so the bottom will stay on . . . the top will stay on to the bottom like that. (Then what?) Then they give it to the shoe salesman and they put it in the store.

A substantial majority of the students was able to respond accurately to the question about what shoes are made of, but only a minority could respond accurately when these initial responses were probed for deeper understanding. Compared to responses likely to be made by adults, the students' responses were less clustered around the prototype notion of a shoe as composed of a leather upper sewn to a rubber or hardened plastic sole. This reflects the fact that most children's shoes do not conform to this prototype, particularly with respect to the uppers (fabric in sneakers, plastic for many types of girls' shoes, wood or cork heels, Velcro™ fasteners instead of laces). With just a few exceptions (paper, cardboard, feathers, tar, tape, clay, gel, and wax) the students' responses concerning what shoes are made of were clearly accurate, at least for some types of shoes. Even most of the listed exceptions might be considered accurate if more were known about what the students meant by some of these terms and what types of shoes the students had in mind in using them.

Students who mentioned leather were asked what leather is. Almost half (49) correctly said that leather is animal skin, cowhide, deerskin, and so on. However, 35 could not respond and 19 said that leather is made from glue and fabric, rubber and tar, wax, or string.

Responses concerning steps in the manufacture of shoes were often vague but accurate as far as they went. Most students mentioned one or more of the steps of cutting the individual pieces, combining them together to assemble the basic shoe, and then adding laces, buckles, or other finishing touches. Clear-cut misconceptions were infrequent, although a few interesting ones emerged: The shoe is a single piece of leather rather than a product assembled by combining separate parts; shoes are made by reprocessing the leather and buckles in old belts; and first one type of machine is used to manufacture a standard-sized shoe and then other machines are used to make these shoes larger or smaller to create additional sizes. Some of the students' descriptions of the actions of machines involved in shoe manufacturing were reminiscent of the black box or semimagical explanations seen in their descriptions of the role of machines in manufacturing clothing.

Overall, the students' responses to questions about shoes paralleled their responses to questions about clothing. They were generally accurate in identifying the raw materials that shoes are made from, but only a minority knew that leather is animal hide and most explanations of the steps in the shoe manufacturing process were vague, frequently relying on black box descriptions of the role of machines. Clear-cut misconceptions were infrequent, so that most incorrect statements reflected good reasoning from a limited knowledge base rather than fundamental and systematic misconceptions.

DISCUSSION

To our knowledge, this has been the first systematic investigation of children's knowledge and thinking about clothing. The findings indicate that the students possessed both more knowledge and fewer misconceptions about clothing than they did about food and shelter, probably because most of what there is to know about clothing is less complicated than much of what there is to know about food and shelter.

Most of the students knew that clothing is a basic need and could talk about different kinds of clothing and why they are worn, but most did not know what clothing actually is. Lacking knowledge that cloth is woven, a majority envisioned cloth as a solid membrane (i.e., animal skin) or a manufactured substance (akin to plastic, rubber, or paper). Many understood that thread is used to stitch together pieces of cloth in manufacturing clothing, but most did not realize that the pieces themselves were woven from thread. Finally, a vast majority of the students, including half of those who understood that cloth is woven from thread, were vague or confused about the nature of thread itself.

Many of the students' ideas about clothing in other parts of the world were troubling because they reflected stereotyped images of people in other countries, frequently accompanied by the ethnocentric suggestion that they dress differently than we do simply because they do not have the knowledge or resources that we have. Several responses suggested incipient bias toward Mexicans, Africans, and even African Americans.

These troublesome themes were especially prominent in responses to the clothing interview, perhaps for attributional reasons. In the shelter interview, students tended to attribute housing differences mostly to differences in access to resources. In attribution theory terms (Weiner, 1992), limited access to resources is an external and largely uncontrollable cause, so it implies that the person is a blameless victim of circumstances. This view also appeared occasionally in the clothing responses, as exemplified by the student who said that "unlucky" people don't have clothes like ours. However, responses to the clothing interview more often attributed clothing differences to differences in style or preference. Attribution theorists classify personal style or preference as an internal and controllable cause, which implies that the person bears responsibility for the behavior in question. The descriptions that some students applied to people who dress differently "than we do" (e.g., describing them as dressing "nasty," "like teenagers," or "weird") suggest that they were making such attributions and associated moral judgments.

Only a few students used language that explicitly communicated a sense of moral superiority to people whom they identified as dressing differently. However, most of those who did comment on differences implied a preference for the familiar and a difficulty understanding how people might prefer something different. A few students spelled out their preference and supported it with relevant arguments (especially those who noted that our clothes are more comfortable or that there are fewer restrictions on girls and women in the present compared to the past and in our society compared to certain other contemporary societies). In most cases, however, preference for the familiar was communicated implicitly through tone of voice or phrases such as "funny little hats" used in describing how people dress differently elsewhere.

Implications for Primary-Grade Social Studies

Information on clothing contained in primary-grade social studies textbooks often is confined to the ideas that clothing is a universal need and that people around the world wear many different kinds of clothes. We conclude that primary-grade students stand to benefit from instruction about clothing that is much more coherent and powerful. The questions in our interview reflect several key ideas that might be emphasized in a unit on clothing. For example, the unit might begin with forms of clothing commonly found in the contemporary United States, especially in the students' own neighborhoods. Instruction would be designed to help students articulate the tacit knowledge that they already possess, as well as to expand on and embed it within a knowledge network structured around powerful ideas (e.g., clothing has several functions in addition to protection, cloth is a woven fabric rather than a solid, thread is spun from raw material, and leather is processed animal hide).

The unit should include a historical dimension illustrating how clothing has evolved from the animal-hide body coverings of the cave dweller days through the mostly course, simple, and homespun garments of the more recent past to the mass production and myriad of fabrics that characterize today's clothes. Technological advances have enabled us to produce clothes that are easier to get on and off, better fitting, more varied, and lighter yet more effective in protecting us from weather and environmental hazards.

The unit also should include a geographical/cultural dimension teaching about how different forms of clothing exist in different geographical locations, in part because of differences in climate and availability of raw materials and in part because of cultural differences. Along with the historical dimension, this geographical/cultural dimension of the unit would extend students' concepts to include examples different from the ones they view as prototypical. This would help them to place themselves and their familiar social environments into perspective as parts of the larger human condition as it has evolved through time and as it varies across cultures. In the language of anthropologists, it would "make the strange familiar" and "make the familiar strange" so that students could appreciate seemingly exotic forms of clothing as intelligent adaptations to local circumstances.

Topic coverage also should include emphasis on applications to students' current and future lives. This can be accomplished through activities designed to raise students' consciousness of choices that they will be making as individuals and as citizens, and of the trade-offs associated with the major choice options. For example, clothing lessons might include discussion of the trade-offs offered by different fabrics or types of clothes, ways to get the most out of limited clothing budgets, the ways that people project personal identity and lifestyle preferences through their choice of clothing (and the ways that schools and society seek to control this), or what might be done to help people who do not have enough money to purchase adequate clothing for themselves and their families.

Such content would help students begin to understand (be able to explain in their own words) how and why things are as they are for them personally as well as for people in very different circumstances. For example, it would help them to understand and respect the decisions their families have made regarding what kinds of clothing to wear, through planned interactions with parents concerning their perceptions of the family's clothing needs, lifestyle wants, financial constraints, and other factors that affected their clothing decisions. Through activities and discourse in class, students would learn about the decisions made by other families in their community and around the world, in ways that would help them to develop empathy for the individuals and appreciation for the diverse cultures that comprise the human condition. Gaining such knowledge and appreciation should help students to become more comfortable with their personal identities and circumstances, and at the same time begin to build their capacity and sense of efficacy for making decisions that will enable them to take charge of planning for their futures. Plans for an instructional unit that incorporates these features can be found in Alleman and Brophy (2001).

4

Shelter

Our shelter interviews asked students:

- to explain why people need homes;
- to talk about Native American and pioneer homes;
- to talk about the trade-offs involved in buying versus renting contemporary housing;
- to address some of the economic factors involved in constructing housing and choosing to buy versus rent a place to live;
- to explain some of the mechanisms and economics involved in supplying utilities to modern homes;
- to describe the locations and key features of their ideal future homes.

For details of the findings, see the technical report (Brophy & Alleman, 1999b).

CHILDREN'S KNOWLEDGE AND THINKING ABOUT SHELTER

Given that shelter is a basic human need, that activities relating to it are commonly emphasized in both geography and anthropology, and that it is a topic addressed in almost all primary social studies curricula, we expected to find at least some scientific literature on trajectories in children's knowledge and thinking about it. However, this was not the case. We were unable to locate any studies that spoke directly to the issues raised in our interview.

Some studies initially appeared to be directly relevant but were found not to be on closer inspection. For example, research on children's science knowledge has focused on topics such as light, electricity, and heat (Driver, Guesne, & Tiberghien, 1985; Shapiro, 1994), so we expected to encounter findings in that literature on children's understanding of home heating and lighting mechanisms. However, the science learning literature is tightly tied to the science disciplines' organizations of science content, so the findings on light concern children's understandings of the spectrum, reflection, and vision (but not manufactured sources of artificial light); the findings on electricity concern their understandings of circuits and resistance (but not how light bulbs work); and the findings on heat concern their understandings of its basic physics, for example, thermal principles, conductivity, and resistance to heat transfer (but not the workings of household heating systems). More generally, these predisciplinary aspects of children's knowledge about science-related phenomena in their everyday lives, especially their knowledge about the built environment and its electrical and mechanical features, have been relatively ignored in research on science learning. It appears that even children in the middle grades have difficulty applying whatever they have learned in science instruction to questions such as, "How does a lightbulb work?" or "How does a microwave oven work?" (Wong, 1996).

Similarly, although there is a notable literature on developments in children's economic understanding, the research is focused on basic economic concepts (scarcity, supply, demand, opportunity cost, etc.) and on the economics of banking and shopkeeping. To date, no research has been done on renting versus buying or other economic aspects of meeting shelter needs in modern society. Even studies focusing on knowledge of the operations of banks have not addressed their financing functions (including their role in providing mortgage loans that allow people to acquire homes without having to wait until they accumulate the full purchase price).

OUR SHELTER INTERVIEWS

Shelter interviews were conducted with 216 students, 54 in each of Grades K–3, stratified within each grade by SES, prior achievement level, and gender. Descriptive statistics and information from analyses of scores derived from the coding are given in Table 4.1.

WHY PEOPLE NEED HOMES

1. Do people live in homes just because they want to, or do they need homes?

TABLE 4.1
Distributions and Phi Coefficients Showing Relationships
of Coding Categories to Grade Level

Response Categories	Total 216	K 54	1 54	2 54	3 54	Phi
1. Rationale: Why people need homes						
0. None	14	4	5	3	2	
1. Home base (only)	41	15	16	5	5	−25
2. Protection (only)	56	12	14	15	15	
3. Home base plus protection	105	23	19	31	32	20
4. Includes protection rationale	161	35	33	46	47	27
5. Includes home base rationale	146	38	35	36	37	
6. Says people need homes in Hawaii	201	48	49	52	52	
2. Rationale: Why people need homes in Hawaii						
0. None	24	9	8	6	1	−18
1. Home base (only)	41	18	12	5	6	−25
2. Protection (only)	72	15	15	18	24	14
3. Home base plus protection	79	12	19	25	23	19
4. Includes protection rationale	153	28	34	44	47	31
5. Includes home base rationale	120	30	31	30	29	
1, 2. Rationale breakdowns						
0. No rationale given	7	2	4	1	0	−16
1. Protection (unspecified)	8	3	4	1	0	−16
2. Protection against rain	80	13	12	25	30	30
3. Protection against cold, snow	122	26	26	33	37	18
4. Protection against sun, heat	53	6	13	10	24	29
5. Protection against the fury of nature	60	7	11	21	21	26
6. Protection against attacks	31	10	5	10	6	
7. Protection against "other" dangers (germs, traffic, etc.)	15	5	3	3	4	
8. Home as place to meet needs	157	43	39	36	39	
9. Home as place to store belongings	54	10	9	17	18	17
10. Total number of rationales mentioned[a]	2.7	2.2	2.2	2.9	3.3	38
3A. Why did different groups of Indians build such different homes?						
1. Doesn't know	65	26	19	12	8	−28
2. Personal preference	11	5	5	0	1	−19
3. Pueblo more durable	57	8	10	14	25	28
4. Size (one type is larger than the other)	63	12	14	19	18	
5. Lack of construction materials	26	4	1	10	11	24
6. Lack of construction knowledge	8	0	1	2	5	18
7. One type was quicker or easier to build	9	1	3	3	2	

(Continued)

TABLE 4.1
(Continued)

Response Categories	Total 216	K 54	1 54	2 54	3 54	Phi
8. Longhouses were temporary, makeshift, or for poor people	19	3	7	5	4	
9. Climate	14	0	2	6	6	20
10. Other relevant responses	19	2	7	5	5	
3B. Could pueblo builders have built longhouses instead?						
0. Yes/maybe	145	41	35	32	37	
1. No—unexplained	22	7	7	5	3	
2. No—lacked knowledge	16	2	5	6	3	
3. No—lacked materials	33	4	7	11	11	15
4A. Knows name "tipi" (0 = *doesn't know*; 1 = tent; 2 = *tipi*)[a]	1.6	1.2	1.6	1.7	1.9	34
4B. Why some Indians lived in tipis						
1. Doesn't know	47	13	18	11	5	−21
2. Unspecified preferences	18	5	6	3	4	
3. Simple/small family home	43	6	10	10	17	18
4. Lack of construction materials or knowledge	44	8	9	13	14	
5. Poverty/low status	2	1	1	0	0	
6. Quick, easy to build	21	2	2	8	9	20
7. Protection from enemies	14	5	1	2	6	
8. Fire for warmth or cooking	18	5	9	1	3	−20
9. Paint, decorate them	13	2	6	4	1	
10. Other relevant response	23	6	4	7	6	
11. Portability—unexplained	9	0	0	4	5	21
12. Portability—explained	9	0	0	7	2	27
13. Mentions portability	18	0	0	11	7	32
5. Log cabins versus modern homes						
1. No response (beyond noting that the cabins were made of wood/logs)	34	20	9	4	1	−37
2. The people built the cabins themselves	39	5	9	12	13	15
3. Cabins were small, cramped	68	7	11	20	30	35
4. Beds, furniture were primitive	54	7	16	19	12	19
5. No paint, color, wallpaper	29	8	11	6	4	
6. No siding, poor insulation, leaky roof	29	2	6	8	13	22
7. Doors, windows missing or primitive	54	8	13	18	17	17
8. No oven/cooked in fireplace	17	2	2	7	6	16
9. No electricity, modern plumbing	46	2	11	13	20	29
10. Wooden/log roof	34	1	4	12	17	32
11. Dirt floor	16	4	3	4	5	

(Continued)

TABLE 4.1
(Continued)

Response Categories	Total	K	1	2	3	Phi
	216	54	54	54	54	
12. One story/no basement or upstairs	15	2	3	2	8	18
13. Easily flammable	9	0	1	4	4	17
14. Other relevant response	40	3	12	10	15	21
15. Level of response (1 = *just describes the illustration*; 2 = *talks about cabins' physical features*; 3 = *also talks about life in them*)[a]	2.1	1.6	2.1	2.3	2.4	35
16. Total number of response categories coded[a]	1.6	0.8	1.6	1.9	2.2	49
6. How did pioneers get their water?						
0. No response or childish guess	21	17	2	0	2	−43
1. Aboveground source	147	31	42	39	35	17
2. Well or underground source	48	6	10	15	17	19
7. How did pioneers heat their cabins?						
0. No response	22	8	7	6	1	−17
1. Gas/electric heat	9	7	0	2	0	−27
2. Blankets; closed door, windows; candles	12	6	2	2	2	
3. Fireplace	155	32	41	41	41	
4. Woodburning stove	18	1	4	3	10	23
8. How did they light their cabins?						
0. No response/other	19	13	4	2	0	−33
1. Electric lights	14	10	2	1	1	−28
2. No lights	53	18	16	12	7	−18
3. Only light from fire	35	5	10	11	9	
4. Candles	51	3	11	19	18	28
5. Oil lamps, lanterns	44	5	11	9	19	23
9A. Do most people prefer a house or an apartment?						
0. Can't decide or mixed	4	1	1	1	1	
1. Apartment	22	9	8	4	1	−20
2. House	190	44	45	49	52	
9B. Why do most people prefer houses to apartments?						
0. No response	24	17	5	2	0	−39
1. More space, bigger	115	15	25	37	38	35
2. Privacy, not crowded with others	54	14	11	12	17	
3. Yours to use, decorate as you wish	50	3	8	15	24	35
4. Easy entry/exit, access to washer/dryer	25	4	6	5	10	
5. Extra features: fireplace, pool, and so on	42	7	7	13	15	17
6. Don't have to keep paying rent	8	0	0	4	4	20
7. Second floor and/or basement	27	7	8	8	4	

(Continued)

TABLE 4.1
(Continued)

Response Categories	Total 216	K 54	1 54	2 54	3 54	Phi
8. Other	47	9	13	9	16	
9. Number of response categories coded[a]	1.7	1.1	1.4	1.9	2.3	44
10A. Why do some people live in apartments?						
0. Not relevant/only speaks to preferences	91	29	34	18	10	−35
1. Doesn't know	11	10	0	0	1	−35
2. Can't afford a house	88	10	10	28	40	48
3. Waiting for house availability	25	5	9	8	3	
11. Why do some people prefer apartments to houses?						
0. Doesn't know	76	24	25	15	12	−22
1. Want to use the money for other things	21	2	1	4	14	32
2. Safer from robbers/tornados	9	1	3	2	3	
3. Only need a small space	37	1	6	15	15	30
4. Don't want work of house upkeep	7	1	1	1	4	
5. Want to live close to others	21	3	3	6	9	16
6. Confuses apartments with hotels	21	4	8	5	4	
7. Apartments have pools, playgrounds, washers and dryers	15	3	7	2	3	
8. Apartments are quieter	9	5	0	3	1	−18
9. Other	77	15	17	20	25	15
10. Number of response categories coded[a]	0.8	0.6	0.7	0.9	1.2	30
12. What type of home does this student live in?						
1. House	181	51	47	43	40	−21
2. Apartment	18	2	3	5	8	
3. Trailer/mobile home	9	0	1	3	5	18
4. Other	8	1	3	3	1	
13. Why are there so many high-rise apartments in big cities?						
0. Doesn't know	37	20	7	5	5	−31
1. Demand for housing	124	23	32	36	33	18
2. Convenience/close to stores, and so on	8	2	1	0	5	18
3. Builders' profits maximized	10	0	3	4	3	
4. Build up to get more out of space	26	2	2	11	11	26
5. Not enough room for houses	23	2	2	5	14	30
6. Easier/quicker to build a few highrises than more houses	19	2	4	7	6	
7. Lack of money, materials, resources	18	2	6	6	4	
8. People want high-rise views	16	3	8	2	3	
9. Environment (saves trees, less pollution, etc.)	7	0	1	4	2	
10. Other	27	7	11	4	5	

(Continued)

TABLE 4.1
(*Continued*)

Response Categories	Total 216	K 54	1 54	2 54	3 54	Phi
11. Number of reasons given[a]	1.2	0.8	1.3	1.3	1.5	38
12. Includes space-saving concept (coded for Category 4 or Category 5)	49	4	4	16	25	39
14A. Do apartment dwellers have to pay to live in their apartments?						
1. Yes	201	46	50	51	54	21
14B. Whom do they pay?						
0. Doesn't know	36	17	9	7	3	−25
1. Owner	102	18	19	34	31	26
2. Apartment manager	54	8	21	10	15	
3. Other	25	12	5	3	5	−20
14C. Why do they have to pay?						
0. They don't have to pay	12	5	4	3	0	−15
1. Fact of life	119	18	31	34	36	26
2. Owner reimbursement or profit	41	8	9	10	14	
3. Other	44	23	10	7	4	−33
15. What is the difference between renting and buying a place to live?						
0. Doesn't know	61	30	16	11	4	−39
1. Short versus long-term housing needs	13	4	4	5	0	
2. Buying lets you own your own place	142	20	34	38	50	42
16. Can a family buy and move into a house before they have the full purchase price?						
0. Doesn't know	11	8	2	1	0	−26
1. No	139	35	40	37	27	
2. Only if owner allows them	6	0	1	2	3	
3. Yes—unexplained	51	11	10	11	19	
4. Yes—explains *mortgage-loan* concept	9	0	1	3	5	18
17A. Where does our water come from?						
0. Doesn't know	24	10	6	4	4	
1. Oceans, seas (saltwater sources)	35	4	12	8	11	
2. Freshwater sources/purified saltwater	128	27	30	37	34	
3. Sewers, drains	20	5	6	5	4	
4. Other	14	10	2	1	1	−28
17B. What is done to the water before it is sent to homes?						
0. Doesn't know	36	19	10	5	2	−32
1. Piped to homes	175	34	43	47	51	32
2. Purified first	48	4	9	12	23	32
3. Sent to water tower first	15	2	2	4	7	15
4. Number of response categories coded[a]	1.1	0.7	1.0	1.2	1.5	40

(*Continued*)

TABLE 4.1
(Continued)

Response Categories	Total 216	K 54	1 54	2 54	3 54	Phi
18A. Where does our heat come from?						
0. Doesn't know	19	9	6	2	2	−19
1. Sun	25	10	4	5	6	
2. Heat/power company	13	0	1	2	10	31
3. Fire/fireplace	28	10	8	5	5	
4. Heat register	39	6	4	13	16	24
5. Heater/furnace (unexplained)	78	22	21	19	16	
6. Forced air from furnace	69	7	13	24	25	30
7. Other	21	7	7	6	1	−16
18B. Student's theory of heat source/production						
0. Doesn't know	42	22	10	6	4	−33
1. Power company sends hot air	17	1	5	2	9	
2. Black box furnace theory	104	20	24	32	28	17
3. Firebox furnace theory	28	2	5	9	12	21
4. Other	25	9	10	5	1	−20
18C. Whom do we pay for our heat?						
0. Thinks we don't have to pay	45	20	17	4	4	−33
1. Doesn't know whom we pay	34	15	7	8	4	−21
2. People who made or fixed our furnace	14	5	1	3	5	
3. Bank or government agency	28	1	5	9	13	25
4. Landlord	14	3	0	7	4	
5. Utility company	70	5	22	21	22	29
6. Other	11	5	2	2	2	
20. How do lights in our homes work?						
0. Doesn't know	46	26	10	9	1	−41
1. Black box electricity explanation	135	21	32	40	42	32
2. Incorrect explanation	23	7	6	4	6	
3. Partly correct explanation	11	0	5	1	5	
21. Whom do we pay for our light?						
0. Thinks we don't have to pay	32	19	8	4	1	−36
1. Doesn't know whom we pay	31	18	7	5	1	−33
2. Pay for bulbs, but not for using them	24	8	9	6	1	−18
3. Bank or government agency	24	0	3	13	8	29
4. Utility company	89	5	24	23	37	43
5. Other (including landlord)	16	4	3	3	6	

(Continued)

TABLE 4.1
(Continued)

Response Categories	Total 216	K 54	1 54	2 54	3 54	Phi
22/23A. Rooms mentioned in describing ideal home						
0. None	87	26	18	25	18	
1. Living/family room	43	8	9	9	17	17
2. Dining room	20	2	3	4	11	23
3. Bedroom(s)	96	19	29	20	28	
4. Kitchen	35	7	4	8	16	22
5. Attic	12	3	5	2	2	
6. Bathroom(s)	33	8	4	8	13	
7. Playroom	22	3	7	2	10	
8. Guest room	9	0	1	4	4	17
9. Office/computer/quiet work room	10	2	4	3	1	
10. Other	20	3	5	5	7	
11. Number of rooms mentioned[a]	1.4	1.0	1.4	1.3	1.9	21
22/23B. Extras (besides rooms) mentioned in describing ideal home						
0. None	147	40	43	36	28	−22
1. Basement	25	6	4	6	9	
2. Porch/deck/patio	10	0	3	2	5	16
3. Swimming pool/hot tub	14	2	3	1	8	20
4. Yard/outside play area	16	1	0	8	7	25
5. Other	33	6	4	13	10	18
6. Number of extras mentioned[a]	0.4	0.3	0.3	0.5	0.7	25
22/23C. General home or location features mentioned						
0. None	56	19	16	12	9	−16
1. Size	78	10	15	27	26	28
2. Style	44	10	14	9	11	
3. Colors	27	11	4	7	5	
4. Wants apartment, not a house	24	10	10	4	0	−25
5. Suburban or semirural location	12	0	1	3	8	25
6. Quality: well built, in good repair	22	2	4	7	9	17
7. Other	26	3	6	9	8	
8. Number of general features mentioned[a]	1.0	0.8	1.0	1.2	1.1	18
24A. Ideal home: What would the student like to live near?						
0. Nothing named	40	19	5	10	6	−26
1. Relatives, friends, neighbors	78	21	20	17	20	
2. Body of water/swimming pool	25	7	8	5	5	
3. Woods	28	5	8	5	10	
4. Food stores/restaurants	48	5	13	12	18	21
5. Places to take children (zoos, theme parks, etc.)	11	3	6	1	1	−17

(Continued)

105

TABLE 4.1
(Continued)

Response Categories	Total 216	K 54	1 54	2 54	3 54	Phi
6. Places for children to play	23	1	8	8	6	17
7. Children's school	29	3	7	9	10	15
8. Parents' workplace	12	2	2	4	4	
9. Mall, bank, nonfood stores	19	2	5	5	7	
10. Government services	16	1	8	3	4	
11. Other	24	5	9	6	4	
12. Number of response categories coded[a]	1.4	1.0	1.7	1.4	1.6	30
24B. Ideal home: What would the student like to live far away from?						
0. Nothing named	93	34	22	22	15	−26
1. City/urban density	26	3	1	7	15	31
2. Crime	16	0	5	5	6	17
3. Factory/junk yard/dump/smoke and pollution	12	2	1	4	5	
4. Traffic/noise	25	3	3	5	14	26
5. Dangerous animals, insects/forests	18	4	8	4	2	
6. People they don't like	12	0	3	6	3	
7. Other	60	14	16	14	16	
8. Number of response categories coded[a]	0.7	0.5	0.7	0.8	1.0	27
9. Quality of response (0 = none/not relevant; 1 = relevant but not substantive; 2 = one substantive response; 3 = more than one substantive response)[a]	1.9	1.1	1.8	2.1	2.6	45

Note.   Underlining indicates that the chi-square for the underlined distribution was statistically signifi-cant at or below the .05 level. In these instances the phi coefficients (with decimal points omitted) are given in the phi column to indicate the magnitudes of linear trends.

[a]Numbers in these rows are means. Numbers in all other rows are frequency scores showing how many students in each group were coded for mentioning the ideas represented by the response category.

2. What about in places like Hawaii where it's warm all year round? Do people still need homes there?

K   1. They need homes. (Why do you think they need homes?) Because they don't have homes. If they don't have an apartment, they don't have a home. (You're thinking about the homeless. What about people who have homes? Why do they need homes?) Because they like to decorate the house and have a tree at Christmas time.

   2. Yes, because they have to live in an apartment. (If you lived in Hawaii, would you want to live in a home?) Um hum. (Why do you think you'd like to live in a home?) Because it's funner to have a bedroom.

1st 1. They need homes. (Why do you think they need homes?) To keep them warm and to have a house for if it was cold in January and February, or because it keeps them warm or because you have cable probably, or . . . you just need a home because it just keeps you warm and comfortable.

2. Yeah, because homes are to live, not to live outside, because when you live outside bats come out or all kind of stuff comes out and probably you'll get cold or you'll get uncomfortable or you don't get to see any light that much. At Hawaii you could roll and roll . . . (Are you talking about sand?) Yeah, you could roll and roll and get into the water. (Any other reasons you need to have a home in Hawaii?) I don't know that much. That's all I think of about Hawaii, and I think in Hawaii about the volcanos. That's what I don't like about it.

2nd 1. They need homes. (Why do you think they need homes?) So they could keep warm and be like safe and all that.

2. Yeah. (Why do you think they need homes?) if it rains, they can go inside their house.

3rd 1. They need homes to keep warm and healthy because if you're like out on the street like for two months, you're dead. (Any other reasons why you need homes?) Yeah, so you can live more than two months, and you have a bed to sleep on instead of cement.

2. Maybe, if it like rains really hard. They can get like a thunderstorm and the people out on the street, you know, thunder can strike them.

All 216 students said that people need homes in response to Question 1, and the vast majority made the same response to Question 2. Fifteen noted that people could survive without homes in Hawaii, but probing indicated that even these students recognized the advantages of homes and would want one themselves if they lived in Hawaii.

Although all students were aware of the basic need for shelter, they differed in the types and levels of sophistication of the rationales they generated to explain why people need homes. Most of the rationales fell into two general categories: (a) protection (against rain, cold, snow, or heat/sun; the fury of nature as expressed in storms, tornados, earthquakes, hurricanes, or volcano lava; attacks by insects, animals, or humans; or other dangers such as germs or traffic that might run over you if you were sleeping on the street), and (b) home as a base for everyday living (a place to live, sleep, eat, stay, be inside, or provide shelter; a place to keep belongings, meet needs through access to food, water, etc., and to enjoy conveniences such as electricity, light, heat, beds, a toilet, or television).

Students who generated protection rationales but not home base rationales often had trouble with the question about whether people need shelter in Hawaii. They usually said yes, but resorted to reasons such as the need for protection from killer bees or hot lava. Few outright misconceptions appeared, although several students had the impression that homeless people live and sleep literally "on the streets" (i.e., actually in the streets rather than in cars, doorways, etc.). Several students linked homes to having money. Some may only have meant that if you are homeless, you have no money, but others clearly implied that you need a home as a place to keep your money or that you wouldn't be able to get a job and live a normal life without a home (or at least an address).

A few students made "family" responses suggesting that people need to live not just in a home but in a family that cares about them and takes care of them. Among students who mentioned dangers, the younger ones mentioned mostly impersonal sources (animals, insects, and natural disasters), whereas the older ones focused more on crime and violence committed by other humans (as well as on protection from germs and diseases).

As a side issue, the students projected interesting images of Hawaii. Some envisioned idyllic scenes of a carefree life on beaches (as most adults probably would), but many depicted Hawaii as a place where people are beset by tidal waves, volcanic lava, or dangerous people, animals, or sea creatures. Some of the latter responses may simply reflect a tendency to feel comfortable in familiar surroundings but view faraway places as exotic and dangerous, but some probably reflect impressions gleaned from television programs or other sources of information about Hawaii.

Rare and unique responses included: You need to have a place for parking your car; you need to throw stuff away and your house is where the trash cans are; you need a place to change your clothes; in a home you can refrigerate food that would spoil outside; if you didn't have a home, you'd get all dirty; you can keep your pets in the house and keep young children from running off; without a home you might have to sleep in the streets and get hit by a car; a home protects you from danger on the streets at night.

Two teaching implications might be drawn from the responses to Questions 1 and 2, even though the data show that all of the students "knew" that people need homes. First, many students need to learn that the primary reason why people need homes is that they need shelter from the elements. About 20% of the students made no mention of shelter as a basic human need.

Second, most students could benefit from elaboration of the idea of home as the base for everyday living. In the process, teachers might help students to see that although it is nice to be able to keep pets, watch television, play with toys, and so on, the really vital features of modern homes are the light, heat, water, and facilities for comfortable sleeping, food preparation, and clothing care and storage that our homes provide for us.

PUEBLOS AND LONGHOUSES

Question 3 was designed to determine whether the students understood that in the past, people not only had to build to suit their climate but had to do so using whatever potential construction materials were readily available in the local area. The students were shown a drawing of a longhouse and a photo of a pueblo and asked to talk about why these two types of Indian homes were so different. [Questions 3 and 4 used the term *Indians* because pilot testing of the interview had established that this term was familiar to the students, whereas the term *Native Americans* usually was not.] Probing was designed to see if the students had any understanding that these contrasting housing types reflected the fact that pueblo dwellers lived in a hot, dry climate that did not support much vegetation but longhouse dwellers lived in a four-seasons climate that supported thick woodlands.

3. Here are two kinds of homes that different groups of Indians lived in a long time ago. Why do you think that some Indians lived in this kind of home but others lived in this kind of home? The Indians who built these homes [pointing to the pueblo]—could they have built these homes instead [pointing to the longhouse]?

K   3. Because they builded it. (What else?) And they had some wood to build it with. (Which one?) This one. (I see. You're pointing toward the pueblo. What else?) This one has straw made out of. (The Indians who built this home, could they also have built this kind of home?) Yes. (Why do you think they didn't?) I don't know.

1st 3. Those are kind of mud houses but those are longhouses where a lot of Indians live in them. We studied about Indians but we didn't study about them in a long time because it was a long time ago. (Why do you think that some Indians lived in this kind of home and others lived in this kind of home?) Because they're a different kind of Indi-ans. (Could the Indians who built this kind of home also have built this kind of a home?) Yeah. The ones who live in those houses— they're used to those kind of homes and the ones that live in other ones are used to those kind of homes. (One could not have built this kind?) Um hum, 'cause those Indians can't build those houses because it'll take a long time, and the other ones can't build those houses be-cause it'll take a long time too.

2nd 3. So they can like have fun and they like it, and they want to be warm if it's cold, for like in the winter. (The Indians who built this home— could they also have built this home instead?) Yeah.

3rd 3. Probably they have a lot more stuff to build with and with the other ones, you don't have that much. These probably live in the desert and these live in the woods or something. (Tell me more about this.) You can see a lot more than this. (A lot more what?) Windows, rooms, shelter—this one is just one big old thing. (Do you notice anything else?) Yeah, these have like sand barrels so if somebody attacks, you just have to go back there and shoot arrows. But with these, they'd just get shot because there's no sand barrels or nothing to go under to shoot. (Could the Indians who built this house also have built this house instead?) Yeah.

Only 70% of the students were able to respond to Question 3. Most responses were accurate as far as they went, but stopped short of developing an explanation for why some Indians lived in pueblos but others lived in longhouses. Many were confined to descriptions of the materials from which the two forms of housing were constructed (clay, mud, or bricks vs. sticks and straw). Others drew accurate comparisons (pueblos were more durable and offered better protection against bad weather, whereas longhouses accommodated extended families), but stopped short of explaining why the different housing styles were constructed by the different tribes. Many students could not say or could only attribute the different behavior to "different cultures." A few thought that pueblos were developed later than longhouses, after Native Americans had learned more about construction techniques.

Other responses included: Pueblos were built by people who lived in the city (they were "apartment buildings"), longhouses by people who lived in the country; pueblos protect against cold but longhouses are cool in warm climates; Indians who built longhouses preferred them because they were easier to get into and out of; longhouses were for people who lived out in the forest—they were temporary shelter that could be hidden from potential enemies; the pueblo was a place where a person took care of a whole bunch of kids (a school or day care center), whereas the longhouse was where the Indians lived; pueblo dwellers built pueblos because they didn't want to use much wood so as to preserve trees. Many students recognized pueblos as sturdier shelter and couldn't see good reasons for making longhouses (or tipis, in Question 4) except that they were quick and easy to make.

Finally, 26 students talked about the local availability of construction materials in their original responses to Question 3, and seven more did so when asked the follow-up question about whether pueblo builders could have built longhouses instead. Thus, even with cueing, only 33 students (mostly second and third graders) mentioned the local availability of construction materials as a reason for the different types of Indian housing, and only a minority of this 15% elaborated by talking about the climate and physical features of the two regions. Some of the best responses were the following:

A high-achieving second grader: Well, some Indians lived in this kind of home because like there was a lot of mud there so they built their house out of mud, and then on this one—it's called a longhouse—they built out of wood because there was more wood in that area. (Could this group of Indians have built that type of house?) No, 'cause they wouldn't have enough wood for the whole tribe to have one.

An average-achieving second grader: Because there was lots of rock where these Indians lived and there was lots of wood where those Indians lived. (Do you think that the Indians who built this home could also have built this home?) No. (Because?) Because they don't have very many trees because they would live in the desert and they (the other Indians) would live out in the woods.

A high achieving second grader: I think it was because of what the homes are made out of, like this one has twig branches and there's not all that many twig branches and there's more stone, and it looks like it's pretty hot in there so they wanted to get into the shade some and it'd be cool, and it wouldn't get very, very hot. (Do you think the people who built this house could also have built this house?) Well, they could have but it would have been harder to do that if you were in the same spot as they are there. (How would it have been harder?) Because it's a lot harder to find the stuff that you need.

Unfortunately, such responses were rare. Overall, the responses to Question 3 were part of a larger pattern of findings that suggest the need for better curriculum and instruction concerning geographical influences on people's housing needs and on the forms of housing that they construct. This point is discussed in more detail following the presentation of findings for Question 4.

TIPIS

Question 4 was intended to determine whether the students understood that the plains tribes used tipis because they were nomadic and therefore needed homes that were portable—easily taken down, transported, and reassembled. The interviewer began by showing a photo of a tipi and asking if the student knew the name for this kind of Indian home. If not, the interviewer supplied the name before going on to ask why these Indians lived in tipis. If the student's response did not include the portability notion (e.g., they lived in tipis because they liked them; they had a lot of animal hides and needed something to do with them), the interviewer kept probing for additional reasons. The question was worded as follows:

4. [Show photo of tipi.] **Some other Indians lived in this kind of home. Do you know what it was called?** [Elicit, or if necessary, give the name "tipi."] **Why do you think that these Indians lived in tipis instead of other kinds of homes? Are there other reasons why these Indians lived in tipis?**

K   4. No. (It's called a tipi. Why do you think that some Indians lived in tipis like this instead of other kinds of homes?) Because they didn't know how to build the houses, but they knew how to make a tipi.

1st   4. A tipi. (Why did some Indians live in tipis?) Because they think it's nice to live in them and they like the tipi and that's the only house they know how to build and they go around and hunt and sing songs, and when they make a fire, the smoke goes up to the top and out of the house, like a chimney.

2nd   4. I forgot. (It's called a tipi. Why do you think that these Indians lived in tipis instead of other kinds of homes?) Because they like it a lot, I guess. (Any other reasons?) No.

3rd   4. A tipi. (Why do you think that these Indians lived in tipis and others lived in these other kinds of homes?) Probably they lived in the desert and they just barely had little sticks and they had a lot of skin and they just did that and you had some rope to put down so it will stay up, and probably it's more protective. (The tipi gives you more protection, you think?) Yeah, like if somebody attacks, like some other kind of Indians attack you, they won't know that you're in there because of that flap. They'll think it's on the other side and they'll go walk over there and try to open it up.

When asked the name of the Indian home shown in the photo, three fourths of the students, including half of the kindergarteners, called it a tipi. Explanations for why some Indians lived in tipis paralleled the responses to Question 3. First, although 78% of the students were able to generate one or more explanations, only 8% of them mentioned portability, and only 4% elaborated in ways that showed that they understood that the plains tribes were nomadic and needed portable housing for that reason.

The remaining students made reasonable guesses about the motives of tipi builders: 44 suggested that these people lacked construction materials or knowledge that would allow them to build any other kind of home; 43 that tipis were built by people who lived alone or in a very small family and thus only needed a small home; and 21 that these people preferred tipis because they were quick and easy to build. A few suggested that these were lazy people who were not willing to put in the time and effort to build more elegant housing.

Other common responses, along with most of the unusual or unique responses, involved naive or fanciful suggestions: These Indians preferred tipis because they could build a fire in the middle of them for warmth or cooking and the smoke would go out the top (18); because tipis were small and hard to see from a distance, so the people could hide in them from their enemies (14); or because they liked to paint designs on them or decorate them (13; the tipi shown in the illustration had such decorations). These responses are not surprising given common depictions of Indians in movies, television programs, and children's literature. In one cartoon described to the authors, for example, Indians are shown carrying around a small tipi, covered with branches for camouflage, and using it to get close to and spy on their enemies, then building a fire in it to send smoke signals to their tribe. Even some of the materials and activities used in teaching about Indians can foster such fanciful thinking. It seems likely that some of the "they liked to paint designs on them" responses, for example, were stimulated by activities involving constructing tipis from paper bags and then painting them decoratively.

Other responses included: You can cook better in tipis so you get to eat better food; by living in a tipi they could avoid having another home right next to them or too close to them; tipis were small and Indians didn't have much stuff; they wanted to sleep outside so they could hear their enemies coming; they liked to sleep in tipis because they could go out and "see the world" whenever they wanted to and be close to animals; a chief might want to live in a tipi because he might want his own separate home; it was easy to kill buffalo to get skins to make tipis; they could hide in them from cowboys; it was part of their religion. Several third graders mentioned religion or not wasting animal parts, although typically vaguely and without much empathy. For them, "they did it for their religion" seemed to be the same kind of all-purpose answer that "they did it because they wanted to" was for some younger students.

Many of the responses reflected stereotyped and often negative views of Indians that many students bring with them to school as they begin kindergarten. Replicating and extending findings from earlier studies, Brophy (1999) interviewed students across Grades K–5 to show how their thinking about Indians progresses from the negative and stereotyped views they hold in kindergarten to the more realistic and empathetic views that they express as fifth graders. As in this study, the changes were most obvious between first and second grade. Brophy found that students' knowledge and thinking about Native Americans tends to proceed through the following stages:

1. No knowledge;
2. Cartoon-like stereotypes of the appearance or behavior of Indians (tipis, feathers, bows and arrows, dancing around campfires, warlike tendencies);
3. Knowledge of Indians as the first people in America, wilderness survivors, and teachers of and learners from the Pilgrims and other early arriving Europeans;
4. Elaborated knowledge about Indians' lives and cultures, including empathy with them as noble ecologists and victims of European aggression and greed;
5. Distancing and loss of empathy in fifth grade as attention shifts to the pioneers and the westward expansion of the United States.

Before they learn about different tribal groups at school, most students' ideas are rooted in a stereotype of the plains tribes: living in tipis, hunting buffalo on horseback with bows and arrows, and fighting with soldiers, cowboys, or other Indians. Some students who failed to mention the portability of tipis nevertheless associated this form of housing with buffalo hunting. Some portrayed tipis as temporary shelters used only during hunting, akin to the igloos used by Inuit hunters. Others conveyed the fanciful idea that tipis were easily hidden because they were small, so hunters could conceal themselves in tipis and wait for unsuspecting buffalo to happen by.

Of the 18 students who did mention portability, nine did not show understanding that tipi dwellers needed portable housing because they followed the buffalo:

> Because they didn't have other things to use to build it. (They built this kind of home because . . . ?) They're different kinds of Indians and they could move their houses wherever they wanted.

Because . . . so they could move their homes around. (OK, Why would they want to move their homes around?) I don't know.

Because they could use them camping and they were better than living in the cold. (Are there other reasons why they lived in tipis?) 'Cause they lived near water so they could catch stuff and they could move the house if they wanted to go somewhere else instead of finding new tipis. (Would there be any reason why they'd want to move their tipis?) So they won't get bored of living in one place their whole life.

They liked to build tipis and they liked to draw stuff on them, and they're easier to build than these two [pueblos and longhouses], and if you wanted, you could easily take this down, and you couldn't take these down very easily. (Any other reasons why they used tipis?) They had to use just a little wood and that's all, and they needed a little cloth, and they needed a lot.

From what I've heard, they traveled, so they could travel and take them apart and put them back together and still keep some of the rain out. (Are there any other reasons why Indians lived in tipis?) No.

Because they also lived in some kind of deserts and they used to kill buffalo and get the meat so they could eat it and instead of wasting the skin, they'd make tipis out of it and they could use it for other uses too. (Are there any other reasons why these Indians lived in tipis?) Because they were easy to pick up if people started attacking and they could easily just take it down and move it somewhere else instead of having to just leave that place there and do it all over.

Because they had to travel a ways and they used like horses and packed the tipi on the backs of horses and whenever it got dark out, they'd stop and set up the tipi. (Tell me more about this.) And if they're outside riding on a horse and traveling far, they need a place to stay in and a place to have food and a place to sleep in. (You're telling me that these people who lived in tipis traveled a lot—I wonder why they traveled?) Hmm . . . I don't know that one.

Maybe because you can pack them up and travel with them or something. (Why would they want to do that?) Because like if there's a flood or something. (Any other reasons why they'd want to pack them up and move?) No.

Because you can fold up the tipi and take it somewhere else. When you have a house, you can't do that. (Other reasons?) Tinier than a house.

Finally, the following nine students did show understanding that portable housing was needed by tribes who periodically packed up and moved to follow the buffalo. Some knew this and said so immediately. Others remembered it later or reached it as a reasoned conclusion in the process of developing their answers:

I don't know. Maybe 'cause they liked it in there. It wouldn't be so hard to build it like the other two homes. (They're easier to build?) And you can move it places. You can move it from one place to another. You can't move big buildings like the stick one (longhouse). It would fall. And a big one (pueblo) would be too heavy. But that's the right kind of . . . depends on how much it weighs. (You tell me this would be easy to move? Why would they want to move from one place to another?) Maybe the lake was too little and they wanted to move to a bigger lake, and maybe there wasn't so many animals, 'cause they had so many animals killed and maybe they wanted to move to another side to get more food. If they stayed in that same place, there wouldn't be so much food. Most of the animals were killed for food. That's why they would move.

Because they hunted buffalo for food and they had to pack up their homes real quick 'cause they had to like go after the buffalo.

'Cause they could take it down and take it where the buffalo are and like if the buffalo move somewhere else, they could move where the buffalo are again.

They could move it to different places. (How would that work? Tell me more.) They could take it down and put it on their horses. (Why would they want to move around?) To better places where there's more buffalo. (What did they do with the buffalo?) Eat them, make tipis out of their skin.

Dakota Indians always hunted buffalo and they had to go where the herd of buffalo was, so they always needed to make their home move. They usually painted the tipi, and I know that the women built the tipis. (Is there anything else you want to add to that? . . . Where did you learn about the Dakota Indians?) At school, and also my mom grew up in North Dakota.

It's more easier to build and you can carry it around. (Oh, you can carry it around?) Like they have horses. They could just put the outside on the horses and then put the sticks . . . (Well, why would they want to carry it around?) Well, 'cause they move a lot following the buffalo so they can have something to eat.

Well, these were traveling Indians and tipis were better to be able to undo and go around carrying them, and they would be better on transportation than other houses that were made with rock and sand and stuff . . . in the drawings there's horses chasing buffalo.

So they could move around with the buffalo and the food that they could eat . . . so they could pack it up easily.

Because they needed to move where their food was. They could take out the poles and take the skins that was wrapped around it off and they could carry it.

Our findings indicate that although most primary-grade students can identify and compare the physical features of different forms of Native American housing, few of them are aware of geographical or cultural factors that help explain why these different forms existed. Few showed appreciation of pueblos, longhouses, or tipis as adaptations to environmental conditions (availability of construction materials) or cultural features (nomadic society). There was little mention of the portability of tipis or the defensive value of pueblos.

Our experiences in developing and field testing a curriculum unit on shelter as a cultural universal have turned up more evidence that primary-grade students often know that different forms of shelter exist, but do not know why they exist. For example, second graders typically already knew or easily learned that stilt houses are situated above marshes or periodic flood waters and thus remain dry, but they did not understand (or even appear to wonder) why people would live in marshes or flood plains in the first place.

To promote these kinds of understandings, primary-grade instructional materials and teachers will need to go beyond showing and describing different forms of housing. They will need to point out functions and cause–effect relationships that explain why the houses are constructed as they are and preferred over feasible alternatives. In the case of portable shelters or stilt houses, explanations will need to include descriptions of the economies of the societies (periodic migration to accommodate animal grazing or hunting, cultivation of crops that grow in marshes or flood plains). In other cases, explanations will need to emphasize adaptations to local climate and geography. For example, the steeply sloped roofs of homes in the mountain valleys of Switzerland are not merely picturesque but functional (they prevent dangerous accumulation of snow on the roof and cause the snow to pile up against the house where it acts as insulation). Other adaptive features of these homes might be pointed out at the same time (building them into the side of a slope and facing the sun minimizes their exposure to cold and wind). In teaching about tropical huts or jungle homes constructed primarily of vines and leaves, students might be induced to appreciate that these forms of housing not only capitalize on locally available construction materials but also incorporate features that make them well adapted to the climate of the region.

LIFE IN LOG CABINS

5. [Show drawing of cabin.] **Two hundred years ago, the pioneers lived in log cabins. What were those log cabins like back then? How were they different from today's homes?**

6. **How did people who lived in log cabins get their water?** [If the student does not appear to understand the point of the question or is unable to respond at all, probe by asking:] **When those pioneers were living in those cabins back then and they decided they wanted a drink of water, what would they do?**

7. **How did they heat up their cabins?**

8. **What about light? After it was dark, did they have light in their cabins?**

K   5. I don't know. (How were they different from today's homes?) They're made of wood and they aren't painted.

6. They got it from ponds. They had buckets to carry the water in.

7. They had a special heater (couldn't elaborate).

8. No.

1st 5. They were like made out of wood 'cause I think there was like no bricks to make it. And those people, they like used to live like cowboys and Indians used to come there and try to get them and they tried to get the Indians, and they had like wars. I think they used wood to build it. They had a lot of wood even in the house in the stove they have.

6. I think they just like go . . . they digged in the ground really deep where all the water is and they get the water. One had mud in it. They would like make the water clean and when the water gets clean they could like drink it and they could stay alive. (Did they have water in-side their cabins?) Probably they took these things and they stabbed them in the ground and then the thing sucks up water and cleans it when it goes through a pipe, and then when they opened up the fau-cet, they would get water.

7. Probably like they'd get fire, or they got this like a stove and then they'd get coal and they'd put it in the stove and shut the door, and then they'd light something and put fire and then they closed it very quick and then they could get warm on the fire. (Tell me more about the fire.) Maybe like they already had the matches [i.e., matches had been invented] and so they just go way out and then they find a store and then they go and give them money, but the money was a different kind of money. (So they used the money to buy the matches?) Yup.

8. Probably. I think like Thomas Edison who invented the light bulb, he probably invented where they put the light bulb. (We're talking about back in the old days when they lived in these log cabins.) Probably when the fire was burning, they leaved the fire on for a little while, and after all the kids go to sleep then the parents just go up there, and when the parents were ready to go to sleep they just go there and put out the fire and go to sleep. (Tell me more about the light.) Well, the light was I guess just made out of fire. The light was out of fire, so they just had to let the fire off and then they just had to go to sleep.

2nd 5. They were like neat and they were . . . I guess people liked them a lot. (How were log cabins different from our homes today?) They're made out of logs and ours is made out of wood. (Tell me more about that— the differences between log cabins and our homes today.) Theirs was built longer than ours and ours was built like after theirs. Ours is like a little bit younger than theirs.

6. They might have had a lake nearby and they went over there to get their water.

7. With a fireplace. (Where was the fireplace?) Over on the side, right here.

8. No. (So it was completely dark inside?) Yeah, they had candles and they had matches to light them up.

3rd 5. Made of wood and not much protection against fires. Indians can make a fire and they'll throw it into the house and it'd burn more and the whole house would be burnt down. (Anything else you notice about the log cabins?) Yeah, you have to build the roof and I think that would be kind of tiring—working on the roof. (How were these log cabins different from today's homes?) You don't have cement and bricks on them, no lights—just candles. Back then they had candles . . . and we have electricity. (Any other differences between log cabins and our homes today?) Our roofs today are made of stone, so like if somebody throws fire onto the top of the house, it won't come shattering down.

6. You had to walk to a stream or a little pond to get it. If it was like a mile away, they would still go get it.

7. They took a pot with a lot of wood under it and burned it—they had water in it so you could put wood in it and put it at the foot of your bed and it would just warm your bed up and your feet.

8. No, they had candles. (Anything else?) Nope. Oh, lanterns.

Responses concerning log cabins were more knowledgeable, more realistic, and less fanciful than responses concerning pueblos, longhouses, or tipis. This probably occurred because the students simply were more knowledgeable about log cabins than about Indian homes, although it should be noted that our log cabin illustration included more details and cues to potential response elements than did our illustrations of Indian homes. The students may have been more knowledgeable about pioneer homes than Indian homes because shared Euro-American ancestry made it easier for them to identify with pioneers and their lives than with Indians and their lives (on this point, see Alton-Lee, Nuthall, & Patrick, 1993). Also, the children's literature, movies, and television programs and the school activities that children experience with respect to pioneer life (e.g., churning butter) tend to be more realistic than those they experience with respect to Indian life (e.g., making paper headdresses or tipis).

Most of the students understood that pioneer families built their log cabins themselves (with help from neighbors), that the cabins tended to be small and cramped, that the beds and furniture tended to be homemade and primitive, and that they lacked modern heat, light, and running water. Most of them viewed cabins as relatively primitive accommodations and pioneer life as difficult because people had to construct and maintain their own homes, fetch water, chop wood, make candles, grow their own food, and fend off Indian attacks. However, a few thought of log cabins as warm, cozy homes or remarked that they were sturdier or otherwise more desirable housing than Indian homes.

About three fourths of the students said that pioneers got their heat from the fireplace, and an additional 18 said that they got it from a woodburning stove. However, 22 were unable to respond, 9 thought that log cabins had modern gas or electric heating, and 12 spoke about the pioneers wrapping themselves in blankets, closing the door and windows, or lighting candles, but not using the fireplace or a woodburning stove for heat.

Concerning how the pioneers lit their cabins, 44 students mentioned oil lamps or lanterns and 51 mentioned candles. However, 35 thought that the pioneers only had light from the fire in the fireplace, 53 thought that they had no way of creating light at all after dark, 14 thought that they had electric lights, and 19 were unable to respond.

Most students thought that the pioneers toted water to their cabins from above-ground sources such as rivers, lakes, or ponds. However, some had the impression that the cabins were located a mile or more away from their water sources. Only a minority (48) mentioned underground sources (usually wells, but also "sewers," or underground springs). As in our pilot study (Brophy & Alleman, 1997), some students thought of wells merely as holding containers for captured rainwater or water toted from a stream. These students did not realize that wells tap underground water sources.

Except for the few who thought that the pioneers possessed electric lighting or modern heating systems, the misconceptions expressed were relatively minor. Some students thought that the cabins were prone to collapse because they did not realize that the logs were notched and interlocked at the corners. Others thought that the fire was built in a wooden fireplace or in a fire pit in the middle of the cabin, rather than in a stone fireplace located along one of the sides of the building. A few thought that you could not build a fire inside of a log cabin because it would burn down the structure. One suggested that the length of the cabin was limited by the length of the longest available logs, and several others who talked about the cabins being small probably had this same idea. These students did not realize that although small log cabins were the norm on the frontier, much larger log structures often were constructed using two or more sets of "long" logs on at least two sides of the building (the method could be demonstrated using Lincoln Logs™).

Several students thought that all log cabins were isolated and built at considerable distance from their nearest neighbors, when in fact neighbors sometimes built close together and the earliest frontier towns often had clusters of business and residential structures that all featured variations on the basic "log cabin" construction techniques. A few thought that the cabins were unheated, so that the people only had warm clothes and blankets (and perhaps candles) to protect them against the cold.

Some students did not realize that pioneers had sources of light available to them after the sun went down, so they assumed that the pioneers slept from dusk (or at least, dark) until dawn. Most students beyond kindergarten realized that the pioneers at least had light from the fire after dark. However, fewer than half (95) mentioned candles, and only one fifth (44) mentioned oil lamps or lanterns. In this respect, as in most others, the students tended to exaggerate the primitive level of everyday life conditions at the time.

These findings suggest at least two implications for curriculum and instruction. First, as they progress through the primary grades, most elementary students develop generally accurate ideas about the characteristics of log cabins and the daily lives of the pioneers who lived in them. However, these ideas are somewhat distorted by presentism. It is true that pioneer lives were generally more difficult than modern lives and that log cabins were a less developed form of housing than modern homes. However, it also is true that log cabins can be appreciated as sturdy and functional homes, and certainly as a cost-effective way for the pioneers to meet their shelter needs given the resources available to them. Like other prototypical homes from past eras (including various types of Native American homes), log cabins can be understood as sensible human adaptation to the time and place, and curriculum and instruction can be designed accordingly.

Second, in teaching about log cabins and pioneer life generally, curriculum and instruction can help students appreciate what the pioneers were able to accomplish, not just what their lives lacked relative to ours. Fireplaces featured stone hearths and chimneys that allowed the people to cook in and heat up their cabins without filling them with smoke or burning them down. The cabins were built near an above-ground water source or else a well was dug nearby, so water did not have to be toted very far. The pioneers made their own candles and were able to use these, as well as oil lamps or lanterns, to light their homes after dark. Most furniture and many implements were made on site using relatively simple tools and thus were primitive by our standards, but if taken in the context of their time and place, they can be appreciated as elegantly designed, functional, and often artistic. Wells were not mere holding tanks but means of gaining access to underground water sources. Modern refrigeration was not available but the pioneers developed creative ways to keep foods cool or preserve them for storing before they could spoil. In these and many other respects, pioneer life can be taught in ways that develop empathy with the people and appreciation for their accomplishments, not just distancing or pity based on the ideas that they lived difficult lives and lacked modern conveniences.

CONTEMPORARY HOME PURCHASE
AND APARTMENT RENTAL

Beginning with Question 9, the interview shifted focus from shelter in the past to shelter in contemporary society, particularly in the urban and suburban Michigan communities in which our interviewees resided. Reflecting housing patterns in the communities served by their schools, 181 of these 216 students lived in houses, 18 lived in apartments, 9 lived in trailers or mobile homes, and 8 lived in duplexes or other forms of housing.

This information was elicited in Question 12, which was embedded in a series (Question 9 through Question 16) that dealt with alternative contemporary housing arrangements, focusing on the two most common forms: home purchase and apartment rental. Question 9 through Question 11 focused on the trade-offs presented by these two forms of housing and on the reasons why people might prefer one over the other. Question 13 through Question 16 focused on the economics involved in housing construction and home purchase or rental arrangements.

9. Let's talk about the homes that people live in today. Some families live in houses and some live in apartment buildings. Do you think that most people would rather live in a house or in an apartment? Why?

10A. [If student says most people would rather live in a house:] **If most people would rather live in houses, why do so many people live in apartments?**

10B. [If student says most people would rather live in an apartment:] **If most people would rather live in apartments, why do so many people live in houses?**

Question 11 was a further probe for the majority of students who first answered Question 9 by saying that most people prefer houses to apartments and then answered Question 10A by saying that people who live in apartments do so only because they can't afford homes or are waiting for a home to become available. It was included to see if these students realized that some people prefer to live in apartments and choose to do so even though they could afford to purchase a house.

11. [If appropriate.] Some people could afford to buy a house but they would rather live in an apartment. Why do you think they want an apartment?

K   9. A house. (Why do you think they'd rather live in a house?) Because they want a big bedroom and a big bed.

10. Because they don't have houses. (Why else would they live in apartments?) I don't know.

11. (Question omitted)

1st   9. I think most people should live in a house, 'cause people who live in apartments and you need your clothes cleaned, they just clean it up and bring it to you [thinking of a hotel's laundry service], but if you live in an apartment, probably your house is very little. But houses—there's all kinds of houses and they're huge. I think they'd rather just live in a house instead of an apartment.

10. Probably because they think that apartments are bigger than houses so they want an apartment. Probably when people get an apartment, they just stay in the apartment one day because the apartments are very small and they wouldn't fit all the people.

11. (Question omitted)

2nd   9. A house. (Why do you think they'd rather live in a house?) Because they don't have to be quiet, and they can go outside and ride their bikes whenever they want and play basketball or hide and go seek and stuff like that.

10. Because they think that they can have like quietness and they think it's fun.

11. (Question omitted)

3rd   9. In a house, because in a house you don't have like people connected to your house, and if you're like having fun, they'll come over and knock on the door. "Be quiet, please." And if you want to have fun, you can just go out in the house. I live in an apartment and it's not really fun. (Tell me more about why most people would rather live in houses.) Because like if they're having a party for friends, and you want to turn up the music real loud, but in apartments you can't do that. You just turn it up enough so you can hear it, but in a house, you can full-blast it.

     10. Because houses cost more than apartments, and the rent on houses goes really high and on apartments you go kind of high. That's all.

     11. It's cheaper, and you could pay the rent easier. Because on a house, it would take a long time just to pay it off, so that's probably why they'd move into an apartment.

A heavy majority (190) of the students stated that most people would prefer a house to an apartment. Of the rest, 22 stated that most people would prefer an apartment and 4 could not decide or gave mixed responses (i.e., some people prefer houses but others prefer apartments).

Of the 190 students who stated that most people prefer houses, 166 supplied at least one reason. Many of their statements were not true as unqualified generalities, although they were accurate in the sense that they reflected the students' experiences. The most common explanation was that houses are bigger or provide more living space than apartments (115). Other common explanations included the ideas that owning your own house affords greater privacy and avoids the problem of having to live in close quarters with others (54); the house is yours to use and decorate as you wish without being constrained by the kinds of guidelines that renters are required to follow (50); and houses offer extra features such as fireplaces, swimming pools, or patios (42). Reasons mentioned less frequently included the ideas that houses offer not just a single floor of living space but a second floor and/or basement (27); houses provide easy entry from and exit to the street and easy access to washers and dryers, without having to use stairs or elevators like in apartment buildings (25); and when you own your own house, you don't have to keep paying rent (8).

When the 190 students who indicated that most people prefer houses were asked why so many people live in apartments, more than half indicated that apartment dwellers live in apartments only because they have to. Eleven could not think of any reason why people would live in apartments. Of the rest, 88 said that apartment dwellers cannot afford houses, and 25 said that they live in apartments only temporarily while waiting for a house to become available (either because they are having a house built or because all houses in the area are currently occupied and they have to wait until a new or existing house becomes available).

Only a minority of the students recognized that some apartment dwellers live in apartments by choice rather than by necessity. The rest were informed of this via the wording of Question 11, but many had trouble accepting its premise and persisted in thinking that people live in apartments only by necessity. More than one third (76) could not supply any explanation for why some people might prefer apartments. The advantages to houses seemed so obvious to them that a preference for apartments was incomprehensible. Another 21 suggested that apartment dwellers want to be able to afford cars, clothes, vacations, or other expensive things and thus are not willing to sink all of their money into a house. These students also had trouble accepting the premise of the question, because their responses implied that apartment dwellers are accepting sacrifices in the housing sphere in order to get what they want in other spheres (so they don't really prefer apartments after all).

Among students who did explain why some people might prefer apartments, the most common reasons were that the people live alone or in a very small family and thus need only a small place (37); or that they want to live in close proximity with others, typically relatives (21). Other explanations were built around the ideas that apartments offer swimming pools, playgrounds, washers and dryers, or other features not found in homes (15); apartments are quieter (9); apartment buildings are safer from robbers or tornados (9); or apartment dwellers don't want the work of keeping up a house (7). In addition, there were 77 miscellaneous "other" responses, including 21 that indicated confusion of apartments with hotels or motels (e.g., suggestions that the people were only planning to stay for a day or two, that they liked having a soft drink or candy machine outside the room, or that they enjoyed having a stocked refrigerator waiting for them inside the room).

In summary, a majority of the students had trouble with Question 11 because they had trouble accepting its premise. Some never did accept it and could not think of reasons why apartments might actually be preferable to houses for some people. Others accepted the premise but had to "reach" to come up with possible explanations, and some of these were farfetched or essentially incorrect. Students who thought that apartments might be safer were thinking that large apartment buildings would be less vulnerable to tornados than single-family homes or less vulnerable to robbers because the buildings feature controlled entry and most of the apartments are above ground level. Those who thought that apartments would be quieter than homes based this notion on their awareness that apartments typically have rules prohibiting loud noise (but without simultaneous realization that these rules exist because apartment dwellers live in close proximity to one another, so noise is often a problem). Finally, those who suggested that apartments offered amenities not found in houses often were confusing apartments with hotels or motels.

Reasons why most people prefer houses included: The water is better to drink and you can do more fun things; houses have better couches; houses have more stuff to play with; houses are warmer; houses have kitchens (student thinks of apartments as motel rooms); with a house, you don't have to worry about remembering where you parked your car; you don't have to go up high and you can live in a neighborhood that has trees and places to play; houses have more windows; you can build onto a house; houses are warmer; people who live in houses have nice neighbors, but in apartments you have bad neighbors, and bad people might come in and shoot you; sometimes they don't let you out of apartments (student seems to be thinking of care facilities for the elderly), and you have a better view (more windows); you can have pets; you get to know your neighbors better.

Reasons why some people live in apartments included: They work there (confuses apartments with office buildings); they are sick and need to get better (confuses apartments with hospitals); they wanted to buy a mansion but didn't because their kid could get lost in it, so they got an apartment; people who don't get along with their parents move to apartments nearby; they want a balcony; they like the numbers on the doors; if the people are handicapped, they could buzz in a visitor without having to go to the door; there is lots of parking in the parking lot; they don't want to cook food or have to go up and down stairs (thinking of a hotel that includes a restaurant and an elevator); because these people don't make much noise (so they don't have to worry about getting evicted); the apartment is all on one floor, so it is easy to get to everything; the apartment might be near where they work; they like the view or they travel a lot; they don't have to spend so much time working on the house, so they can spend more time with their children; they like to live alone and don't want pets; apartments have elevators and some are in buildings with cafeterias downstairs and doctors who can take care of you (student may be thinking of hospitals or institutions or apartment complexes for the elderly); they like loud, rowdy neighbors; it's fun going up and down the stairways.

Many of the younger students lacked clear concepts of apartments or confused apartments with hotels or motels. To the extent that they were familiar with apartments, they tended to base their explanations on relatively trivial aspects: numbers on the doors, balconies, cable TV, or elevators (often mentioned with reference to the fun of riding on them rather than their elimination of the need to climb stairs). Older students showed more familiarity with apartments and gave more sophisticated explanations for why some people might want to live in them (they travel a lot or want to live near where they work). Even so, most of their responses were relatively naive and uninformed, and several involved "reaching" to generate dubious explanations (e.g., the people like loud, rowdy neighbors or choose to live in an apartment because they don't like pets).

We suspect that these responses will prove to be typical for students who live in rural or semirural areas, small towns or suburbs, and even the residential neighborhood areas of larger cities. However, a different pattern might be expected from students residing in urban core areas, especially if they live in apartments or condominiums in large buildings. We investigated this in a follow-up study that involved interviewing students who lived in Manhattan (summarized later in this chapter).

THE ECONOMICS OF BUYING
VERSUS RENTING HOUSING

Question 13 through Question 16 assessed students' understanding of certain economic aspects of shelter. Question 13 was intended to see if students understood that high demand on limited space creates a tendency to build upward as well as outward in big cities, or alternatively, to see if they realized that continuous building of houses would place people farther and farther away from the city center.

Question 14 through Question 16 addressed the economics involved in buying versus renting housing. Question 14 was asked to determine if the students realized that people have to pay to live in apartment buildings, and if so, to whom this money is paid and for what. We were interested in whether the students understood that the people who collect rent in very large apartment buildings usually are not the owners, and that rent money provides the owners not only with reimbursement for their expenses in maintaining the building but also with an addition portion realized as profit.

Question 15 focused more specifically on the difference between renting and buying, to see if the students understood that buying implies ownership and not just longer residence at the housing site.

Question 16 was included to see if students knew anything about mortgage loans, particularly the core idea that a family can borrow money from bank, use it to buy a house, and then pay the bank back over a number of years. Four different follow-up probing sequences were used, according to how the student answered the initial question.

13. **In small towns, most people live in houses or small apartment buildings. But in big cities, many people live in very tall apartment buildings, like this one.** [Show photo.] **Why do you think they have so many big, tall apartment buildings in big cities?** [If student says because there are so many people in cities, ask:] **Well, why don't they just build more houses instead of building those big apartment buildings?**

14. **The people who live in apartment buildings—do they have to pay money to live there? Who do they pay? Why do they have to pay?**

15. **Some people *rent* a place to live, and some people *buy* one. What's the difference between renting and buying?** [If student is confused or unable to answer this question, break it into two separate parts:] **What does it mean to *rent* a place to live? What does it mean to *buy* a place to live?**

16. Can a family buy a place to live and move into it even if they have only part of the money they need to pay for it? How does that work? [If student speaks of the family borrowing from relatives or friends, probe for knowledge about mortgage loans from banks, but without mentioning banks directly:] **What if their relatives couldn't lend them the money—is there some other way that they could buy the house?**

[If student says something about getting a loan or money from a bank, probe for details. In particular, determine whether the student knows that the family gets all of the money it needs now but has to pay it back slowly over several years.]

[If student expresses basically correct ideas about mortgage loans, probe for understanding of the bank's profit motive for making those loans available:] **Why are banks willing to give families money to buy houses, and then have the families pay them back later?**

K   13. I don't know.

14. Yes. (Who do they pay?) They have to pay the person who is the manager. (Does the manager own the place?) Yes. (Why do they have to pay?) Because so they can live there.

15. I don't know. (What does it mean to rent a place?) I don't know. (What does it mean to buy a place to live?) It means to give money. (Anything else?) No.

16. No.

1st   13. Probably because when they go out of the apartment there's probably like a big swimming pool and they like swimming so they like the apartment. And apartments are a lot higher and bigger than houses, so probably they want to go very high and they want to live on the top floor to see the whole place. (Any other reasons?) Probably there's no driveway and they probably don't like parking their car in the driveway because all the time when there's two cars in the driveway and another car comes in and crashes into the other one. So they don't like that. (Why don't they just build more houses instead of these big tall apartment buildings in big cities?) Probably because they want more apartments than houses 'cause they want more money and people.

14. I think they do because my friend, he had a apartment and every time the people come up and bring his stuff, he has to pay the money and give them tips. (Who does he pay?) He pays this guy—the butler, and one of the guys doesn't like him so he uses his dad's credit card for all this stuff. (I see. Why do they have to pay to live there?) Because they just want more money.

15. Renting you just stay in the house for a little time, like one week or a couple of days, and buying you probably could stay there for a lot of years.

16. Probably you have to save money. Whoever is selling the house, they want the money to buy another house.

2nd 13. Because that city has enough room for big buildings, and little cities don't have enough room for big stuff. (You told me that most people like to live in houses. Why don't they just build more houses in big cities for all the people instead of these tall apartment buildings?) Because they . . . because there's so much tall buildings so they can't fit like any houses in there.

14. Yeah. (Who do they pay?) The manager who owns the place. (Why do they have to pay?) So they can stay there until they can find a house if they want to live in a house.

15. Buying is more than renting. Renting is cheaper than buying. (What does it mean when you rent a place?) It means you want to stay there until like until you like get your trailer or something back, because it might have been . . . caught fire, and they had to rebuild it and stuff. (So when you buy, what's that like?) That's like if you don't want to live in that one anymore, then you can buy another house and live in that one.

16. Sometimes they can and sometimes they can't. (How does that work?) It works like . . . I don't know.

3rd 13. Because there's a lot of people in the cities and they can't afford houses, so they just go to apartments. That's how I see it. (Well, why don't they just build more houses in big cities instead of these tall apartment buildings?) You got me there . . . Probably the city thinks houses take up more room instead of tall apartments. But you could make a house just like an apartment. You could have two people, like one of your cousins, like that, in your house and that would be like an apartment.

14. Yes. (Who do they pay?) The manager who owns the apartments. Then he pays the bills for the electricity and everything. He'll pay like half of it off and half of it will come to the people, I guess, and they have to pay that off. (Why do you have to pay if you live in an apartment?) 'Cause if you want to live there, you gotta pay no matter what.

15. Renting costs less than buying. Like I wanted to rent a place and there's a place for sale, say like the house I want. I'll see what the price is for an apartment for sale—it'd be like $50,000 and for a house for rent, it'd be like $100. Between a thousand and one hundred. (What are other differences between renting and buying?) Renting—the bills go down. If you buy an apartment, then the bills go like up to $1,000 if you use the time. For renting, it would just go up to $100 if you used your time. There's a difference between renting and not renting.

16. No, you have to pay the whole thing . . . the money that you have to pay. You can't like pay half of it off and just move in. The manager would just kick you back out again and wait for the rest of the money.

Responses to Question 13 through Question 16 indicated that the students possessed only limited and spotty knowledge of the economics of housing. Most struggled to respond because they were reasoning from limited bases of knowledge (often distorted by incorrect beliefs). Concerning the emphasis on high-rise apartment buildings in big cities, for example, only 26 clearly understood that demand for location in or near the city center creates pressures toward building up instead of out in order to get more human use out of centrally located space (Wiegand, 1993). A majority of the other students said that more people live in cities so more housing is needed there, but they struggled to explain why this housing would take the form of high-rise buildings instead of smaller apartment buildings or individual homes. Some based their explanations on assumptions about the motives of the apartment dwellers (wanting to live close to work sites or stores or to have a panoramic view), others on assumptions about the motives of construction companies (more profitable, or at least quicker and easier, to build a few high-rises than many houses), and still others on assumptions about the motives of city governments (trying to house the most people possible with limited resources, seeking to minimize environmental damage).

Some responses indicated confusion of high-rise apartment buildings with hotels, hospitals, or other facilities. Others revealed naivete concerning the reasons why people might choose to live in high-rise apartment buildings (e.g., because these buildings offer parking spaces or protection from tornados). Still others displayed naivete in attributing the decisions of builders or city governments to humanitarian rather than economic motives (e.g., desires to protect the environment or to accommodate people's housing needs as quickly as possible). Other explanations included: They like all those windows; the building might contain a hospital or clinic that you could take a sick child to without having to drive somewhere; people want good security at midnight; they don't have enough wood to build so many houses; it takes a lot of time to build a lot of houses; they like the view from the top (they can look out and see airplanes); people want height, swimming pools, and parking places; there is more money in the city so they can build whatever they want; building all of those houses would require cutting down more trees and "destroying our earth"; the city doesn't have the money to build houses for everyone; expansion into the countryside would urbanize it and kill more trees; building fewer buildings reduces the amount of smoke in the city, and living high up in a big apartment building shields you from traffic noises and other city noises.

Several students indicated that they were familiar with the concept of *renting* from experiences in renting videotapes (but often unfamiliar with renting housing). Also, several saw renting as arranging to live in a place temporarily to see how well you liked it, and then deciding either to move out or to buy it. A few viewed renting as more convenient than buying because renters can move out immediately if they decide to, whereas buyers have to wait until they can sell their house (these students were unaware of the penalties involved in moving before a lease is up).

More than 90% of the students understood that apartment dwellers have to pay to live in their apartments. About 17% did not know to whom the money was given, but 48% said the owner and another 25% said the apartment manager. Concerning why this rent money must be paid, more than half (119) offered only "fact of life" explanations: Everyone has to pay for housing; nothing is free, they won't let you stay there if you don't pay, and so on. Twelve thought that apartment dwellers did not have to pay to stay in their apartments, and 44 suggested "other" explanations, mostly guesses by younger students (e.g., If they don't pay, they go to jail; if they didn't pay, people would think that they were stealing the house and they wouldn't be friends with the owners anymore; you pay the doorman so he will let you in; you have to pay if you have pets). Finally, 41 students indicated that rent money is kept by the owner of the building. However, these responses focused on expense reimbursement, not profit. Only four students stated or implied that owners might use rent money for purposes other than paying workers, utility bills, or other expenses involved in owning and maintaining an apartment building, and none showed clear understanding that renting is a profit-making business.

For most of the students, the economics of housing boiled down to paying for living space, with owning being more desirable but also more expensive, and renting usually being a short-term arrangement for people currently unable to afford a home. To the extent that they went beyond "fact-of-life" explanations for why apartment dwellers must pay to stay in their apartments, their rationales tended to be rooted more in notions of fairness and justice than notions of economics: Building engineers and other workers need money to live and also deserve payment for their services; owners deserve to be reimbursed for their expenses; it wouldn't be fair to have some people get housing free while others have to pay for it; living in the house without paying would be like stealing.

Most of the students understood the difference between renting and buying a place to live, and about two thirds included the key concept that *buying implies home ownership* when explaining this difference (others explained it only in terms of short-term vs. long-term occupancy). However, even those who noted that buying implies home ownership explained this concept only in terms of ownership allowing owners to use and decorate the home as they wish and to sell it when they decide to move. No student mentioned *build-up of equity*, *appreciation of property value*, or other concepts relating to investment or economic assets.

Most of the students were unaware of mortgage loans. When asked whether a family could buy and move into a house before it had accumulated the full purchase price, only 60 said yes, and 51 of these could not explain. Only 9 students were able to explain the basic concept of a mortgage loan arrangement (the family gets all of the money it needs to buy the house now, then pays the bank back slowly later), and only two of these (the last two quoted below) understood that banks make mortgage loans available because they charge interest and thus make profits from their lending operations:

1st   It's when you pay someone back, and not usually on that day but not like right then. (Why are you paying them back?) Because you borrowed money from them and you used it.

2nd They could get a loan from a bank. (OK, they could get a loan from a bank. Why are banks willing to give families money to buy a house, and the families have to pay them back later?) Well, they give loans because all the people that put their money in the bank . . . they use that money to give to the families and the families pay them back and they put it back in their savings account, whosever money they took out.

2nd Their bank could pay for some of it. (Tell me how that works.) If you have only half of the money that you need, then you can get some from the bank to use and then you have to pay them back. (Are there reasons why a bank would be willing to give people money and then let them pay them back?) 'Cause they need somewhere to live and the bank doesn't really mind, I guess.

2nd Well, it depends if they borrowed money from the bank. (Tell me about that.) Well, if you borrow money from the bank, you still have to pay the bank back. But then at that time you've got the money, so you can buy it, but each month you have to pay that amount, and then finally you pay the bank back all the money and then the house is officially yours. When you haven't paid it all off, it's partly the bank's. (Why are banks willing to give people money and then let them pay it back later?) Because the people in the banks think that it probably will take them a long time and they're probably very generous and nice—the people at the banks.

3rd Yes, they could borrow it from a bank or something, and then they'd have to pay bills. (How does that work?) If you don't have enough money— you only have like a few thousand dollars and the house that you want to buy costs a lot of money, you could like borrow some from the bank and you would have to pay them back for all the money that you borrowed.

3rd Yes, 'cause they can borrow money from the bank. They can save some money and pay it in little amounts, like say $300 a month or something. I have a bike payment and I have to pay $25 a month. (Why are banks willing to give families money to buy houses and then have the families pay them back later?) That's one of the reasons that banks are here—to put money in and borrow money from the bank because they know that you're willing to pay the money back in the same amount you took out. (Are there reasons why banks are willing to give people money and have them pay it back?) Because you have to pay money to get into a bank so the banks . . . probably know if they don't use opportunities of borrowing, they will lose customers, and it's just one of the things that banks do like the same things that schools do.

3rd They can borrow money from the bank and sometimes they can pay the person and then in a little while they can pay the other part of the money to the person. (Why do you think banks are willing to give people money and then let them pay it back?) Because they want to help people and . . . I can't think of anything else.

3rd You can sometimes go to a bank and say, "I don't have enough money for this house," and then they would say "OK," and then they'd give you the money and then you'd have to pay them back that money, but like pay them back for borrowing the money too. So it would be a lot of money to pay back, but it would be . . . you'd have to pay back some money for borrowing it.

3rd They can get loans from the bank. (Tell me about that.) Well, they need to get loans from the bank so then it's basically . . . they pay the bank off until they get enough money to pay them off. (Are there reasons why the bank would be willing to give people money and then let them pay it back later?) Yeah, because when you do that, usually the bank costs more money . . . they charge more money to give you money, and when you pay them back, it's actually more money than you get, most of the time.

The students' responses were slightly more advanced than expected based on previous research. Berti (1995) noted that studies done in different parts of the world have indicated a gradual development in children's ideas about banking as they progress from kindergarten through high school (Berti & Bombi, 1988; Jahoda, 1981; Jahoda & Woerdenbagch, 1982; Ng, 1983; Takahashi & Hatano, 1994):

0. Total absence of ideas on banking.
1. Bank as a source of money: Anyone can go to the bank to get money on request.
2. Banks look after money; they protect it from thieves and give it out only to people who have previously deposited it.
3. Banks also lend money. Children are aware of bank loans but believe that the money comes from external sources such as local or state government; they still believe that depositors' money is kept in individual envelopes or boxes until they come to claim it again.

4. Banks lend depositors' money; children begin to understand connections between deposits and loans but do not know about interest, know about only one type of interest, or do not yet see connections between loan interest and deposit interest.

5. Connection between loan interest and deposit interest; children now are aware of both types of interest and understand that the interest received from loans enables banks to pay interest on deposits, but they may think that the interest rates are the same or even that loan interest is less than deposit interest. They may be well into high school before they understand that loan interest is significantly higher than deposit interest, allowing banks to pay their employees and earn profits.

Previous studies have found that kindergartners and first graders tend to be at the lowest levels in this progression, and even third graders usually are limited to Level 3 or Level 4. Thus, for most primary students, banks are places to get money on demand or deposit it for safekeeping, and transactions involving interest are either unknown or understood only vaguely. Berti (1995) found that a relatively modest intervention was successful in bringing most fifth graders to the highest scale levels, but only partially successful with third graders. A subsequent intervention was highly successful with third graders, although it required 20 hours of instruction (Berti & Monaci, 1998).

For the vast majority of these 216 students, buying versus renting reduced to paying the full purchase price for a home in a single transaction versus paying much smaller amounts of money periodically to continue living in an apartment. Most knew nothing at all about, and most of the rest could not explain, how mortgage loans make it possible for families to buy and move into a house before they have accumulated the full purchase price. Only 2 third graders were able to explain the motives and financial arrangements involved in these transactions (i.e., that the bank charges interest and thus makes profits from mortgage loans, but people are willing to pay this interest because it allows them to move into a home much sooner than they would be able to otherwise).

UTILITIES IN MODERN HOMES

Question 17 through Question 21 assessed students' understandings of the mechanisms and economics involved in supplying our homes with water, heat, and light. Concerning water, we wanted to know whether students understood that utilities collect water from freshwater sources, purify it, and pipe it into our homes under pressure. Concerning heat, we wanted to know if students understood the energy use and mechanisms involved in heating modern homes (in the case of most of their homes, that natural gas is piped in and burned in furnaces that heat air and then circulate it throughout the house). Concerning light, we wanted to know whether students understood that lights require electricity, and if so, what they knew about what makes the light shine when the switch is turned on.

We asked students whether we have to pay for our heat and light, and if so, whom we pay and for what. We wanted to see if they understood that we pay for the gas and electricity that we consume. In our pilot interviews we also had asked about paying for water, but we dropped this question because all students understood that people use water and typically (except for people who have their own wells) pay a utility company for what they use. However, they were less clear about what we use to create heat and light. This difference in understanding was related to the fact that water supplied to homes is used directly without transformation (except for heating some of it to create hot water), whereas transformations are involved in the creation of heat and light (i.e., utility companies do not supply us with heat and light per se; instead, they supply us with energy that is converted into heat and light after it enters our homes).

17. **Inside our homes, we use water when we turn on our faucets. Where does that water come from?** [If student says from pipes under the sink, keep probing for the original source of the water.] **OK, but where is the water piped in from?**

18. **Our homes are heated when the weather is cold. Where does that heat come from?** [If necessary, probe to see if student understands concept of central heating—water or air heated in a boiler or furnace, then circulated around the house. *Individualize your probing as follows.*]

[If student says heat comes from furnace:] **How does that heat get from the furnace to the different rooms in the house?**

[If student says the heat comes from register:] **OK, you can feel warm air blowing out, but where does that warm air come from? Is there something that makes the heat?**

[If it is clear that the student's home is heated with dispersed electrical heaters, portable space heaters, or something other than a central heating system, probe for knowledge of the heating system at school:] **Here at school we have warm air blowing into the room when the heat comes on.** [Show heat register in the interview room.] **Where does that heat come from? What makes the heat?**

19. **When we use heat in our homes, do we have to pay for it? Who do we pay? Why do we have to pay?**

20. **Families light up their homes by turning on lamps or lights. How does that work?** [If initial answer indicates that electricity is involved but does not offer any further explanation, probe by asking:] **What happens when we turn on the switch?**

21. **Do families have to pay for the lighting in their homes? Who do we pay? Why do we have to pay?**

[If student only mentions paying for bulbs, ask:] **OK, we buy light bulbs and then bring them home to use them in our lamps. Do we also have to pay for using them—does it cost us money to turn our lamps on and leave them on?**

K   17. Lakes. (How does it get from the lakes to our house?) I don't know.

18. I don't know. (You're not sure. Where do you go in your house when you want to get warm?) Downstairs in the basement, that's nice and warm. (What's down in the basement that's nice and warm?) There's a heater. (There's a heater down in the basement. How does that heat from the basement get to the other rooms of the house?) There's . . . I don't know.

19. Yes. (Who do we have to pay?) I don't know. (Why do we have to pay?) I don't know.

20. You put a light bulb in it. (Tell me more about that.) You plug it in and it makes light. (What makes it light up when it's turned on?) The little switch will light it up.

21. No.

1st 17. I think there's like a pipe under our sink and all the water comes and it goes seeping into the ground, and the pipe sucks the water up and it'll come out of the faucet.

18. It comes . . . like in the sewer there's this big spot of a lot of heat and when everyone turns on their heat, there's a lot pipes and everyone who lives there, and then the pipes suck the heat up. (Where does that heat come from in the first place?) I don't know, but the heat . . . in the sewer there's this big round spot that just sucks it up.

19. No, you can just turn on something and it sucks up the heat.

20. By electricity and light bulbs. (Tell me more about that.) When you turn on a light, you might be able to get light from electricity. (Well, what happens when you turn on the switch?) We get light and we have electricity.

21. No, they could just turn on a light and it comes from electricity and the light just *zzzzztttt* and it just comes out of the wall, but when you have no electricity no more you have to go over there and pay money to get more electricity. (You have to pay for the lighting you use? Who do you pay?) The people that own the electricity. (Why do you have to pay?) Because they want money to buy a lot of stuff. They want to buy stuff. That's why everybody wants more money than everybody.

2nd 17. Sometimes sewers.

18. A heater. (OK. So then how does the heater get the warm air to different rooms?) It like spreads.

19. No.

20. It works like if you turn on your light, then that's like . . . it lets out more light and if you turn on a lamp, then it don't let out that much light.

21. Yes. (Who do they pay?) The electric people. (Why do they have to pay?) Because it's like wasting energy—light energy.

3rd 17. Ponds, lakes, oceans, rivers. (How does it get to our houses?) There's like this place—I don't know where—it has like big tubes going into the water and sucking it in and they'll clean it out. Then it will go through pipes to your faucet.

18. Whoa! Gas, electricity. It'll keep you warm. When you turn it on, there's like a heater down there that heats up like the water like in the pot. (How does the heat get from the heater to the different rooms in the house?) There's heaters along the walls that go to each room, and it'll warm up that place. (How are they connected to the heater?) Wires.

19. Yes. (Who do we have to pay?) The gas people or the electricity people—you gotta pay that. (Why do we have to pay?) If you want to be warm in the winter or have like cool on a hot day, and you wanted some of your rooms kind of cold and warm, you put it on warm.

20. Electricity. When you turn it on, it's already ready and it just goes on. (How does the electricity get to the lamp or the light?) From this place with wires going into it from the walls. It'll go into them, and when you turn it on, it'll go on. (And it gets to the house by how?) Underground—the wires.

21. Yes. (Who do they pay?) Electricity people. There's more electricity than gas or heaters, because like right now, there's electricity going everywhere. (Why do we have to pay?) If you want light. If you want to live in blackness—the people that want light, they don't care about the people that want to live in blackness.

Students were clearer about water than about heat and light, but even so, only about 60% of them correctly identified lakes, rivers, groundwater, or other freshwater sources in explaining where our water comes from. Many could not respond or named saltwater sources instead of freshwater sources. In addition, almost one fourth made some reference to the water being purified before it is sent to our homes. For some of these students, the concept of *purification* was limited to desalinization (i.e., they spoke of removing salt from the water but made no mention of removing waste products or harmful chemicals). A few students thought of rivers as purifying agents. These students envisioned water as flowing from oceans through rivers into inland lakes, and thought that salt was "filtered" out of the water during the process.

Only 15 students mentioned the water going to a tower before flowing into our homes, and few if any of them clearly understood the role of water towers in

creating hydraulic pressure to power the flow in the system. We were not surprised by this because our tape recordings of lessons on modern housing taught to
first and second graders indicate that one question commonly asked by these students is how water can flow upward from underground pipes into our homes.
These students (and apparently most third graders as well) do not realize that the
water arrives at our homes under pressure or understand the role of water towers
in creating this pressure.

In talking about the flow of water, students referred not only to pipes but to
hoses, sewers, drains, and tubes. Sometimes the alternative terms were used to refer to pipes when students did not know the word *pipes*, but at least some of the
time it was clear that the student was referring to sewers, storm drains, or other
aspects of the drainage system when trying to explain the water collection system. One kindergarten student thought that water was made from a recipe; all
other students understood that water is a naturally found substance.

Responses concerning heat indicated that many students were not very aware
of furnaces or what they do, although most were familiar with the controls for ad-
justing the heat in the house. About two thirds knew that the heat comes from a
heater or furnace located somewhere in the house. Of these, 78 made reference to
a heater or furnace (or to "that thing down in the basement" or some similar description) but were unable to explain further, whereas 69 supplied responses that
were recognizable as descriptions of the workings of a forced-air furnace. None of
these students used the term *forced-air* and only some of them used the term *furnace*, but they all described heat as warm air that originates in a heater or furnace,
circulates throughout the house, and comes into rooms through registers. An additional 39 students depicted heat as warm air and noted that it enters rooms
through heat registers, but they could not say anything about where this warm air
comes from before it reaches the register. [Note: We are using the term *register*
here for clarity of communication. None of the students used this term. Instead,
they used terms such as *grate* or referred to "that thing in the wall with the holes
in it that the heat comes out of," etc.]

In addition to or instead of supplying these heater/furnace/register responses,
smaller numbers of students articulated alternative concepts of *heat* in modern
homes. Of these students, 28 said that this heat comes from a fire or fireplace, 25
that it comes from the sun, and 13 that it comes from a heat or power company.
In addition, 21 students gave "other" responses and 19 were unable to answer the
question.

Probing concerning students' ideas about the source of heat in the home or
the processes involved in producing it yielded three main theories. The most
common response, coded for 104 students, was what we labeled the *black box* furnace theory: These students indicated that the heat comes from a furnace or
heater but were unable to explain how the process works. Many fewer students
were coded for the other two theories. Only 28 (13%) articulated the correct
"firebox" furnace theory: Within the furnace, fire is used to heat air that is then

circulated through the house. Finally, 17 believed that heat (i.e., warm air) is sent directly to the house by the heat or power company. These students thought that heated air is piped underground to our houses, where it is either circulated immediately or else stored in the furnace until it is needed. If they mentioned the furnace, students who held this theory viewed it merely as a holding tank for heat piped in from the utility company, not realizing that the furnace houses a fire that heats air on-site. Another idea, mentioned by several students, was that it is warm under the ground and this underground heat "just floats up" into our homes. Finally, a few students thought that warm air is somehow captured in warm places like Hawaii and then transported to Michigan.

Most students were aware of thermostats (although they didn't use this word) and could talk about using them to control temperature in the home, but couldn't explain anything about how the process works. Similarly, many students could say that a heater or furnace needs electricity but could not explain how it heats the air. In fact, a subtype of the black box furnace/heater theory was to say that electricity makes the heat but students would then be unable to say more. For some of these students, electricity was an all-purpose explainer, much like God is for younger children.

The students often lacked vocabulary or confused terms, referring to registers as heaters, to furnaces as dryers, to fans as air conditioners, and to pipes as tubes, sewers, hoses, or drains. Several students pictured a particular person sending you heat (i.e., hot air), such as by pushing a button in response to some signal received electronically from your home when you use the thermostat. Some of the younger students pictured this heat as captured and saved from hot days in the summer (unexplained further). Unusual explanations included: Heat from the sun goes to your registers; "they catch warm air, put it in a duct and then between your vents"; hot water comes into your house from underground pipes and then "melts into the air" to heat your house; your heater "sucks up" heat from the air when the sun is out; maybe warm air comes from the wind, because it's blowing (out the registers).

Few students mentioned a fan as a mechanism for circulating heated air, whereas several suggested that hot air just "floats" up through the house. Thus, the main progression in students' thinking seemed to be from believing that a utility company supplies heat directly and the furnace is merely a storage place, to knowing that the heat is generated in the furnace but not knowing how, to knowing that the furnace contains a fire that heats air.

Almost 80% of the students understood that we have to pay for our heat, but fewer than half knew whom we pay and few if any understood that we pay for natural gas that is consumed in fires that create our heat. In talking about whom we pay for heat and light, some students said "the city," "the government," or made some other reference to paying a governmental agency rather than speaking of paying "the heat company," "the light company," "the power company," or some other term for the utility company.

Various students said that we pay because it wouldn't be fair not to pay, because people need money (or people deserve pay for their work), or because if we didn't pay, some people would use up all the heat or electricity. Other responses included: We pay the man who fixes the furnace; the "heat guy"; the person who lived in the place before you, or they will shut it off (you have to buy heating equipment as part of the house); the builders of your house when you buy it ($n = 3$); you pay for heaters and materials to make fires; the man who works in the apartment building; the heat manager who runs the home; the president or people in Hawaii who get the heat bills; the mayor; the landlord or the people of the city (2); the boss of the house (landlord or manager); the office of the mobile home park; the person who owns the heating system; the man who made the heater; you pay the landlord and he pays the government (this student also said that heat outside the home comes from rain which contains tiny "pellets" of hot air that are released when the drops splash down); the person you bought the house from; you pay the landlord who pays "somebody" who gives us the heat; the person you bought the furnace from (4); the bank; the guy who installs the heater; the factory that made the furnace (you pay them once a month for using it); you have to pay for the furnace but not for using it; you pay the company that installed the heater (but not for the heat).

About three fourths of the students knew that electricity is involved in creating light, but most of these could only advance a black box theory to explain the process. They knew that one must throw a switch to allow electricity to enter the bulb, but they were unable to explain how the arrival of electricity causes the bulb to light up. Other theories included the following: The power company or manufacturer puts something into bulbs to create light-up potential in them, and the arrival of electricity somehow activates this potential; electricity glows brightly in its natural state but is usually kept covered, whereas in light bulbs, the ends of the wires are uncovered so that they can glow; the ends of the wires running into the bulbs (or attachments to the ends of these wires) glow brightly or spark back and forth to create light when electricity reaches them; fire "just gets into" light bulbs; lighting comes from the power that is in the light bulb (unexplained further); the sun sends light to the bulb by magic when we throw a switch; electricity is made from the sun and since the sun is bright, it makes the light bright; when you throw the switch, fire (literally) goes into the bulb; electricity is like lightning; bulbs are filled with something like fire (adds a magical explanation about what happens when you turn on the light); tells the story of Franklin and lightning but cannot say more; "oil" comes through "cords" from the telephone poles and lights up our bulbs; says that the utility company sends "light" through power lines, but also says that if you opened up the power lines you would see electrical waves; when we throw a switch, "light" comes in and touches "a little thing in the bulb" and makes it shine; electricity in the bulb can burn out; there is a fire in the bulb that can be switched on and off; there is a little fire sealed within the light bulb; there are tiny lights inside the light bulbs; the utility company sends light (literally) through wires to your lamps; fuses are switches that make lights go on; a bulb lights up "because it's got so much energy" after we throw the switch; there are two wires inside the bulb; bulbs contain a little ball of fire that "comes up" when you turn it on (apparently like a pilot light leading to a bigger fire when you turn it on); you put a battery and it lights the wick inside the bulb; the utility company gets electricity by capturing lightning during storms.

Only 34 students were able to go beyond "black box" electricity explanations and articulate some theory of how the lights in our homes work. Of these, 23 provided explanations that were simply incorrect (although often indicative of creative and intelligent thinking), and 11 provided explanations that were at least partly correct. No student provided an unambiguously correct basic explanation for electric lighting. The 11 partially correct explanations, shown now, were quite limited in scope and often included incorrect as well as correct elements.

1st Just turn the little thing and it comes on. (OK. When you turn on that thing, what's making the light come on?) The little thing inside the bulb. (Can you think of anything else that makes that bulb come on?) Fire stuff, 'cause there's little streaks of dust and it's hot and they turn on the light.

1st It works from a light bulb. If you didn't have a light bulb and you got a light bulb from another person and you put it in your lamp, then you can put the top on your lamp and then you can turn it on. The light comes from a wire that is in the light bulb. The light bulb is glass and you can see through it because it's glass.

1st A light bulb is made out of glass with little fusing wire it needs for electricity to come in. (What happens when the electricity goes through those wires?) It will light up the light bulb and you put a little sheet thing over lamps and it'll go down and make light around a big circle.

1st Electricity. Like there's a wire inside and when you touch a switch, it comes on. (So what happens when you turn on the switch?) Then it lights up.

1st It comes from electricity and the electricity leads from . . . it gets lighter. (Can you tell me more about that?) Well, there's like two little wires in the light bulb and when you turn it on, the wires go into it and it makes it light up.

2nd Electricity goes into the light that it's hooked up to. (Then what happens?) Then it lights up. (Do you know how electricity works?) There's little things that are called atoms and they like get into wires and they just flow into the lights and they make the lights glow. (How do you know so much about electricity and lights?) We listened to a book and it had a tape that went with it and it told us about how electricity works.

3rd   Electricity goes into the bulb. There's two little wires and when you turn
      on the knob it makes electricity go through them, it goes in between and
      makes the light. (Do you know how electricity works?) Sort of. It's gener-
      ated by a river. You build a dam, the river's there, the river starts circling
      around and it makes electricity. Well, they put in some electricity in
      some bulbs and then they put them in boxes at stores and then people
      come and buy them and put them in their lamps and the electricity . . . as
      soon as you turn on the lamp, then the electricity gets hot and then it
      lights up. [This was the only response to mention the role of heat in cre-
      ating light.] (Do you have any idea where the electricity comes from?) By
      a switch. The electricity goes through that. There's a bunch of wires in it
      and stuff and you flip it up and down and the lights turn on. The wires
      connect to the lights and stuff. (Do you know why the light bulbs come
      on?) Electricity inside your light bulb. There's like two wires inside.

3rd   Well, first you have to plug it in. If it's just a switch then you turn it on,
      but if it's a lamp and you have to turn it on by hand, then first you would
      have to plug it in. (When you turn the switch, what happens?) There's
      the little wire things in the bulb and somehow—it's like catching on fire
      but it's not. It's really bright and then the bulb lights up.

3rd   The energy goes into the light bulb and it has a wire that creates a lot of
      energy that lets off a lot of light.

A majority of the students was able to respond to the question about whom we
pay for light. They usually gave generally accurate responses, although some confused power lines and companies with cable television lines and companies, and
others confused utility companies with banks or governments. Also, a sizable minority (24 students) thought that we only have to pay for light bulbs (but not for
using them), and a few others thought that we pay only for installation and repair
of power lines or light fixtures. Other responses included: the light people; you pay
for the bulbs and you pay the building engineer for maintenance; the man who
takes care of your lights; the manager; the president and the light company; the cable company (2); the landlord or the community; you have to pay to have electricity lines hooked up to your house and there's a thing attached to your house that
attracts the electricity (lightning rod?); the governor; you have to pay if you have
your lights on for too long, and the money goes to government workers and people
who fix your lights (student goes on to define government workers as people who
don't really get money for doing their job, "like librarians"); the city (3); the IRS;
the person you bought the house from (2); you have to pay the utility company to
fix broken wires (but no mention of using electricity); you pay the landlord, who in
turn pays "somebody who gives us light"; the tax collector; the taxpayers (the government); you pay for wires and light switches, but not for using them.

       Some of the themes emphasized earlier in the students' explanations of why
renters must pay to stay in their apartments reappeared in their explanations of

why we need to pay for utilities. Many included the "fact-of-life" rationale: Just as you have to pay for housing or else face eviction, you have to pay for utilities or else lose your heat or light. Rationales based on notions of fairness and justice occasionally reappeared as well: You have to pay the people who supply you with these utilities because they deserve to be paid for their work and they need money too, because using the utilities without paying for them would be like stealing, and so on.

The difficulties that many students experienced in trying to answer our questions about paying for heat and light were rooted in their lack of knowledge about the processes involved in producing heating and light. Students who did not understand that home heating is created through fires that consume natural gas or other fuel were unclear about what (if anything) a utility company might be supplying to us that makes it possible to heat our homes, and thus unclear about what we might have to pay for. Similarly, students who did not realize that running our lights consumes electricity that is supplied to us by a utility company were unclear about what we might have to pay for that makes it possible for us to light our homes.

Some of the students who said that we do not have to pay for heat or light may have been correct (in a sense), if their responses were based on the assumption that heat or light expenses are included in the rent paid to landlords. Any such "we don't have to pay" responses that were based on this assumption, however, failed to take into account the fact that rents are higher when utilities are included than when they are not.

IDEAL FUTURE HOMES

22. **When you're grown up and have a family of your own, you might want to buy a place to live. What kind of place would you look for?** [If necessary, ask:] **Would you want the home to have any special rooms?**

23. **Is there anything unusual or special about the home you would want?**

24. **What about the location of the home—would you want to live near certain things? Would you want to live far away from certain things?**

   K   22. A home. (What would you want to have in this home? Any special rooms?) No.

         23. No.

         24. A backyard, swings. (What would you like to live far away from?) Poison ivy.

 1st 22. I would look for a place that's very cool and that's good enough if I have kids . . . it would be like a house that's a white house.

         23. Yeah, if I have boy kids, I'd want them to have a room with a wall that's painted green, or if they like . . . if the house was white for ev-

erybody, but not for the boys, we'll buy a piece of green paint and I'll let them paint the room.

24. Well, not like a road . . . like they're digging it and we can't get out of our driveway. (So you wouldn't want to live near a road they're just building—is that it?) Um hm. (Is there anything else you would not want to live near?) Like a car place, 'cause we do live by a car place and every time I go over with my brother, then when we go past the car place, there's always smoke getting in our face. (Is there anything you'd like to live near?) Nice neighbors or like a store so it'll be easier to get to it, or like a toy store for my kids.

2nd 22. A house. (What would you like to have in that house—any special rooms?) A living room, a family room, a kitchen, a dining room, and some bedrooms to sleep in, and a bathroom.

23. No.

24. No. (Would you want to live far away from certain things?) Yeah. (What, for instance?) Like . . . nothing.

3rd 22. A house in the country so my two children can run out and play. If I have pet, he can play with them. And so you can raise horses in the country. 'Cause in the city you can't raise nothing.

23. Yeah. There will be a playroom, a place for kids that have been naughty—we'll put them in there if they don't say "sorry" to the people for what happened.

24. No. (Would you want to live far away from certain things?) Yes, because if you live in the country without nothing around . . . if you live near stores, there'll be a lot of cars around and there will be gas coming through. I'd rather live far away. I don't care if it costs money just to drive.

In describing their ideal homes, some students identified their features (size, style, color, house vs. apartment, etc.), others identified specific rooms or "extras" (basement, deck, swimming pool, yard, etc.), and some identified both. In addition or instead, 160 students identified more general features. Most specified that their ideal home would be a house, but 24 (11%) specified an apartment. Only 78 (36%) made reference to size, but all of these students specified that the home would be large. In addition, 44 students mentioned the style of the home (ranch, two-story, etc.), 27 described the color(s) that it would be painted, 22 specified that it would be well built or in good repair, and 12 that it would be located in a suburban or semirural setting.

Unusual rooms or features included: a reading room; a special place in the attic from which you could watch events going on below in the street; a computer room; a thinking room; a hobby room; a piano room; an all-TV room (a room filled with televisions); a display room for showing expensive crystal and gold; a "time-out" room to send the children when they are disobedient; a tornado shelter; wood-paneled rooms; big windows; tennis courts; balconies off your rooms; a barn; fence and bright lights at night to protect against robbers; fluffy carpets and wooden walls; lots of windows; a bird feeder in the yard; golf and basketball facilities; cross-ventilation; a sliding glass door in back; special passageways through closets to link the children's bedrooms; secret passages. Unusual general features included: a mobile home; a mansion; an apartment with room service; an apartment in a skyscraper, located in New York or Hawaii; a cabin in the woods, near a lake and a hill for sledding; mansion with 50 rooms, pool, and tennis court; a duplex in good repair; vinyl siding; a farm in a peaceful setting, three stories with loft and trap doors, well insulated; a cabin in the mountains—efficient and environmentally friendly rather than big and gaudy.

In talking about what they would like to live near, 78 students mentioned relatives, friends, or neighbors. Other answers included: food stores or restaurants (48); the school that their children would attend (29); woods (28); a body of water or swimming pool (25); places for the children to play (23); a mall, a bank, or other nonfood stores (19); a post office, police station, fire station, hospital, or other government service location (16); their own work site (12); and places to take children, such as zoos or theme parks (11). Unusual responses included: flower shop; nail and hair shop, book shop, and carnival; a big tree (just one, not a woods); babysitters; a light pole (this student feared the dark); a public garden; subway; cemetery; Mount Rushmore; pet store; New York City, the White House; a mall; bait store; Eiffel Tower; the equator. The infrequent mention of the parents' work sites indicates that K–3 students are relatively unaware of the importance that most adults attach to "convenience to the job" as a determinant of housing location.

Concerning what the home would be located far away from, 26 students mentioned the city or urban density; 25 traffic or noise; 18 dangerous animals, insects, or forests; 16 crime; 12 factories, junk yards, dumps, smoke, or pollution; and 12 people whom they didn't like. "Other" things to avoid included: not near a lake because you might fall into it; pricker bushes; China; poison ivy; a volcano; monsters and mean dogs; farms (because they stink); cold climates; dangerous people and things such as bombs, power plants, museums that zap you with electricity, people in wheelchairs, old people who can give you Parkinson's disease, or scary rock concerts; a fairground (because of the noise); railroad tracks; rattlesnakes and the desert; jails. Most of the "far away from" responses were similar to those that might be made by adults, although adults would be less likely to mention living far away from people they didn't like or from insects or forest animals.

Some of the younger students were notably limited or naive in what they were able to say about their ideal homes, and a few older ones playfully depicted mansions equipped with extensive sports or recreation facilities. Most, however, depicted a comfortably large house located in a quiet, family-oriented suburban or semirural neighborhood. Many added that this home would be located near relatives or friends and convenient to places to shop and take children, but removed from urban density, crime, traffic, noise, and so on.

Although some students emphasized childish fears (of insects, bears, etc.) or fanciful ideas (spy holes and secret passages, the all-TV room, 500 refrigerators stocked with goodies, avoiding museums that "zap you with electricity," etc.), most were able to adopt an adult perspective in responding to this question. Consequently, as far as they went, at least, most answers emphasized similar themes to those that would be emphasized by adults. Perhaps the major exception was the fact that only about 6% of the students indicated that their ideal home would be located close to their workplace. Also, only 13% mentioned the children's schools, and all of these focused on the schools' location (near the home) without mentioning the quality of the schools.

A FOLLOW-UP STUDY

The data just presented were elicited from students who lived in Michigan in low-density urban and suburban communities. We recognize that somewhat different patterns of response to at least some of our questions might be elicited from students living in high-density urban environments in inner cities, students living in considerably warmer or colder regions that do not have the four-season climate that Michigan has, students living in sparsely populated rural areas, students whose home heating systems feature boilers and radiators rather than furnaces and heat registers, and so on. To address one of these possibilities, we compared the interviews from the 24 third graders in our main shelter study with interviews from 35 third graders from families living in a primarily vertical, high-density area of New York City (Manhattan). Eighteen of these students were from primarily high SES families living in the Upper West Side, and 17 were from primarily low SES families living in Harlem. Each subsample was stratified according to achievement level and gender. Because the two Manhattan samples were so different, rather than combine them, we tested for differences between three location groups: Michigan (n = 24), Upper West Side (n = 18), and Harlem (n = 17).

These analyses produced chi-squares that reached statistical significance for 36% of the coding categories. In most cases, this was because the Harlem students had less knowledge to bring to bear and therefore were less able to answer the questions (or provided less complete and accurate responses). Otherwise, the response patterns were more similar than different, although each group displayed certain tendencies interpretable as reflective of its geographic location or socioeconomic circumstances.

The Harlem students were less able to explain why people need homes, to supply the name "tipi" and suggest an explanation for why certain tribes used this form of housing, to discuss the characteristics of log cabins, to say where the pioneers living in log cabins got their water, to explain why people prefer houses to apartments, to distinguish renting from buying, to explain home heating and lighting, to explain payments associated with keeping homes heated and lit, to identify general features of their ideal home, and to talk about things that they would like to avoid living near. Harlem students were more likely than students in the other groups to talk about paying rent or utility costs to "the super" (i.e., the building superintendent), mention a boiler or radiator when talking about heating, think that people do not have to pay for heating their living quarters, mention bathrooms in talking about features of their ideal homes, and describe relatively modest (in some cases, minimal) living quarters when describing their ideal homes.

The Upper West Side students displayed more knowledge than students in the other two groups on a few items: They were the most likely to say that pueblo dwellers could not construct longhouses for lack of sufficient large trees, to say that pioneers had light from candles in their log cabins, to say that high-rise buildings are built in order to get more out of the available space in large cities, and to offer an explanation of lighting that went beyond black box electricity theories. In addition, their responses occasionally reflected their generally privileged socioeconomic backgrounds; they identified more "other" rooms and extras in talking about their ideal homes and made more references to travel or to owning more than one residence.

The Michigan students' responses paralleled those of the Upper West Side students for the most part, although they displayed more knowledge than both Manhattan groups on a few items. They were more likely to describe pueblos as more durable than longhouses, to identify freshwater sources when talking about how pioneers got their water, to say that most people prefer houses to apartments because you own the house and can decorate or equip it as you wish, to express the *ownership* concept clearly when distinguishing between renting and buying, to identify freshwater sources when asked where water for our homes comes from, to say that this water is piped to homes underground, and to say that we pay utility companies for our lighting. Some of these responses, especially those dealing with freshwater sources, are attributable to their geographic location. This also applies to a few other instances where the Michigan students made distinctive responses: They were more likely than the Manhattan students to describe log cabins as small or cramped, to think that people who live in apartments must do so because they cannot afford a house, to suggest that some people prefer to live in apartments because they want to live close to others, and to talk about forced-air/furnace systems when discussing home heating.

In general, although each of the three groups showed some distinctive responses reflective of the housing patterns in the locations in which they lived, socioeconomic contrasts produced much larger differences in the students' response patterns than geographic contrasts did. The Michigan and Upper West Side students were mostly similar to each other but very different from the Harlem students in having more, and more accurate, things to say in response to our questions.

The most notable geographic difference appeared in beliefs about whether most people would prefer to live in a house or an apartment. Whereas 96% of the Michigan third graders said a house, this was true of only 47% of the Harlem students and 39% of the Upper West Side students. In contrast, whereas only 4% of the Michigan students said that most people prefer an apartment, this was said by 35% of the Harlem students and 28% of the Upper West Side students. Many more of the New York students than the Michigan students said that they didn't know or couldn't choose because different people have different preferences. In addition, the New York students came up with explanations that did not appear in the Michigan sample: I would want both an apartment in the city and a house in the country; older people might want an apartment but younger people might want a house; people who want to live in Manhattan have to get an apartment, but people who want to live somewhere else can get houses; if you have a house, you can go out in back at night and relax and look at the stars, but if you live in an apartment building, the super will come to fix your plumbing, you are safer from robbers, and there are candy and cake sales in the building; in apartments you don't have to worry about bugs or take action to get rid of them; and apartments offer better heat (several New York students viewed houses as poorly heated or insulated, perhaps from experiences with summer homes). The New York students were generally more knowledge about renting and the Michigan students more knowledge about buying, although neither group understood that banking (specifically, making mortgage loans) and renting are profit-making businesses.

In response to the question about sources of water for our homes, six Upper West Side students mentioned reservoirs. Some of them conceived of a reservoir as an original water source (akin to a lake) rather than a holding place for retained water or a source of pressure. However, two did imply that water reaches homes under pressure. Some thought of reservoirs as catching rain (i.e., believing that rain was the source of all the retained water). A few New York students also mentioned pumping stations.

The students' visions of ideal homes mostly reflected modestly enhanced versions of the lives they were living. Thus, the vision of suburban family living projected by the Michigan students is not a generic contemporary version of the American Dream likely to be articulated by children from any background located anywhere in the country. The Upper West Side students were as likely to mention urban as suburban locales for their ideal homes, and they mentioned "extras" that did not appear in the Michigan interviews (expensive furniture or decor features, or in a few cases, security features). Although some of these students shared the Michigan students' vision of a big house in the suburbs, many depicted well-appointed apartments or condos in New York or some other large city (including foreign cities).

The Harlem students' ideal home depictions were mostly confined to basic rooms and common features. They were much more likely than other students to mention bathrooms, perhaps because they had to share bathrooms with many more other people than the other students did. Concerning things that they would like to live far away from, they focused on crime, without much mention of urban density, traffic, noise, factories, junkyards, and so on. Details of these and other findings can be found in the technical report (Brophy, O'Mahony, & Alleman, 2002).

DISCUSSION

Except for our own pilot study (Brophy & Alleman, 1997), this has been the first systematic investigation of children's knowledge and thinking about shelter. Our findings replicate and expand on the findings from the pilot study by providing more evidence that primary-grade children typically do not acquire all, or even a significant portion, of what is worth knowing about cultural universals through everyday experience, so that they stand to profit from instruction on these topics.

In reporting the findings, we do not just focus on misconceptions but instead seek to characterize the students' thinking about each topic addressed, however it may vary in accuracy, sophistication, embedded values, and so on. For example, the Michigan students' expressed preferences for suburban homes were not relevant to misconception issues, but they did provide information about the students' restriction of purview (e.g., most of them did not know much about alternatives to home ownership and possessed only a "cities are bad" stereotype of urban living). At the time, we did not yet know the extent to which these preferences reflected a tendency for children everywhere to both prefer and value what is familiar versus a particular tendency for most U.S. children to believe that suburban living is the ideal. Our follow-up study with Manhattan students supported the former more than the latter hypothesis. This is but one example of how the findings from our studies can not just inform social studies educators' curriculum and instructional planning but also suggest lines of inquiry worth pursuing by child development researchers, even when they do not involve discovering and analyzing misconceptions.

Our questions were phrased in simple, familiar language and most of them addressed aspects of shelter with which students possessed at least tacit familiarity through experiences in their everyday lives. These considerations, along with claims that primary grade students do not need to be taught about cultural universals because they learn about them in their lives outside of school, would lead some to predict consistent indications of sophistication in the students' response patterns. That is, some might have predicted infrequent coding of categories for "don't know" responses and naive and incorrect responses, but frequent coding of categories for responses indicating complete and accurate understanding. However, such patterns were seen for only a few questions (e.g., all of the students understood that shelter is a basic need and most of them knew the name "tipi"). In contrast, most questions produced the opposite pattern, in which most students were unable to respond or gave responses that were naive or at least incorrect, and only a few were able to generate responses that could be characterized as reasonably complete and accurate. We did observe increases in knowledge associated with increases in grade level, but most of the gains occurred in categories representing lower levels of sophistication about the topic, so that the increases represented shifts from little or no knowledge to partial knowledge rather than shifts from partial knowledge to complete knowledge. Even the second and third graders had very limited knowledge about many of the topics addressed.

The students understood that shelter is a basic need even in warm climates; they could recognize and talk about some of the formal aspects of different forms of past and present homes; and they displayed at least tacit knowledge of current norms and practices (e.g., people need to pay for their shelter and utilities and tend to prefer home ownership over apartment rental). Their beliefs were not always accurate, however, and even when they were accurate, they usually were not embedded within elaborated structures that included knowledge of connections and cause–effect relationships.

Most responses emphasized description over explanation and form over function. That is, the students recognized differences in the sizes, construction materials, durability, and general quality of the shelter provided by different forms of past and present housing, but they did not understand much about the historical, geographical, or cultural reasons for these contrasting housing styles. In thinking about contemporary housing, they focused on what is visible inside and outside the home but did not show much awareness of what is in between the walls or beneath the building. They knew that shelter is a basic and universal human need, but they were less appreciative of modern homes as controlled environments for comfortable living that cater to a great many of our wants as well as our more basic needs. Most showed only very limited awareness of the mechanisms through which modern houses are supplied with water, heat, and light.

The students displayed knowledge about evolution in forms of housing over time, but they did not know much about why particular forms were emphasized by particular groups. There was very little recognition that housing types reflected differences in climate and local availability of construction materials, and the students emphasized the deficiencies of these homes in comparison with contemporary housing rather than appreciating them as inventive adaptations to their time and place (thus displaying a pervasive presentism).

Concerning shelter in today's world, most Michigan students understood that people have to pay for shelter and that most people prefer homes to apartments. If anything, they may have exaggerated the latter preference, which is perhaps to be expected given their ages and the fact that most of them lived in homes located in a suburb that emphasized family living. Most of them had difficulty even accepting that, let alone explaining why, some people prefer apartment rental to home ownership.

The students understood that people have to pay for their housing, and most understood that buying a home implies ownership whereas renting does not. Otherwise, however, they possessed only limited and spotty knowledge of the economics of housing. Only a few understood that renting is a profit-making business or that people can get mortgage loans to allow them to move into a home before they have accumulated its full purchase price.

The students also displayed limited and spotty knowledge about the utilities supplied to modern homes. Almost all understood that water is piped into homes, but many did not appreciate that the water is drawn from freshwater rather than saltwater sources, purified, and delivered under pressure. Most understood that thermostats are used to adjust heating in a home, but were vague about where the heat comes from or how the system works. Only 13% understood that furnaces contain a fire that heats air that is then circulated throughout the house. A majority knew that electricity is involved in creating light, but they were unable to explain how the arrival of electricity causes the bulb to light up. Most students understood that we pay for our utilities, although most were unclear or incorrect about whom we pay and for what.

When asked about their ideal homes, most students depicted single-family homes located in suburban or semirural areas, near relatives and friends but removed from urban density and crime. They emphasized many of the same home features and location considerations that their parents might have, except that only a few talked about locating near the children's schools or the parents' workplaces.

Implications for Primary-Grade Social Studies

The questions asked in this study reflect our notions about key ideas that might be emphasized in teaching about shelter. We recommend powerful treatments that enable students to develop understanding of how shelter works in our society, how and why it got to be that way over time, how it varies across locations and cultures, and what all of this might mean for personal, social, and civic decision making.

Students can learn that people's shelter needs are determined in large part by local climate and geographical features and that most housing is constructed using materials adapted from natural resources that are plentiful in the local area. Other key ideas to which they might be exposed include:

1. Certain forms of housing reflect cultural, economic, or geographic conditions (tipis and tents as easily movable shelters used by nomadic societies, stilt houses as adaptation to periodic flooding, high-rises as adaptation to land scarcity in urban areas).

2. Inventions, discoveries, and improvements in construction knowledge and materials have enabled many modern people to live in housing that offers better durability, weatherproofing, insulation, and temperature control, with fewer requirements for maintenance and labor, than anything that was available to even the richest of their ancestors.

3. Modern industries and transportation make it possible to construct almost any kind of shelter almost anywhere on earth, so it is now possible for those who can afford it to live comfortably in very hot or very cold climates.

4. Forms of shelter that existed in the past and that still exist in some societies today are much simpler than the modern homes that most American students live in, but they typically represent intelligent use of locally available materials to fashion homes that not only meet basic shelter needs but are well adapted to the local climate and reflective of the cultural mores of the inhabitants.

These goals suggest four principles in selecting and developing content. First, using contemporary and familiar examples, the unit should help students to understand how and why the social system functions as it does with respect to the cultural universal being studied. A unit on shelter, for example, might begin with the forms of shelter commonly found in the contemporary United States, especially in the students' own neighborhoods. Instruction would be designed to help students articulate the tacit knowledge that they already possess, as well as to expand on and embed it within a knowledge network structured around powerful ideas (e.g., modern houses are not merely shelters but controlled living environments).

Second, the unit should include a historical dimension illustrating how human responses to the cultural universal have evolved through time due to inventions and other cultural advances. For example, shelters have evolved from caves and simple huts, to sturdier and more permanent homes such as log cabins, to modern weatherproof homes that feature running water, heat, light, and insulation. Technological advances have enabled us to meet our shelter needs and wants more effectively with less personal effort and time investment than in the past.

Third, the unit should include a geographical/cultural dimension that exposes students to current variations in human responses to the cultural universal. Different forms of shelter exist in different geographical locations, in part because of differences in climate and availability of construction materials and in part because of cultural differences. Along with the historical dimension, this geographical/cultural dimension of the unit would extend students' concepts to include examples different from the ones they view as prototypical. This would help them to place themselves and their familiar social environments into perspective as parts of the larger human condition as it has evolved through time and as it varies across cultures. In the language of anthropologists, it would "make the strange familiar" and "make the familiar strange" so that students could appreciate seemingly exotic forms of housing (e.g., tipis, stilt houses, jungle huts) as intelligent adaptations to local circumstances.

Fourth, topic coverage should include emphasis on applications to students' current and future lives. This can be accomplished through activities designed to raise students' consciousness of choices that they will be making as individuals and as citizens, and of the tradeoffs associated with the major choice options. For example, shelter lessons might include discussion of the tradeoffs offered by different housing types and locations (urban, suburban, rural) and the problem of homelessness and what might be done about it. For shelter unit plans that incorporate these recommendations, see Alleman and Brophy (2001).

5

Communication

Our communication interviews asked students about:

- communication as a universal human need and the functions that it fulfills for us;
- methods of and limitations on communication in prehistoric times and among preliterate people who lived more recently;
- the impact of major inventions (writing, the printing press, radio, television, telephones, computers);
- communication by infants and among people who are blind or deaf;
- how people communicate when they do not share a language;
- how the environment and the culture shape vocabulary;
- the invention of new words;
- reasons for using symbols instead of words on certain traffic signs and other public notices;
- how the postal system works;
- why people read newspapers;
- the workings of the television industry.

For details of the findings, see the technical report (Brophy & Alleman, 2001a).

CHILDREN'S KNOWLEDGE AND THINKING ABOUT COMMUNICATION

Not much research is available on developments in children's thinking about communication except for studies of their reactions to television. However, in

the 1960s and 1970s, there was a flurry of research on the development of communication-related social skills, such as gaining adult attention in acceptable
ways, obtaining information effectively, expressing feelings verbally, and inter-
acting with peers (Wood, 1977). In the emerging field of media studies, research
has focused on children as critical readers of media as text.

Children learn gradually about differences in the languages that people use to
communicate. Most American preschoolers understand that some people speak
languages other than English and that different social groups speak in distinct
ways. For example, Hirschfeld and Gelman (1997) found that preschoolers predicted that people from minority races, people wearing unfamiliar clothing, or
people living in unfamiliar dwellings were more likely than other people to speak
an unfamiliar language. Children develop finer distinctions as they get older (as-
sociating dialects with people from particular social or geographical backgrounds).

Children also learn that some people's communication abilities are limited by
sensory deficits (blindness, deafness) or physical impairments to their speech production mechanisms. We were unable to locate studies of developmental trends
in this knowledge, although we did locate curriculum packages that teach children to empathize and interact productively with people who have disabilities
(Del-Val et al., 1981; Lambert, 1994).

Most communication-related research has focused on the kinds of visual images and verbal messages being directed at children through the media, and how
children respond to this input (e.g., the degree to which they understand what is
real vs. fictional, or that advertising is intended to persuade them to purchase
products or services). Media literacy curricula have been developed to teach children to critically understand, question, and evaluate how media work, produce
meaning, and impact our lives (Abdullah, 2000). They seek to inoculate children
against undue persuasion by teaching them to notice the messages being directed
to them, to note the techniques being used to hold their attention and persuade
them to a point of view, and to ask who created these messages and why
(Feuerstein, 1999; Thomas, 1999).

Children are not just passive viewers who merely absorb information from
television. Instead, they actively process what they watch, and their strategies for
doing so become more efficient as their general cognitive skills mature and they
acquire more experience with television. Young children's attention tends to focus on salient stimuli. As they mature, conceptual information and information
seeking become more important than perceptual salience, and they begin to distinguish more efficiently between relevant and irrelevant material and between
what is apparent and what is real. They are most affected by televised events that
are perceived to be realistic or plausible and that involve characters with whom
they identify. Heavy viewers who rely mostly on television as an information
source are the most likely to accept television's version of reality. If they spend
much of their time watching shows that depict violence or stereotypic portrayals

of women and minorities, they may become more fearful, more biased, or less tolerant (Van Evra, 1990).

Wolf (1987) talked with 4- to 12-year-old children about television programs they were watching and found considerable knowledge about conventions involved in television production and viewing. Most children understood that certain types of clothing and mannerisms distinguish "good guys" from "bad guys," that an initial panoramic scene is often used to indicate location, that music is often used to build anticipation, and that commercials are intended to persuade us to buy.

The Annenberg Media Literacy Study found that children ages 6 to 11 showed good awareness of television illusions, with 92% knowing that Superman and Batman cannot really fly, 75% knowing that fights in dramatic programs are not real, and 78% agreeing that television advertising makes items like toys or candy look nicer than they really are. Most knew that fights in adventure shows do not really hurt people and that news anchors are not alone in the studio, but only the older children typically knew that situation comedies are produced on sets (not in regular homes) and that programs are paid for by producers, advertisers, and media corporations (Davies, 1997). Other studies of children's understanding of what is "real" on television were reviewed by Chandler (1997).

A study done in India found that children enjoyed watching ads on television, sometimes as much or more than the regular programming. The main characteristics of television ads that drew children to them included: (a) brevity and repetitiveness (the brevity makes them suited to the concentration spans of young children and the repetition guarantees that they "learn" them); (b) complete capsules (they convey a single main idea that is easy to grasp and remember); (c) music; (d) color; (e) technical superiority (often better than the regular programming); (f) emotional manipulation (emphasis on excitement, fun, sentimentality, mischief, or other emotions and personal problems easily understood and appreciated by children); and (g) role models (attractive people in attractive settings wearing attractive clothes, etc.). The youngest children in the study (8-year-olds) were beginning to recognize that advertisements are intended to sell a product or service. Even so, they expected these advertisements to be essentially honest, so they emphasized an informative role over a persuasive role for these ads. By age 10, most of them had begun to question the fundamental honesty of advertising (Unnikrishnan & Bajpai, 1996).

These naively trusting reactions were found at a time when mass television was just being introduced in India, so they may not hold for children who have grown up with television. A recent study of British children ages 8 to 12 found considerable skepticism and even cynicism about television advertising (Buckingham, 2000). Many of the students understood that celebrities were paid for their product endorsements, questioned the legitimacy of surveys or "before-and-after" tests, or talked about "camera tricks" for enhancing the desirability of the products. Although the children understood that advertisements were attempting to persuade them to purchase, they knew much less about why these ads appeared on television in the first place (i.e., that sponsors paid television stations to air them). Henriksen (1996) also noted that children may not be aware of the profit motives that underlie the development and airing of ads.

Reviews of research done mostly in the United States and mostly during the 1970s and 1980s suggested conclusions that lie in between those based on Indian children somewhat new to television and British children who had grown up with it (John, 1999; Van Evra, 1990). These studies suggested that children from 5 to 8 years of age distinguish between programs and commercials based primarily on perceptual cues (e.g., a commercial is short, but a program is long), whereas older children distinguish the content of the messages (e.g., shows involve stories but commercials involve product selling). Children aged 5 or 6 do not understand many commercials very well, but 7- to 10-year-olds are more vulnerable to television manipulation. Those younger than 7 or 8 show little awareness of commercials' persuasive intent, viewing them as entertainment or unbiased information. By age 9, many children have had experience with products that they were disappointed in and have become suspicious of advertising claims. Awareness of the persuasive intent of commercials rose across childhood, as did knowledge of some of the tactics and appeals used to sell products. However, few children of any age showed high awareness of the larger world of television advertising, including the profit motives of the companies involved.

Reviews that have analyzed across time and cultures have found that children who have grown up from infancy with television are more sophisticated about advertising than children living in countries where television is newly introduced, and within the most developed countries, children are more sophisticated now than they were in the past (Chan, 2000; Chan & McNeal, 2002; Martin, 1997). Nevertheless, concern about advertising directed at children continues, especially with regard to undesired influences of ads for junk foods, as well as the more general role of television advertising in promoting a consumer culture among children (Bandyopadhyay, Kindra, & Sharp, 2001; Bulmer, 2001; Carruth & Skinner, 2001; John, 1999; McNeal, 1987; Wiman & Newman, 1989).

Despite the wealth of research on children and television, we did not find studies relating to most of our questions probing children's thinking about how television works and how its invention changed the world. Nor did we find studies relating to most of our other questions about communication as a cultural universal.

OUR COMMUNICATION INTERVIEWS

Communication interviews were conducted with 96 students, 24 in each of Grades K–3, stratified within each grade by prior achievement levels and gender. Descriptive statistics and information from analyses of scores derived from the coding are given in Table 5.1.

TABLE 5.1
Distributions and Phi Coefficients Showing Relationships
of Coding Categories to Grade Level

Response Categories	Total 96	K 24	1 24	2 24	3 24	Phi
1. What is communication?						
0. Doesn't know/no relevant response	58	22	18	10	8	−49
1. Talking, having a conversation, speech	26	0	2	11	13	52
2A. Do people like to communicate, or do they need to?						
1. They like to	12	6	3	2	1	−24
2. They need to (cannot give examples)	14	5	4	2	3	
3. Need to make plans (to meet, etc.)	11	3	1	4	3	
4. Need to communicate with family members	10	3	2	3	2	
5. Need to participate in school or work activities	16	2	4	2	8	27
6. Need to in emergencies or when something is harming them	30	4	9	10	7	
7. Need to be informed/ask or answer questions	8	1	2	3	2	
8. Need to communicate or understand feelings or needs	15	2	4	4	5	
2B. Would our lives be better or worse if we couldn't talk?						
0. Doesn't know/no relevant response	11	9	1	1	0	−48
1. Worse, no explanation	10	4	5	1	0	−28
2. Physical impediments inhibit speech	6	2	2	1	1	
3. We would have to use sign language, read lips, or write messages	26	6	4	6	10	
4. We wouldn't be able to get help in emergencies or when sick or hurt	8	1	3	2	2	
5. It would be difficult to understand each other; we would not be as well informed, could not get needed information	27	1	5	11	10	37
6. We would be isolated from others, lonely, unable to share thoughts and feelings	13	0	5	3	5	25
7. Talking helps us to learn	6	0	1	3	2	
3. Some animals communicate by making noises, like dogs bark at each other. But we don't have to bark, we can talk. What does talking allow us to do that dogs can't do? Is talking better than barking? Why?						
0. Doesn't know/no relevant response	20	12	3	3	2	−42
1. No difference; barking is just as good as talking	6	1	1	2	2	
2. Barking is noisy, annoying, hurts your ears	6	1	1	3	1	
3. Talking is easier to understand; people can't understand barking	38	4	15	9	10	
4. We can communicate better by talking, say more or more complex things, express emotions and plans, explain about emergencies	26	2	5	8	11	31

(Continued)

TABLE 5.1
(Continued)

Response Categories	Total 96	K 24	1 24	2 24	3 24	Phi
4. Back in time, the earliest people lived in caves. How did these people communicate?						
0. Doesn't know/no relevant response	6	4	2	0	0	−29
1. They talked (like today)	60	17	11	18	14	
2. They grunted, growled, made other vocal noises	16	2	6	3	5	
3. They talked in a different language	13	3	5	2	3	
4. They used sign language or pantomime or acted things out	39	4	9	13	13	31
5. Says that there was a time when people didn't have language, could not talk	57	15	15	11	16	
6. They wrote or drew (typically on walls, ground, rocks)	19	0	1	6	12	50
7. They had to have face-to-face communication because they did not have telephones or mail then	10	1	3	3	3	
5A. Before Columbus discovered America, the only people who lived here were the Indians. How did the Indians communicate?						
0. Doesn't know/no relevant response	10	4	3	3	0	−21
1. They talked (like today)	54	17	12	15	10	−23
2. They talked, but in a different language/their own language	27	1	7	5	14	44
3. They communicated through whoops and hollers	8	1	4	2	1	
4. They used hand signals or sign language	21	5	2	4	10	30
5. They used written or symbolic language (carving on walls, scratching on ground, artwork)	12	0	2	4	6	28
5B. How would the chief of one Indian village get a message to the chief of a village five miles away?						
0. Doesn't know/no relevant response	24	16	5	2	1	−57
1. Modern inventions: telephone, telegraph, tape recorder, mail service	8	1	4	2	1	
2. Send someone with a written message	20	2	9	5	4	
3. Go personally or send someone with a verbal message	56	7	14	15	20	39
4. Smoke signals, drum, light flashes	7	0	2	3	2	
5. Yell	6	0	1	3	2	
6A. Did the Indians have libraries? Why didn't they have libraries?						
0. Doesn't know/no relevant response	18	12	2	0	4	−49
1. Libraries weren't invented yet/they didn't know about them	24	2	7	7	8	23
2. There were no materials to build libraries or they didn't know how to build them	7	0	3	2	2	
3. They couldn't or didn't read (or write)	16	6	5	1	4	

(Continued)

TABLE 5.1
(Continued)

Response Categories	Total 96	K 24	1 24	2 24	3 24	Phi
4. They didn't have schools, libraries or other big buildings	16	4	6	6	0	
5. They didn't have books or access to books	18	0	2	10	6	41
6B. Did the Indians have books? Why didn't they have books?						
0. Doesn't know/no relevant response	16	11	3	1	1	−46
1. Books weren't invented/they didn't know about them yet	24	2	7	10	5	
2. They lacked materials to make books/didn't know how to make them	11	0	2	4	5	25
3. They couldn't or didn't read (or write)	13	5	1	3	4	
4. Student says that Indians did have books	28	5	7	6	10	
7. If Indians couldn't write, how could they pass on what they had learned about hunting or fishing?						
0. Doesn't know/no relevant response	30	18	5	3	4	−55
1. Through language or gesturing	10	1	2	3	4	
2. Visual representations (draw pictures, make carvings, mark on trees, put stick or flag in ground to mark spot)	14	1	3	4	6	21
3. Show them where to go or what to do/bring them to the spot	16	0	2	6	8	35
4. Tell them, teach them verbally	54	5	16	18	15	42
8. For a long time people could speak but they couldn't write. Then alphabets and writing were invented. How did the invention of writing change the world?						
0. Doesn't know/no relevant response/they could write, do ABCs, spell	37	19	11	5	2	−56
1. People started using or needing pens, ink, paper	10	0	4	3	3	
2. People had an alternative or better way to communicate (including stating that it made things easier for people who couldn't speak or hear)	19	0	1	7	11	47
3. People had books/libraries	18	4	3	3	8	
4. Learning became easier or enhanced; it was easier to pass on information	20	2	2	6	10	34
5. People could send written messages or letters	26	0	5	8	13	44
6. People no longer had to be face-to-face in order to communicate	17	0	1	6	10	44
7. People could read	7	1	0	1	5	31
9. If George Washington was in New York and wanted to send a message to Benjamin Franklin in Philadelphia, how could he do it?						
0. Doesn't know/no relevant response	15	7	6	0	2	−33
1. Modern inventions: describes using a device not invented at the time (telephone, telegraph, fax machine computer, etc.)	22	4	7	5	6	

(Continued)

TABLE 5.1
(Continued)

Response Categories	Total 96	K 24	1 24	2 24	3 24	Phi
2. Modern transportation (train, car, bus, plane, etc.)	16	2	3	7	4	
3. Send it by water (ship, bottle, boat, etc.)	7	1	2	1	3	
4. Use the mail: write a letter, "send it," or put it in mail box	28	4	8	13	3	
5. Washington would have to go visit Franklin (or vice versa)	35	8	7	9	11	
6. Someone would be sent with a written message (recognition that today's mail system wasn't in place)	34	4	4	9	17	46
7. A messenger would travel by horseback or wagon	12	0	1	6	5	32
10. What do you think the first books looked like?						
0. Doesn't know/no relevant response	19	12	4	1	2	–45
1. Books were made out of wood, bark, cardboard	14	3	3	5	3	
2. Books had no color or no or few pictures	14	2	2	3	7	24
3. Books looked old, tattered, torn, dusty, rusty, bad	9	1	3	2	3	
4. People used pens, pencils, markers, crayons to make books	14	2	5	5	2	
5. People used feather pens, ink, or paint to make books	19	2	1	5	11	41
6. People used paper	26	1	9	8	8	30
7. People wrote or drew pictures themselves	42	5	11	12	14	28
8. Other (books were carved rather than printed or written by hand, etc.)	36	3	8	11	14	35

11. For a long time, anything that was put down on paper had to be written by hand—even books. Then, the printing press was invented, and people could print newspapers and books like we have today. How did that invention of the printing press change the world?

Response Categories	Total	K	1	2	3	Phi
0. Doesn't know/no relevant response	35	21	7	5	2	–63
1. Printed materials would be easier to read/writing in them would be neater or more permanent	8	0	1	4	3	24
2. You could have pictures or color (or more pictures or color)	9	1	4	1	3	
3. People would not need to write; their hands would not get as tired, and so on	22	2	3	7	10	32
4. The people who made books could work more quickly or would not have as much work to do	18	1	7	5	5	
5. People could make multiple copies of things with greater speed or ease	14	0	1	6	7	36
6. Books could be read or enjoyed by more people; people had greater access to books	8	0	1	3	4	24
7. Books were printed in typeface instead of cursive writing	18	0	6	4	8	32

(Continued)

TABLE 5.1
(Continued)

Response Categories	Total 96	K 24	1 24	2 24	3 24	Phi
12. Another important invention was the telephone. How did that change the world?						
0. Doesn't know/no relevant response	9	7	0	1	1	−40
1. You could call or talk to other people (without further explanation of why this was better)	18	10	6	0	2	−41
2. Responses that do not fit into subsequent categories: you could make plans more easily, call to see if someone was home before visiting, call to order pizza, and so on	6	3	1	1	1	
3. You could talk to people without being face-to-face with them	45	5	9	14	17	38
4. You could communicate with people far away without having to write notes or letters	33	1	9	13	10	39
13A. How do babies learn to talk?						
0. Doesn't know/no relevant response	12	7	4	0	1	−35
1. They learn from older people; people teach them	65	11	14	19	21	35
2. They hear people talking and copy their speech	13	0	4	2	7	32
3. They have conversations with people	7	1	1	3	2	
4. They listen	18	4	4	6	4	
5. Speech develops as babies get older	12	4	5	2	1	−20
6. Learning to speak is like learning to read: phonics, ABCs, and so on	9	0	2	3	4	21
7. School, preschool, day care	10	0	1	4	5	28
13B. Sometimes a young child will know what s/he wants to say but s/he doesn't have the words to say it. What could s/he do?						
0. Doesn't know/no relevant response	14	9	3	1	1	−39
1. Wait until she can say it	8	1	3	2	2	
2. Use baby talk or try to say the word	29	7	10	6	6	
3. Pull or touch the person to try to get his or her attention	12	1	2	3	6	24
4. Go to the door, point outside, gesticulate	63	9	15	21	18	39
5. Cry, whine, use sound to draw attention	23	4	7	6	6	
6. Use sign language	8	0	1	5	2	28
14. Here, we have only a few words that we can use to describe different kinds of snow, like snow or sleet or slush. But up in Alaska the Eskimos' language has a lot of words that they can use to talk about snow. Why is that?						
0. Doesn't know/no relevant response	34	17	11	5	1	−53
1. They are different or their language is different from ours	19	3	3	5	8	21

(Continued)

TABLE 5.1
(Continued)

Response Categories	Total 96	K 24	1 24	2 24	3 24	Phi
2. They have more snow; they have spent more time in snow	48	3	10	15	20	52
3. They know more about snow	11	1	3	5	2	
4. They have more types of snow	9	0	2	2	5	26
15. Can people communicate with each other even if they don't speak the same language?						
0. Doesn't know/no relevant response	11	6	3	2	0	−28
1. No	41	12	11	7	11	
2. Yes	44	6	10	15	13	28
3. They could write it down	14	1	3	5	5	20
4. They could teach or learn both languages	20	5	5	6	4	
5. They could gesture or use sign language	37	7	6	11	13	25
6. They could use an interpreter that speaks both languages	10	0	2	3	5	25
16A. Can deaf people communicate?						
0. No/doesn't know	25	18	4	3	0	−66
1. They can use sign language	57	4	14	17	22	56
2. They can read lips	6	0	0	3	3	26
3. They can write	11	0	2	2	7	34
4. They can talk (spontaneously says that deaf people can talk, before being asked directly)	17	0	6	6	5	27
16B. Can deaf people understand what you say? How?						
1. Doesn't know/says yes but cannot provide any explanation	9	3	2	4	0	
2. No	65	20	21	12	12	−38
3. Read lips	22	1	1	8	12	47
16C. Can deaf people talk? How?						
0. Doesn't know/no relevant response	8	4	2	1	1	−19
1. No	31	9	9	9	4	
2. Yes	47	10	12	12	13	
3. Yes, but their speech sounds different from other people's; not very clear; is hard to understand	10	0	0	4	6	35
4. Some can, some can't	10	1	1	2	6	28
17. Can blind people communicate? Can they understand what you say? How? Can blind people read?						
1. Yes, they can communicate	76	10	20	23	23	55
2. Thinks that blind people can hear but not talk or can talk but not hear	7	5	2	0	0	−33
3. Blind people cannot read as sighted people do	44	23	10	8	3	−62
4. They can read Braille	16	0	0	4	12	55

(Continued)

TABLE 5.1
(Continued)

Response Categories	Total 96	K 24	1 24	2 24	3 24	Phi
18. Are there some words that we use today that didn't exist 50 years ago? What are some examples?						
1. No or doesn't know	10	7	3	0	0	–39
2. Yes (no examples)	32	9	6	14	3	
3. Poor examples (cites words that were in existence 50 years ago)	25	3	8	5	9	
4. Technical examples (cites words related to inventions or new technologies [computer, television, etc.])	16	0	3	3	10	41
5. Popular culture (cites slang words or words used to describe artifacts of popular culture or new practices [compost pile, duh, cool, etc.])	13	0	4	2	7	32
6. Cites both poor and good examples	9	0	3	3	3	
7. Cites good examples only	18	0	3	3	12	48
19. Sometimes communication is done with symbols instead of words. Why are symbols used instead of words?						
1. Doesn't know/no relevant response	36	16	10	5	5	–39
2. Writing would have to be too small to fit on sign	22	1	5	7	9	29
3. Symbols allow the sign to be understood by people who can't read	16	4	4	4	4	
4. Symbols are easier to see/words are harder to read	15	1	4	4	6	21
5. Written signs take longer to read	15	2	4	3	6	
6. Signmaker didn't want to take the time to write out words	14	2	2	7	3	
7. Includes key idea that symbolic signs are quicker/easier to read	35	5	9	9	12	22
20. What do I have to do to send a birthday card to my brother in Chicago?						
1. Doesn't know/no relevant response	10	6	2	2	0	–30
2. Stamps (talks about attaching a stamp to envelope or about how the stamp is cancelled at the post office)	27	1	8	7	11	34
3. Believes mail carrier picks up card and delivers to brother personally	19	11	5	3	0	–42
4. You or your mail carrier take card to local post office	67	7	17	19	24	56
5. Mail is sorted at local post office by destination	15	0	4	6	5	26
6. Card is sent to Chicago by truck, plane, or boat	58	3	16	17	22	60
7. Card taken to Chicago post office and processed there	46	5	10	11	20	45
8. Card taken directly to brother's house	17	1	5	7	4	
9. Complete, accurate response	38	2	9	9	18	48

(Continued)

TABLE 5.1
(Continued)

Response Categories	Total	K	1	2	3	Phi
	96	24	24	24	24	
21A. Why do people read newspapers?						
0. Doesn't know/no relevant response	7	6	1	0	0	−40
1. News in general	49	11	15	10	13	
2. Good news	9	0	1	1	7	40
3. Bad news	19	2	4	11	2	
4. Advertising	19	1	5	4	9	30
5. Announcements	19	2	4	6	7	20
6. Sports	44	5	12	12	15	31
7. Weather	33	3	10	11	9	27
8. Entertainment (puzzles, comics)	24	2	8	5	9	26
9. Death notices	12	1	5	3	3	
21B. Who reads newspapers in your family?						
0. Doesn't know/no relevant response	6	2	1	1	2	
1. Mother or other female relative	49	9	13	14	13	
2. Father or other male relative	80	21	21	22	16	−26
3. Student	21	0	7	1	13	53
4. People read paper when they miss or do not watch TV news	9	1	3	3	2	
5. Mothers and fathers read different parts of paper	7	0	2	1	4	24
22. How is a newspaper made?						
0. Doesn't know/no relevant response	10	8	2	0	0	−45
1. Make paper from wood	21	6	3	5	7	
2. Gather news at the site	15	2	2	4	7	24
3. Get news from the television	12	0	5	3	4	
4. Write text with a pen, pencil, computer, or typewriter	64	7	15	22	20	51
5. Add illustrations	16	2	8	4	2	
6. Machine prints, copies, or stamps paper	59	9	13	16	21	38
7. Papers are delivered	24	3	5	7	9	22
23. How did radio change the world?						
0. Doesn't know/no relevant response	18	13	1	1	3	−53
1. People could listen to music at home	62	8	19	22	13	47
2. People could hear news and announcements about events	40	5	9	12	14	29
3. People could listen to sports	7	0	3	0	4	
4. People could get weather forecasts	22	3	7	4	8	
5. Other	12	0	1	3	8	39

(Continued)

TABLE 5.1
(Continued)

Response Categories	Total	K	1	2	3	Phi
	96	24	24	24	24	
24. How did television change the world?						
0. Doesn't know/no relevant response	8	7	0	1	0	−44
1. Cartoons	28	7	12	4	5	
2. Entertainment shows (no mention of news, weather)	22	4	6	8	4	
3. News or weather reports (no mention of entertainment shows)	10	3	4	1	2	
4. Allowed people to watch videos or movies at home	16	2	6	5	3	
5. Allowed people to witness events without being there	13	2	2	3	6	20
6. Allowed people to learn things from educational shows	6	1	2	1	2	
7. Allowed people to see in addition to hear (compared with radio)	69	9	21	17	22	47
8. Mentions both entertainment and news	36	3	9	10	14	34
25. What would Channel 6 have to do to show an astronaut talking to the kids at the school on the six o'clock news?						
0. Doesn't know/no relevant response	30	17	8	2	3	−53
1. Put it on TV, show it	48	2	11	19	16	54
2. Anchor person would describe event	18	0	2	8	8	38
3. Reporters/camera people would come and tape the visit	62	6	16	20	20	50
4. Videotape is taken back to TV station	23	2	4	6	11	33
5. Videotape is played on VCR or VCR-like machine to broadcast it	21	1	8	7	5	
6. The tape is edited	8	0	1	2	5	28
26. Where is your favorite show made and how do we see it in Michigan?						
0. Doesn't know/no relevant response	24	12	3	5	4	−34
1. Describes the process of making the show	31	5	12	7	7	
2. A video camera or tape machine is played	6	1	3	0	2	
3. Videotapes are sent from where they are produced to the local station	6	1	2	0	3	
4. Radio waves (satellites, radio dishes, antennas transmit the show)	9	1	2	1	5	23
5. TV shows travel through electric wires, phone wires, power lines, cable lines to TV	39	6	12	12	9	
6. A central piece of recording equipment (camera, VCR, machine) is connected to all TVs	7	0	1	4	2	

(Continued)

TABLE 5.1
(Continued)

Response Categories	Total 96	K 24	1 24	2 24	3 24	Phi
27A. Why do we pay for some channels but not others?						
0. Doesn't know/no relevant response	50	22	16	9	3	−60
1. You pay only for good or new programs	20	0	6	8	6	31
2. You pay for new movies	11	2	1	2	6	25
3. Other	24	0	3	7	14	51
27B. Why do TV stations show commercials?						
0. Doesn't know/no relevant response	26	20	6	0	0	−77
1. TV people need time to rest, take a break, correct a problem, rehearse next scene, and so on	34	2	8	11	13	36
2. Breaks are for viewers to get up and do something, make popcorn, and so on	7	1	1	3	2	
3. Commercials give you information	24	1	6	9	8	30
4. Commercials entice you to buy products or services	36	1	8	12	15	45
5. Companies pay to advertise on TV	9	0	2	0	7	41
28. Television programs sometimes get cancelled. The networks take them off the air and put on something else instead. Why do they do that?						
0. Doesn't know/no relevant response	29	15	7	6	1	−46
1. Those on show are tired of doing it and want to quit	15	5	3	6	1	
2. Those who make show make mistakes, do the work wrong, argue, and so on	8	2	3	1	2	
3. Network executives don't like the show anymore	7	2	1	3	1	
4. People who make the show have run out of new ideas	6	0	4	1	1	
5. Viewers don't like the show anymore	33	1	5	9	18	55
6. If people don't watch the show, network doesn't make any money	9	0	2	2	5	26
7. If people don't watch the show, it's taken off	22	2	3	5	12	39
29. Have you ever heard of electronic mail, or e-mail? What is it?						
1. No	43	22	11	7	3	−59
2. Yes (no elaboration)	9	1	3	2	3	
3. E-mail works on the computer	39	1	7	13	18	54
4. E-mail is faster	33	0	8	9	16	50
5. Typing e-mail messages is easier or neater than writing letters by hand	12	0	2	4	6	28
6. E-mail doesn't require putting the message in envelope, taking to mail box, and so on	15	0	3	6	6	29

Note. Numbers in the frequencies columns show how many students in each group were coded for mentioning the ideas represented by the response categories. Underlining indicates that the chi-square for the underlined distribution was statistically significant at or below the .05 level. In these instances the phi coefficients (with decimal points omitted) are given in the phi column as indicators of the magnitudes of linear trends.

WHY PEOPLE NEED TO COMMUNICATE

1. Today we're going to talk about communication. That's a big word—do you know what it means?

If the student could not define communication or suggested an overly constricted or specific meaning, the interviewer explained that it means talking or sending messages to other people.

2. All over the world, people communicate by sending messages or talking. Do they do that just because they like to, or do they need to? When would be a time that people need to talk? How would our lives be worse if we couldn't talk?

3. Some animals communicate by making noises, like dogs bark at each other. But we don't have to bark, we can talk. What does talking allow us to do that dogs can't do? Is talking better than barking? Why?

K   1. No.

2. Need to. (How come they need to?) Just in case they need to talk to people and they wanted to make a plan to go somewhere. (How would people's lives be different if they couldn't talk to each other?) I don't know.

3. Talk on the telephone. (Anything else?) No.

1st   1. No.

2. They like to, and they want to. (When would be a time that people needed to talk?) If someone was sick and they wanted them to feel better. (How would our lives be different if we couldn't talk to one another?) You would have to bring messages to each other so they could know what you wanted to say. (If we couldn't talk to one another, would our lives be better or worse?) Worse. (Why?) Because you couldn't talk and they might not know what you want to say, so you might want to write messages to them.

3. We can and they can't and we can't understand what they're doing. (Is talking better than barking?) A little bit sometimes. (Why?) So they can know more what they're saying and sometimes . . . because you can't understand what dogs are saying but they can understand what we're saying.

2nd   1. Yeah, it means like you can talk to someone else on the phone, like communicating.

2. It kind of depends. (Tell me about that.) Like . . . let's say you're like at work and then you have no car and you're married and you have no car 'cause the father took you, and you like have to have it 'cause

you're having a baby—you might have to call to communicate. Sometimes you might just want to talk to them, like come over, like come
over to play. (How do you think our lives would be different if we
couldn't talk to one another?) Kind of boring, probably. You couldn't
play or anything, all you could do is do stuff by your house and all you
could do is talk to your family and all that. (Well, you wouldn't be
able to talk to them if you couldn't talk, right?) Oh. Kind of be boring
because if you couldn't talk to anybody, like the same thing of having
a baby, you can't talk to anybody.

3. Um . . . maybe like we can laugh and they can't or something (anything else that talking allows people to do that animals can't do?)
Talking on the phone.

3rd 1. Probably how to do things, to talk to someone in a different way.

2. They need to. (Why? When would be a time that people need to
talk?) When it's like an emergency or they feel like it, or somebody
wants you to spend the night or something. (How would our lives be
different if we couldn't talk to one another?) It'd be like . . . we'd be
trying to communicate, but it'd be really hard. We'd have to use our
hands, if we knew how to. (Would our lives be better or worse?)
Worse. (Why?) Probably because it'd be really hard to talk and you
didn't learn how to—you were born without a voice box or something, so you'd probably have to use your hands.

3. It means we don't have to do weird stuff, like do motions [i.e., pantomime, pointing]. Sometimes we just . . . like what I'm doing right
now—talk. (Is talking better than barking?) Yeah, way better than
barking because we're not animals. (But why is it better?) Probably because it's better for you to talk than bark because then people will understand you. We don't understand dogs.

Only 26 students defined communication adequately. Of the rest, 58 were unable to respond and 12 were incorrect or overly specific (e.g., speaking in sign
language or a language other than English, understanding each other or helping
others).

A heavy majority (84) of the 96 students said that humans need to communicate, although 14 were unable to give examples of when or why. The others identified the following situations: in emergencies or when something is harming us
(30); to participate in school or work activities (16); to express or understand
feelings or needs (15); to make plans, such as to meet a friend (11); to interact
with family members (10); and to ask or answer questions (8).

Asked how our lives would be worse if we couldn't talk, students said that it
would be difficult to understand each other, we would not be as well informed, or
we could not get needed information easily (27); we would have to use sign lan-

guage, read lips, or communicate in writing (26); we would be isolated from others, lonely, or unable to share our feelings (13); we wouldn't be able to get help as easily in emergencies or when sick or hurt (8); we wouldn't be able to learn as easily (6); our lives would be boring (5); and we couldn't talk on the telephone (4). Other responses included: You wouldn't be able to say "no" if someone was hurting you; we would be deaf (3); you couldn't tell the dentist what tooth to pull; you would be late for meetings and not know when Christmas was; you would always have to write things, and this would make a lot of work for "our postal service people."

Faced with hypothetical situations, children often respond as if everything else would remain the same except for the changes identified in the question. In this case, the students who said that we would have to read lips or write messages failed to realize that there would be no possibility for lip reading if people did not speak, and the development of written language would be extremely unlikely.

Asked to compare human speech with the barking of dogs, 20 students were unable to respond and another six could only say that barking is noisy, annoying, or hurts your ears. However, 38 recognized that speech is easier to understand than barking and 26 elaborated that we can communicate better through talking, say more complex things, express emotions and plans, or explain about emergencies. Some interesting misconceptions appeared, including the ideas that dogs' thinking is verbally mediated and barking is just as efficient a language for dogs as speech is for humans (6). Other responses included: They're the same because dogs talk in their heads and then talk to other dogs; we can understand what dogs are saying, but they can't understand what we're saying; barking is the same as talking if you understand it; we can move our mouths in all directions but dogs can only move theirs up and down [an interesting but incorrect attempt at physical explanation]; we could communicate with dogs and cats if we taught them how to communicate with people.

The students were generally aware that communication is a basic need, although this was not as clear and obvious to them as it was for food, clothing, and shelter. They recognized the need for communication most clearly with respect to emergencies and situations in which there was a need to communicate information in order to learn or carry out a job. Some thought that lip reading and writing would have developed even if humans did not possess the ability to speak.

A minority said that speech allows for much more subtle and differentiated communication than barking does. Levels of understanding progressed from believing that dogs think and communicate just like humans except that they use a different "language," to not crediting dogs with verbally mediated thought but recognizing that they can communicate different "messages" through different forms of barking, to recognizing that although barking has some communication value, it is much more limited than language. Only two students noted that human speech mechanisms allow us to produce a much greater variety of sounds and sound combinations in our speech than dogs can produce in their barking.

COMMUNICATION AMONG PRELITERATE PEOPLE

The next set of questions addressed the students' understanding that among preliterate people, communication is limited to face-to-face interactions and artistic renderings that do not include writing based on the alphabetic principle.

4. **Back in time, the earliest people lived in caves. How did these people communicate? Did they have any other ways to communicate?** [If the student does not mention speech, ask if cave people could talk to each other. If the student does mention speech, ask if there was ever a time when people did not have language, and, if so, how these people communicated.]

5. **Before Columbus discovered America, the only people who lived here were the Indians. How did the Indians communicate? If the chief of one village wanted to get a message to the chief of a village five miles away, how would he do it?**

6. **Did the Indians have libraries? Why not?** [If yes:] **Tell me about the books that were in the Indians' libraries.**

7. [If necessary, the interviewer prepared students for this question by explaining that Indians did not have libraries because they couldn't write their language, so they had no books.] **If the Indians couldn't write, how could they pass on what they had learned about hunting or farming?** [If necessary, ask:] **Suppose that an Indian man was out hunting and found a new hunting ground. How could he communicate that to the rest of his tribe?**

K   4. Um . . . they talked. (Did they have any other way to communicate?) Do this [makes grunting noises]. (Any other way?) No. (Was there ever a time when people didn't have language—when they didn't know how to talk?) Yes. (Well, how did people communicate then, when they couldn't talk?) I told you. (Oh, you mean by making grunts like that—making noises?) Yeah.

5. I don't know how. (Do you think they talked?) A little bit. (Now, if the Indian chief from one village wanted to get a message to a chief from another village five miles away, how could he do that?) Talk. (But the chief was five miles away.) Walk there. (Is there any other way he could get the message to the other chief?) No.

6. No. (Why not?) Because it was very old when they were alive. (OK, so it was early times. Did they have books?) No. (Could they write?) Yeah. (So they could write but they didn't have books. Is that right?) Yeah. (How come they didn't have books?) I don't know.

7. [pause] I don't know.

1st   4. They growled at each other. (So you think they didn't talk?) Yeah. (Is there anything else they could do besides growl if they needed to communicate?) I don't know.

5. They said different words. (So they talked, but a different language. Any other way they communicated besides talking?) I don't know. (If an Indian chief back then who lived here in a village wanted to get a message to the chief in the next village five miles away, how could he do it?) He would . . . he would send one of his men to go tell him.

6. No. (They didn't. Do you know why they didn't?) Because they didn't know what a library was. (Did they have books?) No. (Why not?) Because they . . . they didn't know if there would be a book to read or not. (They didn't know about books?) No.

7. I don't know. (Well, if an Indian man went out and found a new hunting ground, was there some way he could let the rest of the tribe know about that?) He could go back and tell them.

2nd 4. I don't know. (Could cave people talk to each other?) Yeah. (Was there ever a time when people didn't have language—when they didn't know how to talk to each other?) Yeah. (Well, how did those people communicate?) They do sign language or something.

5. They talked to each other. (If the chief of one village wanted to get a message to the chief of a village five miles away, how would he do it?) They walk or ride horses. (What if he wanted to stay home but he wanted the message to get to the other chief—what would he do?) I don't know.

6. No. (Why not?) Because they didn't have buildings like that. (Did the Indians have books?) Yeah. (What sort of books?) I don't know.

7. I don't know. (Suppose an Indian man was out hunting and found a new hunting ground. How could he communicate that to the rest of the tribe?) I don't know.

3rd 4. By talking. (Any other way?) Sign language. (Do you think there was ever a time when people didn't have language—when they couldn't talk to each other?) Yeah. (Well, way back then when they couldn't talk, how did they communicate?) With their hands.

5. I don't know. (Do you think they talked to each other?) Yeah. (Do you think they communicated any other way, besides talking?) Sign language. (Back then, if the Indian chief from one village wanted to get a message to another chief in a village five miles way, how could he do that?) Ride a horse over there with his message. (Was there some way he could get a message to him without having to go there himself?) No.

6. No. (How come?) 'Cause there weren't any books back then. (How come there weren't any books?) 'Cause no one had any paper to write on and make a book.

7. Tell them. (Is there any other way they could pass on their learning?) Showing them something they found.

About two thirds (60) of the students said that cave people communicated through speech just like people do today, although 57 said that there was a time when people did not have language. The latter response might be considered accurate, depending on one's definition of "people." Among students who said that cave people used spoken language, 13 specified that they spoke in a different language than the one we use today, and 10 that they had to have face-to-face communication because there were no telephones or mail then. In describing how cave people communicated in addition to or instead of using language, 39 mentioned sign language or pantomime, 19 writing or drawing (typically envisioning artwork on cave walls or primitive maps or directions scratched on the ground), and 16 grunting, growling, or other vocal noises. Other responses included: They communicated just like monkeys; when the "first man who stepped on the earth" arrived, he taught the others how to talk [semi-magical explanation for how humans acquired speech]; they communicated like animals do, with smells or something; they chipped letters into wood or rock; they used drums or something to make noises (2); they would jump up and down and yell at each other. Responses to questions about cave people often drew from Alley Oop or Flintstones cartoons, which led many students to say that cave people spoke pretty much as we do today.

The intention of the questions about Indians was to see if the students understood that Native Americans had oral but not written language. Probing was designed accordingly. If the student said that the chief could use smoke signals, the interviewer would ask what the chief would have to do if it were a rainy day. If the student mentioned shouting or beating drums, the interviewer would say that the second chief was too far away to hear this. If the student said that the chief would have to walk or ride to the other village, the interviewer would ask if he could get the message there without leaving his own village. In general, the interviewer would probe to see if the student understood that the chief would have to send someone to convey the message.

Most students knew that Indians talked: Fifty-four said that Indians spoke the way we speak today (presumably in English, although three thought Spanish and one Algonquin), 27 said that they spoke but in their own language, 21 said that they used hand signals or sign language, 12 mentioned artwork, carving on walls, or scratching on the ground, and 8 said that they communicated through whoops and hollers. Unique responses included: American sign language; made paper and wrote messages; used signs when sneaking up on buffalo [so they wouldn't have to make noise talking]; painted pictures on animal skins; communicated by giving gifts [potlatch].

Only 56 students accurately stated that the chief would have to go personally to the other village or send someone to deliver the message verbally. Other students couldn't respond (24); or made reference to a telephone, telegraph, tape recorder, or modern mail service (8); smoke signals, drumming, or light flashes (7); or yelling (6). Other responses included: Drive to the other village in his car;

shoot the message using a bow and arrow; write pictographs on buffalo skin or bark; make paper, make a pencil, and then send a message; make wolf calls, or use a whistle.

When asked if Indians had libraries, two students said yes and 18 didn't know. The others all said no, but only 12 stated that this was because Indians couldn't read or write. Another 4 said that they didn't read (presumably by choice rather than because they lacked written language). Other responses were that libraries hadn't been invented yet or Indians didn't know about them (24), Indians didn't have books or access to books (18), they didn't construct big buildings such as schools or libraries (16), or there were no materials to build libraries or knowledge about how to build them (7). Unusual responses included: They didn't know how to make drawers for books; they didn't have paint to paint the library; they were home schooled, so they didn't read books; they didn't need libraries because they had "ways of knowing things"; there weren't a lot of trees to make paper and books back then.

On the follow-up question, 28 students said that Indians had books, even though only 2 had said that they had libraries. About one fourth believed either that Indians possessed only a few primitive and homemade books for personal or family use or that they had books (presumably comparable to today's books) but lacked libraries because they lacked the knowledge or wherewithal needed to construct large buildings. Unusual responses included: Indians couldn't write because they had no pencils or crayons [reversed reasoning]; they bought books at stores; they had books but only small ones; the books were made out of buffalo skin and if they made a mistake, they didn't have erasers, so they had to keep on getting buffalo; they had recipe books for cooking animals; Indians didn't use books because most books are in English and they didn't read English.

A majority understood that Indians communicated through speech, so 54 said that they would pass on things that they had learned by talking. However, 30 were unable to respond, and the rest said that the hunter would bring other tribe members to the newly discovered hunting ground to show them exactly where it was and how to get there (16); use visual representations such as planting a flag to mark the spot, marking trees along the route to provide visual guidance, or drawing a map on the ground (14); or use sign language or gestures (10). About 10 thought that Indians were unable to communicate through spoken language. Other responses included: He could build a library; he could get some paper and show them [i.e., through drawing]; go to someone who knew how to write and get it written; put a new flag up [presumably referring to the flags planted by explorers to claim land for their nations].

Most of the students understood that Native Americans communicated through speech, although only a minority understood that their languages were spoken but not written, so they did not possess books or communicate across distances by sending written notes. Many thought that Indians did engage in reading or writing, or could have but did not because their interests lay elsewhere.

Others understood that they could not, but thought that this was because they lacked writing materials or the knowledge and wherewithal to make books or build libraries (i.e., rather than because they lacked the alphabetic principle). A few thought that whatever writing Native Americans did involved language, and a few of those who mentioned sign language thought that they used American sign language.

Although knowledge about communication in preliterate societies increased with grade level, the second and third graders were no more likely than the kindergarteners and first graders to know that Indians lacked books because they lacked written language. Based on previous findings about the transformations in elementary students' thinking about Indians (Brophy, 1999), we have a hypothesis about why this was so. Students tend to come to kindergarten possessing either no knowledge about Indians or stereotypes picked up from cartoons and movies. However, as they are exposed to traditional First Thanksgiving instruction, they begin to understand that Indians were actual people (the first people in America) and to develop respect for them as knowledgeable wilderness survivors. As they progress through the primary grades and study representative tribal groups, they typically develop considerable empathy with Native Americans and even come to view them as noble ecologists and victims of European aggression and greed. The instruction does not include claims that these people were literate or possessed books (although it may mention that some of their languages later were rendered into written forms). However, in the process of learning many positive things about the Indians they study, some second and third graders may come to assume that Indians were literate and wrote books (at least, develop this assumption if the question is raised with them, as it was by our interviewers).

Responses to Question 4 through Question 7 indicated mixed and spotty knowledge of communication among preliterate people. Majorities understood that cave people and Native Americans communicated through spoken language, although only minorities seemed aware that the languages spoken by these people were very different from contemporary American English. Some thought that cave people lacked speech, and a few even thought that this was true of Native Americans as well.

Surprisingly few students talked about whoops and hollers or gave other evidence of the "wild Indian" stereotype that many children bring to school. At the other extreme, a few clearly had developed great empathy with Indians and communicated the "wilderness survivor" and "victim of European exploitation" images. Many thought that Indians could have engaged in reading or writing if they had wanted to, or if they couldn't, this was not because they lacked the alphabetic principle but because they lacked writing materials, paper, or the knowledge and wherewithal to make books or build libraries. Only minorities understood that tribal languages were spoken but not written, so that learning had to be communicated, retained, and transmitted primarily through verbal interaction.

Noteworthy misconceptions included: Cave people or Native Americans could not talk; they acquired speech (and later, writing) because it was taught to them by a single individual who somehow knew it or discovered it; the impressions that they made on wood, rock, or dirt included letters and words; they made their own paper from wood and books from buffalo hide; they had books but not libraries; and they couldn't make many books because exploitation by the Pilgrims left them too depleted. Some students communicated ideas that were incorrect but indicated good thinking (Native American books included recipes for cooking animals) or transitions toward more complete understanding of preliteracy (Indians didn't read English).

THE INVENTION OF WRITING

The next two questions addressed students' appreciation for writing as a fundamental, world-changing invention that allowed communication to be accomplished across distances.

8. For a long time, people could speak but they couldn't write. Then alphabets and writing were invented. How did the invention of writing change the world? What did writing bring people that they didn't have before?
9. Let's think about communication in the time of George Washington. If George Washington was in New York and he wanted to send a message to Benjamin Franklin in Philadelphia, how could he do it? [If the student correctly says that Washington would write a letter, ask how he would get it to Franklin. If the student says that he would mail it, ask:] **Did they have mail back then like we do now? So what would he have to do to get the message to Philadelphia?**

K   8. It was different. (How?) I don't know.
     9. I don't know. Send a message? (How could he send a message?) Take it to him. (Is there some other way he could get him a message?) I don't know.

1st 8. It changed it 'cause there's letters and they didn't know what letters were before. (So what did writing bring people that they didn't have before?) It brang them so they could write . . . I don't really know.
     9. Maybe he could . . . maybe he could like send it to him somehow, but I just don't know how he sent it to him. (How could he do that?) I don't really know.

2nd 8. More happier, because someone could like ask you how to spell something, and you could say "I don't know," and if you do, you could like spell it and you'd be like, "Fine." (OK, so people learned how to spell words. Did being able to write make a difference in other ways or change the world somehow?) Yeah, because like they couldn't write,

so how could they write messages? Like if you had a birthday, how could you write messages like "Come to my birthday party"?
9. Send a message or talk on the phone. (Did he have a phone?) . . . Probably not, so he couldn't talk on the phone, so he could send messages. (OK, he could send a message. How would he get it to Philadelphia?) Um . . . sail, like sail on a ship. (Would he do it or would somebody else do it, or what?) He would probably ask somebody if he didn't want to. (So he would have to ask somebody to get the message to him, and you think it might have to go on a ship or something?) Yeah. (OK. So you don't think they had a post office then like we have now?) They didn't.

3rd 8. Because you didn't have to draw pictures anymore to communicate. You got to use pencils and got to write like we do now, like writing letters. (So what did writing bring people that they didn't have before?) Probably they think it's better to write now with letters than drawing pictures and doing motions, 'cause that'd be kind of hard when you're trying to think or trying to do something, like you grew something—a crop. It'd be hard to show them what it was because probably some of the cave men wouldn't know what it is.

9. He'd probably have this map kind of paper that's like cloth, and he'd have a quilled pen that has a feather, and he'd probably write it down, but I don't know if he went to school or not. (Say if he wrote it down, what would he do then to get that message to Ben Franklin?) He'd probably find one of his secretaries, if he had one, and tell them to take it to Benjamin and give it to him and tell him that it's from him—George Washington.

About half of the students couldn't explain why writing changed the world (beyond noting that people began to write or started using pens, ink, and paper). The other half provided responses that were valid as far as they went and sometimes included good insights (such as that writing made it possible to communicate across distances, facilitated learning, and made it easier for people who couldn't speak or hear to communicate with others). The only misconception was one student's belief that writing had been invented specifically for deaf people.

Responses to Question 9 were less impressive and often included misconceptions because the students frequently were unclear about when Washington and Franklin lived and which inventions were available at that time. Fewer than half understood that Washington could send Franklin a written message, and only about one third that the delivery services available to him were a far cry from today's U.S. postal service. A few interesting misconceptions appeared: People had mail boxes then, the Pony Express operated between eastern seaboard cities, and there were no mailboxes because there were no cars (in this suburban student's experience, mail boxes are placed at the curb and accessed from a vehicle—he was unaware of urban mail boxes placed just outside or inside the building entrance and accessed by mail carriers traveling on foot). Other unusual responses included: Use a sign or something; write the message on a cannonball and shoot it there (2); they had mail carriers on bicycles; tell a slave to take the message; put the message in a bottle and float it (2).

The following is quoted as a noteworthy good answer: "Well, they had horses back then. He had to write a note, send it like in the mail, and give it to Benjamin Franklin". (Did they have mail back then like we do now?) "No, they didn't have holders [mailboxes], they didn't have trucks, vans, or post office things." (So what did he have to do?) "Give it to a man on a horse that's like a mail person and tell him to ride it to Philadelphia."

About half of the students were able to explain why the invention of writing was so basic, such as by noting that writing made it possible for people to communicate across distances, facilitated their learning, and made it easier for those who could not speak or hear to communicate with others. The students were less successful in applying this understanding to contrasting the distance communication options available to George Washington with those available to a preliterate Native American tribal chief, primarily because they often were unclear about when Washington lived and which inventions were available at the time. Consequently, some students thought that Washington and Franklin could communicate only through face-to-face interactions, but others thought that they could use communication or transportation devices that were not invented until much later.

INVENTIONS OF THE PRINTING PRESS AND TELEPHONE

10. Think about the very first books that were ever made. What do you think those first books looked like? When the people made those first books, how did they make them?

11. For a long time, anything that was put down on paper had to be written by hand—even books. Then the printing press was invented, and people could print newspapers and books like we have today. How did that invention of the printing press change the world? What did printing bring people that they didn't have before?

12. Another important invention was the telephone. How did the telephone change the world? What did the telephone allow people to do that they couldn't do before?

K   10. I don't know. (The people who made those first books—how do you think they might have made them?) They made them 'cause they maked up a story and then they wrote it down in books and they putted it in libraries or in stores.

11. I don't know.

12. Because they decided to do a telephone so they can call people and stuff without walking over.

1st 10. A little bit like the books now. (When the people made those first books, how do you think they made them?) They wrote them. (With their hands?) No, with a pencil or a pen.

11. They didn't have to use their hands to write it. (That's right. What else, though? Did printing bring people something they didn't have before?) They had a machine that printed out books. (OK, why was that good?) I don't know.

12. They could talk to each other from a long far away.

2nd 10. Maybe like all rusty because they didn't know how. They just tried to do it and it might be like kind of bad. (How do you think the people made those first books?) They like had to write about the book and get like a wooden thing and then like make this cover and then they put it on the top and then . . . or maybe they just took paper and put it there, and then they like colored it what it was, and then they like got paper and writed in it, and then at the last part, they just put "The End" and then they put the colored paper on the back. (When you say they wrote it, do you mean they wrote it themselves with a pen or pencil?) Yeah.

11. Probably happy because they didn't have to take that much time. They might have to go the next day and you might be kind of late and you could just go there and then it might be done the next day and you could just like send it to them and give it out. (So printing would make it quicker to make books?) Yeah, because maybe they didn't have time to do stuff, and now they can have time because all they have to do is like print the book, and then when it's done, they can go back and send it out, so they don't have to waste their time so they can't do anything.

12. Pretty happy, because now you don't have to walk or go on a bike. You can just like talk to them.

3rd 10. Pale colors, old, dusty, really old from being written back then. (When the people made those first books, how did they make them?) Probably they took the paper, and they used it for making a book. They probably used a cover—maybe out of the same thing that they wrote the pages on, but they added something else that's really hard. I don't know what it would be.

11. It would be better because when you don't have to write it, it'd be easier. It would just show up on the paper. You would just type it in and then do it in the size you want it, and when you write it by hand, you can't do all those sizes and cool ways, where if you tried to do

Japanese, that'd be hard if you were an American. (Yeah, it changed the nature of the books, but how did it change the world?) Probably 'cause they added more kinds of stuff to it, like regular paper now and they had harder covers, not just like paper covers but they have cardboard covers. (What did printing bring to people that they didn't have before?) Probably they think that's kind of weird because they were only used to drawing and doing motions of what they did or saw. I don't know.

12. You wouldn't have to tell someone to take a message to give it to them, and walk far to give it to them. Now, they've just got to dial in the number that the other person has and it'll send right across the country.

Some students began by talking about carving on rocks but then switched to better responses when asked about the first books "that looked more like the books of today." Several added covering and/or binding the book as a step in the process, although usually without much clarity about how this would be accomplished. Nine answered (at least initially) not by describing how the earliest books looked at the time but instead how they might look today (old, tattered, torn, dusty, etc.). A few had made books in class.

The students typically depicted the earliest books as written on primitive forms of paper, perhaps using feather pens or ink made from berry juices. Most understood that until the printing press was invented, making books was a laborious process that required printing or writing the text in longhand (and perhaps illustrating it by hand as well). Other responses included: books about Indians; they had no pencils so they used "coloring sticks" to make homemade wooden books; the books had soft covers and were "written by this little machine" [probably thinking of a typewriter]; they drew pictures on pages, then sent the pages out to have a cover put on them; they wrote on stone with "strong sticks"; books about famous people like George Washington or Bush Clash [sic]; made out of tree bark; on brownish paper; big books with lots of pages [Bibles?]; they painted using their fingers because they didn't have pens or brushes; the books looked bold [apparently referring to the big letters being particularly noticeable]; they used animal fur [leather?] for the cover; they bound the book with string going through holes in the pages; they didn't have big humungous words like "communication" then, so you wouldn't learn much from reading the books; they stuck the pages together with ooey, gooey muck or something; they were not big, about five pages, triangular or square, using paste to bind the pages; they used thin wood shavings as pages; they were made of fur or something [leather?]; the words were in code [lines and dots], and the books were printed using the typewriter that they invented; the pages were gold [probably referring to the gold letters on the pages]; they were scrolls.

More than one third (35) of the students were unable to say how the printing press changed the world. Most of the rest spoke of benefits to those who manufactured books (less work required, less tiring on the hands) or improving the appearance of the text (easier to read because it was printed in typeface instead of written in cursive, less likely to get smudged, and more likely to have color or illustrations). Thus, most students emphasized a microlevel purview focused on the individuals involved in manufacturing or reading particular books, rather than a macrolevel purview that included recognition of significant changes in the human condition around the world. Only 16 students noted that the printing press made it possible for people to make multiple copies of text with greater speed or ease and/or for more people to read more books. Unique responses included: They could make bigger books with more pages and have covers on them; they didn't have to kill as many animals to get feathers for pens; if you messed up, you didn't have to write it all over again.

The students were more successful in explaining how the telephone changed the world. More than two thirds understood that the telephone made it possible for people to converse without being face to face and/or to communicate across distances without having to write letters. Apparently, it was much easier for the students to envision the nature and implications of communication in a world without the telephone than in a world without the printing press.

INFLUENCES ON LANGUAGE DEVELOPMENT

13. How do babies and young children learn to speak their language? [If the student says something like "from their parents," ask what the parents do.] **Sometimes a young child knows what s/he wants to say, but doesn't know the words. What can s/he do? For example, if the child wants to go outside but doesn't know the word "outside," what could s/he do?**

14. Here, we have only a few words that we can use to describe different kinds of snow, like snow, or sleet, or slush. But up in Alaska, the Eskimos' language has a lot of different words that they can use to talk about a lot of different kinds of snow. Why is that? Why do the Eskimos have more words for snow than we do?

K 13. Because we teach them to speak our language. (How do we do that?) Every month you say a word and we tell them what name that we call them and tell them what to say. (Sometimes a young child might know what she wants to say but not have the words to say it. What could she do then?) She could ask her parents, and they could tell her what she wants to say when she don't know what to say. (OK, but if she didn't have the words, it would be hard to do that. Like what if she wanted to go outside, but she didn't know the word "outside," what could she do?) She could ask somebody to help her teach it [i.e., teach her the word "outside"].

14. I don't know.

1st 13. I don't know. (Like maybe he wants to go outside but he doesn't know how to say "outside." What could he do?) He could learn to speak and say "outside." (He could do that but that's going to take a long time. Is there anything he could do now before he learns to speak that word?) I don't know.

14. They have lots of snow and they could see lots of different kinds of snow.

2nd 13. From their mom and dad. (Tell me more about that.) Like when they're a baby, they can say mommy, say daddy, and maybe like when they're one they can finally say it. 'Cause they learn it from their mom and dad because they keep on copying it and copying it and then when you get it stuck in your head, you just say it. (Sometimes a young child might know what he wants to say but he wouldn't have the words to know how to say it. What could he do?) He could like point to it maybe. (OK. Anything else?) If he could do sign language, and the mom knew or the dad knew, he could just use sign language . . . they could just point to it or something, and if they didn't know and they just like left him alone, he could like just touch it or something like that.

14. Maybe they know the snow more because like mostly every day it snows, and you have to like cover up. (So maybe they know more about snow than we do?) Yeah, because it snows like twice a day or twice a week, and that other one takes like three weeks, so they might know more.

3rd 13. Probably after their dad or mom says, like the mom says "mommy" or something or "daddy," or "cat," or "dog." I remember I used to say "dog" as "goggie." (So what did your parents do?) They never really told me what they did, but I imagine that they'd probably tell me what I'm supposed to say and I'd try to say it, and I'd keep on practicing. You've got to learn how to do something really good. (Sometimes a young child knows what she wants to say, but doesn't know the words. What can she do?) Probably she could make motions that she'd probably know how to do, or she could maybe do like . . . I think you can just do motions.

14. Probably because they learned it in a different way, I think from their parents, and their parents probably learned when they were kids if they went to America, but they didn't like it there so they'd go back to Alaska and figure out their own words. (But why would they have so many different kinds of words for snow?) Probably because other people have different imaginations, so they probably say they want to have it this way or that way.

The students generally understood that language is acquired both through specific instruction and through general exposure to communication from and among significant others in one's environment. Unique responses included: They take little books, say the words, and keep on until they get it right; use letter-sound flashcards at home; babies learn from seeing adults and older siblings act out the meanings, but this doesn't work for big words; they listen, beginning while they are still in the mother's belly; parents point to pictures in books and ask "What's this?" Some of the references to speech developing with age seemed to imply that this would occur automatically without input from the environment.

The students also showed generally good knowledge about what a young child would probably do if s/he lacked the words to communicate a desire to go outside. More than two thirds (63) said that the child likely would go to the door and use pointing or gesture, 29 that s/he would use baby talk or try to say the word, 23 that s/he would cry, whine, or otherwise use sound to draw attention, 12 that s/he would pull or touch the person to get his or her attention, 8 that s/he would wait until s/he could say the word, and 8 that s/he might use sign language. Other responses included: The child could move his lips and the mother could read them; he could write a note (3); he could use a picture to show what he wants. There was some resistance to the premise of this question, in that some students kept wanting to say that the child would verbally explain his or her needs to the parent, for example, by using a baby-speech version of the word.

The students were less knowledgeable about indirect influences on vocabulary development. About half had no idea why the Eskimos' language has more words for snow. The rest usually said because they live in a snowy environment, although for many, this was a brief guess on which they could not elaborate. Few students noted that the Eskimos needed to pay careful attention to snow and perhaps differentiate various subtypes for survival reasons, and none made a general statement that people need to pay close attention to their environment in order to thrive in it. Unique responses included: They are smarter than us; they invented more words because they couldn't decide which to use; they thought of more just by looking at the snow; they don't have to talk about warm things, so they spend more time talking about cold things; they want to be unique; scientists up there study different kinds of snow and name them.

Few misconceptions were communicated in responses to these questions, although some students thought that language appears automatically without input from the environment; one that a mother could read the lips of her young child; several that infants could write or draw to communicate messages that they could not communicate orally; and one that Eskimos have multiple words because they couldn't agree on just one word to use. Although one thought that Eskimos "are smarter than us," several felt the need to indicate that although Eskimos may have more words for snow, we have more words for other things. [Note: Question

14 made reference to *Eskimos* because the children were familiar with this term, whereas they usually were not familiar with *Inuit*, *Aleut*, or other more contemporary and specific terms for native peoples of Alaska.]

OVERCOMING BARRIERS TO COMMUNICATION

15. Can people communicate with each other if they don't speak the same language? How? [If student says no or cannot explain, ask:] **When Columbus and the Indians first met, were they able to communicate somehow? How?**
16. Some people are deaf—they can't hear. Can deaf people communicate? How? [If student only mentions sign language or other nonverbal means, ask:] **Can deaf people talk?** [Also, if the student fails to mention lip reading, ask:] **If a deaf person was sitting here watching you talk, could they understand what you were saying?**
17. Some people are blind—they can't see. Can blind people communicate? How? [If necessary:] **Can blind people read? How?**

K 15. Yeah. (How can they do that?) I don't know. (When Columbus and the Indians first met, did they communicate?) No. (So what did they do? Did they just stand there and look at each other?) I don't know.

16. No, 'cause they can't hear. (Could deaf people understand what you were saying by watching you talk?) No.

17. Not if they don't know who they're talking to. (But if they did . . . if a blind person was sitting right here with us, could they communicate with us?) Yeah, if they told us. (Could they hear us too?) Yes. (Can blind people read?) No.

1st 15. I think they can. (How do they do that?) By sending messages or something like that. (But wouldn't the messages be in different languages?) Yeah, and the other person might understand what they're saying. (But what if they don't understand? Can they still communicate? When Columbus and the Indians first met, were they able to communicate somehow?) Yeah. (How?) By acting out something.

16. They do it like with sign language. (Can deaf people talk?) No, I don't think so. (Why not?) 'Cause they couldn't hear.

17. I know that they can communicate, but I don't know how. (Can blind people read?) No. (Why not?) Because they can't see that good. (Can they talk?) Yes.

2nd 15. Yeah. (How?) Like one person can talk like this and one can use sign language.

16. Um . . . I don't know. (Can deaf people talk?) I think so. (How do deaf people communicate?) Sign language, like they can use their

hands in sign language. (If a deaf person was sitting here watching you talk, could they understand what you were saying?) No.

17. Yeah. (How do they communicate?) I think they use sign language too. (Can blind people read?) No.

3rd 15. By using sign language.

16. By talking. (OK, they can speak. What else could they do?) I don't know. (If a deaf person was sitting here watching you speak, could they understand what you were saying?) No.

17. By talking and listening to other people. (Can blind people read?) Yeah. (How?) By those little dots that they put their fingers on.

The students found it difficult to visualize and talk about communication among people who do not share a common language. Some resisted the premise of the question by suggesting that the people might have words in common, could communicate through writing, or could verbally explain to the other people that they did not understand their language. Only 37 understood that communication under these circumstances initially would depend primarily if not solely on gesture or sign language (although with time, the people might teach each other their languages). Rephrasing the question to focus on examples (Columbus and the Indians or the student on vacation in France or China) made it easier for the students to respond, but most of their responses still involved attempts to undermine the premise of the question (they could use an interpreter), unrealistic suggestions (they could exchange written messages), or solutions that would not accomplish immediate goals (teach each other their languages). Other responses included: The Indians told Columbus that they didn't have a language but they understood what one another said [i.e., they could interpret other Indians' grunts, groans, whoops, hollers, etc.]; they could look in a book; they could use smoke signals; they could speak slowly.

About one fourth (25) of the students either did not know whether deaf people can communicate or said that they cannot. Of the rest, 57 said that they can use sign language; 17 said that they can talk (spontaneously, before being asked about this in a follow-up probe); 11 said that they can write; and 6 said that they can read lips. Probed concerning whether deaf people can understand what we say, 65 said no, 22 said that they can read lips, and 9 didn't know or said yes but could not explain. When further probed concerning whether deaf people can talk, 31 said no, 8 were unsure and 10 said that some can but some cannot. The remaining 47 said that deaf people can talk, although 10 qualified by saying that their speech sounds different from other people's or is difficult to understand because it is not clearly enunciated.

In summary, a majority understood that deaf people can communicate using speech or sign language, but only a minority understood that they can read lips or communicate through writing. Unusual responses included: Deaf people can use special headphones to hear; they can't hear themselves, but we can hear them; they can talk, but it's hard for them to learn; if they were born like that, they can't speak because they've never heard anything, but if it happened like when they were old, they can speak because they knew those words in their head for a long time; they could watch other people talk and then try to move their jaw like that; deaf people talk inside their minds, but not really—it's hard to teach them, but if they could hear words using hearing aids, then they could learn them; they can talk "if they got deaf when they already knew some words, but not if they were born deaf."

More than three fourths (76) of the students understood that blind people can communicate through speech but only 16 understood that they can read using the Braille system. Almost half (44) thought that blind people cannot read and 7 thought they can hear but not talk or can talk but not hear. Unusual responses included: Blind people cannot communicate because they cannot see your face or know what you are saying [typical response of students who thought of blind people as also being deaf]; no, because they can't see the person they're talking to [one of several responses implying a belief that communication involves conversation between people who can see as well as hear each other as they talk, or at least that it wouldn't be communication if a blind person spoke to somebody that he or she could not see]; they can talk on the phone; they use sign language; they would communicate better if they would take their glasses off because the eyes express feelings.

The students varied considerably in their knowledge about communication abilities of deaf and blind people. The younger ones tended to exaggerate the scope of these deficits, such as by thinking that deaf or blind people cannot communicate at all or that blind people also are unable to speak or hear. Older students usually understood that deaf people may be able to read lips and that they can express themselves through speech, sign language, or writing, as well as that blind people can carry on conversations and read Braille materials. A few students displayed somewhat detailed knowledge, usually based on personal experiences with deaf or blind people. For example, 10 understood that although deaf people can talk, their speech is usually not as clearly articulated as other people's speech, and another 10 understood that people who become deaf after childhood are more likely to learn to speak well than people who were born deaf.

Statements about deaf and blind people tended to be accompanied by expressions of empathy and recognition that these are otherwise normal people who have sensory deficits. There was no disparagement of these people or suggestion that they are generally weird, scary, or mentally defective. Perhaps this is a reflection of movements in recent years toward inclusion of handicapped students in regular classrooms and education of students about the nature of handicaps and how to interact with handicapped people.

ADDITION OF NEW WORDS TO LANGUAGES

18. Are there some words that we use today that didn't exist 50 years ago? What are some examples? [If student says no, probe by asking:] Does anyone ever invent new words? What are some words that might be pretty new?

K   18. No.

1st   18. I do not know. (Does anyone ever invent new words?) I don't think so.

2nd 18. Yes. (What are some examples?) Um . . . I don't know.

3rd   18. Probably laser or strobe light or like surf board or something like that, or like purse or bag, or a tote which would be a bag. (Does anyone ever invent new words?) Yeah, some people if they find them out and make them up and say, "Well, this means this and that means that." If they become a teacher, they can tell the kids that this means that and that means this.

Most of the students understood that languages expand as new words are coined. All but 10 understood that there are some words we use today that didn't exist 50 years ago, although 32 were unable to suggest any examples. In addition, 25 cited poor examples—words that have been in existence for much longer than 50 years. Valid examples typically were either words associated with technological inventions (computer, television, etc.) or words reflecting advances in popular culture (slang terms such as "cool" or "duh," as well as words that describe artifacts or new practices such as "compost pile"). Applying liberal acceptance criteria (i.e., any term introduced within the last century, not just the last 50 years), we determined that 16 students cited only poor examples, 9 cited both poor and good examples, and 18 cited good examples only.

Four students said that new words are coined when new inventions appear. Another four mentioned "Supercalifragilisticexpialadosius," reasoning that this must be a new word because it was introduced in a movie. Other responses: YMCA [apparently because the student had been to a newly built YMCA]; roller coaster; videotape; seahorse; microwave; wanna, gonna [slang]; firewood; store names.

Some students mentioned words that they associated with science (marsupials, tortoise, X-ray fish) on the grounds that most things scientific were discovered recently. Others reasoned sensibly but from incorrect premises ("bank" is a new word because money is relatively recent, "robe" is a new word because we use it when we complete a shower and showers are relatively recent, and the names for specific tribes are new because in the past they just referred collectively to "Native Americans").

The latter response also is one of several confusions we have seen connected with the term *Native Americans*: Some students wondered why Native Americans are called Native Americans if they came here from Asia, others thought that the Native Americans were the early colonists (called such to distinguish them both from Indians and from the British), and one thought that Native Americans (not "Indians") was a generic name that Europeans used to refer to American Indians collectively because they didn't know or care enough to differentiate among them and use their more specific tribal names. Many primary-grade students are confused about the meaning of this term, which is why we used the term *Indians* in our interviews.

COMMUNICATION WITH SYMBOLS

19. [Show illustrations of commonly seen signs that use symbols but not words to communicate "railroad crossing ahead" and "no bicycling":] **Sometimes communication is done with symbols instead of words. Why are these symbols used instead of words?**

K   19. 'Cause they need to know that thing. (Why would they put up a sign like that instead of just a sign that said "No Bikes"?) I don't know.

1st   19. They're used because they don't take up that much room to write it or something. (But if you write "No Bikes," that wouldn't take that much space. So why do you think they use symbols?) I don't know.

2nd 19. It would be easier because maybe they can't read, but they can just figure and use a symbol if you can't. (Any other reason why they might use symbols?) So maybe a kid rides his bike and he went right past it and he doesn't know what it's saying because he went so fast he couldn't read it, and if it's just like that and he goes super fast, he could know because it just has a bike and a line.

3rd 19. 'Cause they're not there to tell people [i.e., to tell them personally]. (Well, instead of putting this sign up here, they could have put up a sign that said "Railroad Crossing Ahead." So how come they put this up instead of a sign with the words?) I don't know.

When shown drawings of "railroad crossing ahead" and "no bicycling" signs, almost all of the students understood their meanings. However, more than one third were unable to suggest a reason why these signs employ symbols rather than words, and 14 others focused on the whims of the sign maker (e.g., not wanting to take time to write out the words). Other responses included: They had to use symbols because the words wouldn't fit on the sign or they would have to be written so small that they would be difficult to read (22); symbols allow the sign to be understood by people who cannot read or who do not know English (16); symbols are easier to see or the words are harder to read than the symbols (15), or written signs take longer to read than the symbolic versions do (15). A few unique responses appeared: The sign would get too big and heavy and fall over if you used a lot of words; the presidents might like it better [i.e., using symbols]; symbols look better. Only 35 students clearly understood that symbols are used on these signs because they are quicker and easier to read than verbal messages (and universally interpretable regardless of the person's literacy level or native language).

THE WORKINGS OF THE POSTAL SERVICE

20. My brother lives in Chicago and I want to send him a birthday card. What do I have to do to send him the card? OK, I put the card in the mail box. Then what happens to it? Then what? Etc. [Probe to see if the student understands the following steps: I put the card in my mail box; the card is taken to my local post office; it is sorted and grouped with other mail headed for Chicago; this mail is trucked to the airport and put on a flight to Chicago; from the Chicago airport, it is trucked to my brother's post office; there it is sorted by mail routes; then the mail carrier assigned to my brother's route delivers the card to his home.]

K   20.   You have to write it and then mail it to Chicago. (How do I mail it?) You put it in your mail box. (Then what happens to it?) The mail person takes it and takes it to the place. (Do you mean where my brother lives in Chicago?) Yeah. (Do you think my mail man takes it all the way to Chicago?) Maybe they stop by the mail place and they could give it to people and then they could drive . . . a mail person could drive it to Chicago, they could drive there and take it. (OK, so you think my mail man takes it to the post office and then somebody else drives it to Chicago?) Yeah. (OK. What does that person do when he gets it to Chicago?) He goes and finds the right person and then they give it to him. (So it goes right to my brother—not to somewhere else first?) Right.

1st   20.   You could probably air mail it. (What do I do? What are the steps?) First you write in it, then check and see if the spelling was right, and then you would put it in an envelope and write it to whatever your brother's name is, and then you'd put the address. Then you would check if the address was right and then you would close the envelope and then you would put a stamp on it, and then you'd mail it to your brother. (How do I do that?) By putting it in the mail box and then the mail man will come and get it. (What does the mail man do with it?) He takes it to the mail place and then there's this machine or something that puts it in and if there's another card to Chicago— there's tons of cards to Chicago, then they put the cards in a big old thing that can carry it by arms, and you just push it, and then you put it in a mail box or mail cart and then . . . then they'll get it to Chicago and put it in his mailbox. (OK, we got it to the post office now, and they put it in with all the other ones that go to Chicago. How does it get to Chicago?) There might be planes there and it might do air mail. (What happens then?) They would fly it to Chicago and they would drop it off at that post office, and then they'll give it to your brother. (At the post office?) I don't know. A post office in Chicago.

2nd 20. Like you put it with the mail and he (the mail carrier) goes to his house and then he gives it to your brother. (That's what I wanted to know. I give it to the mail man. This is a birthday card that's going to Chicago to my brother. So when the mail man takes it from me, what does he do with it?) He goes to his office and he like sorts it and then he like . . . there's these guys that like put it in something and then to Chicago and everywhere in the world, and then it goes through this little hole. It goes through and then it keeps on going until it gets to the man that goes to Chicago, and then he goes and that goes and gets to him. (That man goes to Chicago—when he gets to Chicago, what does he do? Does he take it right to my brother's house or does he take it somewhere else first?) Like he just goes to houses and houses and just keeps on going to houses, and then he looks at it and just gets the mail from it and when he gets to the house, he just takes it up and puts it in.

3rd 20. You first have to write the card and when it's all written, and you'd probably send it to another place, and you'd have to put . . . let's see, if you're in Michigan, you'd have to go through five or six states so you'd have to put like six postage stamps to get it from one place to another. You can't have just one or they'll think you're just going to one state and they'll just take it to one state, but if it was just Chicago, they'd just have to take it to their house by the mail. (But how does it work? I've written my card, I've got the address on it. What do I do then?) You put the six or seven postage stamps and then you take it to the post office and tell them it's going to six or seven states until you get to Chicago, and then they'll know what address it says because you've got the address on the envelope. (I leave it at the post office, right? What happens to the card then?) Oh, they'd probably read the card and they'd put it in the mail carrier thing—box, and then the guy that takes the thing to the airport . . . and it would have to fly over and over and over until it gets to Chicago and then it'll get there, and he'll get it. (So we've got to the Chicago airport. Then what happens?) They probably drive it to the house and they put it in the mailbox and he'll just come out and get it.

Most students were able to provide at least some details but only 38 generated responses that we considered to be both complete and accurate. Most began by talking about obtaining the card, signing it, placing it into an envelope, addressing the envelope, and putting it in the mail box, then went on to say that the card would be taken to their local post office, transported to Chicago, and then processed at a Chicago post office where it would be assigned to a delivery route. Minorities of students added other details. Some were accurate, such as that the sender would place a stamp on the envelope, the local post office would cancel the stamp and sort the outgoing mail, and the card would be placed with other mail headed for Chicago. However, 19 students thought that the same mail carrier who picked up the card at the sender's house would travel to Chicago and delivery it personally; 17 suggested that upon arrival at Chicago, the card would be taken directly to the addressee's house without being first taken to a post office for processing; and several expressed misconceptions concerning how the post office would arrange to convey the card from Lansing to Chicago. Other responses included: Send it by computer (3); your mail man would take the card to Chicago but then give it to a Chicago mail man to deliver; it would be driven to Chicago, with two gas stops on the way; and the Lansing post office would drive it half way to Chicago, then turn it over to people from the Chicago post office to take the rest of the way (2).

Most students conveyed images of postal services being rendered by just one or a very small number of individuals who handle all aspects of the work personally, not images of the post office as a huge organization that employs hundreds of thousands of people who each work on just a subset of the steps involved in picking up, processing, and delivering mail. In general, there was a progression from the idea that your own mail carrier personally delivers the mail picked up from your house to wherever it is going, through degrees of understanding of the post office as a large organization that includes many specialists besides mail carriers (sorters, people who take the mail from one city to another, etc.).

NEWSPAPERS

21. **Let's talk about newspapers. Why do people read newspapers—what's in them? What else is in the newspaper?** [If no response:] **Does someone in your family read the newspaper? Why does _____ read the newspaper?**

22. **How is a newspaper made? What do they do first? Then what? Etc.**

K   21.   Like if you're looking in a newspaper and you want to go to the movies, then you'll see it in there. (OK, so there's ads telling you what movies are playing. Anything else that you might find in a paper?) No. I don't know.

      22.   They make paper. (OK, they make paper. So then you've got the paper. Then what?) I don't know.

1st 21. So you know what's happening. Like there's a ball game and you did-
n't watch it and you could tell who wins or who wins it for the whole
game. (What else is in the newspaper?) Um . . . information about
things. (Is there anything else in the newspaper?) Things that are going to happen like next week or tomorrow. (Does someone in your
family read the newspaper?) Yeah, my dad does. (Why does your dad
read the newspaper?) 'Cause he wants to know what the weather's
going to be like on Sunday, Monday, Tuesday, Wednesday, Thurs-
day, Friday, and Saturday, and he also reads other parts, like the
sports.

22. By old papers. It recircles into newspapers. And then after the newspapers are done, they're made into different kinds of paper, and it
goes in a circle. (But what do they do first to make a newspaper?)
First they write it and for the weather they copy it off the weather
channel. Then they write it on a newspaper and they give it to someone else, and the other person writes lots more than just the weather.
(What happens then?) Then it goes to some people that gives the
newspaper to everyone. (How do they get enough papers to give to
everybody?) They keep on copying and copying. They copy it like a
copier machine that copies . . . they make one and then they know
what to write on the other ones and it copies it, and then they stamp
it on a paper and then it goes to the other machine.

2nd 21. So they know what's happening. Like there might be a new show
that you might like or that you think your child would like. Or
maybe like if there's a thunderstorm or something. (So there's
weather news and there's news about new shows. What else?) Like if
you forgot to watch the football game or the basketball game, then it
says about it. (The sports news. Anything else in the paper?) Like
there's the president. (So news about the country and stuff.) Yeah.
(Do you read the newspaper?) No, my dad tells me. (Does he read it
for any reasons besides the ones you told me already?) Mostly he just
wants to solve the puzzle on the back and he might want to look at
the stories about the Simpsons and that. (OK, so there's puzzles and
there's stories about TV.) And he might want to read about the basketball game. He just wants to read about the games.

22. They like get a tree and do something with a tree, and then paper
comes out and then you like write stuff on the paper, and then you
send it to people. (OK, but let's back up to where you got the paper
and you want to turn it into a newspaper. Do they just write on it or
what do they do?) They make the shape of a paper and then they like
put it through a machine and it'll turn into a paper. (What does that
machine do to turn it into newspaper?) They might like soften it up

and make it kind of straight and put white stuff on it and when it dries, they might like just do something like push it down [i.e., flatten it], and then it just goes through and it's like done. (OK, you have blank newspaper, nice white newspaper, but there's nothing on it yet.) I know. You write on it. (The newspaper at home—does it have pencil and ink on it or what?) You might like print it. (OK, so it's printed. Where do they get the stuff that's printed? How do they know what to print?) 'Cause there's like this guy that like looks at every game to see who wins, and he's the man who like knows who won and stuff, and then knows what to put. (OK, for sports, there's someone who gets the information together.) Yes. (Then what does he do?) He like tells them what to put in the sports. (I see. Then what do they do after he tells them?) They might like print it on the newspaper. (OK, so somebody tells them what to print, and then they fix the printing somehow and print it. Is that what you're saying?) Yeah. (Do you know anything more than that?) No.

22. From wood, like on trees and stuff. (Yeah, that's the paper. But how does the news get in it?) I don't know. (Who decides on the stories?) I don't know.

3rd 21. So they can find out what's going on, what the weather's going to be like, what's happening—if anybody's got injured, or if they just want to read it. (What's in newspapers?) The weathercast, what's happened to kids or families, about fires and kids. (OK, so weather and news. What else is in the newspaper?) Probably new stuff they invent and probably stuff they've done. (Who's done?) Really famous people. Like if the president got fired or something. (Does anyone in your family read the paper?) My brother has to because my dad makes him. My dad does and my mom does, and sometimes I do because I found out about the kid that got stuck in the trees and got cut up in the wood chipper. (Why do the people in your family read the newspaper?) Probably because they want to find out what's going on so nothing happens at the house or nobody's going to get hurt or anything like that.

22. By printing presses and like by an editor. Sometimes they can be in schools. (What does the editor do?) It writes an article and they print it into a newspaper and then they just send it all out and make copies of them.

Responses to questions about newspapers reflected recent shifts in the roles and relative prominence of newspapers vis-à-vis other communication media. Ideas about newspapers were generally valid as far as they went, but most students were vague about how stories are composed, edited, collated, and transformed into printed newspapers. Few understood that newspapers fulfill unique functions by covering a much greater range of information than is covered on the television news and going into greater depth on the material covered in common. In fact, some thought that newspapers get all or at least most of their content from television and that they function as primary news sources only for people who do not watch the news on television.

Only 15 students referred to newsgathering and only a few of these clearly understood that reporters proactively develop stories rather than just receive what people convey to them. Most viewed newspapers as supplements to televised news, read not so much for hard news content as for sports, features, weather, and local advertising and announcements. None mentioned editorials, and only a few suggested that newspapers provide deeper coverage than that found on television.

All but 6 mentioned one or more people in the family who reads newspapers. A heavy majority (80) mentioned the father or another male relative and more than half (49) mentioned the mother or another female relative. In addition, 21 said that they read (at least part of) the newspaper themselves; 9 said that family members read the newspaper when they miss or do not watch the news on television; and 7 said that females focused on different parts of the paper than males. When students themselves reported reading the paper, most said that they only read the comics or looked at the photos (the older ones often mentioned sports). Other responses included: Read about strikes at General Motors and about the stock market; news items (birthdays of famous people, the Arkansas shooting; new towns getting started, and bands coming to town to give concerts); you read a newspaper to know more than you would know from just watching television (2); read about laws, such as the need to be 16 years of age to get a driver's license; the newspaper reports on new things that get invented and famous people; read stories about pets and garage sales; read the kids' contributions (the local paper prints essays and stories written by children in a special section that appears once each week).

When asked how newspapers are made, 10 students could not respond but the others suggested one or more steps, most typically that someone uses a pen, pencil, typewriter, or computer to compose text (64) and then this text is entered into a machine that stamps, prints, or makes multiple copies for distribution. Many of the latter were "black box" responses, in which the student talked about the paper being printed but could not say anything more specific. Other steps included making the paper from wood (21), going to a site to gather news (15), getting the news from television and writing a report of it for the paper (12), adding illustrations to the written text (16), and delivering the paper to people's homes (24). In addition, 4 students mentioned that the originally written story would be given to an editor or rewriter, and several talked about the characteristics of the paper on which newspapers are printed: old or scrap paper (4), gray (2), or recycled (3). Fourteen mentioned the involvement of a computer somewhere in the process of making a newspaper. Other responses included: They use stamps to print it [this and one other student seemed to think that the printing is done with wooden blocks, letter by letter]; they make paper by chopping wood into tiny pieces; editors decide which stories to use; mentions proofreading and correcting the text before sending out the paper; when asked how the typescript becomes newspaper, says "They dip it in hot water." The following third grader is quoted as one of the better responses:

> First they have to find some news somewhere, then they have to write it, and then there's this guy called the editor—he sees if it's good enough for news and he checks all the work to make sure it's not spelled wrong. If it's good enough and it's not spelled wrong, he'll take it to a place called the press where they sometimes type it up on this one kind of paper. They put it in and put all the stories and stuff into these papers and then they put it into a packet and it's called the newspaper.

Most students viewed newspapers as supplements to television news, read primarily as sources of entertainment and information about local sports, weather, and shopping or leisure time options, along with coverage of events not significant enough to be covered on television. This view would have been clearly inaccurate 50 years ago and mostly inaccurate even 25 years ago, but today it is mostly accurate for all newspapers except *The New York Times*, *The Washington Post*, and a few others that invest significant news-gathering and editorial resources on reporting that extends beyond the scope of local news. Even the misconception that newspapers get much of what they print from watching television news broadcasts is not all that inaccurate; much of the content of most newspapers is reprinted or edited from received input rather than developed and written originally by the paper's own staff. The only difference from the children's version is that this input comes primarily via computer from news distribution services, rather than from television.

In summary, although the students were mostly fuzzy or confused about the processes and technology involved in creating a newspaper from written or typed copy, they had generally accurate ideas about what is found in newspapers and why people read them. Most of them clearly subordinated newspapers to television as the primary source for information about major news and depicted newspaper employees primarily as receivers (and in some cases, editors) of information that comes to them, rather than as people who proactively go out and develop stories. No student mentioned editorials, and only a few suggested that newspapers provide more in-depth coverage than can be found on television. This view of newspapers was a far cry from traditional journalistic ideals, but probably realistic given the changes that have occurred in the newspaper business in the United States over the last 50 years, and especially in the last 20 or 30 years.

THE NATURE AND IMPACT OF BROADCAST MEDIA

23. An important invention at the time was radio. How did radio change the world? What did radio bring to people that they didn't have before?

24. Another important invention was television. How did television change the world? What did television bring to people that they didn't have before?

25. Let's talk about how television works. Suppose one of the astronauts came here to your school to talk to the kids. Now if Channel 6 found out about it, they would say, "Wow—that's big news! One of the astronauts is coming to talk to the kids at the school. Let's show that on our six o'clock news!" What would they have to do? [If necessary:] What would a TV station have to do to show that on their news program? [Probe to see if student understands that the station would have to come to the school and videotape the talk, then take the tape to the station to edit. Also, see if the student has any explanation for how the tape then is "put on TV."]

26. Besides the news, television brings us entertainment shows like *Cosby*, or *Jeopardy*, or *Star Trek*. What's your favorite show? OK, let's take _____. Where do they make _____, and how does it get to us, on our TV? [Probe for details, especially to see if the student understands that the shows are taped in Hollywood or elsewhere, then later broadcast through a network to local stations. If the student says that they make videos and then send them to local stations, ask about live shows, such as sports events, that we can watch as they unfold.]

K   23. I don't know.

24. I don't know.

25. They would have to make wires—the TV wires, where it would go through (What else would they have to do?) I don't know.

26. I don't know.

1st   23. You could listen to music and stuff. (What did radio bring to people that they didn't have before?) They could listen to things like songs.

24. You never got to watch things that were happening, like shows. Now you get to watch shows. (What did television bring to the world that they didn't have before?) They could watch things like shows.

25. They might have to videotape it . . . like put a tape in the VCR and then show it on the news.

26. I don't know where they make Pooh Bear. (Well, let's say it's California. How do we see Pooh Bear on television when it's made in Hollywood?) 'Cause it goes by electricity to everyone's homes.

2nd   23. So they could make like songs and they could make sounds and see what they sounded like.

24. So they didn't have to go to the game. They could always just watch it on the TV instead of going all the way to it. Like something might be in Chicago and you could just watch it on TV.

25. The camera guys might go to the room and take a picture and then like show it on there. (OK, then what would they do?) They put it on TV so everyone would know and watch it. (Do you know anything about what they'd actually do to put it on TV?) They would take the picture and then they'd put it in a little box or something or put it to the side and then when they turned the TV on, when they want it there, it's there because they want it to be on TV. And it's there when they put it on.

26. There's like these wires in the street and when you want to watch it, you turn to the channel and the wires are hooked to your TV, and then the wires to go your house, and it's there so you can watch it.

3rd 23. By telling people what was going on. (OK, so it brought the news. Did it bring them other things that they didn't have before?) It told them about sports. (Anything else?) I don't know.

24. You could see what the weather was and the news. (What else did television bring people that they didn't have before?) Nickelodeon.

25. Take a camera there and tape it and put it on.

26. It travels to the cable lines. (OK. Do you know any more about that?) No.

The students were very familiar with radio and television in their current forms, so they could talk about how radio brings us music, news, and weather and television brings us entertainment, news and weather reports, and allows us to watch the events being broadcast. However, their responses showed little awareness of the fact that the broadcasting and instantaneous communication features of these media have "shrunk" and homogenized the world in many respects.

When asked how radio changed the world, 18 students were unable to respond but 62 said that radio enabled people to listen to music at home, 40 said that it brought news and announcements, 22 said weather forecasts, 7 said sports broadcasts, and 12 said other things such as commercial advertising or dramas and other entertainment shows. Many thought of radio as just background music or something to do if you are bored. Other responses included: Radio allowed people to hear things from faraway places (2); you could have a portable radio and take it outside; radio stations have contests for prizes (4); radio made it easier to get information—you could just listen instead of having to read, and this was especially good for blind people. The students did not show much knowledge of how radio changed society when it was first popularized. Only a few were aware that prior to television, radio served the same kinds of nightly entertainment functions for people that prime time television serves today.

Asked how television changed the world, a heavy majority (69) noted that television allowed people to see in addition to hear what was being broadcast. Minorities noted that television brought cartoons (28), mentioned both entertainment and news shows (36), mentioned entertainment shows but not news or weather information (22), mentioned news or weather reports but not entertainment shows (10), or mentioned that television allowed people to witness events without being there (13) or to learn things from educational shows (6). In addition to these responses referring to broadcast television, 16 students said that the invention allowed people to watch videos or movies at home. These responses also were accurate as far as they went, although they reflect the child's (as contrasted with the adult's) perspective on the medium in their emphasis on cartoons and other entertainment shows over news and information shows.

Many students had difficulty comparing television to radio because they lacked a clear idea of what radio was like in the pretelevision days. Several said that television is good if you are bored, tired, or looking for some variety, and several others (probably students whose parents placed tight restrictions on their viewing) suggested that television makes you lazy, tempts you to watch junk like wrestling, and so on. Other responses included: With TV, you could not only read about sports but get to see the highlights of the games; TV brought Nintendo and other video games; TV allowed us to know that the news people weren't lying to us; TV has channels in other languages and you could try to learn those languages by watching those channels; TV brings us news faster than a newspaper, and you can see it happening; TV brought commercials (2); kids often want to keep watching TV instead of starting their homework.

The students possessed good knowledge about the people but not the electronics involved in bringing television shows into our homes. They understood that a local station would send out personnel to videotape an event that it wanted to cover for its news program, and many of them displayed at least some knowledge of how entertainment shows or cartoon shows are made. However, few understood much about what is involved in broadcasting a taped news event, and even fewer understood that broadcasting is accomplished by transmitting wave signals through the air to antennas or other receivers. Some made reference to receiving television programs via cable but did not consider how the programming gets to the local cable company. Others understood that the cameras recording live events would have to be connected somehow to the television sets in viewers' homes, but were vague about what this connection might be. Only nine made reference to transmission of signals through the air, and only a minority of these had clear ideas about the nature of these signals.

About two thirds were able to say that the station would send personnel to the school to videotape the astronaut speaking to the students, then take the tape back to the station to "show it" or "put it on TV." Most were vague about what had to happen to get the video onto the newscast. Some had the general idea but lacked vocabulary. Others were confused by the notion that the tape might be sold in stores and played on VCRs. Unusual responses included: The police might take pictures of the event and send them to the TV station; they would take the tape to "a huge building with this little thing at the top which sends it to any house because of the electricity"; they would tape it using cameras that were "hooked on to all the Channel 6s in the world"; the school would tape the event and send the tape to the television station; after it's recorded, they take it off the tape and put it in Channel 6 so it will show on Channel 6.

This first grader is quoted because her response includes a version of the "the big one supplies the little one" theory that we have seen used to explain many phenomena in our different interviews, as well as for some unique comments about editing the tape and assembling its segments into a program: "They would have to go to the school and film it and then come back." (OK, then what would they do?) "They'd take it and check it and see if there's any mistakes on it and they'd take those mistakes out. After it's all finished and looked exactly right, they'd put it on . . . they'd use the same that they were putting on other stuff— they'd use that same tape to use that other stuff." (What would they have to do to put it on the TV?) "There's this big machine somewhere, it's like a big VCR and they stick it in—they stick a whole bunch of movies of that show on the TV and so everybody gets the channels that they bought" [i.e., people at the station compile a program on tape and then feed the tape into a machine that causes it to be broadcast to the right homes on the right channels].

Finally, when asked how they are able to view their favorite shows on their television sets at home even though the shows originate from somewhere far away, 30 students were unable to respond but the rest generated responses that addressed the question in varying degrees. About one third (31) talked about the processes involved in making their favorite show (some of these were quite well informed, especially responses concerning the making of cartoons). The most popular idea about how the show reaches the viewers was based on the notion of electricity traveling through wires (variously described as electric wires, phone wires, power lines, or cable lines), which was mentioned by 39 students. Other students mentioned signals transmitted through the air (with references to satellites, radio waves, radio dishes, or antennas; 9); suggested that the show was being taped by a camera or VCR that was somehow connected to all of the televisions in the country (7); said that the show is videotaped and then the tapes are sent to local stations where they are played for local viewers (6); or said that a video camera or tape machine was involved but could not explain (6).

Most if not all of the 39 students who mentioned electricity traveling through wires received television programming in their homes via cable, so their responses were correct as far as they went. Still, very few of the students understood that the most basic method of transmitting television programming is through broadcasting signals via waves that travel through the air to antennas or other receivers rather than through wire connections running from the source of a televised event to the homes of the people viewing it.

Most responses coded in Category 5 were for students who mentioned satellites, dishes, or antennas but not waves, and most of the codes in Category 7 were for students who spoke of a "special" camera or video recorder that was somehow connected to all of the televisions in the world, or at least the nation. Other responses included: There's a network that goes all over the United States and shows everyone the movies; tape it, then put the tape in the slot at the base of an antenna tower; spoke of "signals hitting antennas" [one of just a few students who had this idea]; satellite dishes "bring in electricity."

The following third grader is quoted for the best overall response: "They make the show in a studio, and they practice like if they were making a movie. They practice until they get it right, and then they send it to us like in a show by satellites. Satellites bounce from one to another and then it comes to your TV." (What is it that's bouncing from these satellites?) "I think it's the electric stuff. I'm not sure, but I think it's electric waves or something like that."

The students showed little awareness of these inventions as fundamental: that they made it possible to broadcast events around the nation or world, that the ubiquity of such instantaneous communication "shrunk" the world in many ways, and that these innovations in communication (and transportation) eventually homogenized the world to a considerable degree. The purviews of students of these ages are mostly restricted to their personal life spaces and experiences, so they think of radio and television as sources for personal entertainment and information, not as media that facilitate instantaneous and continuing communication among people all over the world. As in all of our interviews, the students showed a great deal of practical knowledge about how to use the things being asked about, but much less knowledge about the nature of those things, where they come from, and how they work.

THE ECONOMICS OF TELEVISION

27. We have to pay for pay TV channels, like HBO, but other channels are free. Why is that—why are some pay and some free? [If necessary, ask:] **You know, another thing about television is that they keep interrupting their programs to show commercials. Why do they have all those commercials on television?** [If the student says that commercials provide a break so that performers can get ready for the next scene, point out that TV channels show commercials during movies that are already made, so they must have some other reason for showing commercials. If the student says that the sponsors want to show commercials because they want people to buy their products, accept this but probe further to ask why the television stations let these companies show their commercials.]

28. Television programs often get cancelled—the networks take them off the air and put on something else instead. Why do they do that? [Probe to see if the student is aware of the importance of program popularity and connects this to ratings and then to income from sponsors. If the student initially talks about reasons why a show would go off the air only temporarily, such as during a tornado, clarify that you refer to permanently getting rid of a show. If necessary, use the student's favorite show as an example:] **Well, you like to watch _____. Someday the people who run the channel that shows _____ might say, "We don't want to show _____ anymore—let's get rid of it." Why would they do that?**

K   27. I don't know. (Do you know why the networks keep interrupting their programs to show us commercials?) No.

28. I don't know.

1st   27. I don't know. (Another thing about television is that they keep interrupting their programs to show commercials. Why do they have all those commercials on TV?) Because there might be a big thing and they might not know some parts and so they just walk out or something like that. (Could you tell me a little bit more about that?) The actor might have to go backstage and another one come and so you don't see how they do it—only the people who are watching at Nickelodeon studios. (Often they show commercials in the middle of movies that are already made, and it's not about changing scenes. So they must have another reason for showing commercials.) Because if you were making popcorn and you didn't see part of a movie, they couldn't really show it or something. (Why does the television channel let people show commercials?) I don't know.

28. 'Cause they didn't want it anymore. (Why?) Because maybe it gets boring and the parents called and said "We don't want Pooh Bear anymore because our kids are getting tired of it."

2nd 27. 'Cause maybe like this wrestling one—it might be like this special one that's really good, 'cause maybe like this one is real good and you might want to watch it so you have to pay for it 'cause it's really good and you can't watch it on TV because it's so good, so you have to pay for it. (So sometimes they have this extra special stuff that they charge you for?) Yeah. (Well, maybe the thing to ask is how come the free channels are free?) 'Cause maybe they're not as good as the other ones. (The TV networks—when they show us these programs, they interrupt them every once in a while to show commercials. Why do they do that?) 'Cause maybe there's like this new stuff that they want people to buy and they interrupt it so they can tell you about it. (OK, that's why the company wants to show us the commercial, but why does the TV station let them show it?) People who want to advertise will come to the TV people and ask them to put their commercials on and the TV people will do that as a favor for them.

28. 'Cause maybe they had a vote and then they said, "Well, maybe I like this show better than Cosby, so they can watch the show they like," instead of putting what the other people liked. So they would have more people that like the other show instead of Cosby. (Are you talking about just the people at the station making this decision or do you mean people everywhere all over the country?) Everybody all over the country. (So you think the shows that they have on are the ones that more people want to watch?) Yes. (Why would they do that?) So they'd be happier so they could watch what they wanted to watch.

3rd 27. 'Cause there are special shows on that aren't on that much. (Anything else you know about why some are pay and some are free?) No. (When we watch our shows, they interrupt the show every once in a while to show commercials. Why do they have commercials on TV?) To tell what's going on at stores and stuff. (OK, so that's why the stores want to show the commercials, 'cause they want people to buy what they're selling. But why do the people who run the TV channel allow the stores to show these commercials?) I don't know.

28. 'Cause they were breaking a new show they wanted to put on TV. (They might have a new show they want to put on. Why wouldn't they just stay with the old one?) I don't know.

When asked why we pay for some channels but not others, more than half (50) of the students were unable to respond. Of the rest, 20 said that we only pay for new programs or especially good programs, 11 said that we pay for movies, and 24 gave other responses: You pay for adult/grown-up/R-rated stuff (4); for programs that come from far away (3); only for the channels that you use the most (2) or for programs that a lot of people want to watch (3); some channels take electricity and some don't; the free stuff is stuff that's not true things that really happened; the people who make shows on the pay channels need money to get on a lot more channels like the free shows [to expand their operations]; cable is more expensive because it has more channels (2); free ones are free because they come with the television when you buy it; you pay if you live too far away for the "tower thing" to reach you; you pay for the shows that are more costly to make; you pay when the people who make the show want money for it; news is cheap to produce but entertainment shows are costly, so you have to pay for them.

When asked about commercials, 26 students could not respond, and the other 70 made one or more of the following statements: Commercials are shown to entice you to buy a company's products or services (36), the actors, news anchors, or other people involved in making the television program need time to rest, take a break, correct a problem, rehearse the next scene, and so on (34), commercials are shown to give viewers information (7), or the breaks are planned to allow viewers time to get up and make popcorn or do something else that they may need to do in between segments of the show (7). Only 9 students (7 of them third graders) knew that companies pay the TV stations to show their commercials. This finding is comparable to that reported by Chan (2000) for fourth graders in Hong Kong. A little more than one third of those fourth graders knew that stations were paid to show commercials, whereas 29% of our third graders knew this.

Many students recognized that commercials inform us about products. Of these, about 40% saw them as purely informative (i.e., as a public service), but the rest understood that they are intended to entice us to buy products or services. Unusual responses included: Commercials teach you stuff so that you will be smart; the company shares the money it makes with the television station [this student thought that television stations get a percentage of the profits generated by ads, rather than a flat fee for each showing]; the TV station lets advertisers take turns [i.e., regulates how often and when they get a turn to run their ads, but doesn't charge fees]; stations agree to show commercials if they are asked [i.e., they are nice people willing to do a favor]; the stations charge for commercials unless their performers need a break, and then they might run them free.

When asked why television programs sometimes get cancelled, 29 students were unable to respond. The others suggested the following reasons: Viewers tire of the show or don't like it anymore (33); the television station finds out that people aren't watching the show and takes it off the air (22); the people who make the show are tired of doing it and want to quit (15); the people who make the show have begun to argue among themselves, make mistakes, and so on (8); the people who run the network don't like the show anymore (7); or the people who make the show have run out of new ideas for it (6). Again, only 9 students went on to say that if people don't watch the show, the network doesn't make money, and these students were thinking of network income from cable subscriptions, not from advertising.

These interviews were done shortly after Jerry Seinfeld announced that he was quitting his show, and this influenced some students who said that the people who make the show might decide to stop doing it. Other responses included: It's a different time of year [and therefore time for some new shows]; the makers of the show are punished or fired because they didn't do nice things; maybe they couldn't keep making the show because their camera broke or they ran out of tape; something was wrong [sickness, injury] with one of the people; viewers held a vote to decide between the shows; network executives are selfish and don't care what other people want; the show was too violent and kids were watching it (2); the show was too rowdy or bad and should have been removed, like *South Park*.

Few students had awareness of commercial television as a business (i.e., a mechanism for delivering viewers to watch commercials). Only nine understood that companies pay television stations to run their advertisements, and two of these held a profit-sharing (rather than fee per showing) theory of the financial arrangements involved. Few if any understood that commercial television stations are profit-making enterprises that generate income from sponsors because they deliver viewers for their advertisements.

Nor did the students understand the importance of ratings and "the bottom line" as influences on networks' and local stations' decisions to replace programs that are not attracting enough viewers. No student said that if a program fails to attract enough viewers, sponsors will not pay for their ads to be shown during it, and the network/station will lose money. Nor did any student show understanding of the facts that stations must pay for the programming they show, that they recoup these costs (and make profits besides) from the monies collected from sponsors, or that how much they get depends on ratings information indicating how many people watch the show.

The students tended to exaggerate the role of writers and performers relative to the role of network/station executives and sponsors in determining what programming is made available to the public. To the extent that they did speak of network/station executives, they depicted them as service-oriented people managing a public trust (much like the people running public television networks/stations), not as people running businesses strongly influenced by bottom-line numbers.

ELECTRONIC MAIL

29. Have you heard of electronic mail, or e-mail? [If yes:] **What is it? How does e-mail work? Why might someone want to use e-mail instead of regular mail?** [Probe for two possible reasons: It's faster and it's less trouble because you don't need stamps, envelopes, etc.]

K   29. No.

1st   29. I heard of e-mail. (Tell me about e-mail.) It can come to you on the computer if you're on the computer. (That's right. Why would somebody want to use e-mail instead of regular mail?) They can just print it on the computer and send it to people. (Why is that better than regular mail?) 'Cause you don't have to go outside and put it in your mail box, and you can just stay inside and print it out and send it to people.

2nd 29. I don't know.

3rd 29. It's where you can type it on the computer and it'll send it. That's what my aunt has. She works here and she sends an e-mail to my uncle at the junior high. As soon as she does, it just shows up on his computer. All she has to do is type the message in and then send it. (Why might someone want to use e-mail instead of regular mail?)

Probably because you don't have to write it and your hands won't get tired doing it, you don't have to lick the envelope shut. And you won't have to put a postage stamp on it either. You can just type it down where it's going and it'll just send it over there.

Almost half (43) of the students had not heard of electronic mail, and another 9 had heard of it but could not elaborate with any specifics. The rest supplied one or more of the following responses: E-mail works on the computer (39), it is faster than regular mail (33), it doesn't require using an envelope or taking it to a mail box (15), and typing e-mail messages is easier or neater than writing letters by hand (12). Unusual responses included: E-mail can go to far places, beyond the range of mail carriers; e-mail can go across the ocean but mail trucks cannot; e-mail is cheaper (3); e-mail is more fun; there is no cost difference because e-mail requires electricity.

Most, if not all, of the students who knew about e-mail did so because they had observed it being sent and received on computers, and some had sent and received it themselves. Even though these interviews were done in 1998, almost half of the students already had acquired basic understandings about e-mail's nature, uses, and advantages. The same question addressed to a comparable sample of U.S. children in the year 2005 might elicit very high percentages of accurate responses.

DISCUSSION

The students' responses to the communication interview displayed many of the same patterns seen earlier in their responses to interviews on shelter, clothing, and food: They knew more about the physical appearances of things than their underlying natures, and more about the uses of products than about how they do what they do or what is involved in creating them. Sophistication of responses was related much more closely to age (grade level) and personal experiences out of school than to achievement level or gender. Knowledge about the past was limited and tinged with presentism (i.e., viewing people in the past as less intelligent or well functioning than we are because they lacked modern inventions).

The students generally had a good sense of the fundamental importance of communication, often including an ability to imagine ways that life would be constricted if certain communication channels were not open to us. In this regard, they showed a better sense of the bigger picture than they did in responding to parallel questions in the transportation interview. Even so, they could profit from activities designed to increase their appreciation for humans' unique language-mediated capacities. For example, most understood that speech is better than barking, but few appreciated the scope of the difference.

Students also could learn about evolution in communication skills from primitive sign language (a far cry from American sign language or other rich modern versions) through pictograms, oral vocabularies, and alphabets. Early histories and cultures were limited to oral communication of stories, and most details were lost when the people who could remember them died (e.g., even if we assume that the explanation about Native Americans traveling across a land bridge from Asia is accurate, we will never know precisely who these people were or why they chose to migrate as they did).

A language needs to develop a standardized vocabulary to become established and spread, and standardized symbols for its words and sounds are needed to support a written version. Vocabularies usually begin with things that are most basic to survival (fire, water, common foods and dangers), but once a language has become established, it continues to grow by adding words for new inventions or things that did not have a name before.

People who lack a shared language can still communicate, although initially mostly through expressions to communicate emotions and gestures to communicate desires concerning things that one can point to or manipulate. A shared language is usually required to communicate more complicated or abstract ideas. Students can get a sense for this by playing charades or other games that forbid or limit the use of oral language.

Students should learn about sensory deficits and other handicaps, preferably through direct experiences with disabled individuals. Although being clear about what their disabilities prevent these people from doing, instruction should emphasize the abilities that they do possess and how they use these to compensate as much as possible for the ones they lack. In particular, students should learn that blind people usually have normal speech and hearing and can read Braille, and that deaf people usually have normal eyesight, can read and write, can communicate using sign language, and in varying degrees can read lips and speak to others.

One way to cross language barriers is through symbols that refer to concepts or experiences that are shared by people everywhere, even though they call them by different names. Publicly posted symbols can make it easier for people to find food or restrooms and walk or drive safely in other countries. International road symbols communicate basic driving and traffic information to people of all nationalities, often more efficiently than signs spelling out the information in the person's native language.

Students are usually interested to learn about the workings of the post office, newspapers, radio and television stations, and other communication industries. Rather than just focus on symbols (e.g., the uniforms worn by postal workers) and the general notion of community helpers, we recommend instruction that will demystify and rationalize the operations of these industries and the jobs of the people who work in them. Our interviews indicated that primary-grade children already have good knowledge about many aspects of what is involved in processing and delivering mail, but they need to learn that different tasks are handled by different kinds of postal workers, each making a unique contribution to the total effort. They also should learn that the post office is part of the federal government, so it is not necessary to purchase separate stamps for each state that a letter will pass through. The U.S. Postal Service cooperates with the postal services from other countries to facilitate passage of mail across international borders.

Concerning newspapers, most students already were aware that they contain puzzles, comics, movie listings, and advertising for local stores, as well as news, weather, sports, and so on. However, they often believed that newspapers simply regurgitate what is shown on TV and phoned in or sent to them from citizens. They need to learn that newspapers initiate stories by sending out reporters to investigate situations and write original reports (which are then edited, fitted with headlines, combined with other stories and with advertising within page layouts, etc.). Newspaper reports often provide more depth and local connection to stories that receive only brief headline treatment on television. Also, in addition to informing people through news stories, newspapers attempt to shape their attitudes and beliefs about civic issues through their opinion pages (e.g., by urging readers to vote for certain political candidates or policies). Finally, many different job roles and mechanical processes are involved in composing, printing, and delivering newspapers (a site visit to a newspaper should be included if possible).

Students should learn about how key inventions such as the printing press, telegraph, radio, and television changed the world by introducing new communication capacities that made it possible to disseminate messages to more people more quickly. The ability to print books was important not just because it eliminated the need for laborious hand copying, but because it allowed a given text to be distributed to thousands or even millions of people. This made cultural diffusion not only much faster but also much more uniform than it had been in the past, and it multiplied the influence of the authors whose works were printed and the nations and languages in which the bulk of the printing appeared. The telegraph, telephone, and radio were important because they made it possible to communicate in real time across great distances, vastly reducing the time needed to learn about events occurring in other parts of the world. These trends have continued to the point that today we have international news networks that allow us not only to learn about but to watch significant events occurring all over the world. Along with parallel developments in transportation, these communication advances have "shrunk the world" to the point that, far more than ever before, people are not just national but global citizens.

Radio and later television also developed as entertainment media, featuring news and variety early in the day and weekly drama and comedy series at night. More recently television has evolved as a major source of news and opinion, joining and sometimes even supplanting newspapers in this role. Increasingly, our ideas about other countries (and even more so, their ideas about us) reflect images seen on television, including both news stories originating in these countries and dramas depicting events supposedly occurring there. Depending on what kinds of television they watch, some people in other countries view the United States as a land of riches and opportunity, but others view it as a place of crime and violence.

Most television stations are profit-making businesses. Companies pay these stations for showing their ads. Most of this money is used to pay for the rights to show the programs on their schedule and to pay the salaries of the people who work at the station, but some is left over as profit to the station's owners. Advertisers are charged more when their ads are shown on programs seen by a great many people than when their ads are shown on programs seen by fewer people. Consequently, stations want their ratings to be as high as possible, so they renew highly rated programs but replace lower rated programs. Ads are shown because the stations are paid for showing them, not because the performers on the show need a break. These ads are designed to get viewers to purchase the sponsors' products or services, not to provide objective information as a public service. Therefore, learn to view them critically rather than passively.

We pay one way or another whenever we use communication media, whether it be reading a newspaper, using a telephone, or watching television. Commercially sponsored television programs are free of direct costs, but we have to accept program interruptions to show advertising, and the cost of that advertising is passed along to us in the form of higher prices for items being advertised. When programs are not interrupted by advertising, they are paid for in other ways. Public television stations are government supported, which means that part of the taxes that we pay to governments is used to purchase the programming shown on these stations. Finally, we can get commercial-free programming from cable television stations, but we have to pay these stations a monthly fee for access to it.

A recent and increasingly popular way to communicate with others is through e-mail, which allows us to type messages that will be sent instantly from our computer to another computer. E-mail is delivered much more quickly and does not require stamps, envelopes, and the other requirements of surface mail. It lacks the immediacy of telephone conversations, but it can be a very convenient way to communicate, especially with people who live very far away (perhaps on the other side of the world), so that telephone calls would be very expensive. E-mail makes it even more important than it was before to learn to type efficiently.

For a unit on communication that incorporates these and other basic ideas suitable for teaching in the primary grades, see Alleman and Brophy (2002).

6

Transportation

Our transportation interview asked students to talk about:

- transportation as a universal human need and the functions that it fulfills for us;
- the evolution of transportation over time and the impact of inventions;
- the tendency for settlements to be built along transportation routes;
- the ways in which improvements in transportation have "made the world smaller";
- the fundamental importance of the wheel as a basic invention;
- how modern life differs from earlier times as a function of improvements in transportation;
- effects of building a highway through a rural community;
- effects of improvements in transportation on farming and consumer access to farm products;
- special forms of transportation found mostly in cities (trains, buses, taxis) and what is involved in using these forms of public transportation;
- how automobiles work;
- problems that exist in places where most people drive cars or trucks;
- the nature and uses of maps;
- the need for traffic control mechanisms;
- considerations involved in traveling across national borders.

CHILDREN'S KNOWLEDGE AND THINKING
ABOUT TRANSPORTATION

Despite longstanding emphasis on transportation in early social studies, practically no information exists about developments in children's knowledge and thinking about the topic. A dissertation study done in 1947 tested fourth through ninth graders' understanding about a variety of social concepts (Bates, 1947). *Transportation* was one of the concepts that the author found to be familiar to students at all of the grade levels included. That is, most of even the fourth graders were able to define the term correctly. Unfortunately, this study did not include the K–3 grade range.

The same was true of a study by Batterham, Stanisstreet, and Boyes (1996) in which British students ages 11 to 16 were interviewed about negative effects of cars on people and the environment. Findings indicated that these students were generally well aware of such negative effects, emphasizing (a) the physical hazards of motor vehicles in creating pedestrian injury, vehicle–vehicle accidents, and vehicle-related mortalities; and (b) environmental damage such as air pollution, respiratory problems, vehicle emissions, and global warming.

Authors writing about children's understanding of sequencing and time concepts commonly use transportation examples (e.g., although they are fuzzy about when key inventions occurred, they understand that transportation progressed from walking to riding on animals and in animal-pulled vehicles to riding in motor-powered vehicles). Although this observation is commonly made, we have not seen quantitative data relating to it.

The only other studies located that touched even indirectly on topics addressed in our interview were studies of children's understanding of public ownership that included questions about the ownership of buses (Cram, Ng, & Jahveri, 1996; Furth, 1980). These studies indicated that children in kindergarten either do not know who owns buses or identify as owners people who are in close spatial contact with them (e.g., passengers). As children progress through the elementary grades, they begin to identify the owner as the person who uses or controls the use of the object (e.g., the bus driver), then the person who controls the use of the object by others (e.g., the bus driver's boss), and only later the local government or transit authority that provides transportation to the area. These studies focused on ownership of buses rather than on the buses themselves, so they did not provide information about children's understanding of this particular form of transportation.

Transportation interviews were conducted with 96 students, 24 in each of Grades K–3, stratified within each grade by prior achievement levels and gender. Descriptive statistics and information from analysis of scores derived from the coding are given in Table 6.1. For detail of the findings, see the technical report (Brophy & Alleman, 2001c).

TABLE 6.1
Distributions and Phi Coefficients Showing Relationships
of Coding Categories to Grade Level

Response Categories	Total	K	1	2	3	Phi
	96	24	24	24	24	
1. What is transportation?						
0. Doesn't know/no relevant response	57	23	23	9	2	−77
1. Names a vehicle or mode of transportation	10	1	0	4	5	28
2. Moving someone or something	9	1	0	4	4	26
3. Changing location, going from one place to another	30	0	1	12	17	65
4. A means of getting around, conveyance, vehicle	12	0	0	3	9	46
2. Is transportation just something that people enjoy, or do they need it?						
1. Says that people need transportation, at least at times	86	21	18	23	24	31
2. People need transportation to get places: stores, school, work, home, hospital, doctor's office, friends' homes, and so on	61	13	12	18	18	24
3. Transportation needed to travel long distances (Florida, California, etc.)	23	4	6	4	9	
4. People need transportation when they don't have a car (cabs, rides from friends, etc.)	7	2	1	2	2	
3A. Let's talk about transportation in the past. How did people get around way back in the days when they used to live in caves?						
0. Doesn't know/no relevant response	15	6	4	5	0	−26
1. They used modern vehicles or "Flintstone" vehicles made of stone	10	3	3	2	2	
2. They rode animals: oxen, horses	10	1	0	5	4	28
3. They used carts, wagons, carriages, buggies	10	2	0	2	6	30
4. They walked	66	13	19	15	19	
3B. How did people get around back in the pioneer days?						
0. Doesn't know/no relevant response	30	13	10	5	2	−38
1. Modern vehicles: cars, taxis, buses, trains	8	4	3	0	1	−24
2. Walked	15	4	4	3	4	
3. Boats or ships	14	2	2	1	9	38
4. Wagons or covered wagons	24	0	3	12	9	46
5. Oxen or horses	15	1	4	8	2	
6. Carriages or buggies	7	1	2	2	2	
7. Mentions animal-pulled vehicles (coded 4, 5, and/or 6)	38	2	7	17	12	48

(Continued)

211

TABLE 6.1
(Continued)

Response Categories	Total 96	K 24	1 24	2 24	3 24	Phi
3C. What forms of transportation do we use now that people long ago didn't have?						
0. No mention of motor vehicles (no response, walking, animals, bicycles, etc.)	5	3	2	0	0	−25
1. Common road vehicles: cars, trucks, buses, motorcycles	59	19	17	15	8	−36
2. Common road vehicles plus trains, planes, or ships	32	2	5	9	16	46
4. For a long time, the Native Americans didn't have horses, but then they got horses. How did horses change their lives?						
0. Doesn't know/no relevant response	22	13	5	4	0	−47
1. They could ride/didn't have to walk (no elaboration)	18	5	4	4	5	
2. They could go further or to other places	21	3	5	5	8	18
3. They could go faster	18	1	6	5	6	22
4. Riding is easier than walking: You don't have to use as much energy, you don't get as tired or foot sore, and so on	26	1	10	8	7	31
5. Riding made fighting, hunting, or finding food easier	14	1	1	7	5	31
5. For a long time, people had only horses and wagons to get around in, but then the railroad was built. What could people do after the railroad was built that they couldn't do before? Why would they choose to do that?						
0. Doesn't know/no relevant response	20	12	5	3	0	−45
1. It's more fun, easier; they don't have to walk	13	4	1	6	2	
2. Comfort: You can just sit and ride, shielded from the elements	7	1	3	1	2	
3. You can get to places faster/more quickly	48	4	17	12	15	41
4. You can get to places that are farther away, or to many more places	24	8	3	4	9	
5. Other: It's cheaper, you can carry more things, there is more space you don't have to stop as often to let horses rest, and so on	11	1	3	2	5	
6. Later, highways were built. What could people do after highways were built that they couldn't do before?						
0. Doesn't know/no relevant response	18	11	2	3	2	−40
1. They could drive cars, trucks, other road vehicles	27	7	8	6	6	
2. They could go different or faraway places; trains only go to stations; you could go across rivers, and so on	18	3	6	4	5	
3. They could stay clean and safe: highways are smoother, no dirt and dust, and so on	8	0	2	2	4	21

(Continued)

TABLE 6.1
(Continued)

Response Categories	Total 96	K 24	1 24	2 24	3 24	Phi
4. They could travel up high instead of down lower (the roads were raised, they were on bridges that took them over other roads, etc.)	7	1	2	2	2	
5. They could get places faster	25	2	8	8	7	

7. Then, airplanes were built. What could people do after airplanes were built that they couldn't do before?

0. Doesn't know/no relevant response	7	5	1	1	0	−31
1. Ride in the airplane (no elaboration)	9	5	1	0	3	
2. Airplanes were more fun, easier, more relaxing	10	2	1	4	3	
3. Airplanes don't have to stop at stop lights, run out of gas, get flat tires, deal with auto traffic, and so on	8	1	3	2	2	
4. They could go to different states or countries (specifically named)	22	5	9	5	3	
5. They could go to faraway places	28	5	4	7	12	28
6. They could go over water/oceans	9	1	4	2	2	
7. They could get to places faster	42	7	14	12	9	

8. Some people say that all of these changes in transportation have "made the world smaller." What do they mean by that?

0. Doesn't know/no relevant response	56	21	17	12	6	−47
1. We have less space now because there are more buildings, vehicles, train tracks, airports, destruction of nature, and so on	30	2	6	8	14	39
2. We can travel more easily/faster now, get places quicker; people are more connected with things and each other	8	0	0	4	4	30

9. Long, long ago, people built cities near oceans or on big rivers. Why was that?

0. Doesn't know/no relevant response	31	10	10	6	5	−20
1. To view the beauty or the water; to listen to the waves	8	1	2	2	3	
2. To swim or play in the water	24	5	9	7	3	
3. To use the water (for drinking or washing)	27	5	4	9	9	21
4. To get food, fish from the water	15	4	1	7	3	
5. To travel by boat or ship	23	3	8	6	6	

10. Later, people built cities along railroad lines. Why was that?

0. Doesn't know/no relevant response	33	12	10	5	6	−25
1. They liked to watch the trains or listen to their noises	9	1	3	2	3	
2. So they could ride the train, go places	24	5	9	3	7	

(Continued)

TABLE 6.1
(Continued)

Response Categories	Total 96	K 24	1 24	2 24	3 24	Phi
3. So they could get to the train more quickly or easily	24	2	3	11	8	35
4. So trains would have a place to stop/people would have a place to board trains	15	4	3	5	3	

11. At one time, mountains made it hard for people to travel. Most people didn't even try to cross mountains, but now we cross them all the time. Why is it easier?

0. Doesn't know/no relevant response	29	10	10	6	3	−27
1. Better climbing equipment: ropes, backpacks, shoes, hooks, and so on	22	5	5	7	5	
2. Modern vehicles: drive cars on roads, take trains through tunnels to cross mountains	33	3	6	10	14	36
3. Airplanes can fly over mountains	10	0	3	4	3	
4. Mountains are smaller or less dangerous now (less snow, falling rocks, etc.)	9	4	3	2	0	−21

12. Why was the wheel an important invention?

0. Doesn't know/no relevant response	18	7	6	3	2	−22
1. People can go faster on things with wheels	20	0	6	5	9	33
2. You need wheels to use vehicles: drive cars, land planes, and so on	57	16	13	16	12	
3. You can travel, move from place to place	21	4	4	4	9	22
4. You can move things more easily, don't have to drag them	27	1	4	9	13	43

13. If the first Pilgrims to come to the New World had cars, could they have used the cars to drive across the country?

0. Yes, they could have	57	18	10	15	14	
1. Doesn't know or mentions barriers other than those coded in Category 2 (they would have to get around water, could get stuck in mud or snow, might run out of gas, etc.)	24	5	8	5	6	
2. They couldn't because trees/forests would be in the way; they couldn't until they made roads	15	1	6	4	4	

14. What if there were no cars today? How would our lives be different if we only had horses and wagons to help us get around?

0. Doesn't know/no relevant response	29	14	5	7	3	−38
1. Lists characteristics of horses: They get scared, tired, need feeding, and so on	14	1	6	4	3	
2. We would have to walk more	12	3	6	2	1	
3. It would be harder to get around	23	2	5	4	12	37
4. We couldn't get around as quickly	42	4	12	12	14	32

(Continued)

TABLE 6.1
(Continued)

Response Categories	Total 96	K 24	1 24	2 24	3 24	Phi
15. What if we had trains but no cars? How would our lives be different?						
0. Cannot respond or says only that we would ride trains	25	16	3	4	2	−54
1. Trains would be faster than horses	8	0	2	2	4	21
2. It would cost money to ride the trains	7	1	0	2	4	24
3. We would walk more	32	5	7	10	10	19
4. The trains would make noise	8	1	5	0	2	
5. Travel would be slower because of all the train stops	19	0	6	7	6	29
6. Talks about the hassle, crowding of train travel	17	1	2	3	11	43
7. Inconvenient because trains usually don't stop at the exact place you wish to reach	23	2	5	7	9	25
8. Trains cannot cross water	7	0	3	1	3	
9. We would want to live near the train station	20	2	8	5	5	
16. Suppose you lived in a small town out in the country and a big highway was built right through the town. How would your town be different after the highway was built?						
0. Doesn't know/no relevant response	26	13	10	3	0	−49
1. Destruction of houses, yards, parks, trees, gardens, nature; some people would have to move	17	2	4	7	4	
2. It would be noisier	24	2	1	10	11	44
3. People could get to other places faster/more easily	29	4	5	9	11	26
4. More or more dangerous traffic, more accidents, and so on	36	5	6	12	13	30
5. More houses and other buildings would be constructed	6	1	0	3	2	
6. Other negative outcomes not included in previous categories: pollution, dust, bad smells, barriers to local travel, and so on	10	1	0	3	6	31
7. Student mentions both positive and negative outcomes	20	2	0	8	10	42
17. Farmers produce food for people. A long time ago, farmers didn't have trucks, but then they got trucks. How did the farming business change after trucks were built?						
0. Doesn't know/no relevant response	32	16	8	6	2	−45
1. They could get places faster	14	1	3	3	7	26
2. They didn't need to carry things by hand or by walking	14	1	5	1	7	31
3. They could use the truck to take things to and from markets	33	4	4	12	13	37
4. They could use the truck to do farm work	22	3	9	5	5	

(Continued)

TABLE 6.1
(Continued)

Response Categories	Total 96	K 24	1 24	2 24	3 24	Phi
18. Apples grow here in the summer, but not in the winter. Even in the winter we can buy apples. Why is that?						
0. Doesn't know/no relevant response	20	9	8	3	0	−38
1. Student talks only about the process of getting apples from trees to stores in the summer	9	7	1	0	1	−40
2. Local apples picked in the summer are preserved for sale in the winter (possibly chilled, etc.)	52	6	14	15	17	35
3. Apples are imported from other states or countries	15	1	1	8	5	34
19A. What kinds of transportation do you find in big cities but not in other places?						
0. Doesn't know/no relevant response	38	16	16	4	2	−56
1. Cars	36	4	7	16	9	38
2. Buses	23	3	2	11	7	35
3. Trains	24	3	2	9	10	34
4. Taxis	13	0	1	5	7	35
5. Planes	16	2	0	6	8	35
6. Trucks and vans	14	1	4	5	4	
7. Other	14	4	3	2	5	
19B. Why do people use buses or subways instead of cars?						
0. Doesn't know/because they want to (without elaboration)	38	18	15	4	1	−61
1. People don't have cars/don't have money to pay for a car	20	0	4	8	8	34
2. Buses, subways go faster than cars	20	3	5	6	6	
3. Traffic and stoplights impede surface travel	11	1	1	3	6	27
4. It's easier to travel on buses or subways/you don't have to drive	9	0	2	2	5	26
5. Other (buses and subways are bigger, have room for more people, etc.)	20	3	3	9	5	
20A. What is a taxi cab?						
0. Doesn't know/no relevant response	12	6	5	1	0	−32
1. Describes taxi as a yellow or checkered car/with taxi sign/number on the back, and so on	52	10	10	17	15	26
2. Something that takes people where they want to go	58	15	11	15	17	
3. A car that someone drives for you	25	4	6	6	9	
4. A car that you pay to use	24	1	5	11	7	35
5. A car that will stop and pick you up if you signal it	13	1	4	4	4	

(Continued)

TABLE 6.1
(Continued)

Response Categories	Total	K	1	2	3	Phi
	96	24	24	24	24	
20B. Why do people use taxis?						
0. Doesn't know/no relevant response	10	7	3	0	0	−39
1. Shows understanding of taxis as car/transportation, but not why people use them (to get places, they don't want to walk, etc.)	37	8	10	10	9	
2. Using a taxi is cheaper than buying or renting a car	7	1	3	3	0	
3. The people don't have a car to use	46	10	8	15	13	
20C. Do people have to pay to use taxis? How does that work?						
0. Doesn't know whether they have to pay or says that they do not	12	8	3	1	0	−39
1. Says "yes" but cannot elaborate or guesses dollar amounts without explanation	18	8	8	1	1	−37
2. The meter tells what the cost is	11	2	2	3	4	
3. Cost is determined by the number of people or the number of stops made	6	1	1	2	2	
4. Cost is determined by the time required	14	3	2	5	4	
5. Cost is determined by how far you go	45	3	9	14	19	50
6. Cost is determined by the driver's boss	7	1	2	4	0	
7. Shows clear understanding of taxis as local transportation that you pay for when you are not driving your own car	81	14	19	24	24	48
21. How does a car work—what makes it go? How does the engine make the car go?						
0. Doesn't know/no relevant response	38	14	14	6	4	−39
1. You use the key to turn on the car and make the engine go	15	5	2	2	6	
2. Pushing the pedal makes the engine go	17	2	3	4	8	25
3. The engine makes the wheels turn	25	4	4	8	9	22
4. The gas makes the engine go	27	3	6	8	10	24
5. Other: wires from the engine make the car go, the battery gives power to the engine, piston motion in the engine is transferred to the wheels, and so on	15	1	3	6	5	22
22. It's nice to have cars and trucks, but they create problems too. What are some problems that exist in places where most people drive cars or trucks?						
0. Doesn't know/no relevant response	21	12	7	1	1	−46
1. Individuals' problems: blown tires, out of gas, and so on (code only if no codes in 2–6)	9	2	4	1	2	
2. Difficult for people or animals to cross the road	8	0	1	2	5	28

(Continued)

TABLE 6.1
(Continued)

Response Categories	Total	K	1	2	3	Phi
	96	24	24	24	24	
3. Traffic jams, congestion, delays	27	3	4	11	9	31
4. Accidents	43	8	8	13	14	23
5. Noise	12	1	3	4	4	
6. Air pollution, dust, gas/oil spills	18	1	2	9	6	34
23. What is a map?						
0. Doesn't know/no relevant response	6	4	2	0	0	−29
1. Something that tells you where places are/a representation of the state, nation, world	35	5	7	12	11	27
2. Something that helps you go where you want to go; tells you how to get from one place to another	80	19	20	21	20	
24. If people want to go to another country, can they just go, or do they have to get permission?						
0. Doesn't know/no relevant response	13	2	7	3	1	
1. Just go	39	8	12	10	9	
2. Need permission	44	14	5	11	14	
3. Permission granted by government officials	17	2	2	7	6	25
25. Why do we need stop lights on our streets? What would happen if we didn't have stop lights?						
0. Doesn't know/no relevant response	6	4	2	0	0	−29
1. Cars would crash if we did not have them	33	7	8	7	11	
2. They control traffic, make sure that people stop for each other	46	7	11	16	12	27
3. Other functions: They tell us if cars are coming the other way, keep people from traveling too fast, prevent traffic jams, and so on	8	3	2	1	2	
4. Without them there would be many more accidents	83	15	21	24	23	43
5. Focuses on pedestrians: They enable people to cross busy streets safely	10	6	1	0	3	

Note. Numbers in the frequencies columns show how many students in each group were coded for mentioning the ideas represented by each response category. Underlining indicates that the chi-square for the underlined distribution was statistically significant at or below the .05 level. In these instances the phi coefficients (with decimal points omitted) are given in the phi column, to indicate the magnitudes of linear trends.

WHY PEOPLE NEED TRANSPORTATION

The first question was asked to determine how the students would define transportation in their own words. If they were not able to do so, or if their definition was incorrect, overly specific, or otherwise problematic, the interviewer defined the term for them before proceeding to Question 2.

1. **Today we're going to talk about transportation. What does transportation mean?** [If student does not know, explain that transportation refers to how people travel or get from one place to another.]

2. **Is transportation just something that people enjoy, or do they need it? What are some times when they need it?**

K   1. I don't know.

     2. They need it. (What are some times when they need it?) To go shopping and get some food and get some clothes.

1st   1. I don't know.

     2. They need it. (When are some times when they need it?) Like when they need to go on vacation and they need to go to the store or something. And they help people get to the hospital and they help people when their car is out of gas; they can go to the gas station with another car.

2nd   1. Like if you go somewhere, like if you ride a train or a car or bus or plane.

     2. They need it. (When are some times when they need it?) If they're like poor and they don't have enough money for a car and they just take a cab or a bus or a train. (What are some times when you have to be able to travel or have transportation?) Like if you're going on a business trip.

3rd   1. Like a bus . . . if you have to go on a bus, then that's transportation because you go from one place to another. So is a car.

     2. They need it. (What are some times when they need it?) When . . . like if their cousin was in the hospital.

More than half (57) of the 96 students were unable to define transportation. The rest defined it as changing location or going from one place to another (30); stated that the term refers to a vehicle, conveyance, or means of getting around (12); named a specific type of vehicle or mode of transportation (10); or said that it means moving someone or something (9). Two students said that transportation is talk (thinking of communication).

A heavy majority (86) understood that people need transportation, at least some of the time. However, 7 were unable to respond and 3 said that people enjoy transportation but do not actually need it. The latter response is defensible, although most observers would say that transportation is a basic need these days, at least for people living in developed countries. When asked to explain why people might need transportation, 61 mentioned local travel (to stores, schools, jobs, doctors' offices, friends' homes, etc.), 23 mentioned long-distance travel (e.g., to Florida on vacation or to visit relatives), and 7 talked about how people sometimes might need to take a taxi or get a ride if they do not own a car or if their car is being repaired. Other responses included: You need to walk to get exercise (2);

you need transportation in bad weather (2) or when you have to get somewhere fast (2); you use transportation on special occasions like holidays (driving to visit relatives).

Compared to their responses concerning food, clothing, and shelter, the students were less likely to say that transportation is a basic need, although 90% of them did so. The minority who were able to define transportation typically depicted it as moving from one place to another or as a conveyance or vehicle used to do so. About two thirds cited local travel in explaining the need for transportation, although some emphasized long-distance travel or said that people need transportation when they do not have a car.

TRANSPORTATION IN THE PAST AND PRESENT

Question 3 assessed students' knowledge about transportation through three time periods: the cave days (prehistoric times), the pioneer days (early 18th century), and the present.

3A. Let's talk about transportation in the past. How did people get around way back in the days when people used to live in caves?

3B. How did people get around back during the pioneer days?

3C. What kinds of transportation do we use now that people long ago didn't have?

K   3A. Walk.
     3B. Walk.
     3C. Cars.
1st 3A. They walked.
     3B. They had these cattle thingies and they still have them and they have a horse, two horses taking them somewhere.
     3C. Cars. (Anything else?) Nothing I can think of.
2nd 3A. They used to use horses.
     3B. I don't know.
     3C. Cars. Buses. Trains. Airplanes.
3rd 3A. They used rocks for tires and more rocks for the sides and wood for the other stuff. What do you call those—like on the Flintstones? (I don't know.) I know they used to have cars that would run on their feet. (OK, but that's from the Flintstones—the cartoon. Do you think the real people in the olden days back when they lived in caves looked like that or do you think it's a story?) It's a story but the cars might be real and true—the cars, I think are true, and

maybe the dinosaurs. [For this student, cars from the Flintstones
were more real than dinosaurs.]

3B.   What were the pioneers' wagons called? I gotta figure out what
      they were called—buggies or something.

3C.   Cars, trucks, buses, skidoos, boats.

Concerning transportation in the cave days, 15 students were unable to respond, 5 said that people rode in "Flintstone" vehicles featuring stone wheels,
and another 5 mentioned cars or other modern vehicles. Most (66) of the rest
correctly said that people walked in the cave days. In addition or instead, 10 said
that they rode animals (oxen, horses) and 10 said that they used carts, wagons, or
other wheeled vehicles. Other responses included: wheelbarrows; dinosaurs (2);
they invented cars and trains; bikes; baby strollers; boats; mammoths.

Concerning the pioneer days, 30 students were unable to respond and another 8 mentioned cars, taxis, or other modern vehicles. The rest spoke of wagons or covered wagons (24), walking (15), oxen or horses (15), boats or ships
(14), and carriages or buggies (7). Other responses included: They rode goats;
bikes (3); airplanes.

Concerning modern forms of transportation, only 5 students were unable to
respond or mentioned only walking, riding animals, or riding bicycles. The rest
almost all mentioned engine-powered vehicles: Fifty-nine only cited common
road vehicles (cars, trucks, buses, motorcycles), but 32 also cited trains, planes, or
ships. Other responses included: Indy cars, monster trucks, jet skis; skateboards;
limos; tractors, horse trailers; baby strollers; scooters; roller blades (2); hot-air
balloons; motor homes; skidoos; go carts.

A few students showed misconceptions induced by the Flintstones and other
cartoon series and a surprisingly large percentage was unable to respond to the
question about travel in the pioneer days, but otherwise most of what the students had to say was accurate or at least defensible in characterizing travel at the
three time periods addressed. More than two thirds said that the cave people
mostly walked, although some thought that they rode animals or used animal-
pulled carts or wagons. Surprisingly, only 38 mentioned animal-pulled vehicles in
talking about transportation in the pioneer days, and more students were unable
to respond to this question than to the previous one about the cave days. The
younger students actually appeared to know more about the cave days than the
pioneer days. Responses concerning contemporary transportation modes were almost all accurate, focusing on motor vehicles. In general, the students seemed to
understand the progression from walking and carrying or dragging things to ani-
mal-powered wheel vehicles to engine powered wheeled vehicles. However,
some of them were badly confused about when these progressions occurred, and a
few believed that cave people used the types of stone vehicles shown in the
Flintstones cartoons.

CHANGES BROUGHT BY INNOVATIONS
IN TRANSPORTATION

Question 4 through Question 8 addressed the students' understanding of the ways that key innovations in transportation brought new opportunities into people's lives and "shrunk the world."

4. For a long time, the Native Americans didn't have horses, but then they got horses. How did horses change their lives?

5. For a long time, people had only horses and wagons to get around in, but then the railroad was built. What could people do after the railroad was built that they couldn't do before? Why would they choose to do that?

6. Later, highways were built. What could people do after highways were built that they couldn't do before?

7. Then, airplanes were built. What could people do after airplanes were built that they couldn't do before?

8. Some people say that all of these changes in transportation have "made the world smaller." What do they mean by that?

K   4. Well, they came to a city—the horses came to a place where people didn't have anything. (How did horses change their lives?) Well, they came to the Indian spot and found them. (What could they do with the horses that they couldn't do before?) They could ride on it.

5. They could go on it. (If they could go on it, what could they do that they couldn't do before?) They didn't have to walk.

6. They didn't have to walk anymore—they drove.

7. They could ride on them and you could ride on a horse if you had one.

8. It means that the world is not that huge anymore.

1st   4. They could take them to other places without them walking and they could take them places that they like if they weren't riding a horse to go get food, they could. And the horses could run. (Well, you've said that the Native Americans could use horses so they didn't have to walk places. Why would they rather ride the horses than walk?) Well, I think it would be easier to go by horses. (And why do you think that?) Because sometimes they get tired of walking. (Are there any other reasons why people would rather ride horses than walk?) Because it's easier to get places. (Why is it easier to get places on a horse?) Because horses are faster than you.

5. They could ride the train. (Why do people choose to ride trains?) Because they could get people places and because they could take people to Chicago and wherever they needed to. (Why do you think people would want to ride trains instead of riding a horse and wagon?) Be-

cause trains are bigger and faster than a horse and wagon. (Can you think of anything else that the trains could do for people that horses and wagons couldn't do?) They could take people places and they could go anywhere they would like to.

6. Well, they could go faster and when the cars were built they could ride on it. And I think that big trucks can go on it. (OK, you said that cars on the highway would be faster than the transportation forms that people had before. Why could you go faster in a car on the highway?) Because you can go fast on the highway and you can get places faster on the highway.

7. Well, if they wanted to they could fly. And they could get places even faster. It would take a couple of days flying in an airplane. (What do you mean that it would take a couple of days for an airplane?) Because sometimes some airplanes are slow. They like want to go really slow to stop and look in the sky. (Anything else that airplanes could help people do that they couldn't do before they were invented?) They're going to take people places that they couldn't go in cars. (What are some places that people couldn't get to in a car?) It would take a pretty long time to get to Florida in a car and they could not go around the world. (Why couldn't they go around the world in a car?) Because it would take them like days and days and days and days and anyway, there's oceans in it going around the world. (Could you go around the world in an airplane?) You could go above people but I don't think you could go around the world in a plane, not outside, but I think you can go like around the world when you're like outside and you go other places in an airplane.

8. Well, like they invent a lot of stuff so the world is smaller. (OK. Did the world actually get smaller?) Well, I can't be sure because I'm not outside on the world right now, but when they build like houses, the grasses are getting smaller because they put houses on the grass when they do that.

2nd 4. Before they could just like walk, and after they usually didn't want to walk because they were tired.

5. They couldn't go on the trains before it was built, and now they can go on trains, because they don't want to go on horses because horses weren't fast enough.

6. Cars. (Can you think of any reasons, any times, when people might choose to use cars instead of taking a train?) Because they don't have a train by their house, or it's a long drive. (Long drive to . . . ?) The train station.

7. They could get places faster. Like instead of doing like the whole day just to get to Florida, it would only take them, like 10 hours. (When

are some times when people might choose to take an airplane instead of taking a car or train?) When they're going somewhere far.

8. Because they take up so much room trying to build the railroad tracks.

3rd 4. A lot because they could go places more fast instead of walking.

5. They could go places easier and not have to walk, and they could go places faster, and sometimes it's fun.

6. If there were cars, they could go on the highway with the cars and you could go lots of places because cars have an engine and the engine makes the car go.

7. They could go somewhere way farther away and it didn't take that long.

8. Because there's more cars and highways and railroad tracks. (How does that make the world smaller?) There are big highways and big places so it makes it a little smaller.

Twenty-two students were unable to respond to Question 4, but the rest suggested a number of ways in which horses changed the lives of the Native Americans: Eighteen said that now these people did not have to walk (without elaborating further); 26 that they didn't have to expend as much energy or get as tired or footsore; 18 that they could now get places more quickly; 21 that they could now go farther or visit places that they could not reach previously; and 14 that riding on horses made fighting, hunting, and finding food easier. Other responses included: They could get to the cowboys and "war" with them; horses helped with the work; they had less food because horses made noise and scared away the buffalo; you can pack "luggage" on horses; horses could pull stuff that they wanted to take with them (2).

Half of the students said that railroads made it possible for people to get to places more quickly, and 24 that trains allowed them to get to more places or farther-away places. In addition, 20 were unable to respond; 13 said that trains made travel easier or more fun; 7 noted that trains allowed people to travel in comfort, shielded from the elements; and 11 gave "other" responses such as that trains were cheaper, could carry more people or things, allowed the traveler more space (compared to a stage coach), and did not require stopping to let horses rest. One kindergartener thought that horses and buggies were faster than trains, and two third graders made unique and insightful responses: Trains could carry coal and things so that people could earn money; trains brought new jobs such as engineer or brakeman.

Concerning Question 6, 18 students were unable to respond and 27 said only that highways allowed people to drive cars, trucks, or other road vehicles. However, 25 noted that this allowed people to get places faster; 18 that they could go to more faraway places (places that trains did not go to directly); and 8 that highways allowed cleaner and safer travel because people were traveling in cars on smooth, paved roads rather than riding horses on dusty trails. Other responses included: Test out new cars; highways brought businesses that provided amenities to travelers (gas, food, drinks); highways are slow because the trips on them take hours (reversed reasoning, based on the idea that you use highways only when you are going on long trips); it is more fun to drive on a highway than to sit in a train all day (2); cars are more comfortable than trains. Finally, 7 students took the term *highway* literally. They said that highways allowed people to travel up high instead of down lower because the roads were raised above the surrounding land. A few students noted that highways include bridges over rivers and thus allow cars to cross rivers, apparently believing that trains are unable to do this.

All but seven students were able to respond to Question 7, saying that airplanes allowed people to get places faster (42), to go to farther away places (28), or to go to different states or countries (22); that airplane travel is more fun, easier, or more relaxing than other forms of travel (10); that people could now ride in airplanes (without further elaboration) (9); that airplanes can travel over water/oceans (9) and that airplanes are preferable to cars because they don't run out of gas, get flat tires, get stuck in traffic, have to stop at stoplights, and so on (8). Other responses included: so you could see things from the sky (several students mentioned the aerial view); you can get food and drinks on planes; if there was a truck full of dynamite about to blow up on the road, you could take a plane and get away from it; you can drink coffee, eat, and read on a plane; planes sometimes fly slow so that people can "stop and look in the sky"; you cannot drive to Florida "because there's water" in the way, but you can fly to it; you can see the clouds; people didn't have to take boats anymore; planes have more storage room than cars; there are lots of seats—planes fit many people.

Young children tend to have difficulties with metaphor, including the notion that transportation has "made the world smaller." When asked to explain this statement, 56 students were unable to respond and another 30 said that developments in transportation take up space (for the vehicles themselves, airports or train stations, train tracks, etc.) and thus have resulted in some destruction of nature and reduction of space available for homes, parks, or other human purposes. This was a thoughtful and accurate response by students who took the statement literally. Only eight students suggested that the term means that now we can travel more easily, get places faster, or are better connected with other people and places. Other responses included: there are more things now than there used to be; a lot of people go to the same places now because there's tons of transportation, so you could see people in the store and say 'This is one small world.' " The best response was made by a second grader who said that this saying is a figure of speech meaning that people are less isolated and more connected, then hinted at the concept of *interdependence*: "They aren't working by themselves anymore, like the Indians who had to build their own fires because they had no matches."

For the most part, misconceptions were minor and infrequent. However, several students thought that trains cannot cross rivers and that all highways are literally "high." Other misconceptions included the notions that Indians found it harder to hunt food with horses because they scared away buffalo, that horse-drawn buggies were faster than trains, that highway travel is slow because it takes hours to get where you are going, and that it is not possible to drive from Michigan to Florida because the way is blocked by a body of water that one must fly over.

In contrast to their generally impressive responses to Question 4 through Question 7, the students were not ready for Question 8. When asked about how transportation innovations had "made the world smaller," the majority could not respond and most of the rest took the statement literally. Only two students grasped the metaphorical meaning of "made the world smaller" and spoke of people now being more connected to one another. None mentioned, for example, that horses allowed the plains tribes to follow the buffalo over much greater distances or that railroads, highways, and airplanes transformed the nation and the world from a collection of mostly isolated settlements into a richly connected social and economic network. Difficulty with metaphor was not the only reason that the students struggled with this question. On all of our interviews, they displayed difficulty imagining and talking about macrolevel social phenomena.

THE HISTORIC EFFECT OF RIVERS, RAILROADS, AND MOUNTAINS ON TRAVEL

Question 9 through Question 11 addressed aspects of understanding that populations tend to concentrate along travel routes and be bounded by geographical barriers, especially mountains.

9. Long, long ago, people built cities near oceans or on big rivers. Why was that?

10. Later, people built cities along railroad lines. Why was that?

11. At one time, mountains made it hard for people to travel. Most people didn't even try to cross mountains, but now we cross them all the time. Why is it easier now?

K 9. Well, because if they didn't have any water, they would have to have water or they couldn't catch any fish.

10. Well, because so they could drive on it and ride on it.

11. Because they can cross it if they wanted to so they don't have to walk. They could go on a bus or a horse and you could go in a car or a bus.

1st 9. Well, because they built like really tiny houses and they don't have water and they don't have electricity and sometimes they don't even have sidewalks. They only have grass, so they could only get out on their driveways. (Can you think of any other reasons why people would want to have cities near oceans or big rivers?) They could go swimming if they didn't have a swimming pool and if the water's clean enough, they could get a drink.

10. Because they didn't know they couldn't go to any other houses. And they could like . . . I'm not sure. (Why would people want to live near the railroad line?) Because they could like go away on the railroad and come back on the railroad. I don't know what else.

11. Well, I think that all the animals that are around, you know, they like brushed their feet marks off there.

2nd 9. So then they could just like get water, right from there, because they don't like live by the grocery store. They have to drive a ways. (Can you think of any other reasons why people would want to live near the water?) To wash their clothes in it.

10. Because if they didn't have a car or anything, they could just like, go to the train station and then they could go on a train.

11. Because like people went up there, and like knocked down rocks, so then the cars can go up there. And they like built roads that went like this, so then they could go up.

3rd 9. Because if they didn't have water, they could get water from oceans and the rivers, and they could fish.

10. Because if they had to go on the train, then they could get on it easier when they wanted to.

11. Because they used to try to walk up mountains and it's really hard because there were oceans right by the mountains, but then people built roads and it makes life easier because the cars can go up the roads instead of you walking across the mountains.

Almost one third of the students were unable to say why people built cities near oceans or on rivers. Of the rest, 27 said that they wanted to use the water for drinking or washing, 24 that they wanted to swim or play in the water, 23 that they wanted to be able to travel by boat or ship, 15 that they wanted to get food (fish) from the water, and 8 that they wanted to view the beauty of the water or listen to the sound of the waves. Thus, most emphasized the more important (functional) reasons (eating, drinking, travel), but some mentioned only recreational or aesthetic reasons. Many were thinking of only casual local boating, perhaps for fishing or swimming, not about transportation linking the settlement to the rest of the world. Other responses included: so they could see if anyone was coming to kill them; so their animals could live—they needed water (apparently not thinking about human needs for water); they wanted to keep cool in the summer; the early Europeans wanted to "explore from edge to edge" rather than walk the interior of the country; they could earn money from fishing; the shoreline was the only open land for building settlements (2); port cities were needed to provide recreation and services to sailors and travelers (2); so they could have some natural resources.

About one third of the students also were unable to say why people built cities along railroad lines. Of the rest, 24 said simply that the people wanted to ride the train or go places, 24 that they wanted to be able to get to the train easily, 15 that settlements were built along the tracks so the trains would have a place to stop and people would have a place to board them, and 9 that the people liked to watch the trains or listen to their noises. Other responses included: so that the trains could stop and the driver could rest and get refreshments; people ride trains to go to cities and do things, so you would have to build cities along the railroad; so trains could stop to get coal and all of the things that trains transported.

Once again, the majority mentioned functional reasons, but a few mentioned only aesthetic reasons. Some of the responses that settlements were built along tracks to provide trains with a place to stop contained elements of reversed reasoning: thinking in terms of the process beginning with the building of the tracks (for no apparent reason) and then settlements being built to serve the needs of the trains, instead of realizing that tracks were laid to link communities to which people wanted to travel and the trains served the needs of these communities.

Almost one third of the students also were unable to explain why it is easier to cross mountains now than in the past. Furthermore, 22 responded, at least initially, within the context of mountain climbing. That is, instead of talking about modern vehicles, they talked about the availability of special climbing shoes, ropes, backpacks, hooks, and other climbing equipment. Only a minority focused on modern vehicles: Thirty-three said that we now drive cars over mountains or ride trains through them in tunnels, 10 that airplanes now fly over mountains, and 9 that mountains are easier to cross now because they are smaller (worn down over time) or less dangerous (there is less snow than in the past, or there are fewer falling rocks because most of the rocks have already fallen). Other responses included: People are bigger now and can do more than the cave people could; ways to cross the mountains have been discovered; people are stronger now; you can grab the rocks easier because they are stiffer now; there are no more bumps or monsters; they cut down the trees and made a road; we have ski lifts; you can use a glider to get up.

Responses to Question 9 through Question 11 were generally accurate or at least defensible, but few students showed much awareness of interactive relationships between transportation and human settlement patterns. Those who were able to generate reasons why people might want to locate near water talked about people wanting to swim or play in the water, travel locally by boat, fish, or simply take aesthetic pleasure in viewing the beauty of the water or listening to the sound of the waves. Only a minority displayed awareness that water is necessary to human survival and only a few conveyed awareness that in the distant past, much exploration and long-distance travel was done on waterways.

Similarly, students generated various reasons why people might want to build cities along rail lines (because they wanted to be able to ride the train to go places, etc.), but few showed awareness of rail lines as vital links to other communities, sources of access to goods and markets, and so on during those times. Furthermore, some showed elements of reversed reasoning in thinking that the tracks were built first and then settlements were built along them. It is true that the opening of a new travel route sometimes stimulates the development of new settlements, but the cause–effect chain usually begins with recognition of the need for a better travel route between existing communities. Finally, the students again generated various reasons why it is easier to cross mountains today than in the past (e.g., better mountain-climbing equipment, engine-powered vehicles), but few showed awareness of mountains as significant barriers to transportation until the relatively recent past.

WHEELED VEHICLES THROUGH HISTORY

The next four questions further probed students' understanding of historical developments in transportation: the magnitude of the changes brought by the wheel; the fact that eastern North America at the time of the Pilgrims was a heavily forested wilderness inhospitable to overland travel, and the many ways in which society was affected by the introduction of trains and then cars to supplant horse-drawn vehicles.

12. Why was the wheel an important invention? What could people do after the wheel was invented that they couldn't do before? [If student starts talking about cars, ask:] **What about before cars were invented—why was the invention of the wheel important?**

13. If the first Pilgrims to come to the New World had cars—could they have used the cars to drive across the country? [If yes:] **How would they have done it?** [If the student says that trees were in the way, ask:] **What if they cut down the trees?**

14. What if there were no cars today? How would our lives be different if we only had horses and wagons to help us get around?

15. What if we had trains but no cars? How would our lives be different? How would that affect where we lived? How would we shop if we only had trains? How would it affect where we went on vacation?

K   12. For driving cars. (Yes, but what about before cars were invented? Why was the invention of the wheel important?) They could be for planes too. It's important to drive somewhere else to another place.

13. No. (Why not?) Because cars weren't built then. (You're right, but let's pretend that they had cars. Could they have driven those cars across the country?) Yes.

14. I don't really know.

15. Don't have to drive. You just sit on the train and ... I forget what else. (Well, if we had trains and no cars, how would that affect where we lived?) You could get to your home. (How would we shop if we only had trains?) The train driver could drive you to the store. (How would it affect where we went on vacation if we only had trains?) By train. I'm going on a jet to Florida—a jet plane.

1st 12. Because they can ... because the wheel is rubbery and they're made of circles and they didn't have no ends. That means they can roll. They put them on the cars and you could drive in them and they rolled. (Well, why was the invention important even before cars?) I don't know. Because they could drive cars faster. The wheels can stop wherever they want and they can't like roll down when they're ... like if there's a circle right here, and I pushed it, it would go right there and it would go round and round and drop.

13. Yeah. (How would they have done it?) They could drive up mountains if it was a very powerful car. They could drive up mountains and go down them and go wherever they wanted.

14. It would be slower because the horses can't go that fast. Like if you wanted to go to Florida and it's a one cattle thing, you could just have another horse and if it was a baby, he couldn't ride it.

15. Because it's on a track and they don't like fall right off of the track. (How would that affect where we lived?) I don't know. (Well, how would we shop if we only had trains?) You could just go there and you can go and you can pick some stuff up and pay for it and the train would be gone. Then you'd have to wait for a little while and the train would come back. (Now, how would it affect where we went on vacation?) You could go wherever you wanted and you can make stops by going "OOHH" and it stops and you can just go off. (So would it change where we went on vacation very much?) Yeah. (Why?) Because you pull a cord.

2nd 12. They could go places. (Why did the wheel make it easier for people to go places?) Because they couldn't like just go on the bottom of a train, because it wouldn't go, so they had to build wheels to fit on the track.

13. Yeah. (OK. How could they have done that?) Like they could just drive to places, and then they could build roads on there, and they go and they could work on that, and then somebody else could drive their car up there and then do work on that.

14. That would take a pretty long time to get places.

15. You would have to walk if you lived far away from a train station. You would have to walk there. (Where would we want to live if there were trains but no cars?) Close to the train station. (OK. How

would we shop if we only had trains?) Then you'd have to like get dropped off, and then you'd have to walk to the store. (Why would you have to get dropped off?) Because trains like just don't go straight to the stores. (How would it affect where we went on vacation if there were only trains, but no cars? Would we be able to go to all the same places for vacation that we can go to now?) No. (Where do you think we wouldn't be able to go?) Like to Florida, because they wouldn't have enough coal to last that long.

3rd 12. Well, it was an important invention because sometimes you have to go somewhere right away and you don't want to be late. (Why does the wheel make it faster?) Because the wheels can go on the road and the engine helps the wheels go and it's really easier.

13. Well, it depends because they might get stuck in the sand and if they go in the water, then the car will sink and they might die. But if they had roads then, then they could go across the ocean. (If they didn't have roads, would they still be able to go across the country?) Yeah, sometimes. (How would they do that?) If there wasn't any snow and if there wasn't any mud puddles and it was summer, maybe they could because they wouldn't get stuck, but sometimes they could, sometimes they can't.

14. It would be really different and it would be really hard to go somewhere and if I went to Florida, then I would have to either have a horse or a wagon and would take really, really, really long, and today, it's like way, way easier.

15. You couldn't go to the exact place, like at your friend's house where she lives in Florida. We would have to have a car to drive from the railroad track where it stops. (If we only had trains, how would it affect where we lived?) You couldn't go to the exact place that you wanted and sometimes you would have to walk like to your friend's house from the railroad train where it stops. (How would we shop if we only had trains?) Sometimes we could walk but it would be really long and sometimes we can take only a few things on the train and then you could only get a little stuff at a time. (How would it affect where we went on vacation? You talked about your friend in Florida. Can you think of other ways it would affect where we go on vacation if we only had trains and no cars?) No.

When asked why the wheel was an important invention, 18 students were unable to respond. A majority (57) of the rest said that wheels are needed for cars, planes, or other vehicles. In addition or instead, 27 said that wheels allow us to move things more easily without having to drag them, 21 that they allow us to travel more easily, and 20 that they allow us to go faster than we can in non-wheeled conveyances. All of these responses are accurate and most show appreciation of the fundamental importance of the wheel. However, most students answered in terms of what wheels do today (e.g., on cars), not how the invention changed the world at the time. There were only a few unique responses: If the wheel had not been invented, there would be no use for cars; the wheel made it possible to open a curtain faster (using pulleys) and eliminated the need to use a bar to turn vehicles; "a car without wheels can't drive, and they probably made cars before wheels, so they had to invent the wheel" (reversed reasoning).

Only 15 students noted that the Pilgrims would not have been able to drive across the country because forests/lack of roads would prevent them from doing so. A majority (57) incorrectly said that the Pilgrims could have driven across the country if they had cars, and the other 24 either said that they were not sure or made reference to barriers such as rivers and lakes, mud or snow, or lack of gas stations (without mentioning the fundamental problem of a roadless wilderness). A few unusual elaborations appeared: Travel would be slow because Indians would keep stopping them wanting to trade; they would have to go in the summer when the car wouldn't sink in snow or mud; they could drive on Indian trails or wagon trails.

When asked how our lives would be different if we only had horses and wagons today, a surprisingly high 29 students were unable to respond. The rest said that we wouldn't be able to get around as quickly (42); said that it would be harder to get around (23); listed troublesome characteristics of horses, such as that they get frightened, get tired, or need feeding (14); or simply stated that we would have to walk more (12). Other responses included: We wouldn't have to make car payments; travel would be boring because you would spend all your time looking for water and food (for the horses); travel would be dangerous because you can fall off a horse; moving things would be harder because wagons can only carry small loads; travel would be bumpy and uncomfortable; some people might be allergic to horses and have to use bikes instead; you would be exposed to the elements when riding horses; trains are noisy and bumpy and the noise gives you a headache; you would have to replace the horses more often than cars because horses die; kids wouldn't get as much exercise because they would be riding horses instead of bikes; people would have to learn how to "drive" horses; every now and then you would hear this "gallop" trot past you. Few responses conveyed any indication that students were visualizing major differences in society as a whole.

When asked how our lives would be different if we had trains but no cars today, 25 students were unable to respond (again, a surprisingly high number). The rest said that we would have to walk more (32); travel would be inconvenient because trains usually don't stop at the exact place that you wish to reach (23); we would want to live near the train station (20); travel would be slower because of all the train stops (19); we would have to put up with the hassle and crowding involved in train travel (17); trains are faster than horses (8); trains would make a lot of noise (8); it would cost money to ride the trains (7); or we would not be able to cross water because trains cannot do so (7). Most answers were sensible as far as they went, but did not show recognition of the scope of the changes in society and everyday life that would occur if we had trains but no cars. Other responses included: We wouldn't be able to travel; we would shop at the railroad tracks; we would have to grow our own food; they would put train tracks by the grocery stores (reversed reasoning); we'd all live in the train station and there would be no schools because schools don't have railroad tracks; we would want to live far away from the train station because of the noise; they would build train tracks to the stores (3); they hadn't invented shops when they just had trains, or if there were shops, they only sold peanuts; stores could call the trains (trains had phones in them) to come when we needed them, like cabs; it would be bumpy riding; you wouldn't be able to listen to the radio or have air conditioning when you traveled; there would be more room to move around and do things than there is in a car; you could only go to places that you don't want to go to, like if you wanted to go to the store but the train took you to Utah; there would be more pollution; maybe there would be special shopping trains that went to shopping centers; you could only go as far as the train would take you until it ran out of coal; they would have carts at the stores that you could use to take your stuff to the trains; you couldn't go to faraway places for vacations.

Responses to Question 12, Question 14, and Question 15 were limited in at least two respects. First, 18, 29, and 25 students (respectively) were unable to provide substantive responses. We found this surprising given the concrete nature of transportation. Second, most responses were confined to microlevel descriptions of personal use of the transportation modes involved, showing little or no awareness of the macrolevel changes in society at large that were stimulated by their invention. Few students showed awareness of the fundamental and far-reaching importance of the wheel or of the ways that society at large (not just personal travel) would be different if we were restricted to horses and wagons or even to trains. They did not yet have enough knowledge of social history or the effects of inventions on everyday living to prepare them to address the macrolevel aspects of these questions.

Only 15 students clearly understood that the Pilgrims would not have been able to drive across the country because the eastern half of it was a heavily forested and roadless wilderness at the time. Asked how our lives would be different if we only had horses and wagons (and later, trains), most of the students who were able to respond said that travel would be slower or more difficult, but few showed awareness of ways that society at large (not just personal travel) would be different.

Several interesting misconceptions or examples of reversed reasoning occurred, especially with respect to the reciprocal relationships between the development of travel routes and the location of settlements along these routes. In general, the students thought more in terms of settlements being built along the routes as service centers for travelers and their vehicles than in terms of travel routes (highways, railroad tracks) being constructed to facilitate transportation between pre-existing settlements. Most of them were familiar with the former, microlevel relationships through long-distance travel experiences with their families (e.g., on vacations), but their purviews did not yet encompass the latter, macrolevel relationships.

The students were more aware of water than of mountains as formidable barriers to long-distance travel, and they were much more heavily focused on personal travel than on the transportation of goods or raw materials. Finally, they were often vague or confused about the reciprocal relationships between the development of travel routes and the location of settlements along these routes.

THE EFFECT OF A HIGHWAY ON A SMALL TOWN

16. Suppose you lived in a small town out in the country and a big highway was built right through it. How would your town be different after the highway was built? How would it be better? How would it be worse?

K   16. You could drive on it. (How would your town be better?) Well, life would be weird and stuff. (How would it be worse?) If it didn't have any trees and no animals and no cars and no trains. (But you're putting in a highway, so how would it be worse if they put a highway in?) That would be good because people could drive on it.

1st   16. I think we could go faster in cars. (Why would you be able to go faster?) Well, because the highway is where people can go faster in cars. (OK, how would your life be different if the highway was built through your town?) They would be better. (Would there be anything that would be worse if you had a highway running through the middle of your town?) No.

2nd   16. There would be like a lot of cars going by, and you like couldn't play street hockey or stuff like that. (Anything else that would be different?) No. (Are there any ways it would be better for your town?) No. (Anything you can think of that would be worse once you had the highway in your town?) That it would be really busy and if you lived by a dirt road, then all the dust would get in your eyes if you were going out in your driveway.

3rd   16. It would be easier to go on the highway but it would be really noisy and there wouldn't be any peace and quiet so you couldn't hardly get any sleep because of the cars going past.

Even though this question doesn't appear to be very challenging, more than 30% (26) of the students were unable to respond. This again underscores the difficulty that children have with hypothetical questions. Most responses emphasized the negative effects of the highway: more traffic and accidents (36); more noise (24); displacement of people or destruction of houses, parks, or nature in general (17); or other negative outcomes such as pollution, dust, bad smells, or barriers to local travel (10). However, 29 students indicated that the highway would allow people to get to other places more quickly or easily, and 6 thought that it would stimulate construction of more houses and other buildings. Both positive and negative outcomes were mentioned by 20 students.

No student mentioned improvement of the economy (more business for stores, more stores built, more jobs, etc.). Unusual responses included: more dust; you could go up on the highway for a vista view of your house; the highway looming over your house would cause you to get less sunshine; the people who build roads are kind of mean because they take down nice little trees and stuff just to build one little city highway, and a lot of houses and churches would probably be knocked down; there would be less room because highways and cars take up space; it would be hot and sticky near the highway; it would be harder to get to a friend's house who lived nearby but on the other side of the highway (3); it would smell bad (2); there would be air pollution (2).

Even though this was a relatively "macro" question, the students again responded mostly at the microlevel, talking about how the highway would affect individuals (making it harder for them to get out of their driveways, creating irritating noise or pollution, allowing them to get out of town more quickly, etc.) rather than how it would change the town as a whole. The students were much more aware of potential negative effects on the town than potential positive effects. Except for a few references to construction of more houses and other buildings (not always viewed as positive), the students seemed unaware of the effect of a highway in stimulating the local economy.

TRANSPORTATION AND FARMING

The next two questions addressed students' awareness of how innovations in transportation have affected farmers and access to farm products.

17. A long time ago, farmers didn't have trucks. Then they got trucks. How did the farming business change after trucks were built? How did trucks make things different for farmers? [If necessary:] **What difference would it make if farmers could take produce to market in trucks?**

18. Apples grow here in the summer, but not in the winter. But even in winter, we can buy apples. Why is that? [If necessary:] **So you think that the apples in Meijer's were grown here in Michigan and then frozen?** [Meijer's is a prominent Michigan supermarket chain.]

K   17. 'Cause they had wheels and pedals . . . not pedals. Let me think . . . I
          forget.

18. Because you could go to a store and buy some apples. (Where does the store get the apples from?) From these boxes. They're inside these boxes. They'll open the boxes and reach a couple and put them inside the bag. (But where do Meijer's get the apples from in the winter?) Apple trees. The apples could fall off. (So you think the apples in Meijer's were grown here in Michigan?) Yeah.

1st 17. They could get corn from the stores instead of just planting corn all the time and they could get milk from the stores. (OK, how do trucks make things different for farmers?) Well, they could get places faster. (OK. What did the farmers do before they had trucks?) They planted things and they got milk from cows. (Now the farmers would grow the crops, is that right? OK, so how would the farmers get the crops to the stores?) Well, they could walk to stores and they could put them in the back. (OK, so how did things change after farmers got trucks?) They could get the food faster to the stores.

18. Because the farmers grow lots of apples and the apple trees grow lots of apples and they bring them to stores, the people who find them sometimes bring them to the stores and they get lots of apples and then they grow again on the trees. (Any ideas about why we can buy apples here in the wintertime even if they only grow in the summer here in Michigan?) No.

2nd 17. Because then the farmers could get in the truck and go somewhere where they had hay and they could pick hay from there and put it in the truck and then they could drive back to their farm. (What difference would it make if farmers could take the things they produce to market in trucks?) Because if they had too much hay, then they might wrap some up in another bag and take it to the store so other farmers could come and get hay.

18. Because before winter comes if it's getting cold, and there's still apples on your trees, you can go outside and pick them. (But I can buy apples now in the shops. Why is that?) Because the shops might get apples from people and they might take it to the store and sometimes schools might have some apples and they might take it to the food bank, and then the food bank might give some of the apples to the market. (The apples I get at the shop, are they the ones that were grown in the summer in Michigan? Are they the same apples or different ones?) They might be different because there's green apples, yellow apples, and red apples, and the green ones taste a little bit more sour than the red apples do. (So the apples I can buy at Meijer's—where did they come from?) They might come from trees in the summer, they might come from other people's homes, they might come from soft, soft grass on the ground.

3rd   17. There's cars and trucks right now to deliver the food to the markets and the markets sell them, and the farmers just help and sometimes they get money for it, and if there were no trucks today, then the market would have to go to the farmer and get it by hand.

      18. 'Cause you can go to the store and in the summer you can just pick it off from an apple tree instead of going to the store because the store charges money for the apples, and sometimes when the apple tree is right in your yard, then you don't have to pay for it. (You said we can get them from stores. Where do the stores get their apples from?) Sometimes from farmers' apple trees but sometimes from other markets if they need it. (So do the apples that we eat now—do they come from Michigan or do they come from somewhere else?) Probably Michigan but sometimes they can come from somewhere else because you can export them. If my grandpa exported some oranges to us in our area, like they brung it but sometimes they could have just mailed it or they could put it on a truck and export it to Michigan and give it to us.

One third (32) of the students were unable to explain how trucks affected farming. The rest said that farmers could use the trucks to take products to markets (33) or do work on the farm (22), that trucks allowed them to get places faster (14), or that they no longer needed to walk or carry things by hand (14). None said anything about trucks increasing the size or scope of farming operations. Unusual responses included: Farmers could now buy some of their food instead of having to grow it all (2); if farmers wanted to go someplace and not have their cow get sick or something, they could put the cow in the back of the truck and take it with them; store employees could use the trucks to come to farms and pick up produce/milk, so the farmers wouldn't have to interrupt their work to take it to the store; the roads built for the trucks would reduce the available land; food could now be transported to other states.

Responses to Question 18 conveyed little awareness of the role of transportation in bringing fresh farm products to our tables all year round. Only 15 students talked about apples being imported from other states or countries when they are not available locally. The rest either could not respond at all (20), talked only about getting apples from the trees to the stores in the summer and fall (9), or thought that the apples sold in the winter had been picked in the summer and preserved (52). Some of the latter students talked about chilling the apples or taking other steps to preserve them, so they at least were aware that apples eventually rot. Nevertheless, they thought that the apples bought in local stores in the winter had been grown locally, not imported from elsewhere.

Some of the younger students thought that stores would just keep getting apples as needed from farmers (not realizing that apples are only available in season). Several expressed the idea that apples will be good indefinitely if you pick them at the right time, but if you wait too long, they will spoil or freeze. Other responses included: They would grow apples in indoor gardens (greenhouses?); special heated gardens kept at the right temperature are used to grow the apples in the winter; greenhouses are used to preserve picked apples (as opposed to being places to grow them); the apples are kept warm indoors to preserve them; some types of apples grow in the winter.

Responses once again focused on the microlevel, with students talking about how individual farmers might use their trucks but not about how trucks transformed farming as a business, and showing little awareness of the role of transportation in bringing fresh farm products to our local stores all year round. A majority harbored the misconception that apples purchased locally in the winter were grown locally, picked in the summer or fall, and then preserved for sale in the winter.

Few students were aware that harvested fruits and vegetables cannot be stored indefinitely until needed (without processing beyond merely heating or cooling them). Thus, here is an instance where lack of knowledge relating to one cultural universal (food—specifically, knowledge that harvested fruits and vegetables must be preserved if not eaten while ripe) contributed to lack of knowledge about another cultural universal (transportation—specifically, the role of modern transportation systems in bringing fresh fruits and vegetables to our local stores all year round).

K–3 students would stand to benefit not only from general instruction on the role of transportation in bringing products from elsewhere to our local stores, but more specific instruction about how fresh fruits and vegetables are only available in season and the ones that we purchase in other parts of the year are imported from elsewhere.

URBAN TRANSPORTATION

The next two questions focused on forms of transportation found particularly in big cities, to see if students were aware that many people in cities do not own cars or do not use them in the cities because of traffic congestion, the scarcity and cost of parking, and so on, and to see if they knew what taxi cabs are, when and why people use them, and how the fare is determined.

19A. What kinds of transportation do you find in big cities but not in other places?

19B. Why do a lot of people in big cities use buses or subways instead of cars?

20A. What is a taxi cab?

20B. Why do people use taxi cabs? Do they have to pay to use taxi cabs?

20C. How does that work? How does the taxi driver decide how much you should pay?

K   19A. A car. (What sorts of transportation do you find in the city that you don't find in other places?) A plane . . . and trains.

19B. I don't know.

20A. I don't know.

20B. To get to other places. (But what is a taxi?) It's a yellow car and has black and white squares on it and you can get to one place from the other.

20C. I think so. (How does that work—how does the driver decide how much you should pay?) I don't know. One dollar or something, or two dollars, or a hundred dollars. (How does he decide?) He has a brain to think with, and . . . I forget.

1st   19A. I don't know.

19B. Because probably they didn't have cars and they had a little money and they could just drop it in when they're on the subway or the train.

20A. A car.

20B. Because probably they're old and they don't have that much money and if it says you have to pay one dollar, and they only had four quarters, they gave them to them and then he would take them someplace and they could drop off and they'd rest.

20C. Yes. (How does that work? How does the driver decide how much you should pay?) Because they say "I want to go to Michigan" and that's a short drive. They said it would say you have to take one dollar or two or something. (But how do they know it's one dollar or two dollars or five dollars or ten dollars?) Because they knew how short their drive was because they've been in there for a very long time.

2nd   19A. They might use trains, because a lot of people I know don't use trains to go anywhere—they use cars. If their cars run out of gas when they get home, they might use their neighbor's car if they're not going anywhere and then they can drive them to a train and they can ride on the train.

19B. I don't know.

20A. It's a car that if someone might be sick and their mom was close by, then they'd call the taxi and the taxi might take them to the school.

20B. Because their car might run out of gas and they might call a taxi to come and they might go to the taxi.

20C. I don't know.

3rd   19A. In big cities you usually find taxis. Sometimes you can find taxis in Michigan.

19B. Because it's fancier, but if they have a clean car or truck then they don't have to worry. And you get food on them maybe, sometimes. (What do you mean?) Like sometimes on an airplane they serve you, and maybe on a subway, but I don't know.

20A. A taxi cab carries you to places. They say, "What place you want to go?" and you go to that place and then you have to pay them.

20B. So they can get around, because if they don't have a car, then they're going to have to use taxis and pay.

20C. He maybe has a thing for each mile you go and it keeps on rolling and rolling.

A surprisingly high 38 students were unable to respond to Question 19A. Furthermore, the most popular response (36) was cars, which is incorrect. Another 14 students incorrectly said trucks or vans. More correct responses included trains (24), buses (23), planes (16), and taxis (13). Finally, 14 students named other forms of transportation: boats (5); bikes (3); limousines; jet skis; subways (3); trolleys (2); dune buggies; monorails.

When asked why people use buses or subways instead of cars in cities, again 38 students were unable to respond. The rest suggested that the people do not have cars (20), that buses and subways are faster than cars (20), that the people take subways because traffic and stoplights impede surface travel (11), or that it is easier to travel on buses or subways because you do not have to drive yourself (9). Some of these responses make more sense for subways than for buses (e.g., the idea that they are a faster or more convenient way to travel in cities). Unusual responses included: People use buses or subways so that they do not have to pay for gas for their own cars (4); these forms of travel don't cost much; their car might be in the repair shop (2); the bus or subway goes just where they need to go, like near their jobs; they go to places where you haven't been to; cars have speed limits but subways don't; many city people are afraid their cars will be stolen; they are afraid they might get into an accident if they drive; trains are faster because they are powered by electricity that comes in at 2,000 volts per minute; people who use them just got to the city and don't have a car yet (parallel to responses to our shelter interview indicating that people who live in apartments are people who just got to the city and don't have a home yet); they don't want to pollute; the city streets are too crowded to accommodate cars for everyone; there are lots of buses and taxis in the city so you don't need a car; city people cannot afford cars because they buy so much from all the stores; because you can't park your car in a big city; because the subways are free; because they make less pollution.

The students were more successful with Question 20. All but 12 were able to say something about taxi cabs, and what they did say was correct. Majorities defined taxis as cars that take people where they want to go (58) and/or described them as yellow or checkered cars with a taxi sign on the top, a number on the back, and so on (52). Other responses included the idea that a taxi is a car that someone drives for you (25), a car that you pay to use (24), or a car that will stop and pick you up if you signal it by waving or whistling (13).

Asked why people use taxis, more than half (46) of the 86 who responded said that people use taxis when they don't have a car to use. Another 37 were less explicit about lack of a car but did describe taxis as auto transportation that people use for local travel. Seven said that using taxis is cheaper than buying or renting a car. Other responses included: Taxis are a way to get home if you forgot where you left your car; they put in their luggage and go to a hotel (i.e., people who have just arrived in town); old people like taxis because you can just rest and be driven around; you can avoid driving in urban traffic where it is hard to even get out of your driveway; you use a taxi when you don't know how to get there on your own; when your car is too small for the group that will be traveling together; if the buses are full; because you don't get squished like on buses; used by people who live in areas not served by buses; taxis are faster because taxi drivers don't get tickets for speeding.

Almost half (45) of the students understood that people do have to pay to use taxies and that the fare is determined by the distance traveled. The remaining responses varied in accuracy: Twelve students did not know whether or not people have to pay or said that they do not, 18 could not explain how the fare is determined or simply guessed a dollar amount without explanation, 11 said that they pay what it says on the meter (but did not explain how the meter arrives at the number), 6 said that the cost of the ride is determined by the number of people in the taxi or the number of stops that it makes, 14 said that the cost is determined by the time required for the trip, and 7 said that the fare is determined by the driver's boss (without further explanation). Finally, one student thought that all riders pay the same amount (flat fee), one that you have to pay more if the taxi looks like a limousine, and one that the cost of the ride depends on how much gas is required.

Responses to Question 19 were surprisingly poor. When asked about forms of transportation found in big cities but not in other places, 40% were unable to respond and more than half of the rest mentioned cars, trucks, or vans. Apparently, the qualification at the end of the question ("but not in other places") didn't register with most of the latter students.

Most of the students understood that city dwellers often ride trains, buses, or subways because they do not have cars or because public transportation may be cheaper, faster, or more convenient for them than driving/parking in a congested inner city. Also, a heavy majority understood that taxis are cars hired for local transportation by people who do not have a car available at the time. Older students usually knew that the fare is determined by the length of the trip, but younger students usually were unable to respond or could only guess how fares are determined.

A few students made reference to crowding and hassle involved in train travel, but most depicted bus and subway riding in a positive light: City people might prefer to ride buses or subways because someone else does the driving for them; it might be a quick and convenient way to get to work or school, and in the case of subways, a way to avoid traffic and stop lights on the surface. No student mentioned having to wait or to walk to and from the bus stop or subway station.

HOW CARS WORK

21. How does a car work—what makes it go?

K 21. The motor and the pedals and the brake, and I forget what else. (How does the motor work?) You put in the keys and twist the keys this way and then the motor goes. (How does it make the car move?) Because of the motor and the wheels and the brake.

1st 21. The wheels and the pedals, and the motor helps it—like connects to the thing and it goes round right here and it connects right here. Then you step on the pedal and the wheel—the back wheels— move. (Probably those move too?) Yeah, and these ones turn, but these ones don't move because these have the . . . (The front wheels have what?) The turning thing. The wheel's connected to the steering wheel, and the steering wheel's connected to this. (To the front wheels?) Yeah, and you can turn but these don't move and this . . . they just roll. (The back wheels just roll?) Yeah, they move the car and the front wheels are connected to the steering wheel and these turn, but these ones don't move, they just roll to get to the other places and stuff. (What makes the back wheels move?) The motor. (How does that work?) I don't know. (That's a great explanation. Is there anything else that makes a car work—that makes a car go?) I think it is the exhaust because when you step on the pedal, the exhaust comes out. And it takes like gas in it and it'll sssshhhh. Yeah, so it won't like go like if you turn the air conditioner on. It doesn't go swwwoooo right in there. And the exhaust takes the gas from this and it goes ffffssss out of the back. (Out of the tail pipe?) Yeah.

2nd 21. The engine. (How does the engine make the car go?) I don't know.

3rd 21. I think it would be the engine because that would make it go real fast, and the radiator would make it go faster, and if they don't have a wheel, it won't turn or nothing. (How does the engine make the car move?) An engine will make it go faster and makes it move. (Yes, but how does it do that?) The oil in it starts up and starts going. It's hooked up to the wheels probably. Yeah, it's hooked up to this thing called disk brakes and that makes the wheels go.

All but three students named one or more car parts: the motor or engine (74), oil or gasoline (62), the wheels (32), the pedals (27), the steering wheel (17), the battery (6), and miscellaneous "other" parts such as wires (22). Probed for explanations, 40% were unable to respond but the rest provided responses that were generally accurate as far as they went in identifying steps or processes involved in "making a car go": Fifteen spoke of starting the car with a key, 17 mentioned pushing on the gas pedal, 25 said that the engine makes the wheels turn, 27 said that gasoline is needed, and 15 made miscellaneous other observations: Wires from the engine make the car go; the battery gives power to the engine; piston motion in the engine is transferred to the wheels; the engine makes "like air" in the wheels and they spin; gas travels to all parts of the car and makes them go; gas goes "somewhere" in the car to make it go; the car burns gas and "once it's burned up, there's enough fuel and it's ready to go"; the engine, which has plugs everywhere, gives power to the car, and then the car gives it to the driver's steering wheel and the car goes; when you step on the gas pedal, "the exhaust comes out"; gas has "lightning power" that makes the car move; the engine "sends a force" and the wheels go; the engine "blows air" or does something else to make the wheels go (analogy to a jet engine); there's a cord in the engine that gets pulled to start it (analogy to lawn mower); the gas tank is at the rear of the car so it can get gas to the rear wheels more quickly; the gas starts at one part of the car and then works its way through the other parts to make it go (one of several "traveling gas" responses).

A good response that contains some unusual elements: "Probably the gas—the gas tank—it goes to the engine." (How does that work?) "It probably has some sort of suction cup that drains the gas out of it. It goes from a tube to the engine. It starts to boil the water in there and the engine warms up and gets going. In old cars, you had to wind it to get it started. Then you pushed the pedal of the car and it will go." (What does the pedal do?) "It puts pressure on it. You might push a little lever and push a button and make it go forwards or backwards. Something like that."

A student who uses specialized terms but nevertheless is confused about the workings of the engine: "You press on this thing called a radiator or one of the brakes that make it go, and that will start the radiator in the engine. That goes to the battery and the battery goes to the fuel tank, so the car starts getting shaky and then it starts moving slowly and then it gets faster."

Perhaps the best response: "The motor works by gas which travels from the gas tank into the generator and then the generator gives it to the motor which has motions [makes up and down piston motions with hands]. They move up and down really fast inside the motor, and sometimes it goes out the exhaust pipe with a fire thingy, and that's how the motor works."

The engine was a black box for the vast majority of the students, even those who mentioned it spontaneously. Consequently, their responses to this question focused more on what the driver does (start it with a key, give it gas, etc.) than on the functioning of the engine or other mechanical parts that "make the car go."

Responses often were less sophisticated than the category labels imply. Students who spoke of "pushing down the pedal to make the car go" were coded in Category 3, even though they may not have mentioned the engine and may not have known what happens when the driver pushes on the pedal (i.e., that this is a gas pedal and depressing it feeds more gas to the engine). Terms often were used in ways that showed that the student did not understand their meanings or functions. No student gave a clear explanation subsuming the key elements that gasoline (mixed with air) is burned within the cylinders to create explosions that move the pistons, and this piston movement in the engine is transferred to the axle to make the car's wheels move. Three students did talk about piston movement in the engine resulting in movement of the wheels and thus the car, but none of them mentioned burning of gasoline or explosions that get the pistons moving in the first place.

Most students understood that gasoline is needed to run a car, but they were vague about why it is needed or what happens to it once it is in the car. Even those who talked about the gasoline traveling throughout the various parts of the car and eventually coming out the exhaust in gaseous form typically had only black-box theories of the engine or the other workings of the car. Only a few mentioned that the gas gets burned, and none described explosions that initiate piston movement.

Most explanations either were simply incorrect or else mixed incorrect elements with correct ones. Most of the latter were black-box responses that spoke of gas traveling to various parts of the car and these parts somehow becoming activated and making the car go. Occasionally a student articulated a more substantive (but incorrect) theory, such as the third grader who first spoke about boiling water in the engine to heat it up and get it going, then went on to offer an explanation of the motion of the car that did not involve the workings of the engine but instead indicated that the driver's foot pressure on "the pedal of the car" was magnified through a system of levers to create sufficient pressure on the wheels to begin turning them.

PROBLEMS CREATED BY MOTOR VEHICLES

Question 22 was designed to assess students' awareness that, besides facilitating travel, motor vehicles create congestion, noise, pollution, and other problems.

22. It's nice to have cars and trucks, but they create problems too. What are some problems that exist in places where most people drive cars or trucks? [Probe for knowledge of noise, traffic, pollution, etc. For students who respond in terms of breakdowns of one's own car, say:] **OK—that would be for your car. But I was wondering if places where there are a lot of cars have problems because there are so many cars there?**

K   22. I don't know.

1st 22. Because it's crowded and it goes vrrrooommm, vrrrooommm and
         they like crash into each other like all the cars crash into each other
         and it's both their fault because they don't know where they're go-
         ing.

2nd 22. They might get in an accident. (OK, anything else that might be a
         problem?) No. (Well, think about a big highway—lots of cars drive
         over it and lots of trucks. Would you want your house to be really
         near that highway . . . ? No? Why wouldn't you want to live near the
         highway?) Because they would be going fast and if there was a ball
         out there, they would be going fast and then you could probably get
         hit [if you tried to retrieve the ball]. (OK, you could get hit. Why else
         wouldn't you want to live near the highway?) Because if it's like a
         dirt road, then all the dirt will fly and then it will like mess up your
         house—all your windows will be all dusty and stuff.

3rd 22. In traffic you could beep the horn where it hurts somebody's ear, or it
         crashes. (So there could be crashes and there could be lots of noise.
         Are there any other problems we have in places where there are lots
         of cars and trucks?) Yeah, New York has a bunch of cars and trucks
         and beeping maybe, and maybe somebody goes too fast to get there
         and it might crash.

The most common problem noted was accidents (43); followed by congestion,
delays, and traffic jams (27); pollution in the form of dust, gas/oil spills, or air pollution (18); noise (12); and busy streets that make it difficult for people or animals to cross (8). A few students mentioned other problems: shortage of parking
places, broken roads and bridges; cars sometimes stall; you have to put gas in cars
and that costs money; sometimes there are gas shortages; the engine could catch
on fire (2); road construction reduces space available for other uses; and you
could accidentally put a manual transmission in reverse and blow it.

Not surprisingly given their previous responses concerning the effect of building a highway through a small country town, most of the students found it easy to
answer our question about problems that exist in places where most people drive
cars or trucks. Most of them named at least one problem and none communicated
misconceptions.

MAPS

23. What is a map? When do people need maps?

K   23. A map is a piece of paper and it has kind of like . . . it's a map of the
         whole world and you can get from one place to the other. (When do

people need maps?) Pirates them need. (Why?) Because to get to their treasure. (When are some other times people need maps?) I don't know.

1st 23. Well, a map is when you're stuck somewhere, and you don't know where you are, you should get a map out because a map helps people know where they should go. (How does the map help people know where to go?) They could go like . . . I don't know. (When do people need maps?) When they're stuck someplace.

2nd 23. It's this big thing that shows you the states and it might have a park like Yellowstone where there's buffalo when you drive to it and there's this stinky smell of smoke. (When do people need maps?) Because sometimes it can show you where to go if you need to get somewhere and you can't remember which way to go.

3rd 23. It shows you where to go. It shows places, like L.A. and you take your truck and you have to bring a boat too, so you bring a boat, and you get there and walk to a place. Or you could use an airplane. (When do people need maps?) They need them when they don't know where to go usually, because when you get lost you have to have a map.

All but six of the students were familiar with maps, at least at the level of their nature and purposes. A heavy majority (80) described maps as resources to use when you need information about how to get from one place to another. They further specified that you would use a map when you didn't know how to find a place (73) when traveling or going to a faraway place (51), or when you were lost (33). Unusual responses included: If you have no idea about places that you might want to visit, you could look at maps for ideas; you use maps on treasure hunts; pirates use them; road racers use them; there are two kinds of maps—one to look at and locate places (atlas or broad geography map) and one to tell you how to get there (smaller scale road map).

In addition to or instead of describing maps as resources to use when you need to know how to get from one place to another, 35 students described a map as a representation of a geographical area (state, nation, world) or as something that shows you where places are. These responses emphasized physical descriptions of maps, whereas the more common responses emphasized their functions. Again, most students understood the nature and function of maps and no misconceptions were expressed.

FOREIGN TRAVEL

24. If people want to go to another country, can they just go, or do they have to get permission? [If they need permission, who do they have to get permission from? If student speaks of a child asking parental permission, ask:] **Do grown-ups have to get permission to go to another country?**

K 24. Permission. (Who do they have to get permission from?) I don't know.

1st 24. They can just go.

2nd 24. They can just go, but if they're at work and they need to do something on the day they need to go, they might ask their boss if they can do it the next time they come when they get off their vacation.

3rd 24. They have to get permission because they have to have this card, because my teacher says you have to have this card. (So you're saying you need a card and your teacher had a card?) Yeah, you have to have a card and you can't bring anything back usually, and you have to have a card to get past, like if you want to go to China, you have to have this card that says . . . and you can't bring any of your . . . I think you might be able to bring some of your money there. I don't know.

Many students initially responded in terms of children getting permission from their parents. Once this was clarified, most said either that adults do not require permission to travel to other countries or that they need permission from airlines, hotels, or people with whom they will be staying. Only 17 understood that travelers require permission from the governments of the countries involved. Only one student mentioned a passport and none mentioned a visa. Unusual responses included: You can leave our country without permission, but in some countries you can't (goes on to refer to Elian Gonzales); to go to Russia, you would have to get a green card if you were going to stay for the rest of your life, but otherwise you could just go; if you are divorced and want to take your children out of state, you need permission from your ex-spouse. The students were relatively vague about the officials or processes involved. Seven referred to getting permission from the police or from officials at the border and various others spoke of getting permission from the government, the king, or the president.

TRAFFIC CONTROL

25. Why do we need stoplights on our streets? What would happen if we didn't have them?

K 25. Because they keep yourself safe. The red light is stop to keep you safe, then the yellow light is slow down to keep you safe, and the green light means go. (How do they keep you safe?) Because even if it's busy and the light's green, stay there until the traffic is stopped and all the cars have gone this way. (What would happen if we didn't have stop lights?) You could crash into another car.

1st 25. Because they tell people if cars are coming other ways. (Any other reasons why we need stop lights?) No. (What would happen if we didn't have stop lights?) Then sometimes we won't have any cars because they're all going to be in a car crash. (Why would there be car crashes if they weren't any stop lights?) Because they wouldn't know if the cars were coming your way because they got to keep their eye on the way they're going.

2nd 25. So then like if somebody's coming like this, so then they don't bash into each other. (OK, so how do the stoplights keep people from bashing into each other?) If there's a lot of traffic coming like this, then this light turns red, and then you have to wait until all the cars go past, and then it turns green and you can go.

3rd 25. Because if we didn't have stop lights, then everybody would crash and it would be a big disaster and everybody . . . most of the people would be killed and we don't want that so we put stop lights up, and now they take turns, but sometimes they don't because they just want to go and sometimes there's accidents, but most of the time there's stop lights and they don't crash, but sometimes they do.

This question proved to be relatively easy for most students. Only 6 of them could not respond, and a heavy majority (83) said that without stoplights there would be many more accidents. Other responses indicated that stoplights control traffic and make sure that people stop for each other (46), that cars would crash if we did not have them (33), that pedestrians would find it difficult to cross busy streets safely without them (10), or that they fulfill other functions such as preventing traffic jams and keeping people from traveling too fast. Although the vast majority knew that stoplights control traffic flow so as to minimize accidents, few if any seemed aware that they also make traffic more efficient, so that people are able to get to their destinations more quickly and easily than they would if traffic were not controlled.

DISCUSSION

Compared to responses to previous interviews (on food, clothing, shelter, and communication), responses to the transportation interview were generally more accurate (as far as they went) and less riddled with misconceptions. Perhaps this was because most of our questions addressed relatively concrete and observable functions and uses of modes of transportation, rather than their underlying natures (with the notable exception of the question about what makes a car go).

However, two major limitations in the responses should be noted. First, on many of the questions, surprisingly high percentages of the students were unable to provide a substantive response. Second, the responses that were provided almost always focused on the microlevel of the activities of individuals or families, without addressing the macrolevel of society in general or the world at large. As a result, students frequently missed the point of or gave only very limited responses to certain questions, especially questions about the impact of inventions.

Instruction about the impact of transportation innovations might begin by establishing that prior to the invention of the wheel, people had to walk everywhere and carry or drag anything that they needed to move. Wheeled vehicles simplified these transportation tasks enormously, especially once people learned to use large animals to pull them. This also enabled people to travel farther and faster, thus coming into contact and engaging in trade with more of the people in their part of the world. This in turn speeded up the spread of inventions and other products of culture.

Even with ox carts or comparable wheeled conveyances, however, travel was slow and difficult; frequently impeded by deep rivers, thick forests, or hilly terrain; and bounded by large bodies of water, deserts, or mountains. Improvements in shipping and the development of ports that linked land and water routes made it possible to overcome some of the water barriers to travel, and sometimes travel between oases made it possible to cross deserts and travel through passes made it possible to cross mountains. Still, these forms of travel were slow and their capacities for moving goods and raw materials were limited. Thus, until recently in human history, most people made do with products grown or manufactured locally and rarely traveled far from their homes.

This changed dramatically with the development of engine-powered vehicles, first trains and later ships, cars, and planes. Once the needed infrastructure (train tracks and stations, port facilities, highways, airports, etc.) developed to allow these forms of transportation to proliferate, it became possible to travel at much more rapid speeds, to move heavy loads of not only people but raw materials and products, and to cross deserts, oceans, and mountains quickly. Communities sprung up along travel routes, not only to service the travelers but to process farm products for shipment to markets and raw materials for shipment to factories. People could not only accomplish local travel more easily but enjoy products brought in from a much broader range of places and migrate more easily if life was difficult for them at their place of birth. Communities became more connected to other communities, and eventually the world became one big network with lots of interconnections.

K–3 students should be able to understand these and related big ideas about macrolevel changes in society, especially if they are presented with frequent reference to microlevel implications and examples. Maps and other artifacts could be used to illustrate the effective size of the "world" inhabited by a child or family living at a particular time and place in history, with emphasis on the ways in which available travel affordances and limitations affected the directions and distances that this "world" extended from the local community (and the implications of this for access to other people, cultures, products, and inventions).

Within this big picture, the instruction might address some of the misconceptions and gaps in knowledge displayed by our interviewees. First, the students should be helped to understand that the transportation of goods is at least as important as the transportation of people—modern living depends on access to steady supplies of goods grown or manufactured elsewhere. Even today, if we lost this access, our lives would be dependent on resource affordances and constraints prevailing in our region of the world.

Although Flintstones and Alley Oop cartoons are enjoyable, they are misleading. Back in the Stone Age, people did fashion primitive tools and weapons from small pieces of stone, but they lacked the knowledge and tools that would enable them to sculpt large boulders into vehicles or houses. The kinds of stone vehicles seen in these cartoons are completely imaginary—they never existed at any time in any culture.

Transportation innovations brought sweeping changes to whole societies, not just to individuals wanting to travel for personal reasons. Once they acquired horses, for example, the plains tribes that hunted the buffalo could patrol a much greater expanse of land from a given location, and could travel much farther, faster, once they decided it was time to pack up and move. Railroads (and subsequently, trucking and air shipping) made it possible to bring the amenities of contemporary living to frontier locations. If they had the money to pay for it, people living in western outposts could enjoy the same kinds of housing, clothing, food, and other luxuries enjoyed by wealthy people in the more established eastern cities. Today, modern transportation makes it possible for those who can afford it to enjoy modern lifestyles and conveniences even if they live in polar regions, high on mountains, in desert oases, or on remote islands.

Instead of being confined by local geography, humans increasingly are reshaping it to suit their needs or desires (e.g., using irrigation to farm in desert climates) and compensating for it by importing what is not available locally. This point might be illustrated through activities involving learning about which foods, raw materials for clothing or heating, and so on are plentiful locally, and which must be imported (and from where). In addition, it is likely that whatever is abundant locally provides the basis for industries that not only supply local needs but export products elsewhere, thus bringing money into the community that can be used for purchasing products that must be imported. Students can learn something about the local economy by studying these import/export relationships.

Students also can begin to understand and appreciate the infrastructure that supports modern transportation. Motor vehicles require a system of good roads to enable them to travel efficiently, bridges are needed to allow cars and trains to cross rivers, tunnels are needed to allow them to go through mountains, and air travel requires not only airports but a system to regulate flight patterns and avoid crashes. As systems develop, more and more things get standardized (traffic signals, shipping containers, railway gauges, the interstate highway system, etc.), which makes the system as a whole more efficient.

Centrality of location continues to be important even today. People living in major transportation hubs such as Chicago or Atlanta have more and cheaper access to consumer goods than people living in Alaska or other more remote areas. Even locally, people living in major cities or communities located on major highways have better access than people living in sparsely populated rural areas. An interstate highway or other major route that brings a lot of traffic through a town will stimulate new businesses and have other economic and social effects (both positive and negative), and the opposite effects will occur in nearby towns located on roads that lose much of their traffic volume once the new highway opens. Even today, some places are still isolated—remote islands, polar communities, roadless wildernesses, and mountain valleys. However, their isolation is much less absolute than in the past, and each year they become better connected with the rest of the world.

Life would be quite different today if we had trains but not cars. There would be many more rail lines criss-crossing populated areas, and they would be better connected to facilitate transfers between one line and another. Even so, door-to-door travel would be much less convenient. People would have to walk or ride bicycles to the nearest train station, then proceed from there to the train station nearest to their destination, then walk again. Most shopping would be very local, and purchases would have to be carried home or transported in wagons or shopping carts. Furniture and other heavy purchases would have to be delivered on horse-drawn wagons. Land along rail lines and especially near stations would be at a premium, and most people would live in high-rise apartment buildings located in these areas rather than in single-family homes in suburbs. There would be no air travel, so fewer people would leave their countries or travel to distant places on vacation. Life would be more local and the pace of change would be slower.

Primary-grade students should be able to follow a basic explanation of engines and how they power wheeled vehicles (controlled explosions in the cylinders move the pistons, and a series of mechanical connections convert the up-and-down motion of the pistons to the revolving motion of the axel, which moves the vehicle). Well-illustrated books written for children are now available on this topic.

Engine power has fueled the transformation from small family farms to modern agribusiness. This can be seen not only in the tractors, combines, and other modern farm machinery that enable families to farm much more land than they could in the past, but also in the trucks and other components of the contemporary delivery system that make it possible to transport a farm's entire crop to a food manufacturing company or supermarket chain shortly after harvesting. Except for orchards that provide seasonal fruit, it is more the exception than the rule now for farmers to sell their crops to local food stores. For an outline of basic ideas about modern agribusiness and the role of transportation within it, see Project 2061 (2001).

Cars provide wonderfully convenient personal transportation for those who can afford them, so they are very popular, especially in the United States. However, they are expensive to own and maintain, require parking places, and contribute to air pollution. These problems are magnified in densely populated urban areas, where many people do not make enough money to afford a car and those who do may avoid driving it in the city because of traffic congestion and high parking fees. Consequently, many urban residents depend on mass transportation to get around in the city. In addition, many people who work in the city are commuters who live in the suburbs. They drive or take mass transportation into the city each morning, work at their jobs during the day, and then return to their suburbs in the evening. In addition to mass transportation (buses, trains, subways), people who live or work in cities (and especially, people visiting cities on business or vacation) can hire taxis to provide personal transportation.

Drivers are subject to traffic laws and rules of the road, which include observing speed limits and responding to stoplights. These regulations are established to keep travelers safe, and in the case of dense urban traffic, to enable people to move more efficiently than they could otherwise. Besides regulating internal traffic, governments regulate travel into and out of their countries. They usually require travelers to present a passport or other photo identification that tells their names, citizenship, and other information about them, and they may impose restrictions on what can be brought into or taken out of their country.

The authors have included these and other basic ideas about transportation in a unit on the topic prepared for primary-grade students. For details, see Alleman and Brophy (2002).

7

Family Living

Our family living interviews asked students:

- to define families and talk about why most people live in families;
- to define grandparents, aunts and uncles, cousins, and step-siblings;
- to talk about ways that families get bigger or smaller and how their needs change accordingly;
- to explain marriage and divorce;
- to talk about ways in which today's families are both similar to and different from families in the past;
- to explain why today's families usually have fewer children than families in the past;
- to make past versus present comparisons concerning the activities of fathers, mothers, and children;
- to talk about why extended families tended to live together in America in the past and still do in some countries today, but this pattern is no longer widespread in America;
- to make past versus present comparisons concerning the amount of time that children spend with their parents;
- to talk about family-related customs in other countries;
- to talk about family life on farms, in small towns, and in big cities;
- to talk about where their ancestors came from and why they emigrated to America;
- to talk about why families today move from one place to another and even from one country to another;

- to talk about how family life might change when a family moves to a new country;
- to explain why children go to school for many more years today than in the past;
- to identify things that children typically learn at home from their families;
- to explain why families need rules;
- to explain how families can get help in emergencies;
- to talk about what families can do to help other families and their communities in general.

RESEARCH ON CHILDREN'S KNOWLEDGE ABOUT FAMILIES

Considerable research is available about some aspects of children's ideas about families and family living (especially their knowledge of kinship relations), whereas little or none is available about other aspects (e.g., their knowledge of changes over time in family structures and activities). Edwards (1984) synthesized the findings of much of this research. She noted that young children are deeply concerned about people's connections to one another and want to know to whom they particularly "belong." Children realize that some of the people they know are special to them. They use kinship terms in talking about their social relationships, but often conflate friendships and family relationships. Adults define friendships as voluntary, self-chosen relationships based on ties of liking, common interests, and so on, but define family relationships in terms of genealogical and legal kinship connections. Young children usually do not understand these connections, so they are more likely to think about family in terms of closeness and support. In addition, the connections are blurred in some subcultures and individual families in which close friends are referred to as aunts, uncles, or cousins.

Fischer, Hand, Watson, VanParys, and Tucker (1984) suggested that children develop from concrete to abstract levels of understanding kinship and family concepts. They identified four steps in this process.

Step 1: Concrete categorical concepts. Children begin to use kinship terms as social labels at about age 3 (Chambers & Tavuchis, 1976; Danziger, 1957; Edwards, 1984; Elkind, 1962; Haviland & Clark, 1974; Jordan, 1980; Piaget, 1946/1971). Typically, they use only the most common terms (*mother, father, grandmother, grandfather,* etc.) and apply them to people both inside and outside the family. They do not understand the kinship relations and cannot coordinate them. For example, they think of a "mother" as a woman and a "son" as a boy, without understanding that in order to be a mother, a woman must have a son or daughter.

Step 2: Early relational concepts. Around age 4 or age 5, children begin to coordinate these social categories. They now understand that kinship terms imply a relationship between two people, but they are vague about its nature. They may think that people are relatives because they live in the same house or like each other a lot.

Step 3: Later relational concepts. Beginning about age 6 or age 7, children start to coordinate multiple kinship roles into a "web of relations." They begin to understand that one person can occupy many kinship roles at once (be one person's wife, another's mother, another's sister, etc.). They begin to move away from the "closeness" definition of a family toward a kinship-based definition, often mentioning a third person when asked to explain the relationship between two people. They also begin to include relatives such as grandparents and cousins on their family lists, and to understand that a family member who moves out of the household still remains related. Kinship concepts that can be understood from the child's point of view (*mother, sister,* etc.) are mastered earlier than concepts that require an adult's perspective (*daughter, granddaughter,* etc.). Age of mastery also is related to the number of logical steps required to define the relationship (e.g., aunt is more difficult than mother, niece and cousin are more difficult than son and daughter).

Step 4: Fully abstract concepts. Children's ability to define kinship terms develops throughout middle childhood. By adolescence, they can understand their culture's kinship system in an abstract way. For example, blood relatives are permanent and given "by nature" but spouses and in-laws that are gained "by law" and are divorceable (except for adoption, which severs the biological kinship and establishes new kinship relations based on law). Adolescents also come to understand that kinship systems are cultural inventions, so that people in different cultures may learn different rules (e.g., concerning whom to refer to as "aunt" or "cousin").

Separation and divorce complicate these understandings. Prior to age 6 or age 7, children conceive of a parent as someone who lives in the household, so they may think that if the parent moves out, he or she is no longer the parent. Also, they may think that when a father divorces his wife, he divorces his children as well.

We found a few additional studies that relate to the kinship findings summarized by Edwards (1984). Thornburg (1983) presented 4 to 8-year-old children with a photograph of four siblings and their parents, then asked questions such as "This is the father. Whose father is it? Are there any other fathers?" Then she gave them abstract figures of various sizes and invited them to make their "very own family" and identify the people in it. Analyses indicated that correct answers to the questions were supplied by 63% of the 4-year-olds, 67% of the 5-year-olds, and 67% of the 6-year-olds, but 81% of the 7-year-olds, and 88% of the 8-year-olds. There were no differences according to gender, race, or family size.

Chambers and Tavuchis (1976) explored the defining characteristics that first- and third-grade children used in conceptualizing 17 American kin terms. They found that the students often were unable to respond to their questions, and that when they did identify relationships, they did not all base their identifications on the same attributes.

Diez-Martinez Day and Remigy (1999) studied the family conceptions expressed by 5-, 8-, and 11-year-old Mexican and French children. They found that the younger children used very concrete criteria for classifying families. Their understanding was focused on partial and fortuitous aspects of social relationships rather than on biologically based kinship.

Mazur (1990) asked children aged 5 to 10 about five themes in reference to a storyline illustrated with paper dolls: marriage, divorce without children, divorce with young children, remarriage, and stepparents. She found that children's understandings were related to their ages but not their parents' marital status. Older children's reasoning was both more concrete and practical and more complex and psychological. Younger children were focused on the obvious and superficial behaviors and appearances of spouses, stepparents, and stepchildren (again, influenced more by proximity and social relationships than by genealogical or legal relationships).

Finally, several studies have addressed understandings of inheritance and parent–child resemblances. Springer (1996) conducted two experiments to evaluate whether young children understand that kinship implies, but does not guarantee, physical resemblance. In the first study, preschoolers showed that they expected adopted babies to share physical characteristics with their biological parents but beliefs and preferences with their adoptive parents. In Study 2, preschoolers expressed recognition that shared physical characteristics do not guarantee kinship: A baby who looks like and lives with a woman is not her biological child if he or she initially grew inside someone else, and babies do not necessarily resemble nor live with their biological parents. In both studies, there was an increase with age in understanding that parents and offspring tend to share physical characteristics, but physical resemblances do not necessarily entail kinship.

Horobin (1997) interviewed K–3 students to determine their understandings of biological inheritance in illustrated stories about animals born and raised under four conditions: normal biological parentage and rearing, adoptive rearing, interuterine transplant parentage and rearing with own species, and interuterine transplant parentage and rearing with transplant species. The results indicated that children thought it most likely that the offspring would resemble their original species, in both physical characteristics and behavior. However, they sometimes perceived the transplant conditions as having biological implications for inheritance.

Solomon, Johnson, Zaitchik, and Carey (1996) reported contrasting findings. In their initial study, 4- to 7-year-old children were told a story in which a boy was born to a man who had green eyes but then adopted by a man who had brown eyes, then asked which man the boy would resemble when he grew up. It was not until age 7 that children consistently expected the boy to resemble his biological father in physical features but his adoptive father in beliefs. Follow-up studies replicated the initial study, leading the authors to question claims that preschoolers understand biological inheritance.

More recently, Richards (2000) argued that understanding of inheritance and the genetic bases for kinship relationships is limited even in adults. Many social (as opposed to genealogical) concepts of kinship developed by children are sustained by everyday social activities and relationships, so they may be particularly resistant to change.

Hirschfield (2001) summarized controversies that have arisen concerning children's naive theories of both biology (including inheritance and family resemblances) and sociology (including family and kinship). He concluded that earlier investigators (notably Piaget) tended to underestimate children's understanding, but more recent ones credit them with "a more nuanced, if covert, understanding of the concept of family" (p. 108).

OUR FAMILY LIVING INTERVIEWS

Family living interviews were done with 96 students, 24 in each of Grades K–3, stratified within grade by achievement level and gender. Descriptive statistics and information from analysis of scores derived from the coding are given in Table 7.1. For details of the findings, see the technical report (Brophy & Alleman, 2001b).

THE NATURE OF AND REASONS FOR FAMILIES

1. **Today we're going to talk about families. What is a family?** [Probe for whatever the student can say about the composition and nature or functioning of a family.]

2. **Why do most people live in families?**

K   1. I have a grandma and a grandpa and I have a brother and a dad and I also have lots of cousins, and me and my mom. (What is a family?) It's where you love all your family. (Can you tell me anything else about a family?) No. (Well, who can be in a family?) Grandmas and grandpas and aunts and uncles and moms and dads. (Anybody else?) I don' t know . . . children. (What things do families do?) They all love each other and they get together. (Anything else?) I don't know. (You told me families get together. Why do they get together?) 'Cause they love each other.

     2. 'Cause they love each other.

TABLE 7.1
Distributions and Phi Coefficients Showing Relationships
of Coding Categories to Grade Level

Response Categories	Total 96	K 24	1 24	2 24	3 24	Phi
1. Today we're going to talk about families. What is a family?						
0. Doesn't know/no relevant response	14	7	6	1	0	–36
1. A group of people who are related (through birth or marriage)	11	1	0	4	6	31
2. Parents and their children (or some larger group centered around this nucleus)	10	3	4	2	1	
3. People who live together	30	8	5	9	8	
4. People who do things together	35	7	8	11	9	
5. People who love/help/take care of each other	37	7	9	10	11	
6. Includes grandparents, uncles, aunts, cousins, stepsiblings or other relatives	38	7	12	10	9	
7. Includes pets	34	7	10	7	10	
2. Why do most people live in families?						
0. Doesn't know/no relevant response (they want to, they're family, etc.)	31	9	10	5	7	
1. To get basic physical needs met (food, shelter, etc.)	14	2	4	5	3	
2. So that they are not alone and have others to live with	12	1	5	4	2	
3. Because they love/want to take care of/want to help one another	27	9	6	5	7	
4. Because people get married/have children	21	2	4	7	8	24
3A. Families include grandparents, aunts and uncles, and cousins. What are grandparents?						
0. Doesn't know/ no relevant response/incorrect response (they are your mom and dad, etc.)	25	13	8	4	0	–46
1. They are old/look old/look like grandparents	14	6	3	3	2	
2. They are your parents' parents	52	5	10	16	21	51
3B. What are aunts and uncles?						
0. Doesn't know/no relevant response	24	12	9	0	3	–46
1. Incorrect response (confuses them with godparents, cousins, etc.)	10	2	3	4	1	
2. Says that they are special to you, love you, and so on, but does not specify relationship	9	4	2	1	2	
3. Can give only partial information (says that they are brothers or sisters but cannot say to whom, that aunts are female and uncles are male, that uncle became uncle because he married aunt, they are related to you, etc.)	13	4	4	2	3	
4. Correctly states that aunts and uncles are sisters and brothers to one's parents (or sons and daughters of one's grandparents, or parents of one's cousins)	41	3	6	17	15	50

(Continued)

TABLE 7.1
(Continued)

Response Categories	Total	K	1	2	3	Phi
	96	24	24	24	24	
3C. What are cousins?						
0. Doesn't know/no relevant response	25	9	11	4	1	−38
1. Friends/playmates (no relationship specified)	19	7	7	2	3	−24
2. Knows that cousins are related but cannot state how	16	6	4	3	3	
3. Correct definition (e.g., your moms and dads are sisters or brothers, so you are cousins; they are the children of your aunts and uncles; they have the same grandparents)	37	2	2	15	18	63
3D. What are stepsiblings?						
0. Doesn't know/no relevant response	42	18	6	11	7	−40
1. Has part of the idea, but does not explain completely or accurately (if you get remarried, they're your stepbrothers or sisters; they're half of your mother's; they are the nephews and nieces of your stepparent, etc.)	15	1	5	5	4	
2. Correct definition (sons and daughters of your stepparent or children that your mother or father has with a new spouse after a divorce)	26	0	7	7	12	40
3. Other (friends, people that you love, they are mean, etc.)	13	5	6	1	1	−28
4A. The number of people in a family can change over time. Sometimes they get bigger. How might a family get bigger?						
0. Doesn't know/no relevant response/answers only in terms of growth in size due to eating or getting older	13	9	4	0	0	−45
1. Birth (new babies, new kids)	71	14	12	23	22	46
2. Marriage (single person/parent takes spouse)	15	1	4	8	2	
3. New stepsiblings (parent's new spouse brings own child(ren) from previous family to new family)	6	1	0	3	2	
4. Adoption of new children	16	1	2	2	11	45
5. Add new pets	10	1	3	3	3	
6. Other (invite/allow someone to live with you, gain more cousins or other extended family members)	19	4	7	2	6	
4B. How do needs change when families get bigger?						
0. Doesn't know/no relevant response	43	18	11	9	5	−40
1. The family will need a bigger house/more stuff or the money to buy it (food, clothing, etc.)	46	5	12	13	16	34
2. Other (student supplies a relevant, substantive response other than responses included in Category 1)	23	1	5	8	9	30

(Continued)

TABLE 7.1
(Continued)

Response Categories	Total	K	1	2	3	Phi
	96	24	24	24	24	

5A. Some families get smaller. How might a family get smaller?

Response Categories	Total	K	1	2	3	Phi
0. Doesn't know/no relevant response/answers only in terms of loss of body mass due to poor nutrition	16	10	4	2	0	−42
1. Death (a family member dies)	53	8	11	14	20	37
2. Divorce/separation (loss of one parent)	26	0	5	16	5	55
3. Normal moving out (children grow up and leave the family for marriage, college, etc.)	27	4	5	6	12	29
4. Traumatic moving out (family member runs away, wanders off and gets lost, discovers that s/he is in the wrong family, etc.)	12	2	2	2	6	22
5. Other	9	3	4	2	0	−21

5B. How do needs change when families get smaller?

Response Categories	Total	K	1	2	3	Phi
0. Doesn't know/no relevant response	67	23	16	17	11	−39
1. The family doesn't need as much living space or as much food, clothing, and so on, or the money to buy them	19	0	5	6	8	31
2. Other (student supplies a relevant, substantive response that is not classifiable in Category 1)	12	1	5	1	5	

6. What is marriage? What does it mean to get married?

Response Categories	Total	K	1	2	3	Phi
0. Doesn't know/no relevant response	9	5	3	1	0	−27
1. You get married/marry someone/take a wife or husband (not explained further)	35	9	8	14	4	
2. Partners will live together, form a family, come into another's family	29	4	9	7	9	
3. Describes ceremony (minister, oath, etc.)	11	1	1	3	6	27
4. Describes other things associated with marriage (formal clothing, reception, dancing, cake, kissing, honeymoon, etc.)	13	3	3	3	4	
5. Motive (couple wants children/wife is pregnant)	27	7	7	6	7	
6. Motive (they like/love each other)	40	7	11	9	13	

7. What is divorce? What does it mean to get divorced?

Response Categories	Total	K	1	2	3	Phi
0. Doesn't know/no relevant response	13	10	3	0	0	−50
1. Physical separation (partners break up/decide to live separately, one moves away, etc.; no mention of dissolution of marriage)	47	10	15	15	7	
2. Marital dissolution (partners get unmarried, are no longer married to each other, etc.)	21	3	3	5	10	29
3. Court actions (student specifically notes that divorce involves going to court, getting legal/ divorce papers, etc.)	9	0	1	3	5	27

(Continued)

TABLE 7.1
(Continued)

Response Categories	Total 96	K 24	1 24	2 24	3 24	Phi
4. Motive (unexplained; unmentioned or confined to the idea that the people do not want to stay married to each other anymore)	36	4	8	10	14	31
5. Motive (hostility or violence; they had a fight, one is mistreating or abusing the other, etc.)	33	3	12	12	6	
6. Motive (incompatibility; spouses are not good for each other, they have different needs and interests, they are not supplying what the other needs, etc.)	18	7	3	2	6	
7. Other (desire to marry someone else, then you have two moms and two dads, you alternate houses, etc.)	11	2	1	2	6	25
9. In what ways are families these days the same as families in the past?						
0. Doesn't know/no relevant response	39	15	14	8	2	−44
1. Response not specific to families (people still need food, wear clothing, etc.)	37	6	4	13	14	37
2. Basic family characteristics (people live in families, family members love and support one another, families share traditions, etc.)	9	0	1	2	6	33
3. Stage phenomena (babies are born and raised in families; they grow up and marry and establish their own household; family members grow old and eventually die, etc.)	7	1	3	1	2	
4. Family composition (families consist of husband/ father, wife/mother, child(ren), grandparents, aunts, uncles, cousins, etc.)	10	2	0	3	5	25
5. Other response specific to families (e.g., family members show physical resemblances)	6	1	3	2	0	
6. Student was coded in Category 4, 5, 6, or 7	29	4	6	7	12	27
10. In the past, most parents wanted a lot of children, but these days most parents want only a few. Why is that?						
0. Doesn't know/no relevant response	32	8	13	6	5	
1. Responses that do not include comparisons of the past with the present (taking care of children is a lot of work, children clutter up the house with their toys, etc.)	42	14	9	8	11	
2. It was easier to have/care for children in the past	7	0	1	3	3	21
3. It cost less to have/care for children in the past	9	0	0	4	5	33
4. Other	7	2	1	3	1	
5. Any valid response (2, 3, or 4)	22	2	2	10	8	35
11A. Everyday life has changed for mothers, fathers, and children. What do mothers do?						
1. Birthing/caring for children (have children, take care of children, feed them, teach them, take them places)	76	18	20	17	21	

(Continued)

TABLE 7.1
(Continued)

Response Categories	Total 96	K 24	1 24	2 24	3 24	Phi
2. Housework and household maintenance (cooking, cleaning, shopping, sewing, dusting, etc.)	65	13	18	14	20	26
3. Work outside the home	41	5	9	12	15	31
4. Relaxation and recreation (sits doing nothing, reads, visits, watches TV, etc.)	27	6	5	9	7	
5. Other (acts as head of family, works with other women to get a man, volunteers at school or elsewhere, does "girl stuff," etc.)	7	2	2	1	2	
6. Student is coded in three or more categories	35	4	8	7	16	38
11B. What did mothers in the past do?						
0. Doesn't know/no relevant response	42	17	14	10	1	−51
1. Birthing, caring for children (have children, take care of children, feed them, teach them, take them places, etc.)	26	6	5	5	10	
2. Housework and household maintenance (cooking, cleaning, shopping, sewing, dusting, etc.)	35	1	6	12	16	49
3. Work outside the home	7	1	2	1	3	
4. Other (sit around, visit, read, etc.)	17	2	4	3	8	25
11C. What did mothers in the past spend a lot of time doing that today's mothers don't do?						
0. Student doesn't draw relevant past versus present comparisons	38	15	14	6	3	−44
1. Past mothers had more work, less time for leisure or spending with children	13	1	2	5	5	22
2. Present mothers have more work, less time for leisure or spending with children	11	3	2	3	3	
3. Today's mothers more likely to work outside the home	17	2	4	4	7	19
4. Names at least one other thing that distinguishes today's mothers from past mothers (volunteers at school, works in a modern office rather than a primitive job shop, etc.)	22	2	4	5	11	33
5. Names at least one other thing that distinguished past mothers (had to make own baby food, worked at growing crops, hand-washed and hung laundry, etc.)	25	3	4	13	5	
12A. What do today's fathers do?						
1. Caring for/helping/teaching children	40	10	11	6	13	
2. Playing with children	20	3	7	3	7	
3. Disciplining or punishing children	6	1	1	1	3	
4. Household chores, shopping, cooking, and so on	34	7	10	8	9	
5. Working outside the home/making money	65	10	16	20	19	35

(Continued)

TABLE 7.1
(Continued)

Response Categories	Total 96	K 24	1 24	2 24	3 24	Phi
6. Relaxing, watching TV, listening to radio, playing computer games, smoking, sleeping	34	7	8	8	11	
7. Activities associated with traditional male role (lifting heavy things, playing sports or rooting for sports teams, cooking on grill, mowing lawn, household repairs, drinking beer, etc.)	30	10	8	6	6	
8. Other (relevant, substantive response that does not fit into previous categories)	6	4	1	1	0	−26
9. Student is coded in three or more categories (1–8)	40	8	10	8	14	
12B. What did fathers in the past do?						
0. Doesn't know/no relevant response	37	15	14	6	2	−47
1. Care for/help/teach children	11	2	0	1	8	41
2. Household chores, shopping, cooking, and so on	13	2	4	4	3	
3. Relaxing, smoking, sleeping, and so on	7	4	1	1	1	
4. Names something else specific to the past (farm work, traveling to get medicine, building home [e.g., log cabin] and teaching children to do so, making shoes or furniture, trading with Indians, etc.)	33	1	5	11	16	50
5. Work outside the home/earn money	8	2	1	2	3	
12C. What did fathers in the past do that fathers today don't do?						
0. No past versus present comparisons made	39	15	16	4	4	−49
1. Past fathers had to spend more time working, had less time for family/leisure	21	2	1	8	10	39
2. Past fathers didn't have to work as much as today's fathers, had more time for family/leisure	10	4	3	1	2	
3. Today's fathers work in offices or do other modern jobs; past fathers farmed or worked as blacksmiths and so on	20	2	5	7	6	
4. Other, questionable (student draws some other comparison that is invalid or at least questionable [fathers play in the snow more today; fathers get married today but in the past they didn't get married; in the past they worked as janitors or policemen, and so on])	9	1	1	4	3	
5. Other, valid (student draws a valid comparison that doesn't fit into previous categories [fathers watch television now; fathers mow lawns today; fathers take kids to parks today whereas there were no parks in the past, etc.])	19	2	3	5	9	28
6. Gender role differentiation: In responding to Questions 11 and 12, student draws clear distinctions between mother's and father's roles	43	10	9	12	12	

(Continued)

TABLE 7.1
(Continued)

Response Categories	Total 96	K 24	1 24	2 24	3 24	Phi
13A. What do children spending their time doing?						
1. Play, relaxation, games, TV, sitting around (no codes in Categories 2 or 3)	35	14	8	5	8	−28
2. School, homework, other school activities	49	7	11	17	14	31
3. Chores, care of self, clothing, room	22	5	9	5	3	
13B. What did children in the past do?						
0. Doesn't know/no relevant response (includes comparison of older with younger children rather than children today vs. children in the past)	28	10	11	6	1	−36
1. Play, relaxation, games, sitting around (no codes in Categories 2 or 3)	23	10	6	3	4	−26
2. School, homework, other school activities	15	3	1	5	6	22
3. Chores (care of self, clothing, room)	35	2	7	11	15	42
13C. What do today's children spend a lot of time doing that children didn't do in the past?						
0. No past versus present comparisons made	26	11	8	4	3	−30
1. Children today have more time for play or other self-chosen activities	30	2	5	11	12	37
2. Children today have modern toys, games, sports equipment that didn't exist in the past	28	5	6	8	9	
3. School (children in the past didn't go to school, went to one-room school, were home schooled, went to school year round)	32	6	9	8	9	
4. Other, questionable (they had no toys in the past, they buried food in the fire, they had more time to play, etc.)	8	1	3	2	2	
5. Other, valid (children in the past had to play with dusty things, had adventures in the woods, gathered firewood, had less opportunity to visit relatives; children today take camping trips, visit their dad, go to a swimming pool instead of a swimming hole, etc.)	8	1	1	2	4	18
14. These days, most kids live with just parents and brothers or sisters, but in the past, they often lived with their grandparents, aunts, uncles, and cousins too. Why did things change?						
1. Student generated a valid response to Question 14	16	2	3	3	8	26
15. In some other countries, even these days, most kids live not only with their parents and brothers and sisters, but also with their grandparents, aunts, uncles, and cousins. Why is that?						
1. Student generated a valid response to Question 15	17	2	2	5	8	27
16. When have kids spent more time with their parents—these days or in the past? Why?						
0. No choice (doesn't know/no relevant response/ says that there was no meaningful difference on this variable between the past and today)	19	3	6	4	6	
1. The past	25	5	4	9	7	

(Continued)

TABLE 7.1
(Continued)

Response Categories	Total 96	K 24	1 24	2 24	3 24	Phi
2. Today	52	16	14	11	11	–18
3. Valid rationale for past (kids didn't go to school then, kids worked alongside their parents, there was no childcare or babysitting available, etc.)	17	1	3	7	6	26
4. Valid rationale for present (parents do not work as many hours these days, kids do not have to spend as much time doing chores, etc.)	10	0	2	5	3	25
5. Other rationale (questionable rationale or one that is not classifiable in previous categories [in the past, parents would go away for a week or two at a time and leave the children at home])	10	1	3	2	4	

17. People all over the world live in families, but different countries have different customs. Do you know of a country where families do things differently than we do here?

Response Categories	Total	K	1	2	3	Phi
0. Doesn't know/no relevant response/initially says "yes" but cannot give one or more examples in subsequent categories	57	19	16	12	10	–30
1. Talks about differences in other places but not differences specific to family living (different language, foods, housing, climate; use of chopsticks; presence of headhunters or slaves; etc.)	33	5	7	11	10	21
2. Gives one or more examples specific to family living (bath time is handled differently in Japan, most families in some places are farmers, some places have less schooling or no schools at all, etc.)	6	0	1	1	4	26

18. What about Japan—do Japanese families do things differently than American families?

Response Categories	Total	K	1	2	3	Phi
0. Doesn't know/no response/no example classified in subsequent categories	43	14	13	11	5	–29
1. Talks about differences not specific to family living (different foods, housing types, language, slanted eyes, different jobs, etc.)	44	10	9	10	15	
2. Gives one or more examples specific to family living (bath time handled differently; partitioned houses that separate the parents from other family members, etc.)	9	0	2	3	4	21

19. How is family life different for people living on farms than for other people?

Response Categories	Total	K	1	2	3	Phi
0. Doesn't know/no relevant response	17	6	7	3	1	–26
1. Farm people have to do more work/chores, feed animals, use tractors to tend to crops, and so on	63	11	14	17	21	32
2. Farm people own bigger properties, have more land, have barns	11	4	1	3	3	

(Continued)

TABLE 7.1
(Continued)

Response Categories	Total 96	K 24	1 24	2 24	3 24	Phi
3. Other, questionable (offers invalid or questionable statement about farm life [houses, barns have to be red, farmers own their own homes but city people do not, city people have bigger houses, farm children do not go to school, etc.])	14	1	5	4	4	
4. Other, valid (offers an accurate or at least defensible statement about farm life [farmers know their neighbors better, farmers need to be sure that animals do not hurt their children, farmers have to put up with stinky smells, farmers need rain, Amish farmers have no electricity, etc.])	22	4	3	8	7	

20. How is family life different for people who live in small towns than for people who live in big cities?

Response Categories	Total	K	1	2	3	Phi
0. Doesn't know/no relevant response	33	13	11	4	5	−34
1. Generic town versus city comparisons that do not specifically address family life (cities are bigger, have bigger schools, more sidewalks, big buildings, more people in the neighborhood, more traffic, more crime, more noise, etc.)	44	5	8	15	16	39
2. Gives one or more reasons for wanting to live in a big city (you get better quality or variety of schools, shopping, etc; you have more friends/playmates; jobs pay more)	9	0	1	4	4	26
3. Gives one or more reasons for choosing to live in a small town (you can live close to your relatives, afford a house, get more house for the money, avoid urban hassles, enjoy flowers/woods/countryside)	15	2	1	3	9	36
4. Other, questionable (invalid or questionable statements not classified in previous categories [town people own but city people rent; cities are full, so you might not get a house; there is/you have more space in the city; bigger families live in bigger cities; most people in cities live in big buildings rather than houses; people in cities have to share housing and don't own cars, etc.])	16	5	4	2	5	
5. Other, valid (valid or at least defensible statements that do not fit into previous categories [cities have playgrounds, if you live in the city you know rich people, cities have trademark places/symbols such as the Statue of Liberty or the lights of Las Vegas, etc.])	13	1	3	4	5	18

21. Your ancestors came to America from somewhere else. Do you know where they came from?

Response Categories	Total	K	1	2	3	Phi
0. Doesn't know/no relevant response	78	22	22	18	16	−28
1. Names at least one country of origin	18	2	2	6	8	28

(Continued)

TABLE 7.1
(Continued)

Response Categories	Total 96	K 24	1 24	2 24	3 24	Phi
2. Identifies a reason for emigrating (escape oppression, obtain freedom, better economic opportunities)	9	0	0	3	6	36

22. Families sometimes move to a different house or even a different city. Why do families move from one place to another?

	Total	K	1	2	3	Phi
0. Doesn't know/no relevant response/vague speculations (they wanted or needed to move, they didn't like or got tired of the old house, etc.)	29	13	6	7	3	−33
1. Outgrew old house/needed more space; old house too big, wanted smaller space	28	5	5	9	9	18
2. Other problems with old house (fleas, disrepair, messy, leaky, etc.)	20	5	6	6	3	
3. Problems with old neighborhood (crime, noise, traffic, etc.)	11	0	5	2	4	
4. Divorce/separation	7	1	4	0	2	
5. Job change/move closer to job site	11	0	1	2	8	41
6. Other (escape high or increased taxes, move closer to relatives, get away from someone they wanted to avoid, move to better school district, etc.)	19	1	3	6	9	32

23. Sometimes families move here from another country where they don't speak English. Why do they do that?

	Total	K	1	2	3	Phi
0. Doesn't know/no relevant response	66	21	17	15	13	−27
1. They want to learn English	17	0	5	5	7	28
2. Escape oppression	9	2	0	4	3	
3. Other defensible explanation (they were disliked in their old country and wanted to come here and meet new friends, they are seeking something that was lacking at home)	8	1	2	1	4	.

24. How does family life change when a family moves to a new country?

	Total	K	1	2	3	Phi
0. Doesn't know/no relevant response	47	19	16	8	4	−50
1. They miss/lose their old friends	13	1	2	4	6	23
2. They meet new people, make new friends	10	1	1	4	4	20
3. They have difficulties understanding and communicating if they don't know the language	21	0	5	8	8	33
4. They will have to get used to new food, clothing, language, and so on	15	3	1	5	6	22
5. Other (valid or defensible explanations not classifiable in previous categories [lower taxes, strange feelings, etc.])	10	1	0	2	7	37

(Continued)

TABLE 7.1
(Continued)

Response Categories	Total	K	1	2	3	Phi
	96	24	24	24	24	

25. In the past, most kids went to school for just a few years, but these days most go for a lot longer. Why is that?

0. Doesn't know/no relevant response (they didn't want to go to school, their parents didn't want them to go, etc.)	66	21	19	12	14	-33
1. Schooling was less available then (fewer schools, fewer grades at the schools, etc.)	16	3	3	4	6	
2. There was less to learn then (teachers didn't know as much as now, etc.)	10	0	2	5	3	25
3. Other (most students came from farm families; didn't need that much education; were needed to work on farms; there were no computers then)	8	0	0	6	2	37

26A. Kids learn things from their families. What are some things that most kids learn at home, from their families?

0. Doesn't know/no relevant response	33	13	11	8	1	-40
1. Academic skills (ABCs, reading, writing, math, help with homework, etc.)	23	3	9	6	5	
2. Manners and morals (how to be polite, how to treat people well, how to act, etc.)	18	4	2	4	8	23
3. Self-care/responsibility (getting washed and dressed, combing hair, taking care of clothes and possessions, cleaning up room, tying shoes, etc.)	15	3	2	3	7	22
4. Health and safety rules (avoiding bad habits or dangerous activities, emergency/9-1-1 rules, avoiding strangers or danger on the street, etc.)	10	1	0	3	6	31
5. Sports/physical activities (playing catch, using jungle gym, using a sandbox, riding a bike, etc.)	6	1	2	1	2	
6. Other (relevant, substantive responses not codable in previous categories [planting, coloring, using computers, how to pick up the dog, how to use toys, family and past history, etc.])	23	5	2	7	9	25

26B. What do kids learn from their mothers?

0. Doesn't know/no relevant response/doesn't speak of learning specifically from female relatives	25	5	6	8	6	
1. Academic skills (ABCs, reading, writing, math, help with homework, etc.)	23	5	9	5	4	
2. Manners and morals (how to be polite, how to treat people well, how to act, etc.)	16	7	1	5	3	
3. Self-care/responsibility (getting washed and dressed, combing hair, taking care of clothes and possessions, cleaning up room, tying shoes, etc.)	8	2	2	2	2	

(Continued)

TABLE 7.1
(Continued)

Response Categories	Total 96	K 24	1 24	2 24	3 24	Phi
4. Health and safety rules (avoiding bad habits or dangerous activities, emergency/9-1-1 rules, avoiding strangers or danger on the street, etc.)	9	1	3	2	3	
5. Sports/physical activities (playing catch, using jungle gym, using a sandbox, riding a bike, etc.)	7	1	2	3	1	
6. Traditional female role behaviors (having and caring for children, how to be a girl/mother, how to act with men, cooking, sewing, other domestic arts, putting a rubber band on Barbie's hair, etc.)	22	4	4	6	8	
7. Other (relevant, substantive responses not codable in previous categories [planting, coloring, using computers, how to pick up the dog, how to use toys, family and past history, etc.])	14	4	2	2	6	
26C. What do kids learn from their fathers?						
0. Doesn't know/no relevant response/does not speak of learning specifically from male relatives	43	15	12	11	5	−30
1. Academic skills (ABCs, reading, writing, math, help with homework, etc.)	11	2	3	2	4	
2. Manners and morals (how to be polite, how to treat people well, how to act, etc.)	7	2	1	0	4	
3. Sports/physical activities (playing catch, using jungle gym, using a sandbox, riding a bike, etc.)	12	2	3	4	3	
4. Traditional male role behaviors (how to be a boy/ father, fixing/assembling/constructing things, boxing, wrestling, football, working with engines, mowing the lawn, etc.)	17	1	4	4	8	27
5. Other (relevant, substantive responses not codable in previous categories [self-care responsibility, health and safety rules, planting, coloring, using computers, how to pick up the dog, how to use toys, family and past history, etc.])	26	4	4	8	10	24
27. Why do families need rules? What would happen if a family didn't have rules?						
0. Doesn't know/no relevant response	12	3	5	3	1	
1. Health and safety (rules help you remain healthy, safe; keep you from getting sick, hurt, kidnapped, etc.)	47	8	12	11	16	24
2. Fairness/morality (rules guide you in treating other people fairly and appropriately, keep you from doing bad things or going to jail, protect us from meanness or bullying, etc.)	29	7	4	10	8	

(Continued)

TABLE 7.1
(Continued)

Response Categories	Total 96	K 24	1 24	2 24	3 24	Phi
3. Underscore responsibilities (without rules, kids might not go to school/do their homework; might dirty up the house or break windows or furniture, etc.)	29	3	4	12	10	35
4. Avoid chaos (without rules things would be wild, crazy, out of control, etc.)	29	1	5	8	15	46
5. Other (so people will know how to act; if we didn't have rules, things might be bad; parents have rules so they can boss you around; if there were no rules, it would mean that your parents didn't love you, etc.)	13	8	3	1	1	−35
28. If families have a fire, a flood, or some other emergency, who can they turn to for help?						
0. Doesn't know/no relevant response	0	0	0	0	0	
1. Relatives, neighbors, family friends	45	7	9	10	19	38
2. Call 9-1-1	25	6	6	9	4	
3. Police	52	13	13	12	14	
4. Fire department	51	13	11	14	13	
5. Hospital, ambulance, doctors, paramedics	30	7	10	7	6	
6. Water person, plumber, lifeguard	7	1	4	2	0	
7. Other (someone who would know what to do, someone who will allow you to live in their home for awhile, insurance company, Red Cross, God, etc.)	19	4	5	6	4	
29. What can families do to help other families?						
0. Doesn't know/no relevant response concerning helping individuals or families	27	7	10	3	7	
1. Give/lend them money, clothing, other things they may need	30	8	4	10	8	
2. Provide direct help with problem (help them get out if stuck in snow, guide lost children home, give needed ride to doctor's office, counsel them with problem, help them move into their home, cheer them up, etc.)	44	10	10	15	9	
3. Take them in (let homeless people live with you, share your high ground in a flood, share your tornado shelter, etc.)	7	2	0	4	1	
4. Other (help the sick/vulnerable by calling to check on them, mow lawns of neighbors when they're away, etc.)	6	1	1	1	3	

(Continued)

TABLE 7.1
(Continued)

Response Categories	Total	K	1	2	3	Phi
30. What can families do to help their communities?	96	24	24	24	24	
0. Doesn't know/no relevant response concerning helping communities	52	23	17	7	5	–61
1. Don't litter/pick up/stop litter bugs	34	1	6	14	13	46
2. Work alone or with neighbors on community improvement projects (get rid of a fallen tree or other hazard, drum up support for a new stop sign, etc.)	10	0	2	3	5	25
3. Other (recycle, keep up your property, obey the laws, work to change the laws, avoid pollution, etc.)	17	0	2	7	8	37

Note. Numbers in the frequencies columns show how many students in each group were coded for mentioning the ideas represented by each response category. Underlining indicates that the chi-square for the underlined distribution was statistically significant at or below the .05 level. In these instances the phi coefficients (with decimal points omitted) are given in the phi column to indicate the magnitudes of linear trends.

1st 1. Me, my brother, my mom and my dad, and my two cats, but I'm going to get a dog. (What is a family?) I don't know. (What people are in a family?) Your mom, your dad, a brother and a sister, twins, triplets, pets, and I forgot. (What does a family do?) They play games and they help you with your homework if you don't know. They go to work and they . . . I don't know.

2. Because they want to. (Why do they want to live in families?) So when you need help on work, someone can help you on it.

2nd 1. The only people living in my house right now is me, my mom, and my dad, and one of my fish, and a cat and a dog. (Do you have any people in your family who don't live in your house?) Yeah, I've got two grandpas and a grandma. I have an aunt and I've got another aunt which has my cousins, and an uncle. My cousins' names are Mike and Johnny and Jake. And I've got another aunt and uncle, and they have a dog named Riley, and my cousin's name that lives there is Charlie. (What is a family?) A family is a bunch of people that are like mom and dad, grandma and grandpa, aunt and uncle, and cousins. (What sorts of things do families do?) Like go out to eat and stuff, and probably like go to see each other and stuff, and probably they go swimming and stuff together, and sometimes they go to each other's houses and stuff.

2. Because when you grow up, you have to learn the stuff that your mom and dad taught you. If a child doesn't learn the things their parents teach them, all they'd do is act mean to other people.

3rd 1. It's like a mom and . . . it's like a family that that loves each other and
plays with each other and they do stuff, like play games usually, board
games usually like Monopoly. (Who's in your family?) My brother in
first grade . . . my parents got divorced and now I have two sisters actually. I have one who's my true one and I have another one but she's
not my sister. She sort of babysits us, like you know. You play games
and stuff—the whole family.

   2. I don't know about that one . . . for shelter and love and care for people and they care for each other and for our shelter too, so they can
live in it, so all of us can live in it—everybody we love . . . like my dad
I love and you'd live in it together and we'd have a bunch of children.

All but 14 of the students were able to define or describe a family. Some offered general definitions: People who love/help/take care of each other (37), people who do things together (35), people who live together (30), or a group of people who are related through birth or marriage (11). In addition or instead, some
described families by listing their members: 10 confined the list to parents and
their children; 38 included grandparents, uncles, aunts, cousins, stepsiblings, or
other relatives; 34 included pets; and one included close friends. Other responses
included: people that you can count on and that you would tell secrets to; your
mother makes a family and your dad helps; a little tiny community.

Asked why most people live in families, almost one third (31) were unable to
respond. The rest said because they love, want to take care of, or want to help one
another (27), want to get married and/or have children (21), need a family to get
their basic physical needs met (14), or want to live with others and not be alone
(12). Other responses included: That's how you "make feelings happy"; we need
to live in a house and not be left out in the streets; you were born with them and
you celebrate your birthday with them; God made them, because if they didn't
have a family, there wouldn't be us; they don't like living in orphanages, so they
live in a house; they want to meet their uncles and stuff.

As in previous research, the students tended to define families and identify
motives for family living in terms of social ties among family members (they live
together, do things together, love/help/take care of one another), rather than in
terms of genealogical or legal ties. Only 11 identified birth or marriage as the basis for the relationship. Similarly, most students said that people live in families
in order to get their basic needs met, so that they will have social companionship,
or because they love/want to take care of/want to help one another. Only 21 said
that they live in families because they get married and/or want to have children.

KNOWLEDGE OF KINSHIP TERMS

Question 3 assessed knowledge about the basis for kinship relationships in extended and blended families. We did not ask about conventional nuclear families

(mother, father, sister, brother) because most children learn the meanings of these terms before they get to school.

3A. Families include grandparents, aunts and uncles, and cousins. What are grandparents?
3B. What are aunts and uncles?
3C. What are cousins?
3D. What are stepbrothers and stepsisters?

K   3A. Grandparents are kind of like a dad or a cousin.

3B. Aunts are mom's children.

3C. Cousins are almost like a friend. (Are cousins related to you?) Yes. (How are they related to you . . . do you know?) No.

3D. They're like a brother and a sister. (Is there anything different?) No.

1st   3A. Grandma and grandpa. (What makes them your grandma and grandpa?) They're old, one is a boy and one is a girl.

3B. Aunts are your mom's sisters and your uncles are your brothers. (Uncles are your brothers?) No, my mommy's brothers.

3C. Cousins are people that are part of your family because they visit you because they're your cousins. (Are they related to you in a special way?) No.

3D. If you have a mom, then you have a different mom that's your stepmom.

2nd 3A. Grandparents are somebody that's like the oldest person in the family. (Are grandparents related to you in a special way?) Yeah, they're related to you because they're your mom's or dad's parents.

3B. Aunts and uncles are somebody that are either your mom's or dad's sister or brother.

3C. Cousins are somebody's mom's or dad's sister's or brother's child.

3D. Stepbrothers and stepsisters I think are people that you adopt or something.

3rd   3A. They're your mom's moms and dads.

3B. They're your mom and dad's sisters and brothers.

3C. They're your mom and dad's brothers' and sisters' kids.

3D. Like if your mom and dad get divorced and they marry another guy and his kids are your stepbrothers and stepsisters, and who he married would be a stepmom.

More than half (52) of the students were able to define grandparents as one's parents' parents. However, 21 were unable to respond, 4 generated incorrect responses (e.g., they are your dad's uncle or your mom and dad), 14 could only say that grandparents are people who are old or look old, and the rest gave "other" responses: Your grandpa is your grandpa because he married your grandma, your mother had you and so you get grandparents too, or they are your grandparents because you share the same last name (5). One third grader articulated several themes that many students brought out when they talked about their grandparents:

> Grandparents are people that are old and they treat you real well and they get lots of sores and stuff and have to take medicine. They will take you to the zoo sometimes and just let you walk around to see what it's like and take you to different places. Sometimes they'll travel to the south in the winter to get away from the cold. They sort of don't have any jobs. (What makes someone your grandpa and not someone else's grandpa?) We're real close and maybe he's not with the other person, and we do lots of things together. We just ride around and play and have fun and go fishing on a boat sometimes, and leave everyone else alone.

An adopted child said,

> When I was first born, my mom adopted me and took me over to meet them and told them that they were going to be my grandpa and grandma. The first time when they were grandpa and grandma was when I was six, and the first time when I went to meet them, I was seven, and when I went to meet them, they became my grandpa and grandma.

The students found it harder to define aunts and uncles. Fewer than half (41) said that they are sisters and brothers to one's parents, sons and daughters of one's grandparents, or parents of one's cousins. Instead, 24 were unable to respond, 13 could only give partial information (such as saying that aunts and uncles are brothers or sisters but not being able to say to whom, that aunts are female and uncles are male, or that an uncle became an uncle because he married an aunt), 9 said that aunts and uncles are special to you or love you but could not specify their relationship to you, and 10 supplied incorrect responses (confusing aunts and uncles with godparents, grandaunts, cousins, etc.).

The students found it comparably difficult to define cousins. Only 37 correctly said that your cousins are the children of your aunts and uncles or that they have the same grandparents as you do. Otherwise, 25 students were unable to respond, 19 described cousins merely as friends or playmates, and 16 knew that cousins were related but could not say how.

The students had the most difficulty defining stepsiblings. Only 19 were able to identify stepbrothers and stepsisters as sons and daughters of one's stepparent. Another 7 identified them as children that one's mother or father has with a new spouse following a divorce (half siblings rather than stepsiblings). We included these as correct responses in analyzing the data because these students at least understood that divorce and remarriage are involved in creating stepsibling relationships. Otherwise, 42 students were unable to respond, 15 supplied part of the idea but did not explain it accurately or completely (e.g., if you get remarried, they're your stepbrothers or sisters; they're half of your mother's; they're the nephews and nieces of your stepparent), and 13 did not include the notion of relationship (e.g., they're friends, people that you love, etc.). A few students described stepsiblings as mean, probably because of exposure to the *Cinderella* story or movie. Other responses included: She has a very young brother who is "not really steppish" yet [i.e., not yet able to walk]; part of your family that doesn't live with you—you acquire them because relatives adopt other children; family members who lived long ago; people in the family that you are not related to; a grown-up brother or sister died, then you would have another; they don't live with you; grown-up siblings who don't live with you but are not married yet; they are your friends, but like sisters; your parents didn't want you anymore so they gave you to someone else; people who are adopted into a family; people who are not really related to you but help take care of you if you get adopted.

Overall, the students found it easiest to define grandparents, harder to define aunts and uncles or cousins, and most difficult to define stepbrothers and stepsiblings. One noteworthy type of family member (variously identified as an aunt or uncle, cousin, or stepsibling) was a brother or sister who had grown up and left home but not yet married and started a family. These individuals were confusing to the students because they were neither moms, dads, nor children (in the sense of children within a nuclear family household).

Knowledge of kinship relationships develops gradually across the age range studied, with the younger students primarily emphasizing social ties among the people involved and the older ones beginning to learn about genealogical or legal ties. Our findings elaborate on earlier ones by indicating that the legal relationships are even more difficult and confusing for students than the genealogical ones. Unless they could speak from direct experience, the students had difficulty talking about adoption or stepsibling relationships.

Attempts to teach young children about kinship relationships can get complicated, especially in contemporary times when we want to define "family" broadly enough to encompass alternatives to traditional nuclear families. The key idea is probably that most kinship relationships are genealogical ones that persist through marriages, divorces, or other changes in household make-up or location. That is, children who share the same parents are brothers and sisters regardless of whether their parents are or ever were married. Their parents' parents are their grandparents, their parents' siblings are their aunts and uncles, and so on, regardless of whether or not their parents stay together. These kinships are based on blood relationships and remain in place whether or not the people involved live together, see one another frequently, or even like each other.

Perhaps depending on the family relationships represented in the class, teachers will have to make decisions about whether and how to address complicated kinship relationships (e.g., whether to identify and distinguish between half siblings and stepsiblings, and how much emphasis to place on formal marriages, adoptions, and other legal proceedings). Kinship ties often exist de facto when people with children begin living together, and especially when they establish a lasting common-law marriage. Other complications are introduced by divorce or separation. The terms *ex-wife* and *ex-husband* are in common use to describe former marital relationships, but we do not have commonly used parallel terms (e.g., *ex-stepbrother*, *ex-aunt*) to describe people who are blood relatives of one's former stepparent. Yet, these relationships (or at least, friendships that originated in these relationships) often persist in children's lives.

Perhaps the simplest solution is to ignore or downplay marriage certificates, adoption papers, and other legal aspects of family relationships and instead explain the bases for two general categories of kinship relations: genealogical relations (blood relatives of one's biological parents) and step relations (blood relatives of one's stepparent). The main point would be that the former relationships persist through changes in marital relationships or households, but the latter relationships can be severed through divorce or separation (although personal friendships and a subjective sense of kinship may persist).

CHANGES IN FAMILY SIZE

4A. The number of people in a family can change over time. Sometimes families get bigger. How might a family get bigger? What is another way that a family might get bigger?

4B. How do families' needs change when they get bigger?

5A. Sometimes families get smaller. How might a family get smaller? What is another way that a family might get smaller?

5B. How do families' needs change when they get smaller?

K   4A. 'Cause people get babies. (Are there any other ways that families can get bigger?) I don't know.

      4B. Because the more birthdays you have, you get bigger and bigger and bigger.

      5A. Well, I have tons of people in my family. I know how they do it. The family gets smaller because a lot of the people died already. (What is another way that a family might get smaller?) Get shot by a gun or something.

      5B. It's a little bit quieter in the house and . . . I forget.

1st   4A. You have to eat food. (How could the number of people in a family get bigger?) If they have more babies and you have more pets.

      4B. They have to go to college and make money. (You told me that a way a family could get bigger is if they had more babies. If a family had more babies, would the things that the family needs change?)

Yeah. (What would they need?) They would need money. (Would they need different things if more people joined the family?) No, because they have too much and there's no more room.

5A. I don't know.

5B. They don't need to change when they have a baby because babies don't know what to do with the money. (Would the family need different things if the family got smaller?) They need toys if they had a baby.

2nd 4A. You might have another brother or something or your mom and dad's sister or brother might have another baby.

4B. When they get bigger, they need bigger clothes and stuff, and they have harder work and stuff. (You told me that one of the ways a family could get larger in number was if it had a new baby. OK, if there were more people in a family, would their needs change?) They would use more money because they would have to buy the baby new clothes and stuff, and sometimes you have to buy other things for your house because when the baby is like two, you like to give them stuff and they break stuff.

5A. When somebody dies or goes away from home and stays and doesn't come home.

5B. They don't use much money and stuff and they don't have to buy that much clothes and stuff, and they can keep more money and they can just . . . they don't have any kids or something and their family is really small and they can do whatever they want without their kids whining or something.

3rd 4A. Like your mom or dad has a kid and the mom and dad's kid has a baby and the baby's grandparents are your mom and dad, and then they got babies, and then the other one could have babies and they could keep going and going and going. (Can you think of any other way that a family could get bigger?) Like if I grow up and marry somebody, then their family gets that big.

4B. Like when they grow really super old and they need people to help them more often. (When families get larger, do the things that they need change?) Yeah, they need more food and more food and more food, and they need more house room, and the kids need more space to play.

5A. Maybe somebody might go to the hospital and they might die maybe, and it would get smaller. Maybe somebody might leave the family.

5B. It's not as much as it used to be . . . they don't need as much money . . . the kids don't need as much stuff as they used to.

All but 13 of the students were able to explain how families can get bigger: the birth of new babies and/or adoption of new children (16); marriage (15); addition of new pets (10); acquisition of stepsiblings (6). Other responses included: If someone died, you might want to replace them with more people; a family might be nice to people so that they would want to come and live with them; the family might discover previously unknown relatives.

Almost half (43) of the students could not tell how a family's needs change when it gets bigger. The only common response was that the family would need a bigger house, more food, and so on (46). Other responses included: There would be more people to care for and kiss good night; the family would have to accommodate a wider range of preferences in brands of cereal, and so on; they would need bottles or diapers for a new baby.

All but 16 of the students were able to talk about how families can get smaller: someone dies (53); divorce or separation (26); normal moving out by children who leave for college, work, or marriage (27); traumatic moving out that occurs when a family member runs away, wanders off and gets lost, or discovers that he or she is in the wrong family (12); or other reasons such as loss/expulsion of pets or parental decision not to have any more children (9). Unusual responses included: A family might not be able to afford a child and would put the child up for adoption; a child might get adopted "because nobody really wants them"; a child might be taken to an orphanage. Again, however, more than two thirds (67) were unable to say how a family's needs would change when it got smaller. The rest said that the family would not need as much living space, food, and so on (19) or gave "other" responses: need to serve only a narrower range of preferences in cereals, and so on; the family would have more money following divorce (mistakenly assuming that fewer people would be sharing the same income).

The students' reasons for why families might get bigger or smaller paralleled those likely to be given by adults, except for the mention of pets and the descriptions of traumatic departures. However, the students were unable to generate many ideas about how family needs would change following an increase or decrease in family size, except for the most obvious answer that needs for space, food, and other resources would increase or decrease. None noted a need for redistribution of chores and responsibilities, that a new baby might mean a change in working hours for one or both parents or a need to arrange for childcare during part of the day, or that the departure of a breadwinner might bring financial pressures. This suggests that students would profit from thoughtful discussion of some of the economic, lifestyle, and system dynamics implications of various changes in family composition.

MARRIAGE AND DIVORCE

6. **What is marriage?** [If necessary:] **What does it mean to get married?**

7. What is divorce? [If necessary:] **What does it mean to get divorced?**

K   6. Marriage is when you get in love. (What does it mean to get married?) I don't know. (Why would people want to get married?) So they could have a baby.

    7. Divorce means you're not in love. (What does it mean to get divorced?) To get love.

1st   6. Marriage is when you get married to somebody . . . a mom and a dad get married to somebody. That's when they have a honeymoon and celebrate and all that stuff. (What does it mean to get married?) It means when they do stuff together and it means you have to be nice and try not to break up and get a divorce with the one you're married to.

    7. Divorce is when you break up, and then your mom and your whole family is not with his family. If you dad breaks up with your mom, then your dad's family is not with your mom's family. (What does it mean to get divorced?) It means you have to go to a court and get divorced. You go to a court and you won't be married anymore and you won't be with each other anymore and you probably won't see them anymore.

2nd   6. Marriage is when a girl or a guy can get married and then a couple of days later, they like have a baby. (What does it mean to get married?) You somehow start to get married to each other. (Why would people want to get married?) Because they want a child and they have to get married.

    7. Divorce is when somebody is starting to get really angry because they get yelled at and stuff. He gets in a lot of arguments and he doesn't like it and he keeps on saying, "Stop it," and arguments keep on happening, and he doesn't want it to happen anymore so he'll go away so it won't happen ever again. (What does it mean to get divorced?) When you get divorced, you're alone and stuff.

3rd   6. It's like when you're about 21 or something and you love somebody and you like really love them very much and you get married.

    7. It means like if you're really mad at each other and you don't want to see them anymore, you just call this one therapy guy and you sort of get these divorce papers and don't see each other no more, and if you have kids and stuff, some people have them on the weekdays and some people have them on the weekends, and sometimes the dad has weekends and the mom has weekdays—something like that.

All but 9 of the students said something about what it means to get married, although only 11 made reference to the ceremony itself. Most simply said that the people get married or take a husband or wife (35) or that they would live together, form a family, or join each other's families (29). Other responses typically referred to things associated with marriage (formal clothing, receptions, dancing, cake, kissing, honeymoons, etc.). Unusual responses included: After they get married they have the same last name (3); marriage means a lot more responsibility; people get married because it would be against the law to do otherwise.

A "male" point of view: "You meet a girl or something and you start dating and you're like 20 years old and you go to this big sort of like a funeral, but no one's dead. And you like walk down the aisle with your bride and you do all this word stuff. Then you give her the ring and then you can kiss [makes disgusted face]."

A "female" point of view: "It means that they live together and talk about mushy stuff. Yuck! And kiss—Yuck!" (Why would people want to get married?) "Because they love each other. Yuck!"

Concerning why people get married, 40 students said that the couple like/love each other and 27 that they want children or the wife is pregnant. A few mentioned other motives such as that the people do not want to live alone. Only 7 included both a description of the marriage ceremony and identification of one or more motives for getting married.

All but 13 of the students were able to say what it means to get divorced, although only 9 referred to the legal papers or court actions involved. A majority (47) spoke of physical separation: The partners break up, decide to live separately, one moves away, and so on (without mention of dissolution of the marriage as such). Most of the rest (21) did refer to marital dissolution: The partners get unmarried, are no longer married to each other, and so on. More than one third (36) of the students were unable to identify a motive for divorce, beyond saying that the people did not want to live together or stay married anymore. The rest cited hostility or violence (the couple had a fight or one was mistreating or abusing the other) (33) or incompatibility (the spouses were not good for each other, had different needs and interests, were not meeting each other's needs, etc.; 18). Other comments about divorce included: the desire to be free to marry someone else as a motive (4); after a divorce (and presumably, remarriage) you have two moms and two dads or you alternate houses; you get in trouble; one wants children, the other doesn't; a brother or sister that you had would become a stepbrother or stepsister; they might still live together if they're not married anymore.

The common responses to these two questions were accurate and did not involve misconceptions, although a few took a child's rather than an adult's perspective (e.g., focusing on the wedding cake, dancing or kissing, or having two sets of parents and alternating houses). Their main focus was on the idea that a couple likes/loves each other and wants to live together as the reason for marriage and that the couple has grown apart or had a fight as the reason for divorce. Few mentioned either the legal papers/ceremonies involved in marriage or divorce or the desire to have children and raise them within a family as a motive for marriage. None said that the actions of the children were the reason for divorce, although there were hints that a few had this in mind. None distinguished between formal marriage and informally living together (common-law marriage), although one was under the impression that the law required a man to have either a girlfriend or a wife (but not both). These results suggest to us that students in these grades might be taught something about the vows that people make as the heart of the marriage ceremony, the legal ramifications of marriage and divorce, and the idea that growing apart and/or incompatibility is the usual reason for separation or divorce (in part simply as information but also as inoculation against a tendency to think that hostility, violence, desire to marry someone else, or the actions of the children are typically involved).

FAMILY LIFE IN THE PAST AND PRESENT

The next series of questions asked the students to make past versus present comparisons concerning family life in general and the roles and/or activities of fathers, mothers, and children. We were interested in the degree to which they were aware that in the past, most people lived on farms in extended families that functioned as economic as well as social units, whereas in modern industrialized countries, most people live in much smaller nuclear families in cities and suburbs, and also that in the past, families tended to be large because children were useful resources (as additional farm workers) and because many of them died in infancy or childhood.

8. In what ways are families these days different from families in the past? What are some other differences? Any others?

9. In what ways are families these days the same as families in the past? How else are families the same as they always were?

10. In the past, most parents wanted a lot of children, but these days most parents want only a few. Why is that?

11A. Everyday life has changed for mothers, fathers, and children. What do mothers do? [Continue to probe until student can no longer respond to the original question, then ask the following more specific probes.]

11B. What did mothers in the past do?

11C. What did mothers in the past spend a lot of time doing that today's mothers don't do? What do today's mothers spend a lot of time doing that mothers didn't do in the past?

12A. What do fathers do? [Continue to probe until student can no longer respond to the original question, then ask the following specific probes.]

12B. What did fathers do in the past?

12C. What did fathers in the past spend a lot of time doing that today's fathers don't do? What do today's fathers spend a lot of time doing that fathers didn't do in the past?

13A. What do children spend their time doing? [Continue to probe until student can no longer respond to the original question, then ask the following specific probes.]

13B. What did children in the past spend their time doing?

13C. What did children in the past spend a lot of time doing that today's children don't do? What do today's children spend a lot of time doing that children didn't do in the past?

14. These days, most kids live with just parents and brothers or sisters, but in the past, they often lived with their grandparents, aunts, uncles, and cousins too. Why did things change?

15. In some other countries, even these days, most kids live not only with parents and brothers and sisters, but also with their grandparents, aunts, uncles, and cousins. Why is that?

16. When have kids spent more time with their parents—these days or in the past? Why?

K   8. Because they were grown up. (Anything else that was different?) No.

    9. I don't know.

   10. I don't know.

   11A. They help children. (How do they help children?) By feeding them, by taking care of them. I don't know. (What else does your mom do?) My mom takes care of me, she takes me shopping, and a lot of different things.

   11B. I don't know.

   11C. I don't know. (What do today's mothers spend a lot of time doing that mothers didn't do in the past?) Today? I don't know.

   12A. Take care of their children and they go to work. (Anything else?) Takes care of his children and feeds his children.

   12B. I don't know.

   12C. I don't know. (What do today's fathers spend a lot of time doing that fathers didn't do in the past?) Not working and I don't know.

   13A. Spend it at school. (Besides going to school, what do children do?) Stay home sometimes. (What do they do when they stay home?) Taking care of their family.

   13B. Going to school and getting teached by teachers. (Anything else?) No.

   13C. I don't know. (What do today's children spend a lot of time doing that children didn't do in the past?) I don't know.

   14. I don't know.

   15. Because. I don't know, but just because. (Do you have any ideas why that might be?) No.

16. These days. (Why?) I don't know.

1st 8. They get old. (Would life have been different for families a long time ago?) Yeah, like if you had a mom and she gets old and then it'll change. (How would it change?) I think she wouldn't look like your mommy.

9. You weren't even born and your grandma and grandpa aren't old, and they didn't even know about your mom and your dad. (How would that be the same?) I don't know.

10. I don't know.

11A. They work and they work in their office because my mom and dad have an office, and when someone is sick in school, their mom and dad can't go to work—they have to stay home so they have to try to remember in their office. My mom goes to work but she has to go to her office first before she goes. (What else do mothers do?) They make you go to sleep, and they make your breakfast.

11B. I don't know.

11C. I don't know. (Can you think of anything that mothers a long time ago might have done that mothers today wouldn't do?) They had to take care of the baby and she really wanted to go to the store and didn't go to the store because the baby would be alone. (Can you think of any other things that mothers a long time ago might have done?) No. (What do today's mothers spend a lot of time doing that mothers didn't do in the past?) Work.

12A. Fathers . . . they work more than moms because . . . I don't know. (What else do fathers do?) They give you medicine, they make you go to the bus stop and then you go to school because they want you to go to school.

12B. I don't know.

12C. Smoke, because my dad promised he wouldn't smoke, but now he's never going to do it again, 'cause he promised. (Can you think of things that fathers a long time ago did that fathers today don't do?) They drive too fast and they used to speed. (A long time ago?) My dad didn't, but some fathers do, but not mine. (What do today's fathers spend a lot of time doing that fathers didn't do in the past?) I don't know.

13A. Working at school . . . they work on handwriting. (What sort of things do you like to do?) I like recess and lunch, and that's the only thing I like because it's fun. (How about when you get home from school—what sort of things do you do?) I have to do my homework, but if I don't have homework I can color or read. (What else do you like to do after school?) I like to go to the after-school program that I'm going to because today's gym day. Tomorrow is movie day.

13B. I don't know.

13C. They don't do their homework. One time I didn't do mine so I had to read a book and then I had to do it. (What do today's children spend a lot of time doing that children didn't do in the past?) I don't know. (Is there anything that you can do now that children a long time ago, way before you were born, things that they couldn't do?) Yeah, because they jumped on the bed.

14. Sometimes your sisters don't live with you anymore because they're grown up. My mom has a sister and she knows a lot about computers.

15. I don't know.

16. These days. (Why?) Because . . . I forgot.

2nd 8. The houses were made different probably, and they didn't have action figures and stuff, and they didn't have cool shows on like Spiderman™ and stuff. (Did families do things differently, do you think?) Like if they wanted to go out and get butter they could either buy it or they could make it, and these days it's really hard to make.

9. You still get to ride bikes and drive cars and stuff, and you still get to have a house, and you still get to watch cartoons and they didn't have cartoons as good as these days.

10. Because back then, probably the kids weren't as pouty and whiny as they are and stuff, and these days they do that a lot because they have more cool toys and stuff and there's more really cool shows on and a lot of other stuff.

11A. [No response]. (What does your mother do?) She works until five o'clock so she can save some money to go to Disney World, and my dad does that except he doesn't stay at work that long. He stays at work I think from like seven at night until 8:30, and my mom gets up at 8:00 and gets around and stuff and she gets home around 5:30 or 5:00. (What else does your mom do?) On some days instead of coming straight home . . . like when I was six she used to just come straight home, but now these days it takes a long time to get home because before she comes home, she goes shopping.

11B. I don't know.

11C. Probably some moms in the past didn't go to office buildings and work and stuff, and they probably didn't have to do as much work and stuff. (What do today's mothers spend a lot of time doing that mothers didn't do in the past?) They probably spend a lot of time working these days and stuff.

12A. They probably do harder jobs than moms do, like men do a lot of building and stuff. (What does your dad do?) My dad, on Sundays, he runs the vacuum and stuff, and my mom on Sundays is a Sunday school teacher.

12B. They probably mostly did gathering up lumber and stuff to make fires.

12C. They spent a lot of time working and stuff and they mostly get things ready, probably like getting the lumber ready and stuff, to carry inside and if their son was around too, they could help the dad probably. (What do today's fathers spend a lot of time doing that fathers didn't do in the past?) I don't know.

13A. Playing with toys and stuff. (What do you spend your time doing?) I spend everyday, if we're not going somewhere, like every single day if I'm home and my friend's home, then we play with each other. (What sort of things do you play?) We pretend we're skydivers, and we pretend we're divers and we swing real high and then jump off into the grass. Sometimes we have weapons and stuff because we pretend we're fighting like bad guys or wrestling sharks or something. (Anything else you do besides play?) No.

13B. They probably were with their father a lot. (What were they doing?) I don't know.

13C. They didn't spend a lot of time playing—they mostly worked and today's children, they hardly have to do any work and they play a lot. Back then they had to do a lot of work, and these days they don't have to do so much, and back then they didn't hardly play a lot, and these days we can play a lot. (What sort of work did the kids do?) They would like help out their father carrying wood for the fire, and stuff. (What do today's children spend a lot of time doing that children didn't do in the past?) They watch a lot of TV and stuff.

14. I don't know.

15. 'Cause there are countries that have a lot of wars, and sometimes in China, they try to break down the Great Wall, and Kung Fu's try to break down the Great Wall. (So how would that make families want to live in larger groups?) In China they want to live in groups so they have lots more babies so they have more soldiers so they can fight off the bad people.

16. In the past because those kids mostly helped their dad a lot.

3rd   8. Like they didn't have TVs and VCRs maybe and they don't have as much stuff as we have nowadays, like probably next year you could do lots and lots of different kinds of stuff, like computers and faxes will change probably. (What would families do if they didn't have TVs or VCRs or computers or fax machines—what would they do?) They'd sort of be bored or something so they'd have books to read and stuff and entertain their selves, or maybe just watching somebody. It may be entertaining to them, but that sounds boring. (Can you think of anything else that would be different about families a long time ago?) Maybe they didn't have as much stuff as we have now . . . like they didn't have much money and stuff was probably smaller, and families were small.

9. We're people and stuff and we all have like mom and dads.

10. 'Cause maybe they like . . . like my brother, they sort of get like a little bit crazy and do weird stuff like Marilyn Manson, and they just don't like that . . . and they don't want us to get involved in drug stuff and they want healthy bodies and they would start to yell at their moms and dads and they would start to take advantage of them and they would like not pay attention anymore and they just wouldn't listen to them. (How would that affect how many kids parents would want?) I don't know. (What would that make the parents think about wanting to have more kids?) They might want more kids because . . . I'm not sure.

11A. They like take care of the kids more than the dad because sometimes when they're little babies, they have to get milk for them and everything so moms take more care of lots of stuff. They do laundry, they clean the house more than dads do usually. The dads usually work all day, but my mom and dad—they both work. (Anything else that your mom does?) She does a lot of stuff. She takes care of everything.

11B. They might have did lots of work, like maybe like the Pilgrims they had to do housework and the guys have to do like field work and tree work.

11C. Working as hard. Now they don't have to do as much work. (What do today's mothers spend a lot of time doing that mothers didn't do in the past?) Working like at a store or something.

12A. They work really hard for their family to survive and have a shelter and have food and clothes—all that stuff, and they protect their family. They're the boss of the family usually, and like if you ask to go somewhere, your mom goes "Ask your dad." So he's like the boss. (What else do fathers do?) They . . . take care of their family.

12B. They might have had a farm or something and had to do all that work. The mom wouldn't do like all the farm work. (What did fathers in the past spend a lot of time doing that today's fathers don't do?) Working like at [the local utility company]—they didn't do that in the past. (How about some things that fathers in the past did a lot that fathers today don't really do?) They probably don't work as hard as they used to—like really hard. (What sort of things would they have done in the past for work?) I don't know.

12C. Like working at shops and stuff, like where you have big buildings. I'm not sure.

13A. Like going to school sometimes and then after they get home, they go and play games with their friends or with their sisters or brothers.

13B. Most of the time going to school because their moms and dads were mostly working and stuff like that, and then their mom would be home before they came home.

13C. Right now we spend a lot of time at school and then we go home and then we play with our friends, but sometimes they don't go to school. (So that's what today's children spend a lot of time doing. What did children back then spend a lot of time doing?) Mostly going to school and then coming back and cleaning their rooms and stuff like that to make it nice. (And what do children today spend most of their time doing?) Playing.

14. Because they're more like attached to each other. (When were they more attached to each other—the past or today?) Today. (So why do you think a long time ago that families lived in larger groups, with kids and parents and grandparents and aunts and uncles and cousins all in one place?) 'Cause there's not like a subdivision anywhere, so it was like a small place back then, so like there were no farms, and there's not like a bunch of houses.

15. I don't know. (Do you have any ideas why it would be different in other countries than it is here?) Maybe because there's probably an accident in the family or probably they had to go to jail or something. I don't know.

16. Maybe these days. (Why do you think that?) I don't know.

Question 8 proved too difficult. Only six students generated valid responses to it—too few to analyze statistically. Others drew past versus present comparisons in general life conditions rather than in factors specific to family living (e.g., that we have more or better food, clothing, and shelter today; that we have television and other forms of entertainment, etc.). A few made vague or questionable responses (e.g., that in the past, grandparents loved their children but then moved away; that all of the sons in the family had the same first name). The six statements contrasting families in the past versus the present included: Families today are more spread out geographically; some people were not allowed to marry in the past (apparently thinking about racial barriers); there is more divorce today; Black people now are allowed to marry; medical treatment and delivery of babies now is done by doctors in hospitals rather than at home by family members (2). Other responses included: People have pets in the family today; their grandpas love them but then they move away; Black and White people like each other now; we no longer have to hunt for food; they didn't go anywhere then because they didn't have any money; they would have fewer kids, just one; they traveled in wagons pulled by oxen and used fob watches; they didn't go bowling; they spent less time cleaning buildings because the buildings were smaller; milk was delivered to people's homes; families today have better businesses and work more (apparently speaking of more opportunities to work away from the home at more pleasant jobs); families were smaller (inferred on the grounds that they had smaller houses and fewer possessions); today it is quicker and easier to get to a doctor's office or hospital; then they had to treat themselves at home because no doctor or hospital was available. No student said anything to the effect that families were larger in the past, that extended families worked together on family farms, or that many children failed to survive to adulthood.

About 40% (39) of the students were unable to identify ways that families today are similar to families in the past, and 37 drew comparisons that were not specific to families (e.g., people still need food, wear clothing, etc.). Comparisons concerning families focused on family composition (families still consist of father, mother, children, grandparents, etc.; 10), basic family characteristics (people still live in families, family members still love and support one another and share traditions, etc.; 9), or stage phenomena (babies are still born and raised in families, then leave to establish their own households; older family members eventually die, etc.; 7). Other responses included: Families still split up; parents still pass on their things to their children (inheritance); families still resemble one another (2); if their house burned down, they could move in with relatives.

Concerning why most parents want fewer children today, 32 students were unable to respond and 42 gave responses that did not include past versus present comparisons (e.g., taking care of children is a lot of work; children clutter up the house with their toys). Only 22 drew comparisons, mostly suggesting that it cost less (9) or was easier (7) to have or care for children in the past. Other responses included: There are more people in the world now, so people no longer feel as pressed to develop the population (3); my mother won't have any more babies because she is taking the pill; if there are too many children or they are too rambunctious, the parents might try to sell them; kids today are harder to handle; modern life keeps parents very busy; in the past, people cared more about their kids, but today there are smaller houses and less room for large families; parents had less out-of-home work then, so more time to play with their children; babysitters are too costly to use as much as in the past; it used to be easier to take care of kids because a lot of them had things to do (chores); kids are more expensive today because back then you could just make whatever you needed but today you have to buy it (3); things cost more now because they are of better quality; children today are disobedient and don't want to listen (2); kids had quiet things to do then, but now they're noisy; everything costs more now; kids have more stuff now, so caring for them is harder.

All of the students were able to talk about the everyday activities of contemporary mothers, emphasizing birthing/caring for children (76), housework and household maintenance (65), working in paid jobs outside the home (41), relaxation and recreation (27), and "other" activities such as acting as head of the family, volunteering at school, or doing "girl stuff" (7). Only 54 could talk about the activities of mothers in the past. They mentioned activities similar to those mentioned for mothers today, although in different proportions: housework and household maintenance (35), birthing and caring for children (26), paid work outside the home (7), and "other" activities (17), including 3 mentions of relaxation and recreation. Thus, those able to respond knew that mothers in the past were less likely to have paid jobs and had less time for relaxation and recreation.

Asked what mothers in the past spent time doing that today's mothers don't do, and vice versa, 38 students were unable to draw relevant comparisons. The others suggested that today's mothers are more likely to work outside the home (17), said that either mothers in the past (13) or mothers today (11) have more work to do and thus less time for leisure or spending with children, named at least one other thing that distinguished mothers in the past (had to make their own baby food, worked at growing crops, hand washed and hung laundry, etc.; 25), or named at least one thing that distinguishes today's mothers (volunteering at school, working in a modern office rather than a primitive job shop, etc.; 22).

All of the common responses can be seen as accurate or at least defensible. Unusual responses included: Mothers in the past would try to find food and water for their children; mothers today yell and scream at their children (says the same thing about their fathers); mothers today discipline their children by sending them to their rooms or giving them time outs; in the past, mothers had to take their children with them whenever they left the house because there were no babysitters (2); mothers shop more today because there are more stores; past mothers worked because they were slaves; today's mothers "work with each other to get a man"; past mothers would churn butter and wash clothes in a tub, but today they use washing machines; mothers today use computers; past mothers cooked a lot and stayed home most of the time; past mothers made clothes for the family (3); mothers today mostly work and don't pay much attention to their kids because they think kids can take care of themselves; past mothers drank a lot and cleaned up the cave; past mothers sewed clothes and gathered corn, but today's mothers are lazy and sit around watching TV; past mothers did the laundry outside; past mothers would grind butter and milk cows but now they buy these things at stores; past mothers had more work to do because they had more kids; today's mothers argue with their husbands a lot about their smoking and drinking; past mothers used wooden bowls rather than the dishes of today; past mothers were neglectful of their children; past mothers had to make a lot of stuff that we buy today; today's mothers do more shopping; past mothers did slavery work—Black women were slaves and White women were bosses; they used covered wagons to shop; past mothers took lots of time to get on complicated dresses, then went to balls and fancy parties, but they didn't brush their teeth because there were no tooth brushes; today's mothers talk on the phone a lot and run errands; past mothers mostly did farm work because there were few jobs for women back then.

Only one student was unable to talk about the activities of today's fathers. Activities identified included working outside the home/making money (65), caring for/helping/teaching children (40), household chores (34), relaxation and recreation (34), activities associated with the traditional male role (heavy lifting, playing sports or rooting for sports teams, cooking on the grill, mowing the lawn, household repairs, drinking beer, etc.; 30), playing with children (20), disciplining or punishing children (6), and "other" activities (6). Concerning the activities of fathers in the past, 37 were unable to respond, 13 mentioned household chores, 11 caring for/helping/teaching children, 8 working outside the home to earn money, 7 relaxation and recreation, and 33 "other" activities such as working on the family farm, building the family's log cabin, or trading with Indians.

Concerning comparisons between the activities of fathers in the past and today, 39 students were unable to respond and there was disagreement between 21 who said that fathers in the past spent more time working and had less time for family or leisure activities, and 10 who said that this was more true of fathers today. Other responses included: Today's fathers work in offices or do other modern jobs instead of working as farmers or blacksmiths (20), other valid comparisons (fathers watch more television today, mow lawns, and take their children to parks; 19), and invalid or questionable comparisons (fathers play in the snow more today, fathers get married more today than in the past, fathers in the past worked more as janitors or policemen; 9).

Unusual responses included: Now they work to make money and buy us food and drinks, so we are not poor people and live outside with nothing; they yell and scream at their children; they are mean; they get angry at their children and go to bars; they take their children to parks (there were no parks in the past); they pick on you; they do boy stuff, like root for football teams; they move heavy things and cheer for the Detroit Lions; he yells at my dogs; today's fathers watch football games on television; they do drag racing; (2); today there is less hunting and fishing but more housework for fathers; they watch TV; they drive mothers to the hospital when they are going to have babies; in the past, fathers invented things; they made shoes and sold trinkets to the Indians; today they work and play sports more, whereas in the past they just sat around the house; they did farm work (5); they gathered firewood; they hunted for food (6); today's fathers spend more time with their kids and going shopping; they pay for houses from their job earnings; they sometimes cook, not just mothers; they are couch potatoes watching TV all day (mothers are not); they built their own homes and taught their children how to do it—there were no schools then; they mow lawns; they went to work at men-only jobs; they used to work for low pay at dirty jobs and were often homeless; they made wooden bowls and clocks for use at home, and worked for the king; they worked as coal miners, store clerks, barbers, or farmers; they would build tipis and make clothes from deer [skins], but today they work with computers, play basketball, and go scuba diving; they take their kids to more places today, be-cause there are more places to take kids to; they were slaves if they were Black or bosses if they were White; they cut wood and built their own homes (2); today's fathers change diapers (adds that in the past, fathers didn't do this because they were "grossed out or something"); they were at home because there weren't many jobs and the jobs cost a lot of money (young children commonly believe that peo-ple have to pay for jobs). Almost half (43) of the students drew distinctions be-tween mothers' and fathers' roles in responding to these questions.

Concerning the activities of today's children, the students emphasized play-ing, relaxing, or sitting around watching television. However, 49 also mentioned homework and other school-related activities and 22 mentioned chores, such as taking care of one's clothing or room. Responses concerning the activities of chil-dren in the past paralleled those for children today, but with different relative fre-quencies: 42 mentioned play and relaxation activities, 15 school-related activi-ties, and 35 chores. The students depicted children in the past as spending a lot of time on chores but children today spending a lot of time on school-related activi-ties and relaxation.

Asked for direct comparisons, 26 students were unable to respond, but the others said that children today have more time for play or recreation (30), as well as modern toys, games, and sports equipment (28). One third (32) made compari-sons relating to school. Most said that children in the past did not go to school or did not attend for as many months of the year. However, a few said that children in the past went to school all year round, and a few made comments about other differences (e.g., that children in the past went to one-room schools or were home schooled). Eight "other" comments were valid or at least defensible (e.g., children in the past had to play with dusty things, had adventures in the woods, gathered firewood, and had fewer opportunities to visit relatives; children today take camping trips, visit their divorced dad, and swim in a swimming pool instead of a swimming hole). Finally, eight responses were invalid or questionable (e.g., children in the past had no toys, buried food in the fire, or had more time to play). Most students took the view that children in the past lived a life of chores and drudgery but today's children have lots of time for play and recreation and lots of modern toys and games to use.

Many students spoke of children in the past as carrying major family responsi-bilities, such as helping to grow crops or build the family home. They often pic-tured these children either as working long and hard or as sitting around with nothing to do (or occasionally both). Several responses concerning modern children mentioned opportunities afforded by modern means of travel (use cars to go shopping, visit relatives, etc.). Unusual responses included: Today's children read books at night; today's kids are spoiled with candy and everything, but in the past, kids had red butts because their moms spanked them hard; today we get our vision and hearing checked and sometimes get glasses, but in the past the girls had layers of bulky clothing, so they couldn't do cartwheels or handstands as easily; they couldn't jump rope or get dogs in the past; they played different games than kids play now; we visit relatives more now; they went to school "for a long day" then; they would have adventures in the woods and go on nature walks with their parents; they were real skinny because they didn't get enough to eat and they didn't have many clothes and sometimes no home; they had more homework and they were more likely to "get biffed upside the head" if they didn't do the homework when their dad told them to; they used to cut out paper dolls to play with; they didn't have clean glasses to drink from and no forks, so they ate with their hands; they didn't have yoyos and probably played with puzzles that were really old and blocks that they would stack up to make castles, and they would spend a lot of time reading and playing games like Fox and Geese and hiding under their beds, and they had to do what they were told or they would be struck with a whip—they used whips in schools like in the 1920s or 1900s; back then they had home schooling.

Asked about the shift from extended families to nuclear families, only 16 students were able to respond, and none cited a drop in the percentage of the population living and working on farms run by extended families. Instead, the students suggested that people in the past didn't have enough money to buy separate houses so they had to live together, that they had older relatives who were sick and needed to be taken in, that they discovered it is easier to care for a smaller family than a larger one, or that they were Indians and living in large families was their custom.

Asked about national differences in family size, only 17 students were able to generate responses. Once again, none referred to the prevalence of family farms. Instead, they suggested: People in these countries have less money and can save money on housing and meals by living together; help is available on site if a parent should die; family members live closer together in these countries than they do here; in China they want big families because they are always being attacked and want to make sure that they have a lot of soldiers from their army—there are always people trying to knock the wall (this child had recently seen the movie *Mulan*); the extended family arrangement makes it easier for cousins to babysit the children; adults in these countries go to lots of different places to work (so they are away from the home a lot and other people must be available to care for the children); in some places like Africa, the people live in tribes, all in one hut because the families want to be together and keep each other company.

A majority (52) of the students said that children spend more time with their parents today, 25 that children spent more time with their parents in the past, and 19 that they didn't know or that there was no difference. Most observers would suggest that children spent more time with their parents in the past when they lived and worked on family farms. Of the 25 students who made this choice, 17 offered valid rationales for it (children didn't go to school then, they worked alongside their parents on the farm, there was no child care or babysitting then, etc.). In contrast, only 10 of the 52 students who said that kids spend more time with their parents today offered a valid rationale (parents do not work as many hours today, kids do not have to spend so much time doing chores, etc.). Most could not offer any rationale, and 10 offered invalid or questionable rationales (e.g., parents in the past would go away to work for a week or two at a time and leave the children at home).

Most of what the students said about past versus present family living was accurate or at least defensible (accuracy was sometimes difficult to judge because the historical time, geographic location, and particular circumstances of the past families that the students were envisioning as they made their responses were not always clear). The students responded readily when asked about today's families, but most had difficulty when asked about families in the past or when asked to draw comparisons. Some did identify general shifts: More mothers work outside the home, fathers are more likely to work in offices now than to be farmers or blacksmiths, children now go to school for most of the year, more consumer products are available, and most people buy the things they need at stores rather than make them at home. However, few if any were aware of the sweeping changes in family living that accompanied the industrial revolution and the shift from extended families living together on farms to nuclear families living separately in cities or suburbs. Many viewed people of the past as sitting around idly with little to do whenever they were not engaged in finding or growing food, and many others viewed these people (more accurately) as working hard all day long with little or no time for schooling, leisure, visiting, or much else other than chores.

Some students kept coming back to certain themes: In the past there was slavery or restrictions on opportunities for Black people to marry and enjoy family life, but things are different today; past families rarely left their farms because their means of transportation were limited or they couldn't get babysitters to watch the children; people didn't buy much then because they didn't have the well-stocked stores that we have today or because they didn't have much money; they grew most of their food and made most of their clothes; they didn't have access to modern medicine and hospitals; the population was sparse at the time, so people felt a need to increase it and therefore tended to have large families; people back then were hardworking and responsible, whereas today we are spoiled and lazy; child rearing and schooling have become more humane; gender roles now overlap more than in the past, and so on. Most of these themes were accurate as far as they went (although often tinged with presentism), but there were exceptions such as the girl who believed that people in the past spent much of their time getting ready for and then going to balls and fancy parties.

References to conflict between the parents or between one or both parents and the child were disturbingly frequent, as were intimations that one or both parents (but typically fathers) did little but sit around all day and watch TV. Some of these students not only did not look up to their parents as role models but held them in contempt. Even though these were relatively young children living in a modest but pleasant community, their comments about family living in general and their own families in particular were characterized much more by realism (and sometimes even cynicism) than romanticism or idealism. Apparently, even children these days are postmodern.

Occasional rare and unique responses were notable for their precocity: Modern grandparents love you but nevertheless often move away (e.g., to Florida); relatives are obligated to take you in if you become destitute; modern parents tend to focus on quality rather than quantity in raising children, although some are too busy with careers or other things to have much time for their children; it is nice to be able to buy lots of things although this complicates our lives; modern jobs involve more pleasant work done in more pleasant surroundings, but they take parents away from their children and require them to make child-care arrangements; women do not passively wait for male attention but planfully pursue desired men; conflict often arises between men and women because men like to drink and go to bars; in the past, children played games that involved little or no equipment, but today they play more with computers and complicated toys; due to a history of invasion, the Chinese are unusually defense conscious; large families present opportunities to take advantage of economies of scale; and modern sports and recreation opportunities are nice but sometimes parents (especially fathers) are more involved in them than in their families.

The frequency of such insights suggests that primary-grade students should be interested in and able to understand discussions of change over time in family constellations and lifestyles (construed as trade-offs rather than as across-the-board improvements). Much of this can be rooted in a single big idea: The combination of inventions that mechanized farming and the industrial revolution that proliferated factory jobs shifted people's life circumstances from extended families working on farms to nuclear families living in cities and suburbs.

GEOGRAPHICAL/CULTURAL CONTRASTS

17. People all over the world live in families, but different countries have different customs. Do you know of a country where families do things differently than we do here? [If yes, probe for explanation.]

18. What about Japan—do Japanese families do things differently than American families? [If student talks about differences in physical characteristics, ask:] OK, so they look different. But what about everyday family life at home? Is that any different?

19. How is family life different for people living on farms than for other people?

20. How is family life different for people who live in small towns than for people who live in big cities?

K   17. I don't know.

18. Yes. (What do they do differently?) I don't know, but they do things differently.

19. They take care of the animals on the farms. (What do they have to do to take care of the animals?) Feed them. (If families have to take care of animals, what does that mean for their life? Is their life different than for other people who don't live on farms?) Yeah. (How?) They both have to take care of pets, but they both don't have to garden. (Who has to garden?) The farmers.

20. People who live in small towns have little houses and people in cities have big houses. (What if your family lived in a very large city—how would life be different for you?) We would have to do things and get all different stuff. (What sort of different things?) We'd have to have new furniture. (How about if your family lived in a very small town—how would life be different?) You'd have a small house and not very much stuff.

1st 17. Yes, in Africa. (What do they do differently in Africa?) They have little huts and sand and it never snows. (What does that mean for the family?) There's different people 'cause the kids have no school. (What do they do if they're not in school?) They don't have recess and everything. (What else is different about life in families of people who live in Africa?) I don't know.

18. Very different. They talk different. (What else is different about families in Japan?) They have eyes like this (lifts outside corners of his eyes).

19. Because they don't have that much pets as farms. (So what would that mean if people on farms had many more pets?) They would have a pig, and a dog and a cat. (So what sort of things would the family have to do if they had all these animals?) They would have to take care of the animals and they would have to get their food and their water and food for pigs, 'cause pigs eat corn. Pigs like corn. (Can you think of any other ways that family life would be different for people living on farms?) They go to school and only if the kids have a field trip is the only time they go to a farm. (How would life be different for the people living on farms?) Their farms have to be red and some

people don't want their house to be red [appears to believe that farm families live in barns, which are required to be painted red].

20. A large city . . . you'd have a big neighborhood and other people don't live in big neighborhoods. I have a big neighborhood. (What would it mean to have a big neighborhood?) There would be a lot more people in your neighborhood. (What about in small towns?) Small towns—they have little houses and in big towns they have big houses. (Anything else that would be different about living in a small town?) They would have small stuff and you would be too big for the house.

2nd 17. No.

18. Yes, because they do a lot of shows and stuff, like a dragon show and stuff.

19. Because when you live on farms you have to do a lot of work or else the cows and chickens and the plants and stuff might die. (So what would be different for people who live on farms than for people who don't live on farms?) They don't have to do as much work as the people that have farms. The people who live on farms—it's not very fun to live on a farm because you'd never get to spend a lot of time with children because the whole time, the only thing you're doing is working.

20. There wouldn't be as much noise and stuff, because we used to live by a highway and my dad could never get to sleep because of all the traffic and stuff going by, so we moved, and now there's not even one sound at night, except for the crickets. (So can you think of any other ways family life would be different if a family lived in a very large city?) No. (What if your family lived in a very small town? How would family life be different?) I don't know.

3rd 17. China, sort of. Usually sometimes on toys, you look at the bottom and it says "Made in China," but other toys are made in the U.S.A. (Right, and how does that affect family life?) We celebrate things differently, like China, French, Great Britain, France. (What do the families do differently?) I don't know. I think one of them makes flags or signs. They make signs, I think. Israel probably. That's a sign. We did it over there in third grade.

18. I'd have to say yes. They celebrate things different, 'cause here we celebrate things like Christmas, and they'd probably have Valentines. They have one thing before us probably. (What about everyday family life at home?) Just sit around and do stuff. (Do you think it's very different from here?) They would usually probably be outside gathering wood or doing something and probably having their birthdays, and we'd be sitting home doing something else, and then when

our birthdays come up they'd probably be doing the holiday coming up next.

19. They have to do a bunch of chores on a farm and they have to feed the pigs, but here in your yard, you don't have to feed anything— only your dogs or cats or any animals you have. You don't want to have too much pets 'cause you have to feed them a bunch.

20. Like in small towns they don't have that much room for a bunch of houses or many buildings, but like in New York City they build a bunch of places. In a small town . . . it's sort of little, 'cause they don't have that much room. (Yeah, but how is family life different?) I don't know that.

Asked about family-related customs in other countries, more than half (57) of the students were unable to give specific examples, and most of the rest (33) drew comparisons that were not specific to family living (different languages, foods, housing styles, climate, etc.). Only six identified differences in family living patterns (e.g., bath time is handled differently in Japan) or in larger social patterns that affect family interaction patterns (e.g., in some places, most families are farmers; some places have less schooling or no schools at all). Unusual responses included: Some countries don't have schools, sidewalks, cars, trees or grass, or even snow; in Mexico, they eat more food and have less night; they don't milk cows like we do; in Africa, they live in little huts and have a lot of sand and no snow and no schools; in Belgium, they call Santa St. Nick, use wooden shoes, and speak Spanish; in China, they eat with chopsticks and use different toys; they have no cars and have to live in the desert and have to hunt for food; in Australia, they drive on the left side of the road and most families are farmers; in China, they eat different food, using chopsticks (2); in Texas, the children play on dirt roads and in Egypt, they live in pyramids; they have no Santa Claus and different customs; in Australia, there are headhunters and they use slaves to cut the grass; in Germany, they celebrate Hanukkah instead of Christmas; in England, they work a lot or take the subway because they don't have many cars, and in France, they drink wine and fly airplanes; in China, they have more people and they live in smaller houses; children are not allowed to play outside the house; in Asia and Africa, they work outside on chores, not in offices; in China, they have different art and writing (script).

Responses were slightly better when the students were asked about Japanese families. Here, 43 were unable to respond, 44 talked about Japanese versus U.S. differences that were not specific to family living, and 9 students cited examples (e.g., bath time handled differently, houses partitioned to separate the parents from the other family members). Unusual responses included: They have Ninjas; they dance and eat funny; they eat from bowls; they have more parades with dragons and fireworks; different holiday celebrations, different Christmas, no piñatas on birthdays; slanted eyes; they dress fancier; they talk and bow differently and use chopsticks; they have different bath times than we do and have lions [dragons?] where they live; they talk "weirder"; different food and eating utensils; different entertainment, with dragons; they make different things at their jobs; they have different festivals, not the same Christmas, and different party customs; they sit on pillows during celebrations; different chairs and no Santa Claus; parents live in their own separate section of the house; they have martial arts and don't invite their extended families to celebrate our holidays; different clothes and they eat a lot of fish; they do a lot of bowing and have dragon parades; they don't know what money is; they do lots of skiing because there are lots of mountains there; they don't live in large communities like we do; they have to grow their own food; they use chopsticks and have less sturdy houses; they use chopsticks and have pandas.

All but 17 were able to respond when asked about how family life is different for people living on farms. A majority (63) said that farm people have to do more work/chores such as feeding animals or tending to crops, and 11 said that farm people own larger properties, have more land, have barns, and so on. Of an additional 36 miscellaneous responses, 22 were judged accurate or at least defensible (e.g., farmers know their neighbors better, need rain, have to put up with stinky smells, and have to make sure that their animals do not hurt their children) and 14 were judged invalid or at least questionable (e.g., their houses or barns have to be red, they own their own houses but city people have to rent, they have smaller houses than city people, and their children do not go to school). These suburban students held generally negative images of farm life, viewing it as difficult (involving more work) and less desirable than city or suburban living.

Unusual responses included: Farms have a bad smell because of the pigs; they don't have homes—they live in barns; they see more stars at night; they have more food but fewer toys; they have to get up early; their kids work all the time and don't have time for play, school, or learning to read; they only have babies so that they can take on their tradition of running the farm; farmers don't usually have kids—they just live alone and raise their animals; some farmers (Amish) have no electricity; farm people are "a little bit stinky" and "they don't have a lot of things that we do"; farm kids can't go to school, "so all the farming children are dumb." In addition, one third grader said, "Farming guys don't have the resources that we do. They don't know how to live like real people do."

Asked for comparisons of life in small towns compared to big cities, 33 students were unable to respond and 44 offered generic comparisons that did not address family life (e.g., cities are bigger and have bigger buildings and more sidewalks, there is more traffic and noise). No single comparison appeared often enough to be analyzed as its own category of response. However, 9 students gave one or more reasons for wanting to live in a big city (e.g., better quality or variety of schools, better shopping, more playmates, higher paying jobs), and 13 gave other responses that we considered valid or at least defensible (e.g., cities have playgrounds, there are more people in the neighborhood, you meet rich people). Unusual responses included: They have smaller houses than in the city (3); there are fewer sidewalks; the roads are less busy; there is danger from bears; city people like to take time doing things and they try to travel a lot, whereas small-town people wear different clothing, pick flowers, and hunt and gather food; city children can get lost easily; rich people live in cities; small-town people are hungrier because there aren't as many stores and therefore less food, and their schools get less money and therefore have fewer supplies; there are more jobs in the city; city people are always in a rush but small-town people may not have cars or electricity; city people have to share a house and often do not have a car; city people drive fast and run stoplights; city people have to live in apartments; city kids have more other kids to play with, so they have more friends, but they have to live in apartments and can't have pets.

Overall, the students' knowledge about family living in different types of communities, and especially in different countries, was very limited. Many were unable to respond and most of the rest identified differences that did not include contrasts specific to family living. Comments about other countries were rife with stereotyping and chauvinism. Some of the stereotypes have (or at least, had) some basis in fact (the English ride subways, the French drink wine, Africans live in huts, the Chinese eat with chopsticks, etc.), but there were numerous confusions and misconceptions (there are no schools in Africa, the Belgians speak Spanish, the Egyptians live in pyramids, Australia is full of headhunters who use bows and arrows, Germans celebrate Hanukkah instead of Christmas, etc.). Chauvinism often was implied in the disparaging way that the students talked about "different" customs, but sometimes expressed more directly through comments such as "they talk weird."

Compared to what adults would say, the students' responses made much more mention of child-oriented things such as holiday celebrations and Santa Claus, toys and games, bath times, and parades. We believe that this tendency is due not only to age-related interests but to the ways that other cultures are often taught at school or conveyed in books and television programs written for children. These exposures often pay disproportionate attention to aspects of culture that are particularly striking or interesting to children, especially celebrations.

Amid the frequent stereotyped and chauvinistic characterizations of foreign customs, there were occasional statements such as that the Japanese people dress "fancier" than we do and that the Japanese spend a lot of time improving their neighborhoods whereas Americans are prone to sitting and watching TV. Also interesting was the observation that the Japanese do not have piñatas on birthdays, like we do. Piñatas have become commonplace enough in the United States that American children are beginning to think of them as American, rather than Mexican (as noted in chap. 2, several respondents to the food interview drew contrasts between prototypical Asian foods and "American" foods such as spaghetti, pizza, and tacos).

We were surprised at the frequency with which chauvinism or serious misconceptions appeared in the responses to our question about farm families. The interviews were done in a suburb located within a modestly sized metropolitan area that was surrounded for miles in all directions by hundreds of farms. Some farms even were located immediately adjacent to (and in a few cases, still within) the community. Yet, most of the students had little or no experience with farms or farm life, and many of them harbored major misconceptions.

In the first place, their images of farm life were almost entirely negative: Farm families have to work most of the time, must endure unpleasant smells, must live in small houses that often lack amenities found elsewhere, and generally don't have much and "don't know how to live like real people do." Some students even believed that farm children do not go to school and are illiterate, that they live in barns (which must be painted red), and that farmers do not have children (or if they do, it is only because they want somebody to carry on the family's farming tradition).

Few such chauvinistic comments and extreme misconceptions were expressed in our food interview, which included several questions about farm-related topics (see chap. 2, this volume). Those questions focused students' attention on the processes and machines involved in farm work rather than on the personal characteristics or family lives of farm people. Responses to the family-living interview suggested that, as much as they may respect farm people for their knowledge and skill in raising crops and animals, many of these students had very negative stereotypes of farm life. The obvious implication for teachers is that such students stand to benefit not only from instruction on land-to-hand relationships and other process and technical aspects of farming, but also from instruction on the motives of farm families, the satisfactions they derive from their work and their lives generally, the fact that their children go to similar schools and learn similar things, and so on. In short, city and suburban children need to learn that farm people are much more similar to than different from themselves and their families.

Stereotyping and misconceptions also were evident in the students' comparisons between small towns and big cities, although to a lesser degree. Many students depicted small towns as backwaters in which not much occurs, and some embellished this with misconceptions (danger from bears, the people hunt and gather for food, they live in small houses and often lack cars or electricity, or they eat poorly because they don't have as many stores). Other students expressed misconceptions about cities, including several that we had seen previously in our shelter interview (the space in cities is all taken up so that you cannot build a house there, confusion between apartments and hotel rooms; see chap. 4, this volume). They also drew some valid contrasts, although usually not about family living (small town people are more likely to live closer to their relatives, there are more sidewalks in cities, money is concentrated in cities, there is a greater amount and variety of shopping and jobs in cities, city life tends to run at a quicker pace, apartment building owners often do not allow tenants to have pets). A general implication here is that students living in any one of the three major types of modern communities (urban, suburban, and rural) need accurate information (and dispelling of misconceptions) about life in the other two.

FAMILY MOVES AND MIGRATIONS

Question 21 through Question 24 focused on what motivates families to move/ migrate and the effects of the move/migration on family living.

21. Your ancestors came to America from somewhere else. Do you know where they came from? [If yes:] Where? Why did they decide to come here?

22. Families sometimes move to a different house or even a different city. Why do families move from one place to another?

23. Sometimes families move here from another country where they don't speak English. Why do they do that?

24. How does family life change when a family moves to a new country?

K   21. No.

22. Maybe because they don't like their house anymore. (Any other reasons why families would move?) Maybe their house is getting old.

23. I don't know. (How about a family from Japan—why would a family from Japan want to move to the United States?) I don't know.

24. I don't know.

1st   21. No, not really.

22. Because maybe that place is getting small and they're getting tired of living in that town with so much noise there and they want to live somewhere where it's going to be quiet, like in the forest where it's very quiet where there's no birds and cars and stuff, or maybe by a street that's not a busy street because there's not too much cars coming past. (Can you think of other reasons why families move?) Maybe because they don't want nobody to know where they live so they move, because maybe somebody comes to their house every day and every minute and says "Hello, are you there?" Maybe that's why, or maybe because it's just too loud there and they want to move somewhere quiet.

23. Oh, they get taught to talk English like us by someone that can teach them really, really good. I read this book and this girl didn't know how to talk English but this boy or someone taught her really good. (OK, but why might they come here?) I don't know.

24. Well, families get bigger and they move to a new country because they get married and maybe the families get smaller.

2nd 21. My mom came from Germany [couldn't say why].

22. 'Cause sometimes the first place they lived in is getting really old and stuff and they want to move 'cause stuff is falling on them and stuff. (Can you tell me again why your family moved from the house by the highway?) Because my dad couldn't sleep because of all the traffic from the highway.

23. Because the United States of America is a lot more fun and other countries . . . I don't know why, but in the United States of America there's a lot of toys and stuff to play with and in other countries almost all you do is work, and in the United States of America you're free and you can do a lot of cool stuff.

24. I don't know. (If a family from Japan moved to the United States, how would life be different for them?) They would have to get used to the stuff that's in the United States.

3rd 21. No.

22. Maybe because the house is getting too small, because our family keeps growing and growing and growing, and we need more room for us, so if you have a small house, you'd need a big house, and maybe because your community is not very nice or something.

23. To check it out to see what's new or something, or to see Mexico and then they come over here . . . they're sort of different, so they might want to check things out, like see how the schools are and see how their stores and stuff like that are . . . maybe see if the concession stands are a lot different and see how different they are maybe.

24. It would be like really sad because they would miss them, sort of. (Who would they miss?) The person that came to a new country.

When asked about what country their ancestors had come from, only 18 of the students named a specific country, and many appeared to guessing rather than speaking from knowledge about the national origins of their ancestors. Only 9 could suggest a reason for the emigration (mostly to escape oppression, obtain freedom, or obtain better economic opportunities). The most credible responses came from two second graders, one who spoke of ancestors coming from Germany to escape oppression and another who spoke of Irish and Russian ancestors who came because relatives already here told them about good farm land.

The students found it easier to say why families move to a different house or even a different city. Even so, 29 were unable to respond or could offer only vague speculations (e.g., the family just wanted to move or needed to move, they didn't like or got tired of their old house, etc.). Common substantive responses included: A change in family size led to a need or desire for a larger or smaller house (28); the old house had fleas, had fallen into disrepair, or had developed leaks or other problems (20); a desire to leave a dangerous, noisy, or congested neighborhood (11); a parental job change or desire to move closer to a job site (11); and divorce or separation of the parents (7). Other responses included: to escape high or increased taxes; move closer to relatives; move to a better school district; get away from someone they wanted to avoid; desire to get new friends; move to a warmer climate; move if the power goes out and you can't fix it; wanting to move closer to someone or something; can't afford to stay where you are (4).

Asked why people from a non-English speaking country would emigrate to the United States, more than two thirds (66) of the students were unable to respond. The rest suggested that the people wanted to learn English (17) or escape oppression (9). Other responses included: to meet new friends; they want to do different things but they can't where they are; to escape Castro; to get something they can't get at home; an enemy used to live next door to them; to get more toys, less work, and more freedom in the United States; to get a bigger house (2); to join family members already living here; better economic opportunities; wanted to meet new people and escape crowded conditions; wanted to learn about life in another country. Most adults probably would focus on better economic opportunities (and secondarily, escape from oppression) in responding to this question, but only a few students mentioned this factor.

Asked how family life changes when a family moves to a new country, almost half (47) of the students could not respond. The rest suggested that the family members would have difficulty understanding people and communicating with them if they didn't know the language (21); would have to get used to new food, clothing, language, and so on (15); would miss/lose their old friends (13); or would meet new people and make new friends (10). Other responses included: better food, more CDs; they would speak with an accent; it would seem weird to them—not like they were used to; they might feel nervous, like "What am I doing here" or "What if I make a mistake and don't even know it?"; they would have to get used to the traffic and stuff; they would pay lower taxes here; at first they wouldn't know their way around.

Few students knew about their ancestors' national origins. The vast majority couldn't say, simply took a guess, or in a couple of instances, recounted the story of the Pilgrims escaping the oppression of the king. This lack of information about the "family story" suggests the value of genealogical activities in early social studies (in which students are asked to interview their parents about their ancestors and perhaps develop a family tree chart).

Most of what the students had to say about why families might move or migrate and about how migration would affect the family was sensible and free of misconceptions, but focused on the child's point of view. Few talked about a change in job or a desire to move to a better school district in explaining local moves, and few emphasized a desire for economic betterment in talking about migrations. Many of them did, however, show an ability to empathize with people who migrate to a new country, understanding that these people would miss their old friends, have difficulty communicating in an unfamiliar language, and feel strange or out of place when dealing with new social experiences and customs.

Unsurprisingly, most of the responses were microlevel ones focusing on the families' satisfaction with its house or neighborhood, rather than macrolevel ones focusing on economic opportunities or political climates in the countries involved. Very few of these students had yet acquired key ideas connected with notions of the United States as a nation of immigrants, a land of opportunity, or a haven for people seeking freedom and democracy. Primary-grade students are ripe for introduction of these ideas, especially in connection with instruction about the Pilgrims (in Thanksgiving units) and investigations of their own "family stories."

LEARNING AT SCHOOL AND AT HOME

Question 25 and Question 26 focused on learning and socialization. We were interested to see if the students would say anything about child labor laws, mandatory schooling laws, and related legislation designed to protect children from exploitation and guarantee their educations, as well as what they would say about things that children typically learn at home from their families.

25. In the past, most kids went to school for just a few years, but these days most go for a lot longer. Why is that?

26. Kids learn things from their families. What are some things that most kids learn at home, from their families? What else?

K   25. Because their school is longer and other schools don't have it longer. (Why would they have school longer?) It's because they don't want to have school that long—teaching.

      26. I don't know. (Have you learned anything from your mom?) Just learning how to tie and zip. (How about from your dad?) Nothing.

1st   25. I don't know.

      26. What they did a long time ago. (What have you learned from your mother?) My mom always wants me to help her cook. (Has your father taught you to do anything?) He taught me how to kick the football high because we have a little fence thingy and I can kick the ball, but you have to kick it under so it can go up high, because my dad used to play football and he kicked it over our fence. (Has your father taught you to do anything else?) How to play soccer.

2nd   25. So they can learn more.

      26. Don't jump off a cliff when your brother or sister says. (Sounds like a good thing to learn. Anything else you learn from families?) No. (Have you learned things from your mother?) Obey the rules. (Have

you learned anything from your father?) Yeah, yelling at him makes him cry.

3rd 25. Because a long time ago, there wasn't a college probably. Before colleges, they went to school for a short time and now you go to one step, and you keep on going until you graduate. Back then they didn't go all those steps . . . just went to kindergarten and first grade. They'd go just five grades and then they stopped.

26. How to talk . . . like if you're a baby and your mom and dad talk a lot, maybe you'd learn some words and stuff like that. I'm not sure. (What are some things you've learned from your mom?) Lots of stuff, like how to draw because I like to draw a lot and she teaches me how to draw and talk and how to behave appropriately, say nice stuff, and stuff. (Have you learned some things from your father?) Yes. How to fix things and stuff. He teaches me a lot of things.

More than two thirds (66) of the students were unable to say why children go to school for more years now than they did in the past. The rest said that less schooling was available in the past (fewer schools, fewer grades at the schools, etc.; 16); said that there was less to learn in the past or that teachers didn't know as much as they do now (10); or gave various "other" reasons, such as: You could learn just by watching things happen around your small town or farm, but today there is more to learn; fewer people wanted to teach in the past; we need more school today because computers give us access to more information; "because long ago a lot of people worked on farms, and so when they had enough education to get out of school, they would go out of school to help on the farm or whatever other jobs they had." Only the last noted that in the past, most people were farmers and received only a basic education because they needed to work on the farm, although three others gave responses that incorporated at least part of this idea.

Surprisingly, more than one third (33) of the students were unable to name anything that kids typically learn at home from their families. The rest named academic skills (23), manners and morals (18), self-care skills and responsibilities (15), health and safety rules (10), sports and physical skills (6), and "other" knowledge and skills such as planting, coloring, or using computers (23). When asked about things learned specifically from mothers or female relatives, 25 students were unable to respond but the rest suggested academic skills (23); traditional female role behaviors such as caring for children, acting female, cooking and other domestic arts, and so on (22); manners and morals (16); health and safety rules (9); self-care skills and responsibilities (8); sports and physical skills (7); and "other" skills (14). Concerning what is learned from fathers or male relatives, almost half (43) could not respond and the rest identified traditional male role behaviors such as how to act masculine, how to assemble or repair things, using machines, and participating in traditionally masculine sports (17); other sports and physical activities (not so identified as masculine; 12); academic skills (11); manners and morals (7); and "other" skills (26).

Responses concerning what was learned from families in general, from female relatives, and from male relatives were generally similar, with two main exceptions. First, all 17 mentions of learning traditional male-role behaviors were made in the context of talking about what is learned from fathers, and 18 of the 22 mentions of female role behaviors were made in the context of talking about what is learned from mothers. Second, students mentioned learning academic skills, manners and morals, self-care skills and responsibilities, and health and safety rules about twice as frequently when talking about learning from mothers as they did when talking about learning from fathers. However, if we only had interviewed students from intact families in which both parents lived in the home, it is likely that most if not all of the differences in frequencies for these "gender neutral" categories would disappear. About 15 students said that they did not have a father in the home and couldn't really say what kids learn from their fathers.

Responses concerning what is learned from female relatives all were covered in the coding categories except for one student's statement that his mother taught him that "Sometimes you can listen to your father, but most of the time he lies." There was more variability concerning what is learned from male relatives: how to play computer games (2); "how to bake stuff" (one of four responses indicating the learning of traditionally female role behaviors from fathers); taking care of people, helping them, giving them their medicine, and helping people that don't got anything (this child had a sick mother and a father who spent a lot of time caring for her); how to hold a camera, work the television, put on a backpack, and put a rubber band on my Barbie's hair; that you have to be strong in the world; how to put things together and make things; how to stay on the couch all day; how to treat women and girls "nice."

Some of the responses were consistent with the traditional ideal of a happily married couple raising children who admire and identify with them. However, a significant minority included negative comments about one or both parents (typically the father), such as contempt for their failure to carry out their personal or parental responsibilities appropriately or resentment for their harsh or neglectful treatment of the child. It is sobering to consider that these comments may have amounted to just the tip of the iceberg; given that they were expressed in response to questions about what is learned from parents, what might the students have said in response to questions about parental behaviors that make them angry or unhappy?

OTHER QUESTIONS

The last four questions raised issues relating to rules, citizenship, and families in society. We asked about family rules to see if students understood that rules are not just constrictions on individual freedom but mechanisms to make it possible for groups of people to live together in harmony. We asked about options available to families in emergency situations to determine the degree to which students were aware of the public services and "safety nets" available in their communities. Finally, we asked about ways in which families can demonstrate good citizenship, both by helping other individual families and by helping their communities in general.

    27. Why do families need rules? What would happen to a family if it didn't have rules?

    28. If families have a fire, a flood, or some other emergency, who can they turn to for help? Who else?

    29. What can families do to help other families?

    30. What can families do to help their communities?

K   27. Because if you're naughty and stuff, you won't get any toys from them, and not from Santa. (What would happen to a family if it didn't have rules?) Some would be good and some would be very, very bad sometimes. (Why is that?) Because sometimes kids are good and sometimes kids are bad, and some kids might be bad and some might be nice.

       28. 9-1-1. (What do you mean by 9-1-1?) If there's an emergency, somebody will come to help.

       29. They have tools and stuff to try to fix some stuff on their house or something.

       30. I don't know.

1st 27. Your life would change funny. (How would it change?) Because you don't know what to do.

       28. Firefighters, a doctor. (Is there anyone else you could turn to for help if there was an emergency?) A policeman.

       29. I don't know.

       30. Have a good house. (How would that help your neighborhood?) Because you can have directions on what to do.

2nd 27. So they wouldn't get hurt or stolen or need to go to the hospital. (What would happen to a family if it didn't have rules?) They would crack their head or trip and hurt theirself. (Anything else?) Or they might get stolen.

       28. OK, a fire—you can get a firefighter or call 9-1-1. (Who else could you call in an emergency?) Like if a tornado is coming, you get down in your basement. (What if someone was ill?) A doctor and a nurse, and your mother.

       29. Like if someone you don't know trips, you help them back up. That would be generous. (What if a family that you knew was having a

problem or needed help?) If they were fighting, I would like, "Guys, guys, guys—stop." Then I would tell someone else that they were fighting.

30. Don't shout, just be quiet.

3rd 27. Because the family would be all bad and say bad things and they would hit each other and you have rules of no hitting and say nice things, and don't be a show-off if your brother's friends come over. (What would happen to a family if it didn't' have rules?) It would be out of control and stuff, and it would be sort of not a very good family.

28. Their neighbors and anyone that would help you—maybe your grandma and grandpa or someone like that or someone really close to you. (How about if there was a fire at your house—who could help your family?) My mom and dad. (Anybody else?) Your brothers or sisters. I don't know.

29. I don't know.

30. Maybe to help their communities they could clean up litter and stuff.

Seven eighths (84) of the 96 students were able to say why families need rules: health and safety (rules help you stay healthy or safe, keep you from getting sick or hurt) (47); fairness or morality (rules guide you in treating other people fairly and help keep you from doing bad things; 29); clarification of responsibilities (rules make it clear to children that they need to go to school, do their homework, keep their room clean, and avoid destructive behavior; 29); and avoidance of chaos (without rules, things would get wild, crazy, or out of control (29). Other responses included: Otherwise it wouldn't be much fun at home; kids would eat too much sugar and get hyper; kids would do whatever they wanted; "when you grow up, you don't want to be a sassy, disgusting butthead, and you don't want to be calling names, and you don't want to say, 'give me that, give me that' and if you don't get it, you start throwing a fit"; no rules could mean that your family doesn't love you; parents want rules so they can boss you around; there would be out-of-control partying and fighting; so they don't go crazy and get in trouble; so kids don't go ballistic; "to be safe and to learn and to be fair. I got that in social studies."

All of the students were able to name at least one person or service that families could turn to for help in an emergency: the police (52); the fire department (51); relatives, neighbors, or friends (45); medical institutions or personnel (hospital, ambulance, doctors, paramedics; 30); calling 9-1-1 (25); or specialists who could be helpful in the event of a flood (plumber, lifeguard). Unusual responses included: Superman; the FBI; God (2); someone who has a home that you could stay in; someone who knows what to do; someone who could help you get another house; a detective; the power company; the Red Cross.

When asked about how families could help other families, 27 students were unable to respond, but 44 talked about providing direct help with the problem (e.g., help them get out if their car was stuck in snow, guide lost children home, help them move into their home, cheer them up, etc.) and 30 spoke of giving or lending them money, clothing, or other things that they might need (e.g., if their home had burned down). In addition, 7 spoke of taking in destitute people and 6 identified "other" ways to help (check in on homebound sick or vulnerable people, mow the lawns of neighbors when they are away).

Only 46 students were able to talk about how families could help their communities: Thirty-four mentioned avoidance of littering or picking up litter dropped by others and 10 mentioned working on some community improvement project (e.g., getting rid of a fallen tree or other hazard, drumming up support for a new stop sign). Other responses included: Start a neighborhood watch; be like Martin Luther King, Jr. and work to change the laws; avoid polluting the water (2); obey the laws; plant flowers; pay your taxes and do what the government says; be a good neighbor (not noisy, not going in other people's yards); work with neighbors and maybe the police to cut down on speeding in the neighborhood; stop cutting down forests.

Almost all of the students understood that rules are needed to promote harmonious living in the group context, and one first grader had the insight that a lack of rules could mean that your family doesn't love you. All had something to say about what families can do in an emergency. The vast majority of these responses were sensible, but a few of the younger students spoke of getting help from Superman, the FBI, or God. Only one mentioned the Red Cross, and none mentioned the Salvation Army or other social agencies, indicating that children in these grade levels do not yet have much knowledge about these agencies. The police were mentioned more often than even the fire department, relatives or friends, or calling 9-1-1, indicating that these suburban children viewed the police at least partly as benign and helpful, not just as authority figures to be feared or avoided. It would be interesting to see how similarly aged minority/inner-city students would respond to this question.

Ideas about how families can help other families varied from one-time assistance (help free a car stuck in snow, guide lost children home, etc.) to helping in significant and often sustained ways (taking in homeless people and letting them live with you). There was a surprising absence of grade-level differences in response to this question.

Disappointingly, fewer than half of the students were able to say anything about how families might be helpful to their communities. However, the 46 students who were able to respond produced sensible and frequently inspiring responses. Several were potential neighborhood activists or office holders, one had been inspired by Martin Luther King, Jr., and one generated a noteworthy list of ways that people could improve their neighborhood through volunteerism and political activism.

DISCUSSION

The students' ideas about families emphasized social bonds over genealogical and legal kinship relationships. A majority could define grandparents, but not aunts, uncles, cousins, or stepsiblings. They could profit from instruction about some of the genealogical and legal aspects of family relationships.

The students usually knew about ways that families can grow or shrink, but had difficulty envisioning ways that these changes would affect the families' finances, interpersonal dynamics, or allocation of chores and responsibilities. Most understood the relationship forming/severing aspects of marriage/divorce, but not the legal or ceremonial aspects. They stood to profit from learning about marriage vows, common reasons for divorce, and implications for relationships (marriage creates and divorce severs legal relationships, but neither affects blood kinships).

Most of the students knew very little, and some harbored misconceptions, about family life in the past or in other cultures today. Furthermore, there were frequent indications of chauvinism in talking about other cultures and occasional indications of presentism in talking about the past. This suggests that comparative lessons on family living will provide many opportunities to develop basic social understandings about life in different historical eras, geographic regions, and cultures. Very good children's literature resources are available for the latter purpose, notably a richly photo-illustrated series of books describing a week in the lives of families living in different contemporary countries. They help children to see that people from different cultures are much more alike than different, especially regarding the things that are most basic to the human condition.

Family living lessons also offer opportunities to help children begin to appreciate some of the implications of major historical events (e.g., after the industrial revolution, more people lived in urban or suburban areas in nuclear families, and fewer lived on farms in extended families), as well as to see connections across social studies topics (e.g., modern transportation brings us a greater variety of food, clothing and other goods, and facilitates personal travel, but it also leads to more job-related mobility that causes extended families to spread out over greater distances and thus have less contact than in the past).

Surprisingly, the suburban students we interviewed often displayed negative stereotypes of people who live in urban areas and (especially) people who live on farms. Here again, instruction emphasizing commonalities and dispelling misconceptions is needed. If parallel patterns of distortion should prove to be common among urban students or rural students, they also will need empathy-fostering instruction. Family living lessons provide many opportunities for this.

The students were surprisingly ignorant of their "family stories" of emigration to America. This suggests the value of activities calling for them to interview their older relatives, compile genealogical charts, find out why their immigrant ancestors left their homelands, and so on, both as introduction to historical data gathering and as input to lessons on why people move or even emigrate.

Study of things learned from parents and other family members is useful for at least two purposes. In studying what they have learned or could learn from their own families, students can develop greater appreciation for the "funds of knowledge" (Moll, 1992) that their family members have developed about topics or activities, ranging from agriculture to business to trades to religion (and teachers can learn a lot about potential ways to connect to their students' lives outside of school and invite parents or relatives to come to class and demonstrate things to the students). Also, by sharing what they have learned and studying one another's families, students can learn about variations in family structures and customs in ways that promote understanding and empathy (Garcia, 1991).

Finally, in lessons relating to our last four questions, students can be exposed to basic social education principles and values relating to citizenship, the common good, prosocial behavior, and community. For an instructional unit on family living that incorporates these and other topics, see Alleman and Brophy (2002).

8

Government

Our government interviews asked students:

- what government is;
- who is the head of our government and how he gained office;
- who can become president;
- differences between presidents and kings or queens;
- totalitarian governments and how their leaders gain office;
- who is allowed to vote in our country;
- differences between the Democratic and Republican parties;
- desirable qualities in a president;
- where the president lives and works and what he does;
- activities of the U.S. Government;
- where the state governor lives and what he does;
- activities of the state government;
- activities of people who work in the capitol building;
- where laws come from;
- whether laws can be changed;
- examples of laws that are being enacted or changed currently;
- what citizens can do if they oppose a law;
- why we need rules and laws;
- the difference between a rule and a law;
- the functions of judges;
- the activities of people who work for the government;
- what government does for people;

- how the government raises money to pay for its activities;
- what taxes are, who pays taxes, what is done with tax money;
- how police and firefighters are paid;
- who owns the school, who pays the teachers;
- differences between public schools and private schools;
- whether the child would like to be president when he or she grows up (with explanation of why or why not).

RESEARCH ON CHILDREN'S KNOWLEDGE ABOUT GOVERNMENT

More is known about children's knowledge and thinking about government than about other cultural universals. However, much of this work was done between 1965 and 1985, mostly in the middle and upper grades. Our work updates earlier findings from the primary grades and addresses aspects of government that have not been included in previous research.

Early Studies

Studies of political socialization were conducted by Hess and Torney (1967) and Greenstein (1969) in the United States and by Connell (1971) in Australia. These studies indicated that young children idealize political authorities. In the United States, they develop deep emotional ties to the president, whom they regard as a benevolent person who can provide individualized assistance to people who telephone or visit the White House. Police officers are more important in children's immediate world than the mayor or other local political leaders. Children usually have very positive attitudes toward the police and regard them as helpers in times of trouble. These positive views of authority figures become less positive as children move through childhood and into adolescence. The *government*, the *president*, and other political concepts and roles are understood initially in personal terms, but these are replaced by more abstract conceptions in late childhood.

In a questionnaire study of children in Grade 2 through Grade 8, Hess and Torney (1967) found that younger children often personalize the government into a single individual, as in referring to government as "the man who signs the checks." Later, images of government shift from individuals to institutions (the offices), and still later to political processes.

Young children's focus on the president includes the belief that he makes the laws. Only a small minority even mentions the Supreme Court, and even fewer mention Congress. Children picture the president as running the country personally; he is the boss of everything, travels a lot, makes speeches, and addresses concerns raised by individual citizens. As children get older, they distinguish between the personal characteristics of the president and the abilities needed to perform the job. They like the president less as a person but respect him more for his abilities. They describe him as knowing more and working harder than most people, being a leader, and making important decisions.

Young children also tend to view the law as helpful and protective, initially keeping people safe and later facilitating the smooth running of the country. They tend to see laws as just and unchanging, believing that most laws were made in the distant past. They expect police officers to enforce the laws but also to help people in need.

Children tend to think of government as benevolent and put their trust in it, so they have difficulty conceiving or approving of pressure groups, parties, conflict, and so on. They are somewhat aware that big corporations influence government, but usually do not think that rich people have any more influence than average people. They tend to idealize elections, believing that candidates should not say unkind things about one another, that the loser should join in support of the winner, and the winner should be gracious and forgiving.

Greenstein (1969) administered questionnaires to students in Grade 4 through Grade 8. He also found that children's ideas about politics were remarkably free of cynicism. Almost all fourth graders could name the president and most could name the mayor of their city (New Haven), but few of them had much knowledge about the roles or duties of the mayor and president. They knew that the president was important but were not sure what he did, and they had little or no knowledge about the governor or the legislature. Those who were able to say something about the president or governor stressed general benevolence (helping and taking care of people) and providing services such as parks for children, snow removal, paying workers, or seeing that people have good homes and jobs. Among fourth graders, 96% could name the president, 92% could name the mayor, but only 33% could name the governor. Other studies have shown that residents of cities and towns with a strong mayoral system are more likely to be familiar with the mayor, whereas residents of smaller communities governed by township boards or town councils presided over by weak mayors tend to be more familiar with the governor.

Children knew a lot more about executives than legislators, often viewing legislators as "helpers" of the executives. They could not even begin to describe differences between the two parties until sixth grade, and expressions of political philosophies were rare. Yet, 60% of even fourth graders declared a party preference, so direction of party affiliation is set prior to understanding of what the parties are all about.

Moore, Lare, and Wagner

Moore et al. (1985) conducted a large study of children's political knowledge and thinking in Grades K–4. It confirmed and expanded earlier findings that children's political orientations are more affective than cognitive, organized around images of political leaders as benevolent parental figures. The children lived in or near Los Angeles. Comparisons across grades indicated that they tended to know first about local government, then the state, and then the nation at the level of governmental activities, but first about the president, then the governor, and then the mayor in terms of political individuals.

The authors described children as developing through *prepolitical, quasipolitical,* and *political* levels of thinking. Most primary-grade children are prepolitical, initially possessing only symbol recognition (the president "signs papers," "makes speeches," or "has meetings") but later acquiring mostly accurate but very general ideas about governmental processes or functions (the president "makes laws," "runs the country," or "solves problems"). There is no awareness of specific functions or division of labor between the president and other political leaders. Children think of a pool of governmental functions that are carried on by important people who help one another in various ways.

Children's political knowledge enters the quasi-political level when they begin to understand the functions of political actors or objects (e.g., the president's interactive role with Congress in lawmaking, how the president governs, or the president's preeminence in foreign affairs). None of the students gave responses beyond this level, but the researchers posited a third, political, level that implied a more comprehensive and detailed knowledge of politics reflecting the content of high-school or college civics textbooks.

The same students were interviewed yearly in each successive grade. The kindergarten findings were described in detail to provide a baseline for assessing knowledge growth later. Questions about who governs the country indicated that one third or more of the students were unable to respond or gave some irrelevant response. The most popular responses were as follows: Asked who is boss of our country, 24% said God or Jesus and 16% said the president (Nixon). Asked who does the most to run the country, 30% said God or Jesus and 15% said Nixon. However, when asked who makes the laws, 24% said the police, 15% God or Jesus, 12% Nixon, 9% other political figures, and 7% "the government." The students had difficulty distinguishing between the office and the incumbent. Some thought that long-dead presidents were still alive, that several presidents held office simultaneously, or that new presidents were picked by Washington or Lincoln.

Only 22% of the kindergarteners had heard of the two major political parties, although 46% gave reasonable answers when asked what a law is. When asked what the president does when he goes to work, 51% did not know and the rest gave miscellaneous answers such as writes, governs, solves problems, helps people, makes speeches, or "tells his secretary to tape" (Nixon).

Asked whether people filling various occupational roles work for the government, 76% said this was true of judges and 67% said this was true of police, but lower figures were obtained for soldiers (49%), teachers (46%), mail carriers (45%), and milkmen (42%).

Only 24% of kindergarteners said that they knew what the word "government" meant, and only 12% generated specific responses when asked what government does. These ranged from helping the president to making pennies, making rules, judging people, and telling you what to do. Ninety percent described what the police do, but only 34% described what soldiers do and none could say what politicians do. Other questions that yielded very low percentages of correct answers included explaining an election (7%), identifying then-Governor Ronald Reagan (2%), and identifying then-Mayor Tom Bradley (1%).

Kindergarten children often confused religious with political authorities and were more likely to know famous presidents of the past than the incumbent president. Few understood the term *election* or could recognize the names of both political parties. Almost half could tell what a law is but fewer than 20% could explain who makes the laws. They were clearer on the functions of the police and soldiers than the duties of the president, and few were able to distinguish consistently between public and private occupations.

There was steady growth across the K–4 range. Occasionally, noteworthy advances appeared at a particular grade, presumably as a result of political content included in that grade's curriculum. Increases in political knowledge included: When asked if a judge works for the government, 76% of kindergarteners answered correctly. Parallel figures for Grade 1 through Grade 4 were 84%, 89%, 90%, and 97%, respectively. Correct-answer percentages for Grades K–4 were 46, 71, 77, 93, and 99 for "What is law?"; 7, 14, 36, 75, and 94 for "What is an election?"; and nonapplicable, 7, 21, 33, and 59 for "What are taxes?" (Kindergarteners were not asked to explain taxes.)

About one third of the children confused utility bills with taxes. When asked about kinds of taxes, the most common response was the sales tax, follow by property tax and income tax. Asked about why people pay taxes, only 19% of fourth graders said that they were used to pay for government services such as schools or aid to the poor. Some mentioned general benefits such as keeping the country running, but 25% mentioned specific private benefits such as retaining one's home or access to utilities.

When asked who can vote, nearly 70% of fourth graders mentioned a required age and 5% said that voters must be citizens. A smaller percentage said that anyone could vote and a few said that the candidates themselves or other people in government could not vote.

Distinctions between the public and private sectors were vague. Police and judges were recognized as government employees more often than mail carriers or teachers. Some students thought that television news reporters work for the government, as part of a belief that television news is presented by the government. Only 1% of third graders and no younger students could define Republicans or Democrats, and only 3% could name a policy difference between the parties. Remarkably, although 60% of Greenstein's 1958 New Haven fourth graders expressed a preference for one political party over the other, this was true of only 7% of 1978 Los Angeles fourth graders.

The authors identified certain items of knowledge that had the highest correlations at particular grade levels and may be thresholds leading to increasing understanding of the political domain. Threshold variables for kindergarten and first grade included knowing something about what the government does, what the president does, taxes, and the electoral process. For second and third grade, three additional threshold variables involved understanding the roles of Congress, the Supreme Court, and senators. Threshold variables for fourth grade included knowing about political parties and what politicians do.

The children knew more about the police, judges, and courts than other aspects of government, presumably from television. When asked about courts, 25% of third graders talked about their punitive function (bad guys go there and have to pay fines); 20% spoke of their adjudicative functions (determine guilt); 21% associated the term with judges, juries, or trials; 14% spoke of courts as facilitating legal proceedings (divorce, adoption, settling disputes); and the rest gave other responses or did not know. When asked about what judges do, 23% mentioned determining guilt or innocence, 18% presiding over a court or running a trial, 17% solving problems, helping people, or solving crimes, 12% determining punishment or jail sentences, and 7% listening to both sides and trying to bring out the truth.

In talking about laws, majorities of younger students mentioned their prohibitive functions. Small but growing (across grades) minorities spoke of prescriptive functions (they are rules that you have to follow). Few students said that laws serve a beneficial or rational purpose such as keeping the world organized. Children tend to believe that laws emanate from a prestigious source (the police, God, or Jesus for kindergarteners and the president or the government for older students). Very few were aware of Congress or other legislators.

Moore et al. (1985) concluded that there was evidence for both developmental phenomena (stages as described by Piaget and by Kohlberg) and social learning phenomena. Developmental phenomena are most obvious in children's tendencies to think about government in terms of particular individual leaders and to endow these leaders with qualities of personal benevolence. Social learning is seen in their knowledge about individual names and issues of the day and about the activities of some governmental workers whom they have opportunities to observe personally (police) or through television (the courts).

Berti's Studies

Although the pace of research on children's political knowledge has slowed since the 1980s, Anna Berti and her colleagues have made noteworthy contributions in recent years through studies done in Italy. Berti (1994) began by probing third graders' understanding of political concepts used in their textbooks. One term was *governing*, addressed in the context of ancient Egypt and the pharaohs. When asked to define the meaning of government, 56% of third graders said that it involved commanding associated with public functions (issuing laws, directing armies, etc.) but 44% restricted the commanding to getting personal services for oneself and one's family. The students were vague about the actual tasks involved in governing. Berti concluded that it is difficult for third graders to imagine the exercise of power in terms of specific functions rather than as generic commanding (ordering servants about).

When asked to define democracy, only 7% of the third graders defined it as an election of representatives. Most could not respond and the rest described it in evaluational terms without actually defining it (e.g., democracy is the best form of government). Most conceptions of government depicted face-to-face commanding rather than hierarchies of offices. Children depicted military commanders as personally leading their armies into battle and supreme court judges as personally hearing criminal cases and assessing punishment to the guilty. Third graders possessed an idea of a chief, but the concept of a *government* featuring political roles ordered hierarchically emerged over the next several years.

Berti and Ugolini (1998) probed first-, third-, fifth-, and eighth-grade Italian students' knowledge of the judicial system. Those who did know about judges thought that their job was to establish guilt and punishment as requested by the victims of a crime. None of these children mentioned laws, either as something to be studied before becoming a judge or as something to consider when making decisions. Also, none said that judges were paid by the state. Some thought that they were unpaid and others that they were paid by the police, the accused, or the plaintiffs. Third graders knew only slightly more about judges. Fifth graders described them as public servants paid by the state. Only by eighth grade did students mention legal studies and basing decisions on the law.

Asked about judges, lawyers, witnesses, prosecutors, and juries, only 8 of 20 first graders correctly described judges, and none correctly described lawyers. The corresponding numbers were 13 and 5 for third graders, and 16 and 14 for fifth graders. Similar numbers appeared for witnesses, prosecutors, and juries. There were common confusions, such as assigning judges the single task of banging a gavel when people got noisy, depicting lawyers as judges or helpers, confusing witnesses with the audience or lawyers, and confusing the jury with the audience or assigning it imprecise tasks such as trying to find out some information. First and third graders either did not know who makes laws or mentioned local authorities such as the mayor, the police, or the judge. Fifth graders spoke more about central authorities such as the prime minister, the government, or lawmakers. Only at the eighth-grade level did most participants mention the parliament.

Berti and Benesso (1998) asked Italian kindergarteners, third graders, and sixth graders to define various terms connected with the concept of *nation–state*.

Kindergarteners tended to define kings by referring to attributes emphasized in fairy tales (crowns, rich clothing, husband of queen or father of princess, etc.), or to commanding servants or slaves. Third graders were more likely to mention commanding the population as a whole, and sixth graders focused exclusively on this response. Asked about taxes, kindergarteners either could not respond or defined them simply as money. Third graders were more likely to define them vaguely as bills that had to be paid, whereas sixth graders were more likely to know that they supplied money to finance the government.

Berti and Andriolo (2001) interviewed a class of Italian third graders about core political concepts before launching a unit of instruction. Prior to instruction, the third graders had very few concepts, either correct or incorrect, about political offices. They were vague about how governmental leaders get their offices or what duties they perform. They knew more about school and the police, but not about the role of government in determining such things as who must go to school or what is studied there. They represented teachers and police as employees but not yet as public servants. Many thought that they were paid by their bosses, using either their own money or money obtained from a bank. Fewer than half could say anything about judges, mostly attributing decisions about guilt, penalties, or disputes to them. Some misattributed functions such as giving money to people, supervising workers, or making laws. The children had difficulty distinguishing laws from rules (by saying that laws are decided by political authorities).

Berti and Andriolo suggested that children's core understanding of the political world develops through a four-step sequence. Before ages 6 through 7, children show little understanding of economic and political institutions. They tend to believe that people perform activities relating to occupational roles because they feel like it (police catch criminals because they want to, bus drivers drive buses so that people don't have to walk, etc.). Understanding of societal institutions begins around ages 6 through 7 with awareness that teachers and other workers cannot do whatever they want (and that people perform occupational roles because these are their jobs and allow them to earn a living). At first, children do not have the notion of an employee, believing that all or at least most people work on their own and are paid by their customers (e.g., teachers by parents, bus drivers by passengers). They do not differentiate public institutions from private ones or distinguish laws from other social rules.

The third stage occurs between ages 8 through 10, when children acquire the notions of a boss who gives orders and pays, and employees who get paid for carrying out these orders. At this time, children start differentiating political characters from other people seen on television, attributing to them the function of commanding. They still lack the notion of political institutions because they do not yet distinguish bosses who are politicians from other kinds of bosses such as business owners, or understand the roles of different political leaders or offices.

They also do not yet possess clear notions of a nation–state, thinking about borders only as mountains, coastlines, rivers, or other physical barriers (walls, moats, etc.) and not understanding what a country or capital city is. They define laws as rules and attribute to laws the functions of preventing crime and disorder, but think of laws as made by the police, local authorities, or the president and announced through the media.

The full emergence of a naive politics that includes the notion of a nation–state at its core does not appear until about ages 11 through 12. At this fourth stage, children distinguish between different political roles (president, governor, mayor) by assigning them different degrees of power and connecting them (incorrectly) within a command hierarchy (e.g., the president gives orders to the governor, who gives orders to the mayor). Children now can see the nation–state as a territory in which a central power makes laws for the whole country and in which the police, army, judges, and teachers are public servants paid by taxes. Laws are seen primarily as restrictions and prohibitions, without much appreciation of their functions for regulating relations between people and guaranteeing rights.

Berti (2002, 2004) synthesized the research on children's political knowledge, indicating that it initially featured studies of political socialization done mostly by political scientists; then featured studies of general stage phenomena done mostly by Piagetian developmental psychologists; and most recently has featured studies by psychologists and educators interested in trajectories of knowledge in specific domains. The latter studies have included younger children than usually studied previously, and sometimes have been accompanied by curriculum development or instructional interventions indicating that the acquisition of domain-specific knowledge typically depends more on learning opportunities (especially, exposure to explicit instruction) than on maturation of generic cognitive structures or processes. Berti has shown, for example, that although Italian third graders usually know even less about law and government than American children of the same age, they can learn networks of explicit and connected understandings (and in the process, overcome common misconceptions), when taught systematically (Berti & Andriolo, 2001).

Other Studies

Along with the major lines of research reviewed so far, other studies done through the years have touched on issues relating to children's knowledge and thinking about government. Barton (1997a, 1997b) described difficulties encountered by fourth- and fifth-grade students attempting to understand the American Revolution that were rooted in their minimal understandings of what taxes are, who establishes them, how they are collected, or what they are used for.

Furth (1980) reported that British children were confused about the nature and purposes of taxes until reaching ages 10 through 11.

Although children's attitudes and beliefs about political offices (especially the presidency) tend to be positive, their attitudes toward specific politicians are often quite negative, especially as they get older. For example, Bronstein, Daily, and Horowitz (1993) conducted focus groups with fourth- and fifth-grade children 1 week prior to the 1992 presidential election. She found that the children articulated negative images of President (George H.W.) Bush and negative ratings of his job performance, although they were unable to supply much factual content to bolster these opinions or support arguments in favor of challengers. Similarly, Bailey (1976) administered a civic education questionnaire to students in Grade 3 through Grade 6 every year between 1973 and 1976, during which Watergate and its ramifications were in the news. He found that attitudes toward President Nixon and his performance in office declined steadily from Grade 3 to Grade 6 and that widely publicized political events impacted these attitudes.

Finally, it is worth noting that in 1999, an ABC News poll of 12- to 17-year-old American students indicated that although 62% of them believed that they or their child could become president one day, only 17% said that they would want this to happen. In comparison, fewer adults (53%) thought that their child could become president, but 30% would want it to happen. The latter figure was down from 35% in a 1992 poll, which in turn was down from 41% in a 1988 poll. The authors speculated that the trials and tribulations of President Clinton during the year before the 1999 poll hadn't "made the job look like a whole lot of fun" (Langer, 1999). Similarly, a Voter News Service (2000) exit poll conducted on election day of 2000 indicated that only 31% of the voters questioned said that they would want one of their children to be president.

OUR GOVERNMENT INTERVIEWS

Interviews were conducted with 96 students, 24 in each of Grades K–3, stratified within each grade by prior achievement level and gender. Descriptive statistics and information from analysis of scores derived from the coding are given in Table 8.1. For a detailed presentation of the findings, see the technical report (Brophy & Alleman, 2002).

WHAT IS GOVERNMENT?

1. **Today we're going to talk about government. What is government?** [If necessary, define government as the people who are in charge of running our country.] **What does government do?**

TABLE 8.1
Distributions and Phi Coefficients Showing Relationships
of Coding Categories to Grade Level

Response Categories	Total	K	1	2	3	Phi
	96	24	24	24	24	
1A. Today we are going to talk about government. What is government?						
0. Doesn't know/no relevant response	62	23	8	11	10	–46
1. Person: Defines the president, the governor, or some other individual as the government	17	1	3	7	6	26
2. People/organization (the government is the people or an organization that makes rules or laws, runs the state or country)	17	0	3	6	8	33
1B. What does government do?						
0. Doesn't know/no relevant response	29	18	10	1	0	–66
1. "Helps people" or gives people money, food, clothes, and so on	16	3	6	4	3	
2. Makes/enforces laws (make laws, keeps us safe, etc.)	36	3	4	12	17	50
3. Run the country (run the state/country, solve problems)	20	0	4	8	8	34
4. Other (makes land, engages in wars or foreign affairs, etc.)	10	0	4	3	3	
5. Person confusion (speaks of the government as an individual person or organization)	14	0	2	7	5	32
2. Who is the head of our government?						
0. Doesn't know/no relevant response	23	10	7	3	3	–29
1. The president	49	6	7	19	17	48
2. Bill Clinton	38	3	3	15	17	56
3. Past presidents (George Washington, Abe Lincoln, John Kennedy)	17	7	6	3	1	–26
4. Other (the governor, John Engler, the people, etc.)	10	2	5	2	1	
3. How did he get to be the president?						
0. Doesn't know/no relevant response	30	17	10	1	2	–58
1. He was elected, won an election	44	1	3	19	21	76
2. Virtuous (hardworking, a good person, speaks the truth, etc.)	14	3	7	2	2	
3. Competent (did well at school, good speaker, problem solver)	8	0	4	1	3	
4. Other (made a lot of money, he signed up for the job, etc.)	12	3	5	2	2	
4. Who can be president?						
1. Anyone/everyone (unqualified) or no relevant response	15	4	2	7	2	
2. Anyone who meets the age qualification	43	4	14	7	18	46

(Continued)

TABLE 8.1
(Continued)

Response Categories	Total 96	K 24	1 24	2 24	3 24	Phi
3. Must have special qualifications (virtuous, well/ specially educated, good speaker or decision maker, etc.)	22	3	9	5	5	
4. Other qualification (be a lawyer, really want the job, etc.)	12	0	2	4	6	28
5. Disqualifying exceptions (the elderly, people who already have jobs, criminals, etc.)	12	2	2	1	7	30
6. Only certain people qualify (couldn't say more)	18	12	3	3	0	–48

5A. Some countries have kings or queens instead of presidents. How are presidents different from kings or queens?

	Total	K	1	2	3	Phi
0. Doesn't know/no relevant response	16	9	5	2	0	–38
1. Kings/queens live in castles, palaces	21	3	6	7	5	
2. Kings/queens wear crowns, jewels, wigs, royal robes, and so on	25	2	8	11	4	
3. Kings/queens live life of luxury, have servants, and so on	11	2	1	4	4	
4. Kings/queens rule all by themselves or are despots (whereas presidents do not have dictatorial powers)	20	1	4	3	12	43
5. Kings/queens have mostly ceremonial jobs	7	2	1	1	3	

5B. How do kings or queens get the job?

	Total	K	1	2	3	Phi
1. Marriage/inheritance	31	0	7	11	13	44
2. Rich (they are rich, own a castle, etc.)	15	3	4	3	5	
3. Other (they are greedy, they are not elected, etc.)	24	9	6	5	4	–18

7. In our country, the president and other government leaders are elected by voters. Who is allowed to vote?

	Total	K	1	2	3	Phi
1. Anyone/everyone (unqualified) or no relevant response	22	11	5	4	2	–33
2. Everyone who is old enough	46	2	9	16	19	55
3. Not everyone old enough to vote is allowed to vote (cannot explain it further)	10	3	4	1	2	
4. Citizens/residents	6	0	1	2	3	19
5. Other qualifications/exceptions (only those who register, the president or criminals can't vote, etc.)	20	8	6	2	4	–23

9. What would you look for in a candidate for president?

	Total	K	1	2	3	Phi
0. Doesn't know/no relevant response/unexplained preference	21	9	7	2	3	–29
1. Names a person (Lincoln, Louis Armstrong, Clinton, etc.)	20	9	3	6	2	–28
2. Generic virtues (nice, kind, helpful, not greedy, not bossy, etc.) All generic virtues except those coded in subsequent categories	50	9	12	15	14	19

(Continued)

TABLE 8.1
(Continued)

Response Categories	Total 96	K 24	1 24	2 24	3 24	Phi
3. Honest, trustworthy	13	0	2	2	9	42
4. Competence (smart, educated, knows the job, experienced, good leader, problem solver, etc.)	21	1	2	6	12	44
5. Vision/policies (has good ideas about needed laws or ways to improve the country, etc.)	21	0	1	14	6	56
6. Treats people fairly or with respect	6	0	1	0	5	35
7. Other (happy, will do what I ask, a female, helps the poor but without raising taxes, pleasing personality, etc.)	23	1	6	10	6	31
10A. Our president right now is Bill Clinton. Where does he live and work?						
0. Doesn't know/no relevant response	24	12	11	0	1	–53
1. White House (specifically)	52	4	8	21	19	60
2. Less specific or incorrect name for the building (big house, president's house, capitol building)	9	4	1	1	3	
3. Washington, DC (specifically)	48	1	5	19	23	77
4. Some other location	10	4	4	2	0	–23
10B. What does the president/government do?						
0. Doesn't know/no relevant response	21	12	8	0	1	–50
1. Generic virtuous behavior (works, does good, helps people, etc.)	15	4	6	5	0	–26
2. Generic office work (reads, writes, has meetings)	19	6	0	6	7	
3. Solves problems (generic [unexplained further, no examples])	28	0	4	13	11	48
4. Solves problems ([unrealistic] stopping riots, cleaning up things, acting as a judge or policeman, setting broken bones, etc.)	12	4	6	1	1	–27
5. Solves problems ([realistic] making decisions about foreign affairs or warfare, recommending or enforcing laws, making policy speeches, vetoing laws, etc.)	17	2	2	5	8	27
6. Other (tries not to get assassinated, keeps the country united, etc.)	14	1	5	6	2	
7. Student is coded in Categories 3 or 5	45	2	6	18	19	62
8. Student generates "virtuous behavior" response (all responses coded in Category 1 plus some coded in Categories 4 or 6)	19	6	8	5	0	–31
11A. We live in the state of Michigan. The governor of Michigan is John Engler. Where does he live and work?						
0. Doesn't know/no relevant response	57	18	19	13	7	–40
1. Capitol building	14	0	0	6	8	42
2. Any other building	8	2	1	2	3	

(Continued)

TABLE 8.1
(*Continued*)

Response Categories	Total	K	1	2	3	Phi
	96	24	24	24	24	
3. Located in Lansing	20	1	2	6	11	40
4. Located somewhere else	11	4	2	2	3	
11B. What does the governor/government do?						
0. Doesn't know/no relevant response	36	14	17	3	2	-57
1. Generic virtuous behavior (Works, does good, helps people, etc.)	33	8	6	11	8	
2. Solves problems (generic [unexplained further, no examples])	28	1	2	14	11	51
3. Solves problems ([unrealistic] stopping riots, cleaning up things, acting as a judge or policeman, setting broken bones, etc.)	9	3	2	1	3	
4. Solves problems ([realistic] recommending or enforcing laws, making policy speeches, seeing that we have street lights, vetoing laws, etc.)	12	1	1	5	5	25
5. Student is coded in Categories 2 or 4	33	2	3	14	14	51
12. What do people who work in the Capitol building do?						
0. Doesn't know/no relevant response	50	20	16	8	6	-48
1. Generic good deeds (help people, do good, work for the governor, solve problems, etc.)	17	2	5	4	6	
2. Generic office work (work in offices, work on computers, write letters, stamp papers, etc.)	10	2	3	3	2	
3. Specific example (respond to questions that people send in, develop rules and laws, act as staff people to governor)	20	0	2	9	9	42
4. Other (clean the building so it will look good for tour groups, etc.)	9	1	2	4	2	
5. Student is coded in Categories 2 or 3	27	2	4	11	10	36
13. Where do laws come from? Do you know about any laws that our government is working on right now?						
0. Doesn't know/no relevant response	13	7	4	2	0	-31
1. The police	10	4	1	1	4	
2. The president, the governor, judges	59	9	16	17	17	29
3. The government	27	1	7	8	11	34
4. Other (bad guys, God, the people, etc.)	9	5	1	1	2	
5. Mentions Congress/legislation process specifically	6	0	0	3	3	26
14A. Can laws be changed?						
0. Doesn't know/no relevant response	6	4	1	1	0	-26
1. No	22	13	6	2	1	-47
2. Maybe/yes	68	7	17	21	23	57

(*Continued*)

TABLE 8.1
(Continued)

Response Categories	Total	K	1	2	3	Phi
	96	24	24	24	24	
14B. How are laws changed?						
1. The president, governor, or judges change them	40	5	9	12	14	29
2. People in the government who made the laws have a "revote"	11	0	3	3	5	23
3. The new law or change in law is publicized	6	0	2	2	2	
4. Other (the president speaks to the government about changing the law, citizens petition, God changes them, etc.)	6	2	1	1	2	
5. Student names one or more specific laws that have been or might be changed/introduced	27	1	4	8	14	45
14C. What can parents do if they don't like a law?						
0. Doesn't know/no relevant response/ambiguous response	33	13	13	4	3	−42
1. Accept it (just put up with it, obey it)	14	3	4	5	2	
2. Defy it (just do what they think is right, disobey the law, etc.)	12	6	2	3	1	−24
3. Contact president, governor, police, and so on	32	2	6	10	14	40
4. Contact your representative	9	0	0	4	5	33
15A. People are supposed to follow rules and laws. Why do we need rules and laws?						
0. Doesn't know/no relevant response	11	5	5	1	0	−30
1. Provide guidance (so people will know how to act, etc.)	9	2	3	1	3	
2. Safety (keep us safe, prevent harm, etc.)	61	14	12	18	17	
3. Create a well-ordered society/avoid chaos	29	3	6	9	11	28
15B. What is the difference between a rule and a law?						
0. Doesn't know/no relevant response/says that they are the same	7	4	3	0	0	−29
1. Gives examples of rules or laws but does not draw a clear distinction between them	6	1	1	4	0	
2. Says something accurate about rules or laws but does not directly compare them	39	18	14	5	2	−55
3. Contrast (you can break rules but you must obey laws)	29	2	1	8	18	61
4. Contrast (rules are made by parents, teachers, etc., whereas laws are made by governments)	9	1	2	1	5	23
5. Contrast (rules apply only to the home, the school, etc., but laws apply everywhere)	24	0	3	12	9	46
6. Draws a contrast (vs. fails to do so)	50	2	7	19	22	69

(Continued)

TABLE 8.1
(Continued)

Response Categories	Total	K	1	2	3	Phi
	96	24	24	24	24	
16. Judges are part of the government. What do judges do?						
0. Doesn't know/no relevant response/vague generality (help the government, talk to people)	36	12	16	5	3	–45
1. Decide criminal cases (determine if people are innocent or guilty)	40	7	6	13	14	30
2. Decide civil cases (make rulings in lawsuits, divorces, etc.)	10	1	1	5	3	
3. "Lecture" defendants about their conduct	8	4	1	1	2	
4. Preside over the courtroom (run the court, keep order, bang gavel, etc.)	15	2	4	3	6	
5. Question to elicit facts, motives (talks to witnesses to clarify what they saw, talks to the accused to clarify motives, etc.)	6	1	0	3	2	
6. Other (speaks very politely to people, reviews jury decisions, etc.)	9	1	1	3	4	19
17. A lot of people work for the government. What are some of the jobs that they do?						
0. Doesn't know/no relevant response/vague generalities (works, helps the government, president, etc.)	58	20	18	12	8	–41
1. Names specific government jobs (president, governor, legislator, judge, makes laws, etc.)	22	1	2	8	11	41
2. Staff/office work (works on computers, goes to meetings, secretary, assistant to executive or legislator, etc.)	14	2	2	4	6	20
3. Other (cleans windows, invents things for the government, works for military or police, etc.)	12	1	2	5	4	20
18. Besides making laws, the government also helps people. What are some of the things that the government does for people?						
0. Doesn't know/no relevant response/vague generalities (helps, does good, etc.)	34	13	13	2	6	–41
1. Speaks of general functions of government rather than specific services to individuals or families (keeps us safe, passes good laws, etc.)	31	2	6	15	8	42
2. Government as all-purpose provider (builds homes, factories, grocery stores, etc., to provide everyone with whatever they need)	8	1	1	3	3	
3. Safety net services (provides assistance to poor people, people who have suffered fires or storm damage, etc.)	16	2	4	4	6	
4. Basic community services (police, fire, paramedics, etc.)	10	3	1	2	4	

(Continued)

TABLE 8.1
(Continued)

Response Categories	Total 96	K 24	1 24	2 24	3 24	Phi
5. Other (certifying the safety of consumer products, providing insurance, renewing run-down neighborhoods, etc.)	10	4	0	5	1	
19. It costs money to pay the people who work for the government. Where does this money come from?						
0. Doesn't know/no relevant response	28	11	9	1	7	−34
1. Government (the president or government prints or coins the money)	13	3	3	3	4	
2. Banks, ATM machines, others places where they have/make money	26	8	9	7	2	−25
3. The people (from people/families/wage earners [does not explicitly mention or describe taxes])	26	8	4	11	3	
4. Taxes (uses the word "taxes" or describes taxation)	29	0	0	14	15	66
5. Sales taxes (when we buy something, a little bit of the amount we pay goes to the government)	16	0	0	7	9	45
6. Transition responses (Coded both 1 or 2 and 4)	10	0	0	5	5	34
7. Mature responses (Coded 4 without 1 or 2)	19	0	0	9	10	50
20. What are taxes?						
0. Doesn't know/no relevant response	37	17	16	3	1	−62
1. Money, bills (taxes are money or bills that you have to pay [can't explain further])	21	6	5	5	5	
2. Bills other than taxes (utility bills, fines, interest or finance payments on cars, etc.)	11	1	1	2	7	33
3. Taxes (money that you pay to the government)	33	0	3	14	16	60
21A. Who owns the police and fire stations?						
0. Doesn't know/no relevant response	31	16	8	4	3	−46
1. The boss, chief, deputy, and so on	19	5	3	7	4	
2. The people who work in the building	14	3	7	3	1	
3. The government/governor/township, and so on	36	0	6	13	17	56
21B. Who pays the police and firefighters?						
0. Doesn't know/no relevant response	28	13	12	2	1	−51
1. Any response other than those coded in Categories 2, 3, or 4 (the people who work there, the bank, etc.)	24	6	6	7	5	
2. People who use the services, including people who get fined for making nonemergency or false alarm calls	8	2	2	2	2	
3. The president, the government, and so on (no mention of taxes)	18	3	3	4	8	22
4. Tax money/taxpayers/the people who pay money to the government	23	0	1	10	12	52

(Continued)

TABLE 8.1
(Continued)

Response Categories	Total 96	K 24	1 24	2 24	3 24	Phi
22A. Who owns the school?						
0. Doesn't know/no relevant response	14	8	3	1	2	−32
1. The principal/boss/assistant principal	57	12	18	16	11	
2. The teachers (or the teachers and principal, the people who work there)	12	4	2	2	4	
3. The superintendent of schools/school board/ school district	7	0	0	3	4	29
4. The government/governor	11	0	1	5	5	30
22B. Who pays the teachers?						
0. Doesn't know/no relevant response	25	12	9	2	2	−42
1. The principal (presumably using his or her own money)	29	6	8	9	6	
2. The principal, but using money that comes from the parents, taxes, or the government	18	1	1	7	9	38
3. The parents of the children who go to the school (i.e., thinks that public schools are paid for like private schools are)	7	3	0	1	3	
4. The president, the government, and so on (no mention of taxes)	9	2	3	4	0	
5. Taxes/taxpayers (via the government)	13	0	2	6	5	29
6. Other (fees for yearbooks or supplies, etc.)	7	0	2	2	3	
23A. What other kinds of schools are there besides public schools?						
0. Doesn't know/no relevant response	64	22	21	7	14	−53
1. Home schools	10	2	1	6	1	
2. Sectarian religious schools	7	0	0	3	4	29
3. Other private schools (reading schools, tutorial schools, etc.)	21	0	2	12	7	47
23B. What's the difference between a public school and a private school?						
1. Makes distinction based on funding source	6	0	0	4	2	29
24A. Would you like to be president when you grow up?						
0. No	56	15	14	11	16	
1. Maybe/undecided/can't say	18	3	3	6	6	
2. Yes	22	6	7	7	2	
24B. What would be good about being president?						
0. Doesn't know/no relevant response	51	18	14	7	12	−33
1. Power (you can make laws, issue orders, make things happen)	12	0	3	6	3	27
2. Service (you can do good for the country, make things more fair, help the needy, etc.)	12	3	3	2	4	

(Continued)

TABLE 8.1
(Continued)

Response Categories	Total	K	1	2	3	
	96	24	24	24	24	Phi
3. Perquisites (you get to live in the White House, have a bowling alley or swimming pool in your house, get free cars, etc.)	21	3	5	7	6	
4. Other (fame, popularity, travel, you get lots of lawyers)	8	1	0	3	4	24
24C. What wouldn't be so good about being president?						
0. Doesn't know/no relevant response	43	19	9	10	5	−43
1. Hard work (work long and hard, little time to be with family, etc.)	31	1	10	7	13	40
2. Work not enjoyable (boring, wouldn't be fun, have to write a lot, etc.)	10	3	1	3	3	
3. Daunting responsibilities (wouldn't want all that responsibility, would be afraid of messing up some important decision)	11	0	2	2	7	34
4. Other (you might get sent to jail or be killed, you might not get reelected, etc.)	13	1	3	4	5	18

Note. Numbers in the frequencies columns show how many students in each group were coded for mentioning the ideas represented by each response category. Underlining indicates that the chi-square for the underlined distribution was statistically significant at or below the .05 level. In these instances the phi coefficients (with decimal points omitted) are given in the phi column to indicate the magnitudes of linear trends.

K   1. I don't know. (The government is the people who are in charge of running our country. What does the government do?) Makes sure we . . . owns Michigan.

1st 1. A president who . . . thinks about things. (OK. What sort of things does that person think about if they're in the government?) How people should act and they make rules about things. . . . He makes sure everything is OK with our country, our parades and stuff. (Is there one person that's government, or are there many people who are government?) There's lots of people.

2nd 1. The government is sort of a place and the governor rules the government. (What does the government do?) It makes land and stuff and it makes rules.

3rd 1. Government is basically a group of people that . . . for example, if someone thinks up a law, you gotta tell it to the government and they'll talk about it with each other and they'll announce it if they think it should or shouldn't be allowed. So the government is basically a group of people that decide on things about the country or city they're running.

Question 1A asked the students to define government. Almost two thirds were unable to respond. Of the rest, half (17) defined it with reference to the president, the governor, or some other individual person, and the other half (17) identified it as the organization or people that make laws or run the state or country. Other responses included: the people who buy stuff for the school; "If a boss in the government dies, we fly our flags halfway up"; the boss of the world; people who own the state; somebody who wants to be president, but there's already a president, so they're known as the government (i.e., the governor).

Asked what government does, 29 students were unable to respond, 36 said makes or enforces laws, 20 said runs the state or country or solves its problems, 16 said "helps people" or gives them money, food, clothes, or other things that they need, and 14 continued to describe the government as a single individual. Other responses included: sends notes to all the people; makes and buys food and medicine for people; keeps people from stealing our money from the bank; keeps people from running across busy streets; makes sure that places are clean; like George Washington or a king, but not that rich; knocks down buildings; takes away your old clothes; tells how many trees, houses, farms and stuff (zoning); builds hospitals; people who could kick you out of your house if you didn't pay for your house; picks new presidents; gives money to young people who don't have a house; makes the taxes (i.e., passes the laws relating to taxes); asks doctors or scientists to find a cure if there's a disease; "They give a lot of orders and are bossy. They make people do what they want, because they don't want to do it themselves."

The majority of the students either could not define government or confused it with the governor or some other individual leader. These trends replicate findings reported in previous research, as do the trends indicating generally benevolent views of the activities of government (solving problems, keeping us safe, helping people, etc.).

Person confusion appeared more frequently in the responses of older students than younger ones because the older students were much more likely to make extended substantive statements about the activities of government. The overall developmental trend progressed from being unable to say anything substantive about government to knowing something about governmental functions and understanding that these are carried out by a group or organization rather than a single individual.

The response trends paralleled those seen in earlier studies indicating that children emphasize either or both of two main ideas: government as a source of authority and power over people's actions and government as a benevolent resource that protects us, solves problems, and helps people in need. However, relatively neutral responses emphasizing making laws and running the country were more frequent than either positive responses depicting government as benevolent or negative responses depicting government as oppressive. Most students were not very clear about who does what, but they shared a general perception that the nation, state, and/or local community were run by competent people who took actions as needed to protect the health, safety, and general welfare of the citizens. A few displayed naivete in describing the extent of governmental benevolence or the motivations behind it (e.g., keep the streets clean to protect birds from choking) and a few others displayed resentment against governmental exercise of authority (e.g., enforcing eviction notices), but most spoke matter-of-factly when describing the nature and functions of government.

THE PRESIDENCY

2. Who is the head of our government? [If student says president, ask for name.]

3. How did he get to be president?

4. Can anyone be president or only certain people? [Follow up by probing for explanations.]

K 2. I don't know.

  3. Because he was nice to other people, and he did good things.

  4. Anybody.

1st 2. Bill Clinton. (What is the name of his job?) To be the . . . president.

  3. He worked hard.

  4. Anyone, except for little tiny babies that are just born and kids that don't pass college.

2nd 2. Bill Clinton. (And what's his job?) To help the world. Like make the world a better place. (And what do we call Bill Clinton?) The president.

  3. People voted for him.

  4. Only certain people get picked.

3rd 2. The president. (What's the name of the current president?) Clinton.

  3. He was elected for being good at certain things, like being good at speeches and stuff and being able to say things and being truthful.

  4. Certain people cannot be president because they don't have the main things they need to be, which is truthful, able to make speeches that are pretty good, and you've got to be able to stand up in front of crowds of people, and the last thing is you've got to be ready to help decide if the government can't seem to decide.

More than half of the students were able to answer Question 2 correctly by saying the president (49), Bill Clinton (38), or both when asked who is the head of our government. Twenty-three students were unable to respond and 17 named George Washington, Abraham Lincoln, or John Kennedy. Other responses included: the judge; Bill Gates; God or someone in heaven; God—Jesus; the boss; the mayor; the secretary.

When asked how the president got to be the president, most of the older students immediately said that he won an election but most of the younger students focused on virtue, competence, or other positive qualities. Several developed scenarios in which the person apprentices for the job (e.g., by being vice president) and then advances when the previous president dies or leaves office. Another common scenario depicted candidates undergoing some kind of examination, interview, or apprenticeship, then being selected for the office by the previous president, by someone else, or by agreement among themselves. Other responses included: They sign up for the job; someone who is out of money needs a job, so becomes president; people ask for the job and then the people who work for the government pick one of them; the president who is about to die chooses his successor; the president dies and the vice president becomes president; the president survives a "war" with his rivals for the job; before Lincoln died, he named Clinton his successor; the old president chooses his successor; each candidate spends a day acting in the job and being observed/mentored by the "president teacher," who then selects one of them; "he got it in a speech"; all of the candidates "practiced" the job but the others found it too hard and agreed that he should be the president.

When asked who can become president, almost half (43) said anyone who meets the age qualification (most guesses were in the 30 to 40 range). In addition or instead, 22 said that the person must have special qualifications (virtues, education, speaking or decision-making ability), 18 said that only certain people qualify but could not identify the requirements, 15 said that anyone could become president or made no relevant response, 12 mentioned some specific qualification in addition to age (being a lawyer, really wanting the job), and 12 mentioned certain disqualifications (criminals, the elderly, people who already have other jobs). Other responses included: people who are old or who already work at another job are not qualified; people "you can be caring about" are qualified; must be male; special people pass certain tests and then get the people to vote for them; a person whose brother is the president; people who "pass college"; people who "win the Civil War or something"; you have to keep your promises; they have to make a speech telling what they are going to do, and they also have to be 38 years old because younger people would "play around and stuff"; they must be 35 and have lived in the country for at least 14 years; must be famous; must go to New York and apply for the job, be interviewed, and give a speech making promises (and then keep those promises); people who are important and who really want the job; people who know what to do and are not afraid to act; those who give things to people, like jobs. Not qualified: people under 35 and presidents who already have had two terms; women and people who don't speak English (no mention of citizenship); people who are too old (near death); people who already have been president three times; criminals and drug users; very poor people (2).

In summary, more than half of the students knew that the president is the head of the government and almost half knew that the president is elected and knew something about qualifications required of candidates. Other students usually were able to construct sensible responses, guessing past presidents or the governor when asked who heads the government, and guessing reasonable qualifications (focusing on virtues and competence) when asked who can become president.

Some of the "virtue" responses, especially those that referred to working hard, probably flowed from the same assumptions that lead young children to equate effort with achievement. Research on children's attributional thinking has shown that 5- and 6-year-olds tend to believe that how much one achieves is a direct function of how hard one works, whereas older children take into account other factors such as ability, luck, or assistance from others (Stipek, 1998).

Although more than half of the students did not realize that presidents are elected, none of them thought that the title was hereditary. Instead, they assumed that the new president would be chosen on the basis of competence displayed in prior government service. Thus, even young children who do not understand much about our form of government have already learned that our country is neither a monarchy nor a totalitarian state, and have been conditioned to view it as a meritocracy.

Third graders showed some exposure to instruction about eligibility for the presidency. They were much more likely than younger students to identify disqualifying factors. Some were accurate (criminality, prior terms in office). Others were technically inaccurate but understandable given our history (no women or poor people). Overall, there was no evidence of widespread, clearcut misconceptions. The differences between inaccurate and more accurate responses were primarily differences between guesswork and accurate knowledge, not differences between crystallized misconceptions and accurate knowledge.

KINGS AND QUEENS

5. Some countries have kings or queens instead of presidents. How are presidents different from kings or queens? [If necessary, ask:] **How does a person become president? How does a person become king or queen?**

K   5. Because presidents don't boss people around. (How does a person become a president?) Because it helps the state that it comes from. (And how does a person become a king or a queen?) Because other people think that they could be a queen or a king.

1st   5. Queens and kings get all this royal stuff and the president doesn't get all this royal stuff . . . he doesn't get jewels and stuff to wear. (So what kind of royal stuff are talking about?) Like gold, jewels, beads, a lot of money. (So why do kings and queens get all that royal stuff and presi-

dents don't?) Because kings and queens are a big ruler across the country and then they make up all the rules and stuff. (So how is that different from presidents?) Presidents make up the rules and they get to
ride in a helicopter every day. (Presidents make the rules too. Why
couldn't they say they should get all the royal stuff?) I don't know.
(How does a person become a president?) Work very hard and you've
got to be very, very smart, like I am. (OK, let's say there are lots of
people who work hard and are very smart. Say there are five people,
and they all want to be president. How is it decided who gets to be
president?) I don't know. (How does a person become a king or a
queen? Do you have any idea?) No.

2nd 5. Presidents are sort of the head of the country of the United States, and
kings and queens are more royal and they have crowns and they don't
get elected—they just are born to be that from a royal family.

3rd 5. Kings and queens have a castle and presidents don't. Kings and queens
can be richer than the president because anybody can be President if
they just tried. (So how does someone become a president?) The same
way as the government [governor]. You have a piece of paper of
choices and you put the one that you want. You just draw the name
and keep on drawing. Whoever has the most names in it wins and gets
to be the president. (OK, so people vote for the president. How does a
person become a king or a queen?) Maybe a king and queen can have
lots of money so they can hire servants and then they can be king and
queen. (Can all rich people become the king or the queen or just a
particular person?) I guess anyone can be a king or a queen.

Eighty students were able to contrast presidents with kings or queens. The
most common responses were that kings and queens wear crowns, jewels, wigs,
royal robes, and so on (25), live in castles or palaces (21), rule all by themselves
or as despots with dictatorial powers (20), live a life of luxury, have servants, and
so on (11), or have mostly ceremonial jobs (7). None of these responses included
reference to elections or inheritance. Instead, they focused on the symbols of luxury and power associated with monarchs, especially in children's literature and
videos.

Only 31 students knew that kings or queens ascend to the throne through
marriage or inheritance. Other responses included: They qualified for the job by
being rich or owning a castle (15); are royalty (7); ride horses, fought wars and
had knights; get the job by being good and asking for it; get the job by getting
good grades; boss people around and get the job because other people think they
should; had knights; are famous (2); kings and queens have castles whereas presidents have "a boat fleet"; kings and queens have a special kind of blood (apparently thinking of blue blood); are from the past (2); kings and queens own more
than one country, but the president owns just one (2); kings and queens have big

castles but George Washington only had a medium castle; kings and queens have knights to fight dragons, but the government (governor) doesn't because there are no dragons in Michigan; the queen gets the job if people think she's pretty (3); kings and queens see their children all the time, but the president is too busy to see them much; kings and queens are heads of state, but the president is the head of a country; kings and queens keep the same last names but presidents have different names; kings and queens are rich people who fool others at first by giving out gold and acting nice, but they "get greedy" once they get the throne; kings and queens aren't always being bothered by questions from people and work that they need to do, like presidents are; kings and queens make taxes, but not presidents (one of several responses influenced by what students had heard about King George III).

The following second grader's response incorporates several common themes:

> Kings and queens kind of get treated more royal and they live in something like the White House but it's better—it's a castle, and the president lives in the White House which is pretty big, but normally kings and queens live there forever, but presidents only live there for about 5 or 6 years . . . They have lots of servants and they have different food to be served and they might have bigger tables and their castle is like bigger and its made out of bricks and stuff. (Why do you think the kings and queens get treated differently from the President?) Well, right now, the president isn't being very good, but normally the kings and queens aren't good because they try to take over places, so they get treated more royally and they get filthy rich and they say, "I want to take over the world." Like the king and queen of England wanted to take over America. (How do kings and queens get filthy rich?) Well, I don't know. They probably do nothing. (You said that kings and queens want to take over the world. How do they do that?) Well, they get their army up and they gain more people so they can like take over every state, country, continent. (How does a person become president?) By getting elected and giving a good speech. (So how do people become kings or queens?) Probably because one of their parents or grandparents were rich and they passed down their richness and they used some of their richness to build the castle, and then they had servants. (So anyone who has lots and lots of money is a king or a queen?) No, not everybody because some people can be richer than others.

Most students focused on what they knew about kings and queens rather than on comparisons with presidents. Most responses reflected images developed from fairy tales and videos about kings and queens, although several reflected exposure to the disputes over taxes between King George III and the American colonists. A few students thought that queens must be beautiful or that kings and queens existed only in the past.

Most students had more to say about castles, crowns, royal robes, and other symbols of luxury than about the exercise of power or leadership, and those who did address the latter topic did not describe kings or queens as benevolent in the ways that they described presidents. Students who did draw comparisons often depicted kings and queens as basking in the trappings of inherited luxury, while depicting presidents as working long hours for the good of the country during their limited time in office.

CANDIDATES AND ELECTIONS

6. Some countries are run by people who were not elected. How did these people get to be in charge of their governments? Do you know any countries that are run by people like that?

7. In our country, the president and other government leaders are elected by voters. Who is allowed to vote? [If necessary, ask:] Can anybody vote, or just some people?

8. In elections, the voters are usually choosing between Democrats and Republicans. How are Democrats and Republicans different? Like in the last election, why did some people vote for Bill Clinton and other people vote for Bob Dole?

9. In an election, why do people vote for one candidate [If necessary, one person] rather than another? What would you look for in a candidate for president? If you could vote for president, what qualities would you be wanting in a candidate?

K   6. Because they wanted to, and they didn't care if anybody else cared. (Do you know any countries that are run by people like that?) No.

7. The president and the other people that helped the place that we live in. (Can anybody vote or just some people?) Everybody can. (Can you vote for the president?) Yeah.

8. I don't know. (Like in the last election, why did some people vote for Bill Clinton and other people vote for Bob Dole?) Because they liked two different people.

9. Because they need to choose the person that they want to be president. (If you could vote for a president, what qualities would you be wanting in a candidate?) The president who was the nicest to the place that we live in.

1st   6. Because they didn't have any other job that they wanted to do. (What if the people in the country didn't want that person to be in charge of the government?) They could vote. (Do you know of any countries where they don't vote for president?) No. (If they're not elected, how do they get to be in charge? Do you know?) No.

7. The other government people. (OK, so people in the government. Are there any other people that can vote?) I don't know.

8. I don't know what Democrats and Republicans are. (Well, like in the last election, why did some people vote for Bill Clinton and other peo-

ple voted for Bob Dole?) 'Cause they wanted that person to be head of the continent. (Why do you think they would want that person to be in charge?) Because he was nice and he . . . I don't know what else.

9. Because that person might just be faking it and he might be a robber and then he might steal all the stuff. (What would you look for in a candidate for president?) I would be looking for a person that was nice, a person that would let you stay at their house if you didn't have a house, and give the other people food if they didn't have food.

2nd 6. They probably ask somebody. (Do you know of any countries that are run by people like that?) Maybe Australia.

7. Eighteen or older people, and in the old days women weren't allowed to vote.

8. Democrats want to give money to the poor, but they raise taxes, and the Republicans are the more richer people who want to save their money. (That's an interesting explanation. How did you know that?) I just knew that.

9. Because they think that's the best one that would be elected. (If you could vote for president, what qualities would you be wanting?) Kindness, not raising taxes, but giving some of your money and other people's money to the poor and lowering taxes, but still keeping your things. (What other qualities should a president have?) They would be very good at something, like have goals to success. (Do you think that men as well as women or women as well as men can be president?) Yes. The next election, I think Bob Dole's wife is going to try to run for president and that will be the first woman president.

3rd 6. Maybe they're the vice government or they're just helping the government [governor] because maybe he's sick. (Can you think of any other ways that someone can become president without getting elected?) No. (Do you know of any countries that are run by people like that?) No.

7. Anybody who is an adult. (How old do you need to be to be able to vote?) I think maybe 20 or 19 or older. (Are there any rules besides being an adult about who can vote?) Kids might be able to vote for their mom and dad because their mom and dad told you what one they want and you could just vote for it. I don't think they can vote any other way.

8. I don't know. (Like in the last election, why did some people vote for Bill Clinton and other people vote for Bob Dole?) Because maybe some people thought Bill Clinton was a better man than Bob and some people thought that Bob was a better person than Bill Clinton and Bob would help everybody and Bill Clinton wouldn't, or Bill Clinton would help people and Bob wouldn't.

9. Maybe because they think one of them is better than the other. (What do you think would make them choose one person over the other?) Because they would think who could help them better or who they think is a little bit nicer than the other one. (What would you look for in a candidate for president?) If he helps people and not do drugs and if he obeys the laws and if he's really nice almost every day and makes laws that he can obey too.

Question 6 did not elicit enough substantive responses to analyze statistically. Most students could say nothing at all about countries run by people who were not elected, and the rest could only make guesses, such as that the ruler was picked by the previous ruler. None said anything about inheritance, military coups, or totalitarian government. Asked the about countries ruled in this manner, most students again were unable to respond and the rest simply guessed place names. These included some accurate responses (China, Egypt, and Iraq), but without any evidence of knowledge about how these countries are ruled.

When asked who is allowed to vote, five students couldn't respond and 17 said anyone or everyone. Of the rest, 46 said everyone who is old enough, 10 said some people old enough to vote are not allowed to (but couldn't explain), and 6 said that only citizens or residents can vote. Other responses included: Parents can vote but childless adults cannot; only people who work for the government vote; presidential candidates are not allowed to vote; voters must have identification; government workers are not allowed to vote; the president cannot vote; only people who can read and write English can vote; voters are those who follow the rules and are good at it—some people "just aren't fit" for voting.

Asked to compare the Democratic and Republican parties or presidential candidates (Clinton and Dole), only 11 students generated substantive responses. Seven made defensible distinctions (e.g., Democrats want to raise taxes and help the poor but Republicans are rich people who want to keep their money), but four made questionable distinctions (e.g., Democrats are bosses and Republicans are underlings who want to become bosses). Other responses included: They wear different clothes; they shouldn't have voted for Clinton because he was telling those bad lies; one likes the president and one likes the other guy; Democrats steal and kill but Republicans are nice; Democrats work for the president but Republicans are "just people" (one of several responses indicating awareness that the Democrats were in power but being unclear about where the Republicans were or what they were doing); there are more Democrats than Republicans, and a lot of people think that Republicans are rich but Democrats are "a little bit poor"; Democrats have the president to take care of them, but the Republicans just watch, or maybe they can be governors; the Democrats are helpers for the president; the Republicans are good people but the Democrats are bad people who might shoot somebody and lie about it.

When asked about qualities that they would look for in a presidential candidate, 21 students could not respond and 20 named individuals rather than personal qualities (including not only Bill Clinton but Abraham Lincoln and Louis Armstrong). The rest identified at least one, and often several, desirable qualities. A majority (50) mentioned generic virtues: nice, kind, helpful, not greedy, not bossy, and so on. In addition or instead, 21 mentioned general competence (smart, educated, experienced, knows the job, good leader, good problem solver, etc.), 21 cited generic aspects of leadership vision or policies (has good ideas about needed laws or ways to improve the country, etc.), 13 said be honest or trustworthy, and 6 said treat people fairly or with respect. Other responses included: happy; planting trees, picking up litter and stuff; helping our world to be clean; able to go to war; strong and good army leader; not littering; would do what I asked; wouldn't allow people in other countries to shoot people; would make good rules and wouldn't let people break them; a girl; how rich they are; would reduce the price of Pokémon™ cards; keep the roads in good repair; help the poor and homeless; good personality; keep their promises; not lying to the wife (laughs); wouldn't vote for someone who promised to give away more stuff (TVs, radios) than he could deliver. In addition, two second graders generated "not someone like Clinton" responses. One said that Clinton had "done many bad things this year, like selling a recipe for nuclear bombs to China, so they could start bombing anytime." The other said that Clinton had "been greedy and not taken good care of his family. In his interview, he promised he would stay with one wife, but he started cheating. He's about to go to jail, I hope."

The following third grader is quoted to illustrate the idealism that typified most responses:

> Because probably . . . maybe they like their personality better or maybe they think what they're going to do for the country is better than what the other guy would do. (What do you think people are looking for when they vote for president?) Like he's going to help our country out and make some right decisions. (Anything else?) No. (What would you look for in a candidate for president?) Like if he helps out the country—like if something's wrong, he'll go there and try to help people out with some of their problems and stuff. (If you could vote for president, what qualities would you want in a candidate?) How kind he is and if he likes and respects the country and stuff, respects other people. (Anything else?) Like if he could make something different out of the country—something good.

Most students could not respond when asked about countries ruled by people who were not elected, and none said anything about monarchies, dictatorships, or other alternatives to representative democracy (about which they had only limited knowledge as well). These findings fit well with earlier findings indicating that primary-grade children do not yet have clear concepts of nation–states and the political structures and offices involved in governing them (Berti &

Benesso, 1998). Instead, their images of political leadership focus on benevolent parental figures assisted by "helpers."

Only 11 students were able to say anything about Democrats and Republicans beyond versions of "they think differently." Most of these responses were based either on the image of Republicans as rich people or on knowledge that the Democrats (Clinton administration) were currently in power. Two responses depicted Democrats as criminals—bad people prone to "steal and kill" or "shoot somebody and lie about it." Several others reflected very negative images of Bill Clinton. Although infrequent, these responses are worrisome. They suggest that the "argument culture" (Tannen, 1998) that has typified our political dialogue in recent years, and more specifically the personal vilification directed at President Clinton prior to and during his impeachment, have filtered down to children in highly emotional and counterproductive forms.

Additional (although less extreme) examples of this phenomenon could be seen in some of the responses concerning desirable qualities of a presidential candidate. More typically, however, these responses focused on generic virtues and the more specific traits of honesty and competence. Only 21 students mentioned the candidate's vision or policies. Most of the students still assumed an orderly society run by benevolent leaders, but some of the older ones were beginning to understand issues associated with political power and competing agendas, and a few had begun to crystallize these around attitudes toward political parties.

ACTIVITIES OF THE PRESIDENT
AND THE FEDERAL GOVERNMENT

10. **Our president right now is Bill Clinton. Where does he live and work? What does he do? What are some things that the United States government does?**

K   10.   He has a big house, and he works in it. (Does that house have a name?) I don't know. (What else does he do?) He works on important papers. (What are some of the things that the United States government does?) He does what he needs to do for his country.

1st   10.   He lives at the White House and he works at the White House. (Do you know where the White House is—what city it's in?) Washington, D.C. (What does President Clinton do?) He works for the government. (Do you have any idea what sort of work he does?) He makes up all the rules and he might be a police officer. They can still be the government—they can still be that person if they wanted to be—if they still wanted to have another job. He might be an officer and he might be able to arrest people and stuff. (What are some of the things that the United States government does?) I don't know.

2nd 10.   In Washington, D.C. at the White House. (What does he do exactly?) He sort of makes rules and goes places to help people and

makes speeches to help our country. (What are some things that the
United States government does?) Makes laws . . . like if you're going
to another country, you need to pay some money and maybe if you're
going to a foreign land, you have to have a passport.

3rd 10. Washington, D.C., and he works at the White House. (What does
he do?) He basically talks to the governors about certain things—
talks to the government people, and so he tries to deal with problems
like if someone plans an attack against them, he'd talk to the governor and see what . . . and then they'd talk to the government of people and that government would call up like all of the Air Force bases
and see what they could use against who's ever bringing up the war.
Basically, what he's doing is he solves the problems that are caused
by other states or problems in his own state. (What are some of the
things that the United States government does?) They probably call
up certain places to solve the problems that need to be solved, and if
there's this really, really hard-to-catch killer on the loose, then
they'd probably call in a couple of army men—they'd call up the nation of armies and they'd say, "I want about 50 people going here and
there and surround this person," and they just keep scooching in and
get him.

One fourth (24) of the students (23 of them kindergarteners or first graders)
were unable to say where the president lives and works. Of the rest, majorities
knew that the president lives in the White House (52) and works in Washington,
DC (48). Smaller numbers of students gave less specific (big house, president's
house) or incorrect (capitol building) names for the president's residence (9) or
identified some location other than Washington, DC as the place where he lives
and works (10). Other responses included: at the United States (3); at his house
(couldn't say more); in Tennessee; in George Washington, DC; New York City
(2); at a government place in Michigan; where George Washington was; Lansing; East Lansing; lives in Washington, DC, which isn't in Washington but in
Delaware; lives in Washington, DC, and works at the capitol (3).

Responses to Question 10B (What does the president/government do?) mostly
focused on the president individually rather than the government generally: no
relevant response (21), generic virtuous behavior (working, doing good, helping
people, etc.; 15), generic office work (reading, writing, having meetings; 19), generic problem solving (says that the president solves problems without explaining further or giving examples; 28), unrealistic examples of problem solving
(stopping riots, cleaning up things, acting as a judge or policeman, setting broken
bones, etc.; 12), and realistic examples of problem solving (making decisions
about foreign affairs or warfare, recommending or enforcing laws, making policy
speeches, vetoing laws, etc.; 17). Other responses included: talk to people about
being good; pound his gavel (judge); help our earth be clean; help people by sav-

ing their lives; stop the riots at Michigan State University; clean up stuff and help people to get better; send people to jail; arrest people; ride in a helicopter; collects and sells old clothes and gives the money to the poor, takes care of animals that need a habitat, and teaches people; gives people presents and judges people; makes people vote; tries to avoid assassination, sets broken bones, goes to war; makes speeches (2); travels the country (3); takes injured people to the hospital; catches people who don't pay their taxes; helps the country to stay united and not break apart; votes; decides questions brought to him by aides, such as "Can we knock down this building?" or "Can we shoot this country?"; government workers make sure that the president doesn't get shot; makes sure that people aren't breaking laws; signs autographs; appoints judges.

Younger students lacked much specific knowledge about the president's identity or location, let alone about what he does. Their responses emphasized general virtuous behavior (doing good, helping people, etc.), and the specific examples they did give were likely to be unrealistic: personally stop riots, clean the environment, or engage in the activities of police officers, doctors, or judges. The older students were much more likely to know that the president lives in the White House and works in Washington, DC. Among the (primarily older) students who were relatively realistic in their depictions of presidential activities, some imagined the president as signing papers and doing office work, others as carrying out daunting responsibilities requiring decisions about important problems, and still others as traveling around the country providing speeches, photo opportunities, and autographs. The prominent grade differences suggested that most of these students had experienced a lesson or unit on the presidency in second grade (focusing on the current president and the activities of the federal government, as opposed to the focus on Washington and Lincoln that occurs in most grades in connection with Presidents' Day).

ACTIVITIES OF THE GOVERNOR
AND STATE GOVERNMENT

11. **We live in the state of Michigan. The governor of Michigan is John Engler. Where does he live and work? What does he do? What are some things that the government of Michigan does?**

12. **What do people who work in the capitol building do?**

K   11. I don't know. (What does the governor do?) He helps all the people. (What are some things that the government of Michigan does?) He gives other things to the people that he's supposed to give them to, and he helps other things.

      12. I don't know.

1st   11. The capital of Michigan. (Do you know where the capital of Michigan is?) It's in Lansing. (OK. What does the governor of Michigan do?) He works for the people. (How does he work for the people . . . what does he do?) I don't know. (What are some of the things that the government of Michigan does?) I don't know.

12. They work with the government. (What sort of jobs do they do?) They work at computers all day and then they go on the internet and if anyone wants anything . . . if he wants anything done, he'll just ask that person to do it, and then they'll try to work it up on the internet, and if they can't find it on the internet, he'll have to ask somebody else. (Do you know where the capitol building is?) In Lansing.

2nd 11. He lives I think in Lansing and he works all over Michigan. (What does he do?) He sort of makes laws of Michigan and helps settle agreements. (What are some things that the government of Michigan does?) They make laws to help people and make speed limits so that if anybody was over the speed that they wouldn't get hurt.

12. They help people like in court to do some things and they help make laws.

3rd 11. He works sort of near Bill Clinton's house but not exactly near it. He works around it, like in certain bases around it and near it and stuff. (What does John Engler do? He's the governor of Michigan.) He goes to the president whenever the president calls him and stuff, and he usually is always ready to go there, and when the president calls him, he'll be driving right up there, or if he's really near, he'll just run right over there and listen to what the president has to say, and then he'll try to think of an answer for it and then go back and talk to the government. (What are some of the things that the government of Michigan does?) They try to stop certain bad people that are just really crazed and police can't catch them and nobody can seem to, and then they have other problems like wars being set against them and so they probably try to fight against the wars and get all the armies and the Marines and stuff like that ready for them, ready to go into that battle, and the third thing is they'd chase down . . . like if there's some sort of disease that's really bad and no one can find a cure, they'll probably call up some scientists and they'll go over and look at who's ever sick with it and try to see what it is, and if they see what it is, they'd go out looking for where the disease came from.

12. Basically, what they do is vote it in and they have people that are good at stuff, certain things that are really good at those, and they have those people there to help the president solve certain problems, like if there's a meteor coming to them. (Is the President here in Lansing?) No, but sometimes the president is, and if the president is there and he calls, some people will come there. Like there's a

meteor coming down and he'd get the government and the government would call up a good person that can look through a good telescope and see things like that.

More than half (57) of the students were unable to respond when asked where the governor lives and works. Of the rest, 14 named the capitol building but 8 named some other building, and 20 named Lansing but 11 named some other location. The capitol building probably should be considered correct for students in the K–3 grade range. Several students named the White House or Washington, DC because they viewed the governor as a presidential aide. Even some of those who were clear about the governor residing in the state of Michigan viewed him primarily as an advisor to the president rather than as the state's chief executive. This replicates previous findings indicating that children confuse different levels of government and tend to construe anyone other than the president as a "helper." Other responses included: Grand Rapids; an old house or something; in a building in New York City; in England; a tall building somewhere; Florida; the White House (4); I saw his house (summer home) on Mackinac Island; he lives in Lansing but his work takes him all over the state (2); Washington, DC (4); in a big white building in Lansing.

Asked what the governor/government does, 36 students were unable to respond, 33 mentioned generic virtuous behavior, 28 mentioned problem solving without giving examples, 12 gave realistic examples of problems that a governor might address, and 9 gave unrealistic examples. Other responses included: clean up, vacuum, and paint houses (adds that "I don't like John Engler"); be on television; get divorced (Engler had gotten divorced) and go to court where the president is; make cities better; tell MSU people not to have riots; advise the president (2); try to make everyone "happy and nice" so they won't try to kill him, and not litter; make speeches; make rules that some people don't like; the governor fights for our country and "governor workers" help by making sure that there isn't war and that the governor doesn't skip papers so he can go in order; bosses people around, travels; makes laws for state (4); hires construction workers, sends out ambulances, hires army and police people; makes food and clothes for people; levies taxes to pay community workers; creates jobs (2); fixes potholes, raises tax money; improves safety, such as by seeing that streetlights are installed; does background checks on people applying for jobs in stores; has to watch the news regularly to keep informed; maintains public order, keeps streets clean; makes schools and roads; goes to court if necessary to solve the state's problems; makes sure that schools "go right"; travels; gives statements (e.g., making a memorial speech when someone dies); orders buildings to be built (3).

Over half (50) of the students were unable to talk about the activities of government employees who work in the capitol building. The rest mentioned generic good deeds (helping people, doing good, solving problems, etc.; 17), generic office work (work in offices, work on computers, write letters, stamp papers, etc.;

10), and specific examples of governmental activities (respond to questions that people send in, develop rules and laws, act as aides to the governor; 20). Other responses included: talk to people who don't have homes (and try to follow up by helping them); build houses; drive around and go to people who have run out of gas to give them gas or give water to thirsty people; decide who will go to jail or not; keep the building clean for tourists (2); make laws and do building inspections; give tours; "They do votes there" (legislators); make laws (2); order the preservation of old buildings; write and deliver speeches; give speeches; respond to questions sent by letter and then arrange to solve the problem (e.g., complaints about littering); take votes (2); hire people; guard the building so no one tries to harm it; arrange for road repairs (by sending notes to the governor asking if they can have permission to fix roads in a certain place—he says "OK, but we gotta get people to do it.").

Responses concerning the governor and state government paralleled those given earlier concerning the president and federal government. Given that these students resided in a suburb of the state capitol, it was surprising that only 14 named the capitol building and only 20 knew that the governor lives and works in Lansing.

Overall, the responses replicated earlier findings that children tend to have more information about the individuals holding office at higher levels of government, but more information about governmental activities at the local or state level. Most images of government work at any level were limited to vague notions of office work or problem solving, and there were frequent confusions concerning the responsibilities and functions carried out by the federal, state, and local levels of government, respectively.

Most examples of governmental activities did in fact refer to governmental (as opposed to private sector) functions. Thus, even though these students were still vague about the political system, the responsibilities of various political offices, and the functioning of governments generally, they did have a sense of the difference between public sector/governmental activities and private sector/business activities.

LAWS

13. **Where do laws come from?** [If necessary, ask:] **Who makes laws? Do you know about any laws that our government is working on right now?**

14. **Can laws be changed? How do they get changed? Do you know of any laws that have been changed? What could your parents do if they didn't like a law?**

15. **People are supposed to follow rules and laws. Why do we need rules and laws? What is the difference between a rule and a law? What happens to someone who breaks a law?**

K   13. From people. (How do people make the laws?) With paper. (Is there anything else you can tell me about how the laws are made and who makes the laws?) Seeds. (Seeds? OK, do you know about any laws that our government is working on right now?) No.

14. No. (Do you know of any laws that have been changed?) No. (What could your parents do if they didn't like a law?) They could cut it down.

15. Because you could get hurt. (What's the difference between a rule and a law?) I don't know. (What happens to someone who breaks a law?) They get in trouble. (What kind of trouble?) Police trouble. (If they're in trouble with the police, then what happens to them?) Then they go in jail. (Does everybody who breaks the law go to jail?) No. (So why do some people go to jail and some people not go to jail?) Because some escape.

1st 13. The government. (Do you know about any laws that our government is working on right now?) No.

14. Yeah. (How do they get changed?) If the government people don't like the law anymore, they can just change it, like when the Black people had to be the White people's slaves. (Do you know what they do to change laws?) No. (Who changes the laws?) The government. (What could your parents do if they didn't like a law?) They could ask the government to change it.

15. So nobody shoots somebody or kills somebody. (What might happen if we didn't have rules or laws?) It would be total chaos. (What sort of things would happen?) People would be getting killed all over the place and then a lot of people would get arrested. (What's the difference between a rule and a law?) A rule is something in your house that your parents don't allow you to do, and a law is something you can't do—ever. (How come?) Because you can get arrested for that. (What happens to someone who breaks the law?) They get arrested. (Does everyone who breaks a law get arrested?) No. (How is it decided who gets arrested and who doesn't?) If they shoot somebody, they get arrested; if they don't shoot anybody, they don't get arrested. (What happens after someone gets arrested?) You go to jail.

2nd 13. The government and the president. (Do you know about any laws that our government is working on right now?) No.

14. Yes. (How do they get changed?) Like the government says you have to be 18 in order to get a car, and now they say you have to be 16 in order to drive it. (What could your parents do if they didn't like a law?) I don't know.

15. Like if you're on a busy street, and then you have to have stop lights and stop signs so people don't crash. (What's the difference between

a rule and a law?) A law is something that you have to follow, like you have to follow the speed limit or else you'll get a ticket, and a rule is just that there's a rule some place but it isn't always every place. (What happens to someone who breaks a law?) If they break a speeding law, then they get a ticket.

3rd   13. Laws are basically things that you shouldn't do. They're laws and if you break them you might get arrested and you could get in deep, deep trouble. (Who makes laws?) Usually the government, but if there's a person and if the thing happens, then they'd probably make a law that that cannot happen, otherwise you'll get arrested, and then they'll send that to the president and the president will talk to the voters and the voters will all vote on if that should be or shouldn't be. (Do you know of any laws that our government is working on right now?) No.

14. Oh, yeah, easily. (How do they get changed?) They easily get changed if they start to stop and die down and just never happen for the millennium or so and then they'd probably decide that everyone understands this. (What could your parents do if they didn't like a law?) They could move out of the state, or for any reason try to change that by voting on . . . because they'll say, "I want to vote for this again," and if they voted for it and say, "OK, this is OK for me," and then suddenly decided it was getting annoying to have the same old law . . . (How would they go about that?) Well, they might let them vote, and then again, they might not. Now, if they let them vote, they'd probably call up one of the best voters and say "Will you please vote for this," and he might not vote for it because he probably might like that law a little more than she thinks, and then they'll vote and see who votes for the most of the things and who thinks they should be, and then the parents are just going to have to see if that will happen.

15. Bsecause if we didn't follow some of them, our world would be trashed by certain things, like there's a law about littering—you cannot litter. You won't get arrested for it, but you just shouldn't litter. That's basically what they're try to say to you. Now, if you do litter, you usually would get in trouble for that by your parents if they see you. (What's the difference between a rule and a law?) A rule is something smaller than a law. Like the school has rules like you can't run in the hall. That doesn't go for the whole state, because there are some buildings that have floors that are made for running on, like there might be this indoor thing where it's got a track indoors that you can run on. So it doesn't exactly go for everything. But laws go for everything. Law are made so that everything in the state, country or that, have to follow those rules and if you don't, you get in some

big trouble. (What happens to someone who breaks the law?) If the law is a really big one and you break it, you get in serious trouble. You'd probably get arrested for that. But if it's like a tiny law like not littering, then you'd probably just get in trouble by your parents.

All but 13 of the students had one or more ideas about where laws come from: the president, the governor, or judges (59); the government (27); the police (10); and Congress or legislators (6). Other responses included: God or Jesus (5); the people (4); bad guys; the law business or George Washington; the legislature passes laws and the president or governor has to approve them (2). In addition, several students described some alternative form of collaboration between the president and the legislature (e.g., presidents meet with legislators to discuss possible laws and negotiate agreement on what to do). These findings replicate previously reported findings that children are much less aware of the legislative than the executive and judicial branches of government, commonly believing that laws are decided and proclaimed by executives or judges rather than developed and voted on through a legislative process.

More than two thirds (68) of the students said that laws can be changed. The majority (40) said that the president, governor, or judges change them. Other responses included: People in the government who make the laws have a revote (11); the new law or change in law is publicized through the media (6); God changes them (4); citizens petition for change; the president speaks to the government about making the change; changes are submitted to popular vote; when a new law is passed, the president sends people to drive around the country, blow their horns to get attention, and then explain the new law to the people; a new president takes office and makes changes (4); a lot of people get together and complain or demand change (3).

The questions about laws that the government was working on at the time and about laws that had been changed yielded few responses, so we considered responses to both questions when coding whether students were able to name at least one specific law that had been introduced or changed. Only 27 students were able to do so. Most of their examples dealt with bicycle safety, seatbelts, or the regulation of smoking, alcohol, or drugs. Other responses included: laws about suicide (the arrest and trial of Jack Kevorkian was widely publicized in Michigan); laws regulating stop signs and the Pledge of Allegiance; speed limits and restrictions on how long truck drivers can drive without rest; laws allowing you to get a car at age 16 instead of age 18; laws banning tobacco ads; laws allowing people to turn right on red lights and banning people from having more than three marriages (because a famous actress had nine marriages and this isn't good for children); laws protecting wildlife; setting a minimum age for using jet skis; gun control and gun safety laws (3); laws to prevent school shootings; raising the driving age from 16 to 17; banning smoking in the capitol building.

Asked what their parents could do if they didn't like a law, a majority of the students either could not respond (33) or said that their parents could contact the president, the governor, or the police official who made the law and request change (32). Other common responses were that nothing could be done and the parents would just have to accept and obey the law (14); the parents could disobey the law and do what they thought was right (12); and the parents could contact their representatives in the legislature (9). Unusual responses included: express frustration by throwing things or punching a wall; go to court and argue for change (2); press charges against the governor; vote against the president in the next election; organize popular resistance to the law. Once again, most responses assumed that laws are promulgated by the executive or judicial branches of government. The 26 students who thought that their parents could not do anything to change a law were split almost evenly between those who said that the parents would just have to accept it and those who said that the parents should defy it. Most of the latter students assumed that there was something wrong with the law that justified an unusual decision, not that people routinely choose to disobey laws that displease them. Other research also has shown that children often believe that law violation is sometimes acceptable, especially if the law is unjust or unnecessarily infringes on personal rights (Helwig & Jasiobedzka, 2001; Sears & Levy, 2003).

All but 11 of the students were able to talk about why we need rules and laws. A majority (61) articulated a safety rationale (laws keep us safe, prevent harm, etc.), 29 said that laws prevent chaos or make for a well-ordered society, and 9 said that they provide guidance (so that people will know what to do or how to act). All of these common responses reflect a positive view of laws—that they are needed and helpful. Students coded for safety rationales tended to focus on traffic regulation, whereas those coded for chaos avoidance tended to focus on crime. Only three students talked about laws making sure that people are treated fairly or have their rights secured. One kindergartener said that it would be OK if we didn't have any laws at all (thinking about speeding laws). The following third grader is quoted as an example of "chaos avoidance" responses:

> Because if we didn't have laws, people would like be breaking windows and . . . hurting people and climbing on people, other people's houses, and start shooting everybody and making fires everywhere and then we wouldn't have any buildings to rest in. Then everybody would start drinking a lot of beer and then driving, because they didn't know that was a law. And then we would just have nothing. The whole earth would be nothing.

All but seven of the students were able to discuss the difference between rules and laws. A majority (50) drew one or more contrasts, typically stating that you can break rules but must obey laws (29), rules apply only in the home or school but laws apply everywhere (24), or rules are made by parents or teachers whereas laws are made by governments (9). Other students either said something accurate about rules or laws but did not compare them directly (39) or gave examples of rules or laws but did not draw a clear distinction between them (6). In general, those students who did draw distinctions depicted rules as applying only in certain contexts and breakable with only minor consequences, but laws as applying everywhere and requiring obedience under penalty of significant consequences (fines, imprisonment). Other responses included: Lawbreakers will get hurt; lawbreakers "won't be Christian and won't go to heaven"; lawbreakers will "go down to the devil"; rules can be changed but laws cannot; laws are made when people can't be trusted to follow a rule (i.e., you need to add sanctions).

Few students knew much about the lawmaking process. Lacking knowledge of the legislative branch, the majority assumed that laws are proclaimed by the president, the governor, judges, or the police.

Examples of laws that have been changed or might be changed or introduced were mostly accurate, focusing on bicycle safety, seatbelts, or regulations concerning smoking, alcohol, drugs, or weapons. It was to be expected that students would be much more aware of laws regulating the behavior of individuals than of laws regulating commerce, corporations, or governmental processes. Although a minority of the students was able to generate generally accurate examples, it should be kept in mind that more than two thirds could not generate any examples of laws that had been introduced or changed.

Very few students had realistic ideas about political organization or lobbying. A few third graders spoke of organizing to create political pressure for new or changed laws, a few spoke about their parents seeking redress in the courts, and one mentioned voting against the incumbent president in the next election. However, the fact that two thirds of them understood that laws can be changed contrasts with previous findings that children tend to think of laws as longstanding and unchanging.

The students' attitudes toward rules and laws were generally positive, reflecting beliefs that they make for a safe, well-ordered society and provide guidance about desired behavior. Several drew apocalyptic visions of the chaos that would result if rules and laws were not in place.

JUDGES

16. Judges are part of the government too. What do judges do?

K   16. They tell if they go to jail.

1st 16. They know who gets arrested . . . they tell them whether to arrest the person or not.

2nd 16. They help settle agreements and they help in the court and they might like say you're innocent, guilty, or have to pay a fine or something.

3rd 16. They judge things. Like if a person comes in and they've witnessed this crime that's been done by a person, they'd tell their story and the judge would think about that, and then a couple more people would come in and tell their story, and the judge would think with the other people, and then finally the person who did the crime or didn't do the crime would walk in and tell his story and then they'd judge it and see which one sounds more better to trust, and it's usually that the only two things that could happen are the witnesses didn't see right and maybe they saw something else that looked like a crime but wasn't, or the person actually committed the crime.

A substantial minority (36) of the students either were unable to respond or could only produce vague generalities (judges help the government, talk to people, etc.). Of the rest, 40 said that judges decide criminal cases (determine if people are guilty or innocent); 15 described them as presiding over the courtroom (running the court, keeping order, banging their gavels, etc.); 10 as deciding civil cases (making rulings in lawsuits, divorces, etc.); 8 as lecturing defendants about their conduct; and 6 as questioning to elicit facts or motives (talking to witnesses to clarify what they saw or talking to the accused to clarify their motives). Thus, those students who were able to respond were quite realistic in their depictions of the activities of judges, most probably reflecting information gleaned from watching television.

Two students referred to Judge Judy and one referred to Judge Brown. These and other stars of television "judge" shows apparently were the models for the students' images of judicial responsibilities, because most depicted judges (as opposed to juries) deciding guilt or innocence and the fate of defendants. Some of the students coded for depicting judges as presiding over civil cases had had family experiences in the divorce courts. Only one student depicted judges as reviewing laws to see if they were good or not, so there was little awareness of the judicial review function. Other responses included: They talk in a very polite way; own the courts; work out solutions to problems of people who come to court (2); make people cry (when they admonish them); listen to all sides and then decide who is telling the truth; review jury decisions and make the final decision (one of two students who depicted juries as advisors to judges); vote to decide who will be the governor or the president; suggest possible new laws to the president.

Responses were generally accurate for courtrooms in which the judge (rather than a jury) is in fact the arbiter who will decide which side wins the case and what subsequent actions will be taken. The few students who did mention juries tended to depict them as advisors to the judge. The few students whose responses indicated personal experience with courts depicted judges as ruling in divorce cases. Grade level differences were less pronounced than usual, presumably because students at all grade levels were familiar with judges depicted on television.

GOVERNMENT JOBS AND SERVICES

17. A lot of people work for the government. What are some of the jobs that they do?

18. Besides making laws, the government also helps people. What are some of the things that the government does for people? How does the government help your family?

K   17. They do other important papers.

18. He helps people so they're not sick. (How does the government help your family?) He helps and I don't know what he helps us with.

1st   17. They give him food and he . . . rings a bell or something, and says, "I need some coffee" or something. And that's why people work for him, and they get paid for it, and they would have lots of money, because they do it every day for him. (OK, are there any other sorts of jobs that people in the government do?) They go answer the door for him and give him packages and stuff.

18. Helps people because their house burned down and they don't have any money, so I think he would loan them some money . . . so they can buy some clothes. (What else does the government do for people?) Brings them food if their house is on fire. (How does the government help your family?) You have to give him checks and when we give him checks he would give us some money back and it would be change. (What else does the government do to help your family?) He says "If your house burns down, I would make you another one, and you wouldn't have to pay because you signed this thing," and some people don't do it, so some people do, some don't. And helps you by doing that.

2nd   17. They are like maybe in the Air Force or they're in the sort of like the Navy to help us in case there was a war or something.

18. Gives them money if they lose money, like if they were blind and someone stole their seeing-eye dog, they would help them by making money to get a new one for them. (How does the government help your family?) It's sort of like an insurance to help our family do things, like get a job and stuff.

3rd   17. Some of them just make laws, they can make rules, or almost anybody in the whole United States can make rules.

18. The government can help people by setting laws, because if they don't set laws then people could get hurt really bad because I know somebody whose mom and dad almost killed themselves because they were fighting so hard and they wanted to get a divorce. Somebody helped them. (What are some other things that the govern-

ment does to help people?) Say that a person was smoking so that that they hurt their lungs. They could help them. They can set laws so people don't get hurt. (How does the government help your family?) If they get hurt, like my dad. He hurt himself and then somebody helped him and that's how I think the government would help.

A majority (58) of the students either were unable to respond or could only speak in vague generalities about work done for the government (working, helping the government or the president, etc.). Of the rest, 22 identified specific government jobs (president, governor, legislator, judge, lawmaker, etc.), 14 mentioned staff or office work (works on computers, goes to meetings, works as a secretary or assistant to an executive or legislator, etc.), and 12 named "other" jobs: Help the president; clean windows; build buildings, give people money; count votes; clean and guard the White House; make sure everyone does their taxes and that roads are good and bridges are safe; teachers; security people for the president; repair the governor's mansion and the roads leading to it; make new inventions and give them to the government, work for the Chamber of Commerce (this student's mother did the latter). Some of the students coded for staff or office jobs depicted these workers as providing personal services to the governor (e.g., getting coffee) rather than performing governmental duties.

The students also had difficulty identifying things that the government does for people. More than one third (34) were unable to respond or could not get beyond vague generalities (helps, does good, etc.). Almost as many (31) confined their response to the general functions of government (keeps us safe, passes good laws, etc.). Of the rest, 16 identified safety-net services (assistance to poor people or people who have suffered from fires or storm damage, etc.); 10 identified basic community services (police, fire, paramedics, etc.); and 8 depicted the government as an all-purpose provider (of homes, factories, grocery stores, etc., to provide everyone with whatever they need).

Few students communicated images of government services beyond safety nets or welfare, and many of the latter responses depicted far more personal forms of help than actually occur. Also, some of them described services that ordinarily would be performed by insurance companies (e.g., paying for a new house after a fire) rather than governments. Other responses included: helps them to get a job, talks to them about swimming and stuff (safety?); gives out food in the winter; helps lost children to get home (2); helps keep people healthy and not sick; gives money or food to poor people (2); gives people houses, money, medicine; tells people what to do; helps businesses; puts up construction signs to warn people about road dangers and reminds them to pay their taxes; prints money; fixes roads, regulates traffic; provides schools and courts; fixes up run-down neighborhoods.

Responses to questions about government jobs and functions were surprisingly poor, given how much was said about government in response to previous questions. Very few students mentioned roads, schools, parks, or other government institutions or services. It is not that children are unaware of these aspects of their lives and surroundings; it is that they do not yet connect them with their images of government. We believe that a major reason for this is that what little students learn about government focuses on government leaders and the symbols associated with them (e.g., the White House), with little attention given to the specifics of government functioning, and especially the provision of government services. We believe that instructional units on government for children ought to provide much more such information, building on the basic idea that governments provide important infrastructure and services that society needs but that are too big in scope, expense, and so on, for individual families to provide for themselves.

TAXES

19. It costs money to pay the people who work for the government. Where does this money come from?

20. What are taxes? Who pays them? Who gets that tax money? What do they do with it?

21. Here in our city, we get services from the township police and firefighters. Who pays the police and firefighters? [If appropriate, probe to clarify where the money comes from.]

K   19. I think it comes from trees.

20. They're money. (Who pays them? Who pays taxes?) My dad pays taxes sometimes. (Why does he have to pay taxes?) He does rentals. (Now, who gets that tax money?) I don't know. (Well, what do they do with it?) I don't know.

21. I don't know.

1st 19. The stuff that you buy, and then like . . . I don't know.

20. The stuff that you owe for the stuff that you have to give to the government because you've had it for a long while, and you have to pay them back like a few hundred dollars of it to get the car and stuff. (Who pays taxes?) Your parents. (Does everyone pay taxes?) No. (Who doesn't pay taxes?) The kids. (Who gets the tax money?) The government. (What do they use the money for?) They use it for the same thing . . . for cars and stuff . . . they give it to poor people so they can have some money.

21. The government. (Where does the government get the money to pay them?) From the people that pay taxes.

2nd 19. From the people . . . like if they just give him money for nothing, they might use that.

20. They're like bills that you have to pay. (Who pays taxes?) Your mom and dad. (Who gets the tax money?) Like these people that send them the letters—they tell them that they have to pay your taxes and then you send the money back in the mail or you take it to them. (The people who get the tax money—what do they do with it?) Sometimes if they have laws, then the boss gets some of the money and he pays some of the money to the workers. (Do you know the name of the people who send out those letters and collect the tax money?) No.

21. I'm not sure. (Well, who pays the police and the firefighters?) Sometimes people have to go to court and like if they get a ticket, they have to pay how much it says on the thing. (Who pays the firefighters?) I'm not sure.

3rd 19. The president which designs the money. They usually design it in new ways, 'cause there is a new dollar bill coming out that glows in the dark, so that no one can try to remake one. (Where does the president get the money from?) He usually tells these certain people to make this money, and usually for his job, that money that he makes, he usually tells people ideas, and the ideas would be put into dollars and he'd get paid for getting that. (So he designs the money as well? Is that one of his jobs?) No, only sometimes does he actually design the money, but his job is to help the country and solve problems.

20. Taxes are sort of like money for poor people, or they add taxes on because that's just what maybe they put down a price and they decide to make it a little higher and add that price on and just say "tax included." (Who pays taxes?) Usually everybody. The president I don't think does, but the government [governor] might or might not, and usually all the other people do. (Who gets the tax money?) Probably some of it—maybe 50% goes to the poor and the other bit goes to the people that need that and the people who really took some time to it and added some things onto it. (What do those people do with the tax money?) It usually becomes money that they probably give to some other people for certain things that they've done to their house, and it keeps going around and around and around.

21. (Who owns the police stations and firehouses?) I think [names a local sheriff's deputy] does the police station, and he does the hospital. (Who pays the police and the firefighters?) Usually the patients that they save will help and they would pay them $10, $15, or $20 for saving their lives or helping them in some way. If that help is used for helping tons of people, they'll get help from the government, usually. (How do they decide that?) Well, maybe more than 50% of the people in that area gets help, then they probably do that.

About 30% (28) of the students were unable to say where the money to pay for government comes from. The rest generated the following responses, listed in rough order of sophistication: The government gets the money from banks, ATM machines, or other places where they have or make money (26); the money comes from the government itself because the president or someone who works for the government prints or coins the money (13); the money comes from people/families/wage earners (stated without mention of taxes; 26); the money comes from taxes (29); the student not only mentions taxes but specifically describes the sales tax by saying that when we buy something, a little bit of the total goes to pay the government (16).

To better distinguish the level of maturity displayed in the responses, we distinguished between transition responses and mature responses. Overall, 28 students were unable to respond, 29 gave relatively immature responses, focusing on government printing of money or getting it from banks, 10 gave transition responses mentioning both printing/banks and taxes, and 19 gave mature responses mentioning only taxes. Other responses included: from kings and queens; banks get "spare money" from rich people; taxes, phone bills, car and house payments (student views the government as a universal lender and provider of utilities as well as services); the president gets the money from another country; the president is rich and also gets money from (rich) former presidents; from a house tax.

When directly asked what are taxes, 37 students were unable to respond, 33 correctly stated that taxes are money paid to the government, 21 described them only as bills that you have to pay (without saying who gets paid or why), and 11 described them as bills other than taxes (utility bills, fines, car payments, etc.). This question had to be clarified for some students who initially began defining "tacks" or "taxis." In addition, there was frequent confusion of taxes with bills or refund checks that come in envelopes, as well as with statements that you have to pay your taxes in order to keep your house. Although 16 students described sales taxes from experiences in stores, only one mentioned income taxes and one other mentioned a "house tax." It was not clear from the latter responses that either student understood the basis for these taxes. These findings replicate previously reported findings indicating a tendency for many children to confuse taxes with other bills.

When asked who owns the police and fire stations, 31 students were unable to respond; 19 said the boss (chief, deputy, etc.); 14 said the people who work in the building; and 36 correctly said the government/governor/township, and so on. Similarly, when asked who pays the police and firefighters, 28 students were unable to respond; 8 said that they are paid by people who use the services (including those who get fined for making nonemergency or false alarm calls); 18 said the president or government without mentioning taxes; and 23 correctly said tax money/taxpayers/the people who pay money to the government. Other responses included: the judge (2); Bill Clinton; the boss; the boss pays the police but the people who get their services pay the firefighters. These findings replicate reports that children often believe that a workplace is owned by the boss, who pays the workers from personal funds or goes to a bank to get the money (merely by asking for it). More students understood that the police and fire stations are owned by the local government than understood that the police and firefighters are paid by the government using tax money.

Older students were more likely than younger ones to confuse taxes with utility bills, fines, interest or finance payments, and so on. This is another case where an incorrect response increases with grade level because of more fundamental differences in the students' ability to generate substantive responses to the question, rather than because accurate knowledge had deteriorated into inaccurate knowledge. The general developmental trend here is from inability to respond at all to responses that confused taxes with other bills, to accurate definitions of taxes as money paid to the government.

Similarly, although older students were more likely to correctly state that the police and firefighters are paid by local governments using tax money, they also were more likely to say that these community employees were paid by the president or the government, without mentioning taxes. Here, the developmental pattern went from inability to respond at all to responses that did not include taxes to responses showing clear understanding that these people are paid using tax money.

Overall, the students' answers to tax-related questions revealed developmental trends similar to those reported in previous research. Some were unable to generate any response at all. Others generated misconceptions, such as that governmental leaders pay employees using their own personal funds or money obtained from banks (simply by going to get it). Some thought that the government could simply manufacture the money needed to pay its employees. Finally, the most mature students understood that governments collect taxes to fund their activities, including construction of police and fire stations and payment of police and firefighters.

Most students who used the word "taxes" understood them as bills to be paid. However, some confused taxes with utility bills, house or car payments, or other bills. Those students who did understand that taxes are money paid to the government usually also understood that most of the money used to fund government activities comes from these taxes.

PUBLIC AND PRIVATE SCHOOLS

22. The kids in this city go to schools like this one. Who owns this school? Who pays the teachers? [If appropriate, probe to establish where the money comes from.]

23. This school is a public school. What other kinds of schools are there besides public schools? [Probe for whatever differences the child can mention, but especially information about who pays for the schools.]

K   22. Mr. Principal. (Well, who pays the teachers?) Mr. Principal. (Where does he get the money from?) He gets it from the bank. (And where does the bank get the money from?) I don't know. (Why would the bank give Mr. Principal money?) You put money in a slot, and then it comes out when you need it.

     23. I don't know.

1st 22. Miss Principal. (Who pays the teachers?) Um . . . Engler [the governor of Michigan]. (Where does Engler get the money to pay the teachers?) From when the people pay him. (And who pays him?) My grandma and . . . tons of people. (And why do they pay him?) So they can have their home. (OK, do they have to pay Engler, or do they want to pay him?) They don't have to, but some people want to.

     23. High schools, elementary schools, middle school. (Who pays the teachers then?) Bill Clinton. (OK, and where does Bill Clinton get the money?) My mom and dad and . . . all the other people. (Why do your mom and dad give Bill Clinton the money for the schools?) So we can keep our school.

2nd 22. Mrs. Principal. (Who pays the teachers?) Mrs. Principal. (And where does she get her money from?) The governor. (Where does the governor get the money from?) The taxes. (Where does the tax money come from?) The people.

     23. There's private schools, there's Catholic schools, there's Episcopalian schools and Christian schools. (How are public schools different from private schools?) Public schools—anybody can come to them, but private schools, you can only go to that one and it's like private and only a certain person can go to a private one. (Who pays the teachers at private schools?) The principal. (Where does the principal get the money from?) From the governor. (So who owns these schools?) The principal, but the governor pays the principal and the principal pays the teachers.

3rd 22. Mr. Principal. (Who pays the teachers?) Mr. Principal and the government, for doing the job and teaching the children useful things for when they grow up. Then kids like me will teach other people and the cycle will go on. (You said Mr. Principal and the government. What do you mean by that?) Well, Mr. Principal pays them for helping kids learn certain things so they can go on to higher grades, so the kids go higher and higher until they finally make it to where he usually is, and if they want to be principal, they'll do so when they grow up. (Where does the money come from?) Usually the government or whoever pays him. (Who would pay him?) Probably the people . . . maybe he helps other schools and those schools would pay him for being good and helping, and that money would be given to them and they give so-and-so back a little. They'd just keep doing that cycle.

23. A religious school and a regular school. (What's the difference between a public school and a regular school?) A regular school could be owned by anyone and anyone can go in it, but public schools usually have older people in that state or area. (What's the difference between this public school and a religious school?) Religious school is they usually teach other things like religion and some sort of regular and some sort of public school things, only it's not a public school. (Who owns this school?) Mr. Principal. He owns this school, and some other people probably owned it before him. (Who owns regular schools?) Usually anyone that's got good skills at that can do that job, as long as they're worthy of doing the things that they're supposed to do. (Who owns religious schools?) People that are really into religion, like if there's this person that reads a Bible a lot or something.

A majority (57) said that the school was owned by the principal (or in a few cases, the boss or the assistant principal). Less frequent responses included: the people who work in the building, the teachers, or the principal and teachers together (12); the government/governor (11); or the school superintendent/school board/school district (7); the janitors; all of us; the superintendent; the people who built it; the city's public community service; the school district.

Concerning who pays the teachers, 25 students could not respond and 47 said the principal (29 implying that the principal would use personal funds but 18 that the principal would use money that comes from the parents, taxes, or the government). Other responses included: taxes/taxpayers (13), the president or government (no mention of taxes; 9), fees collected for yearbooks, supplies, and so on (7), or the students' parents (suggested by students who thought that public schools are funded just like private schools; 7). Unusual responses included: "the people who made the money" come and give it to the school secretary, who puts it in envelopes in the teachers' boxes; the teachers' teachers pay them (couldn't explain who these people were); fees collected for yearbooks and supplies; the governor; rich people; the U.S. government or the PTO [the parent–teacher organization]; the principal gets money from one of the janitors; fees collected for camp and the proceeds from candy sales.

Concerning kinds of schools besides public schools, a majority (64) of the students was unable to respond. The rest suggested home schools (10), Catholic or other church-sponsored schools (7), and a variety of other types of schools. Other responses included: day care; a school in Colorado that had kids getting shot; private schools have sleepovers and harder work; schools of fish; week schools, where you stay there for a week; boarding schools (2); reading schools; private schools where you have to wear uniforms; language schools for immigrants and special schools for the deaf that teach sign language; private schools are smaller and parents have to pay to send their children there; charter schools—a charter school is in a charter township but a public school is "around in the public" (interesting but incorrect theory); academies—they have longer school days and "want you to be prepared" (this student's brother went to one of these academies); private school is where the teacher just teaches one kid; special schools for the handicapped; religious schools where they teach religion; Catholic schools; private schools where they only let in certain people (3); Christian schools where they have to wear uniforms, study the Bible, leave class to go to religion services, and have different science than we do; board schools that have a shorter school year and where the parents have to pay (not sure about public schools); Catholic schools and private schools (goes on to state clearly that private school parents have to pay to send their children there but public schools are free because the teachers are paid by the government from tax money). In addition, the following three second graders made more extensive comments:

"Public school teachers have to follow a curriculum but private school teachers can do anything they want. Private schools cost a lot more (can't say why) and people who have the money are willing to pay it because they think that private schools are better."

"Schools only for boys or only for girls, and boarding schools. At private schools you have to dress nicely, like at church, in a tuxedo or something. My dad went to one and told me that they had metal doors to lock people in."

I went to a private school before, where you have to sign up to enter and you have to pay money for it and you can't just let every kid go there. There's a very little amount of kids. I thought that was pretty nice. (How do they decide to go there?) They don't decide. What they do is make sure the kids are very healthy. They look at their shot cards and all of those kinds of things. It doesn't matter who's Black and White. That's not anything to do with it. They just make sure that they can make friends. They're good at social stuff, and they make sure that they're OK. (So what is the difference between a private and a public preschool?) Public preschools, anyone can go there. They'll treat them the same. But in a private preschool you have to pay more money and you get better service than you would in a public school—no offense to this school, I really like it too. (What do you mean by better service?) There's more teachers and different classes and you get bigger classes (i.e., classrooms). I had a humungous class the size of a church. Actually, it was a church. I thought that was pretty nice and I did get good service. I had two different teachers because at lunch time, if I paid for it, I could go to a different preschool class and they'd take me outside. It was sort of like an afternoon daycare. (You said something about paying money.) You have to pay more money because if you were just going to pay the regular amount for very good service and everything because they work hard to get better people. (Do you pay for public school?) Yes, starting from the beginning. If you leave that school you get your money back for the rest of the grades.

Most students either made no clear distinction between public and private schools or said that religious schools teach religion or do other religion-related things that public schools don't do or that private schools are more exclusive (only certain students can get in). Only six attempted to distinguish public from private schools on the basis of their funding sources. Two said that private school parents support their schools whereas public schools are supported by the government. The other four made transition responses indicating that private school parents paid private school teachers but being unclear about the funding of public schools (thinking either that the government pays all teachers but for some reason private schools cost more, or else that all schools are paid for by the parents of the students who attend them, but for some reason public schools cost less).

Overall, a few students displayed considerable knowledge about the variety of schools available and the nature of their funding, but most could not identify alternatives to public schools and were not clear about how the various types of schools are funded. Only a small minority of students understood that their own public school was owned by the local government and that its teachers were paid using tax money. Many more could not respond or thought that the school was owned by the principal or others who worked in the building and that the teachers were paid by the principal, the president or governor, or the parents. Very few students understood that public schools are "free" because they are supported using tax money, whereas private schools are funded through private sources. The students' knowledge about public ownership and funding of schools was noticeably less developed than their parallel knowledge about police and fire stations.

PRESIDENTIAL ASPIRATIONS

24. Would you like to be president when you grow up? Why or why not?

K   24. No. (Why not?) Because I don't wanna. (What would you rather do?) I would rather be a veterinarian.

1st   24. No. (Why not?) Because I don't want to work that . . . yeah, maybe, because you get a bowling alley in your house and you get a swimming pool in your house, but you have to do very hard work.

2nd   24. Yeah. (Why?) Because it sounds like a special job and I think I can do it. (What parts of it do you think you could do well?) Make some laws and do better things like make people only go to school three days a week.

3rd   24. Not really. (Why not?) I don't know. I just don't want to.

Reflecting the findings of surveys conducted in recent years, a majority (56) of the students said that they would not want to be president when they grew up, 18 were undecided, and only 22 said yes. Follow-up probes yielded responses from 45 students concerning what would be good about being president and from 53 students concerning what would not be so good. Frequently mentioned positive aspects included the perquisites that come with the office (you get to live in the White House, get free cars, etc.; 21), power to issue orders, make laws, and make things happen (12), and the opportunity to do good for the country by making things more fair, helping the needy, and so on (12). Other positives included: You get to have lots of lawyers (thinking of Clinton); it's a lot of money—I also want to marry someone rich; I could tell people to make more toys; you get paid and you get help in your work; every day when the mail comes, it would probably be more money coming in for you; the White House might have secret doors to discover; you get to travel a lot.

Negatives commonly associated with the office included having to work long and hard, with little time for recreation or your family (31), daunting responsibilities (11), and being required to do a lot of work that is not enjoyable because it involves going to meetings and writing a lot, and so on (10). Other negatives included: If you don't follow the rules, you can be sent to jail; I wouldn't like the job because it is too much sitting quietly; some people don't like the president and might try to kill him; you have to make all the rules, and I don't know if I'm smart enough to do that; you have to know what to say when you speak into the microphone; I might be a bad president—like if they said they want some income and I didn't know what to do; you might not get reelected; all the paperwork and traveling; you have guards that follow you around and watch you all time, even when you go to the bathroom; it's a big responsibility and I wouldn't want to mess it up; you can't run again (term limits); if you messed up on something, it would mess up the whole country; it's more of a boy thing—a girl would have trouble getting elected (this was the only girl who said anything like this); someone might ask you a hard question (that you wouldn't be able to answer), and photographers are always taking your picture, even when you don't want them to, like with Michael Jordan.

Clearly, despite most students' tendencies to view presidents as benevolent and powerful leaders, only a minority of them would aspire to the office. One second grader explained why at some length:

No—I wouldn't want to get into all that presidential stuff. I wouldn't like to be a Democrat or a Republican—any of those parties. I just want to be a normal worker when I grow up. I don't want to be president. (Can you think of what would make the job of president difficult?) Well, like you're in charge of the country and you have to do a lot of work. Somebody would think that you just lay back and sit down and watch TV or something, but you can't. You have to run the country, and it's hard. (What would be interesting or good about being president?) Well, when you have time off, you're going to do very fun things. (Like what?) Well, if I ever wanted to be president, I would think of having fun as using videogames, but that would be using taxes for something that you don't need, but if you used your own money, then it would be fine. (You told me you wouldn't want to be a Republican or a Democrat or one of those parties. Why not?) I wouldn't want to get into all that political stuff. Political stuff is like . . . I don't know what political stuff is, but I wouldn't want to get into it.

It is noteworthy that less than a fourth of the students said that they would like to be president when they grew up, and that many of these were more focused on the perquisites attached to the office than on opportunities to use its power for the good of the country. Furthermore, even though most of these students attributed near-omnipotent power to the presidency, more of them associated the office with long hours, daunting responsibilities, and boring work rather than with exciting opportunities to serve the nation and make things happen. Some of this can be attributed to filter-down effects of the "argument culture," particularly the negative responses to "political stuff," the reference to a need for lawyers to keep you out of jail, and so on. It appears to us that the nation in general, the schools in particular, and the social studies curriculum most especially, need to do a better job of emphasizing the common good, helping students to appreciate the many services and functions that governments perform, and socializing students to aspire to public service careers.

DISCUSSION

To the extent that our questions overlapped with questions asked in earlier studies, the responses they elicited mostly replicated trends reported in previous research. Most K–3 students projected images of a benevolent society in which dedicated and competent people working for the government provide individuals and families with whatever they need and address whatever problems face the nation as a whole. They were much more aware of the administrative than the judicial and especially the legislative branches of governments, and they (or at least, the younger ones) tended to view presidents as godlike figures notable for their power to get things done and their benevolence and caring about everyone's needs.

Lacking knowledge about hierarchical levels of government and the specific functions performed at each level, they focused on the president as the key law and decision maker, assisted by governors, judges, and other "helpers." Early images of political leadership tended to be limited to symbol recognition (the president "signs papers," "makes speeches," or "has meetings"). Later images were better connected to governmental processes or functions, but still very general (the president "makes laws," "runs the country," or "solves problems"). There was little or no awareness of the division of labor between the president and other office holders, the roles of political parties or lobbies, or the role of taxes in funding governmental activities. Despite depictions of the president as powerful and benevolent, fewer than one fourth of the students said that they would want to be president when they grew up, and their images of the role stressed daunting responsibilities over opportunities to advance the common good.

A few trends contrasted with findings reported previously: In addition to or instead of portraying the government as a benevolent provider, some students (especially when talking about laws) depicted it as restrictive or oppressive. Also, although a previous study found that children tended to think of laws as long-standing and unchanging, we found that two thirds of the students we interviewed knew that laws can be changed.

Implications for Primary-Grade Social Studies

We believe that primary-grade students stand to profit from instruction about government as part of their social studies curriculum. The questions asked in our interview reflect our notions about some of the key ideas that might be emphasized in teaching about government. They tap networks of knowledge that we believe to be basic for developing initial understandings of the topic.

The students' ideas about why governments are needed and what governments do typically either were vague or were focused on regulating society/preventing chaos or on safety net services for people in need. Very few students mentioned roads, schools, parks, or other government institutions or services that benefit everyone. One reason for this is that primary-grade social studies textbooks and other materials written for children typically restrict their content to leaders and the symbols associated with them (the flag, the White House, the Capitol Building, etc.). Typically, little attention is given to the specifics of government functioning, particularly, the provision of government services.

We believe that units on government for primary-grade students can do a much better job of helping the students understand why governments are needed and what they do for their people. We recommend developing such instruction around the basic idea that governments provide important infrastructure and services that societies need but that are too big in scope, expense, and so on, for individuals or families to provide for themselves. These include national defense and the armed forces; roads, airports, and other transportation infrastructure; education, from kindergarten through university levels; the criminal justice system, including court buildings, jails, and prisons; police and fire protection and emergency services; parks and recreation facilities; the postal service; standards and regulations regarding product quality and safety; safety net services for people with special needs; and so on. The money to pay for these governmental services comes from taxes—money collected from individuals and families to support the common good. Such instruction would delineate a much richer picture of public sector activities than most children possess now, and likely would be of more interest and use to them than some of the more abstract notions often emphasized in lessons on government (e.g., how a bill becomes a law).

We have found that an effective way to develop such appreciation in students is to prepare a photo essay illustrating events occurring in a typical day in the life of one of the students in the class and underscoring the role of government in facilitating these activities. For example, the photos might depict the child getting up in the morning wearing fire-resistant pajamas (per government regulations), washing using running water supplied by local government, changing into clothes inspected for quality and safety, eating a breakfast consisting of foods inspected for quality and safety, boarding a bus required to meet governmental safety standards and be driven by a licensed driver, traveling to school on government-maintained roads patrolled by the local police force, attending school in a government-owned building, participating in learning activities using government-supplied materials assisted by government-supplied teachers and other school personnel, and so on. Such activities help young children see the relevance of government to their lives and broaden their perspectives from a focus on government's restrictive aspects to appreciation of its enabling and supportive aspects.

Primary-grade students also can learn about the three major levels of government (federal, state, local) and their respective responsibilities and functions (especially those most familiar and meaningful to children). The same is true for learning about the three main branches of government (executive, legislative, and judicial). The focus would be on what prototypical government leaders and employees do, not on abstract political science principles or concept definitions.

Initial ideas about alternative forms of government can be developed by contrasting our system of representative democracy (leaders are elected to limited terms and must act within constitutional guidelines) with systems in which leaders ascend to power through other means (inheritance, military power), hold office indefinitely, and exercise totalitarian power. Contrasts can be brought home through discussion or simulation of what it is like to live in countries where there are no elections or at least no secret ballots, access to desired housing and jobs requires continued government approval, and people who resist government policies are subject to arrest.

Some of the details of how our system works are best addressed around election times (national, state, or local), via study of some of the issues and the reasons why different stakeholders would prefer one candidate or policy over another. Also, using examples easily understood by children, instruction can help students learn that debates about laws or policies often focus on means–ends relationships and tradeoffs rather than ultimate purposes (e.g., people who agree with the ultimate purpose of a proposed law or policy might nevertheless oppose it because they do not believe that it will accomplish the purpose or that whatever good it accomplishes will not be worth the costs in higher taxes, new restrictions on individual freedoms, etc.).

Teachers can convey basic information about taxes and address likely confusion of taxes and utility bills by sharing and leading discussions about relevant documents. Most of the students will be familiar with sales taxes at some level, but showing the amounts added to the purchase price as listed on store receipts will help bring home the fact that sales taxes are attached to most purchases and provide a sense of the relative amounts involved. Similarly, sharing property assessments and local tax bills will help students understand how local governments raise money for schools and community services. Support of the federal (and if relevant, the state) government through income taxes can be made concrete by showing paycheck statements indicating that employers keep track of the taxes that their employees owe and deduct this money from gross pay to send to the government.

Once the students have developed some basic knowledge about common forms of taxation, where tax money is sent, and what is done with it, teachers can share utility bills and lead discussion of what is being purchased from utility companies, how it is used, and how the companies keep track of what customers owe them. Class discussion would be followed up with home assignments calling for students to interact with their parents in locating and observing the meters that measure water, gas, and electricity usage, as well as inspecting and discussing tax bills, utility bills, store receipts, and related documents.

Instruction about the civic aspects of government might begin with emphasis that students are members of a classroom community as well as a larger community that incorporates their homes and businesses. As members of communities, they are expected to follow rules designed to help people get along, keep things fair, protect individual and public property, and keep people safe. The larger community has laws for similar reasons. Political office holders make sure that life in the community allows people to carry out their daily activities in a safe and orderly environment. They are paid with tax money collected by the local government. Students might be introduced to local leaders through guest speakers who visit the classroom, field trips to government offices, or studying photos and listening to taped interviews.

The students might learn that the community leaders have three basic jobs: make plans and laws, solve problems, and make the community a pleasant place to live. They make the rules that become laws that need to be followed by everyone. Some laws protect people's rights, some protect property (e.g., zoning ordinances), some protect health (e.g., pollution ordinances), and some promote safety (e.g., speed limits).

Laws help guide our lives and remind us of our responsibilities toward other people. They are enforced by police and judges who are part of local government, but they are intended to make the community a better place, not merely to limit individuals' behavior. To make this concrete, students might select particular laws and discuss why they exist (e.g., considering what would happen if people drove at any speed they wanted and ignored stop signs). Once students have developed a basic understanding of and appreciation for local government, they are ready for lessons on state and national government, voting, and other aspects of responsible citizenship, and comparisons of different forms of government.

Finally, the learning might include encouragement of and opportunities for practicing good citizenship. Some of these might involve government (e.g., writing to appropriate government leaders to suggest new laws or express a position on a current issue). Others might involve volunteer efforts (e.g., participation in antilitter, recycling, or volunteer activities), rationalized with the explanation that governments cannot be expected to do everything and good citizens contribute to the common good as individuals. For a unit on government that incorporates these and other basic ideas, see Alleman and Brophy (2003).

9

Money and Childhood

Along with studying children's knowledge and thinking, we have developed resource units to support teaching about nine selected cultural universals (Alleman & Brophy, 2001, 2002, 2003). Seven of these units drew on the information on food, clothing, shelter, communication, transportation, family living, and government gathered in the large studies summarized in chapter 2 through chapter 8. The other two units focus on money and childhood. We were unable to complete comparably large studies of these two cultural universals, but we did gather information in two smaller studies. The findings are summarized in this chapter.

The data were collected in an elementary school located in a community similar to the one in which most of our other data had been collected—another bedroom suburb adjoining the same city. This second suburb was very similar socioeconomically (i.e., middle/working class) but a little more racially diverse than the first one.

In each of the two smaller studies, we interviewed 12 students—6 first graders and 6 second graders—stratified according to gender and achievement level. These smaller samples were miniversions of the samples used in the larger K–3 studies—smaller in size and confined to first and second graders, but similar in SES and similarly stratified according to gender and achievement level.

CHILDREN'S KNOWLEDGE AND THINKING ABOUT MONEY

Previous research on developments in children's economic understanding has shown that young children tend to believe in a benevolent world in which people get whatever money they need from banks simply by asking for it and shopkeepers sell items for the same price at which they were bought (Berti & Bombi, 1988; Byrnes, 1996; Furnham, 1996). Even when children's economic understandings are valid, they often are limited: They may know that money is printed by the government but do not realize that the amounts of money in circulation are carefully regulated; they may know that banks are places to keep money safely but not know anything about other banking operations; or they may think that the value of an item depends only on the resources that go into producing it. In addition, certain misconceptions are common: The price of an item depends on its size, property is owned by those who use it, or the value of money depends on its color, picture, size, or serial number (Schug & Hartoonian, 1996).

Synthesizing both her own research and studies done by others in several nations, Berti (2002) identified the following trajectories in children's knowledge about economics. Preschoolers typically show no understanding of economic institutions. Lacking prerequisite arithmetical knowledge, they do not understand the value of money and how money is used in buying and selling. Consequently, if offered coins, they may prefer larger, more familiar, or more attractive coins to more valuable ones. They are aware that their parents make money by working, but they also think that money is available on request from banks and obtained as change from shopkeepers. In the early primary years (ages 6 to 8), they develop initial comprehension of the value and function of money and begin to represent banks as places where people deposit their money to protect it from thieves (rather than as sources of money).

Older children (ages 8 to 10) mention several sources of money that owners can use to pay their employees, such as earning it through their own job, getting it from banks, getting it from the government, or even getting it from the employees themselves (who must pay in order to be hired). Knowledge about shop profits and about banking operations (deposits, loans, interest, and their relationships) usually is not acquired until at least ages 9 or 10, although it can be taught earlier (Berti & Monaci, 1998). Until then, children do not realize that employees are paid with money acquired from the sale of goods or services produced by their work, and that retail prices must be higher than wholesale prices to enable shopkeepers to make a living. Most children do not know about bank interest, and even if they do, they usually do not understand how banks make a profit through the difference between deposit interest and loan interest. There are cross-national differences in the speed with which children go through these stages in economic thinking, apparently based on differences in the degree to which children have direct experiences with money and economic activities.

Studies of children as consumers indicate that they are often brand conscious but seldom price conscious when asked to represent shopping or purchases (John, 1999; McNeal, 1992), even though probing may reveal that they know the approximate costs of the items (Pliner, Freedman, Abramovitch, & Darke, 1996). As they progress through the early grades, they gradually become more knowledgeable about the value of money and sophisticated about managing it. These developments emerge sooner among children who are high achievers in mathematics or who have had direct economic experiences (receiving an allowance, saving for a purchase, having their own bank account; Abramovitch, Freedman, & Pliner, 1991; Sonuga-Barke & Webley, 1993).

Given that children in the first and second grade have little understanding of macroeconomics or even fundamental economic concepts such as *profit* or *opportunity cost* (although some of these concepts also can be taught successfully in these grades), we focused our interview on money and other aspects of personal economics that reflected the students' prior experience. The questions featured topics included in our instructional unit on money (Alleman & Brophy, 2003):

- money is a medium of exchange, needed in all but the simplest and most isolated societies;
- several denominations of coins and currency are needed to make it convenient for people to compile exact amounts or make change;
- before the idea of a medium of exchange was invented, people had to rely on trading (barter);
- money eliminates several problems associated with trading and makes economic exchanges much easier;
- early forms of money (such as wampum or precious stones) were less convenient to store and use than more modern coins and paper money;
- U.S. coins and bills include a representation of a past president or another significant American on one side and an American symbol on the other side, words and numbers indicating the value of the coin or bill, and other material such as slogans, information about the depicted person, and information about when and where the money was manufactured;
- money is made in factories (mints) run by the federal government;
- banks not only provide safekeeping for money but also pay interest on accounts and provide loans, checking accounts, credit card accounting, and other financial services;
- budgets are plans for managing finances (and in particular, keeping spending within one's means);
- writing checks and using credit cards allow people to transfer money without having to exchange bills and coins, but they need to keep track of these transactions because the money is deducted from their accounts at their banks;
- when people want to start a business (or buy a home, etc.) and do not have all of the money needed to do so, they can get a loan from a bank (they will have to pay back the loan plus interest, but they are willing to do so because this allows them to start the business or purchase the home now, without having to wait until they accumulate the full amount);
- the value of an item ultimately comes down to what potential purchasers are willing to pay for it;

- most people earn most of their money by working at jobs;
- ordinarily a country's money is good only in that country, but it can be exchanged for an equivalent amount of another country's money which then can be spent in that country.

CHILDREN'S RESPONSES TO OUR MONEY INTERVIEWS

1. Today we're going to talk about money. What is money?

All 12 students generated accurate responses. Eight said that money is used to buy things. In addition or instead, eight described paper money and/or coins. Additional comments were mostly descriptive elaboration: George Washington's face is on the dollar, coins are silver, and so on. Two students mentioned gold coins, possibly thinking of dollar coins, but perhaps thinking that pennies are made of gold.

2. Why are there so many kinds of money? There are $20 bills, $10 bills, quarters, pennies, and so on. Why is that?

For this question, students were shown a $20 bill, a $1 bill, a 50-cent piece, a nickel, and a penny. Four students (all first graders) could not explain why there are so many different kinds of money. Another four expressed the idea that you need a sufficient variety of values to allow you to put together the exact cost of an item (e.g., "We need all different kinds of money so we can pay the right amount.").

Two students conveyed the idea that money would be less convenient if it only came in low denominations: You wouldn't want to have to carry around or count out large sums of money if you had only single dollar bills and pennies. Finally, two students articulated misconceptions. One thought that each U.S. state has its own money, and the other thought that a new bill (denomination) is introduced each time we elect a new president.

3. Long, long ago, there was no need for money. Why was that?

One student said that people didn't know how to make money then and had to use shells instead. The other 11 all said that people then had to hunt for and gather food, make their own clothes, and so on, so there was no need or use for money. One second grader added that people traded things back then.

4. Long, long ago, people often traded for the things that they needed or wanted. How did that work? Trading is difficult. Why is that?

Four first graders could not define or give examples of trading. One second grader's example involved purchase (exchanging money for goods) rather than barter (exchanging goods for other goods). The remaining seven students adequately defined trading or gave examples of it (e.g., exchanging a teddy bear for a toy cash register or exchanging food for clothes).

When asked why trading was difficult, 11 students produced responses that were accurate as far as they went. Five first graders said that you might be unwilling to part with an item that the other person wants (e.g., you wouldn't trade your bike for anything else because you want to keep and use your bike). These responses made no mention of the relative value of the items.

Another three students said that you might be unwilling to accept what you were offered for your item: You wouldn't accept a bad Pokémon™ card for a good one, the other person might not have what you need, or you might not want what the other person has to offer. Finally, three second graders articulated in child language the idea that it can be hard to evaluate the items under discussion (it's hard to tell if it's even; it depends on how much the things are).

5. As more and more trading occurred, people began buying and selling things using money. Why was that?

Only four students suggested explanations, including the three who had just said that it can be hard to determine the value of items offered for barter. Three said that people started using money simply because it was invented (referring to the invention of metal and the means to make coins), and the fourth said that they began to use money after the idea of money was invented. None stated that money was invented because it was easier or more convenient than trading.

6. Indians used money known as wampum. What did wampum look like? Why don't we use it as money today?

These questions about wampum were intended to see if students understood that modern coins and paper currency are easier to carry and use than the more bulky forms of money used in the past. However, none of the students knew what wampum looked like. Nine could not respond, one described it as "little furry stuff," one as a triangle with a dot in the middle, and one as similar to modern coins.

When asked why we don't use wampum today, three students were unable to respond and six others said that wampum is money from the past and we have our own money today. The remaining three students thought that wampum is still used, at least sometimes—by Indians. Two of these meant contemporary Native Americans, but the third said that we don't use wampum because "we don't live in India and are not Indians." Once again, no student said anything about modern money being more convenient or easy to use.

7. Tell me about our money. What does it look like? How do you know
how much it is worth? Tell me about the pictures and writing on the money.

Most students' descriptions of U.S. money reflected the bills and coins they
had been shown; whitish/greenish paper, brown or silver coins. Once again, however, two referred to gold coins. None spontaneously mentioned the numbers or
writing on the money, but one said that George Washington is on the $1 bill
(which he went on to say was carved out of wood and then painted). Another
said that money is needed to pay for things in stores ("or else it's stealing") and to
buy a job (young children commonly believe that jobs cost money).

All 12 students said that the individuals depicted were presidents, and some
identified Washington or Lincoln. No other presidents were mentioned, although one first grader said that the depicted presidents included George Washington Carver, Abraham Lincoln, and George Carvington. Four second graders
thought that the depicted president was the one whose succession number corre-
sponded to the value of the coin or bill—the first president is on the $1 bill, the
20th president is on the $20 bill, and so on. Two expressed puzzlement that
Washington is not on the penny because this is the one-cent coin and he was the
first president.

Two students thought that the presidents make the money and put their own
images on it. One added that this makes sense because the presidents want people
to remember them after they die. Some thought that only presidents can be depicted on money (one added that the money wouldn't look right if someone less
prestigious was depicted on it), but others included other special people such as
"popular guys who lived back then" or "the guy who invented light."

Only four students talked about the tail sides of the coins—two noting the
White House and two noting the eagle. When asked why the eagle was shown,
one could not respond but the other said that it represents "the U.S.A. or freedom." Finally, one first grader said that coins have a head side and a tail side so
you can flip them to start football games. Young children frequently display this
kind of teleological thinking—noting that something can be used for a particular
purpose and therefore assuming that it was specifically invented for that purpose.

Ten students were able to talk about the writing. Four thought that it said
something about the depicted people—explaining that they lived here or honor-
ing their contributions to the country. Three noted that the writing explains how
much the coin is worth ("It says quarter, nickel, or dime."). Other comments included "This says 'Liberty, 1974,' and 'In God We Trust,' " "When the first one
came out it said 'one cent,' so the others put the same thing on the coins they
made," "Some is cursive and some is print; there is different writing because some
of them don't live in the United States," and "If a coin says Los Angeles, then it
means that it was made there."

In addition to these spontaneous comments, some students added elaborations
in response to specific probes. When asked about the word "Liberty," one student

said "That's what it stands for" and another said "Our pledge is about liberty—it ends with 'liberty and justice for all.' " When asked about "In God We Trust," one student could not respond but others said "Because if you break the money, you break the rules, and you are not going to trust anybody or anything," "to show that we trust God and like him," and "Maybe the president believes in God." Concerning how we know how much money is worth, four students could not explain but the other eight noted that the value is stated on the coin or bill. Most referred to the printed words, but three noted the numbers as well. In general, the students' descriptions of money were mostly accurate but indicated that they had not spent much time studying or thinking about the words or images on coins or bills.

8. Who makes our money?

Five students could not respond, three said the presidents, and three said a company or factory (none used the term *mint*). The 12th student said that money is made at the Freedom Coin Shop (a local business) and described watching a television show depicting how coins are manufactured. No student said that only the federal government can make money, that each bill has a unique serial number, that precautions are taken against counterfeiting, or that worn bills are taken out of circulation.

9. What are banks? What kinds of services do banks provide for people? How does your family use the bank? Anything else?

Six students described banks as places to put extra money for safekeeping, and five as places to go to get money (simply by asking for it). Other responses included: Banks manufacture money; banks have money because stores send it to them; you can pay bills there; and each person's money is kept in a separate box, with money put into or taken out of this box every time the person makes a transaction. All of these responses have been observed frequently in previous research on children's knowledge about banking. An exception was the response of a first grader who noted that you can get money just by using the ATM machine, but if you use the drive-through window you can ask for lollipops.

Concerning services banks perform/how banks help people, six students spoke of banks holding your money for you and giving it back whenever you come to ask for it. Another five (four first graders) spoke of banks as places where you can go to get money on request (without specifying that it is your own money). Finally, one first grader spoke of using banks to pay bills and cash checks but did not talk about savings accounts or getting money through means other than cashing checks. Elaborations included: If your bank has run out of money, you would have to go to another bank; the bank holds your money for you and will not steal it; anyone can get money from a bank but you have to show identification; and banks get their money from the money factory. No student said anything about checking accounts, loans, or financial services other than paying bills and cashing checks.

Concerning how their families use banks, most students spoke of the mechanics of operating ATM machines or using drive-through windows (typically describing sending and receiving materials through vacuum tubes). Most depicted families going to banks to get cash, but two spoke of making deposits and two spoke of getting lollipops. Some could not talk about the inside of the bank because they had not been inside (or if they had, not recently or often enough to retain images of what goes on there).

10. What kinds of jobs do people who work in banks have?

Four students could not respond and the others mostly emphasized helping people by giving them money (none used the term *teller*). When probed for details, various students depicted bank workers talking on the phone, using computers, or writing on papers, but they usually could not specify the content of these transactions. Other than giving people the money they asked for, the only specific elaborations were using computers to send money and helping people by "giving them bills that they need to pay." The only nonteller job mentioned was a person who "stands at the front and says 'Good morning,' 'Have a nice day!' and things like that." These responses mostly replicated children's ideas documented in previous studies, especially their notion of the world as a benevolent place where people can get money just by going to banks and asking for it and their tendency to think about banks merely as storehouses for money without knowing much if anything about the bank's other functions and services.

11. What is a budget? Why is budgeting important?

The students were unfamiliar with the term *budget*. Ten could not respond and the other two guessed "like a discount or something" and "a savings account."

12. Some people write checks to pay for things. How does that work? Why do people use checks? Other people pay by credit card. How do credit cards work? Why do people use credit cards?

One student could not respond but the others all gave responses (of varying accuracy and specificity) indicating that people use checks to get money or to transmit money to someone else. Three mentioned only the first of these uses for checks, six mentioned only the second, and two mentioned both.

Among students who spoke of using checks to get money, most referred to writing your own check and cashing it, but one spoke of getting a check from someone else (e.g., as a birthday gift). Among students who spoke of writing checks as a way to transmit money, most mentioned paying for store purchases but some spoke of sending money to someone living elsewhere (e.g., as a birthday present to a relative).

Only four students, all second graders, noted that the money specified on checks that people write is debited from their bank accounts. Explanations of when or why people use checks included: If you don't have enough money with you to pay in cash (2); if you were sick at home and couldn't get out to pay personally; for big amounts like $100; and because it is more convenient—you don't have to count out the money.

When asked about how credit cards work, most students initially spoke of the mechanics of using the cards (e.g., slide it through the slot, sign the slip, etc.) but then went on to describe credit cards as alternatives to cash that can be used when making purchases at stores, restaurants, gas stations, and so on. However, two first graders spoke only of using credit cards to get money from ATM machines.

Half of the students said that you would use credit cards if you didn't have enough money with you or didn't want to spend the cash, and three noted that amounts charged against your credit card are debited from your account at the bank. Other elaborations: Using credit cards is like using checks except that you just get your card back, without money too; credit cards are quicker than checks because you don't have to wait for the bank person to process the paper and count out the money; you could use it at a gas station if you didn't want to go inside to pay; a credit card is like a check except that you use it at a store rather than at a bank; it's the same as with checks except that it works through computers; you can get change back if you wish; and it enables you to buy things without having to carry around a lot of cash that might get stolen. In general, most of the students knew something of the mechanics involved in writing checks and using credit cards, but only a minority understood that the transferred money is debited from your bank account.

13. Imagine you were going to start a business such as a restaurant. What things would you need to think about?

The students gave sensible answers to this question, emphasizing staff hires, food purchases, recipes, prices, and so on, but only two mentioned getting together the money needed to start the business. When asked about this, seven spoke of getting money from a bank, two said that you would have to accumulate savings from money earned in previous jobs, two couldn't respond, and two said that you would have to get it from other people (one couldn't say from whom and the other said from people already in business who had money available in their cash registers). Among students who spoke of getting money from the bank, the first graders thought that you could just go to the bank and ask for it (one spoke of going back many times because a lot of money would be needed), whereas the second graders clearly stated that the money would be from your own account.

No student mentioned getting a loan. One second grader did say that you might not have to accumulate all of the money, but couldn't say more when asked how you would get the rest. These findings support those from our shelter interview indicating that primary-grade students know little or nothing about financing major purchases (whether homes or businesses) by getting mortgage loans from banks.

14. People have garage sales to get rid of things they don't need. How do people know how much to charge?

Students had difficulty with this question. Several began by saying that you would charge what the item originally cost, but all but one of these changed their thinking when probed. One ended up saying only that bigger things would cost more than smaller things, and another that he might be able to charge as much as the store would charge because some people wouldn't know how much they should pay.

The remaining nine students eventually determined that items would (or at least should) cost less at a garage sale than a store. Two could not explain further, three said that this was because the garage sales items were used and the store versions were new, and the rest gave the following rationales: A garage sale is a sale and the store might not be having a sale; you pay more at stores because they have more stuff there; stores charge a lot because they want to make a lot of money, but you could choose to charge less (i.e., be less greedy); and you could really charge whatever you want, but people tend to negotiate at garage sales and expect to pay less than they would pay at the store. No student mentioned supply and demand or said that an item is worth whatever potential purchasers are willing to pay for it, although the student who talked about people negotiating at garage sales appeared to have partial understanding of the latter idea.

15. How do people get money? Any other ways?

When asked how people get money, most students initially said from banks. Only four (all second graders) initially spoke of earning money from jobs, but the others understood that people get money this way when asked about it. Several made reference to payday in talking about money earned from jobs.

When probed about other ways of getting money, various students mentioned getting change in transactions at stores (2); other people might give you money or you might find it on the ground; garage sales; and *alimony/child support* (this student did not use these terms but talked about how her father gave her mother money every month that was used to buy necessities for her mother and herself).

Some students were asked about how they themselves might get money. Most mentioned getting paid for doing chores at home. Other responses included getting an allowance, babysitting, setting up a lemonade stand, and doing good things for others and getting rewarded for it.

16. Is Mexican money good in our country? Can we use our money if we travel to Mexico? Why? Why not?

All 12 students said that Mexican money is not good in our country. Most could not explain beyond saying that it is different from our money, we only take our own money, and so on. Elaborations included: If you tried to use Mexican money, people would think that you were Mexican and you don't dress like they do; Mexican money is good only in Mexico; Mexican money is money after all, so some people might be willing to take it if they were planning to go to Mexico; we don't read their language or know how to work their money, so we can't take it and use it.

Responses concerning whether we can use our money in Mexico were similar. One first grader said yes (but couldn't explain), but the other students all said no (because our money is different, they only take their own money, etc.). Elaborations included: If you tried to use American money, they would think you were American and take you back to the United States; U.S. money is still money so some Mexicans might take it; and Mexicans do not speak our language or know how to work our money, so they wouldn't know what it is worth.

Most students could not explain how one might get Mexican money. One said that you would have to go to Mexico and get a job there, another that maybe you could just find it, and a third that maybe a relative would visit Mexico and bring some back for you. No student showed any awareness of the possibility of exchanging money at banks or currency exchanges, or even of the idea that two currencies can be equated in value and exchanged for like amounts. The students seemed to think that money is of no value outside its own country.

At the conclusion of the interview, students were asked what questions they would like to see answered in a unit on money. Most responses focused on the process of making money (who makes it, where, and how). Other questions included: How much money can there be in a bank? Does the whole world have money, and if so, how many different kinds are there? How do you get money? Why was money invented?

Overall, the students' responses indicated that the second graders knew more about money than the first graders, but none of the students knew very much about the big ideas emphasized in our instructional unit.

CHILDHOOD

Our instructional unit on childhood (Alleman & Brophy, 2003) focuses on childhood as a cultural universal. That is, besides being a time of physical and cognitive development, *childhood* is a social category recognized as such by most if not all societies. Formal laws or informal role expectations charge particular adults with responsibilities for protecting and socializing particular children, and charge society as a whole with parallel responsibilities for children in general. Within the culture as a whole, there are subcultures reflecting the activities of children of different ages (toys, games, etc.), rites of passage marking progress toward adult status, and correspondingly graduated privileges and responsibilities.

Our interview questions focused on these and other basic ideas about childhood that we think are important for children to learn, especially aspects that we thought they might know something about already. Topics included:

- ways in which children around the world are similar and different;
- individual characteristics that make the student different from all other children;
- why we have schools for children;
- why children in some countries work in fields or factories most of the time but children in our country go to school most of the time;
- schooling in other countries;
- how schools in Japan or in Africa differ from our schools;
- how pioneer children spent their days;
- pioneer children's schooling and recreation;
- toys and games used in other countries;
- toys or games used in Japan or in Africa that are different from our toys or games;
- what birthdays are;
- how birthdays are celebrated in other parts of the world;
- birthdays before the invention of calendars;
- why some birthdays are more important than others;
- things that children are not allowed to do until they reach a certain age;
- differences between babies and young children and between young children and older children;
- things that young children sometimes believe that older children do not believe;
- the purposes and nature of advertising directed toward children;
- laws that the government has passed to help protect children;
- special talents that the student possesses that might be used later in a job or career;
- things that the student could do to help others, practice good citizenship, and help get rid of the problem of discrimination;
- choices that students make in their lives.

To date, there have been no systematic investigations of trajectories in children's thinking about childhood as a cultural universal, and very few studies that connect in any way to the questions on our interview. The few exceptions are cited when findings from the relevant questions are discussed.

CHILDREN'S RESPONSES TO OUR
CHILDHOOD INTERVIEWS

1. Today we're going to talk about children and childhood. Children all around the world are the same in some ways and different in others. How are all children around the world the same?

Students had difficulty talking about similarities across children around the world. Only four gave accurate answers (all eat food; have the same body parts; need food and water; and have clothes, shoes, food, and houses), and two of these also gave incorrect answers (all have same skin color and wear the same outfits; all have the same pets). Two other students were unable to respond and one gave an incorrect answer (they all play the same sports).

The remaining five students could only identify ways that children "might" be the same: have the same hair or skin color (2), be twins (2), know the same songs, have friends with the same name, have the same music or sports preferences, have the same appearance or eat the same food, and have the same views on school.

2. What are some ways in which children around the world are different?

In contrast, all 12 students were able to identify ways in which children differ. Eight mentioned skin color (although none used the word "race"), and a ninth said that people "look different." Other responses mentioned by more than one student included differences in foods (5), wealth or material possessions (3), hair color (3), sports (2), languages (2), and clothes (2). Unique responses included differences in need for glasses; countries; eye colors; running speed; preferences for colors, books, music, sports, or games; birthdays; handicaps; and access to schooling. The student who mentioned handicaps had a handicapped sibling.

These responses are typical of young children's self-descriptions in that they focus on physical appearance or specific behavioral preferences or activities, without reference to more abstract qualities such as happiness or generosity (Harter, 1999). The responses also replicate earlier findings indicating that children typically find it easier to identify differences than similarities when asked to draw comparisons.

3. Some things about each child are special. What are some special things about you that make you different from all other children?

Students tended to mention facial features (4), musical or sports talents or skills (3), prized toys or pets (3), having many friends (2), and unique family connections (mother is a school principal; father has many tattoos). Unique responses included: not riding his scooter in the winter (when other kids do), living in a different house, possibly having something different to eat tonight for dinner, sometimes loses her teeth, and has traveled to Kentucky. Once again, these responses mostly reflect physical appearance or behavioral activities rather than more abstract personal traits.

4. Children usually go to school. Why do we have schools for children?

All 12 students said that children need to learn knowledge and skills that will be needed in the future: reading (4), thinking (4), mathematics (2), writing (2), science, music, and learning how to teach by observing the teacher. Four mentioned preparation for jobs and one mentioned preparation for high school and college. Unique elaborations included: teachers want children to go to school; we learn to make friends at school; we learn to be better people; and we learn to be safe and to respect others, including people from other countries.

5. In some countries, children work in fields or in factories most of the time, but in our country, children go to school most of the time. Why is that? If you family wanted you to stop going to school and start working to earn money, could you do that?

Nine students could not respond; two said that in places without schools, people are very poor and do not have money to build schools; and the other said that we go to school in our country because that is how the president wants it (implying that the presidents of some other countries have different ideas). Concerning whether they would stop going to school if they could, all 12 said no. Eight simply repeated that children need to get prepared for the future. Three said that children their age are too young to get a job. One added that she had only a few pennies in her piggy bank, not enough to buy a job. Another said that she would prefer to stay in school because it is more fun than working in the fields, and the one who said that children go to school in our country because that is how the president wants it said that she would stay in school because we all should listen to the president.

Among students who said that children need to stay in school to learn, some were thinking of relatively immediate effects of dropping out, not just future effects. One said that if he stopped going to school, he wouldn't keep learning things that other kids his age were learning. Another said that if he stopped going to school, he would sit around watching cartoons all day and not get smarter like other kids. In general, the students showed good understanding of the fact that schools are established for their benefit. Apparently, even students who are lethargic in school or frequently grumble about requirements understand that learning what is taught in school is in their best interest.

6. Today, children all around the world go to school. Do you know about schools in any other countries? Are the schools in _____ different from ours?

Eleven students could not respond and the twelfth gave a suspect answer. She claimed to have been in schools in Africa and China, describing them as similar to ours (in teaching ABCs and other school subjects) but saying that the people in these schools speak Spanish and talk a lot about dancing and music.

7. What about Japan—are Japanese schools different from ours? Do Japanese children do anything different in their schools than you do in your school?

All but one student generated ideas about how Japanese schools are different from American schools. Six said that a different language is spoken there (although one identified this language as French and another as Spanish). One added that children dance and sing in a circle with an "X" in the middle in Japanese schools, and another said that they eat rice at all of their meals. Otherwise, the students gave "might" guesses: In Japan they might have bigger or smaller schools, different lunch or recess schedules, no music, different rooms, different subjects, a different calendar, or one-room schools (for lack of money to build larger ones).

8. What about in villages in places like Kenya in Africa—are African schools different from ours? Do African children do anything different in their schools than you do in your school?

The students generated similar responses when asked about African schools. One said that these schools are no different from our own, but four mentioned language differences, four suggested that the quality of the buildings or of the students' clothes or equipment was not as good, and three mentioned possible differences in the size or type of organization of the school. Except for language differences, these were mostly "might" guesses. So were most of the unique responses: different homework, using brown paper rather than white paper, smaller beds, no lunch boxes, one recess instead of two, a bigger school or a combination school and college in the same building, a smaller school with no afternoon program and no combined first–second grade classrooms, different arts and crafts, either less or more time in the school day, different activities (they don't have dominoes there), different foods for lunch or snack, and different clothes (clothes were ragged for lack of money for better clothes).

The students' responses concerning schooling in other parts of the world were mostly guesses. They found it easier to respond when asked about specific places (Japan, Africa) than about the world in general. This pattern has appeared in several of our interviews. Although several mentioned possible differences in the sizes of school buildings, none said anything about the materials from which the buildings were constructed or the design of schools or classrooms. Several suggested that African schools might suffer for lack of comparable resources to spend on education, whereas only one raised this possibility in talking about Japanese schools.

9. Here is a picture showing life back in the pioneer days, when most people lived in log cabins and worked on farms. How do you think pioneer children spent their days when they were your age? What was their typical day like?

One student could not respond and another depicted pioneer children as spending the day with their families (without elaboration). The other ten depicted them as working all day or at least most of the day. The jobs they described were mostly accurate: feed pigs, clean house, build furniture, sweep, make bread, gather or hunt for food, gather wood, tend fire, churn butter, stir honey, work in fields, and help mother prepare meals. One student mentioned that pioneers had no electricity and another said that they had no television.

10. Did pioneer children go to school? What were their schools like? Did they do anything different in their schools than you do today in your school?

Eight students said that pioneer children could not go to school because there were no schools then (or at least, none in the wilderness where they lived). The other four described schooling generally similar to ours. However, in elaborating, one said that pioneer schools had fewer toys and less "stuff," so students did more work there and had less time for lunch; a second said that their school was different in some ways such as not using the same calendar; a third said that their studies were mostly similar but they did "French or something"; and the fourth said that pioneer schools didn't have field trips for lack of money to pay for them.

11. Even back in the pioneer days, children played and entertained themselves with toys and games. Did pioneer children entertain themselves differently than children do today? Why?

One student said that things were no different then, four said that they were different but couldn't explain, and the other seven explained with general accuracy. Comments included: Pioneers had to make their own toys "from animals and stuff"; pioneer children didn't have much time to play or much stuff to play with; they played with string, played tag or tic-tac-toe, or wrote in the dirt with sticks because they didn't have chalk or slates or paper; they played tag or hide and seek but had no board games; they just had wooden toys that they found or made at home; and they just had homemade toys such as paper dolls.

These responses about life in the past are similar to those elicited in the family living interview (see chap. 7, this volume). They are typical of children in that they reflect a pervasive presentism, emphasizing what people in the past were lacking. However, they were mostly accurate as far as they went, indicating once again that even first and second graders possess some information about pioneer life (either from units taught at school or from children's literature, television, and videos).

12. Today, kids play with toys and games all over the world. Do you know of a country where kids play different games than in our country? Do you know of a country where kids play with different toys than you play with here?

None of the children said no to this question. However, one did not know, three said yes but could not give examples, two only gave examples of toys or games played in the United States, and two said that in some places they only have homemade toys. Only four gave examples that could be considered valid: Chinese girls play with dolls but boys play with kites; Canadian children use different skateboards and ramps than we do; China has different Pokemon characters than we have; and in some countries they play a "Jado" game (couldn't explain the game or name the country). Of the two students who spoke of homemade toys, one couldn't specify a country but described balls made from animal skins and the other said that Chinese children don't have board games and have to find "a trash can or something" and make a game with it.

13. Do Japanese children have different games than American children? Do Japanese children play with different toys than American children?

Five students said that Japanese children play with different toys or games but could give no examples, two gave only examples of toys or games played in the United States, and none gave valid examples of toys or games played in Japan. One student could not respond and the other four said that Japanese children lack certain U.S. toys or must play with homemade toys. Comments included: Some of them live in the wild and have no money to buy toys; they make toys out of animals, but we get ours out of a box; they don't have bikes and scooters like we do; and they have some used toys donated from the United States, plus they make their own from garbage cans or old wood chips or something like that.

14. Do African children have different games than American children? Do African children play with different toys than American children?

One student said that African children play with the same toys and games that American children do, one didn't know, four said that African children use different toys or games but could not give examples, and one said that African children play with circular dice. The other five said that African children lack certain U.S. toys or must play with homemade toys. Comments included: It is boring there because they don't have many games; there is no money or stores to buy toys; they don't have Connect 4™ games or much other stuff; they play tag in the rainforest, build stuff with leaves using sticky stuff to hold it together, or play with dragons; and they don't have board games and have to make toys out of garbage and dolls out of paper.

Responses to these questions indicated that the students possessed little information about toys or games in other countries. In addition, in contrast to earlier questions about schooling, these questions about toys and games in other places elicited several indications of chauvinism (or at least, of the notion that Japan, Africa, and presumably most other places in the world are not very developed economically and thus unable to offer their children opportunities to purchase the wide range of manufactured toys and games sold in U.S. stores). Like the responses to most questions about life in the past and in other parts of the world across our interviews, these responses indicate that primary-grade students stand to benefit from a broad range of instruction about life in the past and in other places (especially instruction that underscores that people are generally more similar than different).

15. In our country we celebrate birthdays. What are birthdays? What does it mean when you have a birthday?

One student said that a birthday means that you get a year older, four said that you celebrate or get presents, and the other seven said both of these things. No student used the term *anniversary*; instead, they talked about getting older or celebrating the day you were born. One said that some people do not celebrate birthdays because their parents do not believe in such celebrations (this student's family practiced a religion that includes this prohibition). Another said that your birthday is "the day that you were born but in the past," and two mentioned that when you get a year older, you qualify to go on to the next grade at school.

These findings are compatible with those of Klavir and Leiser (2002), who studied 3- to 9-year-old Israeli children's understandings of birthdays. They found that younger children emphasized the social/celebration aspects of birthdays (party, presents, cake, etc.) and sometimes harbored misconceptions (e.g., that age can be affected by multiplying or skipping birthdays). As the children got older, misconceptions faded away and their responses shifted emphasis from celebrations to the idea that you are now a year older than you were on your last birthday.

16. What do you know about children in other parts of the world and how they celebrate their birthdays?

Six students were unable to respond, two described birthday parties like those held in the United States, and the other four said that other countries celebrate birthdays too, but each in its own way. The latter students envisioned the following celebrations: Do something, but probably not have cake or ice cream; sing in a different language and make the cake from different ingredients; maybe have presents but not cakes; and if they were poor, they might have a party at home, but if they had more money, they might have something at a hotel or go on a treasure hunt or something. These were minor variations on familiar forms of birthday celebration. No one mentioned anything specific about forms of celebration occurring in other countries (although in some of our other interviews, students have made reference to piñatas).

17. Did people have birthdays before calendars were invented? [If yes:] **How did they know when to celebrate their birthday?)** [If no:] **Then how did they know how old they were?**

When asked if people had birthdays before calendars were invented, one student could not respond, four said no, one said yes but couldn't explain, and six said yes and attempted an explanation. The explanations all suggested that the people (or their parents) would have to "think really hard," "remember," or "keep track of the days in their head." Two suggested mechanisms that the people could use to help them remember: Keep a running tally of months and days (J1, J2, etc.) or draw boxes with 30 or 31 days on them and just cross them out. Even the latter responses construed the problem as a limitation on memory capacity, without taking into account that people had not yet developed the concept of a *year* as a complete orbit of the earth around the sun. The students understood that people could mark days, but did not yet understand that they couldn't mark weeks, months, or years as we define them today.

18. Are some birthdays more important than others? [If yes, ask for explanation about:] **Which birthdays are especially important and why?**

One student said that your 21st birthday is special because you become an adult. Otherwise, five said no, one said yes but could not explain, and the other five could not respond or said such things as that birthdays are more important in certain countries (without being able to explain) or that his dad's birthday was especially important because his mom buys his dad special stuff. Thus, the idea that certain birthdays mark important rites of passage was not immediately salient to the students, although some of their responses to subsequent questions indicated awareness of it.

19. Children aren't allowed to do certain things until they reach a certain age, like 16. What are 16-year-olds allowed to do that younger children aren't allowed to do? What about 18—what are 18-year-olds allowed to do that younger children are not?

Concerning 16-year-olds, one student could not respond but eight said drive, two said drink, and three said visit with friends or travel far away on their own. Other responses included: do more things with computers, buy things on their own at stores, go to high school, wear slit skirts, sit in the front seat in cars, and walk in the streets instead of having to stay on the sidewalks. Although there were a few errors in certain details (e.g., it is not legal to drink at 16), the students had generally accurate ideas about things that teenagers can do that children are not allowed to do.

Concerning 18-year-olds, one student could not respond, four said drink, three said drive, three said smoke, two said go to a college, and three said make their own decisions about snacks, decorating your room, or doing what you want. Other responses included: Go to scary movies, cuss without getting whipped, date and kiss, travel to distant cities, get a job, have your own money to use in stores, move into your own place (even in a different state), go to gyms or health clubs, get tattoos, and wear make-up and clothing of your own choice. Again, despite a few incorrect details, it is clear that the students had images of freedoms allowed 18-year-olds. It is noteworthy (but probably not surprising) that these responses focused on making their own decisions and participating in activities often viewed as vices, rather than on assuming adult responsibilities such as higher education, marriage, voting, or military service.

20. Children include babies and little kids and bigger kids like yourself. What are some differences between babies and little kids? When do you stop being a baby and start being a little kid? What are some differences between little kids and bigger kids like yourself? When do you stop being a little kid and start being a bigger kid?

Concerning differences between babies and young children, five students mentioned size differences, three said that babies cry, and three said that babies cannot yet walk. Other responses: Babies don't like to watch television and children do; babies are gentle and we can hug them but they can't hug us; children are stronger than babies; babies don't have hair yet; babies are more vulnerable to broken bones; babies can't ride roller coasters yet; babies spend a lot of time napping, cannot play outside alone, and cannot swim without floaties; babies don't do much other than cry, move around, and drink milk, but children can run, play, and hop; children can do more things; and children have different toys, can paint their nails, drink from cups rather than bottles, and can play outside or go to friends' houses.

Three students said a baby starts being a young child when the baby has a birthday and another said when the baby becomes 1 year old. The remaining responses ranged from 2 years old to 5 years old, with most concentrated in the 3- or 4-year-old range.

Concerning differences between younger children and older children "like themselves," one student could not respond and six mentioned size differences. In addition or instead, students also mentioned: Little kids can be bad; little kids can't ride roller coasters; bigger kids get to go to more places; bigger kids can be bossy and little kids nicer, and bigger kids are in higher grades in school; bigger kids go to sports practices, do more things, and use computers; bigger kids have longer hair; bigger kids go to different schools; and bigger kids know how to paint their nails and drink from cups rather than bottles. Many of these responses were similar to those given to the previous question about differences between babies and young children.

When asked when a child stops being a little kid and starts being a bigger kid, three students said "On your birthday" but didn't specify a particular age. One said that your parents tell you because they see that you stop crying as much and you get bigger. The remaining students gave ages or age ranges, with several clustered at ages 4 to 5 but two at ages 6 to 9 and two at ages 10 to 13. We were surprised at the range of ages mentioned as markers between babies and little children and between little children and bigger kids. We wonder if the differences might be related to birth-order differences, with oldest children tending to identify younger transition ages (because they feel like bigger kids) and younger siblings tending to specify older transition ages (because they look forward to privileges enjoyed by their older siblings).

21. Young children sometimes believe things that aren't true because they don't know any better. What are some of those things that young children believe? What are some things that kids your age know that younger children don't know?

Five students mentioned believing in ghosts, monsters, or people coming to get you in the middle of the night. Other mistaken beliefs included: If they break glass, they will get in trouble; the blue cup holds more water than the green cup (he once fooled his younger brother about this); angels and tooth fairies; things depicted in cartoons are real; fear of the dark; they really are eating or drinking when they use pacifiers; things depicted in horror movies are real, Jaws is a real shark, and sharks fear humans and won't eat them; maybe people like them but maybe they don't; and they don't think that God is real or they believe in other gods rather than the real God. Some of these responses touched on the conservation of volume, the distinction between intentional and accidental property destruction, and other emergent concepts studied by child development researchers, but most dealt with fictions deliberately conveyed to children by their parents or by the producers of children's literature and entertainment. When asked what older children know that younger children don't yet know, one student could not respond; four mentioned academic skills of reading, writing, or mathematics; three mentioned manners or morality (not scratching on walls or ripping off posters, going to school the right way and knowing right from wrong, and knowing how to act at restaurants); and two mentioned safety knowledge (being careful around glass, the stove, or when reaching up over a counter; not tasting things when you don't know what they are and being careful with knives or hot curling irons). Unique responses included: There are no ghosts or monsters; how to ride bikes and scooters; knowing about homework and knowing that you have to be 16 to drive; and knowing that there are no ghosts or people coming to take you away in the night. In general, most of what the students said about differences between babies and younger children and between younger children and older children was accurate.

22. Many companies advertise their products on television to try to get you to buy them, like cereals. What are some things that cereal companies do to try to get you and your family to buy their cereals?

Three students could not respond, six mentioned putting prizes in the box, four mentioned depicting the cereal as good tasting or "cool," and two mentioned advertising low prices or sales. However, one who mentioned advertising low prices and one who talked about glowing depictions of the product went on to say that these claims may be lies—that what you find when you get to the store is not the quality of product nor the price that you have been led to expect. Other responses included: Make commercials and show them on television; and put up signs—at the store, in commercials, or on the cereal box itself. Most of the students were not yet very aware of advertising directed at children, but some of those who were aware had already developed skepticism about the claims made in this advertising.

23. What are some laws that the government has passed to help protect children?

Four students could not respond and four mentioned laws against underage smoking or drinking. Other responses included: not allowed to drive until age 16; bikers must wear helmets; laws against picking up children and taking them away in cars, and laws forbidding children to do things that are not safe; laws requiring children to stay in school until they finish learning; laws forbidding children to have guns; required fire alarms and seatbelts; and laws specifying that schools must have principals prepared to intercept potential child molesters and call the police to arrest them. In addition to the two comments about laws forbidding child molesting or kidnapping, two other students spoke of house or school rules against getting into a stranger's car or getting out of the house immediately if there is a fire. The eight students who were able to respond to this question showed good awareness of child safety and protection issues, although they sometimes confused informal admonitions or rules with formal laws.

24. Do you have any special talents or interests right now that you might use in your job or career when you grow up?

Four students could not respond, three said no, two mentioned football or basketball skills, and three mentioned language arts skills. Of the latter, one said that he was a good reader and could become a lawyer, another that she enjoyed writing stories and could become a children's story writer, and a third that she was good at drawing and wanted to become an artist. The substantive responses were good as far as they went, but limited to 5 of the 12 students.

25. What are some things that you can do even as a child to help others and practice good citizenship, either here at school or in your community?

Two students were unable to respond, but the rest talked about either generally doing good and respecting others or helping someone (especially a younger child) with something specific. Responses included: If they need help with spelling or are stuck in the road; help others, like if they are hurt in an accident, pull them out of the car and away from danger; help younger children learn to read; help younger children find a game on the computer; ask their parents to respond to television ads calling for sponsoring third-world children in need; do good things, respect others, and grow up to be a cop; help younger students cross the street, go and get their mom if they get hurt, and help make their food; do your job because that will help others to do theirs; help new classmates learn what we do in our class; and donate old clothes and toys to the poor. These responses were accurate and mostly realistic.

26. Some people suffer from discrimination—they are treated badly because they are different. What can you do as a child to help get rid of this problem of discrimination?

Three students could not respond, three spoke of imitating Martin Luther King, Jr., by growing up to fight unjust laws and telling people to get along, and five spoke of being nice to people who are discriminated against or treating them well (make them feel at home, don't treat people differently by skin color, be nice to them and become their friend (2), learn to be fair, be nice to people who think they are stupid because they are different). In addition, three students spoke of interceding directly: Talk to people who are discriminating and tell them that they shouldn't do it (and if they are little, tell their parents what they did); confront them directly by telling them that they are acting mean when they disparage people of other races (this student claimed to do this with her own father); first ask them not to do that "because it hurts my feelings and I don't want anybody to get killed, because I like these people," and if necessary, say "Don't do that or you'll be in big trouble by the president." We find it encouraging that most of these young students already possessed specific ideas about avoiding discrimination in their own behavior, and that some of them said that they would confront discrimination by others when they encountered it.

27. None of us can do everything, so we all have to make choices in our lives, even children. What are some kinds of choices that you make in your life?

One student couldn't respond, three mentioned food choices, two television program choices, and three choices of what to do during literacy time at school. Surprisingly, eight mentioned choices regarding deportment or following rules (not doing dangerous things, doing the right thing, saying no to offers of cigarettes, choosing to be quiet and be a good listener, doing what you are asked to do at school, not saying bad words or lying, being helpful to classmates, and getting good grades). We think these responses reflect the fact that in recent years, the language of choice and responsibility has been incorporated into many of the socialization messages directed at children by their parents and teachers. Other choices included: when to play the drums at home; which classmate to sit by during free times; things to buy at the store; where to sit; to stick up for myself against bullies; and a joint decision with her mother that on school days she would eat breakfast at the babysitter's house rather than her own house.

Across the interview as a whole, the children's responses usually were accurate as far as they went, but often indicative of very limited knowledge about the topics addressed (especially in questions about childhood in the past or in other countries).

DISCUSSION

Our interview questions, drawn from big ideas stressed in our instructional units on money and childhood, reflect our thinking about basic aspects of these topics to introduce in the primary grades. The responses of the first and second graders we interviewed revealed frequent knowledge gaps and misconceptions about specifics, as well as generic patterns similar to those documented in our large studies (e.g., indications of presentism and chauvinism suggesting the need for empathy-oriented instruction about life in the past and in other countries).

The gaps and misconceptions all point to needed content emphases in teaching about relevant aspects of the topic (e.g., banks provide a range of services besides holding money for safekeeping; rites of passage bring not just new freedoms and pleasure/entertainment options, but also new responsibilities and educational, occupational, family, and citizenship roles). It appears that the home, the media, and the culture generally make children very aware of the hedonistic and materialistic aspects of development toward adulthood, but it is mainly up to the school to nurture their awareness of the personal, social, and civic responsibility aspects.

10

Variation Across Socioeconomic Status, Achievement Level, and Gender

We noted in chapter 1 that the original plans for our large studies called for samples of 216 students, 54 in each of Grades K–3, stratified according to SES, achievement level, and gender. Our first two studies (on shelter and clothing) did in fact reflect these plans. However, analyses of their data led us to conclude that it would not be cost effective for us to continue to sample systematically from communities representing three different SES levels. In this chapter, we explain that decision in more detail and also present our findings relating to student achievement level and gender.

Chi-square analyses were used to test for the statistical significance of obtained variation across stratified subsamples. The Mantel-Haenszel chi-square test for linear trends was used when the subsamples were aligned sequentially (e.g., by grade level, SES level, and achievement level). The conventional chi-square test was used to compare boys with girls because these qualitative gender categories are not sequential steps on a common dimension. These analyses produced statistically significant chi-squares much more often for grade level than for the other three variables (see Table 10.1)

The findings were quite consistent across the seven large studies. The rates at which the chi-squares were large enough to reach statistical significance varied from 56% to 69% for grade level, from 12% to 25% for achievement level, and from 8% to 17% for gender. In the two studies that allowed for analysis of SES level, the corresponding rates were 13% (shelter) and 12% (clothing). To put these rates in perspective, bear in mind that given our selection of the .05 probability level as the criterion for statistical significance, 5% of the chi-squares in each study would be expected to reach the statistical significance criterion even when no corresponding relationship existed in the population as a whole, due to chance sampling characteristics. The observed rates for SES level and for gender

TABLE 10.1
Percentages of Analyses in the Seven Large Studies That Yielded
Statistically Significant Grade Level Trends, SES Level Trends,
Achievement Level Trends, and Gender Differences

Study	% Significant Grade Level Trends	% Significant SES Trends	% Significant Achievement Level Trends	% Significant Gender Differences
Food	59	NA	22	11
Clothing	56	12	25	10
Shelter	63	13	19	9
Communication	63	NA	18	17
Transportation	60	NA	12	8
Family living	56	NA	24	16
Government	69	NA	24	11
Average	61	13	21	12

Note. The data for grade level, SES level, and achievement level were derived from Mantel-Haenszel chi-square analyses for linear trends; the data for gender were derived from conventional chi-square analyses for group differences. The numbers shown are the percentages of the total analyses that reached the .05 level of statistical significance (e.g., the food coding yielded 218 score distributions that were subjected to statistical analyses; of these, 128, or 59%, showed significant grade-level trends). The letters "NA" (standing for Not Applicable) appear in the SES column when the samples were not stratified on this variable.

were not much above this expected 5% chance rate, averaging 13% and 12%, respectively. The rate for achievement level was notably higher at 21%, but still not nearly as high as the 61% rate observed for grade level.

SOCIOECONOMIC STATUS (SES)

SES level analyses were made possible by interviewing 72 students in each of three SES groups. Only about one eighth of the analyses yielded statistically significant linear trends, suggesting that the highest SES students were reliably more likely, and the lowest SES students reliably less likely, to be coded in the category being analyzed (or vice versa, in the case of negative relationships). In the clothing study, all of these significant linear trends indicated that the higher SES students made more sophisticated responses than the lower SES students. Higher SES students were more likely to say that people need clothes to protect them against cold or against dirt, sun, insects, or injury; to describe work clothes accurately; to say that clothes are made from wool or animal skin; to know that cloth is woven or knitted from thread or yarn; to know that thread is spun from raw material; to provide accurate responses concerning pioneer clothes and clothes of the early 20th century; to say that today's clothes are improved because they are more aesthetically pleasing; to say that clothes are easier to take care of today and to attribute this to washers, dryers, or other machines; to mention processing of the raw material as a step in manufacturing a shirt or dress; to suggest that their own shirt or dress was made in a factory located where raw materials are plentiful; and to know that leather is animal hide. These responses all were part of the general sophistication pattern running throughout the interview that was associated even more closely with student grade and achievement level than SES level. Consequently, the pattern appears to reflect differences in amounts of general information held as prior knowledge rather than more specific home background experiences related to social class.

In the shelter study, many of the statistically significant SES trends indicated that the higher SES students had more to say in response to the question than did the lower SES students. That is, they were less often unable to respond and more often coded for more than one substantive response category. Other differences indicated that higher SES students were more likely to say that the Indians who built tipis or longhouses did so for lack of construction knowledge or materials that would allow them to build something better; that longhouses were temporary or makeshift housing for poor people; that pioneers got their water from wells or underground sources and their heat from woodburning stoves; that people tend to prefer houses to apartments because they get extras such as patios, pools, or fireplaces; that highrise apartments in cities reflect pressures to build upward rather than outward in order to get more human use out of the same space; that apartment dwellers must pay for their apartments; that people prefer buying to renting because buying lets you own your own place; and that the ideal home would be large, would include a guest room, and would be located far away from traffic and noise. Concerning the possibility of moving into a home before accumulating the full purchase price, lower SES students were more likely to say that this is possible but be unable to explain how or why, whereas higher SES students were more likely to say that this is because the owner allows you to do so or because you can get a mortgage from a bank. Concerning home heating, lower SES students were more likely to say that money paid for heating goes to a landlord and to describe heat as coming from a heat register, whereas higher SES students were more likely to identify "other" heat sources that did not fit into the categories for common responses. Finally, lower SES students were more likely to say that our drinking water comes from sewers or drains and that the ideal home would be located near food stores or restaurants.

Along with differences in amounts of general information held as prior knowledge, a few of these differences may reflect home background experiences related to social class (especially the ideas that longhouses were for poor people, houses contain desirable extras that apartments do not offer, and buying lets you own your own place, as well as the statements about the nature and location of the ideal home). For example, perhaps location of the ideal home near food stores was important to many lower SES students because this was an issue in their everyday lives, especially if their families had to walk or depend on public transportation to do their shopping.

Although it is tempting to highlight and try to interpret these SES differences, they need to be viewed within the context of the bigger picture: Only 13% of the SES analyses yielded significant chi-squares, and none of the group differences were strikingly large (in contrast to the group differences for grade level). Given the observed ranges for the coding frequencies, the patterns for the three SES groups were much more similar than different. This leads us to conclude that the students' knowledge about topics addressed in our questions was shaped more by their common learning at school and exposure to contemporary U.S. media and culture than by contrasting SES aspects of their home backgrounds. At least within the range of SES backgrounds included in these studies, there was no evidence of strikingly contrasting patterns of knowledge between contrasting SES groups.

However, our sampling in the shelter and clothing studies included only the middle three fourths or so of the SES distribution. If we had included samples from the extremes of the population (i.e., the very rich and the very poor), we might have observed more noteworthy SES differences. Hints of this were evident in the follow-up shelter interviews we conducted in Manhattan, where many of the students in the Upper West Side sample were from highly privileged backgrounds and many of those from the Harlem sample were living in poverty. Even there, however, the observed differences were better described as differences in amounts of knowledge of a mostly common culture than as reflections of two contrasting networks of ideas.

In summary, our investigations of SES differences indicated that they were relatively weak and infrequent, and when they did occur, they showed (as expected) that the higher SES students had more, or more accurate, knowledge of the topic than the lower SES students. This suggests that students from different SES backgrounds were progressing through essentially the same trajectories at slightly different rates, not developing through different trajectories toward contrasting networks of ideas. Although mildly interesting, these observed SES differences do not carry important theoretical or practical implications.

Rather than continue to document such minor differences at a significant cost in time and resources, we decided to shift to studies involving 96 students drawn from the middle of the SES distribution. This allowed us to interview students about twice as many topics as we would have been able to address otherwise, although without the capacity to analyze for SES differences. It also left open the option of pursuing hypotheses about specific subpopulations through smaller side studies (as we did in interviewing Manhattan students about shelter and rural students about food).

ACHIEVEMENT LEVEL

Across the seven large studies, statistically significant achievement level trends appeared in about one fifth (21%) of the analyses. Inspection of the corresponding response frequencies indicated that, as expected, in the vast majority of these cases, the higher achievers had more to say about the topic or made more accurate or sophisticated responses than the lower achievers.

Furthermore, close inspection of the apparent exceptions to this pattern indicated that only a handful of them constituted genuine anomalies. Some exceptions are of limited import and questionable reliability because they involved seldom-coded categories. For example, there was a positive relationship between achievement level and the incorrect statement that everyone everywhere eats the same foods. However, this statement was made by only 6 of the 96 students interviewed about food.

In many instances, what at first appeared to be exceptions turned out not to be so when examined more closely. For example, when asked about foods that we eat today that were not available in 1920, more higher achievers than lower achievers incorrectly listed foods that actually were available in 1920. However, this was a more sophisticated response than being unable to respond at all, saying that there are no foods that didn't exist in 1920, or saying that there are such foods but being unable to suggest any examples. It was the older and (within grade) higher achieving students who at least were able to generate substantive examples, although these examples were more likely to be incorrect than correct. Thus, this seeming anomaly is part of, rather than an exception to, the overall pattern indicating that higher achievers tended to give more sophisticated responses than lower achievers.

There were a few unexpected achievement level trends that do appear to constitute genuine anomalies. For example, lower achievers were more likely than higher achievers to say that certain foods are good for us because they do not have fats or sugars. However, this response was coded for only eight students, and it was just one of several that we consider to be accurate (others included the notions that these foods give you energy, contain healthy stuff/nutrition, or contain vitamins, minerals, etc.). Thus, although lower achievers were more likely than higher achievers to focus on fats or sugars in addressing this question, they were not more likely than higher achievers to provide a sophisticated response to it.

In the clothing interview, high achievers were more likely to be coded for identifying a specific store at which to purchase a shirt but being unable to explain this choice beyond stating that the store sells clothes. It is surprising that more higher achievers did not explain their choice of store more substantively (i.e., by citing low prices, good quality, etc.); perhaps they thought that the appropriateness of the store they named (as a place to buy a shirt) was obvious and didn't need explaining.

When asked if deaf people can talk, lower achievers were more likely to say yes and then elaborate by stating that their speech sounds different from other people's or is hard to understand. Again, however, this was but one of several acceptable responses, and there was no overall tendency for lower achievers to answer this question more sophisticatedly than higher achievers. More generally, it appeared that what the children knew about the communication competencies of deaf and blind people had been learned mostly through contact with deaf and blind people or other out-of-school experiences, except perhaps for knowing that blind people can read text rendered in Braille.

In the family living interview, higher achievers were more likely to include pets when listing family members. We found this surprising because we assumed that including pets would prove to be an immature response. However, this response was unrelated to grade level. Perhaps the achievement level trend reflected nothing more than a quirk of sampling (i.e., a probably unreliable tendency for the higher achieving students in our sample to be more likely than the lower achieving students to come from families with pets).

Higher achievers also were more likely to say that fathers in the past did not have to work as much as today's fathers, and thus had more time for family and leisure activities. This response might be considered incorrect, particularly if students were thinking about fathers in the frontier days. However, it also might be considered accurate, depending on the historical time periods and particular circumstances of the fathers that the students were envisioning as they answered the question. Furthermore, the achievement level trend for this response category was part of a larger pattern indicating that higher achievers tended to have much more to say than lower achievers in responding to this question, and thus were coded more frequently in most of the categories.

In the government interview, lower achievers were more likely to depict judges as questioning people to elicit facts or motives. This pattern is surprising given that such questioning is a salient part of the judge's role (especially as depicted on television). However, the reliability of this trend is questionable because it is based on a total of only six response codes, and there was no general tendency for lower achievers to know more about judges than higher achievers.

When asked who owned their school, higher achievers were more likely to say that they did not know. Although unexpected, this finding was not completely surprising, for two reasons. First, similar findings have appeared occasionally on other items for which very few students possess confident knowledge (so they are faced with either taking a guess or saying "I don't know"). In these situations, higher achievers may be more likely to say "I don't know" than to hazard a guess that they are almost certain is incorrect. In contrast, lower achievers often are less inhibited about taking guesses or even blurting out anything they can think of that may be relevant to the question. Consequently, we interpret this finding as part of a larger difference in familiarity and comfort with answering questions incorrectly. Lower achievers do this frequently and apparently become accustomed to it, but higher achievers often would rather say "I don't know" than verbalize a response in which they have little confidence. Second, in this context, the higher achievers' reticence was justified; most of the substantive responses, especially those of lower achievers, were incorrect (e.g., that the school is owned by the principal or the teachers).

These few anomalous achievement level findings are interesting and puzzling, but it is unlikely that many if any of them will prove to be reliable. Furthermore, they do not cohere in ways that might identify particular knowledge domains as likely to show earlier trajectories in lower achievers than higher achievers. Essentially, they are minor exceptions to an overall pattern indicating that, when statistically significant achievement level trends appeared, they almost always indicated that the higher achievers' answers to the questions were more sophisticated than those of the lower achievers.

Perhaps more surprising is the fact that these statistically significant achievement level trends did not appear more often. However, bear in mind that in structuring our interviews around cultural universals, we were asking students about topics with which they often had personal experience to draw upon, so they were not wholly dependent on knowledge acquired at school in constructing responses. If our interviews had focused more exclusively on content typically learned at school, significant achievement level trends might have appeared more frequently.

We suspect that the trends that did appear were observed for three primary reasons. First, given modest positive correlations between Piagetian cognitive development measures and measures of IQ or school achievement, we can expect a pervasive (although limited) tendency for higher achievers to be a little more cognitively developed than lower achievers of the same age. Second, given correlations between social class and school achievement, it is likely that higher achievers, on average, enjoyed more cultural capital at home and more exposure to educative experiences (trips to museums, travel on vacations, etc.) than lower achievers. Finally, and most importantly, some of our questions did address topics to which the students had been exposed at school, and we believe that the higher achievers were especially likely to do better than the lower achievers in answering these questions.

One additional factor might have contributed to the frequency of significant achievement level trends. On some of our interviews, we showed a photo or drawing while asking a few of our questions. The response patterns that emerged, especially in the shelter interview, led us to suspect that group differences in academic skills may have influenced responses to these items. That is, the higher achievers appeared to be more adept than the lower achievers at studying these illustrations to identify cues to potential responses.

GENDER

Fewer than one eighth of the chi-square analyses yielded statistically significant gender differences. Furthermore, these differences were quite mixed concerning which gender had more, or more sophisticated, knowledge about the topic: 48% favored the boys and 52% favored the girls. The boys did better on the food interview and marginally better on the clothing, shelter, and transportation interviews; the girls did marginally better on the government interview and notably better on the communication interview and (especially) the family living interview. Overall, however, boys' and girls' responses were much more similar than different.

Some of the gender differences are not interpretable because they involved categories for "other" responses that were miscellaneous in content and variable in quality. Others are of questionable import and reliability because they occurred for categories not coded very frequently and were of marginal statistical significance. The remaining differences, shown in Table 10.2, are sometimes but not always interpretable with reference to what is known about differences in gender role socialization and children's interests and activities.

On the food interview, the observed gender differences were infrequent, scattered, and usually impossible to interpret with reference to what is known about gender differences in socialization or interests (e.g., boys knew more about how cheese is made but girls knew more about how applesauce is made). One exception to this generalization was that girls had more knowledge about healthful versus junk foods. This was not surprising given indications that women are more health conscious than men in their eating patterns. Another exception concerned knowledge about developments in farming technology. Boys were more able than girls to identify farming innovations and talk about why today's farmers are more productive than farmers in the past.

On the clothing interview, girls were more likely to describe work clothes as old or worn clothes that you can get dirty, but boys were more likely to talk about them as protecting workers from hazards. Furthermore, girls were more likely to say that we wear play clothes because they are washable. This pattern suggests greater female awareness of factors involved in keeping clothes clean and greater male awareness of the need for protection against job-related hazards. Boys were more likely than girls to mention metal as a shoe component, because most of the boys who mentioned metal were thinking of cleats on sports shoes.

On the shelter interview, boys were more likely to know the name "tipi" and to explain that tipi dwellers needed portable homes. Perhaps they had had more experience with camping in tents or with scouting activities that included supposed "Indian lore." Girls were more likely to talk about the paint or wallpaper on the walls of log cabins and to mention the colors of their ideal homes. These differences suggest, unsurprisingly, that girls were more attuned than boys to the decorative aspects of housing interiors.

More boys said that some people live in apartments because they can't afford homes, but more girls said that some people prefer apartments because they need only a small place to live. Neither difference was expected but potential explanations can be advanced on a post hoc basis. The difference concerning ability to afford a home was part of a larger pattern indicating that the boys had more knowledge about or interest in costs, bills, and other economic aspects of modern

TABLE 10.2
Noteworthy Differences in Frequencies of Responses for Boys Versus Girls

Coding Category	Boys	Girls
Food interview	<u>48</u>	<u>48</u>
We eat food to stay alive or avoid starvation or death	39	29
Lists American foods that people in other countries presumably do not eat	15	7
Says that people in other countries eat generic ethnic foods (Chinese, Italian, etc.)	7	2
We refrigerate certain foods to keep them from making people sick	12	5
Before electricity, people kept foods in storage places or cold places	8	2
Good foods are good for us because they keep us healthy	7	17
Identifies ice cream or milk shakes as junk foods	5	14
Junk foods are bad for us because they do not keep us healthy or make us strong	3	9
Junk foods are bad for us because they could make us sick or kill us	5	11
Unable to say how apple sauce is made	7	1
You need apples	1	5
The apples must be cooked	6	15
Unable to say how cheese is made	18	28
Cheese is made from milk	27	13
Unable to say why farmers raise chickens	1	6
Unable to identify steps that farmers go through to grow corn	1	6
Plant the seeds	46	39
After harvest, clear the field/plow for the next planting	1	8
Farmers of the past did not have the range or quality of animals/plants/seeds that we have now	7	0
Tractors as inventions that have helped farmers	23	14
Unable to say why only a few farmers can now produce all the food that we need	26	34
Farmers can do so because they have more knowledge now	6	1
Clothing interview	<u>107</u>	<u>106</u>
Whether or not people need clothes depends on the climate	7	1
People need clothes to protect against the cold	84	69
Work clothes are old, worn clothes that you can get dirty	80	90
Work clothes are uniforms	1	9
Workers wear work clothes to protect them from hazards and keep them safe	27	16
Doesn't know why we wear play clothes	17	9
We wear play clothes because you can get them dirty/they're washable	65	83
Cave dwellers wore clothes fashioned from animal skins	74	56
The pioneers made some of their clothes and bought others	4	10
Includes processing the raw material as a step in manufacturing a shirt or dress	15	4
The shirt's design or print given as a reason for purchasing it	31	20
Whether the shirt was made for a boy or a girl as a reason for purchasing it	1	5
Lists metal among substances that shoes are made of	19	9
Defines leather incorrectly (made from rubber, wood, etc.)	6	13
Defines leather correctly (animal skin)	30	19
Shelter interview	<u>108</u>	<u>108</u>
Says that people need homes for protection, without further specification	7	1
Unable to say why different Indian groups built pueblos versus longhouses	26	39
Knows name "tipi" (0 = *doesn't know*; 1 = *tent*; 2 = *tipi*)	1.7	1.5
Mentions portability in talking about tipis but does not explain further	7	2

(Continued)

TABLE 10.2
(Continued)

Coding Category	Boys	Girls
Log cabins lacked paint, color, wallpaper	9	20
Log cabins had dirt floors	4	12
Pioneers heated their cabins using blankets, closed door or windows, or candles (no heat source)	3	9
People live in apartments because they cannot afford a house	52	36
Some people prefer apartments because they only need a small space	11	26
Cannot say what is done to water before it is sent to our homes	11	25
Water is piped to homes	94	81
Sent to water tower first	11	4
Describes heat as forced air from furnace	42	27
Firebox furnace theory	20	8
Partly correct explanation of how lights work	9	2
We have to pay for bulbs, but not for using them	7	17
Mentions color(s) of ideal home	6	21
Would like to live near food stores/restaurants	15	33
Would like to live near children's school	6	23
Communication interview	**48**	**48**
People need to communicate in order to participate in school or work activities	11	5
Barking is just as good a form of communication as talking	5	1
Cave people communicated by talking, just like today	34	26
Cave people spoke in a different language	3	10
Cave people used sign language or pantomime	15	24
Cave people wrote or drew on walls, ground, or rocks	6	13
George Washington would get a message to Benjamin Franklin by sending a messenger on horseback or wagon	9	3
People used pens, pencils, markers, or crayons to make the first books	4	10
The telephone enabled people to communicate with others far away without having to write letters	12	21
Cannot say how babies learn to talk	10	2
Babies learn from older people who teach them	27	38
Babies hear people talking and copy their speech	3	10
Cannot say what a young child would do if she knew what she wanted to say but lacked the words to say it	10	4
The child would pull or touch the person to get their attention	9	3
The child would go to the door, point outside, or gesticulate	27	36
Spontaneously says that deaf people can communicate by reading lips	1	5
Spontaneously says that deaf people can talk	13	4
Deaf people cannot understand what you say	39	26
Deaf people can read lips	4	18
Doesn't know whether deaf people can talk	7	1
Blind people cannot read	28	16
Gives both good and poor examples of words that didn't exist 50 years ago	7	2
Symbols used on signs because they are easier to see or words are harder to read	11	4
The birthday card would be taken to the Chicago post office and processed there	18	28
People read newspapers to read about sports	30	14
People read newspapers for puzzles, comics, or other entertainment	16	8
Doesn't know who reads newspapers in his or her family	5	1

(Continued)

TABLE 10.2
(Continued)

Coding Category	Boys	Girls
Father or other male relative reads newspapers	37	43
The newspaper gets the news from television	9	3
Newspaper people write text with a pen, pencil, computer, or typewriter	28	36
Cannot say how television changed the world	7	1
Television allowed people to watch videos or movies at home	5	11
Cannot say how the local television channel would cover the astronaut's visit	10	20
Reporters and camera people would come to tape the visit	36	26
The videotape would be taken back to the television station	16	7
Child can watch favorite television show because videotapes of it are sent from where they are produced to the local station	1	5
Radio waves, satellites, radio dishes, antennas transmit the show through the air	7	2
Commercials allow performers to rest, correct a problem, rehearse, and so on	12	22
Commercials allow viewers to get up and do something, make popcorn, and so on	1	6
Programs get canceled because network executives don't like them anymore	0	7
Cannot explain e-mail	17	26
Transportation interview	**48**	**48**
Transportation is moving someone or something	8	1
Transportation is a means of getting around, a conveyance or vehicle	3	9
People used carts, wagons, carriages, or buggies in the cave days	1	9
People only walked in the cave days	38	28
People used carriages or buggies in the pioneer days	0	7
Railroads allowed people to get places more quickly	28	20
Highways allowed people to travel up high instead of down low	0	7
It is easier to cross mountains now because airplanes can fly over them	8	2
Trucks and vans are kinds of transportation found in big cities but not other places	10	4
Understands taxis as car/transportation but cannot explain why people use them	23	14
Using a taxi is cheaper than buying or renting a car	6	1
People use taxis when they don't have a car to use	17	29
The car goes because the engine makes the wheels turn	16	9
If people want to go to another country, they have to get permission from that country's government officials	12	5
Family living interview	**48**	**48**
Defines family as people who do things together	13	22
Includes grandparents, uncles, aunts, cousins, stepsiblings, or other relatives	15	23
Includes pets	12	22
Most people live in families because people get married/have children	7	14
Grandparents are old/look old	10	4
Grandparents are your parents' parents	22	30
Cannot define "stepsiblings "	25	17
Defines "stepsiblings" correctly	8	18
Cannot say how a family might get smaller	11	5
Cannot define marriage or say what it means to get married	8	1
Cannot say what it means to get divorced	10	3
Incompatibility as a motive for divorce	5	13

(Continued)

TABLE 10.2
(Continued)

Coding Category	Boys	Girls
Today's mothers have more work, less time for leisure or spending with their children	9	2
Today's fathers play with their children	14	6
Today's children spend time playing, relaxing, and so on	22	13
Today's children also do chores, take care of self, clothing, room	7	15
Gives at least one example of ways that families do things differently in another country	6	0
Gives at least one example of ways that Japanese families do things differently than American families	7	2
Farm people have to do more work/chores than other people	27	36
Things that children learn at home from their families include sports and physical activities	5	1
Cannot say what children learn from their mothers	16	9
Children learn academic skills from their mothers	8	15
Children learn self-care and responsibility from their mothers	1	7
Cannot say what would happen if a family did not have rules	9	3
Rules are needed to promote fairness and morality	10	19
Cannot say how families can help other families	18	9
Families can provide direct help with the problem	17	27
Cannot say how families can help their communities	31	21
They can avoid littering or pick up litter	13	21
They can work alone or with neighbors on community improvement projects	2	8
Government interview	**48**	**48**
Person confusion (defines the government as an individual)	4	10
Cannot say who is head of government	6	17
Names Bill Clinton as head of government	23	15
Asked what they would look for in a candidate for president, names a person (Lincoln, Clinton, etc.)	14	6
The president lives and works in the White House	31	21
Names a location other than Lansing in stating where the Michigan governor lives and works	2	9
We need rules and laws to provide guidance about how to act	2	7
Judges decide criminal cases by determining guilt or innocence	25	15
Cannot describe any government jobs	34	24
Identifies staff or office work as government jobs	3	11
Identifies taxes as the source for government money	6	13
Defines taxes as utility bills, fines, interest or finance payments, and so on	9	2
Identifies home schools as alternatives to public schools	8	2
Would not like to be president when he or she grows up	33	23
Would like to be president	7	15
Being able to do good for the country, make things more fair, help the needy, and so on, as good things about being president	3	9
Perks as good things about being president	7	14

life. This may be related to traditional socialization suggesting that males are expected to be the primary providers for the family. The girls' more frequent mention of the idea that some people only need a small place to live may reflect a tendency of girls to be more aware than boys of single, divorced, or widowed people who live in small homes or apartments (more of these people are female than male, especially those likely to have frequent contact with young children).

All of the significant gender differences in knowledge about utilities favored the boys, who were more likely to know about how water is processed and delivered to homes, to know about furnaces, to be able to offer at least some explanation of how lights work, and to know that it costs money not just to purchase light bulbs but to use them. These differences are not surprising given traditional gender role socialization that orients boys more than girls toward interests in machines and mechanical operations.

Finally, girls were more likely to specify that their ideal home would be located near food stores or restaurants and near their children's schools. These differences fit with traditional expectations that females will assume major responsibilities for family meals and child care.

Gender differences appeared most frequently in the communication interview, but they tended to be scattered rather than clustered in interpretable patterns. One exception concerns knowledge about how language is acquired and how young children try to communicate when they lack needed vocabulary. All six of the gender differences relating to these topics favored the girls. Differences in responses to questions about sensory handicaps also favored the girls, because more boys exaggerated the scope of the handicaps (thinking that deaf people cannot understand speech or that blind people cannot read).

More boys talked about people reading newspapers for sports news or for the puzzles, comics, or other entertainment features, and there was an almost significant tendency for more girls to talk about reading the advertisements. These patterns reflect gender differences in interests. Boys knew a little more about how television programs are made and broadcast, but girls knew a little more about the economics of television. Finally, boys knew more than girls about e-mail.

The transportation interview produced few gender differences. Most were for categories reflecting stylistic approaches to responding to a question rather than possession of relevant knowledge. Overall, gender differences were less frequent and less patterned in the transportation interview than in any of the others.

Gender differences were relatively frequent in the family living interview, and the majority of them favored girls. The girls were more able to talk about families and define kinship relations, talk about marriage and divorce, identify things that children learn from their parents, and specify ways that families can help other families or their communities. Most of these differences are compatible with the notion that socialization of girls places more emphasis on family than socialization of boys does. In talking about what contemporary children spend their time doing, boys were more likely to mention only play, whereas girls were more likely to mention chores and marginally more likely to mention school-related activities. These differences might have been expected based on past research indicating that families tend to place more self-care and household maintenance expectations on girls than on boys and that girls tend to spend more time on homework than boys.

In the government interview, boys showed more knowledge about the location and activities of the president and the governor, but girls showed more knowledge about taxes and government jobs. Girls were more positive about the notion of becoming president when they grew up, as well as more likely to identify good things about being the president. The latter differences are a little surprising given that although gender differences do not always appear in research on children's knowledge about government, when they do appear, they tend to favor boys.

Looking across the interviews, it can be said that: (a) the responses of the boys and the girls were much more similar than different; (b) most of the observed differences were scattered and disconnected rather than clustered; and (c) only a minority of the clusters that did appear could be interpreted with reference to research on traditional gender-role socialization or gender differences in children's interests. With the exception of the tendency for more girls than boys to favor the idea of becoming president, none of the observed gender differences are especially surprising.

Estvan and Estvan (1959) interviewed first and sixth graders about their perceptions of pictures showing contrasting socioeconomic situations. They reported that boys had greater familiarity with or a more cognitive response to outside world stimuli, whereas girls concentrated more on home and family aspects. That generalization also appears to apply, although weakly, to our findings.

DISCUSSION

Relative to our findings for grade level, our findings for SES, achievement level, and gender are notably weaker, provide less new information about child development, and suggest few implications for curriculum and instruction in primary-grade social studies. Almost all of the statistically significant SES and achievement level trends, and many of the gender differences, conformed to expectations based on previous theory and research (i.e., that higher SES and higher achieving students would provide more sophisticated or better informed responses than lower SES and lower achieving students, and that differences between boys' and girls' response patterns would reflect what is known about gender differences in socialization and interests).

To the extent that subsample patterns differed, the differences were limited to minor variations on major themes observed in the sample as a whole; there was no evidence that different SES, achievement level, or gender groups were following contrasting trajectories toward distinctly different networks of knowledge. Consequently, although we believe that it is important for teachers to get to know their students and their families so as to be able to connect the curriculum to individual students' personal interests and home cultures, we do not see any need or reason to differentiate early social studies curricula according to students' SES levels, achievement levels, or gender.

11

Overall Trends in the Findings and Their Implications for Early Social Studies

In previous chapters, we presented details of the findings from our interviews on particular cultural universals and discussed them with reference to earlier research on the topics and to potential implications for teaching about them in the early grades. In this concluding chapter, we focus on findings that cut across all or at least several of our interviews.

The most generic of these findings were previewed in chapter 1:

- indications of presentism when talking about the past and chauvinism when talking about other cultures;
- limited awareness of the role of climate and geography in creating affordances to and constraints on people's lives;
- evidence that children possess accessible schemas for recognizing and using objects related to cultural universals, but have not yet embedded these schemas for action potential within well-connected knowledge networks structured around big ideas;
- tendency for knowledge and thought to be predisciplinary or based on psychological analogies (reference to individuals' intentions and goal-oriented actions), without much awareness of macrolevel thinking about the nation, the world, or the human condition in general (or of social scientific modes of thinking that might mediate these ideas);
- tendencies toward partial explanations that rely on black-box or even magical mechanisms to cover the parts not understood;
- teleological reasoning;
- reversed reasoning, and so on.

In this chapter, we consider these and other generic findings with reference to the literature on developments in children's social knowledge and thinking and to the literature on curriculum and instruction in primary social studies.

GENERIC ASPECTS OF STUDENTS' RESPONSES

Little or no previous research was available for most of the topics addressed in most of our interviews, so much of the information we generated is new to the literature. Where there was overlap with previous literature, however, our findings generally replicated (and extended) it, without raising significant contradictions. There were occasional minor contrasts to previous findings (e.g., indications that the American children we interviewed knew more about government than comparable Italian children interviewed by Berti), as well as some evidence that previously identified trends have continued (e.g., reductions in the scope and strength of gender differences and in the percentages of students who say that they would like to become president when they grow up). However, there were no stark contrasts with previous findings and our findings on unresearched topics show many of the same characteristics that have been reported for other developments in children's social knowledge.

Our Interview Method

We believe that our data collection method (primarily verbally mediated interviewing, supplemented with occasional visual illustrations) was generally effective, given our purposes. There were a few instances where questions failed to yield usable data from most students beyond establishing that they did not know the meaning of a key term (e.g., *budget*) or had not yet acquired basic knowledge needed to grasp the point of the question (e.g., Alaska has a very cold climate). For the vast majority of our questions, however, either the wording of the original question (along with any information included within it or along with it), or if necessary the inclusion of prespecified follow-up probes, successfully cued students to the specifics about which we were asking and enabled them to respond to the intended question by accessing whatever articulable information they possessed (if any).

We might have uncovered fragments of not-yet-articulable knowledge by using some of the methods that child development researchers have designed to demonstrate that children possess at least tacit knowledge of some aspects of certain domains several years earlier than previously believed. Rather than require children to generate substantive answers to open-ended questions, these methods present them with narrative scenarios or physical demonstrations and then probe their understanding using questions that require only "yes" or "no" responses or even just nonverbal indications of a choice between two alternatives. We did not include such methods, however, because our purpose was not to establish the earliest appearance of nascent concepts or knowledge. Instead, it was to assess the nature and extent of accessible and articulable social knowledge that K–3 students might bring to bear as they participate in lessons on topics commonly addressed in primary social studies. These lessons typically involve verbal discourse and include (or should include) questions like those asked in our interviews.

Limitations in Children's Social Knowledge

Our findings underscore the need for research about trajectories in children's development of knowledge in these domains, and indicate that children stand to benefit from instruction designed to develop connected understandings about major topics. The knowledge that children do accumulate through everyday experiences is mostly tacit, limited in scope, poorly connected, and frequently distorted by naive ideas or outright misconceptions. It is focused on the more easily observable forms and functions of objects and actions related to cultural universals, without penetrating to include understanding of less obvious cause–effect relationships and explanations. We do not find this surprising because most children's experiences relating to cultural universals are primarily informal and do not include sustained discourse structured around key ideas.

K–3 students typically know more about the physical appearances of things than their underlying natures, and more about the uses of finished products than about the land-to-hand transformations involved in creating those products. Sophistication of responses often is related more closely to personal experiences out of school than to school experiences or achievement levels. There is only limited evidence of historical or cultural empathy (i.e., understanding people's behavior from their perspectives and thus viewing it as sensible adaptation to their time and place rather than as weird, stupid, or incomprehensible). There also is little awareness of the degree to which humans have reshaped landforms, imported flora and fauna, created built-environment infrastructures, and developed transportation and delivery systems that support contemporary life in first-world societies.

Much of children's knowledge about the human activities associated with cultural universals is organized in narrative rather than analytic form. They can explain what they have done or seen and then use that as a basis for reasoning by analogy, but they usually lack awareness of how their experience fits within a big picture that has been analyzed and synthesized. Their fund of concepts is limited, and the concepts they do possess often cannot be accessed and used as tools for reasoning.

Even as children begin to articulate social knowledge, they can easily become confused or acquire misconceptions. The social sciences involve many fuzzy and overlapping concepts, and many of their principles and generalizations are rules of thumb that admit to exceptions rather than universally applicable algorithms.

In addition, some are obsolescent (e.g., national differences in food and clothing preferences).

Some of the input that children receive from adults and the media is fictional, frequently deliberately so (Santa Claus, the Easter Bunny, the Tooth Fairy, ghosts, monsters, Flintstone™ vehicles, fanciful stereotypes about Native Americans or Mexicans communicated in cartoons, etc.). Even some of what they learn from their teachers or textbooks is incorrect (everyone but Columbus thought that the world was flat and feared sailing off the end of the earth, the story of George Washington and the cherry tree, etc.). Much of the rest is accurate as far as it goes, but limited to a single point of view even when multiple points of view would be more appropriate (Eurocentric accounts of the exploration and colonization of the Americas).

Developmental Trends

Although our questions focused on domain-specific knowledge and thus mostly generated findings compatible with recent child development research that emphasizes domain specificity over the generic stage theories emphasized previously, we occasionally encountered patterns of thinking reflective of patterns that Piaget and others have characterized as prototypic of generic stages. The students' difficulties with our question about why a pound of cereal costs more than a pound of apples, for example, revealed the kinds of confusions about mass, density, and class inclusion that Piaget discussed in describing preoperational thinking. Similarly, students' frequent references to fairness or justice in responding to our questions about whom and why we pay for shelter and utilities (if you didn't pay it would be like stealing, people who provide services need money and deserve to be paid for their work, etc.) harkened back to Piaget's descriptions of early stages in children's moral reasoning.

The grade-level analyses often showed a relatively linear trajectory of gradually advancing knowledge across the K–3 range, but some analyses showed a dramatic increase between kindergarten and first grade or between first grade and second grade. Occasionally, the latter patterns could be traced to curricular components commonly included at either first grade or second grade, but more typically, they appeared to be connected to broader developments in children's cognition that have been described as shifts from preoperational to concrete operational thinking (Piaget, 1983), shifts from enactive to cognitive reasoning (Bruner, 1966), or the 5-to-7 shift in children's thinking (Samaroff & Haith, 1996). Much of what the students had to say in response to many of our questions was procedural knowledge focused on action schemas rather than declarative knowledge focused on cognitive schemas.

Examination of grade level trends typically revealed trajectories in the technological aspects of social knowledge that reflected the following progression:

1. No knowledge at all;
2. brief guesses based on associations to the sound of a key word or the meaning of a seemingly related word more familiar to the student;
3. primarily observational knowledge of surface appearances or procedural knowledge of how one uses objects (or other practical applications);
4. partial knowledge of the nature, manufacture, or mode of functioning of the object, but with misconceptions or black-box mechanisms standing in for aspects not yet understood;
5. generally accurate and mostly complete (at least, up to a point) knowledge of the object's nature, manufacture, and functioning.

Parallels to these developments in knowledge about technology and material culture could be seen in responses to questions about people's motivations, beliefs, and actions. As Carey (1985) and others noted, children's domain-specific thinking often uses psychological analogies based on individuals' goals and intentions, rather than as-yet unfamiliar concepts and reasoning patterns identified with other sciences. Our work indicates that this is just as true of the social sciences as it is of the physical sciences. Children are psychologists before they are anthropologists, economists, sociologists, historians, or geographers.

Generic Response Characteristics

We also identified several other generic aspects of children's social knowledge. First, it tends to focus on microlevels represented by individuals, families, and local settings, often rendered in narrative style with emphasis on goal-oriented actions. Even when asked questions such as "How did the invention of printing change the world?" the students tended to say that the people who made books no longer had to copy them by hand or that the people who read them would find the print easier to read than written script, rather than to say that printing made it possible to make multiple copies of books much more quickly, so that many more people would have access to them and knowledge could be stored and disseminated much more easily. They rarely made reference to effects of events on the nation, let alone the world or the human condition at large.

Second, children's knowledge and thinking tends to be restricted to the here and now. Although familiar with human actions relating to cultural universals that they can observe in their homes and neighborhoods, children usually know little or nothing about how and why these practices have developed over time (history) or how and why they vary across locations (geography, culture). Consequently, the major problem facing those who would develop children's knowledge in the social domain often does not involve connecting with a large preexisting network (and thus building on valid knowledge but addressing misconceptions). Instead, it involves extending their purviews by helping them to place the familiar within broader contexts that stretch the temporal and spatial boundaries of their knowledge. For example, children are unlikely to have much knowledge, let alone appreciation, of the affordances and constraints that local geography provides to people living in their region until they develop basic knowledge of the range of local geographies in the world and the trade-offs they embody.

Third, unlike the mathematics and science domains, children's social knowledge does not include many misconceptions developed on their own through their explorations of the physical environment. Children's social knowledge does include many misconceptions, but most of them are embodied in the culture and conveyed verbally rather than acquired through misleading experiences with the physical environment. Children are exposed to a great deal of incorrect information. Some of it is probably easy to correct (e.g., explaining to children that, contrary to what they may have heard, educated people at the time of Columbus already knew that the world was round, so he was not the first, although there was much debate about the size of the world and Europeans did not realize that whole continents lay between them and Asia).

Several sets of responses to our interviews were correct as far as they went but reflected a child's rather than an adult's purview. In talking about the desirable characteristics of a shirt they would buy, for example, the children emphasized style, color, and so on, but typically not quality or price. In talking about desirable features of the location of their ideal home, they seldom mentioned convenience to good schools or to the parents' job sites. Many of them spoke of towns being located on water because people like to swim or along railroads because they might want to take a ride, without mentioning the importance of transportation and connection to other communities. In talking about other cultures, they often focused on such things as holiday celebrations, Santa Claus, toys and games, bath times, and parades (in part because school lessons and children's media often emphasize these same features).

Many of their responses were valid as far as they went (lights require electricity, you need food to survive, the Chinese grow more rice than wheat), but did not extend beyond the level of description to include attempts at explanation. When they did generate explanations, and especially when their explanations went beyond the black-box level, they often included misconceptions such as reversed reasoning (Indians couldn't write because they had no pencils, towns were built along railways to serve the trains and the people who worked on them), and occasionally even invoked magical mechanisms (a can that turns smushed apples into applesauce, flipping a switch to cause the sun to send light into a light bulb). In talking about human behavior, they sometimes relied on broadly applicable default explanations (there were no stores then, they do it because of their religion or their culture), which functioned much like black box explanations for mechanical processes. Some responses contained both black box elements and incorrect beliefs, such as references to machines that "smish" raw materials into cloth or initially make garments all the same size and then shrink or stretch them to create different sizes.

Some responses were restricted to levels of explanation that stopped short of the levels called for by the questions. One example was the "A big one supplies the little one" idea that appeared periodically. Asked where their local food store gets its food, for example, some students referred to a "big Meijer's" (i.e., a food warehouse) that supplied local Meijer's supermarkets, without addressing the question of where the warehouse got the food. Similarly, when asked about the light in a light bulb in his home, one student said that it traveled through electrical wires from the street lamp outside, without addressing how the light gets into the streetlamp. In effect, students who gave these answers converted our questions into easier ones and answered those instead.

Occasionally, students rejected the premise of our questions and answered some other question altogether. This was most likely to happen when questions involved assumptions that contradicted students' firmly held beliefs (e.g., the idea that some people who could afford to purchase a home nevertheless prefer to rent an apartment) or assumptions that students simply could not visualize (e.g., the lack of a shared language in which to communicate when Columbus first made contact with Native Americans).

Our questions about the past revealed several characteristics of K–3 students' thinking about history that reflected trends reported previously from studies conducted with older students, such as orientation toward narrative rather than analysis, toward telescoping long processes into single events, and toward personalizing large and complex systems by focusing on the goals and behavior of a few people or even a single individual. In our data, the latter tendency was also observed in the children's thinking about government (depicting the president or governor as personally doing much of what is involved in government operations, and a single postal employee doing most of what is involved in picking up a birthday card in one city and delivering it in another), geography (images of small family farms rather than the macrosystem of agribusiness), culture (attributing construction of tipis to the preferences of individuals or families but not to the geographical locations and survival mechanisms of nomadic societies), and economics (describing banks as places to keep one's money but not as financial institutions; attributing prices to individual sellers' decisions without taking into account larger market factors).

Limitations in the children's knowledge about the past included not just confusion about dates but spotty images of the progress of the human condition at the time. For example, those who thought that the Pilgrims could have driven across the country if they had cars were responding as if North America then was pretty much as it is now, except that cars had not yet been invented.

Some of the difficulties that children displayed in imagining scenes from the distant past had parallels in their difficulties responding to hypothetical situations. Here again, the children sometimes responded as if everything would remain the same except for the one change identified in the question. For example, when asked how we would communicate if we were unable to speak, many students said that we would read lips or write messages.

Presentism pervaded the students' thinking about the past. They typically exaggerated the differences that they were aware of, thinking in terms of sea changes rather than continuity and in terms of replacement of old patterns by new ones rather than in terms of a proliferation of choices (such that many older technologies or traditions would continue alongside the new ones rather than disappear). They often overgeneralized the notion of progressiveness, so that for example, they tended to think of all changes as improvements, even changes in clothing styles and practices.

Limitations in children's thinking about the past had many parallels in their thinking about other cultures. They showed little awareness of environmental affordances and constraints that help explain alternative cultural and economic practices in different parts of the world or of the land-to-hand progressions involved in processing natural products or creating manufactured ones. Many thought that people living in other parts of the world were unaware of even the existence of certain foods, clothing types, or shelter types, or that if they were aware, they lacked knowledge of how to manufacture them. They typically attributed third-world homes to limited natural resources or money, but attributed third-world clothing to personal preferences, sometimes conveying a sense of moral superiority to people who dress differently than we do. Explanations for food preference and consumption patterns included both of these attributional inferences.

Much of their nascent presentism or chauvinism appeared to reflect guesswork based on ignorance rather than well-formed views. More generally, their incorrect answers ranged from stab-in-the-dark guesswork or incorrect vocabulary usage to fully developed and seriously held misconceptions. Sometimes it could be difficult to tell. For example, many of the students who identified the oceans or seas as sources for the water that is sent to our homes probably had not yet learned much about differences in the origin and nature of fresh water versus salt water. For these students, "ocean" or "sea" responses simply reflected this ignorance and did not imply belief that homes are supplied with salt water rather than freshwater. However, other students gave evidence of harboring this belief, such as by making reference to the need to filter the salt out of the water or by communicating a broader misconception depicting water as flowing from the oceans through the rivers into the inland areas and becoming filtered in the process. Genuine misconceptions often were embedded within these more extensive (but at least partly incorrect) theories or models of the phenomena being explained.

The students sometimes generated misconceptions by working from literal interpretations of words or phrases that no longer carry their original meaning or are meant to be taken metaphorically. In talking about highways, for example, several students communicated their belief that these roads are literally high—

built up significantly above the surrounding land. Later in the same interview, when students were asked how transportation improvements had "shrunk the world," many took this phrase literally and talked about how the construction of roads, railroad tracks, airports, or other transportation infrastructure required the use of a lot of land that then was no longer available for other purposes, and thus shrunk the world in that sense.

The students (especially the younger ones) provided several examples of the previously reported naive trust that the social world is generally a supportive place and things usually work out for the best. Examples include their general tendency to talk about historical progress through the development of inventions and better ideas, depictions of the president and the governor as benevolent leaders willing to help anyone who needs it, depictions of these leaders and other people working for the government as competent at their jobs and dedicated to the general welfare, depictions of banks as eager to help people and willing to give them money if they come and ask for it, depictions of television station managers as public servants and commercials as a provision of information (vs. attempts to persuade), and depictions of animals raised for their meat as well-cared-for pets who are butchered only after they die natural deaths. Even so, there were limits to the students' naive trust and optimism. Many of the older students communicated awareness of the persuasive intent of commercials and the "political stuff" associated with running for and holding government offices, and some students not only did not depict their parents in heroic terms but expressed criticisms of them for vices, irresponsibility, or other inappropriate behavior.

CULTURAL UNIVERSALS AS A BASIS FOR ORGANIZING THE CONTENT OF THE EARLY SOCIAL STUDIES CURRICULUM

Our findings indicate that, to the extent that it is important for children to learn about cultural universals, they stand to benefit from systematic instruction about them. But is it important for children to be taught about cultural universals? Research findings can provide information about the validity of assumptions made in constructing curricular arguments, but debates about what is appropriate curriculum are conducted primarily on the basis of value-based reasoning.

Kliebard (2004) noted that curriculum debates reflect continuing struggles among supporters of four competing ideas about what should be the primary basis for K–12 education. The first group believes that schools should equip students with knowledge that is lasting, important, and fundamental to the human experience. This group typically looks to the academic disciplines, both as storehouses of important knowledge and as sources of authority about how this knowledge should be organized and taught. The second group believes that the natural course of child development should be the basis for curriculum planning. It would key the content taught at each grade level to the interests and learning needs associated with its corresponding developmental stages. The third group works backward from its adherents' perceptions of society's needs, seeking to design schooling to prepare children to fulfill adult roles in society. The fourth group seeks to use the schools to combat social injustice and promote social change, so it favors focusing curriculum and instruction around social policy issues. Past and present curricular debates in social studies can be understood as aspects of the ongoing competition among these four general approaches to K–12 curriculum development.

In the United States, the gradual balancing among these tensions in the early decades of the 20th century eventually produced a de facto national curriculum for elementary social studies. This curriculum encompasses a great range of content, sequenced within the expanding communities framework that begins with a focus on the self in kindergarten and gradually expands to address families in Grade 1, neighborhoods in Grade 2, communities in Grade 3, states and geographic regions in Grade 4, the United States in Grade 5, and the world in Grade 6. Although never empirically validated through systematic research, the expanding communities sequence has retained popularity because it has face validity with teachers and is flexible enough to accommodate various combinations of the traditional curriculum sources as well as most emerging topics (e.g., environmentalism, multicultural education). Nevertheless, various criticisms have been directed at this framework. These criticisms have spawned suggestions, so far mostly unheeded, for radical restructuring of elementary social studies.

As we noted in chapter 1, we believe that the cultural universals traditionally addressed in the primary grades provide a sound basis for developing fundamental social understandings, for two reasons. First, human activities relating to these cultural universals account for a considerable proportion of everyday life and are the focus of much of human social organization and communal activity. Second, children begin accumulating direct personal experiences with most cultural universals right from birth, so that by the time they begin school, they have developed considerable funds of knowledge and experience that they can draw on in constructing understandings of social education concepts and principles. If cultural universals are taught with appropriate focus on powerful ideas and their potential life applications, students should develop basic sets of connected understandings about how the social system works, how and why it got to be that way over time, how and why it varies across locations and cultures, and what all of this might mean for personal, social, and civic decision making.

In summary, our response to the widely recognized content problem in primary-grade social studies is to retain cultural universals as the unit topics but develop these topics much more powerfully and elaborately than they are developed in the textbook series. Others have suggested different responses. We briefly describe the major alternative suggestions here, both to explain why we do not endorse them and to further explicate our own position.

Cultural Literacy/Core Knowledge

E.D. Hirsch, Jr. (1987) proposed cultural literacy as the basis for curriculum development. He produced a list of over 5,000 items of knowledge that he believed should be acquired in elementary school as a way to equip students with a common base of prior knowledge to inform their social and civic decision making. We agree with Hirsch that shared common culture is needed, but we view his list of ostensibly important knowledge as dubiously extensive and fragmented. Furthermore, because it is a long list of specifics, it leads to teaching that emphasizes breadth of coverage of disconnected details over depth of development of connected knowledge structured around powerful ideas.

Subsequently, educators inspired by Hirsch's book have used it as a basis for developing the CORE Curriculum, which encompasses science, social studies, and the arts. The social studies strands are built around chronologically organized historical studies, with accompanying geographical and cultural studies. Thus, first graders study ancient Egypt and the early American civilizations (Mayas, Incas, Aztecs). Second graders study ancient India, China, and Greece, along with American history up to the Civil War. Third graders study ancient Rome and Byzantium, various Native-American tribal groups, and the 13 English colonies prior to the American Revolution.

Because it is divided by grade levels and organized into World Civilization, American Civilization, and Geography strands, the core knowledge curriculum is a considerable improvement over Hirsch's list of assorted knowledge items as a content base for social studies in the primary grades. However, it focuses on the distant past. We think that cultural universals have more to offer than ancient history as a basis for introducing students to the social world. Also, we believe that an approach that begins with what is familiar to the students in their immediate environments and then moves to the past, to other cultures, and to consideration of the future constitutes a better rounded and more powerful social education than an exclusive focus on the past.

History/Literature Focus

Kieran Egan (1988), Diane Ravitch (1987), and others have advocated replacing topical teaching about cultural universals with a heavy focus on history and related children's literature (not only fiction but myths and folktales). We agree with them that primary-grade students can and should learn certain aspects of history, but we also believe that these students need a balanced and integrated social education curriculum that includes sufficient attention to powerful ideas drawn from geography and the various social sciences. Furthermore, we see little social education value in replacing reality-based social studies with myths and folklore likely to create misconceptions, especially during the primary years when children are struggling to determine what is real (vs. false/fictional) and enduring (vs. transitory/accidental) in their physical and social worlds. Fanciful children's literature may be studied profitably as fiction within the language arts curriculum, but it is no substitute for reality-based social studies.

Issues Analysis

Many social educators believe that debating social and civic issues is the most direct way to develop dispositions toward critical thinking and reflective decision making in our citizens (Evans & Saxe, 1996). Most supporters of issues-centered social studies have focused on the secondary grades, but some have suggested that primary-grade social studies should deemphasize providing students with information and instead engage them in inquiry and debate about social policy issues. We agree that reflective discussion of social issues and related decision-making opportunities should be emphasized in teaching social studies at all grade levels. However, we also believe that a heavy concentration on inquiry and debate about social policy issues is premature for primary-grade students whose prior knowledge and experience relating to the issues often are quite limited.

Our Position

We share critics' concerns about the triteness and other problems in the major publishers' textbook series for the early grades, but we do not believe that the solution lies in radically restructuring the curriculum to focus on cultural literacy, history, or social issues, respectively. Instead, we favor an approach that retains emphasis on teaching about cultural universals, but embodies much more powerful curriculum and instruction than what is reflected in the textbook series. We elaborate our argument with reference to several related issues.

TEACHING CULTURAL UNIVERSALS FOR UNDERSTANDING, APPRECIATION, AND LIFE APPLICATION

We advocate teaching primary-grade students about cultural universals in ways that foster understanding, appreciation, and life application. This requires focusing instruction on big ideas and developing these ideas in depth, with attention to their applications. The big ideas that anchor instructional units should reflect an appropriate balance among the three traditional sources of curriculum: (a) knowledge of enduring value (including but not limited to disciplinary knowledge); (b) the students (their needs, interests, and current readiness); and (c) the needs of society (the knowledge, skills, values, and dispositions that our society would like to see developed in future generations of its citizens).

Related principles come from research on teaching for conceptual change. Students' prior knowledge about topics sometimes includes naive ideas or even outright misconceptions that can cause the students to ignore, distort, or miss the implications of new information that conflicts with their existing ideas. Our studies of K–3 students' knowledge and thinking about cultural universals have yielded a great deal of information about accurate prior knowledge that most students are likely to possess as they begin an instructional unit, as well as about important knowledge gaps and noteworthy naive conceptions or misconceptions that will need to be addressed through instruction. It is helpful if teachers are aware of common misconceptions so that they can plan instruction to address these directly, helping students to recognize differences between their current beliefs and the target understandings, and to see the need to shift from the former to the latter. Such instruction is often called *conceptual change teaching*.

Roth (1996, 2002) developed an approach to conceptual change teaching that she applied to science and social studies. She embedded the conceptual change emphasis within a more comprehensive model of teaching school subjects for understanding, working within a learning community context. This approach puts at least as much emphasis on discovering valid prior knowledge that instruction can connect with and build on as it puts on identifying misconceptions that will need to be addressed.

A third set of principles is rooted in our thinking about topical units as appropriate vehicles for introducing young students to social studies. Like others who have focused on the primary grades, we believe that the curriculum should feature pandisciplinary treatments designed to develop "knowledge of limited validity" (Levstik, 1986) or "protodisciplinary knowledge" (Gardner & Boix-Mansilla, 1994) about topics, rather than attempts to teach disciplinary knowledge organized as such. The knowledge of enduring value emphasized in such treatments includes but is not limited to disciplinary knowledge, and it also reflects the needs of students and of society. Within this context, we believe that a pandisciplinary introduction to the social world (past and present, taught with emphasis on developing understanding, appreciation, and life application of big ideas) makes more sense for primary-grade students than premature attempts to socialize them into the academic disciplines.

Following these basic principles, we have developed detailed plans for instructional units on each of the nine cultural universals addressed in our interview studies (Alleman & Brophy, 2001, 2002, 2003). The units are intended for use in primary-grade social studies teaching, although some schools have used some units in the middle grades.

All of the units emphasize teaching for understanding (and where necessary, conceptual change) by building on students' prior knowledge and developing key ideas in depth and with attention to applications to life outside of school. The plans provide a basis for 3 to 4 weeks of instruction, depending on the topic and the degree to which the teacher includes optional extensions. All of the units feature six common components:

1. They begin with focus on the cultural universal as experienced in contemporary U.S. society, especially in the students' homes and neighborhood (this includes eliciting students' mostly tacit prior knowledge and helping them to articulate it more clearly).
2. They consider how the material culture and technology associated with the cultural universal have evolved over time.
3. They address variation in today's world in the ways in which the cultural universal is experienced in different places and cultures.
4. They include physical examples, classroom visitors, field trips, and especially, children's literature selections (both fiction and nonfiction) as input sources.
5. They include home assignments that call for students to interact with parents and other family members in ways that not only build curriculum-related insights but engage family members in enjoyable and affectively bonding activities.
6. They engage students in thinking about the implications of all of this for personal, social, and civic decision making in the present and future, in ways that support their self-efficacy perceptions with respect to their handling of the cultural universal throughout their lives.

Our units focus on elementary and familiar content in that they address fundamental aspects of the human condition and connect with experience-based tacit knowledge that students already possess. However, they do not merely reaffirm what students already know. Instead, they raise students' consciousness of and help them to construct articulated knowledge about basic aspects of the cultural universal that they have only vague and tacit knowledge about now (aspects that can be made comprehensible to them given their limited cognitive structures and prior knowledge; aspects that are too abstract or macroanalytic are not included). The units also introduce students to a great deal of new information, develop connections to help them transform scattered understandings into a network of integrated knowledge, and stimulate them to apply the knowledge to their lives outside of school and to think critically and engage in value-based decision making about the topic.

Experimentation may be needed to find appropriate levels of explanation and elaboration. For example, telling students only that butter is made "by shaking cream" is likely to confuse or mislead them, but so is an overly detailed scientific explanation. Also, emotional readiness sometimes needs to be considered. For

example, experiences with pets, zoos, fanciful children's literature, Disney movies, cartoons, and other child-oriented input sources condition children to personify animals and think in terms of nurturing them and enjoying their companionship. Yet, as part of acquiring realistic social knowledge in the primary grades,
children need to learn that many animals are basic sources for common foods
(and other products). However, this instruction need not include the gorier details of slaughterhouse operations or other content likely to upset some students
unnecessarily.

National Council for the Social Studies (NCSS) Standards

Our unit development plans also have been informed by two definitive standards
statements released by the NCSS during the 1990s, one on curriculum standards
and one on powerful teaching and learning. The curriculum standards are built
around 10 themes that form a framework for social studies (see Table 11.1). The
publication that spells out these standards elaborates on each theme in separate
chapters for the early grades, the middle grades, and the secondary grades, listing
performance expectations and potential classroom activities that might be used
to develop the theme (National Council for the Social Studies, 1994). The
NCSS subsequently sponsored publication of a collection of readings illustrating
how the 10 strands might be addressed in elementary social studies teaching
(Haas & Laughlin, 1997) and a survey of children's literature published in the
1990s that relates to these strands (Krey, 1998).

Along with its curriculum standards, the NCSS released a position statement
identifying five key features of powerful social studies teaching and learning (see
Table 11.2). The publication that elaborates on these five key features frames
them by stating that social studies teaching is viewed as powerful when it helps
students develop social understanding and civic efficacy. *Social understanding* is
integrated knowledge of the social aspects of the human condition: how these aspects have evolved over time, the variations that occur in different physical environments and cultural settings, and emerging trends that appear likely to shape
the future. *Civic efficacy* is readiness and willingness to assume citizenship responsibilities. It is rooted in social studies knowledge and skills, along with related values (such as concern for the common good) and dispositions (such as an orientation toward confident participation in civic affairs; National Council for the
Social Studies, 1993).

CONNECTING CURRICULUM WITH STUDENTS' IDEAS

Our units were planned to connect with students' existing knowledge and address
their knowledge gaps and misconceptions. Connections with existing knowledge
were developed immediately by beginning the units with contemporary experi-

TABLE 11.1
Ten Thematic Strands

Ten themes serve as organizing strands for the social studies curriculum at every school level (early, middle, and high school), they are interrelated and draw from all of the social science disciplines and other related disciplines and fields of scholarly study to build a framework for social studies curriculum.

I. Culture
Human beings create, learn, and adapt culture. Human cultures are dynamic systems of beliefs, values, and traditions that exhibit both commonalities and differences. Understanding culture helps us understand ourselves and others.

II. Time, Continuity, and Change
Human beings seek to understand their historic roots and to locate themselves in time. Such understanding involves knowing what things were like in the past and how things change and develop— allowing us to develop historic perspective and answer important questions about our current condition.

III. People, Places, and Environment
Technical advancements have ensured that students are aware of the world beyond their personal locations. As students study content related to this theme, they create their spatial views and geographical perspectives of the world; social, cultural, economic, and civic demands mean that students will need such knowledge, skills, and understandings to make informed and critical decisions about the relationship between human beings and their environment.

IV. Individual Development and Identity
Personal identity is shaped by one's culture, by groups, and by institutional influences. Examination of various forms of human behavior enhances understandings of the relationship between social norms and emerging personal identities, the social processes that influence identity formation, and the ethical principles underlying individual action.

V. Individuals, Groups, and Institutions
Institutions exert enormous influence over us. Institutions are organizational embodiments to further the core social values of those who comprise them. It is important for students to know how institutions are formed, what controls and influences them, how they control and influence individuals and culture, and how institutions can be maintained or changed.

VI. Power, Authority, and Governance
Understanding of the historic development of structures of power, authority, and governance and their evolving functions in contemporary society is essential for emergence of civic competence.

VII. Production, Distribution, and Consumption
Decisions about exchange, trade, and economic policy and well-being are global in scope, and the role of government in policymaking varies over time and from place to place. The systematic study of an interdependent world economy and the role of technology in economic decision making is essential.

VIII. Science, Technology, and Society
Technology is as old as the first crude tool invented by prehistoric humans, and modern life as we know it would be impossible without technology and the science that supports it. Today's technology forms the basis for some of our most difficult social choices.

IX. Global Connections
The realities of global interdependence require understanding of the increasingly important and diverse global connections among world societies before there can be analysis leading to the development of possible solutions to persisting and emerging global issues.

X. Civic Ideals and Practices
All people have a stake in examining civic ideals and practices across time, in diverse societies, as well as in determining how to close the gap between present practices and the ideals upon which our democracy is based. An understanding of civic ideals and practices of citizenship is critical to full participation in society.

Note. Adapted from *Curriculum Standards for Social Studies: Expectations of Excellence* (Bulletin No. 89), by National Council for the Social Studies, 1994. Copyright © 1994 by National Council for the Social Studies.

TABLE 11.2
Five Key Features of Powerful Social Studies Learning

Meaningful
The content selected for emphasis is worth learning because it promotes progress toward important social understanding and civic efficacy goals, and it is taught in ways that help students to see how it is related to these goals. As a result, students' learning efforts are motivated by appreciation and interest, not just by accountability and grading systems. Instruction emphasizes depth of development of important ideas within appropriate breadth of content coverage.

Integrative
Powerful social studies cuts across discipline boundaries, spans time and space, and integrates knowledge, beliefs, values, and dispositions to action. It also provides opportunities for students to connect to the arts and sciences through inquiry and reflection.

Value-Based
Powerful social studies teaching considers the ethical dimensions of topics, so that it provides an arena for reflective development of concern for the common good and application of social values. The teacher includes diverse points of view, demonstrates respect for well-supported positions, and shows sensitivity and commitment to social responsibility and action.

Challenging
Students are encouraged to function as a learning community, using reflective discussion to work collaboratively to deepen understandings of the meanings and implications of content. They also are expected to come to grips with controversial issues, to participate assertively but respectfully in group discussions, and to work productively with peers in cooperative learning activities.

Active
Powerful social studies is rewarding but demanding. It demands thoughtful preparation and instruction by the teacher, and sustained effort by the students to make sense of and apply what they are learning. Teachers do not mechanically follow rigid guidelines in planning, implementing, and assessing instruction. Instead, they work with the national standards and with state and local guidelines, adapting and supplementing these guidelines and their instructional materials in ways that support their students' social education needs.

The teacher uses a variety of instructional materials, plans field trips and visits by resource people, develops current or local examples to relate to students' lives, plans reflective discussions, and scaffolds students' work in ways that encourage them to gradually take on more responsibility for managing their own learning independently and with their peers. Accountability and grading systems are compatible with these goals and methods.

Students develop new understandings through a process of active construction. They develop a network of connections that link the new content to preexisting knowledge and beliefs anchored in their prior experience. The construction of meaning required to develop important social understandings takes time and is facilitated by interactive discourse. Clear explanations and modeling from the teacher are important, but so are opportunities to answer questions, discuss or debate the meaning and implications of content, or use the content in activities that call for tackling problems or making decisions.

Note. Adapted from "A Vision of Powerful Teaching and Learning in the Social Studies: Building Social Understanding and Civic Efficacy," by National Council for the Social Studies, 1993, *Social Education*, 57, 213–223. Copyright © 1993 by National Council for the Social Studies.

ences relating to the cultural universal, especially experiences likely to occur in the students' own homes and neighborhood. To introduce new topics, the lesson plans typically call for showing photos or artifacts relating to the cultural universal or simply asking questions about related student experiences. The unit on shelter, for example, begins by engaging the students in discussion about common types of homes or living quarters found in their neighborhood, and the unit on clothing begins with examination of the students' own clothes worn to school that day.

The content is organized into clusters structured around big ideas, so these big ideas are the focus of the information presented to students and the questions addressed to them. These foundational ideas are revisited frequently, each time adding some new information, new examples, or opportunities for review. Because so much of the information is new to the students, the units are front-loaded with transmission forms of teaching used to introduce and develop the big ideas. As the students become more familiar with these ideas, they can begin to contribute more to the development of the content, so the lesson formats can shift from an emphasis on transmission to an emphasis on co-construction of knowledge.

We recommend that teachers conduct informal assessments throughout the units, both to monitor learning progress and to identify knowledge gaps or misconceptions that may need to be addressed directly. These assessments can be accomplished using simple strategies such as asking for explanations or likenesses and differences, or by asking students to sequence things in the order in which they were invented or talk about how something might be improved by changing it or adding something to it.

Content Representations

Within the fundamental principle of representing content as networks structured around big ideas, there are basic decisions to be made about what content to represent, at what level of detail, and with what kinds of examples or experiences. Like most educators, we recommend teaching within the students' zones of proximal development—focusing on content and skills that they have not yet acquired and are unlikely to acquire anytime soon on their own, but can acquire if their learning efforts are scaffolded by teachers. It may not be feasible or desirable to attempt to teach primary-grade students everything worth knowing about a topic, but it is important to make sure that what is taught is coherent (a network structured around big ideas and developed with attention to its connections) and valid and useful as far as it goes. Content development should include questions and activities that call for students to apply what they are learning to their lives outside of school.

Examples should be sufficiently varied to communicate the full set of instances to which a concept or principle applies, or at least enough of those instances to counteract tendencies toward stereotyping. For example, teaching about Native Americans should include coverage of the plains tribes (emphasizing that the hunting of buffalo, the construction of tipis, and other salient aspects of their cultures were adaptations to the affordances and constraints of their physical environment, given the knowledge and technology available to them at the time), but also should include exposure to several other tribal groups (Eastern Woodlands, Southwestern, Northwest Coast) who lived in very different environments and developed very different cultures.

Content development also should avoid unnecessary oversimplifications and address at least some of the complexities involved. For example, as part of their progressivist bias toward history, children tend to view all innovations as improvements. To counter this tendency, instruction can be planned to help them understand that some innovations not only are not improvements but may be seen as temporary regressions (e.g., certain fashion fads), that innovations often bring losses along with gains (requiring wrenching adjustments for people whose jobs or entire lifestyles are rendered obsolete; industries creating pollution problems along with the benefits of new products). Also, older technologies do not simply disappear in the face of new inventions but sometimes are kept alive by people who enjoy them as hobbies or make a living by developing specialized products that people are willing to pay extra for because of their artistic or craftsmanship qualities (handmade clothing, furniture, etc.).

Often it is desirable to include field trips or other opportunities for children to have first-hand experiences with activities relating to the cultural universal. In these cases, it is important to plan the activities with an eye toward learning through the eyes and ears of children, and scaffolding their experiences accordingly. In addition to their out-of-class aspect, the experiences should include advance preparation to help the students get the most out of them, as well as subsequent debriefing discussions focusing on the main ideas learned. This scaffolding should include content designed to help the students appreciate that the particular things they experienced are part of a larger picture (e.g., the dairy farm they visited is just one kind of farm, the Native American clothing and customs they saw were valid for the tribes involved but other tribes had different clothing and customs).

Content representations, especially those involving human interactions, often will need to be scaffolded to help students appreciate nonobvious economic or other considerations involved. For example, interactions involving money at supermarket checkout counters are not just ritual exchanges; the person purchasing the food is paying for it and any money returned is just change, not an amount equal to or greater than the amount given to the checker. As another example, money paid to a restaurant waiter or cashier covers not only the cost of the food but the cost of running the restaurant and paying the employees, plus an additional amount realized as profit for the owner. It is important to unpack these hidden aspects of land-to-hand explanations, the cost and benefit considerations that need to be addressed in making decisions, and so on. As discussion develops, it often is helpful to coconstruct charts or other graphic depictions with the students, using them on the spot and again in the future as scaffolds for review of the main ideas or steps involved.

Another aspect of representing content within larger contexts involves drawing attention to exceptions, anomalies, and cultural differences. For example, we think of raw vegetables (properly cleaned) as healthful foods in our country, but we should avoid eating them in certain other countries. White wedding dresses and dark clothing at funerals are traditional in our country, but other countries have very different traditions. Both the clothes used in blue collar jobs and the clothes used in white collar jobs are work clothes in the sense that they are worn on the job, but we tend to call the former "work clothes" and the latter "business clothes." Furthermore, some companies require their employees to wear uniforms for safety or other reasons. Uniforms are another form of work clothes.

It is not always clear whether or how to introduce these exceptions and anomalies. We typically introduce those that are commonly encountered and likely to cause confusions in the minds of many of the students, as well as encourage teachers to address any that are brought up by the students themselves in their questions or comments. Frequently, however, it seems best to focus on prototype examples and ignore anomalies, especially those that are unlikely to enter the students' awareness anytime soon. For example, sometimes people write checks for much larger amounts than what they owe at the supermarket, in effect cashing a check and making a purchase at the same time. Or, if they are using a card to make payment, it is possible that this is a credit card issued by the supermarket rather than one of the more general credit cards, and possible that it is a debit card rather than a conventional credit card. These anomalies and complications do not seem worth introducing to primary-grade students.

Zone of Proximal Development

The *zone of proximal development* is typically defined as the range of things that children do not know now and are unlikely to acquire on their own anytime soon, but are able to learn with mediation from their teacher. The children already know things that are below their current zones of proximal development, and they are not yet ready to learn things that are above it, even with expert scaffolding from their teachers. This concept is clear enough in theory but can be problematic to implement in practice because it includes some hidden cost/benefit assumptions. In effect, we consider content to lie within the zone of proximal development if it can be learned within a reasonable time period given reasonable effort by the teacher and students. Definitions of what is reasonable will vary, but few curriculum developers or teachers would recommend attempting to teach some concept or principle to say, first graders, if only a few of them were likely to grasp it clearly even after several weeks of instruction. Thus, the operat-

ing definition is not what only some of the students can learn and only then under optimal conditions and extended effort, but what all or at least most of the
students can learn within units of typical length and scope taught for typical time
periods under typical conditions. We and others have found that primary-grade
students are interested in and able to learn a much greater range of social studies
content than many educators give them credit for, but we hasten to add that, in
referring to teaching in the zone of proximal development, we refer to developing
content that most students at the grade level can be expected to learn within the
time allocated for instruction.

Such learning will be smoother and more worthwhile if its content is focused
around cultural universals and other topics with which the students have had
some personal experience, if this content is represented as networks structured
around big ideas, and if the teacher scaffolds with an eye toward helping students
make connections to previous learning and to life outside of school. Typically,
such teaching involves a judicious blend of transmission (especially in the initial
stages) and social construction of knowledge (especially in the later stages). Following up in-school lessons by encouraging students to converse about big ideas
with their families through strategic home assignments provides additional opportunities for coconstruction of meaning. Relatively specific understandings can
be developed in single lessons and reviewed occasionally thereafter. More generic
understandings can be developed gradually by continuing to refer back to them
and note connections as the class proceeds through lessons and units.

To take maximal advantage of these opportunities, teachers need to have a
clear grasp of the big picture of the curriculum, both within and across subject areas. It also helps if teachers develop and use a standard set of vocabulary (preferably taken from or at least well connected with the children's own natural language) to refer to ideas that reappear across units (e.g., culture, inventions, needs
vs. wants, etc.). The students' knowledge of these terms will deepen and broaden
as the terms are revisited in subsequent lessons or units and applied to new examples.

Presentism

Students' ideas about the past were frequently tinged with *presentism*, yielding
judgments that people in the past were ignorant or even stupid, that their technologies were crude and weak, and so on. Teachers can counteract presentism by
helping students to develop *historical empathy*—the ability and disposition to view
past lives and events through the eyes of the people who lived them, and thus to
appreciate their activities as sensible adaptations to their time and place and
their techniques as state-of-the-art (Davis et al., 2001). Teaching about developments in a domain through time can incorporate simple timelines (e.g., using the
cave days, the pioneers, and modern times as anchors) and encourage students to
appreciate the ingenuity of inventions as advances in the knowledge or technol-

ogy available at the time, rather than viewing them only from hindsight and thus devaluing them. We recommend interactive discussion around timelines, in which the teacher and students build up the timelines using drawings, photos, or other visual aids to mark significant inventions or events. Where appropriate, the teacher can underscore the idea that people from the past were just as intelligent as we are, but didn't enjoy the accumulated benefits of science and technology that support our lives today. Also, along with appreciating the advantages brought by each new development, students can learn that progress also brings trade-offs and new challenges. By introducing such content and embedding it within such a context, teachers can help students to construct a richer network of understandings than they would if they limited themselves to the content in textbooks and to skills exercises designed only to determine if the students can sequence a series of events correctly.

A broad range of input sources and activities is helpful here. Simulations, role plays, authentic children's literature, well-chosen video clips, and other such sources, laced with explanations sensitizing students to how and why the domain in question developed through time, help personalize history and bring it to life. They also help students to appreciate that all people, including ourselves, are "players" in history and that hindsight is not the only lens for viewing the past.

Chauvinism

A parallel emphasis on developing empathy can be helpful in combating chauvinism. Teachers can begin by capitalizing on the existing diversity within the classroom and school. For example, children in any classroom will be found to celebrate birthdays and holidays in different ways, depending on their family traditions and cultural backgrounds. Exploration of these differences can help establish a mindset that variations are to be expected, and that awareness of, or even participation in, cultural practices other than our own can enrich our lives.

Working from this base, teachers can introduce the concept of *cultural borrowing*, using multiple authentic children's books to portray a variety of traditions and customs. They also can engage their students in sampling foods, learning about unfamiliar traditions, and so on. We encourage teachers to arrange culturally oriented visits to museums or other relevant local sites, as well as to arrange classroom visits by parents or other relatives who can come to display and talk about their culture's food, clothing, and so on. However, it may be better to avoid (or at least be prepared to help students place into a broader context) festivals, fairs, or performances that may induce a limited and stereotyped view of particular cultures. Members of distinctive cultural groups living in the local community and school librarians and bookstore employees with specialized knowledge of children's literature can be helpful in guiding teachers to materials that will help students develop authentic understandings and appreciation of cultural diversity.

Teaching about the United States might emphasize that its history as a land of immigrants has made it a more diverse and stimulating place to live than places restricted to more homogeneous cultures. Furthermore, instead of stressing differences and focusing on what strikes American children as bizarre, teaching about other cultures can place more emphasis on parallels that reflect the commonalities of human nature. Using food pyramids, typical meals eaten in different societies can be compared to illustrate similarities in food groupings. Different forms of bread can be shown with emphasis on the fact that they are all variations on the same basic food, and other food-related parallels can be noted as well (e.g., sugar and honey as alternative sweetening agents; chopsticks and silverware as alternative eating implements).

It also helps to portray differences as variations along common themes; people everywhere have the same basic needs but come to satisfy them differently due to differences in available resources, cultural traditions, or personal preferences. Geographical and climatic aspects of the areas in which people live, the major economic activities engaged in in their societies, their forms of government, and other local factors may help explain their behavior.

CONCLUSION

In this book, we have presented and discussed K–3 students' responses to interviews about nine cultural universals. Our research has extended considerably what is known about the content and nature of children's social knowledge and thinking during those years. We believe that child development researchers will find it useful as a significant extension to the literature in that field, and that it will inform social educators' efforts to develop curriculum for early social studies.

References

Abdullah, M. (2000). *Media literacy*. Bloomington: ERIC Clearinghouse on Reading, English, and Communication, Indiana University. (ERIC Digest D 152)

Aboud, F. (1988). *Children and prejudice*. New York: Blackwell.

Abramovitch, R., Freedman, J., & Pliner, P. (1991). Children and money: Getting an allowance, credit versus cash, and knowledge of pricing. *Journal of Economic Psychology, 12*, 27–45.

Alleman, J., & Brophy, J. (2001). *Social studies excursions: K–3: Book One. Powerful units on food, clothing, and shelter*. Portsmouth, NH: Heinemann.

Alleman, J., & Brophy, J. (2002). *Social studies excursions: K–3: Book Two. Powerful units on communication, transportation, and family living*. Portsmouth, NH: Heinemann.

Alleman, J., & Brophy, J. (2003). *Social studies excursions: K–3: Book Three. Powerful units on childhood, money, and government*. Portsmouth, NH: Heinemann.

Alter, G. (1995). Transforming elementary social studies: The emergence of a curriculum focused on diverse, caring communities. *Theory and Research in Social Education, 23*, 355–374.

Alton-Lee, A., Nuthall, G., & Patrick, J. (1993). Reframing classroom research: A lesson from the private world of children. *Harvard Educational Review, 63*, 50–84.

Atran, S. (1998). Folk biology and the anthropology of science: Cognitive universals and cultural particulars. *Behavioral and Brain Sciences, 21*, 547–609.

Au, T., & Romo, L. (1999). Mechanical causality in children's "folkbiology." In D. Medin & S. Atran (Eds.), *Folkbiology* (pp. 355–401). Cambridge, MA: MIT Press.

Bailey, K. (1976). *Continuity and change in children's attitudes toward the President: Political crisis to political celebration*. (ERIC Document Reproduction Service No. ED 132 109)

Bandyopadhyay, S., Kindra, G., & Sharp, L. (2001). Is television advertising good for children? Areas of concern and policy implications. *International Journal of Advertising and Marketing to Children, 20*, 89–116.

Banks, J. (1990). *Teaching strategies for social studies: Inquiry, valuing, and decision making* (4th ed.). New York: Longman.

Barrett, M., & Buchanan-Barrow, E. (2002). Children's understanding of society. In P. Smith & C. Hart (Eds.), *Blackwell handbook of childhood social development* (pp. 491–512). Hove, England: Blackwell.

Barrett, M., & Buchanan-Barrow, E. (Eds.). (2005). *Children's understanding of society*. London: Psychology Press.

Barrett, M., & Short, J. (1992). Images of European people in a group of 5–10-year-old English schoolchildren. *British Journal of Developmental Psychology, 10,* 339–363.

Barton, K. (1996). Narrative simplifications in elementary students' historical thinking. In J. Brophy (Ed.), *Advances in research on teaching: Vol. 6. Teaching and learning history* (pp. 51–84). Greenwich, CT: JAI Press.

Barton, K. (1997a). "Bossed around by the queen": Elementary students' understanding of individuals and institutions in history. *Journal of Curriculum and Supervision, 12,* 290–314.

Barton, K. (1997b). History—It *can* be elementary: An overview of elementary students' understanding of history. *Social Education, 61,* 13–16.

Barton, K, & Levstik, L. (1996). "Back when God was around and everything": Elementary children's understanding of historical time. *American Educational Research Journal, 33,* 419–454.

Barton, K., & Levstik, L. (2004). *Teaching history for the common good.* Mahwah, NJ: Lawrence Erlbaum Associates.

Bates, F. (1947). *Factors related to children's understandings of social concepts.* Unpublished doctoral dissertation, University of California.

Batterham, D., Stanisstreet, M., & Boyes, E. (1996). Kids, cars and conservation: Children's ideas about the environmental impact of motor vehicles. *International Journal of Science Education, 18,* 347–354.

Beck, I., & McKeown, M. (1988). Toward meaningful accounts in history texts for young learners. *Educational Researcher, 17*(6), 31–39.

Beck, I., McKeown, M., & Gromoll, E. (1989). Learning from social studies texts. *Cognition and Instruction, 6,* 99–158.

Bennett, M., Lyons, E., Sani, F., & Barrett, M. (1998). Children's subjective identification with the group and in-group favoritism. *Developmental Psychology, 34,* 902–909.

Bernstein, B. (1962). Social class, linguistic codes, and grammatical elements. *Language and Speech, 5,* 221–240.

Berti, A. (1994). Children's understanding of the concept of the state. In M. Carretero & J. Voss (Eds.), *Cognitive and instructional processes in history and the social sciences* (pp. 49–75). Hillsdale, NJ: Lawrence Erlbaum Associates.

Berti, A. (1995). Knowledge restructuring in an economic subdomain: Banking. In W. Schnotz, S. Vosniadou, & M. Carrertero (Eds.), *New perspectives on conceptual change* (pp. 113–133). New York: Pergamon.

Berti, A. (2002). Children's understanding of society: Psychological studies and their educational implications. In E. Nasman & A. Ross (Eds.), *Children's understanding in the new Europe* (pp. 89–107). Stoke on Trent, England: Trentham.

Berti, A. (2004). Children's understanding of politics. In M. Barrett & E. Buchanan-Barrow (Eds.), *Children's understanding of society*. Hove, England: Psychology Press.

Berti, A., & Andriolo, A. (2001). Third graders' understanding of core political concepts (law, nation-state, government) before and after teaching. *Genetic, Social and General Psychology Monographs, 127,* 346–377.

Berti, A., & Benesso, C. (1998). The concept of nation-state in Italian elementary school children: Spontaneous concepts and effects of teaching. *Genetic, Social, and General Psychology Monographs, 124,* 185–209.

Berti, A., & Bombi, A. (1988). *The child's construction of economics*. Cambridge, England: Cambridge University Press.

Berti, A., & Bombi, A. (1989). Environmental differences in understanding production and distribution. In J. Valsiner (Ed.), *Child development in cultural context* (pp. 247–272). Toronto, Canada: Hogrefe & Huber.

Berti, A., & Monaci, M. (1998). Third graders' acquisition of knowledge of banking: Restructuring or accretion? *British Journal of Educational Psychology, 68,* 357–371.

Berti, A., & Ugolini, E. (1998). Developing knowledge of the judicial system: A domain-specific approach. *Journal of Genetic Psychology, 159,* 221–236.

Birch, L., Fisher, J., & Grimm-Thomas, K. (1999). Children and food. In M. Siegal & C. Peterson (Eds.), *Children's understanding of biology and health* (pp. 161–182). Cambridge, England: Cambridge University Press.

Black, P, & Harlen, W. (1993). How can we specify concepts for primary science? In P. J. Black & A. M. Lucas (Eds.), *Children's informal ideas in science* (pp. 208–229). New York: Routledge.

Bogdan, R., & Biklen, S. (1982). *Qualitative research for education: An introduction to theory and methods*. Boston, MA: Allyn & Bacon.

Bronstein, C., Daily, K., & Horowitz, E. (1993). *Tellin' it like it is: Children's attitudes toward the electoral process and the '92 campaign* (Unpublished report). Madison: University of Wisconsin–Madison, School of Journalism and Mass Communication. (ERIC Document Reproduction Service No. ED 361 821)

Brophy, J. (1992). Probing the subtleties of subject-matter teaching. *Educational Leadership, 49*(7), 4–8.

Brophy, J. (1999). Elementary students learn about Native Americans: Developing knowledge and empathy. *Social Education, 63,* 40–45.

Brophy, J., & Alleman, J. (1992/1993). Elementary social studies textbooks. *Publishing Research Quarterly, 8*(4), 12–22.

Brophy, J., & Alleman, J. (1996). *Powerful social studies for elementary students*. Fort Worth, TX: Harcourt Brace.

Brophy, J., & Alleman, J. (1997). Second graders' knowledge and thinking about shelter as a cultural universal. *Journal of Social Studies Research, 21,* 3–15.

Brophy, J., & Alleman, J. (1999a). *Primary-grade students' knowledge and thinking about clothing as a cultural universal* (Unpublished report). East Lansing: Michigan State University, College of Education. (ERIC Document Reproduction Service No. ED 439 072)

Brophy, J., & Alleman, J. (1999b). *Primary-grade students' knowledge and thinking about shelter as a cultural universal* (Unpublished report). East Lansing: Michigan State University, College of Education. (ERIC Document Reproduction Service No. ED 437 311)

Brophy, J., & Alleman, J. (2001a). *Primary-grade students' knowledge and thinking about communication as a cultural universal* (Unpublished report). East Lansing: Michigan State University, College of Education. (ERIC Document Reproduction Service No. ED 451 129)

Brophy, J., & Alleman, J. (2001b). *Primary-grade students' knowledge and thinking about family living as a cultural universal* (Unpublished report). East Lansing: Michigan State University, College of Education. (ERIC Document Reproduction Service No. ED 454 150)

Brophy, J., & Alleman, J. (2001c). *Primary-grade students' knowledge and thinking about transportation as a cultural universal* (Unpublished report). East Lansing: Michigan State University, College of Education. (ERIC Document Reproduction Service No. ED 454 151)

Brophy, J., & Alleman, J. (2002). *Primary-grade students' knowledge and thinking about government as a cultural universal* (Unpublished report). East Lansing: Michigan State University, College of Education. (ERIC Document Reproduction Service No. ED 470 388)

Brophy, J., Alleman, J., & O'Mahony, C. (2000). Elementary school social studies: Yesterday, today, and tomorrow. In T. Good (Ed.), *American education: Yesterday, today, and tomorrow* (99th Yearbook of the National Society for the Study of Education, Part II, pp. 256–312). Chicago: University of Chicago Press.

Brophy, J., Alleman, J., & O'Mahony, C. (2001). *Primary-grade students' knowledge and thinking about food as a cultural universal* (Unpublished report). (ERIC Document Reproduction Service No. ED 451 124)

Brophy, J., O'Mahony, C., & Alleman, J. (2001). *Ideas about food production, distribution, and consumption expressed by third graders from New Zealand and from urban and rural communities in the United States* (Unpublished report). East Lansing: Michigan State University, College of Education.

Brophy, J., O'Mahony, C., & Alleman, J. (2002). *Ideas about shelter expressed by third graders from vertical/urban vs. horizontal/suburban communities in the United States* (Unpublished report). East Lansing: Michigan State University, College of Education. (ERIC Document Reproduction Service No. ED 466 435)

Brophy, J., & VanSledright, B. (1997). *Teaching and learning history in elementary schools*. New York: Teachers College Press.

Brown, D. (1991). *Human universals*. Philadelphia, PA: Temple University Press.

Bruner, J. (1966). *Toward a theory of instruction*. Cambridge, MA: Harvard University Press.

Buckingham, D. (2000). *After the death of childhood: Growing up in the age of electronic media*. Malden, MA: Blackwell.

Bulmer, S. (2001). *Children's perceptions of advertising* (Working Paper Series No. 01-05). Auckland, New Zealand: Department of Commerce, Massey University.

Burris, V. (1983). Stages in the development of economic concepts. *Human Relations, 36,* 791–812.

Byrnes, J. (1996). *Cognitive development and learning in instructional contexts*. Boston, MA: Allyn & Bacon.

Cameron, J., Alvarez, J., Ruble, D., & Fuligni, A. (2001). Children's lay theories about ingroups and outgroups: Reconceptualizing research on prejudice. *Personality and Social Psychology Review, 5,* 118–128.

Carey, S. (1985). *Conceptual change in childhood*. Cambridge, MA: MIT Press.

Carey, S. (1999). Sources of conceptual change. In E. Scholnick, K. Nelson, S. Gelman, & P. Miller (Eds.), *Conceptual development: Piaget's legacy* (pp. 293–326). Mahwah, NJ: Lawrence Erlbaum Associates.

Carruth, B., & Skinner, J. (2001). Consumer goals/skills that mothers want their children to learn. *International Journal of Consumer Studies, 25,* 290–298.

Chambers, J., & Tavuchis, N. (1976). Kids and kin: Children's understanding of American kin terms. *Journal of Child Language, 3,* 63–80.

Chan, K. (2000). Hong Kong children's understanding of television advertising. *Journal of Marketing Communications, 6,* 37–52.

Chan, K., & McNeal, J. (2002). Children's perceptions of television advertising in urban China. *International Journal of Advertising and Marketing to Children, 3,* 69–79.

Chandler, D. (1997). Children's understanding of what is "real" on television: A review of the literature. *Journal of Educational Media, 23,* 65–80.

Connell, R. (1971). *The child's construction of politics*. Carlton, Australia: Melbourne University Press.

Contento, I. (1981). Kindergarten through sixth grade nutrition education. In J. Nestor & J. Glotzer (Eds.), *Teaching nutrition: Review of programs and research* (pp. 159–236). Cambridge, MA: Abt Associates.

Cooper, H. (1995). *History in the early years*. New York: Routledge.

Coulson, R. (1990). *Young children's perceptions of the role of food in their bodies*. (ERIC Document Reproduction Service No. ED 338 414)

Cram, F., Ng, S., & Jahveri, N. (1996). Young people's understanding of private and public ownership. In P. Lunt & A. Furnham (Eds.), *Economic socialization: The economic beliefs and behaviours of young people* (pp. 110–129). Cheltenham, England: Edward Elgar.

Danziger, K. (1957). The child's understanding of kinship terms: A study in the development of relational concepts. *Journal of Genetic Psychology, 91*, 213–232.

Davies, M. (1997). *Fake, fact, and fantasy: Children's interpretations of television reality*. Mahwah, NJ: Lawrence Erlbaum Associates.

Davis, J., & Hawke, S. (1992). The seeds of change: Cutting edge knowledge and the Columbian Quincentenary. *Social Education, 56*, 320–322.

Davis, O. L., Jr., Yeager, E., & Foster, S. (Eds.). (2001). *Historical empathy and perspective taking in the social studies*. New York: Rowman & Littlefield.

Del-Val, P., et al. (1981). *Understanding handicaps: A curriculum for changing students' attitudes toward the disabled*. (ERIC Document Reproduction Service No. ED 232 367)

Dickenson, A., Lee, P., & Rogers, P. (1984). *Learning history*. London: Heinemann.

Diez-Martinez Day, D., & Remigy, M. (1999). Mexican and French children's conceptions about family: A developmental approach. *Journal of Comparative Family Studies, 30*, 95–112.

Downey, M., & Levstik, L. (1991). Teaching and learning history. In J. Shaver (Ed.), *Handbook of research on social studies teaching and learning* (pp. 400–410). New York: Macmillan.

Driver, R., Guesne, E., & Tiberghien, A. (Eds.). (1985). *Children's ideas in science*. London: Taylor & Francis.

Driver, R., Squires, A., Rushworth, P., & Wood-Robinson, V. (1994). *Making sense of secondary science: Research into children's ideas*. London: Routledge.

Duke, N. (2000). 3.6 minutes per day: The scarcity of informational texts in first grade. *Reading Research Quarterly, 35*, 202–225.

Edwards, C. (1984). The age group labels and categories of preschool children. *Child Development, 55*, 440–452.

Egan, K. (1988). *Primary understanding: Education in early childhood*. New York: Routledge.

Elkind, D. (1962). Children's conceptions of brother and sister: Piaget Replication Study V. *Journal of Genetic Psychology, 100*, 129–136.

Estvan, F., & Estvan, E. (1959). *The child's world: His social perception*. New York: G. P. Putnam's Sons.

Evans, R., & Saxe, D. (Eds.). (1996). *Handbook on teaching social issues*. Washington, DC: National Council for the Social Studies.

Feuerstein, M. (1999). Media literacy in support of critical thinking. *Journal of Educational Media, 24*, 43–55.

Fischer, K., Hand, H., Watson, M., VanParys, M., & Tucker, J. (1984). Putting the child into socialization: The development of social categories in preschool children. In L. Katz (Ed.), *Current topics in early childhood education* (Vol. 5, pp. 27–72). Norwood, NJ: Ablex.

Foster, S., Hoge, J., & Rosch, R. (1999). Thinking aloud about history: Children's and adolescents' responses to historical photographs. *Theory and Research in Social Education, 27*, 179–214.

Furnham, A. (1996). The economic socialization of children. In P. Lunt & A. Furnham (Eds.), *Economic socialization: The economic beliefs and behaviours of young people* (pp. 11–34). Cheltenham, England: Edward Elgar.

Furnham, A., & Stacey, B. (1991). *Young people's understanding of society*. New York: Routledge.

Furth, H. (1980). *The world of grown-ups*. New York: Elsevier.

Garcia, R. (1991). *Teaching in a pluralistic society: Concepts, models, strategies* (2nd ed.). New York: HarperCollins.

Gardner, H., & Boix-Mansilla, V. (1994). Teaching for understanding—within and across disciplines. *Educational Leadership, 51*(5), 14–18.

Glaser, B., & Strauss, A. (1979). *The discovery of grounded theory: Strategies for qualitative research.* Hawthorne, NY: Aldine.

Gopnik, A., & Meltzoff, A. (1997). *Words, thoughts, and theories.* Cambridge, MA: MIT Press.

Greenstein, F. (1969). *Children and politics* (Rev. ed.). New Haven, CT: Yale University Press.

Guzzetta, C. (1969). Children's knowledge of historically important Americans. In W. Herman (Ed.), *Current research in elementary school social studies* (pp. 392–400). New York: Macmillan.

Haas, M., & Laughlin, M. (1997). *Meeting the standards: Social studies readings for K–6 educators.* Washington, DC: National Council for the Social Studies.

Haas, M., & Laughlin, M. (2001). A profile of elementary social studies teachers and their classrooms. *Social Education, 65,* 122–126.

Hallden, O. (1994). On the paradox of understanding history in an educational setting. In G. Leinhardt, I. Beck, & C. Stainton (Eds.), *Teaching and learning in history* (pp. 27–46). Hillsdale, NJ: Lawrence Erlbaum Associates.

Hart, K., Bishop, J., & Truby, H. (2002). An investigation into school children's knowledge and awareness of food and nutrition. *Journal of Human Nutrition and Dietetics, 15,* 129–140.

Harter, S. (1999). *The construction of the self: A developmental perspective.* New York: Guilford.

Harwood, D., & McShane, J. (1996). Young children's understanding of nested hierarchies of place relationships. *International Research in Geographical and Environmental Education, 5,* 3–29.

Haviland, S., & Clark, E. (1974). "This man's father is my father's son": A study of the acquisition of English kin terms. *Journal of Child Language, 1,* 23–47.

Helwig, C., & Jasiobedzka, U. (2001). The relation between law and morality: Children's reasoning about socially beneficial and unjust laws. *Child Development, 72,* 1382–1393.

Henriksen, L. (1996). Naive theories of buying and selling: Implications for teaching critical viewing skills. *Journal of Applied Communication Research, 24,* 93–109.

Hess, R., & Torney, J. (1967). *The development of political attitudes in children.* Chicago: Aldine.

Hirsch, E. D., Jr. (1987). *Cultural literacy: What every American needs to know.* New York: Houghton Mifflin.

Hirschfeld, L. (2001). On a folk theory of society: Children, evolution, and mental representations of social groups. *Personality and Social Psychology Review, 5,* 107–117.

Hirschfeld, L., & Gelman, S. (1997). What young children think about the relationship between language variation and social difference. *Cognitive Development, 12,* 213–238.

Horobin, K. (1997). *Children's understanding of biological inheritance: Nature, nurture, and essentialism* (Unpublished report). Sacramento: California State University, Sacramento. (ERIC Document Reproduction Service No. ED 406 066)

Inagaki, K., & Hatano, G. (1993). Young children's understanding of the mind–body distinction. *Child Development, 64,* 1534–1549.

Jahoda, G. (1963). The development of children's ideas about country and nationality: Part II. National symbols and themes. *British Journal of Educational Psychology, 33,* 143–153.

Jahoda, G. (1981). The development of thinking about economic institution: The bank. *Cahiers de psychologie cognitive, 1,* 55–73.

Jahoda, G. (1984). The development of thinking about socio-economic systems. In H. Tajfel (Ed.), *The social dimension: European developments in social psychology* (Vol. 1, pp. 69–88). Cambridge, England: Cambridge University Press.

Jahoda, G., & Woerdenbagch, A. (1982). The development of ideas about an economic institution: A cross-national replication. *British Journal of Social Psychology, 21,* 337–338.

John, D. (1999). Consumer socialization of children: A retrospective look at twenty-five years of research. *Journal of Consumer Research, 26,* 183–213.

Jordan, V. (1980). Conserving kinship concepts: A developmental study in social cognition. *Child Development, 51,* 146–155.

Keil, F. (1992). The origins of an autonomous biology. In M. Gunnar & M. Maratsos (Eds.), *Minnesota Symposium on Child Psychology: Vol. 25. Modularity and constraints in language and cognition* (pp. 103–137). Hillsdale, NJ: Lawrence Erlbaum Associates.

Keil, F., Levin, D., Richman, B., & Gutheil, G. (1999). Mechanism and explanation in the development of biological thought: The case of disease. In D. Medin & S. Atran (Eds.), *Folkbiology* (pp. 285–319). Cambridge, MA: MIT Press.

Kelemen, D. (1999). Why are rocks pointy? Children's preferences for teleological explanations of the natural world. *Developmental Psychology, 35,* 1440–1452.

Klavir, R., & Leiser, D. (2002). When astronomy, biology, and culture converge: Children's conceptions about birthdays. *Journal of Genetic Psychology, 163,* 239–253.

Kliebard, H. (2004). *The struggle for the American curriculum, 1893–1958* (3rd ed.). New York: Routledge.

Krey, D. (1998). *Children's literature in social studies: Teaching to the standards.* Washington, DC: National Council for the Social Studies.

Lambert, T. (1994). *Deaf awareness: A program to increase student awareness of what it is like to have a hearing impairment.* (ERIC Document Reproduction Service No. ED 384 160)

Langer, G. (1999). ABC News for Kids poll: Presidents' Day. Retrieved June 26, 2001, from http://www.icrsurvey.com/icr/president.htm

Lapp, M., Grigg, W., & Tay-Lim, B. (2002). The nation's report card: U.S. History 2001. *Education Statistics Quarterly, 4,* 21–34.

Larkins, A., Hawkins, M., & Gilmore, A. (1987). Trivial and noninformative content of elementary social studies: A review of primary texts in four series. *Theory and Research in Social Education, 15,* 299–311.

Lee, P., & Ashby, R. (2001). Empathy, perspective taking, and rational understanding. In O. Davis, Jr., E. Yeager, & S. Foster (Eds.), *Historical empathy and perspective taking in the social studies* (pp. 21–50). New York: Rowman & Littlefield.

Leiser, D. (1983). Children's conceptions of economics: The constitution of a cognitive domain. *Journal of Economic Psychology, 4,* 297–317.

Levstik, L. (1986). The relationship between historical response and narrative in the classroom. *Theory and Research in Social Education, 14,* 1–15.

Levstik, L., & Barton, K. (1996). They still use some of their past: Historical salience in elementary children's chronological thinking. *Journal of Curriculum Studies, 28,* 531–576.

Marker, G., & Mehlinger, H. (1992). Social studies. In P. Jackson (Ed.), *Handbook of research on curriculum* (pp. 830–851). New York: Macmillan.

Martin, M. (1997). Children's understanding of the intent of advertising: A meta-analysis. *Journal of Public Policy and Marketing, 16,* 205–216.

Masterman, E., & Rogers, Y. (2002). A framework for designing interactive multimedia to scaffold young children's understanding of historical chronology. *Instructional Science, 30,* 221–241.

Mazur, E. (1990). *The development of children's understanding of marriage and divorce.* (ERIC Document Reproduction Service No. ED 321 856)

McKeown, M., & Beck, I. (1994). Making sense of accounts of history: Why young students don't and how they might. In G. Leinhardt, I. Beck, & C. Stainton (Eds.), *Teaching and learning in history* (pp. 1–26). Hillsdale, NJ: Lawrence Erlbaum Associates.

McNeal, J. (1987). *Children as consumers: Insights and implications.* Lexington, MA: Lexington.

McNeal, J. (1992). *Kids as customers: A handbook of marketing to children.* New York: Lexington.

Michela, J., & Contento, I. (1984). Spontaneous classification of foods by elementary school-aged children. *Health Education Quarterly, 11,* 57–76.

Miller, J., & Bartsch, K. (1997). The development of biological explanation: Are children vitalists? *Developmental Psychology, 33,* 156–164.

Moll, L. (1992). Bilingual classroom studies and community analysis. *Educational Researcher, 21,* 20–24.

Moore, S., Lare, J., & Wagner, K. (1985). *The child's political world: A longitudinal perspective.* New York: Praeger.

Morris, S., Taplin, J., & Gelman, S. (2000). Vitalism in naive biological thinking. *Developmental Psychology, 36,* 582–595.

Mugge, D. (1963). Precocity of today's young children: Real or wishful? *Social Education, 27,* 436–439.

National Council for the Social Studies. (1992). The Columbian Quincentenary: An educational opportunity. *Social Education, 56,* 248–249.

National Council for the Social Studies. (1993). A vision of powerful teaching and learning in the social studies. Building social understanding and civic efficacy. *Social Education, 57,* 213–223.

National Council for the Social Studies. (1994). *Curriculum standards for social studies: Expectations of excellence* (Bulletin No. 89). Washington, DC: Author.

Ng, S. (1983). Children's ideas about the bank and shop profit: Developmental stages and influences of cognitive contrast and conflict. *Journal of Economic Psychology, 4,* 209–221.

Ordan, H. (1945). *Social concepts and the child mind.* New York: King's Crown Press.

Palmer, J. (1994). *Geography in the early years.* New York: Routledge.

Pappas, C. (1993). Is narrative "primary"? Some insights from kindergarteners' pretend readings of stories and information books. *Journal of Reading Behavior, 25,* 97–129.

Patton, M. (1990). *Qualitative evaluation and research methods* (2nd ed.). Newbury Park, CA: Sage.

Payne, H., & Gay, S. (1997). Exploring cultural universals. *Journal of Geography, 96,* 220–223.

Piaget, J. (1971). *The child's conception of time.* New York: Ballantine. (Original work published 1946)

Piaget, J. (1983). Piaget's theory. In P. Mussen (Ed.), *Handbook of child psychology* (Vol. 1, 4th ed., pp. 702–732). New York: Wiley.

Piaget, J., & Weil, A. (1951). The development in children of the idea of the homeland and of relations to other countries. *International Social Science Journal, 3,* 561–578.

Pliner, P., Freedman, J., Abramovitch, R., & Darke, P. (1996). Children as consumers: In the laboratory and beyond. In P. Lunt & A. Furnham (Eds.), *Economic socialization: The economic beliefs and behaviours of young people* (pp. 35–46). Cheltenham, England: Edward Elgar.

Project 2061. (2001). *Atlas of science literacy.* Washington, DC: American Association for the Advancement of Science and National Science Teachers Association.

Ramadas, J., & Nair, U. (1996). The system idea as a tool in understanding conceptions about the digestive system. *International Journal of Science Education, 18,* 355–368.

Ravitch, D. (1987). Tot sociology or what happened to history in the grade schools. *American Scholar, 56,* 343–353.

Ravitch, D., & Finn, C. (1987). *What do our 17-year-olds know? A report of the first national assessment of history and literature.* New York: Harper & Row.

Richards, M. (2000). Jack Tizard Memorial Lecture: Children's understanding of inheritance and family. *Child Psychology and Psychiatry Review, 5,* 2–8.

Roth, K. (1996). Making learners and concepts central: A conceptual change approach to learner-centered, fifth-grade American history planning and teaching. In J. Brophy (Ed.), *Advances in research on teaching: Vol. 6. Teaching and learning history* (pp. 115–182). Greenwich, CT: JAI.

Roth, K. (2002). Talking to understand science. In J. Brophy (Ed.), *Social constructivist teaching: Affordances and constraints* (pp. 197–262). New York: Elsevier Science.

Rozin, P. (1990). Development in the food domain. *Developmental Psychology, 26*, 555–562.

Rutland, A. (1999). The development of national prejudice, in-group favouritism, and self-stereotypes in British children. *British Journal of Social Psychology, 38*, 55–70.

Sameroff, A., & Haith, M. (Eds.). (1996). *The five to seven shift.* Chicago: University of Chicago Press.

Schmidt, W., McKnight, C., Houang, R., Wang, H., Wiley, D., Cogan, L., & Wolfe, R. (2001). *Why schools matter: A cross-national comparison of curriculum and learning.* San Francisco: Jossey-Bass.

Schug, M. (1991). The development of students' economic thought: Implications for instruction. In W. Walstad & J. Soper (Eds.), *Effective economic education in the schools* (pp. 137–152). Washington, DC: National Education Association.

Schug, M., & Hartoonian, H. (1996). Issues and practices in the social studies curriculum. In M. Pugach & C. Warger (Eds.), *Curriculum trends, special education, and reform: Refocusing the conversation* (pp. 106–122). New York: Teachers College Press.

Sears, D., & Levy, S. (2003). Childhood and adult political development. In D. Sears, L. Huddy, & R. Jervis (Eds.), *Oxford handbook of political psychology* (pp. 60–109). Oxford, England: Oxford University Press.

Seixas, P. (1994). Students' understanding of historical significance. *Theory and Research in Social Education, 22*, 281–304.

Shapiro, B. (1994). *What children bring to light: A constructivist perspective on children's learning in science.* New York: Teachers College Press.

Shim, S., Snyder, L., & Gehrt, K. (1995). Parents' perception regarding children's use of clothing evaluative criteria: An exploratory study from the consumer socialization process perspective. *Advances in Consumer Research, 22*, 628–632.

Siegal, M., & Peterson, C. (1999). *Children's understanding of biology and health.* Cambridge: Cambridge University Press.

Solomon, G., Johnson, S., Zaitchik, D., & Carey, S. (1996). Like father, like son: Young children's understanding of how and why offspring resemble their parents. *Child Development, 67*, 161–171.

Sonuga-Barke, E., & Webley, P. (1993). *Children's saving: A study in the development of economic behavior.* Hillsdale, NJ: Lawrence Erlbaum Associates.

Springer, K. (1996). Young children's understanding of a biological basis for parent–offspring relations. *Child Development, 67*, 2841–2856.

Stevens, O. (1982). *Children talking politics: Political learning in childhood.* Oxford, England: Martin Robertson.

Stipek, D. (1998). *Motivation to learn: From theory to practice* (3rd ed.). Boston: Allyn & Bacon.

Takahashi, K., & Hatano, G. (1994). Understanding the banking business in Japan: Is economic prosperity accompanied by economic literacy? *British Journal of Development Psychology, 12*, 585–590.

Tannen, D. (1998). *The argument culture: Moving from debate to dialogue.* New York: Random House.

Teixeira, F. (2000). What happens to the food we eat? Children's conceptions of the structure and function of the digestive system. *International Journal of Science Education, 22*, 507–520.

Thomas, E. (1999). Skills and strategies for media education. *Educational Leadership, 56*(5), 50–54.

Thompson, D., & Siegler, R. (2000). Buy low, sell high: The development of an informal theory of economics. *Child Development, 71*, 660–677.

Thornburg, K. (1983). Young children's understanding of familial concepts with implications for social studies units. *Social Education, 47*(2), 138–141.

Turner, S. (1997). Children's understanding of food and health in primary classrooms. *International Journal of Science Education, 19*, 491–508.

Unnikrishnan, N., & Bajpai, S. (1996). *The impact of television advertising on children.* Thousand Oaks, CA: Sage.

U.S. Department of Education, National Center for Education Statistics. (1995a). *NAEP 1994 Geography: A first look.* Washington, DC: Author.

U.S. Department of Education, National Center for Education Statistics. (1995b). *NAEP 1994 History: A first look.* Washington, DC: Author.

Van Evra, J. (1990). *Television and child development.* Hillsdale, NJ: Lawrence Erlbaum Associates.

VanSledright, B., & Brophy, J. (1992). Storytelling, imagination, and fanciful elaboration in children's historical reconstructions. *American Educational Research Journal, 29*, 837–859.

Voter News Service. (2000). *Exit poll results—Election 2000.* Retrieved June 26, 2001, from http://www.udel.edu/poscir/road/course/exitpollsindex.html

Weiner, B. (1992). *Human motivation: Metaphors, theories and research.* Newbury Park, CA: Sage.

Wellman, H., & Gelman, S. (1992). Cognitive development: Foundational theories of core domains. *Annual Review of Psychology, 43*, 337–375.

Wiegand, P. (1992). *Places in the primary school: Knowledge and understanding of places at Key Stages 1 and 2.* London: Falmer.

Wiegand, P. (1993). *Children and primary geography.* New York: Cassell.

Willig, C. (1990). *Children's concepts and the primary curriculum.* London: Paul Chapman.

Wiman, A., & Newman, L. (1989). Television advertising exposure and children's nutritional awareness. *Journal of the Academy of Marketing Science, 17*, 179–188.

Wolf, M. (1987). How children negotiate television. In T. Lindlof (Ed.), *Natural audiences: Qualitative research of media uses and effects* (pp. 58–94). Norwood, NJ: Ablex.

Wong, E. (1996). Students' scientific explanations and the contexts in which they occur. *Elementary School Journal, 5*, 495–509.

Wood, B. (Ed.). (1977). *Development of functional communication competencies: Pre-K–Grade 6.* (ERIC Document Reproduction Service No. ED 137 858)

Woodward, A. (1987). Textbooks: Less than meets the eye. *Journal of Curriculum Studies, 19*, 511–526.

Wooster, J. (1992). Choosing materials for teaching about the Columbian Quincentenary. *Social Education, 56*, 244–247.

Zajonc, R. (2001). Mere exposure: A gateway to the subliminal. *Current Directions in Psychological Science, 10*, 224–228.

Author Index

Subject Index